Evolutionary Dynamics
of Organizations

Evolutionary Dynamics
of Organizations

EDITED BY

Joel A. C. Baum
Jitendra V. Singh

New York   Oxford
OXFORD UNIVERSITY PRESS
1994

Oxford University Press

Oxford   New York   Toronto
Delhi   Bombay   Calcutta   Madras   Karachi
Kuala Lumpur   Singapore   Hong Kong   Tokyo
Nairobi   Dar es Salaam   Cape Town
Melbourne   Auckland   Madrid

and associated companies in
Berlin   Ibadan

Published by Oxford University Press, Inc.
200 Madison Avenue, New York, New York 10016

Oxford is a registered trademark of Oxford University Press

Library of Congress Cataloging-in-Publication Data
Evolutionary dynamics of organizations /
edited by Joel A. C. Baum and Jitendra V. Singh.
p. cm.   Includes bibliographical references and index.
ISBN 0-19-507736-9.
ISBN 0-19-508584-1 (pbk.)
1. Organizational change—Congresses.
2. Organizational sociology—Congresses.
I. Baum, Joel A. C.
II. Singh, Jitendra
V., 1925-   .   HD58.8.E97   1994
302.3'5—dc20   93-17284

Larry Johnson's "Evolution of Man" cartoon is reprinted
courtesy of *The Boston Globe.*

2 4 6 8 9 7 5 3 1

Printed in the United States of America
on acid-free paper

to

Katherine Hick and Sara Beatrice and Bartholomew Baum

and

Marlies and Ambika Stefanie Singh

for putting up with us

Preface

This book was conceived to encourage new thinking on questions of organizational evolution at multiple levels of analysis. The volume presents innovative recent work done by some of the key scholars in the field. We do not attempt in this collection of essays to present a coherent synthesis of ideas on organizational evolution. Since the domain is still taking shape, such a synthesis is currently premature. Instead, we offer here a diverse set of new theoretical analyses, state-of-the-art empirical research, and critical commentaries covering a wide range of topics all broadly grouped within the domain of evolutionary inquiry in organization science.

The principal focus of this volume is the hierarchical nature of organizational evolution. We think a hierarchical approach is needed because organizational systems are hierarchically arranged. Accordingly, the four main sections of the book address *intraorganization, organization, population,* and *community* evolution. The selections assembled here are presented to document the current intellectual energy of organizational evolution researchers with a view toward stimulating future research, which in turn may contribute to an integration of the currently disparate ideas and approaches at these four levels.

In an introductory chapter we attempt to arrange ideas on organizational evolution into a more comprehensive hierarchical conceptual framework. This is followed, in part I, with essays by Donald Campbell and James March, two influential pioneers in the field of organizational evolution. The balance of the book is divided into four main parts, each focused on evolutionary processes and events at a particular level of analysis. Part II consists of three chapters focused on *intra*organizational evolution; part III includes four selections dealing with different aspects of evolutionary processes at the organization level. The five chapters in part IV examine different aspects of population-level evolution. Part V presents five analyses of community evolution, three of which emphasize the *coevolutionary* character of change processes in organizational communities. Each part (except the first) concludes with two commentaries. While these commentaries frequently refer directly to the preceding chapters, their main objective is to identify critical challenges and research questions related to the study of organizational evolution at a particular level of analysis.

The chapters of this book reveal important challenges facing organizational evolution researchers as well as emerging themes that hold promise. In the two final sections of our introductory chapter, we highlight some important challenges and themes that are further developed in the individual chapters and make explicit suggestions for future research.

The genesis of this book was a conference held at the Stern School of Business, New York University, in January 1992. The conference was hosted jointly by the Management Department, Stern School of Business, and three research centers from the Wharton School, University of Pennsylvania: the Huntsman Center for Global Competition and Innovation; the Reginald H. Jones Center for Management Policy, Strategy, and Organization; and the Sol C. Snider Entrepreneurial Center.

The Huntsman Center serves as a focal point and catalyst for Wharton research and teaching on the role of innovation in enhancing competitiveness in global markets. This research embraces such topics as the influences of the innovation environment, management of the innovation process, design of innovative programs, and performance outcomes of innovative activities. The Jones Center supports research and academic and executive workshops in policy analysis, corporate strategy, and organizational behavior. In addition, the Jones Center annually supports a dozen or more active research projects that fall within its broad domain. The Snider Center is the oldest entrepreneurial center, focusing on three major activities: entrepreneurship education at undergraduate, M.B.A. and doctoral levels; research under the general umbrella of expanding our knowledge of the process of wealth creation; and outreach through providing consulting and funding assistance to over seven thousand businesses annually. Two major research thrusts of the Snider Center are the study of emerging enterprises and corporate revitalization.

It is unlikely that this project would ever have taken off without the support and urging of Oscar Ornati, who was chair of the Management Department at the Stern School of Business until his death in December 1991. We were deeply saddened that Oscar was unable to participate in the conference with us and share in the fruit of his inspiration.

We also received consistent and enthusiastic support from Dean Richard Brief, the Stern School; George Day, director of the Huntsman Center; Ned Bowman, director of the Reginald Jones Center; and Ian MacMillan, director of the Snider Center. We thank them for their continuing support of such scholarly activities.

We are also indebted to all our contributors, who, in a real community effort, commented on each other's manuscripts, made numerous revisions, generally adhered to unreasonable deadlines set by us and, as a result, produced exciting essays of a very high quality. We would particularly like to single out Paul DiMaggio for a very special debt of gratitude. In addition to re-revising his own commentary to perfection, Paul provided detailed comments on many chapters by the other authors in this book—but, then, Paul is unusual, as we all know by now. For their generous assistance in helping us conceive the conference, we are grateful to Howard Aldrich, Terry Amburgey, John Freeman, and Jim March.

Financial support for the conference came from both the Stern School of Business, New York University, and the Wharton School, University of Pennsylvania. At the Stern School, grants were provided by the Dean's office, the Management Department, and Bill Starbuck. At the Wharton School, financial support came from the Huntsman, Jones, and Snider centers. We also gratefully acknowledge the support of the universities that sponsored their faculty members' attendance at the conference.

Finally, we would like to thank Mary Sutherland, Henry Krawitz, and Herb Addison of Oxford University Press for trying to keep us on track—whether or not they succeeded.

New York   J. B.
Philadelphia   J. S.
April 1993

Contents

Part III   Organizational Evolution

Part IV   Population Evolution

Part V   Community Evolution

Contributors

Howard E. Aldrich University of North Carolina–Chapel Hill

Terry L. Amburgey University of Kentucky

William P. Barnett Stanford University

Joel A. C. Baum New York University

John J. Beggs Louisiana State University

Jack W. Brittain University of Texas–Dallas

Robert A. Burgelman Stanford University

Donald T. Campbell Lehigh University

Tina Dacin Texas A & M University

Jacques Delacroix Santa Clara University

Paul J. DiMaggio Princeton University

Charles J. Fombrun New York University

John Freeman Cornell University

Raghu Garud New York University

Ari Ginsberg New York University

Heather A. Haveman Duke University

Dawn Kelly Northwestern University

Ita G. G. Kreft California State University–Los Angeles

Theresa K. Lant New York University

Daniel A. Levinthal University of Pennsylvania

Alessandro Lomi University of London

James G. March Stanford University

Bill McKelvey University of California–Los Angeles

Marshall W. Meyer University of Pennsylvania

Stephen J. Mezias New York University

Anne S. Miner University of Wisconsin–Madison

Brian S. Mittman RAND Corporation and University of California–Los Angeles

Joseph Porac University of Illinois–Champaign–Urbana

Hayagreeva Rao Emory University

Lori Rosenkopf University of Pennsylvania

Zur Shapira New York University

Jitendra V. Singh University of Pennsylvania

William H. Starbuck New York University

Udo H. Staber University of New Brunswick–Fredricton

David J. Tucker University of Michigan

Michael L. Tushman Columbia University

Andrew H. Van de Ven University of Minnesota

Sidney G. Winter University of Pennsylvania

Catherine R. Zimmer North Carolina State University

Lynne G. Zucker University of California–Los Angeles

Evolutionary Dynamics
of Organizations

1

Organizational Hierarchies and Evolutionary Processes: Some Reflections on a Theory of Organizational Evolution

JOEL A. C. BAUM AND JITENDRA V. SINGH

If you have an apple and I have an apple and we exchange these apples then you and I will still each have one apple. But if you have an idea and I have an idea and we exchange these ideas, then each of us will have two ideas.

—GEORGE BERNARD SHAW

In this chapter we combine a number of ideas on organizational evolution into a more comprehensive conceptual framework. We introduce the idea that organizational processes—*interaction* and *replication*—act on two kinds of organizational entities—*ecological* and *genealogical*—at a variety of hierarchically nested levels of organization. The framework provides (1) an articulation of the domain of evolutionary inquiry in organization theory, (2) a context for the chapters that follow, and (3) a basis for identifying aspects of evolutionary theory in need of further investigation. We conclude by linking each chapter to the proposed framework, identifying some important challenges and themes revealed in the volume as a whole and making explicit several directions for future research that appear to hold promise for advancing an evolutionary theory of organizations.

The Evolutionary Dynamics of Organizations

What is it that evolutionary theories of organizations seek to explain? Such theories have three major foci: (1) *entities* (e.g., routines, comps, jobs, organizations, ecosys-

We are grateful to Paul DiMaggio, James March, Arthur Stinchcombe, and Sidney Winter for their helpful comments on an earlier version of this chapter.

tems), (2) *processes* (e.g., replication, mutation, recombination, random drift, learning, institutionalization, convergence, reorientation, entrepreneurship, competition, natural selection), and (3) *events* (e.g., birth, death, transformation, speciation, extinction). Organizational evolution is concerned with the events in the histories of these entities that are produced by these processes.

To date, organization theorists do not have a fully developed theory of organizational evolution (Hannan and Freeman, 1989:20). Therefore, in this introductory section, we attempt to link some key ideas on organizational evolution and provide a general representation of it that organizes and articulates its currently disparate parts. We begin by describing the two basic approaches to studying organizational evolution: *organizational ecology* (e.g., Hannan and Freeman, 1977, 1989), which seeks to understand the dynamic interactions within and among organizational populations and communities, and *organizational systematics* (Baum, 1989; McKelvey, 1982), which aspires to develop a theory of organizational differences that explains the processes by which the practices and structures of organizations and organizational forms persist over time. We then explore a framework for organizational evolution that combines these approaches.

Here we conceptualize organizational evolution as the complex interplays between two kinds of processes, *interaction* and *replication* (Hull, 1980, 1988), acting on two kinds of entities, *ecological* and *genealogical* (Eldredge, 1985, 1989), at a variety of levels of organization. We characterize the world of organizations as composed of two *hierarchies* of entities, one ecological (e.g., jobs, work groups, organizations, populations, and communities), focused on the structure and integration (i.e., resource exchange and transformation) of organizational systems and the mutual interactions within them, and the other genealogical (e.g., routines, comps, species, and polyphyletic groupings), concerned with the conservation and transfer of production and organizing skills and knowledge. (See the section entitled "Ecological and Genealogical Hierarchies" in this chapter.) Genealogical entities pass on their information largely intact in successive replications. Ecological entities, the structural and behavioral expressions of the genealogical entities, interact with the environment and this interaction causes replication to be differential. This "natural selection vector" (Eldredge, 1989), the differential success of ecological entities that causes the differential perpetuation (through replication) of genealogical entities over time, is the core of the evolutionary connection between the ecological and the genealogical systems. Thus, organizational evolution is the result of genealogical entities replicating, ecological entities interacting, the net effect of these interactions being the differential persistence of the genealogical entities that produced them.

A theory of organizational evolution—indeed, any evolutionary system—minimally requires these two kinds of processes (i.e., interaction and replication) and two kinds of entities (i.e., ecological and genealogical) (Boyd and Richerson, 1985; Eldredge, 1985, 1989; Eldredge and Salthe, 1984; Hull, 1980, 1988; Salthe, 1985).[1] No theory of evolution can be complete without a careful consideration of the structure and function of moment-by-moment ecological systems. Neither can a theory of evolution be complete without a consideration of the source of the information that supplies the entities to the ecological arena. In the evolutionary view, history and current function are intricately related. We need an understanding of the integration of the interactive processes of resource exchange and transformation, on the one hand, and the historical processes of information conservation and transmission on the other. In the *dual-hierarchy* framework, we account for historical effects through the processes of the genealogical hierarchy and ecological effects through the forces that act on each generation of the ecological hierarchy.

Organizational Ecology and Organizational Systematics

Ecological and systematic approaches to organizational evolution are focused on what happens to different kinds of entities over time. Organizational ecology emphasizes entities involved in resource exchange and transformation, while organizational systematics emphasizes those entities engaged in the conservation and transmission of (hereditary) information. With few exceptions (e.g., Baum, 1989; McKelvey, 1982; Ulrich and McKelvey, 1990), studies of organizational evolution have, to date, been much more focused on the ecological perspective than on systematics.

Organizational ecology seeks to understand the mutual interactions within and among the populations and communities comprising organizational ecosystems and the mechanisms and processes underlying their growth, regulation and decline (Carroll, 1984; Hannan and Freeman, 1977, 1989). The primary emphasis is on the influence of selection processes on the dynamics of organizational diversity (Hannan and Freeman, 1989:21). Most variability in organizations is seen to come about through the creation of new organizations and organizational forms and the demise of existing ones (Hannan and Freeman, 1977, 1989:12). However, new studies are providing evidence that organizations can and do change (e.g., Amburgey, Kelly and Barnett, 1993; Baum, 1990b; Baum and Oliver, 1991; Delacroix and Swaminathan, 1991; Ginsberg and Buchholtz, 1990; Haveman, 1992; Kelly and Amburgey, 1991; Miner, Amburgey, and Stearns, 1990; Singh, House, and Tucker, 1986; Singh, Tucker and Meinhard, 1988), and that these changes are important to understanding what organizations do as individuals, as populations, and as communities. Thus, the emerging ecological view is that organizational evolution can best be studied by examining how social and environmental conditions and interactions within and among populations influence the rates at which new organizations and new organizational forms are created, the rates at which existing organizations and organizational forms die out, *and* the rates at which organizations change forms (Hannan and Freeman, 1989:7; Singh and Lumsden, 1990:163). In addition to organizational selection processes, several researchers have analyzed *intraorganizational* ecologies that focus on selection processes internal to organizations and are concerned with rates of birth, transformation, and death of organizational strategies (Burgelman, 1983a, 1983b, 1990, 1991) or formalized jobs (Miner, 1990; 1991).

Organizational systematics, too, is focused on the study of organizational diversity. It involves the study of the kinds and diversity of organizations, and of any and all relationships among them. Systematics seeks to understand and explain why organizations are structured the way they are and behave the way they do (McKelvey, 1982:12). Organizational systematics is composed of three interdependent domains of inquiry: (1) *taxonomy,* (2) *classification,* and (3) *phyletics* (McKelvey, 1982:27–30). Organizational taxonomy involves the development of a theory of organizational differences for delimiting organizations, including an understanding of the causes of stability and change of organizational forms, and the forces isolating different kinds of organizational forms from each other through time. Classification involves the description of different kinds (i.e., species) of organizations, their relation to more or less similar organizations, the identification and assignment of real entities to classes, and the construction of a classification scheme.[2] Finally, organizational phyletics involves tracing out the origins and evolution of organizations. It is the study of evolutionary lines of descent of organizational entities from their ancestors for the purpose of discovering delimitable groupings of organizations and explaining their origins. Supporting inquiry into organizational phyletics are conceptualizations of *organizational inheritance* (Baum, 1989; McKelvey, 1982; Nelson and Winter, 1982; Winter, 1990), which involve the genealogical processes by which production and organizing competencies, organizations, and organizational forms are transmitted (i.e., replicated) through time.

Combining Ecology and Systematics

Organizational evolution begins with the differential proliferation of alternative forms within populations, that leads ultimately to foundings, the product of entrepreneurial thought (Lumsden and Singh, 1990), that jump out of established populations to create new forms, and ends with the extinction of the last member of the population that imitation creates around the founding organization. Although research in organizational ecology has informed us about selection processes within organizations and populations, and is beginning to deal with the community-level problem of the emergence and disappearance of organizational forms (e.g., Aldrich and Fiol, 1992; Astley, 1985; Barnett, 1990; Barnett, chapter 16, this volume; Barnett and Carroll, 1987; Brittain, chapter 17, this volume; Brittain and Wholey, 1988; Lumsden and Singh, 1990; Romanelli, 1991a; Rosenkopf and Tushman, chapter 19, this volume; Van de Ven and Garud, chapter 20, this volume), by and large, organizational ecologists have not attempted to link ecological processes of interaction and genealogical processes of replication. Consequently, we still know very little about the *other side* of the evolutionary process—the structures of organizational inheritance and transmission (Baum, 1989). How are organizational structures and practices perpetuated through time? What is inherited and how?[3]

For biological organisms, inheritance is based ultimately on the propagation of genes (and for a few species, social learning along lines of descent). Inheritance processes of social organizations appear far more complex than those of biotic organisms (Baum, 1989; Boyd and Richerson, 1985; Hannan and Freeman, 1977, 1989; Lumsden and Wilson, 1981; McKelvey, 1982; Singh and Lumsden, 1990).[4] Information about organizing and production can be inherited from potentially diverse sources and the flow of information continues throughout the life of organizations as generations of members come and go (McKelvey, 1982). Copying mistakes occur frequently, and information is rarely transmitted exactly (Csányi, 1989; DiMaggio and Powell, 1983; Nelson and Winter, 1982). Information can be inherited in many different directions among generations of organizational members and organizations: *vertically forward* (i.e., young can copy old); *horizontally* (i.e., young can copy young, old can copy old); and even *vertically backward* (i.e., old can copy young) (Baum,

1989). Transmission within generations of organizations occurs because the production or organizing routines being spread reproduce rapidly and have short generation lengths compared to the generation length of the "host" organizations (Cavalli-Sforza and Feldman, 1981).

Trial-and-error learning as well as more elaborate methods of adaptation (i.e., rational calculation based on the collection of information about the environment, estimation of the outcomes of various alternatives, and evaluations of the desirability of the estimated outcomes according to some preference criteria) are forces that guide patterns of organizational inheritance (Levitt and March, 1988). For example, in the last fifty years the Japanese have studied American mass-production systems and figured out ways to improve their own though Americans have been slow to bring back to the United States what the Japanese have done (Levin, 1992). At the same time, however, organizational inheritance patterns are *frequency-dependent* (Abrahamson, 1991; Boyd and Richerson, 1985; Campbell, chapter 2, this volume), that is, varying with the commonness or rarity of organizational practices and structures; *path-dependent* (Arthur, 1989, 1990), that is, sensitive to the effects of self-reinforcing positive feedback on small, fortuitous events; and *reputation-dependent* (DiMaggio and Powell, 1983), that is, large and successful enough to provide attractive models for imitation.

These features of organizational inheritance suggest evolutionary effects and levels of organizational diversity and variation that are strikingly different from those expected with purely genetic transmission. The pace of organizational evolution is generally very much faster than that of biotic evolution (Lumsden, 1989; McKelvey, 1982). Although they clearly exist, organizational isolating mechanisms are not as strong as the reproductive isolation of biological species (McKelvey, 1982; Hannan and Freeman, 1989). Since inheritance is not as completely isolated socioculturallly as it is biotically, *hybridization* is likely to be more frequent among organizational than biotic forms (Blute, 1979). In this regard, Campbell (1979) suggests that the extent of "cross-lineage" borrowing that occurs in sociocultural evolution is the major disanalogy between it and biological evolution. Transmission barriers can be set up and taken down quickly, increasing the pace of divergence and convergence in organizational evolution (Powell, 1991). Consequently, quantum (Simpson, 1944, 1953) and punctuated (Eldredge and Gould, 1972; Stanley, 1979b) evolutionary patterns may be more readily applicable to organizational than biotic evolution (Gersick, 1991; McKelvey, 1982; Miller and Friesen, 1980a, 1980b; Tushman and Romanelli, 1985).[5] In combination, transmission after birth and organizational learning may result in a preponderance of *Lamarckian* (versus *Mendelian*) inheritance in the sense that production and organizing competence acquired through learning can be *re*transmitted (Baum, 1989; Boyd and Richerson, 1985; McKelvey, 1982; Nelson and Winter, 1982; Singh and Lumsden, 1990; Winter, 1990). Consequently, the genealogies of organizations may often be equivocal and it may not be feasible (or sensible) to seek direct genetic analogies because there may be nothing close to what exists in the biological world (Hannan and Freeman, 1989; McKelvey, 1982; Singh and Lumsden, 1990).

Nevertheless, it is certainly not true that social transmission and recombination in the organizational world are completely unrestrained (Baum, 1988; Blute, 1979; Hannan and Freeman, 1989; Hull, 1988; McKelvey, 1982). The emergence and maintenance of diversity among organizations require barriers to the exchange of production and organizing competence. Without a stabilizing memory of something akin to an inheritable "genetic code" organizations could not become or remain meaningfully different from each other over time. Instead, they would form a normal distribution of slightly varying forms with some average properties that were not heritable. In the world of organizations, it is obvious that differences can and do become deep enough that the gaps between them are rarely (if ever) bridged (Baum, 1988; McKelvey, 1982:192; Hannan and Freeman, 1989:54). Thus, while probably not rooted in a system of inheritance in the biological sense (i.e., propagation of genes), if the current diversity of organizational forms is to be conceived as a reflection of the "cumulative effect of a long history of variation and selection" (Hannan and Freeman, 1989:20), then an explanation of how organizational forms become different and remain different through time is required (Hannan and Freeman, 1989; McKelvey, 1982).[6]

Fortunately, Darwin's idea of evolution—descent with modification—is not tied to the particular features of biological inheritance (Boyd and Richerson, 1985; Campbell, 1965b; Hannan and Freeman, 1989; Hull, 1988). Natural selection is a very general mechanism, one likely to operate in any system of inheritance that meets the following two conditions: (1) there is heritable variation in form (i.e., phenotype) and (2) the variation in form is related to variation in survival and replication. Whenever these conditions are met, the forms with the highest probability of being transmitted to the next generation will tend to increase in number.

Ecological and Genealogical Hierarchies

The structure of organizational evolution is frequently conceived as hierarchical (Aldrich, 1979; Baum, 1988; Burgelman, 1991; Burgelman and Singh, 1987; Campbell, 1974a, 1974b, 1990a; Carroll, 1984; Csányi, 1989; Hannan and Freeman, 1977, 1989; Hawley, 1950, 1986; Lumsden and Singh, 1990; McKelvey, 1982; Miner, 1991; Singh and Lumsden, 1990). A hierarchical theory is needed not just because theories that cover intraorganization, organization, population, and community levels of organization are too numerous and diverse to fit into a single statement, but, more importantly, because organizational systems are themselves hierarchically arranged. As Simon (1962) has pointed out, hierarchical ordering is one of the most natural ways of organizing complexity.

The hierarchies that seem relevant to the process of organizational evolution are *inclusive*. The hierarchical levels are nested one within the other. Wholes are composed of parts at lower levels of organization, and are themselves parts of more extensive wholes. For example, communities are composed of populations, which are composed of organizations, which are composed of work groups, and so on. The nesting of entities into larger entities at a higher level of organization creates a system of levels. The entities at higher levels are not merely aggregates of lower-level entities. Each level constitutes a discrete class of entities, particular instances of which are all individual entities, each with its own unique origin, history, and end.[7]

Consider the entities that evolve in organizational evolution: routines (Nelson and Winter, 1982), comps (McKelvey, 1982), jobs (Miner, 1990, 1991), workgroups

(Cherns, 1976, 1987; Gersick, 1988, 1989; Trist, 1981), organizations (Aldrich, 1979; Miller and Friesen, 1980a, 1980b; Tushman and Romanelli, 1985; Weick, 1979), populations (Hannan and Freeman, 1977, 1989), species (McKelvey, 1982; Romanelli, 1991; Lumsden and Singh, 1990), communities (Astley, 1985; Barnett and Carroll, 1987; Brittain and Wholey, 1988), polyphyletic groupings (McKelvey, 1982), and ecosystems (Hawley, 1950, 1986). Clearly, this list is partial rather than exhaustive. There may well be additional classes of entities that belong here.[8]

An inspection of this list reveals two functional classes of entities. One, the *genealogical* class of entities, is formed by components of *institutional memory* engaged in the preservation and dissemination of production and organizing information. It is composed of *lineages,* entities that persist through time in either the same or an altered state as a result of their replication (Hull, 1988:409). The other, the *ecological* class of entities, reflects the economic structure and integration (i.e., resource exchange and transformation) of organizational systems, and takes part in the ecology of organizations. It is composed of *historical* entities, the result of the cumulative effect of variation and selection over time, and the structural and behavioral expressions of entities of the genealogical class. These entities form the various class levels of the two inclusive hierarchies, one *ecological* and the other *genealogical,* presented in Table 1.1. Descriptions of the entities forming the levels of each hierarchy are also given in the table.

Notably, organizations constitute a level in both hierarchies. As members of species (i.e., genealogical entities), organizations are packages of routinized competence, temporary repositories of production, and organizing knowledge (McKelvey, 1982:196; Winter, 1990:280). However, as members of populations (i.e., ecological entities), organizations are the external manifestation of the production and organizing competence they carry at any given time (McKelvey, 1982:196). Thus, organizations are the transmitters of the routines, the bearers of adaptations, and the expressors of variation in populations. Varying among one another, they are shuffled as units of selection. Thus organizations have both ecological and genealogical roles: they are the nexus of environmental interaction and the conservation of production and organizing capabilities.

The elements of these two hierarchies interact, regulating change within one another, and, as by-products, create the patterns of organizational evolution. There are processes within each level of each hierarchy. There are also interactive effects among levels within each hierarchy. But it is the interplays between the two hierarchies that integrate all the entities taking part in the process of organizational evolution. The processes within each of these hierarchies plus the interactions among them produce the patterns of persistence and change in the ecological and genealogical entities over time.

Ecological and Genealogical Processes

Two classes of processes, *interaction* and *replication,* distinguish the ecological and genealogical hierarchies, respectively (Eldredge, 1985, 1989; Hull, 1980, 1988). The processes in the ecological hierarchy are concerned with the mutual interactions between ecological entities at the same level of organization (e.g., between jobs within

TABLE 1.1   Ecological and Genealogical Entities

Genealogical Hierarchy	Ecological Hierarchy
Polyphyletic grouping. An aggregate of one or more organizational species descended from two or more immediate common ancestors, though ultimately from a common ancestor (McKelvey, 1982:278).	Ecosystem. A group of coevolutionarily interacting communities and its social, technical, and economic environment between which energy and resources are regularly cycled (Hawley, 1950, 1986).
Species. A polythetic group of competence-sharing populations of organizations (McKelvey, 1982:192). A set of highly probable combinations of competence elements that are temporarily housed at any given time among the members of an organizational population (McKelvey, 1982:195). A collectivity (i.e., compool) of the adaptive properties (i.e., comps) of all its included organizations (McKelvey, 1982:196).	Community. A group of coevolutionarily interacting organizational populations connected by the effects of one population on the demography of the other (Barnett, 1990; Barnett and Carroll, 1987; Carroll, 1984).
	Population. A group of coevolutionarily interacting organizations that embody similar combinations of key production and organizing knowledge and skill (Baum, 1989; McKelvey, 1982).
Organization. A repository of production and organizing knowledge (i.e., routines, comps) temporarily embodied in the employees of the organization at any given time (McKelvey, 1982:196; Winter, 1990:280).	Organization. A group of coevolutionarily interacting work groups and jobs. External expression of configurations of routines/comps temporarily embodied in the employees of the organization at any given time (McKelvey, 1982:196).
Routine/Comp. An element of production and organizing knowledge and skill (McKelvey, 1982; Nelson and Winter, 1982).	Work group. A group of coevolutionarily interacting jobs (Cherns, 1976, 1987; Gersick, 1988, 1989; Trist, 1981). External expression of the routines/comps held by the group members at any given time.
	Job. A set of tasks or pattern of activity performed by a single individual (Miner, 1991). External expression of the routines/comps held by the employee at any given time.

work groups, work groups within organizations, organizations within populations, and populations within communities)—interactions that are connected to the resource exchanges that propel ecological entities. The effect of social (DiMaggio and Powell, 1983; Fombrun, 1986; Meyer and Rowan, 1977), technical (Tushman and Anderson, 1986), and economic environmental conditions, strongly implicated in patterns of organizational persistence and change (Hannan and Freeman, 1977, 1989; McKelvey, 1982), have their effects on organizational evolution through the entities of the ecological hierarchy—indeed forming part of the ecological hierarchy at the ecosystem level.

The dynamic interactions at each level hold the entities at the next-higher level of the nested ecological hierarchy together. Interactions among jobs bind work groups together (Gersick, 1988, 1989), which in turn bind organizations together (Cherns, 1976, 1987; Trist, 1981). Interactions among organizations of the same kind form populations (McKelvey, 1982; Hannan and Freeman, 1989). Competition, mutualism, collective action, collective learning, and other ecological processes at this level are the characteristic phenomena responsible for producing the variables most frequently studied by organizational ecologists—density, rates of founding, failure, and growth. When we become concerned with the interactions of organizations of different populations, we have moved up to the community level. Populations, not organizations, interact to shape communities (Astley, 1985; Barnett and Carroll, 1987; Brittain and Wholey, 1988). Ecological processes at this level include predation, interpopulation competition, symbiotic interactions, and changes in carrying capacities. Finally, organizational communities interact to form ecosystems (Hawley, 1950, 1986).

In the genealogical hierarchy, processes are those related to the production of new entities from old: the replication of routines, organizations, and species. Each level of the genealogical hierarchy is maintained by the production of lower-level entities: routines must reproduce themselves for organizations to persist, organizations must produce more organizations for species to persist, and species must fragment for polyphyletic groupings to endure.[9] While interactions occur at all levels of the ecological hierarchy, replication appears to be concentrated primarily at the lower levels of the genealogical hierarchy. That is, because they have short generation lengths compared to those of higher-level entities, most replication is replication of lower-level entities (e.g., routines, organizations). We also need an understanding of the sources of variation (e.g., mutation, recombination, hybridization), resulting in the production of new kinds of routines and organizations.

Replication occurs through different processes at each hierarchical level. Within an organization, existing routines serve as templates for producing copies, making their replication (e.g., through observation, more formal training and education, or, alternatively, hiring new employees already proficient in the routines by virtue of their professional status) possible with some precision from day to day and over generations of the organization's employees (McKelvey, 1982; Nelson and Winter, 1982).[10] Such inheritance processes are a regular feature of organizations. For as Bandura (1977:38) has pointed out, "once the capacity for observational learning has fully developed, one cannot keep people from learning what they have seen."

What employees acquire is *rules of behavior,* rather than the behaviors that result from the rules (Bandura, 1977; Boyd and Richerson, 1985; McKelvey, 1982; Nelson and Winter, 1982; Weick and Gilfillan, 1971; Zucker, 1977). This permits the replication of behaviors even when appropriate behaviors depend on environmental contingencies.[11]

However, organizational routines not only record history, they shape its future course. Each time an organization uses a certain routine, it becomes more proficient at that routine and more likely to repeat it in the future (Levitt and March, 1988). While this self-reinforcing process contributes to organizational stability, efficiency, and reliability, it can lead to competency traps that make the exploration of potentially adaptive alternatives difficult (Ginsberg and Baum, chapter 7, this volume; Levinthal, chapter 9, this volume; Levitt and March, 1988; March, 1991; Nelson and Winter, 1982).

Nevertheless, as the result of personnel transfers, and the inventiveness as well as the mistakes of an organization's members, ideas for new or modified production and organizing routines emerge all the time and are tried out (March, 1991; Nelson and Winter, 1982). For example, the workers at a single Toyota plant submitted twenty-thousand suggestions for improvement during a one year period. Typically, more than half these suggestions are used (Levin, 1992). Modification of routines can also result from imitation attempts by *other* similar organizations (Nelson and Winter, 1982). In this case, the routine is not readily available for direct observation, and gaps must be filled by independent effort. Consequently, copies produced through imitation may constitute substantial mutations. Of course, mutations are not always harmful. Presumably, organizations can frequently achieve successful imitation through trial-and-error learning or more elaborate methods of adaptive modification.

Within species, organizations retaining similar bundles of routines are also reproduced over generations of employees and organizations as the result of barriers to the inheritance of production and organizing competence from organizations in other species (Baum, 1989; Hannan and Freeman, 1989; McKelvey, 1982; Pantzar and Csányi, 1991).[12] These barriers include the following:

- *Technological interdependencies.* The dependence for successful performance of one element of organizational competence on the successful completion of others means the introduction of new kinds of production and organizing competence is potentially disruptive (Hannan and Freeman, 1989; McKelvey, 1982; Miller and Friesen, 1980a, 1980b).

- *Institutional processes.* Coercive, normative, and mimetic processes (DiMaggio and Powell, 1983) and taken-for-grantedness (Meyer and Rowan, 1977) operate to accentuate and maintain the diversity of organizations.

- *Complexity of learning.* The more difficult an organization's production and organizing competence are to learn and transmit socially (as a function of its complexity and distinctness), the less likely it is that organizations in different species will be able to acquire and comprehend enough of the competence to implement it successfully (McKelvey, 1982).

- *Resistance to learning.* Organizations tend to prefer to employ routines of the past (even beyond their point of usefulness) or to focus on refining current routines (e.g., updating and/or managing more effectively the routines already held) rather than to try out ideas invented elsewhere (McKelvey, 1982; Nystrom and Starbuck, 1984; Milliken and Lant, 1991).

- *Imprinting.* The features acquired by organizations at the time of their founding, for example, by mimicking of those features that are taken as the natural way to organize a particular form of collective activity, or as the result of environmental conditions, are retained into the future (Boeker, 1989; Carroll and Hannan, 1989; Stinchcombe, 1965; Tucker, Singh, and Meinhard, 1988, 1990).

- *Social, professional, and personnel network closures.* Groups of organizations that repeatedly hire each other's employees (because they possess required skill and knowledge) develop a high degree of inbreeding with respect to production and organizing competence and tend to become different from other groups of organizations (Hannan and Freeman, 1989; McKelvey, 1982).

While such *isolating mechanisms* help prevent the breakdown of adaptive combinations of production and organizing knowledge, prevent worthless combinations from forming, and foster the stability of organizational species, they also decrease variability, limiting the ability of the organizations in a species to explore new ways and means of adapting. However, as we discussed earlier, these isolating mechanisms are not so strong and stable that they are never bridged, and organizational species do fragment to produce new organizational species through several processes.

Organizational speciation can result from hybridization, in which several previously existing forms are mixed (McKelvey, 1982). Hybridization can result from entrepreneurial acts that create new organizational forms to handle new services or products (Lumsden and Singh, 1990) or from deinstitutionalization that removes barriers to transmission (Hannan and Freeman, 1989; Powell, 1991). Ecological interactions can also result in speciation. For example, disruptive selection processes, in which organizations with features at the center of a species distribution on some dimension (e.g., size, specialism-generalism) are selected against, can operate to split the species into distinct forms (Amburgey, Dacin, and Kelly, chapter 12, this volume; Baum and Mezias, 1992; Hannan and Freeman, 1977; Hannan, Ranger-Moore, and Banaszak-Holl, 1990; Carroll, 1985). Quantum or punctuated speciation can result from a sudden mutation of production or organizing competence (e.g., a technological discontinuity) that results in strikingly superior organizational performance (Aldrich, 1979; McKelvey, 1982; Tushman and Anderson, 1986). Speciation can also occur less dramatically as the result of random drift when purposeful or accidental changes in productive or organizing competence that occur independent of environmental selection processes accumulate from one generation to the next among an isolated group of like organizations (Hannan and Freeman, 1989; McKelvey, 1982). The process of organizational speciation creates polyphyletic groupings that constitute the highest level of organization in the genealogical hierarchy. These groupings are historical entities formed by the production of new organizational species from old.

There are, of course, considerable obstacles to the emergence of new organizational species. The survival prospects of emergent species are low because they suffer a liability of newness and lack external legitimacy (Hannan and Freeman, 1984; Meyer and Rowan, 1977; Stinchcombe, 1965). Moreover, unless new organizational species can rapidly acquire mechanisms that isolate them from their parent population(s), their distinctive characteristics are unlikely to be maintained over time.

Interactions of the Ecological and Genealogical Hierarchies

The processes within each level of each hierarchy (e.g., the replication of routines, the dynamics of competition), when taken alone, constitute only a small portion of the overall evolutionary process. There are also interactive effects among levels within each hierarchy. While there is a degree of autonomy of event and process within each hierarchical level, and each level is taken to represent a dynamic system in its own right, there is also both upward and downward causation (Campbell, 1974a, 1990a; Eldredge, 1985, 1989; Salthe, 1985; Singh and Lumsden, 1990). Interactions among different levels constrain the kinds of processes that can occur at a given level and regulate the processes that do occur. For example, people constitute, and are acted upon by, organizations and interactions among organizations. Their understanding of, beliefs about, and attitudes toward organizations help shape the decisions from which organizations themselves are formed. These decisions (variations) are injected into the higher level of the population, where selection and random drift take over as dynamics (Singh and Lumsden, 1990). These interactions are likely to be strongest across contiguous levels and their significance declines as the levels involved become increasingly remote. Thus, what goes on at one level of the hierarchy affects processes and events at other levels, with the dynamics connected most strongly at adjacent lower and upper levels. Systems of this type, in which underlying constituents compose and react to the overall organization, are termed *heterarchies* (Hofstader, 1979). They are hierarchical structures with feedback.

However, in the dual-hierarchy framework, it is the interplays between the ecological and genealogical hierarchies that integrate all the entities taking part in the process of organizational evolution. The elements of these two hierarchies interact, regulating change within one another, and, as by-products, create the patterns of organizational evolution. Processes within each hierarchy plus the interactions among them are conceived to produce the patterns and events of organizational evolution: the persistence and the modification of the entities comprising the ecological and genealogical hierarchies over time.

At any point in time, organizations, the members of populations, operate with other populations of organizations in integrated communities. From a genealogical point of view, these ecological communities are collections of organizations drawn from various species. Polyphyletic groupings provide the species, which in turn provide the organizations observed in each community, which are themselves integrated into the larger ecosystems of the ecological hierarchy. Thus, the genealogical hierarchy supplies the entities of the ecological hierarchy, whose continued existence and characteristic features depend on what is available in the genealogical hierarchy. However, it is the ecological entities, the visible structural and behavioral expressions of genealogical entities, that are shuffled as units of selection. And it is these ecological interactions that determine what exists in the genealogical hierarchy, which particular lineages of routines, organizations, and species survive over time and in what form.

The interaction between the two hierarchies can be seen in the unequal results of the interactions among ecological entities that lead to differential representation of genealogical entities in the next generation. In general, the interaction that results in the differential perpetuation of genealogical entities occurs at the same level or higher levels of the ecological hierarchy. For example, within organizations, the ongoing selection of jobs results in valuable routines being retained and less valuable routines being rejected (Miner, 1990, 1991), while within populations, the ongoing selection of organizations results in valuable configurations of routines being retained and less valuable configurations of routines being rejected (McKelvey, 1982; Nelson and Winter, 1982).

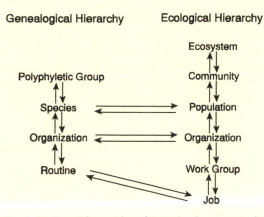

FIG. 1.1   Two hierarchies of organizational evolution

Thus, the source of change in the composition of the interacting entities of the ecological hierarchy is the genealogical hierarchy, and the births, deaths, and persistence of elements within the genealogical hierarchy are to a very great degree reactions to processes and events in the ecological hierarchy. This suggests that most of the regulation of retention and modification of production and organizing competence over time results *not* from processes in the genealogical hierarchy, but from those in the ecological hierarchy. Consequently, anything contributing to the differential births and deaths of the ecological entities is material to an understanding of evolutionary processes. However, this does not mean that one hierarchy is causally prior to the other. To the contrary, both are necessary for a theory of organizational evolution.

The dual-hierarchy framework is summarized in Figure 1.1. The figure shows the class levels of entities of the ecological and genealogical hierarchies. It also depicts the patterns of upward and downward interaction that constrain and regulate processes at adjacent levels within each hierarchy (e.g., the pool of available routines limits the range of organizational variation expressed within a population on which natural selection then acts). In addition, there are processes of interaction among entities within each level of the ecological hierarchy, as well as processes of replication at the various levels of the genealogical hierarchy.

Figure 1.1 also illustrates one possible version of the interactions that take place directly between the entities of the ecological and genealogical hierarchies. In the particular scheme presented, we conceive three points of direct contact between the hierarchies: job-routine, organization-organization, and population-species. In other words, the ongoing selection of jobs within organizations (Miner, 1990, 1991), organizations within populations (Hannan and Freeman, 1977, 1989) and populations within communities (Astley, 1985; Barnett and Amburgey, 1990; Barnett and Carroll, 1987) is seen to affect directly the entities of the genealogical hierarchy, which in turn directly affect the variation among jobs, organizations, and populations (McKelvey, 1982). Others may be possible. For example, selection among organizations may directly affect species when organizations coincide with populations (see DiMaggio, commentary to part V, this volume).

As we have characterized it here, organizational evolution involves the complex interplays between two kinds of processes (interaction and replication) acting on two kinds of entities (ecological and genealogical) at a variety of levels of organization. Organizational evolution is the result of genealogical entities replicating and ecological entities interacting, the net effect of these interactions being the differential persistence of the genealogical entities that produced them.

The Dual-Hierarchy Framework and Its Application to the Other Chapters

The various selections in this volume deal with many aspects of the dual-hierarchy framework discussed earlier in this chapter. In the introductory essays in part I, March addresses both ecological processes of interaction and selection and genealogical processes of the transmission, retention, and retrieval of the "lessons of history," while Campbell focuses his attention on the implications of studying ecological selection processes at individual versus group levels of analysis. In the chapters in part II on intraorganizational evolution by Burgelman and Mittman, Miner, and Winter, ecological processes (e.g., internal selection of managers and projects) and genealogical processes (e.g., replication and modification of routines) within organizations— as well as their interactions—figure prominently. Among the chapters on organizational evolution in part III, Haveman highlights the influence of the ecological interactions among organizations in a population on rates of organizational change. The remaining chapters by Ginsberg and Baum, Levinthal, and Mezias and Lant examine the ecological interactions among organizations or among activities within organizations as well as genealogical processes related to the replication, imitation, and modification of organizational routines either within or between organizations. The chapter by Aldrich et al., which begins part IV, is primarily ecological in orientation, examining the effects of selection processes on population vital rates (i.e., founding, failure, and change). The other chapters in the population evolution section attend to processes and events in both ecological and genealogical hierarchies. Amburgey et al. show how an organizational population can be split into distinct forms (i.e., speciate) as the result of disruptive selection processes. Delacroix and Rao implicate ecological processes of reputation-building and infrastructural development and genealogical processes of social learning and imitation in the legitimation of organizational forms. Freeman and Lomi and Zucker and Kreft go one step further and examine the interaction of genealogical and ecological processes. They do this by examining the ecological consequences of institutional processes that create the conditions for the production and persistence of organizational forms. In the community evolution section (part V), the three chapters by Barnett, Brittain, and Baum and Singh present ecological studies of the mutual interactions among populations and between populations and their environments within organizational communities. The chapters by Rosenkopf and Tushman and Van de Ven and Garud attend to both ecological processes of selection as well as genealogical processes of variation and retention in the evolution of new institutional, technological, and organizational forms.

Challenges and Emerging Themes in Organizational Evolution

There is a need to specify more clearly the nature of organizational evolution. Approaches are diverse, ranging from Darwinian to more Lamarckian views, as well as a variety of others (see March, chapter 3, this volume), although the meaning of the term "evolution" is rarely stated explicitly. Indeed, McKelvey (commentary to part IV, this volume) observes that there may be as many definitions of organizational evolution as there are researchers. Clearly, there is a need for some consensus on a definition of organizational evolution. In our earlier discussion of the dual-hierarchy framework, which draws on recent thinking in evolutionary biology (e.g., Eldredge, 1985; Eldredge and Salthe, 1984; Salthe, 1985) and sociocultural evolution (e.g., Hull, 1988), we characterized organizational evolution as the complex interplays between two kinds of processes (interaction and replication) acting on two kinds of entities (ecological and genealogical) at a variety of levels of organization. Organizational evolution is the result of genealogical entities replicating, ecological entities interacting, the net effect of these interactions being the differential replication of the genealogical entities that produced them. From this view, elaborating the specification of organizational evolution requires an examination of how interactive processes of competition and mutualism studied in organizational ecology research are related to historical processes of information conservation and transmission. Given the extent to which our past achievements in organizational evolution are based on analogical thinking, we think attempts to specify processes of interaction and replication as they pertain to organizational evolution will profit from current concepts and models from evolutionary biology and sociocultural evolution. In addition to the ideas applied here, we think an examination of recent work in areas such as community complexity, stability, and coevolved patterns of diversity (Pimm, 1991; Pimm, Lawton, and Cohen, 1991), projective evolution (Campbell, 1985), cultural group selection (Campbell, chapter 2, this volume; Campbell, 1991; Soltis, Boyd, and Richerson, 1992), and replication of social organization (Csányi, 1989; Pantzar and Csányi, 1991), has a role to play in advancing our understanding of organizational evolution.

A second key challenge is the underexplored area of organizational taxonomy and classification. Until now, most researchers have defined populations as aggregates of fundamentally similar organizational entities (Carroll, 1984; Miner, 1991). While this approach has provided a practical and productive starting point, a more thoroughly grounded evolutionary approach is needed. What is required is a theory of organizational differences that provides a conceptual framework for describing and understanding organizational diversity. Development of a theory of organizational differences requires research examining the causes of stability and change in organizational entities at a variety of levels of organization and the forces isolating different entities from each other. Amburgey, Dacin, and Kelly's study (chapter 12, this volume) of disruptive selection is pathbreaking work in this area at the level of the organizational form. Taxonomy and classification research grounded in a theory of organizational differences would assist in decomposing populations of organizational entities into their separate and potentially countervailing subpopulations, and permitting incorporation of variation in models of population dynamics and intraorganizational evolution (e.g., Baum and Singh, 1992, 1993; Miner, 1990, 1991). Understanding the role of variation is central to an evolutionary theory of organizations. Differences in the adaptive capacities of organizations within a population provide the basis for processes of selection and population change. This research would also provide a theoretical framework for sampling that produces better-defined and replicable samples, increasing the applicability of research findings (McKelvey, 1982; McKelvey and Aldrich, 1983).

A third and closely related challenge is the development of an understanding of the structures of organizational inheritance. In the dual-hierarchy framework, two classes of processes, interaction and replication, characterize the ecological and genealogical hierarchies, respectively. Although the mutual interactions among ecological entities (e.g., jobs, work groups, organizations, and populations) have received considerable research attention, with few exceptions, processes related to the production of new genealogical entities (e.g., routines and organizations) from old remain largely unexplored. Whereas biological inheritance is based primarily on the propagation of genes, inheritance processes for social organizations appear very different and suggest evolutionary dynamics strikingly different from those expected with purely genetic transmission. And, as we pointed out earlier, although it may not be feasible to seek direct genetic analogies, if current organizational diversity is to be interpreted as a reflection of a long cumulative history of variation and selection (e.g., Hannan and Freeman, 1989), then an explanation of how organizational forms come to be different and remain different through time is required. We foresee an approach that embodies a preponderance of Lamarckian inheritance mechanisms in the sense that production and organizing competence acquired through learning can be *re*transmitted. Such social learning–related inheritance mechanisms have the added advantage of easily admitting change in individual organizations and attending to the hierarchical nature of organizational evolution (Singh and Lumsden, 1990). Research on organizational inheritance processes would support inquiry into organizational phyletics—tracing out the origins and evolutionary lines of descent of organizations.

In addition to some key challenges identified previously, which future research would do well to attend to, it is important also to note some of the themes that have emerged in recent work (including this volume). Here we comment briefly on three such themes that, in our opinion, also constitute promising avenues for the future.

A first emerging theme concerns the hierarchically nested nature of organizational evolution emphasized in the dual-hierarchy framework. Much earlier research had focused on single particular levels of analysis. For example, the key focus of organizational ecology research on the density dependent of founding and mortality rates (Hannan and Freeman, 1987, 1988a) was at the population level, and Miner's (1990, 1991) innovative work on evolving jobs dealt mainly with jobs per se. But more and more work recognizes the value added by paying explicit attention to the nested nature of multiple levels of analysis in the study of organizational evolution. Several chapters in this volume elaborate on this theme in some way (e.g., Campbell; March; Burgelman and Mittman; Winter; Shapira; Ginsberg and Baum; Levinthal; Mezias and Lant; Amburgey, Dacin, and Kelly; Freeman and Lomi; and Zucker and Kreft). It is our view that a more complete view of organizational evolution would benefit significantly from pursuing this theme.

A second important emergent theme concerns ideas that attempt to synthesize aspects of the ecological and genealogical hierarchies of the dual-hierarchy framework presented earlier. From an evolutionary standpoint, history and current function are intricately related. Yet, for the most part, earlier research had tended to focus on one hierarchy or the other. Thus, for example, the emphasis of most work in organizational ecology was related to the ecological hierarchy (e.g., Hannan and Freeman, 1989). On the other hand, the work on evolutionary economics (Nelson and Winter, 1982) was much more concerned with the genealogical hierarchy. Exceptions were rather rare; for example, Levinthal (1991b) combined an ecological focus on age dependence in mortality rates with the contribution of learning processes to inertia, which is a basis for selection. However, several chapters in this volume take such a synthetic approach (for example, those by Burgelman and Mittman; Miner; Winter; Ginsberg and Baum; Levinthal; Mezias and Lant; Delacroix and Rao; Freeman and Lomi; and Zucker and Kreft). This direction holds significant potential for enrichment of research on organizational evolution. We think further pursuit of the emerging convergence of ecological, institutional, and organizational learning theories in several recent analyses (see, for example, Mezias and Lant, chapter 10, this volume) will help advance this synthesis.

Finally, the study of organizations using a coevolutionary approach appears to hold enormous potential. Since roughly the 1960s, the study of organizations as open systems has emerged as the prominent view in organization theory. Although each theory differs in the specific treatment of the environment, structural contingency theory (Lawrence and Lorsch, 1967), strategic contingency theory (Hickson et al., 1971), resource dependence theory (Pfeffer and Salancik, 1978), institutionalization theory (Meyer and Scott, 1983), and population ecology theory (Hannan and Freeman, 1989), all take such open systems views. Whether through processes of adaptation or selection or both, organizations, it is argued, become isomorphic with their external environments. Less studied systematically are processes by which organizations influence their environments, even though such a flavor does permeate some theoretical discussions (see, e.g., Pfeffer and Salancik, 1978). We think treatment of the environment as exogenous is a useful starting point and a relatively appropriate one when a system of variables is in equilibrium. But under different conditions, it is more useful to take a coevolutionary approach which eschews the usual focus on independent and dependent variables in favor of viewing each variable as influencing the other. Three chapters in this volume (Baum and Singh; Rosenkopf and Tushman; and Van de Ven and Garud) take coevolutionary approaches even though they focus on different phenomena. A coevolutionary approach may not add value to the study of all organizational phenomena, but we think there is considerable potential in the study of systems of relationships that are not in equilibrium and somewhat complex.

Notes

1. The main reason we are interested in using the ecological-genealogical analogy is practical. To the extent that organizational and biotic evolution are similar processes, we can examine well-developed concepts and models from evolutionary biology and explore how these con-

cepts and models, suitably modified, may illuminate organizational problems. We think the works of Aldrich (1979), Campbell (1965), Hannan and Freeman (1977, 1989), McKelvey (1982), and Weick (1979), among others, demonstrate the potential for such analogical thinking. However, we are as interested in the *disanalogies* (Boyd and Richerson, 1985; Nelson and Winter, 1982:11) between organizational and biotic evolution as in their similarities. If organizational and biological evolution were exactly analogous, organizational evolution would pose few interesting problems. Organizational evolution is interesting *because* there are important dissimilarities between organizational and biotic evolution.

2. Important questions of taxonomy and classification exist at intraorganizational and superorganizational levels as well (Baum, 1988).

3. Powell (1991:190) suggests that the failure to attend to the issues of institutional persistence and reproduction is a significant limitation of institutional theory as well.

4. Although, as Hull (1988:397–431) argues, biological transmission is not simple either. He suggests that, while we are familiar with the complexities of sociocultural transmission, we have an overly simple view of biological transmission.

5. Use of these terms by some organizational scholars differs from their use in biology. In biology, the punctuational hypothesis is that rates of evolution are accelerated by rapidly divergent speciation. Species are conceived to change little during most of their history, but events of rapid speciation occasionally punctuate this stability, resulting in concentrated periods of change (Eldredge and Gould, 1972). The punctuational model explains the rapid speciation as a result of the rapid appearance of new attributes in emergent populations (Stanley, 1979). By comparison, organizational conceptions of the punctuational hypothesis typically entail the progression of single organizations (Miller and Friesen, 1980a, 1980b; Tushman and Romanelli, 1985) or work groups (Gersick, 1988, 1989) through a pattern of alternating inertial and revolutionary periods of change.

6. We pursue this problem in the section entitled "Ecological and Genealogical Processes" in this chapter.

7. Salthe (1985) provides an excellent discussion of the general nature and structure of hierarchies.

8. Other organizational entities that may be relevant to evolutionary processes include repertoires (Simon, 1957), rules and programs (March and Simon, 1958), standard operating procedures (Cyert and March, 1963), strategies (Burgelman, 1983, 1990, 1991), dominant designs (Anderson and Tushman, 1990), dominant competencies and demes, (McKelvey, 1982).

9. The levels of the genealogical hierarchy are also linked by death processes. Deaths of genealogical entities are potentially a major source of asymmetry in this hierarchy (Campbell, 1974a, 1990). This is because the death of an entity at any level may result in the death of all its component *lower-level* entities. For example, the death of a species implies the deaths of all that species' organizations, and the death of an organization can kill off (but need not) all that organization's routines. However, the reverse is not also true. We think the death of lower-level entities will, in general, have a far less profound effect on upper-level entities than is the converse.

10. For a more detailed discussion of routines and their replication by organizations, see Nelson and Winter (1982:96–136).

11. Boyd and Richerson (1985:43) have compared such "rules of behavior" to the contingent effects of genes that lead to different phenotypes in different environments.

12. For more detailed discussions of mechanisms that act to isolate or segregate the transmission of production and organizing knowledge of different kinds of organizations, see Baum (1989:25–33, 44–48), McKelvey (1982:196–202), and Hannan and Freeman (1989:53–57).

I

INTRODUCTORY ESSAYS

2

How Individual and Face-to-Face-Group Selection Undermine Firm Selection in Organizational Evolution

DONALD T. CAMPBELL

A fully optimistic evolutionary theory of the firm and our encompassing economic institutions is patently wrong. We must avoid Herbert Spencer's passive panglossian evolutionism: Let things alone and everything will optimize. Nor must we adopt the interventionist's optimism, for when one intervenes by changing laws or discount rates, and so on, one is changing the selective system in many ways, most often unanticipated, and often destructive. We must avoid these extremes by a more complete and more vigorous selectionism. One must examine *all* of the selective and retentive forces at work, *not just those that would predict improved adaptation.*

Where we find "clearly" effective organizational form, then selection at that level of organization, for that efficacy, is probably the best explanation. But this must not lead us into thinking that *all* selection processes lead to optimal organizational form. There are also selection processes at all other organizational levels. Those at the individual and face-to-face-group levels may lead to firm-level dysfunction, and may be parasitic or entropic in effect.

This chapter is strongest in presenting the evolutionary and sociobiological issues I feel are most relevant to the evolutionary dynamics of business organizations. I will concentrate on two complexities, already encountered in the application of selection theory (or a panselectionist orientation) in biological and cultural evolution: (1) individual versus group selection (or, more generally, the conflict over selection at different levels of organization), and (2) vicarious selection (selection by proxy-variable). After presenting these issues, I will speculate (with much less competence) on applications to the organizational theory of business firms.

"Groups Are Real" Versus "Methodological Individualism"

Methodological individualism dominates our neighboring field of economics, much of sociology, and all of psychology's excursions into organizational theory. This is the dogma that all human social group processes are to be explained by laws of individual behavior—that groups and social organizations have no ontological reality—

that where used, references to organizations, and so on, are but convenient summaries of individual behavior. So pervasive is this dogma that even in a group of social scientists focused on laws of social organization (such as those represented in this book and in the exciting conference it represents) adhere to it, or at least have not self-consciously rejected it. To get into the issues of this chapter we must reject methodological individualism as an a priori assumption, make the issue an empirical one, and take the position that groups, human social organizations, *might be* ontologically real, with laws not derivable from individual psychology. Indeed, some principles of organizational form cannot be in any sense attributes of individual persons. One of my favorite early papers (Campbell, 1958) explicitly sides with that strident minority of sociologists who assert that "Groups are real!" even though it finds human organizations "fuzzier" than stones or white rats.

Group Versus Individual Selection in Biological Evolution

A dogma somewhat similar to individual selection dominates evolutionary biology, although here it is argued on empirical and theoretical grounds, rather than as a methodological a priori: Evolutionary change is produced only by the selection of individuals, rather than by selection by demes, populations, species, or organized social groups. In my pioneer paper that provides the slim justification for my appearance in this book, I was unaware of this issue (Campbell, 1965a), and in a contemporaneous paper (Campbell, 1965b) I naively assumed the biological group selection of traits adaptive for organized social groups. Since then my contributions to the theory of cultural evolution and sociobiology have emphatically adopted the general rule of the dominance of individual selection, at least in most vertebrates. It was Williams' (1966) great book that turned me around. In abbreviated form, the biologist's argument is as follows:

While group selection no doubt occurs, its effects are undermined by individual selection. For example, individuals may sometimes have genes that lead to effective, group-survival-enhancing, self-sacrificial altruism. The chances of survival of the group as a whole are improved because of their presence. But the net benefits of this group-selection are greatest for the nonaltruists. For the altruists, their group-selection gains are reduced by the risks they run. No such costs, but only the benefits, accrue to the nonaltruists. Thus the relative frequency of non-altruists increases in the group in future generations. This obstacle to the biological evolution of self-sacrificial altruism has been noted since Haldane (1932). I summarize the problem by the phrase "genetic competition among the cooperators."

The social insects provide a contrast with vertebrate sociality that serves to dramatize the problem. The ants, bees, and termites are *more* social than any vertebrate, save urban humankind. They communicate and cooperate more effectively. Their soldiers are more unambivalently brave, their workers more unambivalently dutiful. These cooperators are sterile. "Genetic competition among the cooperators" has been eliminated, and because of this, selection for the effectiveness of the organized-social-unit is *not* undermined by individual selection. This fascination with the ultrasociality of the social insects and the role of sterility is old-fashioned, 1880–1930. (See Campbell, 1975.)

I should warn of my unorthodoxy at this point. The dogma of *only-individual-selection* is currently so strong that the leading theorist of social evolution, William Hamilton (1964), denies any role to selection-by-colony (nest) for the social insects. For this, and subsequent discussion, the reader needs two technical concepts, for which I offer nontechnical definitions. *Inclusive fitness* refers to the individual organism's "fitness" defined in terms of the proliferation of that individual's genes in future generations, whether achieved by the individual's own fertility or by that of close relatives sharing those genes. (I find that I use this term as a substitute for "self-interest," as a sociobiological expansion of self-interest to include nepotism.) *Kin-selection* refers to the furthering of inclusive fitness through the fertility of kin. To oversimplify Hamilton, the sterile worker furthers her own inclusive fitness by increasing the fertility of her mother or sisters. For Hamilton, such kin selection is *sufficient* to explain caste sterility in the social insects. In contrast, while I join those who regard kin-selection as a prerequisite to the ultrasociality of the social insects, I do not find it sufficient. Colony or nest selection is also essential. So important is the point that I borrow from some previous documentation:

> E. O. Wilson (1968, p. 41) says, "In fact, colony selection in the social insects does appear to be the one example of group selection that can be accepted unequivocally." Boorman and Levitt (1980) explicitly define group selection so as to exclude the social insects: "Mating does not normally take place between reproductives produced by the same social insect colony. Insect colonies are therefore not reproductively closed populations and accordingly cannot be treated as demes for the purposes of group selection. In turn, this means that group selection is largely ruled out as an explanation of most cases of insect sociality (pp. 13–14)." However, they do not mean to rule out selection by cooperating social unit. In fact they also say, "If selection is mostly at the colony level, workers can be altruistic to the remainder of the colony (p. 41)." While they do not explicitly mention that "net selection primarily at the colony level" can only take place when selection at the individual worker level has been eliminated, it is probable that they would agree.
>
> J. B. S. Haldane, the most explicit founder of the individual-selectionist emphasis, was clear on the special case of the social insects in his founding book: "In general, qualities which are valuable to society but usually shorten the lives of their individual possessors tend to be extinguished by natural selection in large societies unless they possess the type of reproductive specialization found in social insects. This goes a long way to account for the much completer subordination of the individual to society which characterizes insects as compared to mammalian communities" [Haldane, 1932:130]. (Campbell, 1983:21)

The individually selectionist orthodoxy is being challenged (e.g., D. S. Wilson, 1983; Sober, 1984; Wilson and Sober, 1989). But I am *not* challenging it for most vertebrates, for whom genetic competition among the cooperators (with the resulting severe limitations on biologically based cooperation and self-denial) sets the problem that moral norms have been socially evolved to solve (a partial, incomplete solution). For the social insects, however, the scenario involves biological evolution by means of colony selection.

Attention to the social insects reveals the great obstacles to complex social coordination that are produced by genetic competition among the cooperators. The social

insects have achieved ultrasociality by the drastic route of sterility among the cooperators. The only nonhuman vertebrates that achieve some degree of ultrasociality
are the African naked mole rats, and they, like the social insects, achieve this by
sterility among the cooperators (Sherman, Jarvis, and Alexander, 1991; Honeycutt,
1992; Sherman, Jarvis, and Braude, 1992). Socially organized human beings achieve
much greater ultrasociality than do the naked mole rats—much greater division of
labor, collective action, self-sacrificial bravery in warfare, fully comparable to those
of the most caste-ridden of the ants. And we do this *without sterility among the cooperators*. There results a continual ambivalence as well as a continual competition
between the individual goals of the members and the goals of the social organization
of which they are a part:

> The natural instinct of aggressiveness in man, the hostility of each one against all
> and of all against each one, opposes this programme of civilization. . . . Why do the
> animals, kin to ourselves, not manifest any such cultural struggle? Oh, we don't
> know. Very probably certain of them, bees, ants, and termites, had to survive for
> thousands of centuries before they found the way to those state institutions, that
> division of functions, those restrictions upon individuals, which we admire them for
> today. It is characteristics of our present state that we know by our own feelings that
> we should not think ourselves happy in any of these communities of the animal
> world, or in any of the roles they delegate to individuals (Freud, 1930, pp. 35–36).
>
> In principle, the whole system of ant aggression is clearly designed to ensure
> complete peace within the nest and merciless hostility to all potential rivals of the
> community as a whole. There could not be a more complete contrast with monkey
> bands, more prone to internal dissension than war, or human communities, oscil-
> lating between civil and foreign conflict, and requiring every encouragement of mass
> redirection to make them engage in warfare. (Russell and Russell, 1968:236)

Cultural Group Selection of Social Organizations

Accepting the dogma of *no biological group selection of human traits,* I (Campbell
1975, 1979, 1982, 1983, 1991) have attributed the capacity of organized human
beings for ultrasociality to cultural evolution. I have argued that the culturally
evolved moral norms are predominantly preaching against the very sort of personality that biological individual selection would produce—tendencies for selfish and
nepotistic cheating on the social contract, free-riding and freeloading on the altruistic
products of others, etc. This argument has been made more plausible by the very
important theoretical work of Boyd and Richerson (1985).

Of the many important features of their great *Culture and the Evolutionary Process,* I will make use of only one: conformist frequency-dependent nonlinear (mul-
tiple-parenting) transmission ("conformist transmission" for short). Like their major
predecessors (Ginsberg, 1944; Waddington, 1960; reviewed by Campbell, 1965a),
Boyd and Richerson note that cultural evolution makes use of cross-lineage borrowing (they call it "multiple parenting") in sharp contrast with biological evolution
(save for a few isolated exceptions). Under conditions of ecological diversity and
migration, they find, it would be optimal for the learners to adopt the majority (or
plurality) position of the mentors (i.e., the "conformist" version of frequency-depen-

dent cultural transmission). (Their demonstration of advantageousness assumes individually beneficial traits.) Add to conformist transmission the condition of stable small groups semiisolated from each other. In a dozen generations, these groups will be moved to internal homogeneity on all traits. Chance pluralities on neutral traits will become polarized into near-unanimities. In different groups the chance pluralities will be in different directions, in a cultural analogue of genetic drift.

Several points can be noted about this outcome. Cultural unity on a trait need not be interpreted as a product of adaptive selection. Cultural differences between nearby tribes need not be interpreted as adaptations to different ecologies. This is a great emancipation for the believer in cultural evolution. Previously (in my 1965 model) my anthropology friends would challenge me. "In our people, twins are put to death at birth. In the neighboring people, twins are given special treatment and reared for shaman roles. Both live in the same mosquito-ridden yam culture. Are you going to claim that this can be explained as different adaptations?" (Nancy and Phil Leis, personal communication). Cultural evolutionists have been at least as much burdened by excess adaptationism as have the sociobiologists criticized by Gould and Lewontin (1984). Indeed, such excesses in the interpretation of culture have been the major reason for the rejection of the older functionalism in sociology and anthropology.

The new functionalism which I advocate attempts to prevent this excess adaptationism by requiring for each functionality which is posited a plausible selection process at the organizational level of the function (Campbell, 1974a, 1990a). This new restrained functionalism is greatly helped by the nonfunctional, or afunctional explanation of intracultural uniformities which the Boyd and Richerson (1985, especially chapter 7) model provides. This new functionalism does, however, still retain the concept of "latent" functions (functions not obvious to those who practice and transmit the custom, or rationalized by them in other ways), even though it was the concept of latent function that so relaxed the self-critical discipline of the old functionalists, making it possible for them to treat *every* feature of archaic and contemporary societies as functional. Now with Boyd and Richerson's help, functional theorists are forced to distinguish between "accidental" cultural uniformities and "selected," or functional, ones. This distinction requires that a plausible theory of selection at that functional level be provided. The functional level upon which this essay focuses is that of the coordinated social group.

These "neutral" homogeneities within groups, in the context of sharp differences between nearby groups, provide the possibility of group selection. But (expanding on Boyd and Richerson) they almost certainly have an additional function whatever the specific content of the homogeneity, and even if this function was not involved in the selection for the difference. Trivers (1971) in one of sociobiology's most important papers has presented the concepts of "reciprocal altruism" and "moralistic aggression." Reciprocal altruism is also the key to Axelrod's (1984) influential book on the evolution of cooperation. For Trivers and Axelrod, the tendency to form reciprocally altruistic cliques (whose members on successive occasions trade off in being altruistic to the other) is explicable in terms of purely individual considerations. The reciprocal altruist pairs or cliques are precarious, and vulnerable to selfish defection. For them to emerge requires long-lived individuals, who are likely to encounter the same specific others again and again, and who have the capacity to identify and remember the specific others. Given these conditions, an innate readiness to form such cliques could emerge. Trivers posits that under such conditions there would also evolve an innate tendency to "moralistic aggression" against partners who violated reciprocity.

It has been pointed out (Campbell, 1979:42–43; Brewer, 1981) that a culturally inherited membership in such a reciprocal altruist pact would reduce the risks involved in negotiating a new one. It would be in the biological inclusive fitness interests of the biological parents to force such culturally inherited membership upon their offspring. All group uniformities on trait-specifically neutral features would be useful signs of comembership in such a reciprocal altruist pact. *Easily perceivable* homogeneities in dialect, dress, rituals, and scarification would be particularly useful. Thus the Luo of Kenya knock out two front teeth of their men, while the adjacent Kipsigis enlarge a hole pierced in their ears to a two-inch diameter. Moralistic aggression becomes death-to-traitors in this functional explanation of the roots of tribal ethnocentrism.

From this point of view, the accidental in-group homogeneities produced by conformant cultural transmission play a role comparable to that of the unique nest and hive odors of ants, bees, and naked mole rats. They provide signals as to who is to be admitted and who excluded. The complexity and integration of the ingroup cooperative system seem to require sharp group boundaries. As a result, the ingroup homogeneities (and, therefore, the sharpness of the intergroup differences) are no doubt sharpened beyond what conformant transmission would produce, further enhancing the possibilities for cultural group selection.

It is the internal group homogeneity and intergroup variability which set the stage for group selection, were any of the traits involved to provide a group level advantage. This is a central concept for the cultural evolution of group attributes, ideologies, organizational traditions, and so on. It is important to emphasize that this is an organized (or at least face-to-face) social group (rather than some nominal group, type, species, etc.). It is important to emphasize that this is a selection of culturally transmitted, not biological, attributes. (For biological evolution, this chapter tentatively accepts the dogma of the dominance of individual selection.) Groups (social organizations) can "die," with all of their biological individuals joining other groups, becoming converted to other ideologies and organizational structures. Defeated groups can retain continuity of biological personnel but adopt a new religion or political structure. The selective process could be pure emulation by unsuccessful groups of successful. Or it could be the forcible imposition of the victor's culture upon the vanquished. Biological extinction of weak groups, excess biological fertility of successful ones, could also further the selective reproduction of ideologies but is not essential. The "group selection" posited is a selection of culturally transmitted beliefs, social-organizational structures, religious ideologies. It is not a "group selection" of genes. This cultural organized-social-group selection would make possible social norms and behavior that lead individuals to override their own *individual* maximization of "inclusive fitness." (Such overriding might lead to the maximization of the *average* individual inclusive fitness of the members of the group, but the only-individual-selection dogma precludes a biologically innate tendency to achieve this.) I believe that such culturally based group selection of norms and organizational forms has taken place. It is thus with regret that I noted that the most recent analysis of the problem by them (Soltis, Boyd, and Richerson, 1992) reduces the likelihood. Nonetheless, I will persist in assuming it in the remainder of this chapter.

Three more evolutionary concepts are needed before getting into my speculations on the evolutionary theory of the firm.

Face-to-Face-Group Solidarity

Groups of persons who are regularly in face-to-face contact develop an in-group solidarity and have the power to discipline, to reward and punish, even the designated leader of the group, in the service of the collective interests of the group. Theory of social groups (and the theory of the business firm) should pay particular attention to these face-to-face groups (the "primary groups" of the older sociology). As I have argued (Campbell, 1982), social control through culturally transmitted moral norms with sanctions is no longer efficacious, and legal controls were never effective without such support. What is left is primary group mutual inhibition, and this is likely to work against, rather than for, the purposes of larger collectives.

Even though the primary message of my chapter requires a continual ongoing conflict between behaviors that optimize organized groups and behaviors that optimize an individual's personal and nepotistic interests (which I pose as a conflict between the products of biological and cultural evolution), I do not want to deny that our biological evolutionary history, way back into its prehuman primate roots, has been increasingly social, and that our biological human nature contains innate adaptations furthering some forms of sociality (possibly the products of biological group selection). The earlier discussion of Trivers' reciprocal altruism refers to several possible biological adaptations, innate tendencies to forming reciprocally altruistic cliques (clique selfishness); moralistic aggression; and pressuring of one's offspring into group conformity. The following quotation presents mutual monitoring as a double-edged sword for the theory of organizational control:

> *Mutual monitoring* covers most of the "primary group" or "face-to-face-group" social controls described in the older sociology. The anthropological concept of "shame" culture overlaps. Primate sociality as reviewed by Boehm (1982), Goodall (1982), Gruter (1982), and Itani (1982) exists at this level. . . . The ecological study of human facial expressions, the autonomic nervous system and hormonal reactions associated with face-to-face disapproval, opinion-minority status and lying all fit in here.
>
> In my judgment, it will turn out that many of the mechanisms that make mutual monitoring effective are stubbornly innate in human beings, and that they can be counted on to be at work creating a kind of ingroup solidarity, homogeneity of belief, and discipline in even arbitrarily assembled aggregates of persons who repeatedly interact in small groups. Indeed, research on social processes in experimental and social psychology laboratories shows that such group formation processes begin to occur in as little as two hours. This fact is of extreme importance in understanding the dynamics of bureaucracy and large-scale organizations, but is still overlooked in human organizational theory.
>
> In practice, reciprocal altruism can be translated as *clique selfishness.* While it may be true that a complete theory of games analysis would show cooperation to

be mutually beneficial even if everyone were in the cooperating group, in practice, reciprocal-altruist pacts and the inhibition of parasitical free-riding by mutual monitoring are most common and most feasible for small groups, as the economist Olson (1968) has shown. In addition, both the lower primates and humans achieve their group solidarity in a context of competition with, or threat from, other groups of conspecifics. The formation of an ingroup solidarity is always accompanied by an outgroup hostility, as ubiquitously noted in studies of ethnocentrism (LeVine & Campbell, 1972). One of the most ubiquitous principles of that literature is that ingroup social control is enhanced under conditions of outgroup threat.

It is the common circumstance of modern social organization, in public or private bureaucracies, that they are made up of many separate face-to-face groups, connected by messages and messengers. It follows from our mutual monitoring principle that each face-to-face assemblage tends to become an ingroup whose solidarity tends to be motivated by treating other units as outgroups. . . . Given human nature, both as observed and predicted from evolutionary tendencies, such occurrences are not occasional, isolated instances, but are unavoidable, universal tendencies. If they fail to produce major problems for large organizations it is because other factors keep them in check, not because they are absent.

Thus *mutual monitoring* as a means of social control is effective at the small group level, but can easily become organized around purposes that are contrary to the larger group's collective interests. Keeping these interests co-aligned is one of the major unsolved problems of organizational design. Max Weber gave us a theory of bureaucratic rationality that failed to take these processes into account. Some such optimistic assumption that "as it is planned so shall it be carried out" seems endemic among legislators and administrative designers as even larger bureaucratic structures get created. Yet actual studies of bureaucracies (e.g., Blau, 1963) support the popular concept of inflexible, lethargic, self-serving bureaucracy. Sociobiology thus provides two grounds for predicting distortions of bureaucratic rationality. The first is the individual's selfish and nepotistic biases, particularly biassing when exemplified by those in high administrative rank. The second is this clique selfishness, the tendency for face-to-face ingroup formation with clique solidarity interests athwart those of the larger collective. (Campbell, 1982:435–36)

Creative Thought as a Source of Group Adaptations

While my basic model is supposed to work *even if* the group-to-group variations upon which selection operates have been generated at random, I do not mean to exclude "intelligent" variations such as Boehm (1978) has emphasized. While I am notorious in evolutionary epistemology for my stress on *blind* variation, my nested hierarchy of blind-variation-and-selective-retention mechanisms explicitly incorporates creative thought:

1. A blind-variation-and-selective-retention process is fundamental to all inductive achievements, to all genuine increases in knowledge, to all increases in fit of system to environment.

2. The many processes which shortcut a more full blind-variation-and-selective-retention process are in themselves inductive achievements, containing wisdom about the environment achieved originally by blind variation and selective retention.

3. In addition, such shortcut processes contain in their own operation a blind-variation-and-selective-retention process at some level, substituting for overt loco-motor exploration or the life-and-death winnowing of organic evolution. (Campbell, 1960:380)

Creative thought is a prime example of such a short-cut process using fallible vicar-ious selectors, as envisaged in points 2 and 3. Not at all do I deny the importance of creative thought. But I insist upon an explicit model for how it operates and require that this model fit in with radical selection theory (Campbell, 1990b).

Innovations coming from the "intelligent" problem solving of leaders would of course still have to be cross-validated in group-versus-group competition. Such creative problem solving is not based on "reality" directly, but only on incomplete memory and simplified extrapolation. Even where wise, the wisdom reflects past realities, not the current or future ones directly relevant to group survival. Boehm (1978) finds such processes even in primates. Certainly when we come to business firm–level adaptations, creative thought rather than blind chance will most often be the source of the group-level variations upon which selection of firms operates. I have expanded natural-selection analogies into a general selection theory, and from this expanded perspective, the occurrence of intelligent planning as a source of group-level adaptations is not in conflict with our shared evolutionary perspective.

Vicarious Selectors

A final addition to my evolutionary toolkit is the concept of vicarious selectors. For this I can go back to that first paper which earned me my invitation to this conference volume:

> A major emphasis of the more general model (e.g., Campbell, 1956, 1959, 1960) is that in the course of evolution, both biological and social, more economical vicarious exploratory and selective systems have been evolved where they were possible. It is also important that each of these vicarious systems embody within themselves the three essentials of a blind variation process, a selective criterion, and a retention-propagation process. Thus instinct-formation involves a trial-and-error of the life and death of whole mutant animals. A learning process may end up providing a very comparable behavioral repertoire, but does so by trial-and-error of responses within the lifetime of a single animal, and using memory rather than genetic structure as the storage process. The encounter with environmental realities is now more indirect, being represented by pleasure and pain senses, the activation of which winnows out the responses. The indirectness is indicated by such illustrations as the rat's willingness to selectively retain responses leading to non-nutritive saccharine. (Campbell, 1965a:41–42)

The communications systems of the social insects can be subsumed under vicarious selectors:

> The economy of cognition is clearly shown in the scouting activities of the social insects in which the trial-and-error encounter of a food supply by one worker leads to a direct locomotion to the food by the other workers. In the ants, this may be

mediated by a scented back-tracking. In the honey bees, it is achieved by a linguistic instruction. Through the wagging-dance described by Frisch (1950) the successful scout indicates range and course, so that the other worker bees can fly directly to the new food source. Here too, honesty and trust or the functional equivalents are required. Hives with scout bees that keep the good news to themselves, or that dance of non-existent treasures, or that give erroneous bearings, undoubtedly occur from time to time, and fail to survive. Similarly, trust, gullibility, belief, or their functional equivalents are required of the recipients of the messages, and have survival value even if occasionally deceived. The ecological pressure of the economy of cognition keeps honesty and trust as effective values. It is hard to see how it can be exploited without them. (Campbell, 1965a:45)

But in human social organizations the group-level selection system which keeps valid the vicarious selectors (message honesty and trust) is likely to be absent.

Applications to the Evolutionary Theory of the Business Firm

In the remainder of this chapter, I will be speculatively applying the framework presented previously to possible applications to the theory of business organizations. In these conjectures, I will be much less well informed than in the first part of the chapter. It may well be that what I suggest has already been done. If not, then I offer sketches of issues that I believe would profitably be examined by future scholars seeking to exploit more fully the implications of an evolutionary approach to organizational dynamics. But I will not be providing any of that scholarship.

The pattern of argument in what follows is to get away from the all or none question of whether or not firm-level, cultural group selection ever occurs; to assume that it sometimes does; and then to speculate on how different conditions would favor its occurrence and retention, versus allow group-level selections to be eroded by individual and face-to-face-group optimizing. Just because I am likely to neglect the point in my dialectical pessimism, correcting the overoptimism of the past, readers should also be reminded that many firm-level innovations will be favored by both firm and individual selection and will *not* involve the conflicts on which I focus.

Firm-Level Selection of Firm-Optimal Firm Organization

This awkward title is intended to be an unambiguous label for the point of view that the competition of business firms, with selection by bankruptcy and by voluntary going-out-of-business, systematically selects for organizational forms, rules, collective atmospheres and customs that *improve the longevity and prosperity of the firm, per se* (with no necessary relation to the optimization of the economic well-being of the CEOs or other individual personnel). This point of view is a subspecies of the view that there are general principles of better and worse industrial organization and management (e.g., such as might be taught in schools of business, and departments of business policy, management, and organizational behavior). Firm-level selection is one proposed explanation of how such superior traits might come to be prevalent. While this point of view is being challenged (Amburgey, Kelly, and Barnett, 1990; Baum, 1990b; Baum and Oliver, 1991; Delacroix, Swaminathan, and Solt, 1989;

Miner, Amburgey, and Stearns, 1990; Singh, House, and Tucker, 1986; Singh, Tucker, and Meinhard, 1988; Swaminathan and Delacroix, 1991), even in the present volume (see the chapters in parts II and III on intraorganizational and organizational evolution), firm-selection-for-firm-longevity is a prevailing assumption of our area, going back to its founders (e.g., Weick, 1969; Aldrich, 1979; Hannan and Freeman, 1977, 1984; McKelvey, 1982). This perspective abrogates methodological individualism in favor of giving ontological status to at least some social organizations.

Geoffrey Hodgson (1991, 1992, 1993), in contributions that all readers of this book should attend to, notes (1991) that Hayek has explicitly abrogated his explicit methodological individualism to adopt firm-selection and (1992) that our most influential methodological individualist Milton Friedman (1953:22) seems also to have done so in arguing the general likelihood of rational optimality in the behavior of firms. The distinction between Hodgson's important and well-informed work and my position is that his argument for group selection at the level of the firm seems to depend to a considerable extent on accepting the point of view of those few evolutionary biologists who argue for the existence of biological group selection, implicitly even for human beings. To some degree, I am in sympathy as long as we are left with selfish and nepotistic individuals who as members of a firm will unconsciously and consciously tend to undermine the products of firm-selection in the direction of their own well-being and that of their families—ambivalence about duty to the firm will adequately serve my purposes, and I do not expect that Hodgson would disagree with what follows. (Herrmann-Pillath, 1991, and Pantzar and Csanyi, 1991, provide further examples and generous citations to the contemporary European ferment in evolutionary theories of the firm.)

My basic assumption is one of potential conflict between (1) the interests of the firm per se and the interests of each individual at every level of the organization; (2) the interests of one person and his or her colleagues at every level in the organization; (3) organizational levels within the organization; and (4) face-to-face groups within the organization. The first two have already been discussed. It is usually in each individual's best interests if all other group members dutifully behave so as to maximize the firm's interests, and only oneself be the selfish free-rider (or the one who distorts one's behavior in favor of maximizing self and family over firm). The third I will not elaborate here, but will merely point to the special privileges that strata or specialties seek out for themselves, clique selfishness transcending organizational bounds, illustrated by the self-serving solidarity of lawyers across firms and by the U.S.S.R.'s special-privilege private stores available only to the nomenclatura, the higher levels of the bureaucracy. The fourth is a second manifestation of clique selfishness, but so important organizationally that it needs separate description.

Conditions Favoring the Acquisition and Retention of Firm-Level Adaptations

A thorough survey of the literature on cultural evolution, and especially Boyd and Richerson (1985), is needed. In advance of that, here are some preliminary observations.

A large number of similar firms, operating in a similar ecology and with stable selection over long periods, is needed. Neighborhood laundries are a better setting in which to look for cultural adaptation than large conglomerates with heterogeneous subunits. "Populations" are required for the adaptive stabilizing by negative feedback. Contrariwise, if there are very few units, and if these are imitating each other's innovations before validating selection by differential bankruptcy has taken place, a runaway positive feedback can occur that can be establishing nonadaptive or even deleterious traits.

Whereas for the numerous small firms in the parallel ecologies, bankruptcy can probably be assumed to be selecting on average for competence (we need to look at the very small adaptive selection ratios, the very large chance component, employed by the population geneticists for adaptive effects in biological evolution), for the large heterogeneous conglomerates, subfirms may be protected from the bankruptcies they deserve. Very large firms in few-firm environments (think of Chrysler for automobile manufacture, Lockheed for aircraft) may have the political power to be saved from overdue bankruptcies. And leveraged buyouts may bankrupt firms in deliberate efforts to milk them of cumulated capital symptomatic of their prior organizational adequacy.

In Boyd and Richerson's models, the conditions for group selection are best when the shift of individual persons from firm to firm is low. (This both increases the likelihood of firm-to-firm differences, the raw material for selection, and preserves adaptive differences once selected.) One thinks immediately of the much greater personnel stability in Japanese firms. Does the unionization of an industry increase the firm-to-firm exchange of personnel? And through union standards, reduce firm-to-firm differences upon which selection can operate? Are not privately held firms more likely to create the conditions for the firm-level selection of adaptive variants? Do shareholders have interests in dividend level and stock market prices that are inimical to firm-level adaptations? What is the effect of professional CEOs who have no identification with the firm's tradition nor the specific industry? Does the professional training of business administrators support the spread of firm-level adaptations in net? Or does the resulting homogeneity reduce the raw material of firm-level differences upon which firm-level selection can operate? Does the world's highest level of pay for U.S. CEOs reflect the real value of the individual differences in managerial skill (in contrast to firm traditions or optimal managerial policy, i.e., firm-level adaptations), or does it reflect the cumulate effect of the individual interests of executives as a class, in the absence of firm-level adaptations that would curb such excesses?

Hiring executive-level personnel from the most apparently successful rival firm in the same industry would seem to be an important means of diffusion of firm-level adaptations, *when the selection is based upon the firm's reputation*. When based upon the individual executive's reputation, the adaptive value may be more problematic: Too frequently the individual executive's reputation is based upon his or her success in *introducing* a change, and the hiring away (or promotion within) takes place long before the gains or harms from the change can be ascertained. (This discussion overlaps proxy variables and vicarious selectors, discussed later.) Note that success in introducing an innovation (whether or not it has firm-level adaptive value) is so generally regarded as a symptom of executive efficacy that a new head of a department or firm feels called upon to make changes whether needed or not, often destroying valuable practices and replacing them with inferior ones. Thus mythology about individual managerial ability is inimical to preserving firm-level adaptations.

Diffusion of a Firm-Level Adaptation

A firm-level adaptation of considerable efficacy due almost certainly to creative thought is illustrated in the following case, which is worthy of a Ph.D. dissertation or a major monograph if it has not already been done. While a first-term assistant professor at Ohio State University (1947–50), I was affiliated with Carroll L. Shartle's Leadership Studies program. While most of the research was supported by, and done in, the U.S. Navy, Shartle was also working with the local Farm Bureau Insurance Companies. They were undergoing a major internal reorganization that had originated with the Prudential Insurance Company of Newark, New Jersey, and was gradually spreading west to other insurance companies, a major firm-level adaptation that reputedly cut the number of clerical employees needed by one third or one half. Whereas previously the clerks and typists had been organized into work groups by type of work done (new accounts, claims, billing, etc.) with the result that the work groups were not comparable, in the new arrangement each clerical section did all types of work for a small group of agents and their clients. There resulted 20 or so work sections that were highly comparable. This enabled higher management to offer prizes to the most efficient sections, and to put pressure for greater productivity on the supervisors of the worst performing sections, a section scoring and pressure that had not been possible under the previous arrangement of work assignment. (An analysis of the retention of this innovation once adopted might provide a case study of the erosion of a group-level adaptation by the cumulate effects of the individual preferences of the typists and the supervisors, although the later computerizing of the bulk of the clerical work might make such retention studies uninterpretable.)

What would add zest to such a study is the fact that a once famous study of leadership styles and group efficacy (Katz, Maccoby, and Morse, 1951; Kahn and Katz, 1962) was done in the Prudential offices after the change. As naive experimental psychologists rather than cynical streetwise sociologists, the researchers were pleased by the excellent quasi-experimental conditions they found (numerous quite comparable sections and weekly group productivity records) and never asked why these were in place. In comparing the "leadership" behavior of the supervisors of the high-productivity sections with that of the low-productivity sections, they naïvely assumed that the leadership behavior caused the productivity, rather than the reverse; that the poor productivity of the section, combined with the weekly humiliation and the pressure from higher management, caused the leadership behavior. Many features of their findings, plus the knowledge that the reorganization had greatly increased section efficiency, support the hypothesis that low group productivity caused leader behavior: Low-productivity section supervisors did more typing themselves, were less lenient in granting time off for family emergencies, and so forth. The plausibility of my interpretation is increased when it is noted that a subsequent experimental transfer of the supervisors of high-productivity sections failed to transfer the productivity that had previously characterized them (Morse and Reimer, 1956).

How Management Information Systems Lose Their Validity

While these comments probably apply to all management information system (MIS) control variables, I have in mind especially internal reporting systems, self-reports, evaluations of others, and evaluation of subgroup status and products. All such MIS systems produce "proxy variables" that are componentially (and/or factorially) complex, with not all of the components that determine scores relevant to the variable the indicator is intended to monitor. Once any such proxy variable becomes used in managerial control, "irrelevant" components that will produce the desired score come to dominate, and validity is undermined. There is a longstanding literature on the harmful effects of setting quantitative goals in U.S.S.R. Five-Year Plans, in U.S. employment agencies, and so on. The classics are Ridgeway (1956) and Blau (1963). The literature is reviewed by Campbell (1979:83–86) and Ginsberg (1984).

While I am a distant observer of the field, it is my impression that MacNamara's introduction of "scientific management" into government in the 1940s and 1950s (PPB and S) and its successors in government and industry, such as "management by objective," implemented by "MIS" has greatly increased the red-tape paperwork of standardized reporting forms at all levels in government and business, forms that those filling them out and receiving them regularly suspect of invalidity and irrelevance. Once again, I suspect that the forms have been designed by worldly-unwise experimental psychologists who assume that the only motive in filling them out is to report accurately. Instead, our evolutionary analysis leads us to expect at least the following three motives:

1. To describe accurately. (There is widespread evidence of a general preference for not lying if nothing else is at stake. If this is innate, is biological group selection required to explain it?)
2. To influence the decisions one anticipates will be based upon the reporting form in one's personally preferred direction.
2a. For the good of the firm.
2b. For the good of one's own face-to-face group within the firm or the individuals within it (e.g., too favorable evaluation of face-to-face group subordinates).
2c. For one's own well-being and that of one's family (job retention, promotion).

Once the use of such reporting forms has been routinized, we would have to expect that motives 2b and especially 2c will dominate.

In 1988, I borrowed nine texts in MIS from my business school colleagues, hoping to pick up the most used. Of these, seven (Cash et al., 1988; Hartman et al., 1968; Laudon and Laudon, 1988; Mathews, 1981; McLeod, 1986; Mintzberg, 1979; Prince, 1975) had no discussion of the problem at all. Anthony et al. (1984) had a few pages of attention to the problem. And even though Rappaport (1982) reprints Ridgeway's (1956) classic article, plus his own important analysis of the problem (Prakhash and Rappaport, 1977), no awareness is shown in the other selections which make up 80 percent of his collection.

Vicarious Indicators of Firm Effectiveness

In public stock companies, the evaluation of the CEO is done on a short-term basis using indicators of firm effectiveness such as dividend size and value of stocks on the stock market. It becomes essential for the CEO's short-term job maintenance and bonus magnitude (individual selection) that these imperfect proxy variables of firm longevity, growth potential, and long-term profitability (firm-level selection) be kept at high readings, even at the expense of underlying long-term firm-level efficacy. Thus maintenance and modernization of production facilities are deferred in favor of short-term "profitability." The U.S. steel industry provides a shocking example when viewed close up (e.g., Strohmeyer, 1986). In their concept of "information inductance," the tailoring of recordkeeping and reporting to the desired decisions wanted from the important information recipients, Prakhash and Rappaport (1977) have provided a valuable analysis of firm-level indicators and their modification by anticipated use. The fact that they imbed their analysis in a general systems theory should make it assimilable to our evolutionary perspective.

The environment of taxation, regulation, tariffs, and foreign labor costs is also an important part of the ecology of organizational evolution. (It may seem as though evolutionary concepts have been expanded to cover too much. For me, what is important is a very general "selection theory," and its call to examine what is actually being selected for at each level of individual, subgroup, and firm-level selection of courses of action. Within that totality, my main emphasis, from current evolutionary theory and sociobiology, is on the conflict between optimizing the person-family system versus the firm-level system.)

Firm-Level Organization Adaptations to Keep Face-to-Face Group Interests Aligned with Firm Interests

In most of this chapter, I have made use of but two levels of organization, two levels of selection. In my general framework (Campbell, 1990a), I posit a node of selection for each node of organization in a complex, hierarchical organization such as a firm and would recognize several intermediate levels between the individual-family system and the firm. Of intermediate levels, the face-to-face work group, within which persons spend the great bulk of their working hours, seems to me of particular importance.

The face-to-face group, or the primary group as it has also been called in the older sociology, is likely to have been the level at which biological evolution produced innate mechanisms of social control, as reviewed previously. Laws and religious belief systems are cultural, not biological, adaptations and characterize early city-states, and so on, combining many primary groups (Campbell, 1982, 1991). The face-to-face groups a person regularly participates in have a powerful ability to control individual behavior and to create a group solidarity at this level.

As has been noted, the mutual monitoring, nonverbal and verbal expressions of approval and disapproval, most naturally is devoted to creating solidarity in favor of the face-to-face group's preferences for comfortable, pleasant working conditions. In the sociological literature, this has been observed to include punishing (ostracizing) those who work too hard, the rate-busters. Higher management can be seen as an out-group (just as can customers, or groups in different buildings). It is conceivable that unions, strikes, and labor/management conflict also predispose this alignment of face-to-face-group interests against those of higher management and/or (not synonomously) those of firm-longevity.

Firm-level inventions which would correct such misalignment would be of great value. Sidney Winter (chapter 6, this volume) draws our attention to "quality groups," and they may represent such a firm-level innovation controlling face-to-face group undermining of firm-level interests. Japanese management techniques (even if learned from Elton and Mayo, or Roethlisberger and Dickson) that reward and punish the face-to-face work group *as a whole,* as with bonuses and with fines for imperfectly assembled products, would mobilize the mutual-monitoring always available, for the purposes of improved product quality and perhaps productivity. (It is, of course, in the spirit of this chapter to predict that such innovations will be under strong erosion pressure from the persistent individual and face-to-face-group preferences.)

It is perhaps surprising that this collective-product organizational device should emerge from the recent decades' most successful capitalists. In December 1985 I lectured at a hydraulic pump factory in Shanghai to a scientific management group which included a few faculty from business and engineering universities, the factor managers, and a few leaders of the Shanghai labor unions. It was at the most open and optimistic period of the first Deng reforms. The agricultural communes had been disbanded and the land leased to individual farmers who were free to sell surpluses in privatized markets. This had greatly increased the food available in the big cities and made prosperous the farmers living near them (as shown by new two-story masonry houses on the farms and motorcycles for the farmers' sons). An enthusiasm for individual incentives had spread to the industrial sector, along with artificial and probably dysfunctional "worker of the month" awards to one member of the face-to-face work group. (My U.S. China-watching colleagues were already reporting that wise supervisors were promising that each member of the work group would get this award in turn.) But none of these problems had affected the group I lectured. They were shocked to learn that individual incentives were absent in the typical U.S. assembly line, and to learn of the shift to collective sanctions in the modern Japanese management techniques.

The use of evolutionary theory in management science should not be limited to cultural evolutionary analogues focused on the selective survival of firms. It should also pay attention to the human nature produced by biological evolution, especially by the genetic competition among the cooperators so conspicuously absent in the ultrasocial social insects and the naked mole rats. This mixture of cultural-level of group selection and biological individual selection means that firm-level adaptations will be under continual undermining pressures from individual and face-to-face group preferences.

3

The Evolution of Evolution

JAMES G. MARCH

In the organizational research literature the word "evolution" is ordinarily used in a relatively narrow sense, referring to a set of ideas about change in a population through variation and selection of a particular sort. In the present essay, that usage is located in an older and larger context in order to explore some implications of the evolution of evolution that are not limited to Darwinian natural selection models but extend to a wide range of theories of organizational adaptation.

The arguments are simple: As ideas about evolution have developed, they have moved from outcome conceptions of evolution to process conceptions. They have moved from conceptions of evolutionary processes as "efficient" instruments of adaptation to an appreciation of their "inefficiencies." And they have moved from an emphasis on using evolutionary theories to predict history to an emphasis on the engineering of history.

Evolution as Outcome and Process

Evolution as an Outcome of History

One traditional meaning of "evolution" is ordered change in species, individuals, or social systems. Within this meaning, historical sequences are not arbitrary. Rather, the state of an organism, organization, technology, or society at any particular time is a "natural" step in an historical path. Evolutionary history is described in terms of such natural developments, and theories of evolution are theories of these ordered paths.

In this spirit, we describe the development of the human embryo, observing how it evolves along a path toward a recognizable human being. Or we describe the development of the human species, observing how it evolves along a path of increasing capability. Or we describe the development of organizations, human civilizations, technologies, science, or knowledge as evolving through a set of orderly stages that can be observed in histories of similar units of adaptation. These paths of develop-

Research for this essay, first presented as a talk at New York University, was supported by the Spencer Foundation and the Stanford Graduate School of Business. I am grateful for the comments of Derek Scissors and Jitendra Singh. The style of a talk, without references, has been retained here.

ment can be seen as unfolding toward a destiny that is implicit in the unit that is developing or in its environment or both.

In theories of historical progress or in theories that trace the elaboration of a technology from a vague idea to a finished and economically successful product, the destinies reflect relatively exalted states. Ordered change is described as leading from relatively simple structures to more complex ones, from relatively crude practices to relatively sophisticated ones. Evolution is described as following a path of greater and greater elaboration, beauty, civility, or fit with the environment. The essential element, however, is not that development leads to higher and higher states but that it inexorably leads somewhere. For example, theories of entropy, as found in some theories of information "development" by transmission through a series of channels, are theories of inexorable degradation. They presume that the evolutionary destiny of information is noise.

Evolution as a Process of History

"Evolution" is also used to refer to the processes that produce history. The development of a species, individual, organization, or society occurs through a set of historical mechanisms. Much of contemporary interest in evolution is in describing the mechanisms that generate a path of history. These include reproduction, learning, choice, imitation, and competition.

Many of the most common ideas about the evolution of institutions and organisms have historically been ideas that describe the present state of an institution as implicit in its future. For example, the evolution of the embryo can be seen as an unfolding in the biological present of the future destiny of the infant. The forms and procedures that an organization uses in the present can be seen as shaped by expectations and intentions for the future.

The logic is anticipatory. Change stems from the imposition of the future on the present. Engines for the process are found in conceptions of destinies and necessary steps toward their fulfillment. The destinies may be imagined to be inventions of human actors, in which case the theory is one of rational individual or institutional choice, reflecting wills, desires, and intentions. Alternatively, the destinies are sometimes portrayed as extrahuman, in which case evolution is seen as teleologically linked to usefulness within some ultimate purpose or design.

The idea that organisms evolve in order to achieve their destinies is embedded deeply in the history of thinking about evolution and still retains vitality in contemporary talk about evolution. Most such ideas were originally linked to conceptions of "God's will" or "the unity of nature," and evolution was associated with improvement in the fit between organisms and institutions and God's vision. More recently, God's will has been replaced for the most part by the will of individual humans. The idea that the expectations and willful actions of human beings enact the future into the present is a central presumption of much of modern social science. It is reflected in theories of rational action, including theories of rational conflict (e.g., game theory), in theories of strategic action, and in theories of power. The substitution of the intentions of individual human actors for the intentions of God retains a conception of history as being a realization in the present of necessary steps toward a preexistent destiny.

A second set of ideas about the evolution of organisms and institutions emphasizes the ways in which the present is a residue of the past. Present organisms and institutions are summaries of past experience. For example, the evolution of a population can be seen as the coding in the biological present of the past reproductive experience of members of the population. An organizational past can be seen as imposing itself on the present through retention of organizational experience in organizational routines.

The logic is not anticipatory but historical. The past is retained in rules that guide the present. The possible adaptive units in history-based evolution are any that can be imagined to accumulate information from history, but the more familiar examples in practice include such elements as gene pools, individual organisms, organizational forms and routines, cultures, institutions, or systems of knowledge. The fact that some of these evolving units are nested in other evolving units is a troublesome complexity.

Historical processes by which the present encapsulates the past are the mechanisms of modern theories of evolution, as found in theories of learning, culture, and natural selection. The theories differ, most conspicuously in how they imagine the informational consequences of history to be sustained and diffused within a population of evolving units, but they belong to a common family. In each case, the past is experienced through a combination of exploration and exploitation. Exploration produces variety in experience (experimentation, variation, diversity). Exploitation produces reliability in experience (selection, consistency, unity). The engines of evolution include mechanisms for interpreting, retaining, transmitting, and retrieving these lessons of the experienced past.

The Efficiency of History

Expectations about the future and experiences of the past are both ordinarily seen as instruments of the environment. They match attributes of the unit of adaptation to attributes of the environment so that the former can be predicted from a knowledge of the latter. If (on average) expectations about the environment come to match the true environment, actions based on such expectations are implicit in the environment. If (on average) experience in the world leads to forms and actions that come to match the environment, such forms and actions are implicit in the environment. This is, of course, the first thing that a child learns about any kind of evolutionary theory, namely, that an organism or institution adapts to its environment.

In early forms of evolutionary theory (e.g., in the ideas of Alfred Russel Wallace) the environment was seen as imposing itself primarily through scarcity. Where an environment was relatively munificent, environmental pressure was weak and the tie between an organism or institution on the one hand and its environment on the other was loose. In organization theory, this notion has its counterpart in concepts of environmental munificence and organizational slack. Slack buffers an organization from fluctuations in resource availability in its environment, thus weakening immediate environmental pressure. One of the major contributions of Malthus and subsequently Darwin was to recognize the role of competition for environmental resources in tightening the control of the environment over the evolution of species.

Competition plays a similar role in organization theory, but its effects are often complicated by the extent to which organizations use satisficing, rather than optimizing, decision rules.

For much of the history of evolutionary thinking, the competitive processes of history were seen as efficient. That is, they were seen as leading to unique and stable equilibria that were (in some relatively uncomplicated sense) optimal. As a result, evolutionary outcomes were treated as unambiguously implicit in environmental conditions, and the distinction between talking about evolution as a process by which experience is encoded and used (learning, development) and talking about evolution as a mechanism for maximizing fit (performance, maturity) was unimportant. A process that encoded experience in a reasonably systematic and adaptive way was assumed to lead to improvement in fit and ultimately to the one best fit. This was Spencer's vision, and it continues to be a familiar one in the modern literature.

The litanies are familiar. Given competition among intentional actors trying to do well, rationality drives organisms or institutions to behavior that is both uniquely determined by the environment and optimal. Given competition among learning actors trying to improve, learning drives organisms or institutions to uniquely optimal behavior. Given competition among actors selected by differential reproduction, selection drives a population of organisms or institutions to a mix of behaviors uniquely matching the environment. Although the manifest procedures may appear to reflect any number of kinds of adaptive processes, the competitive coercion of the environment assures that evolutionary outcomes are implicit in the environment and are optimal.

Inefficient Histories

Assumptions of efficient histories are appealing, but they are assumptions that have long been suspect. Many of the developments in modern understandings of evolutionary processes involve identifying the inefficiencies of history, the many ways in which evolutionary outcomes are not implicit in evolutionary environments or are not optimal. They highlight the dangers in confusing outcome and process meanings of evolution.

Histories in Exogenous Environments

The history by which organisms or institutions evolve within exogenous environments makes the realization of uniquely required optimal outcomes problematic. There are *lags in matching*. Evolutionary adaptation (e.g., incremental learning, selection) takes time. Although we might imagine that evolutionary processes act to improve the match between the current form of an organism or institution and the environment, there is no guarantee that convergence will have been achieved by any particular time. If the environment changes, there is not even any assurance that adaptation will be fast enough to improve the match.

There are *multiple equilibria*. Most theories of learning or selection are theories of local adaptation. They assume a process in which relevant factors are localized in time and space. Considerations that are close in time and close in cognitive or organizational distance dominate those that are more distant. Such adaptation is essentially "hill-climbing," responding to local feedback, and is subject to becoming stranded at any one of a number of local (rather than global) maxima.

There is *path dependency.* Many models of evolutionary processes represent them as branching processes. The outcomes in a particular environment depend not only on that environment but also on previous environments and the ways in which they have been experienced. The historical path makes some outcomes unrealizable in the future, including some previously realized. Relatively unlikely events, if they occur, change the structure in permanent ways. History is nonrecursive, dynamic, and nonlinear.

There are networks of *diffusion.* Outcomes depend on the ways in which the information from historical experience spreads. Evolutionary processes of diffusion (e.g., sexual reproduction, networks of management consultants) create information structures that isolate some parts of the population and produce outcomes (e.g., speciation, cultural differentiation) attributable to elements of isolation and integration. In the organizational context, this makes the outcomes of an evolutionary process sensitive to patterns of connection in information networks, to changes in information technology, and to the ease with which information is incorporated into receiving organizations.

Histories in Endogenous Environments

One of the more important post-Aristotelian developments in evolutionary theory is the emphasis on endogenous environments, on the ways in which the convergence between an evolving unit and its environment is complicated by the fact that the environment is not only changing but changing partly as part of a process of coevolution.

There is *mutual adaptation* between the unit of evolution and the environment. Rats learn from experimenters, but experimenters also learn from rats at the same time. Through experience, organisms learn what parts of the environment are exploitable by them. But the exploitability of the environment changes as a result of the experience. Organizations receive social approval or disapproval as a function of adopting particular practices. But the level of approval or disapproval shifts as the number of organizations adopting the practices changes. These forms of mutual adaptation are likely to lead to stable outcomes that are not uniquely predicted by the initial environment.

Units of adaptation are located within *ecologies* of other units. Organisms and institutions exist in communities of other organisms and institutions. Their histories are intertwined by competition, cooperation, and other forms of interaction. These interactions considerably complicate the idea of evolution. History cannot be seen as simply a product of the organism and its own exogenous environment. Species coevolve, as do institutions.

Units of adaptations are *nested,* so that some adapting units (e.g., individuals) are integral parts of other adapting units (e.g., organizations). The structure of relations among them arises from an interaction among the various nested units responding to a shifting environment and their own internal dynamics. These features of organization considerably complicate any multilevel evolutionary story.

Implications of Inefficient Histories

The idea that history is a locally adaptive, branching process with multiple equilibria is a central feature of modern biological theories as well as theories of organizational change. There is considerable ecological complexity, and how the various units of evolution fit together is significant to the development of each and to the collective course of history.

History is portrayed as a meander. There are irreversible branches, thus path-dependence and decisive minor moments. The branch-points, involving such factors as mutations, mating, communication contacts, and fortuitous opportunities often seem almost chancelike in their resolution, yet decisive in their effects on subsequent history. Though the path of development is explicable in terms of a comprehensible process, the realized course of natural evolution is difficult to predict.

When history is pictured as a path-dependent drift rather than a unique developmental path implicit in the environment, the link between evolution as an outcome and evolution as a process has to be demonstrated rather than assumed. History as a process is not guaranteed to have a unique, optimal result. It may have a unique equilibrium that is nonoptimal. It may have multiple "optimal" (in a Pareto sense) equilibria. Rationality (as a process) may or may not lead to decisions uniquely required by the decision situation. Conflict (as a process) may or may not lead to uniquely predicted resolutions. Learning (as a process) may or may lead to forms and practices uniquely required by the environment. Knowledge accumulation (as a process) may or may not lead to a uniquely appropriate comprehension. Natural selection (as a process) may or may not lead to uniquely adapted species.

This innocent change has some significance for thinking in history and social science. Much of the style of social science is basically comparative statics, the exploration of the ways in which individual behavior, institutional practices, and cultural norms match the demands of the environments in which they are found. The basic strategy is to predict features of the units of adaptation (organisms, institutions, cultures) from attributes of their environments. The "invisible hand" of evolution is imagined to provide the link. Conspicuous examples in organization theory are the various forms of contingency theory, from studies of technology and structure to transaction cost analysis.

A meandering, locally adaptive history provides only a relatively weak link between attributes of the environment being adapted to and attributes of the units doing the adapting. Differences among institutions are traceable not only to differences among their contemporary environments but also to a history of interaction with a changing environment. That history is one in which each step is both problematic and decisive in defining possibilities at the next step.

A connection between environmental conditions and evolved forms remains, and under some circumstances the process may yield a match that is broadly predictable. For example, despite a speciation process resulting in considerable history-dependent species heterogeneity, there are observable consistent differences between water-based species and land-based species. Similarly, despite cultural differentiation resulting in considerable history-dependent organizational heterogeneity, there are observable consistent differences between market-based organizations and those based on political constituencies.

These consistent differences are important, but inefficient histories undermine the strong "functionalist" tone of many modern interpretations of comparative institutions. Implicit presumptions of historical efficiency underlie much of the literature on organizational structure, comparative organizations, the economics of organizations, and organizational change. Their inferences depend on a unique matching between evolutionary processes and evolutionary outcomes that is not assured.

The Engineering of Evolutionary History

A meandering evolutionary history is not easily predicted. Its course depends on the sequence of particular historical branches that are realized along the way. Precisely for this reason, however, it is possible to imagine decisive intervention in history. The classic case is the breeding of species. By managing mating, critical branch-points of biological evolutionary history, breeders change species in decisive ways. Similar examples can be drawn from the evolution of cultures (e.g., colonial intervention), the evolution of knowledge (e.g., the introduction of the printing press), and the evolution of political systems (e.g., the introduction of instruments of governance). In each case, relatively conscious attempts have been made to transform units of evolution by intervening in the evolutionary process. In each case, there have been major effects. History has been changed.

Engineering Basics

The natural speculation is that organizations, like species, can be engineered. The idea is not that any imaginable organization can be designed and built but that natural developmental processes of organizational histories can be affected significantly by relatively small, timely interventions. The engineering of evolution involves understanding those processes well enough to intervene in history and produce organizational effects.

Our theories of organizational evolution provide some basic strategies for intervening in history. They include three broad kinds of interventions. The first involves altering the possibilities for *transmission, retention, and retrieval* of the lessons of history. The invention of the printing press, the construction of computer data bases, and the institutionalization of professional standards are conspicuous examples. The second kind of strategic intervention involves altering the *structure of interactions* among units of evolution. Increasing the intensity of competition or the patterns of cooperation is a conspicuous example, as is the building or breaching of organizational boundaries. By shifting the structure of interactions, we change the advantages that accrue to alternative organizational forms or practices. The third kind of strategic intervention involves managing the *exploration/exploitation balance*. Manipulating the level of risk taking, or the salience of diversity relative to unity, or the amount of organizational slack is a conspicuous example of the ways by which history can be affected by changing the level of variation or the effectiveness by which lessons and opportunities of the environment are exploited.

Ambiguities of Improvement

Producing effects is necessary for engineering, but it is not sufficient. Engineering is not simply the art of making changes. It is the art of improvement. The engineering of transportation is an effort to improve outcomes by intervening in the processes of movement. The engineering of health is an effort to improve outcomes by intervening in the processes of disease. The engineering of history is an effort to improve outcomes by intervening in the processes of history. We ask not only whether we can produce change—which within a branching, meandering history may be relatively easy—but whether we can produce change that can be relied on to be an improvement.

Engineering traditions have ordinarily treated the definition and measurement of improvement as unproblematic. In fact, of course, improvement is difficult to define and measure, and every experienced engineer knows it. If one accepts the dictum that an engineer is simply an agent of a client, there nevertheless are numerous occasions on which engineering involves trying to persuade a client that a desired change involves long-term or second-order consequences that may be unacceptable. If one adds the stricture that good engineering also involves attention to broader social concerns and virtue, the conception of improvement becomes murky indeed. The history of engineering is cluttered with examples of steps that seemed to offer short-run improvements in some domains but in retrospect were deemed to have created greater problems in the long run or in other domains. Engineering history is filled with effects. It is also filled with unanticipated and complicated consequences.

Theories of evolution elaborate these ambiguities more than they resolve them. A central feature of evolutionary history is the way in which local or short-term improvements often turn out to be distant or long-term disasters. In ecologies of interacting and evolving units, improvements in the short-run survival prospects of one part of the system do not reliably lead to improvements in the survival prospects over the longer run or of another part.

These "social welfare" aspects of defining an objective function for evolutionary engineering are implicit in the "unit of adaptation" problem. That problem, as it is usually discussed, is seen as a problem for a descriptive theory of evolution. What is it that adapts to the environment? The individual organism? The gene pool? The species? The ecological community? Or in the case of economic organizations: The individuals? The firm? The industry? The market? The society?

The choice of unit is complicated by the fact that the units are nested in space and in time. Firms are nested in industries which, in turn, are nested in societies. The short-run future is nested in the long-run future. Adaptation involves a complicated mosaic of evolution over time by interacting nested units within an environment that is also evolving. Characteristically, the survival of a unit at one level and at one time is affected by the survival of a unit at another level or at another time. Contemporary disputes over "altruism" and over the role of phenotypic organization in evolutionary models are symptomatic of the difficulties.

These are profound problems for developing a descriptive theory of evolution. They are also profound problems for developing an engineering improvement or history. If evolutionary engineers are supposed to improve prospects for survival, they need to know for what part of a nested system they should make improvements, and over what portion of a nested future. Specifically, in an organizational context, it is not obvious that improvement is achieved by preserving any particular organization or organizational form. And there is no obvious metric for comparing long-run and short-run consequences. Theories of evolution make the difficulties clear without providing any clearer specification of improvements than do concepts of Pareto "optimality" in welfare economics or justice in political philosophy.

Strengthening Evolutionary Processes

Evolutionary engineers seem to be left with two possible approaches to improvement, neither fully satisfactory. The first is to emphasize strengthening evolutionary processes without any commitment to particular outcomes. This approach suffers a bit from obscurity about what it means to "strengthen" the processes, but a few things can be said.

For example, it is possible to argue that organizational engineering involves simultaneously improving the processes by which organizations seek out or generate new options (exploration) and improving their capabilities for implementing options that prove effective (exploitation). Organizations are engineered so as to facilitate experimentation and protect deviant ideas from premature elimination. At the same time, they are engineered to allow the identification, routinization, and extension of known good ideas. With inadequate exploration, an organization suffers from not having experiments with new options from which it can learn about new possibilities. With inadequate exploitation, an organization suffers from not eliminating bad experiments and not utilizing good ones.

An engineering strategy of maintaining a balance between exploration and exploitation is an attractive goal. Unfortunately, some of the more obvious mechanisms of adaptation accentuate, rather than reduce, imbalances between exploitation and exploitation. Organizations can be trapped in either excessive exploration or excessive exploitation through short-term adaptive responses to experience.

Exploration can become a trap for a failing organization. If failure usually leads to exploration and exploration usually leads to failure, an adaptive unit can be trapped in a cycle of exploration, trying one new thing after another without spending enough time exploiting any innovation to secure the gains from experience that are necessary to make it fruitful. When adaptive processes lead to a string of inadequately exploited experiments, they are likely to be improved by interventions that inhibit exploration.

Exploitation can also become a trap. The returns to exploitation tend to be more certain, more immediate in time, and more proximate organizationally than are those to exploration. Consequently, strategies of exploitation that lead to locally positive outcomes are likely to come to dominate exploratory strategies that are globally better. In this way, adaptive processes can easily tip the balance in favor of exploitation, toward excessive stability of organizational practices, forms, and technologies. In such cases, adaptive processes are likely to be improved by interventions that protect or stimulate exploration.

Although determining the optimal balance to be sought between exploitation and exploration is not ordinarily feasible in an organizational setting, it may be possible to anticipate some of these ways in which adaptive dynamics lead to imbalances. Such awareness is a basis for timely interventions based on knowledge about risk preferences, communication, and conflict in organizations.

Visions of Destiny

A second approach to defining objectives for evolutionary engineering involves identifying a desired course of history—a vision of progress. Few concepts in social theory are currently as disreputable as the concept of progress. Conceptions of human progress suffer from a consciousness of the many ways in which progress has historically been defined to confirm the virtue of a particular historical meander and particular historical accidents of survival, dominance, and subordination.

Moreover, the self-referential quality of evolutionary theory undermines the meaningfulness of conscious engineering for progress. Evolutionary engineers are part of the process in which they intervene—and their desires to intervene are as easily seen as a consequence of the process and as a factor in changing it. Seeing visions of progress as themselves part of the process that they are imagined to evaluate or control weakens their status as prescriptive commands.

Nevertheless, one point that seems obvious about human evolution is the persistence of human hope for engineering significance. For the most part, we have abandoned creationist myths and metaphors of God's will. But the will to intervene in history in pursuit of a vision of destiny is built deeply into our souls (or wherever such information codes are retained). Destiny myths of direction (the idea of vision and its implementation, the idea of strategic action) are important parts of contemporary human belief.

Conceptions of destiny do not exist in an evolutionary vacuum. For example, they can be pictured as having coevolved with human rational consciousness. In the presence of a myth of rationality, a myth of human destiny becomes a vehicle for exploration, and the two myths are jointly favored in a world in which exploration is precious. Such a coevolution argument provides a speculative explanation for the evolutionary dominance of ideas of destiny within our specific ideological path, but it is difficult to find justification for any particular vision of future destiny within a meandering theory of history. Indeed, the role of conceptions of destiny as vehicles of exploration would seem to speak to the desirability of conflict over changing conceptions of destiny rather than convergence on one.

Neither ideas of strengthening evolutionary processes nor ideas tied to specific visions of destiny can claim profound justification. Consequently, although evolutionary engineering often seems able to change the course of history, it cannot give assurance that the changes will be desirable. Relative to post hoc assessments of improvement, our interventions in history seem likely to be almost as haphazard as mutations.

Where We Have Been and Where We Are

Theories of evolution have become well-recognized frames for organizational analysis. The frames include theories of rational action, theories of rational conflict, theories of experiential learning, theories of confrontation and contradiction, theories of the development of knowledge, theories of variation and selection. They can be well specified; they can be translated into well-defined sets of procedures for observing and analyzing empirical data; they have been associated with a number of reasonable data sets.

These evolutionary theories carry their histories with them, and traces of those histories are sustained within our current thinking. Three conspicuous historical ideas have been mentioned: the idea of a prototypic developmental path with a preexistent destiny, the idea that process and outcome are closely connected, and the idea that evolutionary histories can (and ought to) be engineered.

For the most part, the meandering drift of thinking about evolution has moved away from the idea of a prototypic destiny and the idea that evolutionary processes have unique outcomes. Although there are regularities within an evolutionary process (e.g., the development of the embryo, the elaboration of forms of life), the course of history has no destiny and no fixed path. And although the evolutionary process involves processes of matching between environments and units of evolution, the outcomes of those processes are not uniquely defined by the environmental context. Nevertheless, conceptions of destiny and uniqueness are part of our linguistic and worldview baggage. Their marks remain in life-cycle stage theories of development and in the generality of comparative statics and functionalism as fundamentals of contemporary social science.

The evolution of evolution has, on the other hand, sustained and supported a vision of evolutionary engineering. Evolutionary theories of history are invitations to interventions in history. By emphasizing the path-dependent branching and local feedback of historical processes, evolutionary theories define opportunities for changing the course of history by relatively modest interventions at decisive places and moments. The possibilities have attracted people from cattle breeders to philosophers of science, from environmental and political activists to consultants in strategic management.

Small, precise changes can be imagined to be achievable by modest, timely interventions and to produce large, permanent effects. Small structural changes in organizations can be imagined to change the likelihood of such interventions and of their having significant consequences to the realized path of history. It is an appealing notion that grants a role to consciousness and thus fits comfortably within a human-centered ideology.

At least in the realm of organizations, however, we have to suspect that our judgments about which changes would be desirable are not likely to be very good. A conspicuous feature of our current condition is that we know enough about evolutionary processes to affect history significantly without knowing enough to be confident that the effects we produce will be intelligent ones. The complications of resolving the trade-offs across space and time are formidable, as is the frequency with which our models of evolutionary complexity are incomplete. Much of modern technological, biological, and social history is testimony both to those problems and to the capabilities of human beings for underestimating them.

II

INTRAORGANIZATIONAL EVOLUTION

4

An Intraorganizational Ecological Perspective on Managerial Risk Behavior, Performance, and Survival: Individual, Organizational, and Environmental Effects

ROBERT A. BURGELMAN AND BRIAN S. MITTMAN

During the last fifteen years, organization ecology has become a major paradigm in the study of organizations (e.g., Carroll, 1988; Hannan and Freeman, 1989). To date studies in organization ecology have been conducted primarily at the organization, population, and community levels of analysis, while phenomena within organizations have largely been ignored. This results, in part, from the fact that organizational ecology is premised on relative inertia of organizations, implying that change processes within organizations are largely irrelevant.

A few studies have used the logic of organizational ecology to examine phenomena within organizations. For instance, Langton (1984) has elucidated the evolution of the Wedgwood pottery firm in the United Kingdom; Miner (1990, 1991) has studied the role of idiosyncratic job development within organizations as a means of adaptation; and Burgelman (1991) has suggested an intraorganizational ecological perspective to explain the transformation of Intel Corporation from a memory company to a microcomputer company. These studies suggest that organizational ecology provides a powerful intellectual perspective which need not exclude the study of intraorganizational phenomena.

The research on intraorganizational phenomena has mostly relied on in-depth field studies of organizations. But such research is time consuming, and gaining access to sites is difficult. Hence, sample sizes have been small. To overcome the limitations of field research, some scholars have combined field research with survey methods (e.g., Bourgeois and Eisenhardt, 1988) while others have proposed laboratory experiments as a useful complement (e.g., Schwenk, 1982).

The approach taken in this chapter relies on computer simulation techniques to explore further ideas and conceptual frameworks generated by field research. Computer simulation has a distinguished history in the development of the behavioral theory of the firm and organizational decision theory (e.g., Cyert and March, 1963; Cohen, March, and Olsen, 1972; Hall, 1976; Levinthal and March, 1981; Hall and

Menzies, 1983; Herriott, Levinthal, and March, 1985) and is beginning to be used in strategic management as well (e.g., Silhan and Thomas, 1986; Lant and Mezias, 1990).

This chapter documents a series of simulation experiments using the CORPSTRAT model, a discrete event simulation model developed for studying individual and organizational decision making and related processes (Burgelman and Mittman, 1991; Mittman and Burgelman, 1991). The CORPSTRAT model is based on the formalization of a conceptual framework obtained through field research (Burgelman, 1983a, 1983b). This framework has posited a correspondence between strategy making in large, diversified firms and the variation-selection-retention paradigm of cultural evolutionary theory (Campbell, 1969; Aldrich, 1979; Weick, 1979). Strategy making is viewed as an intraorganizational ecological process in which variation derives from managers' initiatives competing for limited resources, selection is exerted through corporate context mechanisms governing resource allocation, and retention takes the form of a corporate strategy which defines the areas in which the firm has learned it can operate successfully (Burgelman, 1991). This framework also views the strategy making processes of a firm as an important part of the opportunity structure for managerial career advancement: managers understand that they can advance their careers in the firm through successfully proposing and completing strategic initiatives. Depending on their risk orientation they will decide, at any given time in the evolution of their career, to pursue such strategic initiatives in the *induced* or *autonomous* process. In the induced process, managers propose strategic projects—projects that commit a significant amount of the organization's resources— that fit with the current corporate strategy. In the autonomous process, managers pursue strategic projects that are outside the scope of the current corporate strategy. Induced strategic projects are less risky than autonomous strategic projects because they allow managers to take advantage of existing organizational learning. Autonomous projects involve new individual learning efforts.

CORPSTRAT provides a tool for studying the complex interplays between individual and organizational decision behavior under risk, corporate context, and environmental conditions, which cannot currently be captured by a set of mathematical equations amenable to analytic solution (Averill and Kelton, 1982). It also offers the opportunity to build on work concerning individual and organizational behavior under risk and decision framing (e.g., Kahneman and Tversky, 1979, 1984); March and Shapira, 1987; March, 1988a, 1988b), the role of organizational slack, (e.g., Singh, 1986; Bateman and Zeithaml, 1989) and sustainable growth, (e.g., Donaldson and Lorsch, 1983) in determining decision behavior, and research on organizational learning (e.g., Fiol and Lyles, 1985; Burgelman, 1988; Levitt and March, 1988; Ginsberg, 1990). The model also incorporates a conceptualization of environmental change adopted from organizational ecology (e.g., Hannan and Freeman, 1977; Freeman and Hannan, 1983).

Patterns and Processes of Managerial Risk Behavior, Performance, and Survival

Different theories of managerial risk orientation imply different fundamental behavioral assumptions. The general research question underlying the simulation experiments reported here is, How do managerial risk orientations, decision rules, and related behaviors affect individual and organizational performance?

The advantage of computer simulation models such as CORPSTRAT is that they can be run repeatedly and with different sets of behavioral assumptions. Assumptions about each of the decision processes included in the model can be readily varied, allowing the researcher to illuminate their causal connections and disentangle their separate and combined effects on outcomes at the individual and organizational levels. Such work may help better elucidate both the decision behavior of individuals and organizations in and of themselves, and the outcomes that result when individual and organizational decision behaviors interact under different environmental conditions.

The experiments reported here were designed to address the following specific research questions:

1. How do the frequency and pattern of environmental change affect the relationship between managerial risk orientation and performance?
2. How do firm-level decision rules and risk orientations influence these relationships?
3. How do firm-level outcomes depend on managerial risk orientations?

In addressing these questions we used the CORPSTRAT model in a series of formal simulation experiments. In the next section we provide a basic introduction and overview of CORPSTRAT. We then present the experimental design and analytical methods used to conduct the simulation study.

CORPSTRAT: A Computer Simulation Model of Strategy Making

Burgelman and Mittman (1991) provide a more thorough discussion of the theoretical and conceptual foundations of CORPSTRAT and details of its design. In the remainder of this section we describe key elements of the model, focusing in particular on those elements relevant to managerial risk behavior, performance, and survival.

Model Overview

Figure 4.1 provides an overview of the logic of the CORPSTRAT model. CORPSTRAT combines elements of descriptive and illustrative quasi-realistic simulation models (Cohen and Cyert, 1965). Its general structure is similar to Crecine's (1967) model of the municipal budgeting decision process: like the Crecine model, CORPSTRAT is a formal, abstract statement of a sequence of decisions and processes which recur annually in a business firm. For simplicity the model assumes a simplified discrete sequence of events, even though the decision behaviors, learning patterns, and other processes modeled in CORPSTRAT generally occur in a continuous, overlapping sequence. CORPSTRAT is currently implemented in a computer program written in BASIC and is run on a VAX under the VMS operating system. In the following

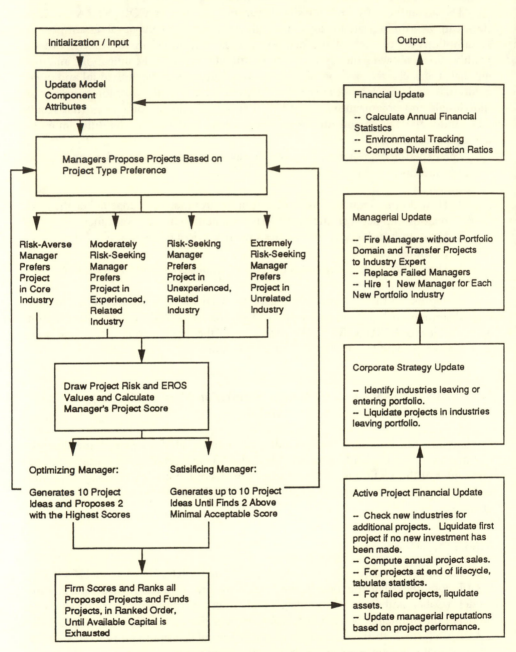

FIG. 4.1   CORPSTRAT computer simulation flowchart

sections we describe each element of the model, followed by the primary decision processes, learning mechanisms, and associated logic incorporated in CORPSTRAT. A complete listing of the CORPSTRAT code and a User's Guide are contained in Mittman and Burgelman (1991).

Model Components

The building blocks of CORPSTRAT are a set of model components which include the environment, the firm, projects, and managers. The *Task Environment* in CORPSTRAT consists of the set of product markets in which the firm operates. Markets are defined in a categorization system derived from the U.S. Standard Industrial Classification (SIC) system. In CORPSTRAT a set of 10,000 industries comparable in scope to four-digit SIC industries represent the basic classification. The industries are grouped into 100 two-digit groups. Each industry is broken down into 10 product market segments which correspond to five-digit SIC categories. As we discuss further later, the firm's productive activities occur within segments, while the firm's concept of strategy is operationalized at the industry and group level.

Each industry is characterized by a variable environmental munificence level. The frequency and amplitude of fluctuations in munificence (Freeman and Hannan, 1983) are determined by model parameters; their effects on individual- and firm-level outcomes can be studied experimentally. Munificence affects the rate of return the firm experiences in each industry, although this return is also affected by several other factors to be discussed later.

The *Firm* in CORPSTRAT consists of a corporate-level (collective) decision-making mechanism, a set of middle-level managers (individual decision makers) who oversee the firm's business activities, and a set of projects which comprise those activities. Individual middle managers' characteristics and decision-making processes govern initial selection and submission of projects for funding. Corporate-level decision rules constitute the firm's strategy and govern final project selection and funding.

A *Project* in CORPSTRAT consists of a specific new product development or an investment in the improvement of an existing product. All projects have a fixed 10-year life cycle and begin with an initial investment equal to a fixed percentage of total firm sales (generally 1 percent). Each project is confined to a single industry segment; the specific segment proposed depends on the characteristics of the manager generating the project, according to the rules described later. In addition to its segment, each project is characterized by two additional dimensions: risk and return. Return is operationalized by a project's annual return on sales (ROS), while risk is operationalized by variability in ROS. Each project has an expected return on sales (EROS) and a realized return. Realized ROS is affected by environmental fluctuations and by project risk, in addition to environmental munificence. The EROS and risk parameters associated with each project are drawn randomly from normal distributions, whose parameters vary with the characteristics of the manager proposing the project and the project's segment: projects in segments within the firm's core businesses are generally lower risk than those in segments outside the core businesses, for example.

The firm begins with an inital set of approximately 100 projects. During the course of a model run, these projects expire as they reach the end of their 10-year life cycle. New projects are generated by the middle managers, who propose these projects for corporate funding and then supervise those which are funded. *Managers* in CORPSTRAT are characterized by a reputation level, an expertise or experience level, and a preferred risk level. Each manager also has one or more areas of expertise. Each of these attributes can vary during the course of a model run. The firm begins with an initial set of approximately 20 managers, each responsible for one or more initial projects, and each generating one or more project proposals during every annual cycle in a model run.

A manager's area of expertise corresponds to one or more industries. Each industry has only one manager who is an expert in that area. Managers develop additional areas of expertise by proposing and leading successful projects in industries that are outside their current areas and outside the firm's current business portfolio. Managers can also lose areas of expertise. Managers who lose their sole area of expertise are fired and replaced by new managers. Managers are also fired and replaced when their reputations drop to zero. The characteristics of replacement (i.e., newly hired) managers are drawn from distributions determined by the characteristics of existing managers. This rule reflects a power or coalitional model of organizational behavior (Cyert and March, 1963); key decisions such as new hires are assumed to reflect the preferences of the existing set of managers, and hiring manager types in proportion to their current representation reflects the relative power of the current groups of managers. This proportional hiring rule is also consistent with the assumption that the existing composition of the managerial corps reflects the effects of enviromental selection pressures and therefore represents an optimal configuration for the current environment.

Managers and their staff generate proposals for new projects based on the manager's personal attributes each year. In general, risk averse managers favor projects within their areas of expertise and in other industries in which they have past experience. Each manager's exact preferences regarding new projects depend on such factors as the manager's reputation, risk profile, and other attributes, however. Project generation and proposal mechanisms are discussed later in greater detail.

Model Strategic Processes and Annual Cycle

Strategic processes in CORPSTRAT include individual-level project generation and evaluation mechanisms, firm-level project ranking and funding, annual updates of projects, managerial reputations, firm-level financial outcomes, and revisions of concept of strategy. Each of these is represented in the flow chart (see figure 4.1) and is discussesd in greater detail later in this chapter.

The annual cycle in CORPSTRAT consists of the primary processes shown in figure 4.1. These processes occur in a fixed sequence each year; during each year projects are generated, evaluated, funded, and tracked as their financial outcomes are realized. Project generation, evaluation, and funding involve decisions at the level of middle managers and at the level of corporate management. Individual middle managers evaluate projects generated by them or their staff and determine which they would like to propose for corporate funding. Corporate management evaluates projects proposed by middle managers and determines which will receive funding. Corporate-level rules also select projects for liquidation and determine how and when the firm's concept of strategy will be amended and how managers' reputations will be adjusted and how and when managers will be hired and fired.

The *Project Generation* process begins with the generation of new project proposals by middle-level managers and their staff, and the evaluation of these proposals by the middle manager. Four types of projects can be generated: (1) projects in industries that are part of the current corporate portfolio and in which the manager already has existing projects and expertise (core business); (2) projects in industries which are outside those encompassed by the current portfolio but in which the firm has existing activities which have yielded positive results and which are located in groups containing industries that are in the current portfolio (experienced, related industries); (3) projects in industries in which the firm has no direct experience, but has positive experience in other industries located in the same group as the project's industry (unexperienced related industries); and (4) projects in industries located in a group in which the firm has no previous experience (unrelated industries). Managers avoid generating projects in industries outside the current business portfolio which have yielded negative experience in past activities.

New projects have three primary attributes: industry segment, expected return, and risk. The industry segment is selected randomly from the set of industries meeting the criteria listed earlier for the four project types. For example, if manager x generates a core business project, the project's segment will be one of the 10 segments associated with one of the manager's areas of expertise. The EROS and the project risk value are drawn from normal probability distributions. EROS is drawn from the same distribution for all project types, while risk is drawn from a distribution corresponding to the project type, and then adjusted according to the manager's experience in the project's industry. Projects generated and pursued in the induced process (core business projects) are less risky than projects generated and pursued in the autonomous process (related and unrelated industry projects), since induced projects benefit from the accumulated knowledge and experience the firm possesses in industries in its business portfolio. Thus, the risk value for induced projects is drawn randomly from a normal probability distribution with the lowest mean.

The risk associated with autonomous projects is randomly drawn from one of three normal probability distributions whose means are a function of the firm's experience with that particular segment: The mean risk for experienced related projects is less than the mean risk for unexperienced related projects. The latter, in turn, is less than the mean risk for projects in unrelated industries in which the firm has no previous experience. The risk value drawn from the appropriate distribution is then further reduced according to the manager's experience in the project's industry; the amount of reduction is directly proportional to the amount of experience. The standard deviations of the risk distributions for autonomous and induced projects are the same.

The type of project generated by each manager depends on that manager's present risk attitudes, or *Managerial Risk Behavior.* Induced projects allow managers to pursue new activities with very little risk. Autonomous projects allow managers to pursue activities with greater risk; these projects also allow managers to compete with each other in industries outside the current business portfolio and to develop additional areas of expertise. The mix of project types each manager favors depends on the manager's risk attitude or risk orientation.

Managers' strategic behavior is assumed to reflect their desire to maximize their performance and reputation. Performance and reputation are associated with material and symbolic rewards and affect managers' chances to continue to garner support for their projects. A manager's success, however, depends not only on the particular strategies he or she pursues, but also on those being used by other managers and the relative frequency with which each is employed. CORPSTRAT thus incorporates Cohen and Machalek's observation that "the dynamics of social interaction among strategists become a crucial force shaping emergent patterns of behavioral diversity" (1988:472).

From the perspective of individual managers, the induced and autonomous strategic processes can be considered part of the organization's opportunity structure for career advancement. Induced strategies represent the least risky opportunities for advancement in the organization because they allow managers to take advantage of the available organizational learning and do not require them to incur the cost of individual learning. The propensity for managers and for the firm to support more or less risky strategic behavior depends on their risk orientations.

Individual-level risk behavior may depend on the values of possible outcomes relative to levels of aspiration and may result from a tendency of managers to focus on targets and from the adaptation of those targets to experience rather than from fixed "traits" regarding risk (March, 1988a). CORPSTRAT may be used to model fixed risk preferences or to model variable risk preferences such as those described by March (1988a). In this case, CORPSTRAT views individual risk orientations as depending on several factors. Risk preferences are assumed to increase as (1) a manager's reputation falls below the xth percentile of the population of managers in the firm, (2) a manager's portfolio value (and hence prospective reputation) decreases, whether or not his or her current reputation is above the xth percentile of the population, and (3) a constant reputation value that managers strive to attain whether or not they are above the xth percentile of the population. Managers are expected to choose portfolios of induced and autonomous projects that satisfy their risk preferences at a particular moment. In the model results reported here, CORPSTRAT was run under an assumption of fixed managerial risk preference.

An additional set of rules governs project selection from nonportfolio industries in which managers have positive experience (experienced related industries). At any time there may be several industries that fall into this category for various managers. In such cases, the managers are guided by the desire to see one or more of these industries incorporated in the portfolio. Thus, they seek to concentrate all of their autonomous project activities in order to build sales levels to reach the portfolio inclusion threshold. Managers concentrate their autonomous activities in these promising industries as long as their risk attitude remains the same. When they become more risk seeking, they cease their activities in the experienced related industries and generate projects in unexperienced related industries or unrelated industries.

After generating up to 10 projects, managers evaluate them for possible proposal to corporate management through the *Managerial Project Evaluation* process. CORPSTRAT incorporates two alternative mechanisms for managerial evaluation. In the satisficing mechanism, managers propose the first two projects that meet their criteria (discussed later). In the optimizing mechanism, managers rank the 10 projects and select the top two for proposal to the firm. (The results reported in this chapter were run with the optimizing assumption.) The proposal process consists of seeking funding for the projects.

Managerial project evaluation entails a comparison of each projects's risk and expected return to the manager's preferred levels. All managers favor higher returns.

In the *Firm-Level Project Ranking and Funding* process, corporate management ranks all proposed projects according to their potential performance and their fit with the firm's concept of strategy and objectives. The actual ranking depends on *Firm-Level Risk Behavior.*The firm's risk orientation may be fixed or may vary according to a prospect theory process. (The results reported in this chapter were produced by using a fixed firm risk orientation assumption.) The project funding process uses a procedure analogous to managerial risk assessment. The firm evaluates each project on the basis of its inherent risk, its sponsoring manager's reputation, and its expected return. The firm's risk orientation determines both the ratio of induced and autonomous projects the firm desires to fund and the level of risk it prefers for these projects. Since typical risk levels for induced and autonomous projects differ, the use of a single preferred risk value for both induced and autonomous projects results in a significant number of projects being funded with risk levels that differ substantially from the preferred level.

Research Methods and Experimental Design

To address the research questions presented earlier we conducted a series of simulation runs using four environmental conditions and two firm type conditions. We also examined four managerial risk orientation categories.

The four environmental conditions studied were as follows:

1. Complete stability: fixed environment
2. Moderate stability: varying environment, with environmental shifts occurring once every 10 years.
3. Moderate instability: varying environment, with environmental shifts occurring once every 5 years
4. Extreme instability: varying environment, with environmental shifts occurring at random intervals, where the number of years between shifts is a normal variate with mean 3 years and standard deviation one year

The two firm risk behavior conditions were as follows:

1. Weak, moderate risk orientation (preferred risk level 0.5);
2. Risk neutral

The four managerial risk orientation categories were as follows:

1. Risk Averse: managerial risk preference in the interval (0.0, 0.4)
2. Moderate Risk Orientation: managerial risk preference in the interval (0.4, 0.6)

3. Risk Seeking: managerial risk preference in the interval (0.6, 0.8)
4. Extremely Risk Seeking: managerial risk preference in the interval (0.8, 1.0)

We studied environmental conditions and firm risk behavior by varying the model parameters for these factors explicitly. We crossed environmental condition (four values) and firm risk behavior (two values) for a total of eight different combinations. In each of these eight runs we classified managers into one of the four managerial risk behavior categories. (In future work we will examine risk neutral managers, as well as variable risk preferences.) Thus, we examined the effects of environmental conditions and firm behavior by comparing different model runs. We examined manager risk behavior differences by comparing managerial performance and survival results for each manager risk behavior category.

In addition to the environment and firm risk behavior, input parameters varied in each simulation study, (i.e., the *experiemental* or *independent* variables); we also varied several *sensitivity analysis* parameters. The full research design consisted of 288 experimental runs: 8 primary experimental runs, and an additional 280 sensitivity analysis runs. (A full listing of the sensitivity analysis parameters and values used, as well as complete results from all 288 runs, is available from the authors.)

We ran 20 model iterations for each combination of input values; each iteration consists of a single 20-year model execution. Each model run required approximately 30 minutes of CPU time on a VAX running VMS. Because of the availability of sufficient computing time, we were able to perform each of the 288 runs in a complete factorial design (Neter and Wasserman, 1974; Box, Hunter, and Hunter, 1978), in which all combinations of factor levels were examined.

Results at the manager level were examined by pooling across all 20 iterations and were limited to the 8 primary experimental runs. For each 20-iteration experimental run we examined the mean reputation, project portfolio growth rate, and project portfolio return-on-sales (ROS) value for managers in each of the four managerial risk behavior categories, as well as several other manager- and firm-level output measures described further later. The primary model outputs of interest at the firm level include growth rates, return, final diversification, and variability in growth (and other outputs). We also examined the changing composition of the entire manager corps of the firm, as differential success rates of managers in each category led to increases or decreases in the representation in the firm.

We examined selected firm-level results for the entire 288-run experiment, performing sensitivity analyses on our primary outcome variables. These analyses were performed by using ANOVA and General Linear Modeling (GLM) approaches, allowing us to model the effects of qualitative and quantitative factors on the model outputs of interest. All analyses were conducted with the SAS software package. The ANOVA and GLM analyses were based on output data sets containing one case per iteration per scenario. The analysis essentially partitions the total variance in the output data into three categories: across-scenario experimental effects (due to experimental factors), across-scenario sensitivity analysis effects (due to sensitivity analysis factors), and within-scenario random error (due to sampling variation in the random numbers drawn for use in various functions in the CORPSTRAT model).

The input variables for the full experimental design include the experimental variables (i.e., the key variables capturing differences in the firm types of processes we are studying) and the sensitivity analysis variables. The latter are model constants and parameters whose values should not affect the findings of our experiments; they are examined to ensure that this is the case. Our hypotheses are tested by examining the relationship between differences in model outputs and differences in organizational processes as specified by the model inputs. If such relationships are found across all values of the sensitivity analysis parameters, we know that our findings are not simply a statistical artifact of the specific values chosen for these nonsubstantive parameters, but instead reflect true differences between the scenarios we are studying.

Results

On the following pages we present results of various analyses conducted on disaggregated data produced by the model. The analyses were conducted at the level of individual managers and/or managerial risk behavior categories and at the firm level. Since the research reported in this chapter was exploratory and intended primarily to illustrate CORPSTRAT's potential role in research, we do not view the simulation experiments reported here as rigorous hypothesis tests. For this reason—and because the precision of the results reported varies with the number of iterations run and the values used for nonexperimental parameters—we report our results without formal tests for statistical significance. Future CORPSTRAT experiments will involve more extensive stability and sensitivity analyses, permitting us to report meaningful significance test statistics.

Manager-Level Results

Our initial set of analyses examined the first research question, regarding the effects of environmental conditions on the relationship between managerial risk orientation and managerial performance (including survival). To answer this question we collected several measures of managerial performance and survival and examined how they varied by manager type in different environmental conditions. We examined these relationships in both of the firm types we studied, thereby addressing the second reasearch question as well, about the effects of firm-level rules and risk preferences on these relationships.

Weak, Moderate Risk Orientation Firm. Tables 4.1–4.5 provide managerial performance results for the first firm type (moderate risk orientation): Tables 4.6–4.8 provide results for the risk neutral firm. We first describe results for the moderate risk orientation firm, which are followed by findings for the risk neutral firm.

Table 4.1 contains a summary of managerial performance results using three different measures of performance; (a) Mean Annual Reputation Change, (b) Mean Annual Portfolio Sales Growth, and (c) Mean Annual Portfolio Return on Sales. Each measure is presented in a separate panel in the table. Each panel, in turn, provides performance data for each of the four manager types or risk orientation cate-

TABLE 4.1   Managerial Performance: Moderate Risk Orientation Firm

Environmental Condition	Managerial Risk Orientation Category				
	1	*2*	*3*	*4*	*All*
(a) Mean Annual Reputation Change (reputation units)					
1	0.002	0.020	−0.031	−0.010	0.003
2	0.002	0.012	−0.034	−0.011	0.001
3	0.004	0.019	−0.017	−0.034	0.004
4	0.006	0.014	−0.022	0.002	0.003
All	0.004	0.016	−0.026	−0.013	0.003
(b) Mean Annual Portfolio Sales Growth (percentage)					
1	6.639	32.916	21.534	−8.540	18.795
2	2.951	28.027	23.384	−9.010	16.992
3	5.011	35.224	16.795	−4.017	17.484
4	13.186	25.345	19.379	−7.249	17.313
All	6.987	30.423	20.309	−7.073	17.662
(c) Mean Annual Portfolio Return on Sales (percentage)					
1	12.641	14.012	12.856	12.193	13.058
2	13.010	13.385	12.820	12.492	12.982
3	12.422	12.898	12.951	12.588	12.792
4	12.542	12.747	12.702	13.114	12.714
All	12.648	13.271	12.832	12.602	12.889

NOTE: Definitions for Managerial Risk Orientation categories and environmental conditions are provided in the text; see the section entitled "Research Methods and Experimental Design."

gories (Risk Averse, Moderate Risk Orientation, Risk Seeking, Extremely Risk Seeking) in each of the four environmental conditions (Complete Stability, Moderate Stability, Moderate Instability, and Extreme Instability).

Examining the first two panels (for Reputation Change and Portfolio Sales Growth) reveals significant performance differences across manager risk orientation categories. On the basis of both of these measures of performance, Moderate Risk Orientation managers perform better than all other manager groups under all environmental conditions. Results for Return on Sales are less clear, however: Moderate Risk Orientation managers achieve higher ROS rates than the other three manager types under the first two environmental conditions. Under Moderate Instability, however, Risk Seeking managers outperform Moderate Risk Orientation Managers slightly, while Extremely Risk Seeking managers outperform all other manager types under Extreme Instability. Averaged over all enviromental conditions, however, Moderate Risk Orientation Managers show the highest performance as measured by ROS.

In interpreting the findings in table 4.1, particularly the modest differences between the ROS results and those using the first two measures, it is important to note that ROS displays a more limited range of variation and also serves as a less reliable measure of performance. The limited variation is due to the firm's funding and liquidation rules: funding rules ensure that the expected returns for funded projects are not far below the average return, while the liquidation rule ensures that projects with actual returns significantly below the firm's average return are liquidated. The lower level of reliability of this measure is due to the fact that it is more closely tied to random environmental fluctuations and thus displays greater variance than the other measures. However, since it is constrained by the liquidation process, the net result is that the ROS measure carries less information concerning managerial performance than the other measures.

The results in table 4.1 indicate that Moderate Risk Orientation managers are generally more successful than other manager types irrespective of environmental conditions. Focusing first on the Mean Reputation Change measure, this result has two possible explanations. Reputations vary with project success or failure: a manager's reputation is incremented by a small amount each year for each project receiving continuing funding (i.e., avoiding liquidation). Reputations are also incremented for each project that successfully reaches the end of its 10-year life cycle. Reputations are decremented, however, when projects are liquidated. Thus, reputation change is proportional to the number of successful projects a manager controls. Managers with positive reputation changes, therefore have been successful in achieving funding for new projects and have also proposed and achieved funding for projects that have high expected returns and/or are located in positive munificence industries, the two key factors contributing to adequate project ROS and, therefore, to continued funding.

The portfolio sales growth rate performance measure is similar to reputation change in that it depends both on the number of projects a manager controls in his or her portfolio and the performance of those projects. Sales growth follows a fixed pattern in CORPSTRAT. Thus, higher levels of portfolio sales growth are achieved through the addition of new projects to the portfolio—not through differences in project performance. Thus, managers who succeed in achieving funding for new projects are more likely to experience increases in sales growth than managers who are unable to obtain such funding. In contrast, portfolio ROS depends on the ROS of each project in a manager's portfolio. In fact, higher levels of portfolio ROS may be achieved through cuts in portfolio size (by liquidating projects with low return rates).

The central role of new project funding success in managerial performance directs attention to the project funding process. In the CORPSTRAT model project funding is based on a firm-assigned score. This score is based on a project's EROS, the munificence level of the industry, the sponsoring manager's reputation, and the project's risk level relative to the firm's preferred risk. Since project risk is the only factor that varies directly with manager type, and since Moderate Risk Orientation managers generate projects with risk values between 0.4 and 0.6 (exactly straddling the firm's preferred risk value of 0.5), it is possible that the higher performance of this group of managers is a direct result of their risk orientations. We return to this question later when we examine the risk neutral firm, in which project risk plays no part in funding decisions.

Table 4.2 provides another measure of managerial performance: managerial tenure and survival. The first panel in this table presents average tenure (years between hiring and firing) for managers hired prior to the initial model run (i.e., managers active when Year 1 begins). Moderate Risk Orientation managers show

TABLE 4.2   Managerial Tenure and Survival: Moderate Risk
Orientation Firm

Environmental Condition	Managerial Risk Orientation Category				
	1	*2*	*3*	*4*	*All*
(a) Mean Tenure: Managers Hired Prior to Year 1					
1	7.63	12.81	6.24	4.93	8.71
2	8.00	11.52	6.19	4.85	8.38
3	7.73	12.38	6.43	4.93	8.63
4	7.88	12.01	6.41	4.97	8.56
All	7.81	12.18	6.32	4.92	8.57
(b) Survival Rates (percentage): Managers Hired During Years 1–18					
1	8.08	7.02	38.37	10.96	14.66
2	5.60	5.57	41.53	19.35	12.44
3	6.33	7.28	35.56	17.69	13.72
4	7.68	6.17	36.31	7.79	13.27
All	6.94	6.46	37.79	13.56	13.52

NOTE: Definitions for Managerial Risk Orientation categories and environmental conditions are provided in the text; see the section entitled "Research Methods and Experimental Design."

significantly higher mean tenure than other manager types, indicating greater survival rates. The second panel of table 4.2 contains tenure data for managers hired during years 1–18 of the model run. We do not examine data for managers hired in Year 20 because all hiring is performed at the end of the year. Therefore, Year 20 hires are not given the opportunity to generate new projects. We exclude Year 19 hires because managers are given a full two years to achieve funding for a new project before they are fired. Thus, all Year 19 hires are still active when the model run ends.

Because tenures are truncated at Year 20 of the model run, and because the proportion of managers hired in each risk orientation category varies across the 20 years, we cannot use mean tenure for all managers as a summary measure of tenure and survival-related performance. Instead, we compute tenure and survival rates by manager category for each year and examine differences across categories and environmental conditions. In addition, we distinguish between two types of survival and compute two different measures: (a) proportion of managers who survive past 2 years (i.e., who succeed in obtaining funding for at least one project and therefore avoid being replaced before their third year) and (b) mean tenure for managers who are successful in obtaining funding and therefore survive past two years.

These survival and tenure results for the first firm are contained in the lower panel of table 4.2. Panel (b) indicates the proportion of all newly hired managers who survive more than two years. Category 3 managers show an average survival rate significantly greater than that of all other manager types, while category 4 managers have roughly twice the survival rate of categories 1 and 2, on average. In additional analyses, however, we discovered that tenure values for surviving managers show a different pattern: conditional on survival past two years, category 2 managers show significantly greater tenure than others, under all environmental conditions. To explore this finding further, we examined tenure data for each annual entry cohort separately (i.e., mean tenure for managers hired during Year 2 who survived more than two years, mean tenure for 2-year surviving managers hired during Year 3, etc.). These disaggregated tenure data (not shown here) revealed that category 2 managers hired during Years 2–11, 13, and 15 all achieved higher mean tenures that all other manager types, while category 1 managers hired during Years 12, 14, and 16–17 achieved higher tenure than other managers. All managers hired in Year 18 survived to the end of the model run.

The results in the lower two panel of table 4.2 are somewhat confusing and were unexpected. On the one hand, newly hired Risk Seeking managers are significantly more successful in obtaining funding for at least one new project, thereby avoiding firing and replacement. On the other hand, the small percentage of Risk Averse and Moderate Risk Orientation managers who do succeed in obtaining funding for new projects are more successful in the long run, achieving higher total tenure than their more risk seeking colleagues. This paradoxical result has several possible explanations. First, the initial project funding hurdle, as described previously, requires at least one project whose EROS and/or industry munificence is higher than that of most other proposed projects, and/or it requires a high managerial reputation and/ or a project risk rating that matches the firm's risk orientation. The survival advantage displayed by Risk Seeking managers may be attributable to their propensity to explore industries outside the firm's current core businesses—thus increasing their likelihood of identifying high munificence industries. Since optimizing managers propose the two best projects from among the 10 generated—and the set of 10 projects they select from has a wider variance in munificence than the projects (i.e., industries) proposed by risk averse managers, they are somewhat more likely to offer the firm projects with greater possible returns.

To explore the performance and survival differences between the four groups of managers further we examined performance variablity within each category. Although Risk Seeking and Extremely Risk Seeking managers appear to have lower mean performance and tenure, we speculated that focusing only on mean values obscures interesting variation. Table 4.3 illustrates differences in the variability of one performance measure, mean reputation change. Although not as consistent as

TABLE 4.3   Managerial Performance Variability

Environmental Condition	Standard Deviation of Mean Reputation Change Managerial Risk Orientation Category			
	1	*2*	*3*	*4*
1	0.1017	0.1067	0.1402	0.0960
2	0.0875	0.1546	0.1392	0.0915
3	0.0670	0.1123	0.1217	0.2250
4	0.0609	0.1033	0.1231	0.0340

other findings, these numbers provide some evidence of increasing variability across manager groups. This phenomenon requires further exploration before definitive conclusions are possible.

We also examined performance for various other subsets of managers. For example, table 4.4 shows the managerial performance measures reported in table 4.1, but for the subset of managers who achieve 20-year tenure (i.e., who are hired prior to the start of the model run and survive through to the end of the run). The most obvious difference between table 4.4 and table 4.1 is that no managers in Categories 3 or 4 survive the full 20 years: the survivors are in Categories 1 and 2 only (see table 4.5 for a summary of survival rates). The differences between Category 1 and 2 managers in table 4.4 are similar to those in table 4.1, however. The surviving managers (table 4.4) show significantly higher performance than that shown by all managers (table 4.1), of course. The reputation results are similar in both tables: Category 2 managers outperform Category 1 managers. The sales growth results are very different, however: surviving Category 1 managers are very similar to surviving Cateogry 2 managers, despite the significant differences between these two groups shown in table 4.1. Finally, the portfolio ROS results show only small differences in tables 4.1 and 4.4.

TABLE 4.4 Managerial Performance: Moderate Risk
Orientation Firm Managers with 20-Year Tenure Only

| Environmental Condition | Managerial Risk Orientation Category | | | | |
	1	2	3	4	All
(a) Mean Annual Reputation Change (reputation units)					
1	0.216	0.404			0.368
2	0.175	0.481			0.384
3	0.168	0.372			0.328
4	0.146	0.320			0.285
All	0.176	0.389			0.340
(b) Mean Annual Portfolio Sales Growth (percentage)					
1	24.697	27.220			26.737
2	30.258	28.156			28.820
3	23.933	26.951			26.289
4	21.615	25.374			24.605
All	25.521	26.847			26.543
(c) Mean Annual Portfolio Return on Sales (percentage)					
1	14.774	14.383			14.458
2	13.418	13.863			13.722
3	13.302	13.113			13.155
4	13.338	12.986			13.058
All	13.686	13.596			13.617

NOTE: Definitions for Managerial Risk Orientation categories and environmental conditions are provided in the text; see The section entitled "Research Methods and Experimental Design."

TABLE 4.5 Managerial Performance: Moderate Risk Orientation Firm (Managers Surviving 20 Years) (Number of Survivors/Number of Managers at Time 0)

| Environmental Condition | Managerial Risk Orientation Category | | | | |
	1	*2*	*3*	*4*	*All*
1	9/140	38/140	0/80	0/60	47/420
2	12/140	26/140	0/80	0/60	38/420
3	9/140	32/140	0/80	0/60	41/420
4	9/140	35/140	0/80	0/60	44/420
All	39/560	131/560	0/320	0/240	170/1680

Risk Neutral Firm. Results for the Risk Neutral firm are presented in tables 4.6–4.8. The format and contents of these tables are equivalent to those of tables 4.1, 4.2, and 4.4 for the Moderate Risk Orientation Firm. In the discussion that follows we do not repeat the detailed explanation of the contents already provided.

Table 4.6 indicates that in the Risk Neutral firm, Moderate Risk Orientation managers' performance is not as consistently superior to that of managers in other categories as was seen in the Weak, Moderate Risk Orientation firm. Although Cat-

TABLE 4.6 Managerial Performance: Risk Neutral Firm

| Environmental Condition | Managerial Risk Orientation Category | | | | |
	1	*2*	*3*	*4*	*All*
(a) Mean Annual Reputation Change (reputation units)					
1	0.009	0.018	-0.056	-0.018	-0.002
2	0.001	0.022	-0.039	-0.024	-0.002
3	0.002	0.013	-0.056	-0.050	-0.010
4	0.004	0.017	-0.033	-0.029	-0.001
All	0.004	0.018	-0.046	-0.031	-0.004
(b) Mean Annual Portfolio Sales Growth (percentage)					
1	15.301	12.285	25.717	13.852	17.327
2	14.228	9.934	15.239	18.300	14.206
3	13.368	9.566	20.512	17.254	15.061
4	12.611	9.883	20.964	13.680	14.330
All	13.877	10.426	20.823	15.915	15.242
(c) Mean Annual Portfolio Return on Sales (percentage)					
1	13.009	13.062	13.107	13.376	13.129
2	13.005	13.153	12.922	12.962	13.003
3	12.397	13.161	12.816	12.844	12.807
4	12.869	12.917	13.028	13.054	12.969
All	12.815	13.075	12.972	13.039	12.975

NOTE: Definitions for Managerial Risk Orientation categories and environmental conditions are provided in the text; see the section entitled "Research Methods and Experimental Design."

TABLE 4.7   Managerial Tenure and Survival: Risk
Neutral Firm

	Managerial Risk Orientation Category				
Environmental Condition	1	2	3	4	All
(a) Mean Tenure (years): Managers Hired Prior to Year 1					
1	13.53	10.09	6.81	5.90	10.01
2	13.80	10.04	7.28	5.55	10.12
3	13.40	9.56	6.74	5.77	9.76
4	14.34	9.42	6.74	5.47	9.99
All	13.77	9.78	6.89	5.67	9.97
(b) Survival Rates (percentage): Managers Hired During Years 1– 18					
1	4.62	6.27	42.16	43.79	15.29
2	4.05	6.37	36.56	45.91	13.96
3	5.67	8.06	43.55	52.51	17.68
4	4.37	6.13	42.86	45.99	14.32
All	4.64	6.69	41.19	47.30	15.26

NOTE: Definitions for Managerial Risk Orientation categories and environmental conditions are provided in the text; see the section entitled "Research Methods and Experimental Design."

egory 2 managers outperformed all other managers on reputation change, this group of managers displays significantly worse performance on portfolio sales growth, while ROS results show only small differences.

The results in table 4.6 provide additional support for our speculation that the match between managerial risk preference and firm risk preference plays an important role in the Moderate Risk Orientation managers' success in the Moderate Risk Orientation firm. As noted, success in achieving funding for new projects plays a significant role in portfolio sales growth and, to a lesser extent, reputation change. Since the Risk Neutral firm's decisions regarding new project funding do not consider project risk, Category 2 managers have no advantage over other managers: the project funding competition is based on managerial reputation, project EROS, and industry munificence only. Without the risk preference advantage, Category 2 managers must compete solely on the basis of their performance.

The managerial tenure and survival results for the Risk Neutral firm (table 4.7) are generally consistent with the other performance measures in table 4.6; Risk Averse managers outperform all others on initial tenure. Survival rates for newly hired Risk Averse managers are lower than those of Moderate Risk Orientation managers.

Firm-Level Results

After our examination of manager-level results, we analyzed several firm-level outcome measures to explore the third research question, regarding the relationship

TABLE 4.8 Managerial Performance: Risk Neutral Firm
(Managers with 20-Year Tenure Only)

Environmental Condition	Managerial Risk Orientation Category				
	1	*2*	*3*	*4*	*All*
(a) Mean Annual Reputation Change (reputation units)					
1	0.245	0.439			0.297
2	0.152	0.341	−0.034		0.191
3	0.088	0.260		−0.055	0.121
4	0.097	0.266			0.129
All	0.143	0.336	−0.034	−0.055	0.184
(b) Mean Annual Portfolio Sales Growth (percentage)					
1	24.009	26.286			24.614
2	23.546	24.447	20.864		23.662
3	21.657	21.535		18.894	21.594
4	22.455	22.169			22.402
All	22.894	23.862	20.864	18.894	23.080
(c) Mean Annual Portfolio Return on Sales (percentage)					
1	14.110	14.343			14.172
2	13.790	13.862	13.403		13.792
3	12.915	13.055		12.490	12.938
4	13.025	12.975			13.016
All	13.438	13.634	13.403	12.490	13.479

NOTE: Definitions for Managerial Risk Orientation categories and environmental conditions are provided in the text; see the section entitled "Research Methods and Experimental Design."

between Managerial Risk Orientations and firm performance. We began our analysis by focusing on changes in the composition of the manager corps in the two firm types and four environmental conditions. We then examined the effects of composition on firm performance.

Figure 4.2 provides an overview of the changing composition of the managerial corps over the entire 20-year model run in both firm types. Each of the four panels in figure 4.2 shows annual changes in the fraction of all managers in the Moderate Risk Orientation firm that are in each risk behavior category ("MTyp"). In each panel, manager type 2 (Moderate Risk Orientation) increases from 33.3 percent of all managers to over 50 percent, while the other types decline or increase at a much lower rate. The four panels in figure 4.2 provide the equivalent results for the Risk Neutral firm.

The change in manager type representation shown in figure 4.2 occurs for two reasons. First, differential managerial performance leads to higher death rates (i.e., fire rates) among managers in categories other than Category 2 (Moderate Risk Orientation). In addition, as discussed previously, the model hires new managers (to replace those who have been fired) from the available categories in proportion to their

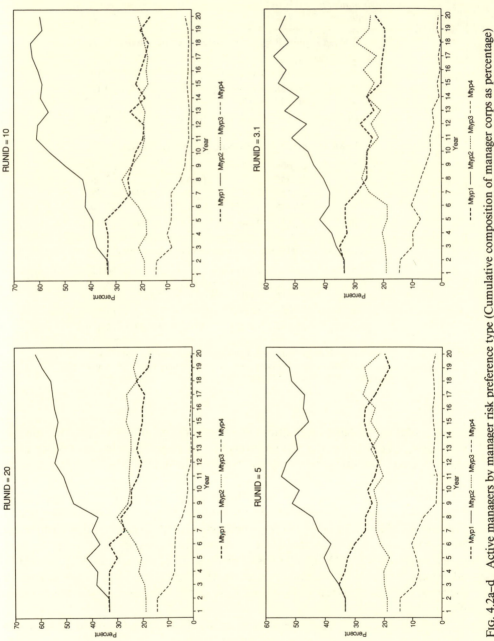

Fig. 4.2a–d Active managers by manager risk preference type (Cumulative composition of manager corps as percentage) Moderate risk orientation firm

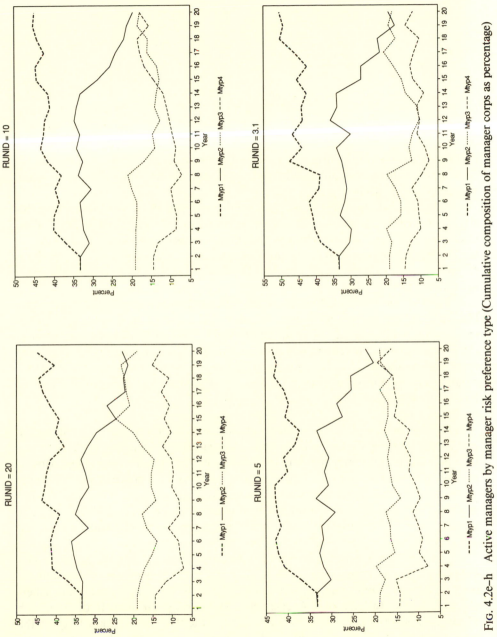

Fig. 4.2e–h Active managers by manager risk preference type (Cumulative composition of manager corps as percentage) Risk neutral firm

TABLE 4.9   Firm-Level Results: Performance by
Environmental Condition by Risk Orientation

| | Moderate Risk Orientation | | Risk Neutral | |
Environment	Mean Growth	Mean ROS	Mean Growth	Mean ROS
20.0	16.56	14.07	16.01	13.81
10.0	15.25	13.55	15.01	13.61
5.0	14.50	13.15	13.17	13.01
3.1	13.83	12.84	14.03	12.98

representation within the firm at the time of the hire. Thus, birth rates also change over time: birth rates of successful manager types increase, while those of less successful managers decline.

Further analyses of firm-level results indicated that the firm benefits from this change in managerial composition: as the proportion of Moderate Risk Orientation managers increases, the firm's annual performance improves somewhat. In particular, regression analyses (not reported here) relating annual changes in composition to annual performance levels support the conclusion that compositional factors influence firm behavior.

Table 4.9 provides additional firm-level performance results for both firm types. Interestingly, the firm-level results indicate that the firm is more successful under most (but not all) environmental conditions when it exercises a strict risk preference rather than selecting potential projects purely on the basis of expected return. Using both Growth and ROS as the measure of firm performance, the Moderate Risk Orientation firm performs better than the Risk Neutral firm in all but one environmental condition (see table 4.9).

The findings presented here provide several interesting observations on managerial and corporate behavior and performance and suggest several intriguing hypotheses. One potentially interesting hypothesis suggested by the present study is that Moderate Risk Orientation of individual managers has very high survival value across a wide range of environmental conditions and corporate contexts. While this hypothesis is perhaps not counter to intuition, it would be useful to see it confirmed in large sample research. This might lead to further empirical research with real data and real subjects.

The simulation model is especially interesting for examining the links between individual-level and organizational-level behavior and performance. The results for both firm types indicate that managers with Moderate Risk Orientations are generally more successful than Risk Averse and Risk Seeking managers. In the firm with Moderate Risk orientation this result is due in part to the firm's funding rule and the match between managerial and firm risk preferences. In the Risk Neutral firm, however, the firm lacks a risk preference and allocates resources solely on the basis of performance. Thus, in this firm the success of Moderate Risk Orientation managers results from the performance of their portfolios, rather than their inherent attributes.

Nonetheless, managers whose risk preferences match those of the firm do possess an inherent advantage in project funding; it would be interesting to examine whether matching Managerial Risk Orientation with firm orientation in general is associated with improved managerial performance—and under what conditions individual and organizational performance will be coaligned and when not. For instance, it might be of interest to study firms in the steady state with low turnover management groups (where individual managers try to maximize their reputation by proposing projects that match the firm's risk orientation but with somewhat low expected ROS) versus firms with high turnover management groups (where individual managers try to maximize their reputation by proposing highly risky projects but with very high expected ROS).

An obvious next step in our research is to repeat the present study with variable managerial and organizational risk preferences. Several behavioral assumptions are of interest. Under a prospect theory assumption, managers and firms would be expected to be Risk Seeking when in the domain of loss and Risk Averse when in the domain of gain (e.g., Tversky and Kahneman, 1979). Under a reverse prospect theory assumption, successful managers and firms would be expected to be Risk Averse (e.g., March and Shapira, 1987).

In still another type of study, Managerial and Organizational Risk Orientation might depend on whether the focus is on risk or on survival (March and Shapira, 1992). In the current version of CORPSTRAT managers make resource allocation decisions independently of their current reputations and, hence, their survival chances; all managers have constant risk orientations and hence do not modify their behavior on the basis of current performance. Running the model under a prospect theory assumption would undoubtedly produce different results: Risk Seeking managers with above-average performance would eventually become more Risk Averse, while Risk Averse managers performing poorly would become more Risk Seeking. The current version of CORPSTRAT creates other limitations on managerial behavior under near-failure, however. For example, managers choose between further investments in their portfolio (core) business(es) on the basis of their risk orientations and these businesses' performance levels. Thus, a manager with Moderate Risk Orientation and a relatively poor performing portfolio will likely direct future resources toward promising related experienced industries. However, if in doing so the manager fails to maintain sufficient sales levels in the portfolio industry, and that industry falls below the minimum sales level necessary to remain in the firm's portfolio, then the manager is at risk of being fired as a result of lack of a portfolio industry. The manager will survive only by successfully growing an alternative business sufficiently to witness its entry into the firm's portfolio. This can be accomplished through dedicated resource allocation to the industry most likely to reach this threshold—not to the industry with the highest anticipated ROS.

The present study and the further studies we envision suggest that CORPSTRAT is a useful tool for exploring interesting research questions which could not be pursued easily by traditional research methods. The capacity of the model to explore complex, multilevel phenomena under a very wide range of parametric variations, and the interpretation puzzles posed by the unexpected results that are generated by model experiments, may be useful to sharpen the intuition of empirical researchers before they set out to undertake studies in real settings.

5

Seeking Adaptive Advantage: Evolutionary Theory and Managerial Action

ANNE S. MINER

Observers of outstanding high-technology organizations report that senior managers often set vague goals, embrace simplistic slogans, propel internal teams into cutthroat competition, set up processes but no outcome standards, and permit employees to use time on unapproved projects (Quinn, 1986; Van de Ven, Angle, and Poole, 1989; Nonako, 1988). These practices seem to violate crucial management principles such as setting clear goals, enhancing cooperation, and assuring that each employee efficiently focus on top priorities.

In this chapter, I suggest that such high tech practices may not violate good management principles, but illuminate instead a potential integrating framework for managerial action. In particular, I explore a simple evolutionary framework for conceptualizing a wide variety of potentially valuable managerial practices. A basic evolutionary model of an organization envisions it as a collection of routines, or stable bundles of activities. Over time, both intentional and unintentional variation occurs in the routines. Some of the new routines are selected into the ongoing practices. This simple variation-selection-retention cycle repeats continuously (Weick, 1979; Baum, 1988). This cycle can also be seen as a form of organizational learning but will be referred to as the evolutionary framework in this chapter.

In this framework, the manager's role is to enhance the probability that these processes will generate organizational survival and prosperity—to seek adaptive advantage. The high tech manager who permits employees to pursue individual projects or directs two research teams to pursue the same question has basically decided to strengthen the variation process. In accepting inconsistencies and local inefficiency created by this practice, the manager chooses to sacrifice some retention (or consistency) in return for the possible benefits of enhanced variation.

In the first section I outline some of the evolutionary model's potential implications for internal managerial action, drawing especially on findings from field investigations of the management of technology. In the second I explicate four promising research areas suggested by this framework: (1) competency driven action; (2)

I appreciate the suggestions of Theresa Lant and Joel Baum.

recombinations of organizational routines as a source of variation; (3) acquisition of external routines; and (4) second-order interactions between organizational routines. I also discuss the importance of incorporating the social bases and the symbolic nature of organizational routines. I conclude by noting some of the disadvantages and advantages of adopting an evolutionary approach to normative theory.

The Manager's Role

The evolutionary perspective envisions organizations as evolving systems nested in other evolving systems at higher levels of analysis (Aldrich, 1979; Singh and Lumsden, 1990). Individual organizations can be seen as collections of routines which continuously go through the variation-selection-retention cycle. At a higher level of analysis, populations of organizations also go through variation, selection, and retention processes (Schumpeter, 1934; Hannan and Freeman, 1989) and may coevolve with technological and social systems. For example, some organizations introduced home video systems based on discs, while others developed tape technologies during a period of early technical variation in video reproduction systems. Market and social forces eventually selected the dominant design of VCR tape systems. Organizations whose fate rested on alternative designs—such as disc technologies or inclusion of the unit inside TVs—failed.

In this setting, the manager's two primary roles are (1) to adjust the organization's relationship to higher level evolutionary processes (including sometimes directly intervening in those processes) and (2) to influence the internal evolutionary process. The manager seeks organizational survival and organizational prosperity. This chapter focuses on the internal evolutionary system. There, managers affect the individual levels and forms of variation, selection, and retention. In addition, they continuously seek adaptive balance of the *relative* levels of (a) variation and retention (including the degree of incremental versus radical change) and (b) competition and mutualism.

Responsibility for Adaptive Variation, Selection, and Retention

Variation. Much literature on organizational innovation has an "innovation" bias which assumes that innovation itself is useful (Clark, 1987). Innovation in routines can be random or harmful, however, especially if current routines are the product of trial and error learning in a stable setting (Holand, Levitt, and March, 1988; Miner, 1991). In general, then, the organization is more likely to survive and prosper when **potentially valuable** innovation occurs.

For technology driven organizations this presents a familiar but difficult problem. If a manager could specify *exactly* in advance what needs to be discovered to produce a new product or solve a known technical barrier, the discovery—and high priced scientists to make it—would not be needed. On the other hand, the organization can affect the types and levels of variation and/or innovation in several distinct ways.

One thing organizations do to facilitate useful variation is engage in *institutionalized experimentation.* Formalized research and development has existed, of course, since the end of the last century (Freeman, 1982). In firms, it may range from highly unstructured research to very focused projects designed to solve quite specific technical problems. More recently, the roles of "champion" and "entrepreneur" have been made explicit, providing a conscious engine of variation within some organizations (Maidique, 1980; Quinn, 1986). Several total quality management statistical control practices also embody institutionalized experimentation (Deming, 1981). Finally, some firms create parallel projects in which several teams work on the same general technical problem, generating intentional variation among potential new technologies. In the development of the VCR, for example, Sony is reported to have had more than five teams working on development of early VCR prototypes.

Firms also provide *direct and indirect incentives* for individuals to produce valuable variation. Many firms seek to establish that useful innovation is part of normal employee duties. Total quality programs emphasizing continuous improvement through employee suggestions seek to establish such expectations. In scientific areas, firms sometimes intentionally create direct competition between individual scientists, for example with competitive rewards of status and scientific resources. Others also provide specific material incentives for discoveries such as a percentage of licensing fees from patents produced by the new ideas. In exteme cases, venture divisions are set up in which employees involved in risky projects share an equity interest in new products to be developed.

Finally, firms sometimes even tacitly acknowledge the value of unfocused variation or pure *playfulness* (March, 1976). Research labs embrace informality in part because they cannot keep good scientists in other ways, but also because informal contact may encourage completely unplanned variations in ideas. "Skunkworks" are tolerated or even encouraged, in which small groups of employees work informally on unapproved projects. Organizations may tolerate a certain level of slack resources as a form of hidden permission for variation to occur (March, 1976, 1991). Table 5.1 summarizes these activities along with examples of mechanisms used for selection and retention.

Management theory has tended to see many of these practices to induce promising innovation as a special activity required of scientific or artistic organizations whose immediate survival depends on innovation. In an evolutionary framework, they simply represent points in a continuum of ways in which management in all organizations facilitates variation. At one extreme of the continuum lies classical rational planning. Here, the manager sets a goal, examines alternative actions available to meet a goal, chooses the best actions, and assures their implementation. The variation process occurs as alternatives are considered *before* action. The variation occurs symbolically or vicariously. The selection process then occurs when a choice is made between the symbolized alternatives. Rational planning and choice, then, represent one mechanism for variation and selection.

At the other extreme of the continuum lies permission for playfulness, in which management encourages variation with almost no control and no direct involvement in its content. Variation mechanisms differ in terms of how much management directly produces the specific content, whether the content is symbolic or enacted, and whether the entire process is intentional or not. However, the role of stimulating appropriate variation is universal.

TABLE 5.1　Sample Organizational Variation-Selection-Retention Processes

Variation	Selection	Retention
1. Institutionalized experimentation 　a. Research and development 　b. Champion and entrepreneurial roles 　c. Some total quality experiments 　d. Parallel projects	1. Goals	1. Active controls 　a. Budgets 　b. Information systems 　c. Audits
2. Direct and indirect incentives 　a. Innovation norms 　b. Professional individual incentives 　c. Material individual incentives value 　d. Equity interests	2. Values	2. Formalization 　a. Rules 　b. Job descriptions 　c. Procedures 　d. Research protocols
3. Playfulness 　a. Informality 　b. Skunkworks 　c. Slack resources	3. Project criteria	3. Social values
	4. Project checkpoints 5. Competition 　a. Shoot-outs 　b. Managerial competition for resources	

Selection. In the rational choice model of management, selection occurs through deliberate managerial choice among alternatives for future action. Once more, however, there is a continuum of approaches management may use to execute or facilitate adaptive selection processes. *Setting goals* but not determining the methods to reach them represents a first move away from complete advance selection of action by the manager. Goals can be seen as a device for providing selection criteria for lower levels of employees to use in determining what they should do (Quinn, 1980; Imai, Nonaka, and Takeuchi, 1985). Employees can ask the question, Does this action or routine further progress toward goals X? as the criterion for selection actions to take and routines to retain. The goals establish premises for decisions made by others in the future (Simon, 1976).

Where fundamental uncertainty or ambiguity is involved, however—as in basic science, some areas of product design, artistic ventures, or times of powerful exogenous change—management may lack the knowledge to specify clear goals in advance.

Managers in high tech companies sometimes eschew narrow goals and *establish broad values* instead. The values can be instrumental—"Will this project further our general value of completing profitable innovations?"—in which case they verge on goals. But they may also be broadly normative—"Is this what a world class biotechnology company would do?" For example, observers note that upper management exerted indirect control at Epson through promoting a value of "thinking the unthinkable." This slogan helped sustain an unwritten rule of thumb that the next generation project should represent a 40 percent improvement in the last generation

(Imai, Nonaka, and Takeuchi, 1985). Values may permit actors to follow a logic of appropriateness rather than instrumentality (March and Olson, 1989).

Management may put in place *preidentified checkpoints* or establish very *basic screening criteria* for project survival. Quinn (1986), for example, describes "chaos within milestones," in which managers give only very broad goals but specify certain decision points at which they will intervene, along with a few critical technical limits. Large firms dependent on new product development routinely attempt to use screening criteria such as minimal level of anticipated return on investment or maximum time intervals before the break-even point.

In some cases, it may even be inappropriate to establish criteria before the actual selection process. In technology management, organizations often set up powerful competitive processes with only modest specification of ultimate selection criteria to be applied. For example, a firm may use parallel teams to generate variation and then arrange for formal "shoot-outs" between the teams (Quinn, 1986). Part of the final shoot-out may include *competition over what standards should be applied* to the product choice. Teams working on different early VCR technologies, for example, needed to persuade upper management that the features on which their design excelled were most relevant to commercial success.

More broadly, individual managers have long set up informal competition between divisions and departments for budget allocations, attention, and institutional legitimacy (Pfeffer, 1981a). Strategic contingency theory argues that departments that mediate critical external dependencies and uncertainties tend to receive more resources over time (Salancik and Pfeffer, 1977). The political struggle within the organization then becomes the selection mechanism that leads to the dominance of certain departments and routines. Senior managers consciously facilitate such a process, providing funds and legitimacy to several units, designing the rules of the game, and waiting to see who makes the best case for further funds and investment. The evolutionary framework would regard these processes as one possible selection system whose effectiveness would vary under different conditions.

Retention. The crucial concept underlying the retention process is that of consistency. Constant innovation prevents the system from harvesting the value of prior innovation, a crucial competency for adaptive systems (Holland, 1975). In rational planning, variation and selection occur in the planning phase. Implementation and control systems then constitute the retention process: the manager seeks to maintain consistency beween the actions outlined in the plan with the actual behavior of individuals and groups. The formal plan may itself work as a mechanism to create consistency across time and units. Active review through budgets, management information systems, and audits is used to seek consistency by controlling behavior across time and subunits. Once more, however, alternative devices can also sustain retention.

Formalization or codification of apparently effective routines—whether planned or not—serves as a retention process. Management may formalize apparently successful actions into rules, policies, organization charts, job descriptions, or research protocols, moving the practices into the "taken for granted" part of organizational life. The U.S. Army, for example, provides its members with handbooks of explicit, illustrated microroutines for literally hundreds of situations (Department of the Army, 1990). Total quality efforts to identify "current best practices" similarly seek to enhance the chances effective routines will be followed by all. Specific routines may even be codified physically through such practices as redesigning equipment to encourage specific behaviors or drawing lines at the place a worker should stand at a particular machine.

Technological organizations have long contended that their need for effective and rapid variation forecloses using written formalization as the primary retention mechanism. Many high tech firms seek to sustain consistency through company "cultures" and informal socialization into particular *values*. One can argue that Japanese firms can avoid detailed narrow job descriptions precisely because lifetime employment enhances such shared values (Miner, 1990). Thus while values can serve as a selection device for future action, they also serve as a retention mechanism.

Responsibility for Balance

Managerial action affects not only the specific modes of variation, selection, and retention, but also the continuous balance between internal evolutionary processes. Two relationships are especially crucial: (1) the balance between variation and retention, including questions of incremental versus radical variation, and (2) the balance between competition and mutualism.

Variation and Retention. The manager who increases the relative level of investment in research and development for product innovation has decided that variation must be increased relative to retention. Many observers have noted that the potential value of new discoveries must always be weighed against the value of harvesting current knowledge (Holland, 1975; Levitt and March, 1988; Miner, 1990; Leonard-Barton, 1991).

In a stable, clear environment variation in the world can be represented rather well in "thought experiments" in the planning process and in traditional managerial control mechanisms used for retention. Even if causal processes are not known, effective trial and error learning can occur. Visibly effective procedures, machines, policies, or people can be selected and sustained for long periods, although the reason they are effective is unknown. The crucial task is to maintain high consistency in organizational action (Deming, 1981; Hannan and Freeman, 1984). Thus, in a stable environment the retention system should be very strong relative to variation, and selection mechanisms can be stable and stringent (Miner, 1990).

A changing or ambiguous setting can shift the required balance, however. If no current routine will be effective for long, higher levels of variation are needed to provide sufficient candidates for new routines. If the effects of routines are very ambiguous, higher levels of experimentation are needed to permit organizational learning. Traditional expectations about 'organic' organizations under uncertainty reflect these ideas. In addition, strategic management theorists have noted for some time that senior managers play a crucial role in designing the overall balance of discovery versus continuity (Mintzberg, 1973; Burgelman, 1983). The specifically evolutionary perspective implies in addition that (1) *all* managers must continuously assess this balance, (2) hidden factors may crucially affect the balance, and (3) managers must address issues of incremental versus radical change.

Levels. The evolutionary perspective implies that managers at all levels need to address this balance continuously (Weick, 1979; Robey, 1982; Miner, 1990) because variation and selection are continuous at all levels of the organization. Operational managers in high technology firms that use cross-functional teams for product development, for example, have reported that one crucial task is to achieve the correct balance of variation—through new team members and diversity in functions—and continuity—through experienced team members and fewer functions (Imai et al., 1985; Williams, 1991, personal communication). In a study of university administrators Miner (1990) observed a midlevel development officer who steadily generated well-researched mathematical plans for future fundraising efforts but also put together unusual groups of volunteers in surprising settings and encouraged irrelevant topics in meetings. He believed he needed a minor but consistent flow of such inefficient activities to maintain a successful fundraising program in the long run.

Hidden Factors. Deciding how much to invest in research and development relative to manufacturing is a decision that obviously affects the balance of variation and retention. Decisions on organizational structure, accounting systems, and human resource policies also affect the balance, however. They may be especially powerful, because their effects are pervasive but invisible.

Some high technology firms, for example, make many natural experiments in structural revisions with high impact on the relationship between variation and retention (Peters, 1990). Consider a firm whose leadership acquires a small innovative scientific firm. To keep the innovative culture, they turn this firm into a research driven division which balances the original manufacturing core of the original company. To hold key high risk research scientists from the new division, however, the firm creates a scheme in which scientists with high risk new ideas can help create a venture subsidiary partially financed by the company. The scientists then hold equity interest in the subsidiary they work for. If the new ideas pay off, the firm reintegrates the subsidiary and the scientists realize exceptional gains.

After ten years the firm finds that the subsidiary system designed to foster innovation (variation) creates problems in the main firm that threaten the entire firm's survival. The firm cannot maintain sufficient morale or consistency within the manufacturing division and reintegrated subsidiary personnel. Yet it cannot survive without these core divisions which produce the products and incremental research. The firm then gets rid of or reduces funds allocated to the subsidiary system to adjust the balance of variation and retention in the total system.

Similarly, choices of accounting and human resource practices affect the ongoing balance and mechanisms for variation and retention. Activity based accounting, for example, can change the apparent cost basis for innovative products and provide visibility to the effects of process innovations. Internal promotion and training policies profoundly affect not only the levels of retention but the types of consistency and variation in the organization. Information and decisionmaking structures can be modeled in which beliefs and values can themselves can evolve as a function of experience (Cohen and Axelrod, 1984).

Incremental Versus Radical Change. Punctuational theorists have argued that in most organizations, long periods of strong retention or incremental change are followed by occasional bursts of major variation and reselection (Tushman and Romanelli, 1985). Others (March, 1982) have suggested that continuous replacement of small routines may have major impact. Although wars, major technological advances, and social revolutions may lead to periods of radical variation outside managerial control, managers can affect the balance of incremental versus radical variation and retention shifts. Indeed, much writing on the management of technology focuses precisely on ideas about how managers can replace inertial patterns with sufficiently strong incremental variation (Nonaka, 1988).

Competition and Mutualism (Cooperation). By competition I refer to situations in which two or more players have incompatible goals or requirements. The parties may or may not be aware of their conflicting interests. I define mutualism as occurring when each party's behavior enhances the other party's interests. When mutualism is intentional, it can be called cooperation. Much traditional theory has assumed that (1) mutualism should dominate relationships *within* organizations, while (2) competition should dominate relationships *between* organizations. The evolutionary framework implies that (1) competition and mutualism should regularly occur both between and within organizations, and that (2) an organization's balance between competition and mutualism at both levels will affect its survival and prosperity.

If an organization has clear, consistent goals, internal conflict and competition needlessly waste energy and reduce efficiency. We know, of course, that conflict routinely marks ordinary organizations (Strauss, 1978; Edwards, 1979; Pfeffer, 1981b). Current management texts also acknowledge that a certain amount of conflict can stimulate healthy action, internal cohesion, and invention (Aldag and Stearns, 1991; Dunham and Pierce, 1989). This prescription is typically grounded in heuristics, however, and is hard to link to rational planning models.

In an evolutionary perspective, the competition-mutualism conflict can be conceptualized as a special case of balancing variation and retention. The crucial concept in the process of retention is consistency: across time and across units. Competition, by definition, represents a form of inconsistency between existing routines or people (variation). Mutualism represents one type of consistency (retention). Looking inside organizations, we saw earlier that managers in high technology organizations sometimes (1) intentionally enhance conflict to generate innovations from current practices (variation), (2) use direct competition to select between variations (selection), and yet, and (3) seek cooperation and congruence in exploiting the innovations (retention).

Looking at the organization's external links, it has become a cliché to note that firms in many fast-moving technological areas now form a variety of cooperative organizational arrangements such as formal joint ventures, research consortia, complex subcontrasts, and joint technological projects. Interorganizational mutualism has always existed, however, including direct cooperation in trade associations, educational associations, private elite clubs, and professional associations. The complex relationships among high technology firms are not a new phenomenon but simply reflect a shift in the balance and forms of interorganizational mutualism.

The evolutionary framework highlights the fact that competition and mutualism routinely occur within a single relationship. Firms in successful joint research projects, for example, may jointly develop 'precompetitive' findings which will help one country's industry survive international competition. Each firm must simultaneously guard its distinctive competencies, however, because of direct economic competition from the other firms in the consortium.

Research Implications of the Evolutionary Model of Managerial Action

The evolutionary perspective suggests several areas for research, including: (1) the value and dangers of competency driven action, (2) recombinations of organizational routines as a source of useful innovation, (3) acquisition of external routines, and (4) second-order interactions between organizational routines. Such research should prove fruitful if it is closely linked with research on the relationships of social interaction routines and the nature of symbolic routines.

Competency Driven Action. For the most part, management theory aggressively cautioned managers about the danger of using current competencies to pick future actions. There are solid theoretical grounds for this position, of course. Managers may fail to see obviously better practices because they do not search beyond current routines. In addition, "competency traps" may arise in which the organization are aware of alternatives but fail to choose them because of switching costs (March, 1991). The short-term lure of exploiting current competencies takes the organization down a path which ultimately leads to failure (Starbuck, 1983; Levitt and March, 1988; March, 1991).

For example, when only firms that have competency in a new technology will survive, action based on old competencies by other firms can lead to their failure. Indeed, it is widely believed by students of the management of technological innovation that firms with a highly developed competency in one generation of a technology may be least likely to survive in the next round of competition, because the temptation to exploit their existing base will be too strong to overcome (Cooper and Schendel, 1976; Peters, 1990).

On the other hand, competency driven action has consistently been observed (Cohen, March, and Olsen, 1972) and can clearly represent an intelligent practice. Change can be costly and lead to unintended destructive outcomes. Reliability or consistency in and of itself may enhance survival (Hannan and Freeman, 1984). With an abundance of both problems and opportunities, it may be efficient to "build capabilities and then encourage the development of plans for exploiting them" (Hayes, 1985:118). Miner (1985) argued, for example, that building jobs around existing employee competencies may be a sensible strategy in the face of uncertainty and ambiguity and found some evidence consistent with this idea. Strategy research in general has increasingly argued that firms should try to identify and exploit core competencies. Quinn (1980) stressed "logical incrementalism" in which the firm generally exploits current competencies, making incremental adaptations as exploratory probes of alternative pathways.

In general, the management literature has combined a theoretical preference for avoiding competency based action with the field based observation that it sometimes makes sense. The evolutionary framework provides a theoretical rationale for both competency based action and its dangers. The organization is a bundle of routines, some of which constitute crucial competencies (Aldrich, 1978; McElvey, 1982; Winter, 1987). Competency driven action focuses on capturing value from existing routines, the underlying purpose of retention processes. Research, then, should focus on conditions enhancing the likely value of competency based action (retention) versus that of the search for new competencies (variation).

Recombination of Organizational Routines. Theorists have long noted that systems may be more efficient if they are composed of stable subunits which can be reassembled, if necessary, after shocks (Simon, 1957). More recently studies of adaptive systems have emphasized that recombinations of routines or subunits have powerful adaptive potential (Holland, 1975). Indeed, while early models of genetic evolution focused on individual mutations as a major engine of change, later work emphasized recombinations of genes and groups of gene fragments as the source of importance genetic innovation. Similarly, early theorizing about organizational innovation focused on wholly novel individual practices.

Increasingly, field research points to recombinations of existing routines as an important source of fruitful change (Schroeder et al., 1989). Product innovation, for example, may consist of recombinations of existing products. Manufacturing flexibility, innovation, and speed may depend directly on the use of preidentified subunits or technological modules. Crucial innovation also arises for new combinations of preexisting products and marketing channels. For example, Timex combined certain watch technologies with the new marketing channel of drugstores (instead of jewelry stores) (Abernathy and Clark, 1985). Administrative reorganization may consist of reassigning old sets of duties to existing employees in new ways that lead to substantial change.

The idea that recombinations of old routines may have important impact has powerful implications. It implies we cannot deduce the original scale of managerial intervention from the scale of impact. Small interventions—if they produce crucial recombinations—could have major impact. Similarly, innovations may have little or no impact unless combined with other routines. If so, we may need to remain agnostic about the ultimate impact of particular practices which research has shown to have little effect when studied separately. For example, Kochan, Cutcher-Gershenfeld, and MacDuffie (1992) suggest that employee involvement may indeed have little reliable impact when implemented by itself, but powerful effects when combined with other new managerial practices.

Studying recombinations or organizational routines should prove somewhat more tractable for quantitative empirical work than studying the formation of initial routines themselves. While recombinations of technical routines offer an obvious starting point, recombinations of administrative routines may yield more fundamental results. Fruitful questions include both the degree of evidence that recombination is an important source of variations and insight into how managers might design routines to offer the highest promise for recombinations.

Incorporation of Routines from External Sources. While studies of the diffusion of innovations track routines moving from one organization to another, they have not yet yielded a comprehensive, empirically supported theory about the processes and impact of importing routines (Clark, 1987). The evolutionary perspective directs attention to imitation as an intelligent way of acquiring new routines (generating variation). It can be more efficient than invention or trial and error learning, allowing others to absorb the costs of search and experimentation (Dutton and Freeman, 1985; Teece, 1987).

Because the organization is nested in a dynamic system of interacting organizations, however, imitation may or may not be a consistently effective tool for organizational survival. Among other things, imitation may lead the organization to copy faulty practices, may attract it into areas that have already been exploited, or may cause it to wait when fast action would be preferred (Dutton and Freeman, 1985; Bourgeois and Eisenhardt, 1988; Lant and Mezias, 1990). Although recent related work has included field studies and simulation studies, clearly additional empirical research is needed on the impact of importing routines. In addition, much work remains to be done on the actual processes and costs of being able to import external routines (Van de Ven and Poole, 1989; Cohen and Levinthal, 1990).

Many observers have noted that benign opportunism and improvisation routinely occur in organizations (Alinsky, 1971; Quinn, 1980; Miner, 1987). The evolutionary perspective should permit us to move from rediscovering the existence of such behavior and explore when such behavior is most likely to be productive and what skills support effective scanning and importation.

Second-Order Interactions. Existing theory already identifies many more complex ecologies of interacting organizational routines above and beyond the simple variation-selection-retention model (Nelson and Winter, 1982; Levitt and March, 1990; McKelvey, 1982; March, 1991). The validity of intuition falls away quickly when we consider second-order effects of interactions of routines. Qualitative researchers have already documented in careful ethnographic research the banality of surprises (March and Olsen, 1976; Strauss, 1978; Van de Ven, Angle, and Poole, 1989), accidental combinations of people and events (Allison, 1971; March and Olsen, 1976), and the role of serendipity in even major organizational change (Allison, 1971; Quinn, 1980). Even simple models of interacting routines can and most likely will produce unexpected—even startling—outcomes (Schelling, 1978).

Simulation studies are attractive for studying these interactions, because they permit one to model multiple elements interacting over multiple trials, with specifically stochastic elements built into the process these studies serve the useful function of testing our intuition against the actual implications of particular mathematical assumptions and suggest important possible second-order effects (e.g., March, 1991). However, the sensitivity of simulations to assumptions and their degrees of freedom make them unsatisfying as the primary tool for exploring this area. Direct field research on the interaction of routines over time is called for at this time (Hutchins, 1991; Miner, 1991; Van de Ven and Garud on coevolution, chapter 20, this volume).

It will be particularly helpful to try to identify circumstances under which small variations may cascade into systemwide outcomes, or in which patterns of effects are counterintuitive (Starbuck, 1976; Weick, 1979; Van de Ven, Angle, and Poole, 1989;

March, 1991; Ginsberg and Baum, chapter 7, this volume). At a minimum, field research may provide a warning about where prudence is most needed. At best, it could point to circumstances in which small interventions (or lack of intervention) could have large positive consequences.

Linkage with Other Current Perspectives. Although research on the themes described should prove fruitful, it could lapse into a sterile exercise unless it builds on and extends current work on the role of social interaction and the role of symbolic routines.

Social Interaction and Organizational Routines. Some theorists have argued that crucial variation and selection processes operate over individual human beings (Starbuck, 1976; Aldrich, 1979; McKelvey, 1982; Boyd and Richerson, 1985). Variation occurs among individuals, some of whom are selected to remain or be given more influence. New organizational patterns arise from the activity of these new individuals.

For the most part, however, most evolutionary discussions of organizational change discuss routines as though they exist independent of individual human beings (Cyert and March, 1963; Aldrich, 1979; McKelvey, 1982; Nelson and Winter, 1982). "Standard operating procedures," assembly lines, accounting practices, rules of war, and strategies, for example, evoke images of disembodied entities removed from day-to-day human interaction. Like structural and rational theories, evolutionary models can easily lapse into ignoring social interaction (Granovetter, 1985).

Most observers of technology transfer, for example, have concluded that personal interaction plays a central role in the fruitful transfer of new technologies. But the processes are likely to be more complex than simple communication of information across known dyads. "Information" does not move about in organizations as a disembodied, atomistic entity (Granovetter, 1985; Leonard-Barton, 1990; Papa, 1990). Competencies may also be embedded in the day to day functioning of informal social networks of practice (Barley, 1988; Brown and Duguid, 1991; Hutchins, 1991). Networks of practice may even function outside the full awareness of their members (Hutchins, 1991). Imitation may occur through structural rather than direct mechanisms.

What is needed now is more precise theory on the subtle ways through which social ties relate to organizational routines. Two issues deserve attention. First, how does individual behavior—which may or may not be the product of stable traits—create and support organizational routines (Berger and Luckman, 1967; Zucker, 1977; Strauss, 1978; Barley, 1988; Miner, 1991)? Second, how do social networks themselves function as agents or objects of selection (Baum, 1988)?

Symbolic Routines. Although Weick (1979) put the active human interpretive role of organizations at the forefront of his evolutionary model of organizations, empirical research on this theme has proved difficult. Two directions offer substantial promise at this time, however. First, we can use a variation, selection, and retention framework to study symbolic routines. In doing so, we will need to incorporate the instability in the meaning of events as well as uncertainty about which particular event will occur, however (Weick, 1979; Dutton, 1993). Early research on innovation, for example, tended to treat innovations as though they were stable collections of fixed technical routines passively absorbed by adopters. Later work showed that developers and adopters of innovations often unbundle and reinterpret the meanings of subroutines (Van de Ven, Angle, and Poole, 1989; Dougherty, 1992). An evolutionary framework suggests looking for events which affect the unbundling of combinations of symbols or open unclaimed fields of meaning. These periods permit variation and competition over the meaning of routines. In a work setting, for example, Barley (1988) describes periods in which radiologists and technicians actively negotiate the meaning of their own actions after the introduction of new technology. At other times, the meaning of certain actions becomes part of a take-for-granted set of stable roles (retention) (Berger and Luckman, 1967; Barley, 1988). Current work on knowledge structures within organizations provides an important foundation for this line of inquiry (Walsh, 1990).

Second, we need to study how symbolic and material routines interact. Symbols, of course, have quite material impact in human affairs. Legitimacy facilitates the flow of actual resources; symbols enhancing trust lead to real actions of generosity. In the technology area, observers have noted that the fate of new products can be influenced by the precise way they are linked (or not linked) to dominant beliefs about firm competencies (Leanard-Barton, 1991). Most observers of organizational change note that linking a new routine to existing core competencies or values enhances its legitimacy. On the other hand, managers sometimes consciously sharpen the distinctions between new projects and current core competencies as part of a broader renewal process (Leonard-Barton, 1991).

Interestingly, the existence of ecologies of symbolic routines implies there may be more degrees of freedom for managers than implied by traditional models of technological evolution. If managerial innovation involves active interpretation of ambiguous internal and internal events, then managers can introduce variation not only by introducing a new practices or products, but by reinterpreting old practices and products in ways that carry new meaning (Daft and Weick, 1984).

Nearly a decade ago, Pfeffer (1982:1) lamented, "The domain of organization theory is coming to resemble more of a weed patch than a well-tended garden." The internal evolutionary perspective has generally been regarded as an amusing but marginal theory in this garden: useful perhaps as a metaphor for arts and scientific organizations, or for irreligious questioning of ideologies of managerial control. In this essay I suggest in contrast that the evolutionary perspective represents a strong candidate for an integrated general theory of managerial action.

In this framework, managerial action can affect the organization's internal evolution, the evolutionary system in which it is nested, and the coevolution of organizations and their contexts (Tushman and Rosenkopf, 1992; Baum and Singh, chapter 18, this volume). Managers appropriately seek adaptive advantage through increasing the probability that their organization both survive and prosper over time. Focusing on the internal processes, I have described managerial action as affecting variation, selection, and retention processes both separately and in relation to each other. Close examination of these steps indicates that in many cases one can reframe apparently contradictory current theoretical models—including rational, political, and learning models—as special cases of the more general evolutionary framework.

Adoption of the evolutionary framework as an overarching normative theory carries obvious dangers. Empirical research on internal evolution has proved difficult. A new literature with complex theoretical elaboration but little solid empirical research is not needed. In addition, it is easy to lapse into dangerous functionalism when using this perspective, blindly assuming that whatever is, must be good (Hannan and Freeman, 1977; Gould, 1980).

On the other hand, this framework offers several advantages. First, it is inherently dynamic and interactive, consistent with many seasoned observers' intuition regarding processes underlying organizational action. Second, although at first glance it appears contradictory to several current theories, it can actually incorporate and suggest links between the theories. A textbook grounded in this framework, for example, could begin with an overarching vision of nested evolutionary systems and treat traditional planning, organizing, directing, and controlling steps as appropriate vehicles for variation, selection, and retention under conditions of some stability. Organizational change, entrepreneurship, and technology management—which sometimes appear as awkward appendages to the planning model—could describe the alternative variation, selection, and retention devices managers use under less stable or clear conditions.

Third, the evolutionary framework generates potentially fruitful research questions, including (1) the role of competency based action, (2) innovation through recombinations of routines, (3) acquisition of routines from outside organizations, and (4) unintended outcomes of organizational practices. Such research would appropriately incorporate issues of social ties and symbolic organizational routines. An obvious additional area for immediate attention is the link between organizational evolution and organizational learning (Miner, 1991).

In terms of applied research, this framework offers an intellectually responsible structure for research on current trends such as total quality practices, problems in product development, technology transfer, and interorganizational cooperation. Managerial practices in high technology organizations are themselves organizational routines that have diffused over time and may represent both superstitious and appropriate learning, for example.

Finally, the evolutionary framework may assist managers not only through applied research, but through influence on their conception of management's role. The evolutionary approach described here implies managers can affect organizational outcome, but only on a probalistic basis, and only by using highly varied influence techniques including process design, political processes, improvisation, and symbolic routines. The approach does not reduce the stature of the managerial role but implies a fairly subtle but heroic managerial mission. A realistic understanding of this mission may better equip current managers to deal realistically with the current explosion of competition, international communication and trade, social diversity, and technological change.

Overall, then, the evolutionary framework offers refreshing verisimilitude, and the potential for integration of multiple theories, rich research, and potential practical value. In terms of Pfeffer's concern about the ill-tended garden of organization theory, evolutionary theory may offer a previously hidden underlying pattern for the existing plantings, while also providing fertile ground for promising new growth.

6

Organizing for Continuous Improvement: Evolutionary Theory Meets the Quality Revolution

SIDNEY G. WINTER

The producers of management advice operate in an economic environment where the tides of fad and fashion run strong. Frameworks, slogans, and buzzwords are brought forth in great profusion with attendant fanfare and claims of novelty. Although large rewards often accrue to successful fashion leaders, it is open to question whether organizations actually perform much better as a result of this activity. To the jaded eye, the latest widely acclaimed insight often looks suspiciously like a fancy repackaging of some familiar platitude or truism. Alternatively, it may be that this year's fashionable ideas are genuinely valuable—but largely because they help to correct a misallocation of attention that was itself produced by an excess of enthusiasm for ideas fashionable in the recent past.

Quality is now a very fashionable word in the management vocabulary. Not too long ago, *Business Week* devoted a special issue to "The Quality Imperative," declaring in its introduction that a focus on quality is producing a "global revolution, affecting every facet of business" (1991:7). Skeptics are not hard to find, however.

If the quality revolution is as significant as its proponents claim, it may well be the most important management innovation of the 20th (and early 21st) century. If its significance is only a fraction of what is claimed, it could still be quite important. In either of these cases, its importance would relate not merely to the theory and practice of management, but also to the assessment of the long-term economic outlook. For example, a major part of the "competitiveness" problem of the U.S. economy might be attributable to the follower status of the United States in the diffusion of quality management innovations. On the other hand, if quality management is merely a collection of buzzwords, it is safe to tune out—unless one has a stake in being in touch with current fashion.

That quality management should be taken seriously is the major conclusion of this chapter, but also, in a sense, its major premise: the chapter would not exist if I

Thanks are due to Jitendra Singh and Don Kash for helpful comments on earlier drafts of this chapter; the usual caveats apply.

had reached the opposite conclusion. Quality management ideas provide an interesting perspective on the nature of productive knowledge and the processes by which it is maintained and improved in organizations. It seems clear that their importance as a source of improvement in organizational performance is substantial; how far the revolution may go and what its consequences may be are important and interesting questions. I seek to explain and assess the quality revolution in terms that link its principal ideas to the characterization of firm behavior in evolutionary economic theory (Nelson and Winter, 1982). Many of the perspectives offered here are specifically and obviously *economic* perspectives—but the evolutionary, ecological, and organization-theoretic aspects of evolutionary economic theory also inform this appraisal in significant ways. In particular, the final major section of the chapter sketches some general hypotheses about the ecology of quality management—the characteristics of the organizational and economic niches in which this management innovation is likely to grow and prosper. The chapter may thus serve, indirectly, to link quality management ideas to economics, evolutionary theory, and organization theory generally.

In discussing these ideas, I attempt to minimize the use of quality management jargon and acronyms. Quality management maxims and statements of the recognized "gurus" of the subject are sprinkled in occasionally for clarification and seasoning. One has to concede that "Seek out the low-hanging fruit first!" has a certain appeal relative to its proximate equivalent in economic theory, "Allocate effort to where its marginal product is the highest!"[1]

The ideas and literature of the quality revolution derive from a number of different sources and involve a number of major themes. Most current accounts of the history of thought in the area emphasize the influence of two Americans, W. Edwards Deming and J. M. Juran. There are numerous parallels between the careers of these two men, including their becoming influential in the United States after first being so in Japan, and the fact that both remain vigorous and active in the quality movement at advanced ages. It is clear, however, that the Japanese themselves have not only led the way in making the quality revolution a reality, but have also contributed fundamentally to its intellectual foundations.[2] Further, not only have there been many "follow-on inventions" in the quality field, but there have been numerous precursors, foreshadowers, and independent coinventors of major themes. As a result, attributions of ideas involve more than the usual hazards.

I make only occasional attributions; the principal focus is on the ideas themselves, not on their sources. As a corollary, the account of quality management here is more my own synthesis of what seems particularly interesting than an attempt to reproduce accurately a particular school of thought.[3]

Evidence and Interpretation

The available evidence that supports the effectiveness of quality management methods is of several kinds. Some of the world's most successful competitors are acknowledged leaders in the practice of quality management and emphatically state their full allegiance to quality management principles—Toyota is perhaps the leading example. Also, there are strong adherents of quality management among executives of struggling or moderately successful companies as well as of highly successful companies. These adherents from less successful companies do not typically blame the quality management tools for their problems; they blame themselves and their fellows for making a late start.

The time required for quality management methods to produce results is, in fact, a key issue. For external observers interested in checking the claims made for quality management, it would be convenient if these tools were touted as the functional equivalent of a magic wand that produces instant, companywide performance improvements. Assuming that the waving of the wand were itself an observable event, it would then be relatively easy to check the validity of the claims. Inconveniently for external observers, the magic wand claim is rarely if ever made. Instead, the usual account is that the introduction of quality management is an incremental, time-consuming (even never-ending) process.

It is not surprising, therefore, that some of the most interesting evidence about quality management methods comes from a very microscopic level, relating to improvements achieved in particular processes. Much of this evidence consists of quantitative anecdotes—accounts of improvements by large factors that were made in particular performance indicators. Among the type of indicators often featured in these stories are defect rates and cycle times. For example, the *Business Week* special issue contains the following story from Hewlett-Packard: "At one HP factory a decade ago, four of every 1,000 soldered connections were defective, not bad for those days. Engineers were called in, and they cut the defect rate in half by modifying the process. Then, HP turned to its workers. They practically rebuilt the operation—and slashed defects a thousandfold, to under two per million" (1991:16).

As illustrated by the examples of defect rates and cycle times, the performance indicators that typically appear in quality management success stories are not direct measures of profitability.[4] Neither do they relate directly to variables like unit cost or market share, whose links to profitability are familiar themes in economic discussion. In some cases, the indicators may be regarded as proxies for what economists call technical efficiency (at the process level). They are imperfect proxies, however, because the improvements reported in "output" measures typically occur at the expense of increases in some inputs. Further, some investment of resources is always required to bring about the improvement in the first place. Regardless of whether this investment is treated as R&D expenditure for accounting purposes, in economic substance it is process R&D expenditure.

To any individual success story, therefore, a skeptical economist might reasonably respond with "So what?" Not enough information is presented about the bottom-line value of the improvement reported, or about the investment costs and continuing costs of the improvement, to permit an assessment of its economic merit. Further, an economic assessment of the general methods whose power is supposedly illustrated in the success stories would have to address the obvious sampling problem: there are failure stories as well as success stories, and those must be given appropriate weight in an overall assessment. That quality management methods have produced positive results in some organizations is beyond dispute; that these methods are generally economically effective by conventional standards has not been demonstrated.

The phrase "by conventional standards" implicitly invokes an important assumption. Although there is continuing debate about the appropriate goals of the large corporation, economists generally take a narrow view of the matter: they think that private sector managers should concern themselves with profit or present value or perhaps the market value of the firm. Efforts to lower defect rates (for example) may or may not contribute to success in this sense. If they do, fine. If not, the costly pursuit of such technical goals is ill-advised.

Two aspects of this assessment need to be considered, one relating to the actual preeminence of the profit goal and the other to its explicitness. The first involves basic questions about the role of the corporate form in economic organization. If the fundamental social rationale of the corporation is strictly to help investors make money, there may be correspondingly fundamental limits to the efficiency gains achievable by imbuing managers and workers with a culture of mutual trust and cooperation. This issue is discussed further, though of course far from comprehensively, later in this chapter.

The explicitness aspect can again be divided into two parts. First, there is a further perspective on the profit goal. If long-run profit maximization is the goal of the investors who are ultimately in control, it is conceivable that their interests are served by keeping that fact as secret as possible. Perhaps such a deceit is the most effective way to approach the fundamental efficiency limits referred to earlier. There is a school of thought regarding quality management that interprets it as the latest manifestation of a recurring pattern in which owners and/or managers pursue their own interests by attempting to deceive workers—talk of efficiency and cooperation masks an attempt to induce workers to work harder while conceding as little as possible of the resulting product.[5]

There is also the question of whether explicit attention to ultimate goals is otherwise desirable, apart from the fact that it may involve the sacrifice of gains attainable through obfuscation or deceit. In its emphasis on the pursuit of a large number of narrow technical goals, quality management doctrine often appears indifferent to the economic logic of resource allocation. Such indifference may lead to overinvestment in the pursuit of technical achievements that do not actually matter very much. Although this observation has some force, it is simplistic to assume that explicit attention to ultimate goals is always instrumental in achieving those goals. Should the receiver, leaping to catch the pass from the quarterback, be thinking about advancing the ball and winning the game—or should he focus on *catching* the ball? Common wisdom on the subject advises the latter. Similarly, quality management's emphasis on proximate goals and measurable achievements may be sound advice in a world where the effective allocation of scarce attention is a real issue.

Quality Management as Heuristic Problem Solving

In the following section, I characterize quality management methods in terms of specific attributes. For present purposes, I require only the following broad characterization of what "quality management" refers to: Quality management is the quest for improvement in organizational routines through the application of a particular collection of problem-solving heuristics and techniques. An important premise underlying most of these heuristics and techniques is that key information required for the improvement of a routine can be obtained only with the active cooperation of those involved in its performance.

A problem-solving heuristic is an approach to problem solving that is useful in spite of limitations deriving in part from vagueness and in part from uncertainty regarding its domain of application. Because of these limitations, shared with all heuristic methods, quality management cannot be expected to *optimize* routines in the sense that optimization is understood in formal economic theory.

At an abstract level, "optimization" means getting the right answer to the problem, and no other approach can logically surpass it. Realistically, however, no approach guarantees getting the right answer, even supposing the formulation of the right question. When real world problems are attacked with optimization methods, it is not the theoretical kind of optimization but optimization-as-heuristic that is at work (Nelson and Winter, 1982:133, 381).

The optimization heuristic advises that the real problem be described and represented in a way that maps it into the known domain of some well-defined optimization method—an optimization algorithm—and that the algorithm then be applied. The processes of identifying the criterion and the constraints gathering relevant data, and achieving the required representation are part of the optimization heuristic, but they are not part of any algorithm. The cost-benefit analysis of the selection of a particular algorithm, with its associated implementation requirements and costs, is also not within the scope of any algorithm. The optimization heuristic is vague about these matters and offers little guidance regarding the limits of its own applicability.

Assessing the practical merits of any body of heuristic methods is inevitably a chancy business. If there is a leap of faith involved in the adoption of quality management as a problem-solving approach, some such leap is also involved in the practical application of linear programming, capital asset pricing, or computable general equilibrium models.

One difference, important to economists if not otherwise, is that the latter methods carry the cachet of economic theory, whereas quality management in its present form is largely a body of methods that have emerged from practice. A corollary observation is that quality management is more explicit in its guidance regarding practical implementation than are problem-solving techniques whose intellectual roots are in economics or operations research.

Key Features of Quality Management

The quality revolution may constitute a major peak in understanding of organization and management, but it is a peak that is often shrouded in a fog of confusion and misunderstanding. A number of conditions contribute to the formation of this fog. The quasi-religious fervor of some advocates is by itself enough to put a reasonable person on guard, and the more so if the advocate is also a seller who stands to profit from a successful pitch. The "empowerment" of employees is a major theme in quality management discussion, and for the casual listener such discussion may be reminiscent of all-too-familiar ideological controversies (just when we thought that chapter of history was safely closed). There is proliferation of jargon, there is aggressive product differentiation effort by purveyors, and there is sectarian controversy—reminiscent, again, of ideological ferment of a political or religious nature. (*Business Week,* 1991:53).

Above all, the word *quality* itself invites misunderstanding. Quality in the sense of reliability, durability, product features, and so forth, is clearly important, but does it deserve attention to the utter exclusion of other economically significant measures, such as cost, price, and productivity? The answer is that no such exclusion is involved. Indeed, it is quite possible that the most important contributions of quality management might fall under the familiar heading that economists label "cost reduction" rather than "quality improvement" in the conventional sense.

Process Orientation

This potential for misunderstanding of "quality" derives directly from the most important feature of modern quality management: it directs attention to the improvement of production processes, and not simply to the characteristics of the products. To a degree, it involves a rejection of the original formulation of quality control, which sought assurance that the characteristics of the end-product fell within preassigned tolerance limits. The critical shortcoming of that approach is that it offers a very limited range of responses when instances of inadequate quality are discovered. Defective products can be discarded, but this implies the waste of the labor and capital services that went into their production, and in most cases of materials and components as well. Or additional costs can be incurred to bring the defective units up to standard—repair and rework costs. Deliberately or otherwise, some below-standard products may be delivered to market, where they will ultimately inflict warranty costs, damage to the producer's reputation, or both. Quality management experts and practitioners assert that these various costs associated with poor quality—not just in final products but at any point in the organization's functioning—are, in combination, very large.[6]

By contrast, a quality control approach that treats the entire production process as within its purview can incorporate quality checks and generate diagnostic information at every stage. The intermediate quality checks serve to limit the amount of faulty production generated when individual processes go out of tolerance, prompting corrective action before the units affected encounter the final quality check. More importantly, intermediate checks are directly useful in locating the source of the difficulty and can be supplemented with additional aids to diagnosis. This information can guide not only immediate short-term corrective action, but long-term efforts at improvement. In both the short and long term, the result is not merely the enhancement of the quality of the final product in conventional terms, but also the reduction of production costs by saving resources formerly devoted to producing discards, or to repair and rework.

Customer Focus

Complementing the concern with the production process "upstream" from its nominal end-point is an enhanced sensitivity to what happens "downstream" from that point—to how well the product or service meets customer needs. This involves a rejection of a narrowly technocratic and inward-looking definition of quality in favor of a more comprehensive and outward-looking definition, a switch from "quality is what our engineers say it is" to "quality is what our customers say it is." In this respect the quality management literature follows a long tradition in economic thought, which insists that the truest indicator of quality is provided by the buyer's utility function.

To implement this approach, information on customer needs and reactions must be gathered. A variety of methods are employed to this end, with the mix depending to some extent on the context. In markets where firms supply innovative products produced to order for other firms, design teams may be expanded to include customer technical representatives. In other markets, the channels of communication to customers may be opened by surveys and focus group discussions, or by 800 numbers to facilitate complaints and comments. It is often recommended that management, at all levels, devote some time to receiving customer feedback directly rather than relying entirely on summary information that has been filtered through the system.

There are limitations, ambiguities, and pitfalls in the notion of customer-defined quality. These derive primarily from the limitations of the customer's information and, relatedly, from the distinction between the customer's satisfaction in the short run and in the long. Some attributes that are actually quite important to the customer—such as safety features—may be difficult for the customer to assess. The most obvious candidate for the role of customer—for example, a purchasing agent—may not fully reflect the long-run interests of the more remote customers who are importantly affected by the product. Customers may be overly conservative, perhaps because they have little idea of what options are actually on the menu, or because they are wary of the risks and inconvenience associated with being early users of innovative products.

Finally, from a social point of view, the notion of customer-defined quality is subject to the same critiques applicable to the closely related idea of consumer sovereignty. Warning labels on cigarettes and alcohol, or motorcycle helmet laws, illustrate the expression in the public policy realm of skepticism about the social merits of choices that individual consumers often make.

These concerns are important qualifications to the simple formulation that "the customer is the final arbiter of quality." There is not, however, much sign that the progress of quality management has been seriously impeded by simplistic notions of customer satisfaction. On the contrary, many companies seem quite flexible and creative in their willingness to expand the concept of "the customer" and seek useful information from behind the facade that they directly encounter in the marketplace.

An important link between the process orientation and customer focus of quality management is the concept of the internal customer. This concept emphasizes that relationships within the producing organization—particularly among successive stages in the production process or in new product development—are akin to relationships at the "market interface" between the organization and its customers. The same techniques that are used to enhance the responsiveness of the organization to its customers are applicable to the internal relationships—particularly, the attempt to meet the needs of internal customers better through improved communication between them and their internal suppliers.

The "internal customer" may be viewed as quality management's counterpart to the financial management device of establishing "profit centers." Like the profit center approach, it seeks to infuse the internal relations of a large organization with an element of market discipline, at the same time heightening appreciation of the fact that the success achieved by the organization as a whole is the sum of many smaller successes or failures. In contrast to the profit center approach, it emphasizes measurement and communication to facilitate horizontal relationships among sub-units, rather than to establish marketlike incentives for subunits and to facilitate performance evaluation from the top.

Analytical and Factual Basis

Quality management techniques facilitate a *disciplined* quest for process involvement. Random tinkering is not advised; neither is the impulsive implementation of a bright idea, whether from top management or from the shop floor. (Suggestions are strongly encouraged, but for study, not immediate implementation.) These familiar methods of seeking improvement are considered inadequate because of their failure to probe the causes of process shortcomings in sufficient depth or to take adequate account of contextual factors. The consequences of such attempts are expected to be small, temporary, and possibly adverse. "Think of the chaos that would come if everyone did his best, not knowing what to do" (Deming, 1986:19).

The techniques employed to guide and structure the quest for improvements constitute the heart of quality management, and they are too numerous for a detailed survey here.[7] Quality consultants and quality management literature offer a wide selection of quite detailed recipes for implementing quality management—or at least attempting to do so. These recipes describe roles, required actions, and rough timetables for action at all levels of the organization. Whether the effort ultimately succeeds or fails depends, however, on the cumulative effect of a large number of individual quality improvement projects. Such projects address particular problems or "opportunities for improvement"; they are typically conducted by project teams composed at least in part of individuals regularly involved with the subprocess in which the problem arises.

In a variety of formulations, quality management authorities and practitioners urge that the first step toward improvement is to achieve understanding of the process as it currently exists. ("If you want to improve a system or process, you must first understand how it works now.") Flowcharting of the current process is a conceptually simple but powerful tool that often produces surprising insights. ("We cannot improve any process until we can flowchart it.") To encounter difficulty in describing and measuring the current "process" is more ominous than to describe successfully an obviously flawed process. It suggests that there *is* no current process; a portion of the organization is simply adrift. ("Adherence precedes improvement.") Identification of the sources of defects or delays and measurement of their frequency and magnitude serve to focus attention on areas where the payoff to improvement may be greatest. Consultation with internal customers and suppliers of the process under examination may permit identification of parts of the process that serve no significant purpose and provide a context for review of proposed changes. Measurement and analysis must continue beyond the identification and attempted implementation of a recommended process change, to determine both whether anticipated favorable results have actually occurred and whether *un*anticipated *unfavorable* results have occurred. If the answers are no, yes, or both no and yes, the quest for improvement must be renewed. The refusal to accept "implementation gaps" is built in.

Leadership and Participation Issues

Much of the intensity and fervor associated with quality management derive from its implications for the roles of managers at various levels, as distinguished from the roles of "hands-on" employees. A distinctive feature of quality management doctrine—especially in the Deming formulation—is that it places responsibility for malfunctioning organizations squarely at the door of top management. ("Export anything to a friendly country except American management" [Deming, as quoted in Walton, 1990:13]). Of the many nostrums profitably peddled to American management over the years, few indeed have so clearly identified the clients themselves as the principal culprits in the difficulties their organizations were suffering.

Management is responsible for the problems because management is responsible for the systems, and it is the systems above all that generate the problems. Deming's "85-15 Rule" holds that 85 percent of what goes wrong is with the system, and only 15 percent with the individual person or thing (Walton, 1990:20). A related idea is that "the people who know the work best are those who perform it" (Walton, 1990:22). Finally, the general assumption about worker motivation is that pride of workmanship is a powerful motivator: "Give the work force a chance to work with pride, and the 3 per cent that apparently don't care will erode itself by peer pressure" (Deming, 1986:85).[8] On the other hand, people may not know how to do a good job, much less how to do a better job in the face of the numerous constraints the organization imposes on them.

These three propositions—that process problems are predominantly attributable to system flaws, that the experts on the work are the people who do it, and that people are fundamentally motivated to do a good job—together imply a need for major recasting of managerial roles in the interests of organizational effectiveness. Although there may be other significant grounds for favoring such a change, they are redundant once the need for improved organized performance is acknowledged. Management must behave so as to provide a supportive structure within which people at lower levels can act effectively to improve performance. It cannot achieve significant performance improvements by its own unilateral action, for it lacks the detailed knowledge required to do so. It might attempt to force the required knowledge to the surface by fiat, but what is likely to surface instead is an account that is brief, abstract, and simple enough for management to understand, and bowdlerized to conform to perceptions of what management is believed to think should be going on. If the real thing were somehow made to surface, management would immediately collapse from information overload—or perhaps from despair.

From this assessment, the need to involve and empower employees becomes apparent, granting only the premise that the need to improve performance exists. The involvement and empowerment of employees are not, of course, objectives that can be accomplished by announcing them one morning as the new corporate policy. Managers must behave in new ways that neither they nor their subordinates fully understand, and they must overcome a long heritage of distrust and justifiable cynicism about change.[9]

Routines, Quality Management, and Evolutionary Theory

Quality management ideas provide an interesting perspective on what organizational capabilities are like in the first place, quite apart from any attempt to improve them. This perspective is similar in many ways to the view of the same issues taken in evolutionary economic theory.

A basic point of contention between the evolutionary theory and orthodox economics is the degree of reality that should be imputed to the orthodox concepts of production sets and production functions—especially long run production functions. As discussed by Nelson and Winter (1982, chapter 3), there are three challenging questions to be raised about the orthodox approach: (1) Where does the knowledge reside? (2) What real considerations could produce a sharp distinction between "technically possible" and "technically impossible" production activities? (3) How does the knowledge possessed by one firm relate to that of others, and to the knowledge environment generally?

On the first point, the orthodox commitment is vague in its details but clearly carries the implication that knowledge is represented in the firm in a form that makes alternative ways of doing things accessible to an effective survey, leading to a choice founded on economic criteria. There is no status quo way of doing things that has special prominence so far as knowledge is concerned; only a costless act of optimizing choice distinguishes the production technique actually used from an alternative that would have been used if prices were different. By contrast, evolutionary theory sees organizational capabilities as fragmented, distributed, and embedded in organizational routines. No individual knows how the organization accomplishes what it actually does, much less what alternatives are available. Although elements of economic choice are built into some routines, the routines themselves are not the consequence of an antecedent choice from a large menu, but of organizational learning.

The quality management perspective is entirely congenial to the evolutionary view but virtually incomprehensible to the orthodox view. Quality management stresses the importance of first *finding out* what process (routine, technique of production) the organization is currently using. Further, this task cannot be approached in a comprehensive way, but only in a fragmented and incremental way that corresponds to the actual distribution of capabilities in the organization. As subprocesses are flowcharted and analyzed, unexpected discoveries are made about how the organization works.

On the second point, the orthodox view sees business firms as operating in a technically efficient manner—right on the cliff edge where the known leaves off and the abyss of the unknown begins. It may be possible to move the cliff edge by investment in research and development, but it is still a cliff edge. Once the engineers have defined the cliff edge, economic choice determines where on that edge the firm operates. On the evolutionary view, there is no cliff edge, and also no sharp distinction between the economics of technical change and the economics of everyday performance. The prevailing organizational routines do not mark the edge of the feasible, but the point where learning stopped—or, more optimistically, the point that learning has now reached.

On the evolutionary view, therefore, it is not particularly surprising that systematic critical scrutiny directed to prevailing routines might turn up major opportunities for improvement in both "technical" methods and "organizational" arrangements. (Evolutionary theory and quality management concur again on the point that the line between the technical and the organizational is not sharply drawn.) There is no general presumption that the prevailing routines ever had such scrutiny in the past. And while "critical scrutiny" may sound simple in principle, quality management teaches that it is anything but simple in practice. Evolutionary theory and quality management doctrine concur again on many specific observations regarding resistance to change—including the important point that such resistance is often functional.

On the third point, evolutionary theory emphasizes that the capabilities of individual firms are not selections from a common technical handbook, but idiosyncratic outcomes of unique firm histories. While imitation across organizational boundaries is a powerful mechanism spreading change through the economy, it is hampered by the general factors tending to stabilize prevailing routines of the imitator and sometimes by attempts at secrecy by the imitatee. The result is something far short of homogenization of method, even within narrowly defined industry categories. The quality management literature takes it for granted that a firm can understand its own methods only by systematic (though fragmented and decentralized) self-study. Methods used by other firms are an important source of ideas for improvement; indeed "competitive benchmarking" is an important branch of quality improvement technique. Effective imitation of the routines of another organization requires, however, at least as much careful analysis and planning as are needed for "home grown" improvement ideas.

In short, there is much common ground between quality management doctrine and evolutionary economic theory with regard to the characterization of organizational capabilities. The improvement program offered by quality management raises somewhat different issues and there is less overlap as a result. (Since evolutionary theory is not a normative approach to management, it is silent on many of the issues that quality management forcefully addresses.) There are, however, some interesting points of contact.

Tacit Knowledge

Evolutionary theory emphasizes that much of the knowledge that underlies organizational capabilities is tacit knowledge; it is not understood or communicable in symbolic form. Two different senses in which this is true have been identified. First, individual skills have large tacit components, and organizational routines involve tacit knowledge to the extent that they involve the exercise of such skills. The second sense relates to the point that organizational knowledge is fragmented. Knowledge that is articulable by some individuals may be inaccessible to others, and to top management in particular. The fact that the organization functions reasonably effectively and is more or less responsive to direction from the top is somewhat mysterious when contemplated from the top—in a sense akin to the CEO's mysterious ability to control his or her car or golf swing, without conscious awareness of how it happens.

The quality management approach to understanding the process as it exists suggests a third, somewhat different perspective on the tacitness of routines. Aspects of a routine that are unknown to any participant may become both known and articulable if the participants get together and talk it over (something they have no occasion to do under routine operation). Together, comparing notes and piecing things together, the team may create an account of how the routine works that simply did not exist before. Such an account provides a framework for predicting the consequences of alterations of the routine and hence an opportunity to plan a successful intervention. Viewed in this light, the injunction "first understand how it works now" calls for an attack on the obstacles to improvement that derive from the tacitness of routines.

This appraisal helps to explain the promise of the method but also suggests some vulnerabilities. There is no chance of articulating all the knowledge that underlies the routine; important areas of tacitness will inevitably remain and can be the source of unintended consequences from improvement efforts. Also, by casting top management in a supporting role in the improvement process, quality management offers relatively little to mitigate the tacitness problem at the top of the organization. It would presumably be helpful for top management to have a better idea of what the organization as a whole can and cannot do; quality management largely defers that problem to some future date—perhaps wisely, perhaps not.

The Ecology of Quality Management

The preceding discussion suggests that quality management is a promising innovation. More accurately, it is meta-innovation, a loose collection of heuristic methods for producing improvements in organizational routines. In a world of imperfect information and understanding, latent opportunities for performance improvement are always abundant. Quality management methods provide some novel ways of converting a portion of these latent opportunities into recognized opportunities, and recognized opportunities into actual improvements. An attempt to assess the likely future influence of these methods, and to identify their most promising niche in the managerial environment, is in order.

In this connection, the general understanding that has been achieved of the processes of diffusion of innovation is clearly relevant. More specifically relevant—and perhaps discouraging for the prospects for successful prognostication and systematic hypothesis testing—is the literature on the diffusion of relatively "soft" innovations that are characterized by substantial ambiguity of definition. Such innovations mutate as they infiltrate differentiated environments, leaving a puzzling trail of definitional issues for the analyst (Walker, 1969; Downs and Mohr, 1976). Given the diversity and complexity of quality management ideas, this problem looms as a serious one.

Leaving this difficulty to one side, the following discussion explores some of the factors that may shape the application and development of quality management.

The "Buy-In" Problem

It has been argued that the need for a major transformation of managerial roles is an implication of quality management insights regarding the locus of productive knowledge in organizations. While this observation provides sufficient justification for the transformation at the theoretical level, it certainly does not sufficiently motivate it at the practical level. Proponents and practitioners of quality management agree that this transformation is unlikely to occur in the absence of a strong commitment at the top of the organization.[10] The innumerable instances of resistance to change in the organization as a whole can be overcome only if the transformation is fully embraced, supported, and enacted at the top.

In principle, such a commitment might arise from a purely intellectual recognition of the possibility of improved performance and the necessity of organizational change to achieve the improvement. Perhaps the early adopters in Japan were motivated in this way. At the present time and in the American context, however, it seems that the commitment is more likely to arise when it is the necessity of improved performance that is clear and quality management doctrine offers one of the few promising paths available. For example, the willingness of Motorola's management to "buy in" to quality management was stimulated by the discovery that its Japanese competitors had vastly superior quality: "Basically, you had better demonstrate the need or the fear or something that's emotional up front. . . . we put on something we called 'Rise to the Challenge.' The intention of 'Rise to the Challenge' was to make it evident to everybody that there was a need: in fact, this scared the heck out of everybody"—George Fisher, Motorola CEO (Dobyns and Crawford-Mason, 1991:130).

If fear is indeed the most reliable motivator for the adoption of quality management, some significant implications follow. First, an answer is suggested for the economist's perennial question of whether the favored management nostrum of the moment is an offer of free lunch, and if not, who is paying for it. The answer is that quality management is not a free lunch. It requires costly and risky investments in the effort to improve existing routines. Some of these costs may be reflected in a temporary decline in the measured profitability of the organization as resources are diverted to the quality management effort, but much of the finance comes "out of the hides" of organization members, particularly managers.

The desire to assure organizational survival probably looms large among the several motivating factors that lead people to contribute extraordinary effort to quality management.[11] The willingness of individuals to contribute such efforts may depend on assurance that the gains from any improvement in organizational performance will be shared with the contributors. When specialized knowledge that defines a worker's role relates to routines that need dramatic change, or when the quality management task group confronts the possibility of eliminating some of the roles occupied by its own members, the quality management effort may lose its motivational traction and stall.

The Ecology of Inefficiency

Inefficiency in prevailing routines is like high-quality ore for quality management to mine. The more of it there is, the higher the returns to digging it out. Other factors equal (including particularly the commitment to improvement), quality management methods are most likely to deliver good results in organizations where the existing situation is the worst.

Where are the most ample funds of waste likely to be found? To address this question it is helpful to consider the origins of routines in more detail. Under the general interpretation offered here, routines emerge in an organization through a protracted process of organizational learning (Levitt and March, 1988). Although this process may be initiated and partially guided by plans and overt deliberation, a functioning routine involves more details than it is possible to settle at the symbolic level. The initial learning phase ends or fades away when performance that is deemed satisfactory is achieved. Or, to put the point somewhat differently, learning stops when the improvement of the routine is an issue that no longer successfully competes for attention of the kind that is actually needed to produce improvement.[12] The pressure for improvement falls because performance reaches a level that satisfies criteria deriving from general considerations that are remote from the costs and benefits of further improvement in the particular routine—the satisfactory profitability of the organization as a whole, or market acceptance of the final product. It is entirely possible that attractive opportunities for further improvement lie just around the corner when the search for them is abandoned.[13]

The nature of the processes that end an initial learning phase would be of little significance if the timely renewal of improvement efforts could be taken for granted. Attractive opportunities that were missed in the first learning phase would likely be recognized and developed in the second or third. The importance of renewing the search—or maintaining it continuously—is the key admonition of modern quality management. This admonition is far from redundant in the context of typical organizational practice; on the contrary, one of the stronger generalizations about typical patterns in organizations is to just the opposite effect. As Cyert and March (1963) observed, organizational search is "problemistic"—initiated in response to perceived problems, including shortfalls relative to familiar performance standards, and, focused (at least initially) in the vicinity of the problem and its symptoms.[14]

If the environment changes over time in ways that enrich the field of search for improvements, large and widening gaps may develop between actual performance and what could be accomplished if learning were renewed. While the shelf of potential improvements in a given routine becomes increasingly laden with contributions from new technology, new modes of organization, and observable innovations adopted elsewhere, an organization that searches only "problemistically" does not look at the shelf until it suffers a breakdown in that particular routine, or overall performance deteriorates to the point where threats to long-term survival are finally acknowledged and *all* routines are open to question.

The foregoing considerations suggest the following hypothesis about quality management: its potential contribution is the greatest in organizations that have survived longest without being required to reinitiate learning but are now challenged to do so. In such organizations, many routines remain in much the same form they were in when they first stabilized. Few occasions for change have occurred, and a large backlog of opportunities for improvement has accumulated.

More specifically, quality management methods are likely to find their most fruitful application in large organizations marked by long histories of consistent but gradually waning success. An industry founder that went virtually unchallenged for a long period because of its strong position in basic patents, and has encountered serious competition only recently, would be an illustrative candidate. A company that was a vigorous competitor and strong survivor in some now-remote shakeout phase in its principal industry, and has had only gradually mounting challenges since, would be an alternative prototypical example of fertile ground for quality management. Both of these prototypes portray companies that were excellent by the standards of an earlier era, but whose more recent history has been an accumulation of minor disappointments—portending more significant disappointments in the future. Never having received a "wake-up call," these companies have had the maximum opportunity to continue on as living museums for managerial choices that were made long ago—choices that have long hindered rather than guided any quest for improvement.

Although the profile just sketched could fit companies over a wide size range, it is the larger companies that seem most likely to offer the best targets for quality management. Size and complexity make the organization's problems less transparent to top management (there is greater tacitness in the second of the senses identified previously). A larger fraction of the organization's productive knowledge involves routinized relationships, as opposed to personal knowledge held in the heads of a few key individuals. But the stability of relationships and expectations that permits the large organization to function may itself be the most formidable barrier to change. As J. M. Juran remarks,

> Some . . . deficiencies are of an *intra*departmental nature; the symptoms, causes and remedies are all within the scope of one departmental manager. However, the major wastes are *inter*departmental in nature. The symptoms show up in department X, but there is no agreement on what are the causes, and hence no agreement on what remedial action should be taken. Neither does there exist any organizational mechanism that can help the department managers deal with those interdepartmental problems. (1989:34)

Finally, large size may provide buffers against adversity that postpone the day when a general alarm sounds for the organization as a whole. Selling off a business unit now and then can provide the resources to sustain "business as usual" satisficing behavior in the remainder of the organization.[15]

Organizational Versus Individual Goals

It has been suggested that the most reliable source of fundamental commitment to quality management is a perceived long-term threat to the survival of the organization. At the level of narrow economic motivation, investment in quality management initiatives can be "financed" by extraordinary efforts that are put forward because participants at all levels are prepared to sacrifice a portion of their current well-being to protect their long-term well-being—when the latter is intimately tied to the survival of the organization. This logic does not track unless the "investors" have reasonable assurance that they will in fact be among the beneficiaries of their investments.

This observation connects the ecology of quality management to a broader set of institutional questions concerning corporate goals and corporate governance. In the 1980s, a surge of activity in the market for corporate control, and of hostile takeovers in particular, was accompanied by a surge of academic commentary endorsing this activity as one of capitalism's most fundamental defenses against managerial sloth and malfeasance (Jensen, 1988). Other commentators, however, took quite a different view. They argued that much of the gain ascribed to the efficiency-demanding discipline of the capital market could equally well be characterized in terms of breach of (implicit) contracts (Shleifer and Summers, 1988). Incumbent—or formerly incumbent—top management was a party to an implicit contract that declared the jobs of middle managers and of key employees at lower levels secure so long as the survival of the corporation itself was not threatened.

Since I have discussed the interpretation of this episode elsewhere (Winter, 1993), I will not address it fully here. Two *Business Week* covers provide a concise metaphor for the issue raised. Five years before the special issue "The Quality Imperative," *Business Week*'s cover story was "The End of Corporate Loyalty?" The story noted the possible threats to morale and productivity resulting from the breakdown of longstanding implicit contracts between middle managers and large corporations. Indeed, nothing that is understood about the requirements for successful response to "The Quality Imperative" suggests that it is compatible with the end of loyalty.

Technical Perfectionism Versus Economizing

The pursuit of improvement relative to measurable, analyzable proximate goals is the heart and soul of quality management. It is this conceptualization of the improvement task that provides the crucial impetus for decentralization and employee empowerment, driving the quest for improvement down the hierarchy to where the relevant resources of knowledge and imagination actually reside. And it is this same conceptualization that makes it possible to prescribe and elaborate a quality management tool kit—teachable methods that actually yield results in pursuit of those proximate goals. It is a view that correctly challenges the comfortable but crippling assessment, shared by corporate bureaucrats and most academic economists, that anything that has been done the same way for a long time is presumptively being done about right. Finally, this conceptualization supports a managerial rhetoric that urges the productive forces ever onward in the quest for improvement, and in so doing provides valid and emphatic warning against the dangers of smugness in an environment that is increasingly competitive in increasingly unpredictable ways. These are potent virtues.

Still, there are some inherent problems in quality management ideas that may limit their influence in the long term. As was noted previously, quality management is at least superficially indifferent to the economic logic of resource allocation. For example, many proponents emphatically reject as a fallacy the proposition that improving quality raises unit costs. On the contrary, they say, effectively addressing quality issues generally lowers costs. The preceding discussion gives the reasons why (and the sense in which) they may be right about this. It seems reasonable to assume, however, that sustained attack on the waste in existing routines will ultimately deplete the "ore body"—the fund of chronic waste. At that point, further quests for improvement may resemble, more and more closely, tentative probes in one direction or another along a transformation frontier relating unit cost to quality of the final product or service. Whether a particular probe promises improvement may seem clearer to the project team that proposed it than to the rest of the organization. While the quest for improvement could continue, the effectiveness of the effort might dwindle and its costs rise in subtle as well as obvious ways. In particular, the problem of "interdepartmental" sources of waste, described by Juran, is as much a hazard for quality management as for any other activity. While a project team attempts a coordinated solution to a problem involving the relationship between departments A and B, the quality management effort itself may be generating new costs diffused through departments H, I, J, and K. Indeed, the doctrine that quality can be improved costlessly may actually encourage team members to focus on solutions that generate relatively diffuse and invisible cost increases. For example, the costs may be covered "out of the hides" of numerous participants not represented on the team, who did not volunteer their hides for that purpose. As the quest for improvements demands more trade-off choices and broader participation, effective quality management will itself become more costly and challenging.

While the enthusiasm for quality management is partly a fad and partly the fruit borne by aggressive promotion, the idea of a quality revolution is not merely a media event hyped by the business press. The organizational ailments and dysfunctions that quality management addresses are real phenomena, with sources that lie in the fundamentals of what productive competence is, how it is created, and how it is maintained and improved. Many other observers had noted the existence of these phenomena before the term "quality management" gained currency.

The prescriptions offered by quality management involve more novelty, and also more uncertainty regarding their validity, than the diagnoses. They derive credibility, first, from the fact that they do not directly offer solutions, but a collection of methods for pursuing answers. Also, they are not directed simply to the corporate boardroom or to the offices of top management, but to the entire organization. Finally, they strongly encourage maintaining focus on the quest for problem solutions and attempt to discourage investment in figuring out whom to blame. For these reasons, quality management methods have a much stronger claim to being applicable methods for producing real change in real organizations than the typical management consultant's nostrums of years past.

Substantial investments are being made in the implementation of quality management methods, both in the companies that have adopted programs and in the new service industry that supplies quality management programs and consultation. These investments are being made in full recognition of the fact that quality management does not promise near-term results and that its greatest benefits are achievable only through profound cultural transformation of business organizations.

In this chapter, I have offered some predictions—or theoretically grounded speculations—as to where the principal successes of quality management methods are likely to occur. To assess the likely overall impact of this management innovation is a more hazardous undertaking. It is obvious that there are many identifiable complexities and pitfalls; much winnowing will have to occur to identify the most valuable parts of the contribution, and it is conceivable that the valid core of quality management might be discredited by the bursting of some speculative bubble of extravagant claims. In my view, powerful forces in the global economic situation favor the wide diffusion of quality management methods. With increasing globalization, expanding technical possibilities, and rising sophistication concerning organizational options, few companies will find it possible to compete successfully without committing themselves to continuous improvement. While labels may change and fine points of doctrine remain in dispute, much of what has been identified here as central to quality management will prove indispensable in the struggle for competitive survival.

Notes

1. The "low-hanging fruit" maxim is the first of several quality management slogans and aphorisms that are quoted in this chapter without attribution. I encountered these phrases in one or more discussions, briefings, or speeches on quality management but cannot at this point provide a citation to a written source.

2. Deming (1986:486–492) provides a brief account of the origins of the quality movement in Japan after World War II.

3. A GAO report on quality management (U.S. General Accounting Office, 1991) was issued on May 2, 1991. By September 25, 1991, more copies of that report had been distributed than of any other report in the GAO's history, and requests for copies were then coming in at a rate of 1,000 per week. The overview of quality management given here draws on that report as well as other sources.

4. For other examples of success stories, see the "quality stories" sections in several chapters of Walton (1990).

5. See Adler (1993, especially pp. 80–93) for an excellent discussion of this issue set in the context of extensive interview data from the NUMMI plant (the GM-Toyota joint venture in Fremont, California).

6. For example: "In the United States, probably about a third of what is done consists of redoing what was done previously, because of quality deficiencies" (Juran, 1989:78).

7. For discussion of many of these techniques, see Deming (1986), Feigenbaum (1991), Juran (1989).

8. On this point, quality management is aligned with the human relations approach to management, generally, and with "Theory Y" in particular (McGregor, 1960). For a review and critique of the human relations model, see Perrow (1986). The interventions that quality management proposes in order to unleash presumptively constructive worker motivations are quite different from those proposed by the human relations school, although there is significant overlap.

9. See Juran (1989:77) on the "Here-comes-another-one" syndrome as an obstacle to change.

10. The meaning of "top" in this connection is somewhat ambiguous. In a large organization, quality management may succeed at the division, business unit, or plant level without necessarily being embraced at the peak of the full organization. But there is at least a require-

ment for tolerance at the peak and commitment at a level that has substantial authority and autonomy in day-to-day operations.

11. Adler (1993) discusses the role of the survival motivation (i.e., fear of unemployment) at NUMMI (pp. 25–26).

12. That is, the end of initial learning may be the result of a satisficing decision (Simon, 1955, 1956, 1987) or something more akin to a lapse of attention. In either case, it reflects the bounded rationality of those whose attention is needed to push learning forward.

13. Of course, even greater benefits might be attainable if commitments made early in the learning process could somehow be reversed and the resources devoted to elaborating those commitments recovered. Chance events early in the process may commit the organization to a learning path that in the long term is markedly inferior to some alternative. Learning itself then reinforces the commitment and makes escape improbable—a "competency trap" (Arthur, 1984; Levitt and March, 1988; Levinthal 1992).

14. To say that search is "initiated in response to perceived problems" is to say that the satisficing principle applies to the initiation or renewal of search as well as to its termination (Winter, 1971).

15. Some of the points made in the foregoing discussion have been addressed in a large and diverse literature dealing with organizational slack (or "X-inefficiency") and its relationship to risk-taking behavior, performance, and organizational change. See, among others, Cyert and March, 1963; Leibenstein, 1966; Bowman, 1982; Singh, 1986; Meyer and Zucker, 1989; Bromiley, 1991.

COMMENTARY

Turning Evolution
Inside the Organization

MARSHALL W. MEYER

Question: What do you do when you see a rhinoceros?
Answer: Give him what he wants.

The preceding is the full text of a reviewer's evaluation of a research proposal submitted to the National Science Foundation in the early 1980s. I won't divulge the names of either the reviewer or the investigator. All I will say is that both the reviewer and the investigator are highly respected researchers, and that the advisory panel recommended full funding of the proposal. The investigator almost certainly appreciated the very personal and, indeed, touching humor of the review, but I can't explain why without disclosing his or her identity.

Aside from demonstrating that social scientists are capable of a good joke from time to time, the review and the advisory panel's recommendation show that rhinoceroses often do get what they want rather than what the world would otherwise dish out to them. Much of evolutionary theory, at least as it is applied to organizations, does not seem to appreciate this fact or, for that matter, to acknowledge the existence of rhinoceroses or their organizational equivalents. The population ecology version of evolutionary theory, which asserts that organizations are inertial, for the most part incapable of internal change, posits a selection process whereby differential rates of birth and death cause populations of organizations, not individual organizations, to accommodate to the environment. The internal evolution perspective, which is reflected in the chapters by Burgelman and Mittman and by Winter and is central to Anne Miner's chapter, posits processes of variation, selection, and retention within individual organizations leading, again, to accommodation to the environment. The differences between the population ecology and internal evolution perspectives are not trivial in that (a) they focus upon very different units or levels of analysis, populations, or species of organizations in population ecology, individual organizations in internal evolution; (b) the internal evolution perspective admits the possibility of change within organizations, whereas population ecology does not; and (c) the internal evolution perspective admits the existence of owners, managers, and the like, the rhinoceroses of organizations, and their capacity to accelerate or delay the evolutionary process within organizations, whereas, again, the population ecology perspective does not. But these differences are not so great as to mask what the two perspectives have in common, namely, that (a) the environment drives organizations in a nondeterministic way involving a lot of variation and, eventually, selection and retention of relatively few alternatives, and (b) the preferences of owners, managers, and the like, may have little to do with ultimate outcomes given that the environment drives adaptation (in internal evolution) or selection (in population ecology).

In this brief commentary, I shall ask whether the internal evolution version of evolutionary theory has misconstrued the dynamics of internal change in organizations. Population ecology, at least in its pristine form, has only a minor role here since it denies the possibility of internal change and hence assumes away the problem of internal evolution. My concern with the theory of internal evolution arises, in part, from its portrayal of managers as prescient yet powerless. To caricature the theory, it seems to be saying the following: managers know when to induce variation in organizations, but once they have done so, the environment and internal political processes determine the selection and retention portions of the evolutionary cycle. Somewhat differently, managers aid and abet the evolutionary process but are unable ultimately to influence its course. A more fundamental concern is that the theory of internal evolution is principally concerned with adaptation to the environment and overlooks the kinds of adaptations taking place within organizations. These adaptations may occur independently of what is going on in the external environment and may be either adaptive or maladaptive as far as the external environment is concerned. The basic proposition I wish to advance is that internal evolution is driven as much or more by excessive adaptation of people to organizations as by maladaptation of organizations to their environments. After developing this proposition and its corollaries, I shall use the quality revolution to illustrate it.

Internal Adaptation and Evolution

Let me begin with a few general notions about internal adaptation and evolution, which differ somewhat from the ideas developed in earlier chapters. (I shall develop these ideas *seriatim*.)

- What people adapt to within organizations may be very different from what organizations adapt to in environments.

- As a consequence, internal adaptation (the kind made by people) may be independent of external adaptation (the kind made by organizations), and sometimes inimical to it.

- Good managers recognize that excessive internal adaptation challenges their ability to exercise control and for this reason induce internal evolution, that is, dramatic and occasionally random variation into organizations.

- Since managers induce internal evolution primarily as a means of bolstering internal control and only secondarily a means of adapting to the external environment, internal evolution is least needed when the environment is most turbulent.

What Do People Adapt To?

The first principles of organizational theory tell us that people do not adapt to organizational environments, at least not directly. This occurs for several reasons. To begin, the larger environment is often inchoate, and individual adaptation would yield the antithesis of ordered action. Secondly, even if the larger environment were understood, bounded rationality limits would impede effective individual adaptation. People would still not know what to do. Third, assuming away inchoate environments and bounded rationality limits, adaptation to the environment is impeded by an absence of feedback. The environment rarely tells people what do to and what not to do with sufficient frequency and in sufficient detail so that fine-grained adjustments are possible. Most people, then, adapt to organizational cues rather than to the environment. Adaptation takes the form of acceptance of goals, subgoals, sub-subgoals, and the like, as defined by organizations, and pursuit of organizationally based rewards for attainment of these goals. The rhinoceros who gets what he wants, or, better, who gets what he thinks he wants, is the organization itself or the organization's management. The rhinoceros is not the environment.

It is interesting that the process of organizational adaptation to environments is much less well understood than individual adaptation to organizations (e.g., there are no how-to-do-it organization-level counterparts to motivation theory). What we *think* we know is that organizations erect buffers to absorb uncertainties arising externally, deploy resources to meet critical contingencies in the environment so that some semblance of organization-environment fit is maintained, and tend, other considerations being equal, to imitate other organizations doing roughly the same things. At the same time, the population ecology perspective on evolutionary theory reminds us that adaptation at the organizational level sometimes fails utterly and with disastrous consequences, and that patterns that were once adaptive can turn maladaptive without warning. For example, firms regarded as well managed during the 1970s, those with ample cash reserves and little debt, were the most likely targets of takeover attempts during the 1980s.

Is Internal Adaptation Good for External Adaptation?

We have tended to assume that what is adaptive internally is also adaptive externally. But there is some reason to believe that the opposite is sometimes the case—that excessive internal adaptation can erode an organization's competence. A venerated but largely forgotten tradition in bureaucratic theory reminds us of goal displacement whereby rules and regulations become ends in themselves and impede the achievement of organizational objectives. The same tradition reminds us of dysfunctional vicious circles whereby centralization and rule-boundedness spiral upward while managers' discretion vanishes. Goal displacement and vicious circles are normally understood as maladaptive for organizations—indeed, the very terminology suggests maladaptation—but these strategies can be very adaptive for individual people who use rules and regulations to preserve a modicum of certainty and power over their own lives. The same logic applies in settings where power is self-perpetuating and hence institutionalized: what is maladaptive for the organization is adaptive for at least some of the people in it.

Problems akin to goal displacement, vicious circles, and institutionalized power are more pervasive than is generally understood and are not limited to bureaucracies. Modern agency theory has led us to believe that the right set of incentives is capable of aligning managers' (and by implication workers') interests with the interests of owners. What agency theory has not recognized is the tendency of any incentive to run down or to lose power as those subject to it adapt to it. The classic case, perhaps, is the use of earnings per share (EPS) managerial incentive schemes during the late 1960s and 1970s. A 1982 survey by McKinsey and Company (Rich and Larson, 1984) found that firms using EPS-based compensation actually did worse than similar firms not using EPS incentives. McKinsey, needless to say, concluded that EPS is not a valid measure of performance. This conclusion missed the point, however. EPS was probably a good measure when it was first used, but it become a bad one as managers adapted to it by finding easy ways to inflate reported earnings (e.g., by deferring maintenance, depreciation, and R&D expenditures). Precisely the same running down has occurred with other incentive schemes and strategies, such as management by objectives (MBO) and divisionalization. While they were initially effective, performance differences between adopters and nonadopters of MBO and divisionalization have all but vanished—indeed, MBO seems to have disappeared from the repertoire of most managers.

I do not mean to argue that all internal adaptations are dysfunctional, but I do think that people will adapt to almost any set of procedures or incentives laid out by their bosses by delivering exactly what is desired—the rhinoceros gets what he wants—regardless of the consequences for what is not being paid attention to, and increasingly so over time as adaptation becomes fine-tuned. Because much internal adaptation consists often of twisting and bending organizational constraints to fit the preferences of people subject to them, it has little to do with and may sometimes be inimical to the external adaptation of the organization to its environment.

Responses to Internal Adaptation

As ironic as it may seem, internal evolution driven by managers is the normal response to internal adaptation. Internal evolution occurs in two steps. First, managers realize that existing control systems are not working because people have adapted to them (e.g., EPS incentives no longer promote performance because people have learned how to maximize EPS and little else). Second, managers put in place new controls that are fundamentally different from existing controls. In the vernacular of evolutionary theory, considerable variation is induced into existing control systems. Neither of these steps is recognized in conventional and highly rational thinking about organizations. Conventional thinking, which is derived largely from experience with physical systems, focuses on optimal design of control systems rather than peoples' adaptation to them and their concomitant running down. And when conventional thinking does recognize failures of control, it seeks a rational solution in more control of the kind that has already run down rather than fundamentally new and different solutions.

Some evidence supports the proposition that internal evolution in organizations tends to follow a jagged course rather than the smooth course characteristic of rational, ordered change. The best illustration of jagged internal evolution, perhaps, comes from the experience of the General Electric Company (G.E.) in the United States. From the late 1970s and through the 1980s, G.E. had a policy of weeding out business units not meeting very high profitability standards. During this period, G.E. shed its weaker business lines and their employees, and the firm's profitability grew substantially. But limits to restructuring have now been recognized, and new and very different values for G.E. have recently been enunciated:

> General Electric's chairman, Jack F. Welch, Jr., who earned the nickname Neutron Jack on his reputation for eliminating people while leaving buildings standing, has gone through a conversion and is now preaching corporate pacifism.
>
> "We cannot afford management styles that suppress and intimidate," he said in the company's new 1991 annual report. Instead, he called on managers to adopt a set of "soft concepts" including such warm, fuzzy notions as having "the self-confidence to empower others and behave in boundaryless fashion." . . .
>
> In the 1980s, Mr. Welch exemplified the relentless executive willing to mow down any employees standing between him and a brighter bottom line. Through layoffs, plant closings, and the sale of business, he eliminated 100,000 jobs, leaving 284,000. As his company's profits increased, his style was widely respected and imitated.
>
> Now Mr. Welch has arrived at a "set of values we believe we will need to take this company forward, rapidly, through the 1990s and beyond." Trust and respect between workers and managers is essential, he said. Managers must be "open to ideas from anywhere."
>
> In Mr. Welch's view, the sort of manager who meets numerical goals but has oldfashioned attitudes is the major obstacle to carrying out these concepts. "This is the individual who typically forces performance out of people rather than inspires it: the autocrat, the big shot, the tyrant," he said (*New York Times*, 1992).

The G.E. case is particularly apt because no environmental imperative is clearly driving this change in corporate philosophy—G.E. remains very profitable. Rather, the old system of values seems to promise few further gains, partly because employees who could not adapt to it left the firm, partly because those who remain have adapted to it so well that short-term profits no longer separate good from bad performance.

Internal Evolution and Environmental Turbulence

If it is the case that internal evolution is a response to excessive internal adaptation rather than to external imperatives, then it follows that internal evolution will occur in inverse proportion to external change. This proposition, although heterodox from the perspective of received macroorganizational theory (as well as Anne Miner's chapter), is consistent with several quite disparate kinds of observations. The first is that some organizations, especially those known to be rigid and hierarchical and hence averse to internal evolution, function well only when challenged externally. The military is a prime example, but it is conceivable that the same logic holds for much of Japanese industry, which is floundering uncharacteristically now that few new markets remain to be conquered. The second observation is that bad news often causes organizations to lock into dysfunctional patterns. Just as external threat often triggers rigidity rather than responsiveness, initial low performance is often followed by sustained low performance or permanent failure rather than internal reform.

Although the processes giving rise to threat rigidity and permanent failure differ—the former is mainly psychological, the latter mainly political—both suggest that internal evolution is suppressed when circumstances are difficult. A third observation is simply that organizations that are doing well are better able to bear the risks associated with internal evolution than highly stressed organizations.

The experience of Motorola during the 1980s illustrates internal evolution under conditions of environmental munificence. Keep in mind, in reading the following, that disorderly, unplanned change was deliberately induced in the company:

> Galvin set Motorola's change course initiative in motion through a speech he gave on April 24, 1983, at the biennial meeting of the company's top 153 officers. Although the company's performance was good and immediate prospects were bright, Galvin thought things were not as rosy as they seemed. . . . Galvin's speech called for managers to take a fresh look at their organizations in order to create smaller, more focused units, eliminate layers of management, and get management closer to the product and market.
>
> The reaction to his speech was one of confusion: what was he talking about? . . . While the dust was still setting, Galvin clarified matters somewhat. To begin, he wrote a memo about the need for "change in managing." He elaborated the need for a more responsive organization, but again did not specify particular actions or the expected results of these actions. . . . Finally, the guidelines paper listed not a forty-eight step action plan, but forty-eight *questions*. . . . (Eccles and Nohria, 1992:285–87)

A Note on Quality Management and Internal Evolution

I want to outline but not to elaborate in detail a conjecture about quality management, as follows: where quality management has the characteristics of internal evolution described—a response to excessive adaptation intended to reestablish managerial control—it is much likely to be successful than where it is understood mainly as a response to external exigencies. Certain characteristics of the current push for quality are consistent with this notion of internal evolution. To begin, I think that many U.S. firms have adapted too well to the financial orientation of their executives (and their executives' adaptation, in turn, to financial markets) and have suffered in some respects, including product quality, as a consequence. U.S. firms, it should be noted, remain unusually profitable compared to their Japanese and European counterparts. At the same time, the overall growth of U.S. business has been much slower than world standards, especially in the last decade. The irony of the current recession is that corporate profits are still increasing even as business shrinks. The quality proponents, or, more aptly in some cases, the quality zealots have argued that their methods offer a means of recapturing lost sales without adverse consequences for earnings. Dramatic increments in profitability are not promised, certainly not in the short run. Indeed, some of the quality gurus, such as Juran, believe that the costs of quality management will exceed its payback in its early years.

Second, the kinds of performance measures promoted by quality proponents (or zealots) tend to shift power downward and away from financial managers. Quality measures, for example, describe processes expected to yield future profits rather than profits that have already accrued, and in this respect bear some resemblance to cost accounting measures and very little resemblance to measures used for financial accounting purposes. Quality measures taken at the operating level of firms are, additionally, somewhat technology-specific and are not easily aggregated to higher levels. Comparability of results, the essence of financial management, is sacrificed in favor of the kind of fidelity and of detail that is most helpful at operating levels. Quality measures are also somewhat more stable and less prone to distortion than financial ones. They are usually true ratio scales with known zero points, the latter sought if not achieved. Under quality management, optimal performance is defined as zero buffer inventory, zero wait time for replenishment, zero defects, zero waste, and zero complaints. (Winter's caution that achieving these zeroes can prove quite costly is acknowledged.) This is in sharp contrast to financial management, where expected levels of performance (e.g., profits, ROI, cash flow, shareholder wealth) are subject to continual upward revision, and where idiosyncratic events (e.g., shortages and surfeits, interest rate fluctuations, tender offers) and accounting legerdemain can affect measured performance.

Third, and perhaps most important, quality management all but mandates internal evolution. Not only are quality measurements taken at the operating level, but it is assumed that knowledge of how to improve performance is embedded in people at that level. The role of intermediate managers shifts accordingly: rather than analyzing results and administering rewards and punishments, they become responsible for unlocking the tacit knowledge of subordinates, which is not a once-and-for-all event but rather an ongoing learning process called continuous improvement. One should keep in mind that managers whose job is to analyze and then to reward or punish are quite vulnerable to displacement, whereas opportunities for displacing managers are limited when they have idiosyncratic knowledge of operations and change processes.

Clearly, talk of quality abounds, and there are external imperatives pushing almost all organizations in the direction of quality rhetoric if not quality performance. My sense, however, is that the quality movement is directed at removing control from financial managers, an arrangement to which many firms are too well adapted, and putting it back in the hands of operating managers, and that any firm that tries to follow the path of quality without becoming more operationally managed and less financially driven is likely to find its quality efforts more myth and ceremony than substance.

My overriding concern is that notions of internal evolution threaten to render the organization or the firm a hollow vessel by overlooking that to which most people adapt—the organization itself and its rhinoceroses, not its environment. As Davis-Blake and Pfeffer (1989) have observed in their critique of dispositional research, organizations are strong situations. The same critique can be applied to claims that evolution within organizations occurs in response to external imperatives: if organizations are strong situations, then they shape behavior more powerfully than the environment. Quality management is, I believe, a test case for my argument that internal evolution is a response to excessive adaptation internally rather than a means of adaptation externally. If it can be shown that the rhetoric and tools of quality move from the environment to managers to the work level of firms, and that this sequence occurs most often in firms otherwise maladapted to their environments, then I should withdraw much of what I have said here. If, however, it can be shown that managers implement quality management in order to stimulate change and thereby to regain control of organizations that are otherwise too well adapted internally, where the level of comfort was perhaps too high, then my argument stands. Ask yourself this question: Were struggling, marginal firms the first to adopt quality management, or did quality management appear earliest among large firms that had been successful in the past but were showing early signs of flab and complacency?

Evolution, Externalities, and Managerial Action

ZUR SHAPIRA

In the organizational sciences, the evolutionary approach of the population ecology perspective has gained a dominant position. Since its introduction (Hannan and Freeman, 1977), a debate on what constitutes proper and fruitful research in and on organizations started. In particular, questions about the proper level of analysis ensued. Research in the population ecology tradition has concentrated on studies of entire organizational populations over long periods, and ignored the role of the individual within organizations. Recently, however, some researchers have begun to examine the significance of microlevel processes for macrolevel dynamics (see for example, Burgelman and Mittman, chapter 4, this volume; March and Shapira, 1992). In this spirit, and to facilitate cross-pollination among the different levels of analysis in organizational research (cf. March and Shapira, 1982), I pursue here the idea that microlevel processes have macrolevel effects that may contribute to an increased integration of evolutionary dynamics at different levels of analysis. To explore this idea I discuss some methodological problems associated with the level of analysis question, the importance of externalities, and the emergent role of managerial action. Such an endeavor, if successful, may enhance our understanding of actions within and by organizations. For, if process (rather than content) is the focus of evolutionary analysis of organizations (see March, chapter 3, this volume), then all levels of analysis should be considered, the micro as well as the macro. Potential aggregations of interactions among these different levels should be a central theme of evolutionary analysis.

It is interesting to note, in a brief historical comment, that meager mutual recognition among scholars dealing with different levels of analysis is not unique to the organizational sciences. In an enlightening commentary, Lederberg (1988) noted that at the time Darwin's evolutionary theory was creating stormy debates, another giant of biological research, Louis Pasteur, was working in his lab in Paris. Lederberg continued his analysis by saying that

> there is no record that he (Pasteur) ever achieved a sympathetic understanding of Darwinian evolutionary theory; and he seems always to have been hostile to a meth-

The comments of Joel Baum and the hospitality of the Jerusalem Van Leer Institute are acknowledged.

odology of inference, like Darwin's, that deviated from the grain of laboratory experiment. On Darwin's side, for all his appreciation of Pasteur's medical contributions,
he seems never to have incorporated microbiology into his natural history.
(1988:344–45)

Lederberg laments this unfortunate situation:

> What lost opportunity! Darwin might have found, as present investigators do, mar-
> velous experimental material for the study of evolution in populations of
> microbes—where generation time is measured in minutes, and where natural (or
> artificial) selection can be applied to tens of hundreds of billions of unicellular
> organisms at small cost and less ethical compunction. Pasteur and his successors in
> microbiology might have avoided decades of muddled thinking about variation in
> bacteria. (1988:345)

The Level-of-Analysis Question

Studies that represent the evolutionary dynamics perspective in organizational
research are most likely applications of population ecology models. These studies are
focused primarily on the organizational population level of analysis, emphasizing
mainly such phenomena as birth and death of organizations. The potential role of a
microlevel process was ignored for one of the following related assumptions: One,
that while microlevel processes exist, analyzing them does not matter. That is, since
what should be considered is the aggregate, namely, the macrolevel, analyzing the
microprocesses cannot add much. Or two, that the phenomena of interest are only
at the macrolevel; therefore, microprocesses are irrelevant. To highlight the differences and similarities between these two assumptions, let us consider the level of
analysis issue in economics.

The Notion of Aggregation

The issue of aggregation is very salient in economic theory. Classical economics
makes the assumption that consumers are rational and then derives several properties on market equilibria. Furthermore, Friedman's (1953) famous "as if" dictum
suggests that the assumptions about the individual consumer are not of interest as
long as they lead to verifiable derivations about behavior at the aggregate (i.e., market) level of analysis. Unfortunately, the empirical analysis of markets is not satisfactory on several grounds as demonstrated by the small firm effect (cf. Banz, 1982)
and seasonally effects on share prices (see, e.g., Thaler, 1991). Clinging to Friedman's
positivist view has led many economists to ignore new developments in behavioral
decision theory that may explain some of these deviations from the normative view
(see, e.g., Kahneman and Tversky, 1979; Thaler, 1991; Tversky and Kahneman,
1986).

   Disregarding the microlevel of analysis may lead to biased conclusions regarding
the causes of behavior at the aggregate level. For instance, Darwin's idea of competition appealed to scientists in various disciplines such as economics, sociology, and

sociobiology. While competition is clearly central to theories of evolution, other phenomena such as altruism cast some doubt as to the singular stature of competition. Indeed, there are arguments for the central role cooperation plays in evolution in the field of biology (cf. Margulis, 1981) as well as in economics (cf. Dawes and Thaler, 1990), and political science (cf. Axelrod, 1984), and organization theory (Astley and Fombrum, 1983).

It is intriguing to consider competition in the context of the level-of-analysis question. Although biologists consider competition mainly at the species level, others assume that competition is an unavoidable constraint whether one analyzes the behavior of individuals, firms, or nations (cf. Porter, 1980, 1990). However, competition at the microlevel may sometimes lead to a disadvantage at the aggregate level (Spence, 1985). Conceivably, different modes of behavior at the microlevel (namely, competition versus cooperation) may lead to differential success in competitive behavior at the aggregate level (see for example, Miner, chapter 5, this volume) For example, there are suggestions that the cooperative mode in which the Japanese industries are organized may be partially responsible for their superiority over several U.S. industries. Thus, even those interested only in the aggregate level of analysis may benefit from studying microlevel phenomena.

The Issue of Relevance

The other key question is whether microlevel processes explain part of the variance at the macrolevel. If this is not the case, researchers interested in the macrolevel should not be concerned with findings in studies focusing on the microlevel. Some recent examples, however, indicate the potential relevance of microphenomena for macroanalysis. For instance, Burgelman and Mittman's (chapter 4, this volume) analysis shows how risk taking tendencies of managers can affect the risk taking policy of a firm. March and Shapira (1992) demonstrated how the composition of a population of risk takers is affected by the different ways in which individual risk takers update their aspiration levels. In addition, it has been argued recently that incentive systems may lead to short time horizons of U.S. managers as compared to their Japanese counterparts. This may eventually explain part of the demise of some American industries (Stein, 1989). In addition, the idea that market behavior is a consequence of activities by individual consumers is central in economic analysis. As Campbell (1986) noted population genetics and econometrics share an interest in "models in which populations of individual decision makers that are optimizing utilities, produce macro effects" (S355).

Even if aggregation per se does not increase our understanding of macrolevel phenomena, we may benefit from seeing a more complete picture, one that encompasses different levels of analysis. A potential problem, however, in linking the different levels of analysis may be the methodology used in the micro- versus the macrostudies. Even if the conceptual issues discussed previously were resolved, methodological differences may obscure the potential benefits of linking the levels of analysis. Nevertheless, applications of methodologies similar to those used at the macrolevel to study microlevel processes are increasing. Examples are Fichman's (1989) analysis of absenteeism behavior and Miner's (1991) research in which event analysis was employed to study the social ecology of jobs.

It should be noted, however, that organizational research need not be limited to large sample designs. There are times when small sample studies may be beneficial even at the macrolevel. One solution proposed by "macro" investigators for such cases is to use "event" analysis, thereby increasing the sample size. However, different methodologies may be appropriate when other questions are investigated such as the intraorganizational analysis of managerial risk taking (Burgelman and Mittman, chapter 4, this volume). At times, focusing on small samples, using case study methodology may prove useful for understanding intrafirm processes that may enhance our understanding of organizational responses to environmental variations (e.g., Burgelman, 1983a, 1990). Such analyses may be fruitful in studying decision making by managers in the context of research and development, innovation, and other intrafirm entrepreneurial issues (cf. Van de Ven and Garud, chapter 20, this volume).

Externalities

A major problem in analyzing social or biological systems is the likelihood that external forces might be affecting what appears to be "within-system" causal phenomena. In dealing with causal explanations one should always be cautious and consider the possibility of external effects before arriving at "within-system" causal explanations. Even orthodox Darwinists had a problem in explaining the disappearance of dinosaurs from the planet, using a simple natural selection argument. Later explanations suggesting that external effects such as the consequences of a meteorite collision with earth might have led to the demise of dinosaurs were deemed more plausible. Gould (1980, 1989) suggested that such random events play an important role in evolutionary dynamics. He also pointed at the fragility of the "survival of the fittest" dictum, arguing that the criteria for the "fittest" may not be well defined, as is delightfully illustrated in Larry Johnson's cartoon.

There is a major difficulty in arriving at causal explanations when a large part of what appears to be an ordered process may actually be due to randomness (Gould.

THE EVOLUTION OF MAN

1989; March and March, 1977). In the face of randomness the definition of what constitutes success versus failure depends to a large extent on the determination of external effects. In a sense there's a contrast between believing in natural selection and the notion of free will. The Talmudic statement "All is foreseen and freedom of choice is given" reflects that idea rather well. If everything is determined what's left for individual choice?

This paradox is central in lay persons' versus experts' beliefs about the operation of financial markets. Most economists believe that the process that describes sequential movements of security prices is a random walk model (cf. Fama, 1970), although the behavior of most investors doesn't reflect a belief in this assumption. A major part in developing such beliefs is the role played by "external" agents. In evolution theory this role is played by the environment while in economics the role is played by the "invisible hand." If the "invisible hand" shapes the market it means that no one has control over the market activities. Unfortunately, several recent scandals in securities markets led investors to believe that the invisible hand might actually belong to some real Wall Street personalities.

The contrast between the need to believe in a world controlled by some "causal agent" and the view imputed by the natural selection/invisible hand perspective is crucial for understanding human behavior. This conflict was reflected in the uproar that followed the publication of Darwin's ideas about evolution as contrasted with religious explanations. It is also reflected in the daily interpretations one hears in the media about the behavior of financial markets. Statements such as "a trend for profit taking sent the market prices down" are puzzling if one believes in the existence of efficient markets, which can be manipulated only by the invisible hand. Yet, normative considerations are often at odds with human decision behavior.

A belief in the invisible hand may not be compatible with the behavioral description of human judgment. Human aversion to ambiguity and uncertainty and its effect on choice and decision are well documented (Ellsberg, 1961; Kahneman and Tversky, 1979). A central feature of the efficient market hypothesis is that if there were a bias in the system someone would have detected it and profited from it. Since, in efficient markets, information is disseminated immediately and simultaneously, such "inefficiencies" would be immediately eliminated. This feature of the market should strengthen the belief in the role of the invisible hand, though current research in finance is examining claims that there are often opportunities for arbitrage that, according to the theory, should not exist (cf. Fama, 1991).

The belief in natural selection or in the invisible hand is a belief in randomness and in no control. Sorting out externalities from pure random effects is therefore crucial. It also points at the importance of human judgment since making inferences about causal versus random effects involves judgment. Human judgment can be fallible; it is also prone to many biases that make the ability to sort externalities from randomness rather problematic.

Evolutionary Dynamics and Managerial Action

What are the implications of evolutionary dynamics for managerial action? It appears that the message may have a dual meaning. Consider Lederberg's (1988) analysis of the evolutionary significance of AIDS. On the one hand Lederberg sounds pessimistic in suggesting that this epidemic may be just one manifestation of many potential plagues about which we know very little. Indeed, alluding to a general notion of equilibrium and natural selection, Lederberg comments, "At evolutionary equilibrium, we would continue to share the planet with our parasites" (1988:350). However, he continues: "No theory lets us calculate the (equilibrium) details; we can hardly be sure that an equilibrium for earth even includes the human species. Many prophets have foreseen the contrary, given our propensity for sophistication harnessed to intraspecies competition" (1988:350). At the same time, Lederberg laments the status of public policy that ignores the many plagues in the third world, arguing that such policies are both unjust and shortsighted.

Lederberg's (1988) analysis seems applicable to managerial action. It implies that in general, the world should be considered random as our knowledge is dismal. However, "locally" we can engage in policies that minimize the negative consequences of "plagues" about which we have information. In other words, in a world that is characterized as random, the best that members of the human species can do is to learn, accumulate knowledge, and act accordingly, not losing the perspective that we may actually be participants in a random game whose consequences are beyond our understanding and control.

Managerial Cognition

In attempting to make sense of a seemingly random world it is important to consider processes of change. To analyze the ways managers deal with change one needs to consider managerial cognition on the one hand and organizational procedures on the other. The interesting question is how managers conceptualize randomness. It appears that although managers are familiar with uncertainty and risk in making decisions, they distinguish between gambling (which is the statistical conception of dealing with uncertainty and risk) and risk taking. Managers argue that in taking risks in managerial decision making, they can gain control and use their skills (March and Shapira, 1987). While it is apparent to an outside researcher that oftentimes managers do act as if they are gambling, relating risk taking to control and skills is pervasive in managerial culture and is rather immune to rational argumentation (Shapira, in press). The problems of externalities and the invisible hand raised earlier may enhance managers' beliefs in their ability to exert control in making risky decisions. These beliefs may be sustained even in the face of evidence about the uncertain relations between action and outcome, resulting from externalities and randomness.

It is not clear, however, that managers would do better if they embraced the notion of natural selection and acted in full accord with it. For instance, the high rate of new venture failures would probably discourage all "rational" entrepreneurs if they counted only on representative statistics and not their own idiosyncracies. As March and Shapira (1987) pointed out there may be some intelligence to managers' conception of risk taking as an active endeavor as opposed to choices based on passive calculation of probabilities. Of course this does not mean that managerial actions are error free. On the contrary, managers commit many mistakes. Perhaps some combination of a realistic belief in the role of randomness on the one hand and in the ability to exert control and use one's skills on the other may serve managers better.

Another determinant of the quality of managerial response to environmental changes is the incentive schemes that are at work in their organization. In considering projects for investment, managers are affected by the likelihood of success and failure as well as the rewards and penalties attached to such outcomes (Shapira, 1993). A rather common consequence is the inflated risk aversion managers display, primarily since they feel that penalties for failure supersede rewards for success (Shapira, in press). This leads them to commit more type II errors (rejecting "would be" successful projects) since such mistakes often go unnoticed. Such an unhappy situation is a consequence of top management's inability to separate process from outcome, focusing on the latter and ignoring the former. The term selection has a dual role in decisions about investment in one out of many projects. In the first stage, projects are screened and the best one is "artificially" selected by management. The selected project later competes with other projects, in a particular market, where "natural" selection presumably "sorts" out the winners from the losers. However, even in the latter stage, externalities play a role and may make the process of making inferences about randomness a tough one.

Organizational Routines

Organizational procedures are important in understanding how managers respond to dynamic changes in the environment. As Miner (chapter 5, this volume) noted, organizational routines should be considered along with managerial cognition. Routines may be both functional and symbolic and should not be dismissed as insignificant. They may represent some intelligent form in which organizations store the history of their experience. However, they often appear as a nonintelligent response. Consider the following story: I went to my bank to deposit some travelers' checks, that were drawn in my name, to my account. I needed the money in my account immediately as I was writing a check against the deposit. I asked the teller when would this deposit show in my account and he said it would take one day. I asked for the reason and he said that these were "checks" and would not clear immediately. I reminded him that travelers' checks were essentially cash, but he stood firm in his opinion that it would take a day. At this moment I was upset and thought about talking to the teller's superior. Instead, I asked the teller whether I could cash those travelers' checks and he answered positively. I then cashed the checks and deposited the cash in my account (using the same deposit slip) and was assured by the teller that this cash deposit was going to be posted in my account immediately.

In reflecting on such an experience one may be tempted to consider the case as organizational ineffectiveness. Obviously, routines can be dysfunctional at times. However, in analyzing organizational action we should consider the role of cognition as well as routines. The latter may reveal some ways in which organizations deal with dynamic change. As Winter (chapter 6, this volume) noted, it is quite interesting to analyze the ways organizational routines change in a dynamic environment. Routines may actually be an important force in constraining organizations from adapting too rapidly to environmental changes.

If the world is indeed random, then fast, noncareful adaptation may be detrimental. In a cautious attempt to adapt to environmental changes managers need to be able to sort out systematic changes from random ones. They can do a better job of selection if they are able to notice phenomena that depart from noise. Hence, *noticing* should be the first stage in the variation-selection-retention scheme. Managers should build mechanisms that would help organizations notice the aspects that differentiate systematic from random environmental changes. Routines may play an important role in enhancing this capacity since they reduce the space of events that managers should scan in order to avoid bad surprises and take advantage of good ones (Radner, 1974).

In summary, it is clear that evolutionary dynamics has been gaining popularity as a major framework for research on organizations. Within the field, the major applications have been ecological analyses of populations of organizations. However, applications of evolutionary dynamics to other levels of analyses have also been demonstrated (see, e.g., Burgelman and Mittman, chapter 4, this volume; March and Shapira, 1992). In this chapter, the potential implications of "microevolutionary" dynamics to managerial action were considered. Furthermore, the discussion of the level of analysis suggested that managerial action may have significant effects on "macroevolutionary" phenomena, such as the behavior of firms and collections of firms. In addition to discussing the aggregation problem, I focused on two issues: the belief in randomness on the one hand and the role of externalities on the other. The major theme has been an attempt to show the complexity that can result when managers endorse these ideas, believing simultaneously that in taking risks one can also exert control and use skills. Lederberg's (1988) analysis has shown us that this particular dilemma is not unique to managers of business firms but may be a general characteristic of living in an uncertain and random world.

III

ORGANIZATIONAL
EVOLUTION

7

Evolutionary Processes and Patterns of Core Business Change

ARI GINSBERG AND JOEL A. C. BAUM

During much of this century, corporate growth and diversification have been central objectives for managers of American corporations. Yet, there is a paucity of systematically developed theory and empirical research addressing the evolutionary dynamics of firms' core businesses. This is largely the result of conceptual obstacles and the difficulty of conducting longitudinal research (Ginsberg, 1988). Addressing this deficit requires the advancement of a *process* theory of core business change that explains whether, for example, the occurrence of particular kinds of changes early in a process makes a difference in the overall pattern of change or whether certain sequences of events provide more rapid results.

In this study, we develop an evolutionary process model of core business change that attempts to specify the forces producing core business elaboration and extension events. We refer to the model as *evolutionary* because it specifies processes of variation, selection, and retention over time (Campbell, 1965b). In the model, theories of organizational routines (Nelson and Winter, 1982) and organizational learning (Cyert and March, 1963; Levitt and March, 1988) are used to explain patterns of momentum (Amburgey and Miner, 1992; Miller and Friesen, 1980), imprinting (Stinchcombe, 1965), inertia (Hannan and Freeman, 1977, 1989), and change or, in the extreme, reorientation (Tushman and Romanelli, 1985) in core business change.

To test our evolutionary process model, we analyze historical data on the growth and diversification activities of forty-two bank holding companies incorporated since the passage of the Bank Holding Company Act in 1956. We then identify different evolutionary paths of core business change and assess the extent to which they are produced by the processes specified in the dynamic model.

We define growth and diversification activities of bank holding companies in terms of two types of corporate strategies identified by Mintzberg (1988). The first— *elaboration of the core business* within the firm's own industry boundaries—involves

We are indebted to Clifford Nass for many helpful discussions on sequence analysis and for the optimal matching program used in this study. We are also grateful to Anne Miner, Charles Fombrun, and Bill Starbuck for helpful comments on an earlier version of this chapter. For assistance with data collection and coding we thank Jose Brito. This research was funded in part by the Tenneco Fund Program, Stern School of Business.

such activities as acquiring competitors, promoting existing products in new market segments, and carrying the existing product to new geographical areas. The second— *extension of the core business* beyond the firm's basic mission—involves such activities as vertical integration along the value chain, related or concentric diversification, and unrelated or conglomerate diversification. We examine the core business elaboration and extension activities of bank holding companies reflected in three types of actions: *related* acquisition of banks, *unrelated* acquisition of nonbank businesses, and divestment.

Existing studies of the dynamics of strategic change generally assume that sequences of strategic events are produced by stochastic processes. The likelihood of the occurrence of a particular event at any point in time is specified to be a function of exogenous variables such as organizational characteristics, environmental conditions, and the prior occurrence of change (Amburgey and Miner, 1992; Baum 1990b; Delacroix and Swaminathan, 1991; Ginsberg and Buchholtz, 1990; Haveman, chapter 8, this volume; Kelly and Amburgey, 1991). In general, such sequence generation research is concerned with understanding the occurrence of one particular kind of change rather than with identifying typical patterns of change. In contrast, sequence pattern research examines whole sequences of events and uses techniques such as optimal matching, which produce measures of dissimilarity between sequences, to determine whether ordered patterns exist. In this study, we examine the dynamics of core business change by combining both *sequence generation* and *sequence pattern* analysis techniques (Abbott and Hrycak, 1990). By analyzing both the underlying dynamics and resultant patterns of core business change together, this chapter attempts to link the mechanisms of core business change to patterns of corporate strategy through time.

Evolutionary Dynamics of Core Business Change

Uniform Motion: Momentum and Imprinting

As an enterprise grows from a single-product firm to a complex, diversified corporation, it reveals an institutionalized ability to learn (Kazanjian and Drazin, 1987). Although trial-and-error learning and elaborate methods of adaptive modification based on rational calculation are certainly important forces in organizational evolution, theories of organizational learning suggest that substantial organizational action occurs through the repetition of programs (March and Simon, 1958), search rules (Cyert and March, 1963), and routines (Nelson and Winter, 1982). These features of organizations, through which organizations retain and make use of prior learning, guide their behavior by affecting the way changes in the environment are perceived, the menu of possible alternatives considered, and, ultimately, the actions taken.

From a learning perspective, making a change furnishes an organization with the opportunity to routinize the change. Each time an organization engages in a particular kind of change it increases its competency in making that type of change. The more experienced an organization becomes with a particular type of change, the more likely it is to make further changes of a similar nature—because it knows how to make them. If a particular kind of change becomes causally linked with success in the minds of organizational decision makers, irrespective of whether such a causal link in fact exists, reinforcement effects will make repetition even more likely (Levitt and March, 1988). Once change is initiated, the change process itself may become routinized and subject to inertial forces as well (Burgelman, 1983a; Cyert and March, 1963; Nelson & Winter, 1982; Levitt and March, 1988). This creates organizational momentum, that is, the tendency to maintain the direction and emphasis of prior actions in current behavior (Amburgey and Miner, 1992; Kelly and Amburgey, 1991; Miller and Friesen, 1980). Amburgey and Miner (1992) have identified three types of momentum: *repetitive,* in which the same event is repeated; *positional,* in which a current position is strengthened (e.g., diversified firms become more diverse); and *contextual,* in which organizational factors result in consistent action (e.g., decentralized firms diversify).

While favorable outcomes certainly increase the likelihood that an action will be repeated, and breed more success, unfavorable outcomes can increase repetition as well (Milliken and Lant, 1991; Staw, 1981; Staw, Sandelands, and Dutton, 1981). For example, Levitt and March (1988:322) suggest that "favorable performance with an inferior procedure leads an organization to accumulate more experience with it, thus keeping experience with a superior procedure inadequate to make it rewarding to use." Coupled with their observation that organizations frequently face performance ambiguity, Levitt and March (1988:324) conclude that advocates of an action "are likely to interpret failures less as a symptom that the policy is incorrect than as an indication that it has not been pursued vigorously enough." Of course, in the face of ambiguity, momentum can protect organizations from adjusting routines too quickly and detrimentally to idiosyncratic events. Thus, successful or not, experience with actions of a *particular type* will tend to increase the likelihood that actions of the *same type* are repeated in the future.

Once initiated, momentum acts as a selection-retention mechanism that guides patterns of organizational variation (Boyd and Richerson, 1985) and makes exploration of alternatives difficult (Levitt and March, 1988; Starbuck, 1983; Wildavsky, 1972). Empirical evidence supports the proposition that momentum drives substantial organizational action in a variety of empirical settings (Amburgey and Kelly, 1985; Amburgey, Kelly, and Barnett, 1993; Amburgey and Miner, 1992; Delacroix and Swaminathan, 1991; Kelly and Amburgey, 1991; Miller and Friesen, 1980b).

Our focus in this study is on repetitive and positional momentum in core business change (Amburgey and Miner, 1992). However, we do not distinguish between these two forms of momentum because repetitions of acquisitions that elaborate or extend a core business have qualities of both types: recurrent elaboration entails repetition of the same action to strengthen a diversified position; recurrent extension entails repetition of the same action to strengthen a focused position. We expect that the likelihood of a *particular type* of core business change will increase with the number of prior occurrences of a core business change of the *same type*. Specifically:

Hypothesis 1A: The cumulative occurrence of acquisitions that *elaborate* a core business increases the likelihood of further acquisitions of the same type.

Hypothesis 1B: The cumulative occurrence of acquisitions that *extend* a core business increases the likelihood of further acquisitions of the same type.

In addition to the *frequency* of repetition, organizational learning theory also suggests that early actions will often be most fateful. The routines to which organizations become committed tend to be determined more by initial actions than by information gained from later learning situations (Amburgey et al., 1993; Hedberg, Nystrom, and Starbuck, 1976; Levitt and March, 1988; Nystrom and Starbuck, 1984; Stinchcombe, 1965; Wildavsky, 1972). Organizations are imprinted by their first actions as self-reinforcing momentum processes commit them to repeating routines shaped by early and often arbitrary successes. Consequently, patterns of organizational action are likely to be very sensitive to the effects of early chance events. Thus, in addition to prior frequency, the probability of particular actions should depend on the *primacy* of such actions in an organization's life. As a result, the introduction of an acquisition that elaborates or extends the core business early in an organization's history should provoke an enduring tendency to further acquistions of the same type. Amburgey et al. (1993) provide preliminary evidence of such a primacy effect.

Hypothesis 2A: Early occurrence of an acquisition that *elaborates* a core business increases the probability of subsequent acquisitons of the same type.

Hypothesis 2B: Early occurrence of an acquisition that *extends* a core business increases the probability of subsequent acquisitions of the same type.

Stasis and Change: Forgetting and Unlearning

The presumption that organizational change is propelled by momentum and imprinting does not necessarily imply that organizations never enter a stationary state or change their strategic direction. Indeed, there is ample evidence that organizations advance from periods of momentum to periods of inactivity (Miller and Friesen, 1980; Mintzberg and Waters, 1982; Mintzberg and McHugh, 1985). There is also evidence that organizations enter short periods of reorientation in which they are fundamentally transformed (Miller and Friesen, 1980b, 1984; Mintzberg and McHugh, 1985; Tushman and Romanelli, 1985).

To reconcile these phenomena with those of momentum and imprinting, Amburgey et al. (1993) examined several forces that slow momentum in organizations. To explain how momentum is damped, Amburgey et al. (1993) propose that the effect of prior change is itself dynamic. Since organizational search processes begin with the most recently utilized routines (Cyert and March, 1963), the likelihood of repeating particular actions should be highest immediately after their occurrence, but the grip of momentum should be weakened as the time since the actions were last taken increases. In other words, the longer the period of inaction, the lower will be the likelihood of the actions being repeated. Consistent with this argument,

Amburgey et al. (1993) found that the likelihood of repeating a particular action jumped immediately after an action of that type, but declined with increase in the elapsed time since that type of action last occurred. Delacroix and Swaminathan (1991) also recently found some support for a dynamic effect of prior change. We therefore expect the following:

> Hypothesis 3A: The likelihood of an acquisition that *elaborates* a core business declines with the elapsed time since the last acquisition of that type.

> Hypothesis 3B: The likelihood of an acquisition that *extends* a core business declines with the elapsed time since the last acquisition of that type.

In addition to *forgetting,* a second potential source of damping is *unlearning* (Hedberg et al., 1976; Nystrom and Starbuck, 1984; Starbuck, 1983). Learning theory suggests the impetus for change is triggered by performance below aspiration levels: satisfactory performance will tend to result in the reinforcement of lessons drawn from prior experience, while the tendency toward momentum will be mitigated when unsatisfactory performance calls existing routines and practices into question (Cyert and March, 1963; Lant and Mezias, 1992; Levitt and March, 1988). Consequently, the experience of performance failure may be extremely important in setting the stage for organizational change (i.e., the search for an exploration of new routines rather than the continued use [and refinement] of old ones). Yet, for a variety of reasons organizations tend to resist change, preferring to employ routines of the past well beyond their point of usefulness, and wait until a series of events have explicitly disconfirmed routines before seriously exploring alternatives (Hedberg et al., 1976; Milliken and Lant, 1991; Nystrom and Starbuck, 1984; Starbuck, 1983; Staw, Sandelands, and Dutton, 1981; Tushman and Romanelli, 1985). Therefore, we expect the occurrence of repeated *divestments* that *contract* or *narrow* a core business, signifying the accumulation of evidence discrediting an organization's acquisition routines, to counteract the forces perpetuating the repetition of acquisitions that elaborate or extend the core business as the organization unlearns and searches for new routines to guide its action.[1]

> Hypothesis 4A: The cumulative occurrence of divestments that *contract* a core business decreases the likelihood of an acquisition that *elaborates* the core business.

> Hypothesis 4B: The cumulative occurrence of divestments that *narrow* a core business decreases the likelihood of an acquisition that *extends* the core business.

The foregoing arguments imply that the momentum-damping effects of organizational forgetting and unlearning will diminish with time. After a series of unsatisfactory performance outcomes, organizations may become relatively inactive. However, they may become increasingly likely to undertake further acquisitions again with the passage of time. This is because organizational performance returns to acceptable levels, past failures are forgotten, or new routines incorporating information from the learning situation are developed and tried. Therefore, we expect the time lapsed since the last occurrence of divestment activity to influence the rate of acquisition activity. Specifically, we hypothesize the following:

> Hypothesis 5A: The likelihood of an acquisition that *elaborates* a core business declines with the elapsed time since the last divestment that *contracted* the core business.

> Hypothesis 5B: The likelihood of an acquisition that *extends* a core business declines with the elapsed time since the last divestment that *narrowed* the core business.

Patterns of Core Business Change

Evolutionary Patterns

The combined influences of momentum, imprinting, forgetting, and unlearning on organizational activities provide a set of mechanisms that can produce the characteristic repetition, inaction, and reorientation of organizational evolution. Hypotheses 1 through 5 have two important implications. First, organizational routines and learning not only record history but shape its future course. Second, the direction of that course depends greatly on the processes by which organizational routines are maintained. Each time an organization makes a change of a particular kind it increases its competency in making that type of change and becomes more likely to make further changes of a similar nature. This self-reinforcing feedback creates a momentum that leads organizations to become committed to routines that are formed around early, possibly arbitrary successes. Consequently, patterns of change are likely to be very sensitive to the effects of initial actions and early fortuitous events, which endure though their repetition. Once initiated, momentum serves as a selection-retention mechanism, guiding patterns of organizational action and making exploration of alternatives difficult. However, increases in the time since an organization last made a particular kind of change and performance failures weaken the grip of momentum as routines of the past are forgotten, or patterns of organizational action are redirected as old routines are unlearned and new ones created.

Our evolutionary process model suggests that, rather than evolving through a standard set of stages, organizations may achieve their respective strategies through different patterns of change and convergence (Filley and Aldag, 1980). Sometimes cycles of change and convergence are of shorter duration and are balanced between periods of activity and inactivity, and sometimes they are of longer duration with an emphasis on continuity, which is interrupted by occasional brief, but highly disruptive revolutions (Miller and Friesen, 1980b; Mintzberg and McHugh, 1985; Tushman and Romanelli, 1985). The arguments developed previously suggest that evolutionary patterns of core business change are the result of variation-selection-retention sequences produced by processes of momentum, imprinting, forgetting, and unlearning. Consequently, we posit the following:

> Hypothesis 6: Momentum, imprinting, forgetting, and unlearning generate distinct evolutionary paths of core business change.

Methods

Data Description: Bank Holding Companies

To test these hypotheses, our study examines the core business change activities of bank holding companies founded after the passage of the Bank Holding Company Act of 1956. Bank holding companies are corporations that own one bank and perhaps other businesses, or they may own several banks.[2] Historically, bankers have used the holding company form to provide flexibility denied by law. For example, to circumvent laws against branching, bankers have formed multibank holding companies to create or purchase new bank offices in neighboring communities. For many years, bank owners also used holding companies to engage in business activities denied to banks by federal legislation.

The U.S. Congress passed the Bank Holding Company Act of 1956 to remove excessive exploitation of the Banking Act of 1933, which had allowed bank holding companies to invest in virtually any business except the securities industry. In 1948 the Board of Governors of the Federal Reserve System began federal prosecution of Transamerica Corporation for violating the Clayton Antitrust Act through its bank holding activities. After the court ruled in favor of Transamerica, congressional pressure to regulate bank holding companies escalated. A flurry of legislative activity in Congress between July 1949 and July 1955 culminated in the Bank Holding Company Act of 1956, which was designed to control the expansion of bank holding companies in three important ways (Gup, 1984). First, it defined a bank holding company as any corporation controlling 25 percent or more of the voting stock or the election of the majority of the directors of each of two or more banks. Second, it required registered bank holding companies to divest themselves, with certain exceptions, of their nonbanking activities. Third, it required bank holding companies to receive the Board of Governor's approval before acquiring more than 5 percent of the voting shares of any bank.

Although the Bank Holding Company Act of 1956 limited the activities of multibank holding companies (by restricting them from engaging in unrelated businesses and from acquiring banks in more than one state), it exempted one-bank holding companies from similar constraints. As a result, such companies began to proliferate in the 1960s, as larger banks rushed to form one-bank holding companies, engaging in both related and non-bank-related acquisition activities in a conglomerate manner. By 1970, one-bank holding companies had investments in approximately 100 different nonbanking activities (Doti, 1990).

In 1970, concerned that problems in other industries could harm commercial banks, Congress passed the 1970 Amendments to the Bank Holding Company Act, which brought one-bank holding companies under the provisions of the 1956 act and also gave the Federal Reserve Board of Governors the power to regulate the activities of all bank holding companies (Doti, 1990). Under the new amendments, the Board of Governors defined control with respect to a bank holding company as an interest between 5 and 25 percent. The amendments required that all nonbanking subsidiaries acquired after June 30, 1968, be divested before year-end 1980; a grandfather clause provided selected exemptions for non-banking subsidiaries acquired earlier.

One of the first tasks charged to the Federal Reserve Board was to establish a list of permissible business activities that "are closely related to banking or managing or controlling banks . . ." (Gup, 1984). By the 1980s, these included such activities as investment or financial advising, management consulting to depository institutions, discount brokerage, issuance and sale of traveler's checks, and credit, life, accident, and health insurance underwriting. Activities denied by the board include underwriting life insurance not related to credit extension, general management consulting, real estate syndication, and computer output microfilm services.

Our study examines the growth and diversification activities of a sample of forty-two bank holding companies formed after 1956 (all of which were formed as one-bank holding companies), the year of the Bank Holding Companies Act. We use only a subset of the base population because of missing data in variables central to this study. Information in *Moody's Banking and Finance Manual* (1988) was used to construct a monthly activity history of acquisition and divestment for each bank holding company for the term beginning with the month in which it was incorporated and ending with December 1988. For bank holding companies, the elaboration of the core business is reflected in the *related* acquisition or divestment of a commercial bank in the same or a new geographical area. Extension of the core business is reflected in the *unrelated* acquisition or divestment of a firm in a permissible nonbank business. During the observation period, the 42 sample firms engaged in 365 related acquisitions, 106 unrelated acquisitions, 17 related divestments, and 38 unrelated divestments.

Analytical Techniques

Testing our hypotheses required two distinct analytical techniques: event history analysis and optimal matching. To test hypotheses 1 through 5, we used event history analysis to model the timing of all moves in a sequence (Tuma and Hannan, 1984). We used optimal matching to produce measures of resemblance between sequences of events to test hypothesis 6, which predicts the existence of different evolutionary paths of core business change.

Event History Analysis

Our event history analysis focused on explaining rates of occurrence of two types of acquisitions: related (banks) and unrelated (nonbanks) to the core business. Rate models have the advantage of being able to make use of information on right-censored cases (i.e., firms that do not have an event of a particular type before the end of the observation period), without assuming that it will never have such an event. We used a multivariate point-process approach (Amburgey, 1986), which can examine recurrent events over time. We estimated the following model:

$$r(t) = \exp [\beta X(t)] \tag{1}$$

where $r(t)$ is the rate of occurrence of an acquisition activity of a given type, $X(t)$ is a vector of independent variables, and β is a vector of coefficients for the effects of the independent variables. For the analysis, we organized the data for each bank holding company in the form of a series of monthly spells. We considered each spell right-censored unless an acquisition activity of a given type occurred during the month. We used RATE (Tuma, 1980) to estimate the vector of coefficients by the method of maximum likelihood.

Empirical Specification of the Evolutionary Process Model. To test hypotheses 1A and 1B, we generated cumulative counts for each type of acquisition activity (i.e., related and unrelated) throughout the observed history of a firm. Each firm begins with a value of zero events of each type and receives a count of one after the first event of a given type, two after the second occurrence, and so on. The cumulative value for each type of acquisition at any given time is the independent variable used to analyze the effect of prior acquisition activity on later activity. To test hypotheses 2A and 2B, which predict that early occurrences of a type of acquisition increase the likelihood that that action will be undertaken throughout the organization's life, we used a count of the number of each type of acquisition that occurred within the first two years of each firm's existence.[3]

To estimate the dynamic effects of prior change on the future risk of change specified in hypotheses 3A and 3B, we created time-clock measures that counted the time elapsed since a bank holding company experienced an acquisition event of a particular kind. For each firm, we set the time clock for each type of acquisition activity equal to zero until an event of that kind occurred. After the event, the time clock counted the natural logarithm of the number of months since the event occurred (Amburgey et al., 1993). We reset the counter if the event recurred. In combination, the cumulative count (described previously) and time clock measures permitted an examination of both immediate and longer-term effects of prior acquisition activity on the future probability of a firm's undertaking these activities. Finally, to test hypotheses 4A–4B and 5A–5B we created measures for the cumulative counts of related and unrelated divestment as well as the time elapsed (natural logarithm of the number of months) since the last occurrence of each type of divestment activity. These measures were computed identically to the acquisition measures described earlier.

More formally, the empirical specification of our evolutionary process model is

$$r_i(t) = \exp\,[\beta_1 \mathrm{NACQ}_i(t) + \beta_2 2\mathrm{YRNACQ}_i + \beta_3 \mathrm{TSACQ}_i(t)$$
$$+ \beta_4 \mathrm{NDIV}_i(t) + \beta_5 \mathrm{TSDIV}_i(t)], \quad (2)$$

where $r_i(t)$ is the rate of occurrence of acquisition type i, $\mathrm{NACQ}_i(t)$ is the cumulative number of acquisitions of type i at time t, $2\mathrm{YRNACQ}_i$ is the number of acquisitions of type i that occurred in the first two years of a firm's existence, $\mathrm{TSACQ}_i(t)$ is the time elapsed since the last occurrence of an acquisition of type i at time t, $\mathrm{NDIV}_i(t)$ is the cumulative number of divestments of type i at time t, and $\mathrm{TSDIV}_i(t)$ is the time elapsed since the last occurrence of a divestment of type i at time t. In the analysis reported later, in addition to the *same-type* effects of prior core business change, we also controlled for *cross-type* (e.g., elaboration through acquisition on extension through acquisition) effects. In terms of model [2], support for hypotheses 1 to 5 requires $\beta_1 > 0$; $\beta_2 > 0$; $\beta_3 < 0$; $\beta_4 < 0$; and $\beta_5 > 0$.

Control Variables for the Event History Analysis. The first control variable was the age of a bank holding company. Age was set equal to the natural logarithm of the number of months since the time of a bank holding company's founding. Previous research shows that the natural logarithm of age best represents the functional form of age dependence in exponential models (Hannan and Freeman, 1989). Structural inertia arguments (Hannan and Freeman, 1984) suggest that aging lowers rates of change. Second, to examine whether observed patterns of growth and diversification activity were simply a function of the passage of time, a time trend variable was included in the analysis.

We also included several control measures to model the effects of relevant legislation. During the period of this study three legislative events influenced the activities of bank holding companies. The first was the Bank Merger Act of 1966, which amended the Bank Merger Act of 1960. Although the Bank Merger Act of 1960 had previously established a set of criteria for the three banking agencies to follow when considering bank applications, it did not indicate which criterion should be given the greater weight—banking factors and convenience and needs or competitive factors. In contrast, the 1966 amendments brought about the increased tendency to incorporate antitrust factors into banking law, as reflected in the increasing number of bank merger applications challenged by the Department of Justice after 1966 (Gup, 1984). The second relevant legislative event occurring during the period of this study was the Bank Holding Company Act of 1970, discussed earlier. The third relevant legislative event during this period was the Federal Reserve Reform Act of 1977, which provided for expedited board approval of bank holding company acquisitions, consolidations, and mergers in emergency situations, or when immediate action was necessary to prevent the probable failure of the bank or bank holding company involved in the transaction. We controlled for the impact of these legislative events with three period-effect variables. The periods were 1967–70, 1971–77, and 1978–88. These variables were coded 1 during the specified period and 0 otherwise. The 1956–66 period was excluded as a comparison.[4] Dynamic effects of each legislative period were also examined with time clock variables. Each time clock was set to zero until the legislative change occurred, counted the natural logarithm of the number of months that had passed since the legislation was enacted, and reset to zero upon subsequent legislation.

Optimal Matching Analysis

Optimal matching is a measurement method that produces direct measures of resemblance between sequences of events,[5] given a matrix of dissimilarity between the elements in the sequences, that quantify the minimum extent of *modification* in one sequence required for it to be transformed into another (Abbott, 1990; Abbott and Forrest, 1986; Abbott and Hrycak, 1990). In optimal matching, three basic types of modifications are (a) the *substitution* of one element for another at the same position in the sequence, (2) the *deletion* of an element from a sequence, and (3) the *insertion* of an element into a sequence. Each modification is assigned a "cost," a real number greater than zero that reflects an a priori decision as to the severity of the modification; the less severe, the smaller the cost. Optimal matching techniques have been shown to be relatively stable even when substitution costs are dramatically altered

(Abbott, 1990). Substitution costs are defined for each pair of potential elements, with greater substitution costs assigned to pairs that are judged to be more dissimilar. The substitution cost of an element for itself is zero, and it is conventional to standardize substitution costs to a maximum of 1 (Bradley and Bradley, 1983). Insertion and deletion costs are set equal to each other and may be any value greater than half the minimum, nonzero substitution cost (since an insertion and a deletion is equivalent to a substitution). As the strings are converted until they match, the costs of the transformation are summed.

Because there are multiple sets of transformations, there are multiple costs that will make sequences match. In computing the optimal matching result, one uses algorithms to compute the least costly method of matching the sequences.[6] Although it is conventional to divide the total cost by the length of the longer string, following Levitt and Nass (1989), the total cost is standardized to a maximum of 1 by dividing it by the maximum total cost that could be obtained from an optimal match of two sequences of the same length as the compared sequences.[7] After standardization, a distance of zero means the two sequences are identical; a distance of one means the two sequences are maximally different. We use this approach because it has the advantage of not giving undue influence to the differences in the length between two sequences (Levitt and Nass, 1989). A brief illustration follows.

Illustration of Optimal Matching Analysis*

Assume we have sequences whose elements are letters of the alphabet. Let the substitution cost for a given pair of letters equal the difference in position of the alphabet divided by 25. Thus, the substitution cost between "C" and "H" is $(8 - 3)/25$; the maximum substitution cost between "A" and "Z" is $(26 - 1)/25 = 1$. Let the insertion and deletion costs equal 0.15. To convert the sequence "WAR" into "PEACE" in the least costly fashion, one would do the following:

Modification	Cost
Substitute "W" for "P"	$(23 - 16)/25 = 0.28$
Insert "E"	0.15
Leave "A" alone	0.00
Insert "C"	0.15
Delete "R" and Insert "E"†	$0.15 + 0.15 = 0.30$
TOTAL	0.88

The maximum cost is $[(3 * 0.3) + (2 * 0.15)] = 1.2$. Therefore, the distance between "WAR" and "PEACE" is $0.88/1.2 = 0.733$.

---

*This illustration is based on an example in Levitt and Nass (1989).
†This modification is less costly than changing "R" into "E" since $(15 - 5)/25 = 0.4$.

For the optimal matching analysis we coded the core business elaboration activities of each bank holding company into one of two categories: (1) *related acquisition* (coded A) and (2) *related divestment* (coded C); the core business extension activities of each bank holding company were, likewise, coded into two categories: (1) *unrelated acquisition* (coded B), and (2) *unrelated divestment* (coded D). We constructed sequences based on the yearly activities of each firm with respect to these types of core business elaborations and extensions. For each year we coded a firm according to the type or types of actions it took. For example, a firm undertaking a related acquisition and an unrelated divestment in a given year would be coded AD for that year. We coded firms undertaking no core business elaboration or extension in a particular year as *inactive* (coded Y) for that year.[8] Table 7.1 presents the core business change sequences for each sample firm.

Substitution costs between any core business activity and inactivity were defined as 1.0. While optimal matching is generally robust to changes in substitution costs, we examined the effects of three settings for the substitution costs between the different core business elaboration and extension activities. In the first, all activities were assumed equally different and all substitution costs were set to 1.0. In the second, substitution costs between elaboration and extension activities (e.g., A and B, AC and D) were set equal to 1.0, and substitution costs between acquisitions and divestments of the same type (e.g., A and C, B and D) were set equal to 0.5. In the third, substitution costs between acquisition and divestment (e.g., A and C, A and D) were set to 1.0, and substitution costs between elaboration and extension activities (e.g., AB and B, C and D) were set equal to 0.5. For the second and third settings, the substitution costs between partly overlapped activities (e.g., BC and B, AB and BC) were defined as 0.75. The optimal matching results were robust to these variations in substitution cost settings. Therefore, in the analysis presented later, all substitutions were simply assigned a cost of 1.0. Insertion/deletion costs were also defined as 1.0 in the following analysis. Resetting these costs to equal 0.5 and 1.5 did not substantively alter the results from those reported later.

Results

Event History Analysis Results

The first step in the analysis was to determine the extent to which processes of momentum, imprinting, forgetting, and unlearning influenced the rates of bank holding company acquisition. Table 7.2 presents the results of the dynamic analysis for related and unrelated acquisitions separately.

The estimates provide strong support for the predicted effects of momentum (H1A and H1B) and imprinting (H2A and H2B) on rates of bank holding company acquisition activity. Rates of related and unrelated acquisition are each positively related to the number of prior acquisitions of the same type. Moreover, as indicated by the significant positive estimates for the number of related and unrelated acquisitions in the first two years, bank holding companies that engaged in a larger number of related or unrelated acquisitions in their first two years subsequently exhibited higher rates of acquisition of the same type.

Support for hypotheses 3A and 3B is more equivocal. White rates of both related and unrelated acquisition *increased* with the number of prior acquisitions of the same type, only related acquisition rates *declined* with the time elapsed since the last occurrence of an acquisition event of the same type. The rate of unrelated acquisition is not significantly influenced by the time since the last acquisition of that type.

These effects of the frequency and recency of prior acquisitions of the same type

TABLE 7.1   Bank Holding Company Core Business Change Sequences

Firm	Sequence
1	Y A A A A A A Y A Y A Y A A A A A Y A A
2	AB B B Y
3	A Y Y Y A
4	A Y B A Y Y B A A A A A Y A B A Y
5	A Y Y Y Y B Y Y Y B Y Y B Y B D Y D C D D
6	Y A A A A B A Y A A A Y A Y A Y Y Y C D C C Y Y
7	A A A B A A A B A D Y Y Y Y A A B Y C Y Y AB
8	Y A A A A A A A Y A A A A Y C Y A A B A
9	A Y Y A A A B A B B Y B Y Y Y Y Y BD Y Y A
10	Y A Y Y Y Y Y Y Y Y B Y D B A Y A B Y A B
11	A A Y A Y
12	A Y Y Y Y Y Y Y Y Y Y Y Y Y Y Y Y Y Y Y
13	Y A Y Y Y Y Y C A Y A A A A B
14	A Y A Y A A Y B A A A Y Y Y A
15	A AB AB A Y Y Y Y Y Y Y A Y A A
16	A B B A Y Y Y Y Y Y Y Y Y A Y Y D A B
17	A Y A Y AB AB Y A BD Y Y Y Y Y Y Y Y Y A Y Y Y Y Y
18	A Y Y Y Y A A AB A A AB A A
19	A AB A A A Y Y A Y A A Y A Y Y A A A AB
20	A B Y B B Y B Y Y Y Y D A D Y A Y D AB
21	A Y A A Y Y Y Y Y Y Y Y Y Y Y Y Y A
22	B Y Y Y Y Y Y Y Y Y Y D Y D Y Y Y Y Y
23	A Y Y A Y Y Y Y Y Y Y C A A Y Y A
24	A A Y A Y A Y
25	Y A Y A Y Y A Y A A A A A A A A A AB
26	Y A Y A Y Y Y A Y A A A Y Y A A A A
27	A Y Y Y A Y A Y Y A
28	A Y Y Y AB Y D Y Y Y Y Y A Y Y Y Y Y
29	A B AB Y D D Y D Y D Y D D Y Y Y Y Y Y Y
30	A Y A Y Y Y
31	A Y Y Y Y Y Y Y Y Y AB AB A Y Y AB
32	A A Y A Y Y Y A Y Y Y Y AB Y Y Y C BC AD
33	A Y Y Y C Y Y
34	A B Y B B B Y Y B Y Y Y Y Y Y B B A B B
35	A Y Y Y Y Y Y Y Y Y Y Y Y Y Y A A A A A
36	A Y Y A A B Y B Y Y Y Y B Y B Y B Y Y Y
37	Y Y Y Y Y Y Y Y Y Y A C A A B A A A Y Y A A Y A Y A A A A AB AB
38	A Y Y Y Y Y Y Y Y Y Y Y Y Y Y Y Y Y Y Y
39	A B Y A B A B A B B B AB AB AB AD AB D
40	A Y Y Y Y A A Y Y A Y Y Y Y Y Y A A A B Y AB B
41	Y A A Y Y Y Y Y Y Y Y A A A Y Y A
42	Y A Y A A AB Y A A A B AB AB A A A D C Y Y A ABD Y Y A A AC

NOTE: A = related acquisition; B = unrelated acquisition; C = related divestment; D = unrelated divestment.

are graphically illustrated in figures 7.1 and 7.2. Each figure shows the effects of repeating acquisitions of the same type *once* per year and *three* times per year. In the figures, a multiplier of greater (less) than one indicates that the acquisition rate is increased (decreased) relative to firms that have not changed by a factor equal to the multiplier. Note the damping effect of time since prior related acquisition on the

TABLE 7.2   Models of Bank Holding Company Acquisition†

Variable	Model	
	Related Acquisition	Unrelated Acquisition
Constant	−35.88	−9.312
	(33.50)	(25.64)
ln(organizational age)	−.227*	−.033
	(.158)	(.216)
# prior related acquisitions	.050*	−.006
	(.012)	(.023)
# prior unrelated acquisitions	.039*	.133*
	(.020)	(.019)
# prior related divestments	−.360*	−.559
	(.216)	(.525)
# prior unrelated divestments	−.281*	−.492*
	(.168)	(.269)
ln(time since related acquisition)	−.257*	.034
	(.051)	(.088)
ln(time since unrelated acquisition)	−.098*	.066
	(.035)	(.069)
ln(time since related divestment)	.211*	.216
	(.075)	(.164)
ln(time since unrelated divestment)	−.047	−.044
	(.079)	(.131)
# related acquisitions in 1st two years	.100*	—
	(.051)	
# unrelated acquisitions in 1st two years	—	.312*
		(.167)
1967–88 period	48.34*	42.44*
	(14.06)	(23.67)
ln(calendar time)	−2.896*	−5.007*
	(1.245)	(2.453)
ln(time 1956–66)	6.826*	4.969
	(3.090)	(5.525)
ln(time 1967–70)	.185*	.512*
	(.104)	(.227)
ln(time 1971–77)	.330*	.579*
	(.150)	(.314)
ln(time 1978–88)	.636*	1.058*
	(.236)	(.483)
x^2	182.46	65.71
df	16	16
Diversification events	315	97
Monthly spells	7516	7516

NOTE: * <.05; standard errors in parentheses; —not estimated.

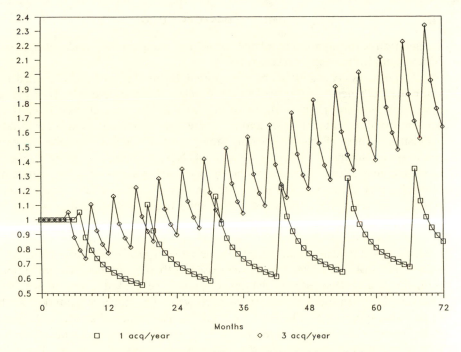

FIG. 7.1   Related acquisition: Effects of prior related acquisition

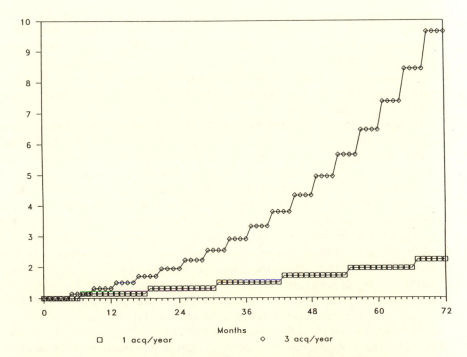

FIG. 7.2   Unrelated acquisition: Effects of prior unrelated acquisition

acceleration of momentum in related acquisition compared to unrelated acquisition, which is not influenced by recency.

Hypotheses 4A and 4B are both supported. Rates of related and unrelated acquisition are both negatively related to the number of prior divestments of the same type. However, the positive effects of increases in the time elapsed since the last occurrence of divestment (H5A and H5B) are only supported in the case of related acquisition. These effects of repeating same-type divestments *once* and *three* times per year are illustrated in figures 7.3 and 7.4. Note the rebound in the momentum in related acquisition produced by the effect of time since prior related divestment. Note also that after six divestments of the same type, rates of related and unrelated acquisition both fall to approximately one tenth the rate of acquisition among firms with no prior divestments.

Several control variables also exhibited significant influences on rates of bank holding company acquisition. Parallel to the same-type effects of prior related acquisitions, rates of related acquisition increased with the number of prior unrelated acquisitions and declined with the time elapsed since the last unrelated acquisition, although the magnitudes of these cross-effects were of a smaller magnitude than those of the same-type effects. The rate of related acquisition also declined with increases in the number of unrelated divestments. However, for unrelated acquisitions, there were no significant effects of related acquisition and divestment activity. These asymmetric cross-effects may reflect underlying asymmetries in organizational learning. Since unrelated activities occur in a variety of nonbank businesses, learning from related acquisitions and divestments may not be easily transferred to the realm of unrelated activities. However, unrelated activities, though in a variety of nonbank businesses, may afford learning situations that are potentially applicable to related activities in banking. Therefore, core business extension experience may influence both further extension and elaboration activities, while core business elaboration experience only influences further elaboration activities. This suggests a hierarchy of core business change routines: learning to implement core business *extension* may require a higher level of managerial capability than learning to implement core business *elaboration* successfully.

Organizational age was unrelated to the rate of unrelated acquisition, although older bank holding companies exhibited lower rates of related acquisition. Notably, combined with the insignificant cross-type effects of related acquisition on the likelihood of unrelated acquisition, the results of this study provide no evidence that bank holding companies engaged in unrelated diversification either later in the organizational life cycle or after the organization had first attempted to grow through related diversification. The legislative period variables and associated time clocks also significantly influenced rates of acquisition activity. The estimates for the 1967–88 period indicated that rates of related and unrelated acquisition were significantly higher after 1966. In addition, the positive estimates for the time elapsed since the most recent legislative change time clock measures indicate that the rates of acquisition activity fell immediately after each legislative change, and then increased with the passage of time until the next legislative change. Finally, the negative estimates for the calendar time variable mean that rates of acquisition activity slowed over time. This effect of calendar time serves increasingly to dampen the positive effects of the elapsed time since the most recent legislative change.

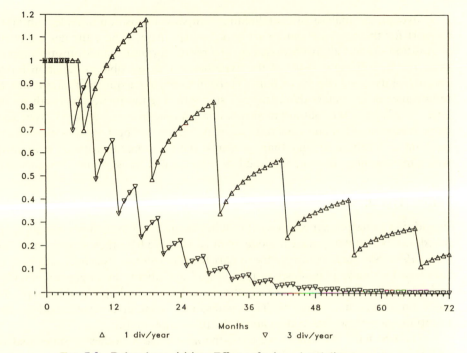

FIG. 7.3   Related acquisition: Effects of prior related divestment

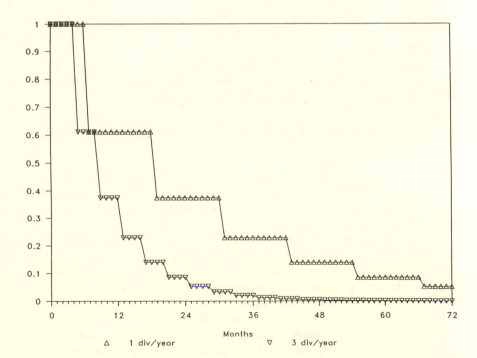

FIG. 7.4   Unrelated acquisition: Effects of prior unrelated divestment

Overall, the analysis of bank holding company acquisition provides substantial support for the study's evolutionary process hypotheses. The estimates for related acquisition support all five hypotheses. The results for unrelated acquisition support three (H1B, H2B, and H4B) of the hypotheses. One possible explanation for the absence of dynamic effects (H3B and H5B) in unrelated acquisition rates is that the importance of recency in dampening or strengthening momentum depends on the-*generalizability* of the routines involved. For example, recently used (or discredited) bank (i.e., related) acquisition routines may have a stronger influence on further banking acquisition activity than nonbank (i.e., unrelated) acquisition routines, which may be more idiosyncratic and less generalizable across nonbank acquisitions.

Naïve Hypotheses

In addition to testing hypotheses 1 through 5 against null hypotheses, we also compared our evolutionary process model with two "naïve hypotheses" (Pant and Starbuck, 1990; Starbuck, commentary to part III, this volume). Starbuck suggests that tests based on naïve hypotheses instead of null hypotheses are of greater credibility and substantive significance. Like a null hypothesis, a naïve hypothesis is simple, but while a null hypothesis generally has no substantive content, a naïve hypothesis tries to capture one or two basic ideas about the process of interest.

The first naïve hypothesis we test—the *no-change* hypothesis—states that the next value of the rate $r_i(t)$ will be the same as the current value, that is, $r_i(t) = r_i(t - 1)$. This hypothesis captures the idea that causal processes are inertial. The second naïve hypothesis we test—the *linear-trend* hypothesis—states that the trend in the rate observed since yesterday will continue until tomorrow, that is, $r_i(t) = r_i(t - 1) + [r_i(t - 1) - r_i(t - 2)]$. This hypothesis expresses the idea that causal processes are inertial in trend as well as state.

We use Bayesian analysis (Jeffreys and Berger, 1992) to compare the fit of the naïve and theoretical hypotheses to the data. To do this, we first compute the probability density of the data given a particular hypothesis:

$$\text{Prob} \ (Data \mid Hypothesis) = \sum_t C_{y(t)}^{n(t)} \ r(t^{y(t)} \ (1 - r(t))^{n(t) - s(t)}, \tag{3}$$

where $n(t)$ is the number of events possible during period t, $y(t)$ is the number of events observed during period t, C_y^n, the number of ways of positioning the y change events among the n trials, is $n!/y!(n - y)!$, and $r(t)$ is the estimated rate (i.e., probability of an event during period t).[9]

The probability densities of the related and unrelated acquisition data for the no-change, linear-trend, and evolutionary process models are given in table 7.3. What is of interest, however, is not the probability density of the data given the various hypotheses, but rather the probabilities of the hypotheses' being true given the data. It can be shown from Bayes' theorem that the ratio, $B = \text{Prob}(Data \mid Hypothesis \ 1)/\text{Prob}(Data \mid Hypothesis \ 2)$, called the Bayes factor, gives the odds of favoring hypothesis 1 over hypothesis 2 arising from the data (Jeffreys and Berger, 1992). When B is greater than 1, the data favor hypothesis 1, and when B is less than 1, they

TABLE 7.3   Probability Densities: No-Change, Linear-Trend, and Evolutionary Process
Hypotheses

Event	Probability Density			Bayes Factor(B)	
	No Change Hypothesis (NC)	Linear-trend Hypothesis (LT)	Evolutionary Process Hypothesis (EP)	(EP/NC)	(EP/LT)
Related Acquisition	3.446×10^{-59}	5.747×10^{-44}	1.525×10^{-39}	4.425×10^{19} (6.585)*	2.654×10^{4} (1.529)
Unrelated Acquisition	1.363×10^{-27}	3.532×10^{-26}	1.713×10^{-22}	1.257×10^{5} (1.631)	4.850×10^{3} (1.424)

NOTE: The values in parentheses give the Bayes factors for each six-month interval. This value gives the percentage improvement in the prediction in each period.

favor hypothesis 2. The ratios of the probability densities for the theoretical and naive hypotheses are given in table 7.3 indicate that the evolutionary process model is strongly favored over both naïve hypotheses. Thus, in addition to rejecting the null hypothesis that related and unrelated acquisition rates do not vary with the variables in the evolutionary process model, we have also shown this model to provide a better fit with the data than two naïve hypotheses about organizational change.

Optimal Matching Results

Given the strong support for the evolutionary process model, the next step in the analysis was to examine whether, as predicted in hypothesis 6, bank holding companies exhibited distinct evolutionary paths of core business change. To do this, we first calculated an optimal matching distance matrix. The mean of the distance matrix for the forty-two core business change sequences is 0.487. This means that on average about half of the activities would have to be changed to make the sequence of one company conform to those of another.

We used the optimal matching distance matrix as input to cluster analysis to analyze the substructure of core business event sequences in the bank holding company sample and to identify clusters of similar sequences of activity. In cluster analysis, sequences are agglomerated into small groups on the basis of highest resemblance; then the small groups are joined into larger groups, repeating the sequence until all are joined in one large group. This produces a hierarchy of ranks consisting of groupings of sequences that do not overlap.[10]

Table 7.4 presents the results of the cluster analysis. The table shows the core business change sequence clusters and the average optimal matching distance between the sequences in each group. Three of the sequences are sufficiently different from all others that they are not included in the resultant groupings. The effectiveness of these groupings was tested using the mean within-group and between-group inter-sequence distances, which are 0.280 and 0.539, respectively (*t*-value = 5.484, 42 degrees of freedom, $p < 0.001$). This test indicates that the clusters of core business change sequences are significantly different, thereby offering preliminary support for hypothesis 6.

TABLE 7.4   Bank Holding Company Core Business Change Sequence Clusters

Firm	Cluster	Sequence	Average Distance
1	1	Y A A A A A A Y A Y A A A A A Y A A	
8	1	Y A A A A A A A Y A A A A Y C Y A AB A	
19	1	A AB A A A Y Y A Y A A Y A Y Y A A A AB	
25	1	Y A Y A Y Y A Y A A A A A A A A A AB	
26	1	Y A Y A Y Y Y A Y A A A Y Y A A A A	.267
2	2	AB B B Y	
3	3	A Y Y Y A	
11	3	A A Y A Y	.370
4	4	A Y B A Y Y B A A A A A Y AB A Y	
13	4	Y A Y Y Y Y Y C A Y A A A AB	
14	4	A Y A Y A A Y B A A A Y Y Y A	
15	4	A AB AB A Y Y Y Y Y Y A Y A A	
18	4	A Y Y Y Y A A AB A A AB A A	
39	4	A B Y A B A B A B B B AB AB AD AB D	.345
5	5	A Y Y Y Y B Y Y Y B Y Y B Y B D Y D CD D	
7	5	A A AB A A AB AD Y Y Y Y A A B Y C Y Y AB	
9	5	A Y Y A A AB AB B Y B Y Y Y Y Y BD Y Y A	
10	5	Y A Y Y Y Y Y Y Y Y B Y D B A Y AB Y A B	
12	5	A Y Y Y Y Y Y Y Y Y Y Y Y Y Y Y Y Y Y Y	
16	5	A B B A Y Y Y Y Y Y Y Y Y A Y Y D A B	
20	5	A B Y B B Y B Y Y Y Y Y D AD Y A Y D AB	
21	5	A Y A A Y Y Y Y Y Y Y Y Y Y Y Y Y Y A	
22	5	B Y Y Y Y Y Y Y Y Y D Y D Y Y Y Y Y	
23	5	A Y Y A Y Y Y Y Y Y C A A Y Y A	
28	5	A Y Y Y AB Y D Y Y Y Y Y A Y Y Y Y Y	
31	5	A Y Y Y Y Y Y Y Y Y AB AB A Y Y AB	
32	5	A A Y A Y Y Y A Y Y Y Y AB Y Y Y C BC AD	
34	5	A B Y B B B Y Y B Y Y Y Y Y B B AB B	
35	5	A Y Y Y Y Y Y Y Y Y Y Y Y Y Y A A A A A	
36	5	A Y Y A AB Y B Y Y Y Y B Y B Y B Y Y Y	
38	5	A Y Y Y Y Y Y Y Y Y Y Y Y Y Y Y Y Y Y Y	
41	5	Y A A Y Y Y Y Y Y Y Y A A A Y Y A	.244
6	6	Y A A A AB A Y A A A Y A Y A Y Y Y CD C C Y Y	
17	6	A Y A Y AB BD Y A AD Y Y Y Y Y Y Y Y A Y Y Y Y Y	
29	6	A B AB Y DD Y D Y D Y D DD Y Y Y Y Y Y Y	
40	6	A Y Y Y Y A A Y Y A Y Y Y Y Y A A A B Y AB B	.318
37	7	Y Y Y Y Y Y Y Y Y Y Y AC A AB A A A Y Y A A Y A Y A A A A AB AB	
24	8	A A Y A Y A Y	
30	8	A Y A Y Y Y	
33	8	A Y Y Y C Y Y	.264
27	9	A Y Y Y A Y A Y Y A	
42	10	Y A Y A A AB Y A A AB AB A A A D C Y Y A ABD Y Y A A AC	

NOTE: A = related acquisition; B = unrelated acquisition; C = related divestment; D = unrelated divestment.

Next, we estimated the variance in patterns of related and unrelated acquisition in the four main sequence clusters (i.e., clusters 1, 4, 5, and 6) explained by the effects of momentum, imprinting, forgetting, and unlearning.[11] This provides a more direct estimate of the extent to which these evolutionary processes account for the divergent sequence patterns of core business change in table 7.4. Figures 7.5 and 7.6 present estimates of average rates of related and unrelated acquisition for bank holding companies in each major sequence cluster for 12 years at six-month intervals. We used the parameters for the evolutionary process variables in table 7.2 to compute these estimates. Control variable effects were held constant at their mean values for a cluster. Thus, the figures depict the *independent* effects of the evolutionary process variables on rates of related and unrelated acquisition. In figure 7.5, note how the momentum in related acquisition in cluster 1, comprising firms characterized by short periods of inactivity and an absence of divestment, increases virtually unrestrained. In figure 7.6, note the marked decline in the average rate of unrelated acquisition in cluster 6 that follows the unrelated divestments that occur in this cluster.

We regressed the estimates in figures 7.5 and 7.6 on values of the average rates of related and unrelated acquisition in each sequence cluster computed directly from the data. The average variance in the actual rates accounted for by the estimates was 0.381 for related acquisition and 0.465 for unrelated acquisition.[12] These results support hypothesis 6, that the dynamic effects specified in the evolutionary process model played a substantive role in producing the divergent sequence patterns of bank holding company core business change.

The clusters of core business change in table 7.4 vary in terms of two major characteristics: (1) the extent to which holding companies emphasized an *elaboration* pattern (expressed primarily through related acquisitions) versus a *conglomerate* pattern (expressed through related acquisitions as well as an extensive number of unrelated acquisitions) and (2) the extent to which activity is *patchy* and *uneven* versus *systematic* and *smooth*. Whereas firms in cluster 1 reflect elaboration patterns involving primarily related acquisitions that are systematic and smooth, clusters 4, 5, and 6 reflect conglomerate patterns that are patchy and uneven and occur through both related and unrelated acquisitions. Among clusters 4, 5, and 6, there is substantial variation in the patches of activity and inactivity. Periods of activity are shortest and inactivity longest among firms in cluster 5, while periods of activity are longest and activity shortest among firms in cluster 4.

We think these clusters help confirm the findings of previous case studies that identified two key *strategy making modes* (Mintzberg, 1990; Mintzberg and McHugh, 1985; Mintzberg and Waters, 1982). The patterns of sprints and pauses in clusters 4, 5, and 6 appear to characterize an *entrepreneurial* mode of strategy making: a firm leads with a primary strategy, usually related to elaboration of the core business, then pauses to rethink and recombine what has been done (Mintzberg, 1988) or brings up lagging strategies, then leads again, and so on. This approach to core business change is opportunistic; that is, it probes the future without full consideration of the consequences (Mintzberg and Waters, 1982). By comparison, the firms in cluster 1 appear to follow a *planning* mode of strategy making, systematically elaborating their core businesses at continuous rates. Thus, rather than reflecting characteristic strategic trajectories, the clusters appear to reflect different strategy

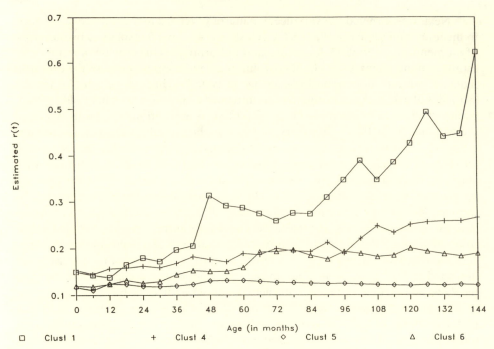

FIG. 7.5   Related acquisition rates

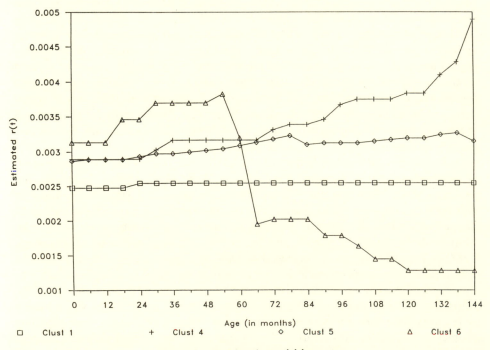

FIG. 7.6   Unrelated acquisition rates

making modes along a continuum that stretches from perfectly *deliberate* at one pole to perfectly *emergent* at the other.

By analyzing both the underlying dynamics and resultant patterns of core business change together, we have attempted to link the mechanisms of core business change to patterns of core business change through time. However, we underscore the preliminary nature of our investigation. We analyzed only a subsample of the population of bank holding companies because of data availability constraints. We did not examine acquisitions of firms in industries completely unrelated to financial services because of the regulations that restrict such activities. Our study also omitted concentric diversification activities because of their rare occurrence in this sample. Finally, our event history model did not include potentially important organizational and environmental control variables such as organizational size, executive succession, and competition. Future research should, therefore, extend our study in three ways: first, by examining core business elaboration and extension patterns in other industries and among firms that were not originally incorporated as holding companies; second, by studying a wider range of sequence events; and third, by analyzing a richer and more extensive set of control variables.

In this study, to increase our understanding of *why* core business elaboration and extension events occur, we used event history analysis to examine an evolutionary process model of core business change. We advanced an evolutionary process model that specified processes underlying the dynamics of core business elaboration and extension over time. The model drew extensively on theories of organizational routines (Nelson and Winter, 1982) and organizational learning (Cyert and March, 1963; Levitt and March, 1988) to explain how variation-selection-retention sequences produced by processes of momentum, imprinting, forgetting, and unlearning dynamically influence rates of core business change. Analysis of historical data on the business elaboration and extension activities of firms in a sample of 42 bank holding companies supported the model. The frequency, primacy, and recency of related and unrelated acquisition fostered momentum effects that encouraged further acquisitions of the same type. However, the frequency and recency of related and unrelated divestments slowed the rate.

To increase our understanding of *how* core business elaboration and extension trajectories develop over time, we used optimal matching analysis to identify different evolutionary paths of strategy making. Previous longitudinal studies of corporate strategy have used narrative studies of single firms to examine patterns of events over time (e.g., Burgelman, 1983a, 1991; Mintzberg and McHugh, 1985; Mintzberg and Waters, 1982). In contrast, our study used optimal matching analysis to determine whether ordered patterns of core business change existed across multiple firms. The optimal matching results provided evidence of the existence of groupings of bank holding companies with distinctive core business change sequences. We showed that the variables in the evolutionary process model accounted for a substantial portion of the variance in rates of related and unrelated acquisition among these clusters. We think future studies of the roles of momentum, imprinting, unlearning, and forgetting in producing different strategy making modes would help clarify the relationship of these evolutionary processes to emergent and deliberate patterns of organizational action over time.

Of the three elements of Campbell's (1965b) variation-selection-retention model of evolutionary processes, most population ecology research has studied processes of selection and retention (i.e., organizational mortality and survival). Far less emphasis has been placed on exploring sources of variation. Yet organizational variation is central to evolutionary theory at the population level. Our study begins to redress this imbalance by examining how organization-level processes of learning and unlearning create dynamic patterns of core business variation among firms. These organization-level variations are introduced into the higher level arena of the population, where interactions among firms influence their differential selection and retention at the population level. By affecting the fates of organizational actions (i.e., variations), these population level processes, in turn, shape the future actions of organizations. Therefore, we think future studies will make important advances in the study of organizational evolution by linking the interrelated dynamics and patterns of organization and population level change.

Notes

1. Our data indicate that, almost invariably, the divestment activities of bank holding companies represent the retraction of prior actions. Consequently, we think it is reasonable to assume that the repeated occurrence of divestments of a particular type will contribute to an accumulation of evidence disconfirming the efficacy of prior acquisitions of that type.

2. A holding company is a parent corporation that owns all or the majority of the stock of its constituent subsidiaries, or a corporation whose lesser holding of stock in other corporations is based on control and/or investment motives. The holding company organization has both financial and managerial advantages: Financially, it allows for concentrating control of large properties with a minimum of investment required and for consolidating financing for the system as a whole, thereby achieving efficiencies in financing costs and terms. Managerially, the holding company form of organization makes it possible to decentralize operations with full responsibility and accountability, each subsidiary's management being accountable for implementation of policies and for success of operations on a profit and loss basis (*Encyclopedia of Banking and Finance,* 1990:454).

3. Amburgey et al. (1993) test a related hypothesis using a measure of the elapsed time since an organization first undertakes a change of a particular type. We use a different approach here since the high correlation between elapsed time since first change and organizational age (all but two of the sample firms undertook an acquisition within their first two years) caused serious problems of multicollinearity. Therefore, we used a cumulative count of events in the first two years. To examine the possibility that excluding the events occurring in the first two years of each firm's history biased the estimates for the other theoretical variables, we compared the estimates obtained from an analysis that included all observations for each firm with one that excluded observations for the first two years of each firm's history. There were no substantive differences in the estimates.

4. Preliminary analysis showed that, while significant, the estimates for the period-effect dummy variables were of similar magnitudes. This indicated that separate intercept terms were not required for each legislative period, only for the periods before and after 1966. Therefore, for reasons of parsimony, in the analysis reported later, the 1967–70, 1971–77, and 1978–88 period-effect dummy variables are collapsed into a single 1967–88 dummy variable.

5. These sequences consist of strings of well-defined elements that may or may not be repeated.

6. The program used here is the Beldings Program Series written by David Bradley (1976) at Long Beach State University and modified by Clifford Nass and Barbara Levitt (1989) at Stanford University.

7. If the length of the sequences is l_1 and l_2, and the insertion/deletion cost is i, the maximum possible cost is $Cost_{max} = min (l_1, l_2) * min(2 * i,l) + abs (l_1 - l_2) * i$ (Levitt and Nass, 1989:201).

8. Our assumption about the meaning of time is that one year is equivalent to another year. Other assumptions are possible. For example, a logarithmic time metric assumes that the wait between 2 and 4 years is more important than the wait between 22 and 24 years (see Abbott, 1990; Abbott and Hrycak, 1990).

9. We calculated probability density functions for the naive hypotheses and theoretical evolutionary process model using a six month time interval, and assuming that the number of trials n was equal to the number of firm-months in each six month period. We used the parameters in table 7.2 to compute estimates for the theoretical model. Control variable effects were held constant at their mean values for the sample. Thus, the estimates for the theoretical model capture the *independent* effects of the evolutionary process variables on rates of related and unrelated acquisition.

10. Although a variety of clustering algorithms are available, most researchers use one or more of three common techniques: (1) single linkage, (2) complete linkage, or (3) group average method. On the basis of a review of the literature, McKelvey (1982) concluded in favor of the group average method. We conducted a preliminary analysis using all three methods because of the possibility that one method might outperform the others. Since there were few substantive differences in the clusters produced by the different methods, we report clusters based on the group average method.

11. We also attempted to provide additional evidence that the variables specified in the evolutionary process model accounted for the different sequence clusters by reestimating the models in table 7.2 at the sequence cluster level of analysis. If these clusters are produced by the processes specified in hypotheses 1–5, then disaggregating the data by cluster should control for the effects of these processes, attenuating or eliminating their effects. In the reanalysis, which was performed on clusters 1, 4, 5, and 6 (unrelated acquisition clusters 4 and 6 only), there was considerable attenuation of the estimates.

12. The estimates of R^2 in each cluster were as follows: Related acquisition: cluster 1 = 0.329; cluster 4 = 0.346; cluster 5 = 0.645; cluster 6 = 0.204. Unrelated acquisition: cluster 4 = 0.626; cluster 6 = 0.305. There was insufficient variance in rates of unrelated acquisitions in clusters 1 and 5 for meaningful estimation.

8

The Ecological Dynamics of Organizational Change: Density and Mass Dependence in Rates of Entry into New Markets

HEATHER A. HAVEMAN

Campbell (1969) and Aldrich (1979) outlined a three-part evolutionary model involving variation, selection, and retention. Most research in organizational ecology has studied organizational failure, thereby focusing on the process of selection. Although variation is an equally important process in organizational evolution (Hawley, 1987; Fombrun, 1987), there have been comparatively few studies of this process, except the small number of studies of organizational founding. Variation is a necessary precondition for selection: without the diverse products of variation, selection would have no raw material upon which to operate (Campbell, 1969). One important source of variation in organizational populations is change in organizational structure and activities, which has recently become a topic of interest in organizational ecology and organizational evolution. Previous research has studied the effects of organizational characteristics on change and stability: age (Singh, Tucker, and Meinhard, 1988; Baum, 1990b), possession of specialized assets and vulnerability of existing domain (Mitchell, 1989), and past experience with change (Amburgey, Kelly, and Barnett, 1993; Delacroix and Singh, 1991; Ginsberg and Baum, chapter 7, this volume). Some work has also modeled the impact of competitive and institutional factors on rates of organizational change, such as population density and differentiation (Swaminathan and Delacroix, 1991), fluctuations in environmental munificence (Delacroix and Swaminathan, 1991; Singh, Tucker, and Meinhard, 1991), the uncertainty that follows exogenous shocks (Amburgey, Kelly, and Barnett, 1993; Delacroix and Swaminathan, 1991), and conditions at time of founding (Romanelli, 1991b).

This chapter extends the evolutionary research program to examine how the

The research reported here was supported by a Social Sciences and Humanities Research Council of Canada Doctoral Fellowship, and by the Fuqua School of Business, Duke University. I thank Nancy Wallace for providing data and Glenn Carroll for his advice on my dissertation research. Helpful comments on earlier drafts were made by Joel Baum, Charles Fombrun, Huggy Rao, Elaine Romanelli, and Anand Swaminathan.

structure of the competitive environment influences variation through organizational change. Change is defined as shifts in organizational domain and operationalized as product-market diversification. The environmental forces studied are market density (the number of organizations in a market) and mass (the total size of those organizations).

An Ecological Model of Organizational Change

Any ecological model of variation in organizational structure and activities must be reconciled with the concept of structural inertia (Hannan and Freeman, 1977, 1984, 1989). If organizational forms are strongly inert, then organizations will respond slowly to perceived opportunities and threats and will not change quickly enough to keep pace with shifting environmental conditions.

Inertia is posited to be the outcome of performance pressures favoring organizations that consistently reproduce desired behaviors and that account rationally for their actions (Hannan and Freeman, 1984, 1989). This model of selection-induced inertia assumes that achieving reliable performance requires keeping structure and activities stable; hence, organizations are inert. However, the model does not take into account the possibility that organizational change may be necessitated by shifts in environmental resources and demands. If the conditions that affect performance fluctuate greatly, then organizations that reproduce their previously effective structures will perform inconsistently. If the outputs required change frequently and by large amounts; if the inputs available changed in quantity, quality, or relative proportions; or if the technologies used change, then organizations will be forced to alter their structures and activity patterns in order to achieve consistent performance. In volatile environments, societal pressures for reliable output will result in flexible rather than inert organizations. Informality and instability can become familiar to organizations that face volatile environments (Starbuck, 1965). Organizational flexibility can derive from stable processes that routinize change (March, 1981). In unstable and uncertain environments, selection pressures will favor flexible organizational forms—forms that adjust to perform consistently.

What is it about organizations that changes or remains stable? The ecological model, like earlier structural contingency models, distinguishes between core and peripheral features. The organizational core consists of goals, authority structure, technology, and marketing strategy (Hannan and Freeman, 1977, 1989). The organizational core is its domain, meaning the claims an organization stakes out for itself in terms of the clients it serves, the products it offers, and the technology it employs (Thompson, 1967). Diversification—the introduction of new products, often to new clients and frequently requiring mastery of new technology—represents change of domain, a means of transcending the constraints of an organization's original sphere of activity by entering new markets and new competitive arenas.

Hypotheses

Within the ecological framework, density has been used as a proximate measure of the processes of legitimation and competition (Hannan and Carroll, 1992). According to this model, legitimacy grows monotonically with density, but at a decreasing rate, while competition grows monotonically, but at an increasing rate. The organizational founding rate is predicted to have an inverted U-shaped relationship with density. This follows from assuming that the founding rate is proportional to the degree to which the organizational form is legitimate and inversely proportional to the level of competition. A parallel argument can be made for the mortality rate by assuming that it is proportional to competition and inversely proportional to legitimacy. This assumption leads to a U-shaped relationship between density and the mortality rate. Empirical support for this model comes from studies of a wide variety of organizational populations, including labor unions, newspapers, breweries, cooperative associations, trade associations, Manhattan banks, and New York life insurance companies (see Hannan and Carroll, 1992 for a review).

The density-dependence model has implications beyond organizational founding and failure, however. It can also be applied to the process of change in existing organizations, specifically to diversification—entry into new product or client markets. The number of organizations operating in any market should affect both that market's perceived legitimacy and its level of competition. Market density thus influences both external legitimacy considerations and general competitive dynamics, two sources of organizational inertia (Hannan and Freeman, 1977, 1984). An inverted U-shaped relationship will exist between the number of firms operating in a market and entry into that market. At low levels of market density, an increase in the number of firms operating in any market will increase market legitimacy and thus raise the rate of entry. In contrast, at high levels of market density, a crowding or competitive effect dominates and further increases in the number of firms operating will lower the rate of market entry.

Hypothesis 1A: There will be an inverted U-shaped relationship between the number of firms operating in any market and the rate of entry into that market.

Research in economics suggests that both the number of firms operating in a market and the size of these firms will influence entry decisions by potential newcomers. Bain (1956) laid out a model of barriers to entry that was extended by Caves and Porter (1977) to include barriers to mobility across subgroups in an industry, thereby addressing the phenomenon of domain shift through diversification. According to this model, oligopolistic markets, which are dominated by a few large competitors, are more difficult to enter than atomistic markets, which are "contested" by many small firms (Bain 1956; Baumol, Panzar, and Willig, 1982), because both direct and diffuse competition are stronger in oligopolistic markets than in contestable markets.

Direct competition occurs when a pair of organizations reduce each other's performance and viability (Hannan and Freeman, 1989). In oligopolistic markets, large incumbents reap economies of scale that are not available to small firms (Bain 1956), so they operate more efficiently, have lower cost structures, and tend to possess more slack resources. Because incumbents in an oligopolistic market are large and few in number, each firm has substantial impact on market policy and price structure. The existence of a few, large-scale, low-cost competitors in oligopolistic markets makes it likely that incumbents will act collectively, building excess capacity and adjusting prices to thwart entry of new competitors, thus increasing direct competition (Edwards, 1955; Bain, 1956).

Diffuse competition occurs when organizations reduce the viability of other, similar organizations by depleting a limited, common supply of resources (Hannan and Freeman, 1989). Large organizations operate on a larger scale than do small organizations, so they use more common resources: labor, capital, suppliers' capacity, distribution channel volume, and clients' demand. Hence, large organizations generate more diffuse competition and decrease the viability of competitors more than do small organizations (Barnett and Amburgey, 1990). Oligopolistic markets will be unattractive to potential entrants because oligopolists are large and generate strong diffuse competition.

This model predicts that both the number of firms operating in a market (density) and their size (mass) will affect barriers to entry and thus rates of entry. The impact of density is not independent of the impact of mass. Note that with market density controlled, market mass estimates the effect of average incumbent size.

Hypothesis 1B: Rates of entry will be high when density is high and firms are small, and low when density is low and firms are large.

Research Design

Research Setting: The Savings and Loan Industry

Since 1831 savings and loan associations have acted as the primary lenders for home mortgages and as the primary depositories for small savers in the United States. These interrelated tasks have, until recently, remained the core business activities of savings and loans. The strong focus on gathering deposits from individuals and lending money for home purchases is reflected in the use of the term "thrift" to describe these organizations.

The regulatory environment of the thrift industry has recently undergone dramatic change in response to volatile environmental conditions. The allowed scope of savings and loan activities was broadened by legislation enacted between 1978 and 1982, which extended the domain of savings and loan associations to include real estate development, commercial lending, consumer nonmortgage financial services, and mortgage banking.

This chapter studies the ecological factors that influence diversification by savings and loan associations, operationalized as entry into six new markets: real estate held for development and resale, nonresidential mortgages, mortgage-backed securities, consumer loans, commercial loans, and service corporation subsidiaries. These markets differ in many respects. Modeling rates of entry into such an array of nontraditional markets offers a broad picture of the process of organizational change through product-market diversification. This research design also allows for repeated tests of the hypotheses, which is unusual. Such replication is seldom done in organizational theory research.

Real estate investment has been identified by some critics as a risky move away from thrifts' traditional strengths (Strunk and Case, 1988; Eichler, 1989). The potential returns are great but are accompanied by high probability of failure. Investment in real estate entails shifting both product portfolio and client base, and so involves considerable reorientation of the technical core. In contrast, moving into *nonresidential mortgage lending* involves offering a familiar product (mortgages) to new clients (commercial establishments). Thrifts entering this market must adjust to new client demands but already possess considerable knowledge about product and technology. *Mortgage-backed securities* are composed of residential mortgages. Diversification into securitized mortgage instruments involves products similar to the traditional residential mortgage but different clients and somewhat different technology—the securitization of bundles of mortgages rather than the management of an aggregate of many individual mortgage loans. The fourth new market, *consumer nonmortgage lending,* is attractive to thrifts because the average maturity of consumer loans is short. Entering this market enables thrifts to achieve a closer match between the maturity of their liabilities and their assets. Because the clientele is familiar, offering consumer loans seems to be a relatively low-risk way for thrifts to diversify. *Commercial lending* includes very short-term unsecured commercial paper and longer-term secured loans. Moving into commercial lending offers thrifts higher interest rates and shorter-term assets: in other words, greater potential profits and greater flexibility. However, thrifts' primary competitors in this market—commercial banks—have strong ties to commercial clients. Hence the conditions of competition in the commercial lending market are very different from those in the traditional residential mortgage market (Eichler, 1989). Finally, *service corporation subsidiaries* represent vehicles for movement into activities not otherwise allowed to thrifts; for example, property management, insurance, accounting and tax services, escrow and trust services. Many service companies cater to traditional thrift clients, offering products that complement residential mortgage lending, such as escrow services.

Model Specification and Estimation

Questions about change are best addressed by dynamic research methods applied to longitudinal data. I analyze discrete change events (entry by thrifts into each of the six new markets), using data covering the period June 1977 to March 1987. Because 1977 is the year before deregulation began, it is an appropriate starting point for this study.

In this chapter I take an organizational perspective, studying diversification by existing organizations. An alternative perspective is that of the market: studying market entry by any organization, newly founded or established. The difference between the two points of view boils down to (1) whether newly formed organizations are included in the sample of firms that are "at risk" of entering a market and (2) whether models of market entry control for the characteristics of individual firms. Studying change from the market perspective makes it possible to examine differences in behavior between established and new firms. Caves and Porter (1977) argue that established firms will be the chief entrants to market niches that are composed of oligopolistic cores of dominant firms protected by product differentiation and absolute-cost barriers. In contrast, newly founded firms will sprout up in the competitive fringe, in more "contestable" market segments (Baumol, Panzer, and Willig, 1982).

On the other hand, studying change from the focal organization perspective makes it possible to control for variations in firm characteristics and past experience. The choice between the two perspectives must be based on theoretical interest. Which is the more pressing question: How do markets and industries change? or How do firms change? Although there is a wealth of literature investigating change in industries over time, relatively little empirical research has been devoted to following shifts in the strategy and structure of individual organizations (Dunne, Roberts, and Samuelson, 1988). This chapter takes the less-traveled road.

I use event-history methods to study change. The dependent variable is the rate of entry into a new market, the hazard rate of change, which is defined as

$$r(t) = \lim_{dt \to 0} \frac{Pr \,(\text{change } t, \, t + dt \mid \text{no change at } t)}{dt},$$

where $Pr(.)$ is the probability of entry into a new market between times t and $t + dt$, given that the firm has not yet entered that market at time t. Entry into each new market is modeled separately. I first build a baseline model of the effects of organizational characteristics on change rates and then add variables representing the competitive and institutional environment. The model used is

$$\ln r(t) = \beta X + \gamma Y,$$

where X is a vector of organizational control variables and Y is a vector that includes market density and market mass. This modeling strategy makes it possible to determine the impact of environmental forces on organizational change, after controlling for diversity due to organizational characteristics. I use Tuma's maximum-likelihood program RATE to estimate these models (Tuma, 1980).

Analyses of entry into new markets cover the entire period from 1977 to 1987, since many firms were active in these markets before deregulation began, albeit on a very small scale.[1] I set a threshold of 5 percent of total assets to mark significant investment in each nontraditional market. For each market, the sample of thrifts analyzed includes only those firms that had not yet invested at least 5 percent of total assets in the market at the beginning of the observation period. A firm remains in the analysis until the period after it invests over 5 percent of its assets in the new market. Because I study change in existing firms, rather than replacement of traditional thrifts by new forms, I eliminate from my samples those firms that have investments over 5 percent of total assets in the focal market at the time of founding. I also perform sensitivity analysis, modeling rates of entry at several different thresholds: 0, 1, 2, 3, and 4 percent of total assets.

Data Sources

The Federal Home Loan Bank of San Francisco regulates savings and loan associations in California and publishes annual *Directories of Members,* which contain summary data on the industry and financial data on each thrift. These *Directories* formed the basic data used to construct the life histories of all California thrifts operating from 1977 onward. *Financial Reports* are filed by all regulated thrifts. These reports were gathered semiannually through 1983 and quarterly thereafter. These *Financial Reports* provide extremely detailed balance sheets and income statements. They were used to determine timing of first entry into the six nontraditional markets.

The data gathered from these two sources cover the period June 1977 to March 1987. The data are semiannual (measured at the end of June and December) for the years 1977 through 1983 and quarterly (measured at the end of March, June, September, and December) from 1984 onward. All variables are updated at the end of each period. Independent and control variables are measured at the beginning of each period; dependent variables, at the end of each period.

Measurement of Variables

The *rates of entry* into the six new markets are the dependent variables in this analysis. For each new market, I observe whether or not a firm has entered the market, that is, whether or not a firm has invested 5 percent of its assets in the market. I code a firm's behavior zero if it has not yet reached the 5 percent threshold and one if it has. For each market, a firm remains in the data until the period after it reaches the 5 percent threshold.

The independent variables are measured as follows. *Market density* is a count of savings and loan associations operating in each of the product markets in each period, including both new firms (which entered the market at birth) and established firms (which entered the market later in their lives). *Market mass* is measured in terms of the dollar value of assets and includes both new and established firms.

Baseline models were built using several organizational control variables: age, size, slack resources, past performance, legal form, and diversity of investments. *Organizational age* has been shown to influence rates of organizational change (Singh, Tucker, and Meinhard, 1988; Baum, 1990b). I measure organizational age as years since incorporation. Previous research has proposed that *organizational size* is an important determinant of organizational change (Caves and Porter, 1977; Haveman, 1993). If scale economies exist, large firms can use excess capacity to facilitate entry into new markets and can purchase inputs common to old and new markets at low prices. Assets can thus lower barriers to entry, although they may not eliminate these barriers completely. Because the size distribution is skewed, I take the natural logarithm of this variable. To operationalize the degree to which *slack resources* are available to facilitate entry into new markets, I use net worth, which measures capital not committed to cover current obligations or to meet regulatory requirements and therefore available to invest in new businesses. I control for *financial performance* with net income, the difference between income and expenses. *Legal form* has two dimensions: capital structure and type of charter. Capital structure distinguishes between mutual and stock companies, while charter distinguishes between firms with state and federal charters. Finally, I control for *diversity of investments*. Thrifts' decisions to enter various markets are not independent of each other; instead, thrifts show consistent patterns of diversification (Haveman, 1990: table 4.2). For example, thrifts tend to move simultaneously into lending mortgages on undeveloped land and into real estate development; those that remain focused on residential mortgage lending also tend to move heavily into consumer nonmortgage lending. The interdependence of different diversification events is controlled with

Blau's (1977) index of heterogeneity, D, calculated as $D = 1 - \Sigma(P_i^2)$, where P_i is the proportion of assets invested in market i.

Results

Table 8.1 presents descriptive statistics on California savings and loans showing how rapidly these firms have moved into nontraditional markets. Nonresidential mortgage lending (NresM) shows considerable market density at the beginning of the observation period: almost half of California thrifts had investments in this market over the 5 percent threshold. This market continued to grow after deregulation. The market for mortgage-backed securities (MBSs) also shows strong growth, peaking in 1983 with 109 of 183 thrifts active. The market for consumer lending (ConsL) grew fastest between 1980 and 1981 and plateaued around 20 participants. Other markets grew later and were still growing at the end of the observation period: real estate (RE), after 1981; service corporations (SCo), after 1982; commercial lending (CommL), after 1983.

TABLE 8.1   Diversification Trends in the California Savings and Loan Industry

Year	RE	NresM	MBS	ConsL	CommL	SCo	Density
1977	1	79	16	11	4	1	166
	1	6	6	2	1	0	
1978	1	76	11	10	2	1	173
	0	7	2	2	1	0	
1979	1	76	13	17	2	0	180
	1	6	3	8	1	0	
1980	0	66	17	25	4	0	202
	1	4	5	15	3	0	
1981	5	72	34	20	0	0	202
	4	15	14	9	0	0	
1982	13	86	78	17	1	3	184
	13	27	58	8	1	3	
1983	32	111	109	21	4	10	183
	22	21	26	9	2	11	
1984	32	157	96	21	7	22	201
	16	38	14	7	6	15	
1985	43	176	58	20	14	23	227
	11	16	10	3	7	8	
1986	40	168	59	20	13	18	218
	19	6	12	4	8	6	

NOTE: The top row of figures presents the number of thrifts with investments above the 5% threshold in each nontraditional market at the end of each year: real estate (RE), nonresidential mortgages (NresM), mortgage-backed securities (MBS), consumer loans (ConsL), commercial loans (CommL), and service corporations (SCo). The second row presents the number of thrifts entering each nontraditional market for the first time; thrifts that have entered before, exited, and then reentered are not counted. The last column presents total savings and loan industry density at the end of each year.

TABLE 8.2 Entry Into New Markets by California Thrifts, 1977–87

Market	Real Estate			Nonresidential Mortgages			Mortgage-Backed Securities		
Constant	−5.47*	−4.53*	−5.47*	−7.34*	−1.28*	−7.68*	−4.20*	−1.81*	−4.07*
	(.961)	(.899)	(.962)	(1.32)	(.601)	(1.49)	(.634)	(.535)	(.632)
Log assets	.262*	.255*	.262*	−.142	−.122	−.142	−.043	−.083	−.014
	(.094)	(.093)	(.094)	(.080)	(.080)	(.079)	(.070)	(.068)	(.068)
Stock	1.69*	1.69*	1.69*	−.367	−.456	−.375	.149	.401	.244
	(.612)	(.624)	(.612)	(.394)	(.391)	(.395)	(.310)	(.318)	(.316)
State	1.11*	1.11*	1.11*	.787*	.938*	.790*	−.166	−.401	−.249
	(.453)	(.456)	(.453)	(.345)	(.337)	(.345)	(.275)	(.283)	(.285)
Net worth	−.048*	−.029*	−.031*	.002	.002	.002	.002	.003*	.002
	(.007)	(.007)	(.007)	(.003)	(.003)	(.003)	(.001)	(.001)	(.001)
Net income	−.005*	−.005*	−.005*	−.028	−.031	−.027	−.001	−.008	−.0002
	(.001)	(.001)	(.001)	(.021)	(.023)	(.021)	(.005)	(.005)	(.006)
Diversity	−2.80*	−3.69*	−2.80*	−1.18*	−1.72*	−1.15*	.577	−1.02	−.327
	(.934)	(.910)	(.934)	(.571)	(.580)	(.575)	(.614)	(.647)	(.652)
Age	.003	.002	.003	−.008	−.010	−.008	−.0005	−.002	−.003
	(.006)	(.006)	(.006)	(.006)	(.006)	(.006)	(.004)	(.002)	(.004)
Mkt density	.104*	.022	.104*	.120*	.006	.129*	.095*	.032*	.128*
	(.031)	(.012)	(.031)	(.022)	(.010)	(.028)	(.012)	(.006)	(.014)
Mkt dens²/100	−.193*		−.193*	−.044*		−.045*	−.068*		−.079*
	(.063)		(.068)	(.009)		(.010)	(.011)		(.011)
Mkt mass/1000		−.021	.0002		.009	−.005		−.015*	−.021*
		(.019)	(.021)		(.011)	(.011)		(.006)	(.005)
#f, #s, #e	303	3999	91	200	1297	148	267	2367	153
χ^2	141.6	132.9	141.6	121.7	99.0	121.9	123.9	86.9	143.0
d.f.	9	9	10	9	9	10	9	9	10

(continued)

NOTES: Standard errors are below parameter estimates. * $p < .05$, two-tailed t tests. #f is the number of firms; #s, the number of spells; #e, the number of entries. d.f., degrees of freedom.

Direct Investments in Real Estate

Table 8.2 presents the analysis of entry into all markets, starting with real estate. The first model shows that the effect of market density on the rate of entry is curvilinear, supporting hypothesis 1A. As the market for direct investment in real estate opens for savings and loan associations circa 1981, the more thrifts that enter this market, the more legitimate it becomes, and the faster other thrifts are to follow. But when many savings and loan associations have acquired real estate investments, competition by incumbents slows further entries. This model fits the data significantly better than does a baseline model containing only organizational control variables, according to the χ^2 likelihood ratio test: $\Delta\chi^2 = 12.3$, Δ degrees of freedom = 2, $p = .002$. The next two models add market mass. Mass has a nonsignificant effect; moreover, the effect of market density is inverted U-shaped rather than positive. These results fail to support hypothesis 1B, which predicts that rates of entry will be greater when markets have a large number of small incumbents.

TABLE 8.2   (continued)

Consumer Lending			Commercial Lending			Service Companies		
−4.52*	−1.16	−4.29*	−1.28	−1.04	−1.39	−4.30*	−2.91*	−4.28*
(1.97)	(.883)	(1.92)	(1.23)	(1.17)	(1.23)	(1.15)	(1.05)	(1.15)
−.219*	−.152	−.152	−.318	−.302	−.314	−.035	−.032	−.036
(.104)	(.104)	(.103)	(.166)	(.165)	(.165)	(.143)	(.142)	(.143)
.173	.458	.376	−.991	−.947	−.952	.580	.686	.582
(.445)	(.453)	(.452)	(.806)	(.765)	(.803)	(.638)	(.652)	(.637)
−.651	−.810*	−.767	1.06	1.03	1.02	.920	.781	.924
(.400)	(.413)	(.412)	(.763)	(.765)	(.763)	(.546)	(.555)	(.545)
.003	.002	.002	.005	.005	−.005	−.005	−.005	−.005
(.002)	(.002)	(.002)	(.004)	(.004)	(.004)	(.004)	(.005)	(.004)
−.002	−.002	−.002	−.005	−.004	−.005	.0001	.0005	.0001
(.003)	(.004)	(.004)	(.016)	(.016)	(.016)	(.006)	(.007)	(.006)
−.005	−1.48	−1.10	−4.77*	−4.84*	−4.68*	−3.96*	−5.33*	−3.97*
(.839)	(.900)	(.908)	(1.56)	(1.55)	(1.55)	(1.43)	(1.40)	(1.43)
−.011	−.014	−.014	−.006	−.006	−.006	.018*	.018*	.018*
(.007)	(.008)	(.008)	(.012)	(.012)	(.012)	(.007)	(.007)	(.007)
.354	.048	.440*	.231	.126	.273	.274*	.053	.263*
(.222)	(.028)	(.214)	(.164)	(.069)	(.168)	(.074)	(.047)	(.078)
−1.02		−1.17	−1.15		−1.00	−.975*		−1.01*
(.670)		(.636)	(1.06)		(1.04)	(.268)		(.285)
	−.063*	−.067*		−.290	−.270		−.043	.020
	(.020)	(.021)		(.260)	(.258)		(.049)	(.055)
301	3834	68	305	4501	30	308	4463	43
23.4	31.3	34.9	32.5	33.1	34.1	59.0	46.3	69.1
9	9	10	9	9	10	9	9	10

The impact of market density can be better understood with a picture. Figure 8.1 shows how the number of thrifts investing in real estate affects the rate of entry into that market by other thrifts. The full inverted U-shaped effect occurs within the observed range of market density, showing that density has both legitimacy and competitive effects. The maximum impact occurs when density is about 28, which occurs sometime in 1983.

Nonresidential Mortgages

The next three models in table 8.2 estimate entry into the nonresidential mortgage market. The first model shows that market density has an inverted U-shaped relationship with the rate of entry into this market. This result supports hypothesis 1A. This relationship is shown graphically in figure 8.2. Again, the full inverted U-shaped effect occurs within the observed range of market density. The next two models show no statistically significant relationship between market mass and entry rates; moreover, the relationship between market density and entry rates is curvilinear rather than linear. Together, these results fail to support hypothesis 1B.

Mortgage-Backed Securities

The next three models present the analysis of entry into the market for mortgage-backed securities. The first model shows that the impact of the number of thrifts operating in this market has an inverted U shape. This finding supports hypothesis 1A. The impact of market density on entry rates is illustrated in figure 8.3, which shows that the downturn for entry rates occurs within the observed range of market density. Market density declines from a peak after 1983, indicating a shakeout. The effect of market mass on rates of entry into this market is negative and statistically significant, and the effect of market density is positive and statistically significant, supporting hypothesis 1B. However, the third model shows that the effect of density is actually inverted U-shaped. This model significantly improves on the fit of the second model: $\Delta\chi^2 = 56.1$, Δ degrees of freedom $= 2$, $p < .001$. Although the presence of larger firms deters potential entrants, rates of entry are highest when density is intermediate, rather than when density is high. This suggests that density has a strong legitimating effect as well as a competitive effect.

Consumer Nonmortgage Loans

The next three models analyze entry into the consumer loan market. The first model estimates the effect of market density and shows a curvilinear effect, as predicted by hypothesis 1A. But this effect is not statistically significant. The second model shows that the average size of savings and loan associations offering consumer loans has a significant negative effect, offering partial support for hypothesis 1B. The larger the average incumbent in this market, the more likely other thrifts are to attempt entry. When incumbents are large, the market is legitimated and other firms are more likely to enter. Moreover, the effect of density is positive, as predicted by hypothesis 1B, but only marginally significant ($p < .09$). When a quadratic term for density is added, an inverted U-shaped relationship between density and entry rate is seen, with a statistcially significant linear term and a marginally significant quadratic term ($p < .07$). The third model significantly improves fit to the data over a model containing only control variables and market mass: $\Delta\chi^2 = 6.5$, Δ degrees of freedom $= 2$, $p < .04$. Figure 8.4 shows the curvilinear effect of market density on entry into the consumer loan market. The market for consumer loans resembles the market for mortgage-backed securities in that the rate of entry is greatest when incumbents are small and density is intermediate.

Commercial Nonmortgage Lending

The next three models present the analysis of this market. The first model shows a curvilinear, inverted U-shaped relationship between rates of entry into commercial lending and market density; however, this effect is not statistically significant. Also, this model fails to improve on the fit of the baseline model containing only organizational characteristics ($\Delta\chi^2 = 3.3$, Δ degrees of freedom $= 2$, $p > .10$). This result fails to support hypothesis 1A. Moreover, the other two models show no support of hypothesis 1B. The effect of market mass is negative as predicted, but not statistically significant; neither the linear nor curvilinear specification for density is statistically significant. Neither model significantly improves upon the baseline model. Together, these results suggest that entry into the commercial lending market is not affected by either the number or the size of thrifts already operating here.

Service Corporation Subsidiaries

The last three models in table 8.2 show the pattern of effect estimates for rates of entry into service corporation subsidiaries. Density has a statistically significant, inverted U-shaped effect on the entry rate, which supports hypothesis 1A. This relationship is illustrated in figure 8.5, which plots entry rate versus density. Market mass, which indicates average firm size, has a negative effect, consonant with the prediction of hypothesis 1B, but this effect is not statistically significant. The linear effect for density is also in the predicted direction, but is not statistically significant. The last model, which includes a quadratic term for density, shows that the effect of density is indeed curvilinear and is inverted U-shaped. These results indicate no support for hypothesis 1B.

Sensitivity Analysis

All models were reestimated using varying thresholds for investment in new markets: 0, 1, 2, 3, and 4 percent of total assets. As the threshold drops toward zero, the number of firms and the number of spells decline. The number of entry events generally, but not always, rises. For instance, for the real estate market at the 5 percent threshold, there were 3,999 spells, 303 firms, and 91 entry events. At 2 percent, there were 3,171 spells, 289 firms, and 128 entries; at 0 percent, there were 1,021 spells, 189 firms, and 148 entries.

The model testing density dependence is not sensitive to choice of threshold. Effect estimates are stable and there are only a few instances where significance levels change; for example, significance levels increase in models of commercial lending as the threshold drops. In the model testing the joint impact of density and mass, however, all parameter estimates are unstable, especially at low thresholds. This is easy to explain: Parameter estimates are unstable in markets where they are not statistically significant. Finally, in the full model, which contains linear and quadratic terms for density and a linear term for mass, density estimates are stable, but mass estimates are not. Instability generally occurs in markets where the effect of mass is not statistically significant.

This chapter investigated one source of variation in organizational evolution: change in the activities of existing organizations through diversification into new markets. The research presented here is part of a growing stream of evolutionary literature studying change in the structures and activities of individual organizations.

Hypothesis 1A predicts that the relationship between market density and rates of market entry is inverted U-shaped. Analyses of entry into five of six new markets—real estate, nonresidential mortgages, mortgage-backed securities, consumer nonmortgage loans, and service corporation subsidiaries—show inverted U-shaped effects, supporting hypothesis 1A. These results suggest that the number of firms active in a market is a good indicator of the competitive and institutional forces that

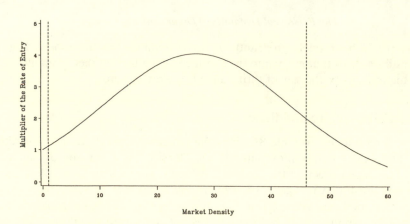

FIG. 8.1 Effect of market density on rate of entry into the real estate market (vertical lines enclose the observed range)

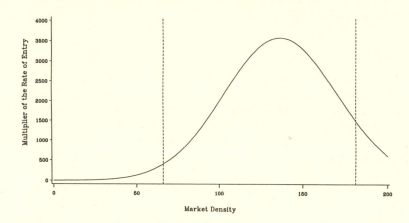

FIG. 8.2 Effect of market density on rate of entry into the nonresidential mortgage market (vertical lines enclose the observed range)

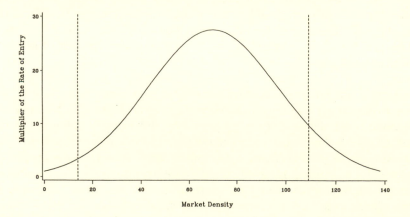

FIG. 8.3 Effect of market density on rate of entry into the mortgage-backed securities market (vertical lines enclose the observed range)

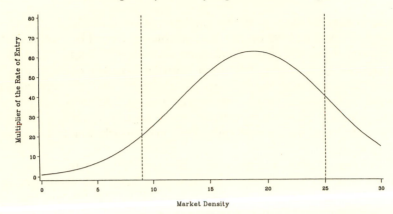

FIG. 8.4 Effect of market density on rate of entry into the consumer nonmortgage loans market (vertical lines enclose the observed range)

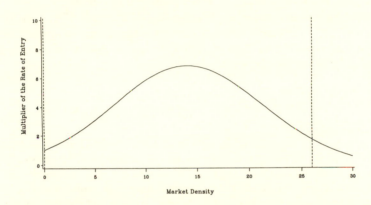

FIG. 8.5 Effect of market density on rate of entry into the service corporation subsidiaries market (vertical lines enclose the observed range)

impel or impede potential entrants. These findings give greater weight to the density-dependence model formulated by Hannan and Carroll (1992) and investigated empirically in a myriad studies, extending the scope of the density-dependence model beyond organizational birth and death processes to the process of change in existing organizations.

For the fifth market—commercial nonmortgage loans—estimates for density were in the predicted directions but were nonsignificant. (However, sensitivity analysis showed statistically significant results when lower thresholds for market entry were used.) These results suggest that when other organizational populations are large players in a market, as commercial banks are for commercial lending, the number of thrifts operating in the market does not fully capture market density. In such cases, data are needed on all populations, not just on the focal population. Unfortunately, data on the number and size of banks and other financial services firms operating in the six nontraditional markets are not available, or are available only for the end of the observation period (1985 on), so market structure cannot be specified fully.

Following the reasoning of Hannan and Carroll (1992: chapter 7), market entry can be expected to have a positive linear effect on a market whose history has not progressed enough to show the full life cycle of growth, peak, and decline. For late-developing markets—real estate, commercial lending, and service corporations—I analyzed what is in essence a right-truncated data set. A longer time-series of data would provide greater variation in density and mass, which would allow a better test of the hypotheses.

The effects of density remain strong after controlling for market mass, and in one case (consumer lending), density effects become statistically significant only after controlling for mass. These results offer partial support for the idea that both the number and the average size of competitors are important forces impelling or impeding diversification. Neither size nor density alone indicates barriers to market entry that derive from market structure. Therefore, neither can explain fully the process of organizational variation through diversification into new markets.

Finally, the research presented here assessed the impact of market structure on rates of entry into six different markets, thereby offering repeated tests of density and mass dependence in rates of organizational change. Such replication is seldom seen in organization theory research.

Notes

1. In June 1977 savings and loan activity in these four markets was as follows: Of the 165 thrifts operating, 103 owned real estate (averaging 0.4% of assets); 77 invested in mortgage-backed securities (averaging 2% of assets); 150 had investments in nonresidential mortgages (averaging 5% of assets); almost all held consumer nonmortgage loans (averaging 2% of assets); 62 held commercial loans (averaging 0.4% of assets); and 136 had investments in service corporations (averaging 0.2% of assets).

9

Surviving Schumpeterian Environments: An Evolutionary Perspective

DANIEL LEVINTHAL

There is what at this point has become a rather considerable body of research documenting the dynamics of the Schumpeterian process of "creative destruction" (see Majumdar, 1982; Tushman and Anderson, 1986; Tilton, 1972; Malerba, 1985). While the collapse of market position and exit of established firms may constitute the main effect of a discontinuity in an industrial market, what this chapter considers is essentially the residual error term of such an event. The process of creative destruction is often not complete; that is, some established firms may survive such a discontinuity in their environment (Abernathy and Clark, 1985). Is this "residual" merely a purely random effect or are there some systematic forces influencing the set of established firms that persist?

This question is of considerable practical importance, as well as an intriguing context in which to explore some recent debates on the nature of organizational and industry evolution. Instances of technological discontinuity and, more generally, of market disequilibria are occasions for the establishment of potentially long-enduring competitive positions. While business strategy is of importance even in situations of stable market conditions, the opportunity to change one's competitive position fundamentally is far greater at times of change when former sources of competitive advantage decay and new opportunities for establishing competitive position emerge.

With respect to the development of the academic fields of business strategy and organizational theory, examining periods of turbulence in industries due to rapid changes in the external environment provides an opportunity to link externally based and internally oriented perspectives on firm and industry evolution. In particular, the organizational theory literature has been animated in recent years by arguments regarding the relative importance of change processes at the level of individual organizations and change at the population level in terms of differential failure and entry

The research was supported by the Reginald Jones Center at the Wharton School, University of Pennsylvania. I have benefited from the comments of participants at the ASSI Foundation Conference on the Evolution of Organizations and Strategy, the NYU/Wharton Conference on Organizational Evolution, and the seminar series on Competition and Technology at the Harvard Business School. I would like to acknowledge, in particular, the comments of Sidney Winter in his capacity as a discussant of the paper at Harvard, which stimulated a substantial revision, as well as Joel Baum, Richard Nelson, and Jitendra Singh for their comments on a prior draft of this chapter.

rates among alternative organizational forms (Hannan and Freeman, 1984; Astley and Van de Ven, 1983). Within the field of business strategy, the locus of attention has shifted from an analysis of firm-level strengths and weaknesses (Andrews, 1980) to subsequent efforts at industry analysis (Porter, 1980) and, most recently, to a reemergence of the firm-level perspective in the context of a resource view of the firm (Rumelt, 1984; Wernerfelt, 1984). Examining the Schumpeterian dynamics of creative destruction encourages, if not forces, one to bridge these analyses of organizational level processes with an examination of population level or market forces.

Consistent with these internal and external perspectives on firm and industry evolution, there are two classes of explanations that one can pursue in explaining firm survival in Schumpeterian environments. First, one can examine the survival of some subset of incumbent firms as the result of a process of differential selection. Alternatively, this variation in outcomes can be viewed as the result of differential adaptation. That is, some firms may respond either more proactively or more effectively to the challenges posed by such changes in the competitive environment.

The initial sections of this chapter consider the issue of organizational level change. First, it is argued that whether change is observed at the organizational level is a function of competing risks: The risk of organizational failure and the risk or likelihood of change. Thus, evaluation of change processes is subject to the problem of right-censoring in that the firm may fail prior to the realization of the change event. It is important to consider not only the fact of whether change occurs, but the survival implications of such changes. Arguments suggesting that organizations are largely inert (Hannan and Freeman, 1984; Hannan and Freemen, 1989) are not statements that change does not occur, but rather more subtle claims about the content of the change, such as core versus periphery, and the survival implications of such changes. By the same token, arguments regarding the fluidity of organization (March, 1981) are quite sensitive to the ambiguity of the survival implications of such changes.

In order to address the relationship between organizational change and organizational survival, a distinction is made between processes of learning and adaptation. While often treated as equivalent terms, they refer to quite distinct processes of change, which differ as well in their survival implications in periods of discontinuity in an organization's environment. The path dependent nature of learning processes is an important basis for organizational inertia. As a result, the inability of an established firm to respond to changes in its environment need not reflect a lack of adaptation but, in some sense, may be interpreted as resulting from having adapted too well to prior environments. The subsequent section evaluates arguments in the organizational theory literature regarding the magnitude of organizational change; in particular, whether processes of organizational change are likely to be incremental (Lindbloom, 1957; March, 1981) or radical (Tushman and Romanelli, 1985).

The latter part of the paper addresses the nature of selection environments. Schumpeter's argument is, in some sense, a testament to the power of selection forces. The technological discontinuities to which he refers lead to substantial changes in the basis of selection. For instance, as Majumdar (1982) observed in the calculator industry, where previously firms in the calculator industry differed in their survival chances on the basis of their expertise in electromechanics and the scope and quality of their dealer network, design skills and low-cost manufacturing capa-bilites in electronics became the critical attributes over which selection occurred.

However, for a variety of reasons firms may be buffered from selection pressures (see Singh, Tucker, and House, 1986; Baum and Oliver, 1991; Miner, Amburgey, and Stearns, 1990). In particular, the selection forces that confront the firm are not solely the result of economic efficiency. To an important extent, organizations are buffered from selection pressures as a function of the institutional environments in which they operate. Expanding on the work of Abernathy and Clark (1985), firms have a variety of attributes that may influence their probability of survival. Those firms that survive a disruption in their technical environment may be the ones that pose distinctive capabilities that are still of value in this new epoch of competition. In addition, features of the firm's institutional environment may shield it from selec-tion pressures. As DiMaggio and Powell (1983:149) state, "a wide range of factors—interorganizational commitments, elite sponsorship, and government support in terms of open-ended contracts, subsidy, tariff barriers and import quotas, or favor-able tax laws—reduce selection pressures even in competitive organizational fields." Thus, while a pure market system would rely heavily on change via the death of existing firms and the birth of new firms, most firms face more complex institutional environments involving a variety of interest groups that may have considerable stakes in fostering the survival of the firm apart from its economic viability (Meyer and Zucker, 1989).

Organizational Evolution

Organizational Evolution and Right-Censoring

As Hannan and Freeman (1984) point out, the question of whether change occurs at the population level or at the level of individual organizations is an issue of the rate of change of organizations relative to the rate of change in their environment. One may fail to observe an organization respond to its changing environment either because the organization is unable or unwilling to make such changes or because it fails prior to the realization of such efforts.

Thus, organizational change may be more likely to be observed if firms are, at least partially, buffered from selection pressures. Firms may be buffered from selec-tion pressures for a variety of reasons. As suggested, buffering may result from firm attributes that retain their value or linkages with important external actors. The pres-ence of either form of buffer, ceteris parabis, increases the likelihood of observing evidence of organizational level adaptation. These buffering mechanisms, however, may also influence the impetus for organizational level adaptation (Miner et al., 1990). If pressures for organizational level adaptation result from feedback from an organization's environment (Levitt and March, 1988), then those factors that shield the firm from selection pressures may also impede adaptation. For instance, suppose that a firm is insulated from selection pressures as a result of being sheltered from product market competition; such a firm may have little impetus to change as well.

In considering processes of organizational change and survival, it is useful to recognize that some factors that drive these processes are essentially "stock" variables while others reflect current outcomes and can be characterized as "flows." For instance, Levinthal (1991a:398–9) models organizational survival as being driven by an organization's stock of organizational capital, where the notion of organizational capital "represents the many financial and nonfinancial 'stock' variables that influence a firm's viability, such as 'stocks of customers, employees, and advertising or R&D capital' (Winter, 1987:163)." Models of organizational learning (Cyert and March, 1963; Levitt and March, 1988) generally assume that change is driven by the relationship between the organization's current performance and its aspiration level.[1] As a result, such models involve flow processes, such as current performance, and, to the extent that aspiration levels reflect both past outcomes as well as the current outcome, these models have some "stocklike" elements as well. The issue remains as to how quickly current performance changes with changes in the firm's environment and how rapidly a firm's aspiration level changes to reflect these new performance levels.

If the likelihood of organizational change is negatively associated with the degree of organizational capital due to the buffering provided by the firm's existing resources and the likelihood of organizational mortality is also negatively associated with the level of organizational capital, then change would largely occur at the population level and only rarely at the level of individual organizations. Organizations with a modest level of organizational capital would feel the greatest impetus to change, but such organizations would have a very high base rate of failure. Organizations with abundant levels of organizational capital would be likely to persist for some time but would also be more resistant to change. In contrast to Hannan and Freeman (1984), this argument for change at the population level is not based on any claim regarding the survival implications or organizational level change.

Following this line of argument, an important managerial task for large, established enterprises would be to generate pressures for change on the basis of flow processes, such as the organization's current performance, while benefiting from the luxury of reduced immediate selection pressures such organizations have. Indeed, much of the recent initiatives regarding benchmarking (Winter, this volume) and other such efforts at performance evaluation have the property of identifying a variety of outcome measures and continually adjusting upward the organization's aspiration levels with respect to these measures so that the impetus to change is more a function of current performance than of past successes.

Organizational Evolution: Learning and Adaptation

In considering the relationship between organizational evolution and firm survival in changing environments, it is important to address the distinction between processes of organizational learning and adaptation. The terms "learning" and "adaptation" are often used interchangeably. However, the slight differences in nuance between the two terms may, in some instances, imply quite distinct processes. "Learning" is typically taken to mean the cumulative development of skills and knowledge, whereas "adaptation" generally refers to a response to feedback from one's environment. In the context of many discussions of organizational change, the terms are closely related. For instance, Levitt and March's (1988) characterization of organizational learning is that organizational behavior is based on routines and that these routines change in an incremental manner in response to feedback about outcomes. An important attribute of this feedback is how organizational outcomes compare to the aspirations associated with those outcomes.

If we take adaptation to mean a change in a significant organizational attribute, such as basic business strategy or organizational structure, in response to an environmental change, then the two terms are quite distinct. In this interpretation, adaptation is essentially a comparatively static (Samuelson, 1979) statement of contingency theory (Lawrence and Lorsch, 1967) and does not refer in a direct way to processes of learning. That is, adaptation is defined to have occurred when an organization changes its strategy, structure, or some other core attribute to fit some new enviornmental contingency.[2]

When viewed in this manner, the processes of learning and adaptation may be antithetical. Again, drawing from the work of March and colleagues (Levinthal and March, 1981; Levitt and March, 1988), we see that processes of adaptive learning may result in a competency trap whereby increasing skill at the current procedures makes experimentation with alternatives progressively less attractive. In this sense, organizational learning contributes to organizational inertia, which, in turn, provides a basis for selection processes as an important source of change.

This issue is illustrated as well in Cohen and Levinthal (1989, 1990), who argue that the ability of firms to evaluate and utilize outside knowledge is a function of their level of prior related knowledge. This prior related knowledge confers an ability to recognize the value of new information, assimilate it, and apply it to commercial ends, which they suggest collectively constitute a firm's "absorptive capacity." In particular, they argue that a firm's own R&D activity enhances this learning capability.

This simple notion that prior knowledge underlies a firm's absorptive capacity has important implications for the development of such capabilities over time, and, in turn, the innovative performance of organizations. First, these learning capabilities may be subject to increasing returns in that accumulating absorptive capacity in one period will permit its more efficient accumulation in subsequent periods. Second, the possession of related expertise permits the firm to understand better and therefore evaluate the import of intermediate technological advances that provide signals as to the eventual merit of new technological developments. These two features of absorptive capacity—cumulativeness and its effect on expectation formation—imply that its development is path or history dependent.

Furthermore, these same forces will tend to confine firms to operating in a particular technological domain and, in turn, may lead to the neglect of new technological developments. As a result, these self-reinforcing features of learning provide some intuition for the difficulties firms face when the technological basis of an industry changes. A firm without a prior technological base in a particular field may not be able to acquire one readily if absorptive capacity is cumulative. In addition, a firm may be blind-sided by new developments in fields in which it is not investing if its updating capability is low. Accordingly, firms may not realize that they should be developing their absorptive capacity because of a catch-22 associated with its valuation; the firm needs to have some absorptive capacity already to value it appropriately.

The notion of a competency trap suggests that organizations may reduce their search activity prematurely or, in the case of a changing environment, not renew search activity despite the fact that new opportunities may be present. Thus, with respect to a competency trap, the process of learning is antithetical to adaptation if the term "adaptation" is interpreted according to the second definition that was posed. Alternatively, with respect to the notion of absorptive capacity, prior knowledge facilitates the acquisition of new knowledge; however, the fact that a firm's absorptive capacity is domain specific implies that prior learning is not sufficient for adaptation if the new relevant knowledge domains are sufficiently distinct from the firm's current knowledge base.

More generally, while processes of adaptation and selection are often posed as conflicting perspectives on change, to some extent such characterizations misconstrue the nature of adaptation in that processes of organizational learning contribute in important respects to the stable sources of organizational heterogeneity that, in turn, form the basis for processes of differential selection (Levinthal, 1991b). As a result, some processes of organizational level change enhance the likelihood that established firms will fail, given a significant change in their environment.

Organizational Evolution: Frequency and Extent of Organizational Level Change

The prior discussion of right-censoring raises the issue of the both the speed and the extent of organizational level changes. If change occurs infrequently and in modest steps, then organizations are likely to fail prior to adapting to a shift in their environment. The possibility of radical change in an organization (Tushman and Romanelli, 1985) offers the prospect of timely adaptation; however, the survival implications of such changes are unclear. Indeed, both theoretical arguments (March 1981; Hannan and Freeman, 1989), as well as empirical findings (Singh, House, and Tucker, 1986; Amburgey, Kelly, and Barnett, 1993; Baum and Oliver, 1991; Delacroix and Swaminathan, 1991; Haveman, 1992), suggest that the implications of organizational change for survival are ambiguous.

Tushman and Romanelli (1985:178) argue that organizations undergo occasional radical "reorientations" in response to (1) a lack of consistency, either among internal structures or, more prominently, between external forces and the internal structure and processes of the organization, or (2) major changes in the "competitive, technological, social and legal conditions of the environment that render a prior strategic orientation, regardless of its success, no longer effective." The two classes of forces are importantly related in that changes in the external environment are likely to lead to inconsistencies between the new environmental context and the existing structure, processes, and personnel of the organization.

This focus on change via reorientations seems at odds with the prior section of this chapter and the more general literature (cf., Nelson and Winter, 1982) on the development of organizational capabilities, which suggests that capabilities evolve slowly over time and are, therefore, not amenable to abrupt changes. Similarly, the rich body of work on organizational decision making associated with James March suggests that patterns of change would tend to be incremental. In a summary piece articulating this perspective, March (1981:564) notes that "most change in organizations results neither from extraordinary organizational processes nor forces, nor from uncommon imagination, persistence or skill, but from relatively stable, routine processes that relate organizations to their environments."

The discrepancy between the transformational vision of change developed by Tushman and Romanelli and more incremental, or adaptive, perspectives (March, 1981) is more understandable when one considers what attributes are the foci of attention in the two streams of research. Tushman is concerned with what is essentially the political structure of the organization: which individuals have influence in the organization; and what systems of control they impose on the organization.

It seems quite plausible that political structures in organizations may change discontinuously. Furthermore, the focus in Tushman's work on the role of executives and, in turn, executive change (See Tushman, Virany, and Romanelli, 1985) is appropriate in trying to understand changes in the internal power structure of firms.[3] Indeed, in the modern business corporation, which provides the empirical context for much of this research, it is hard to conceive of changes in organizational power as the result of emergent or adaptive forces from the lower ranks of the organization. Political power results from the control of critical resources (Pfeffer and Salancik, 1978), the authority of one's position, or the force of individual leadership (Weber, 1968). Such attributes are unlikely to change in an incremental manner. In fact, one does observe revolutions in both governments and business firms.

In addressing these issues of both the frequency and the extent of organizational change, it may be useful to build on Parsons' (1960) characterization of the three basic levels of organizational structure: the technical, the managerial, and the institutional. The technical level refers to the skills and capabilities associated with the organization's operating activities, while the managerial level corresponds to the coordinating and resource allocation functions. The institutional level refers to broader notions or organizational goals and values and the legitimacy of the organization within the society in which it operates.

Change occurs across these elements of the organization at different frequencies, and, furthermore, when change does occur in a particular domain, the degree of change varies in the extent to which it tends to be incremental or more radical. Change at the technical level occurs continuously as a result of first-order learning processes. Furthermore, characterizations of organizational learning (Nelson and Winter, 1982; Levitt and March, 1988) suggest that, while frequent, such changes tend to be incremental. In contrast, changes at the managerial level are typically driven by changes in the power structure of the organization and, therefore, are less frequent. However, the degree of change in managerial systems, given that change does occur, can be substantial. For instance, organizations may change their fundamental structure, as Chandler (1962) depicts in his account of the transformation of industrial firms to the multidivisional form. Lastly, change at the institutional level tends to be quite rare and typically occurs in response to a crisis associated with financial performance or organizational survival.

Therefore, the conflict in perspectives with which this subsection starts is suggested to be a difference in unit of analysis. Tushman and Romanelli (1985) are not making any claims that an organization's set of capabilities are changing in a discontinuous manner. In contrast, the political structures of organizations may indeed change discontinuously.

Given that the two perspectives are not mutually inconsistent, there remains the possibility of reconciling the two sets of views, that is, of discontinuous change in power relations and incremental changes in capabilities. Indeed, there is useful complementarity between them. The change in the internal power structure of a firm implies that there may be a substantial change in the internal allocation of resources (Bower, 1970). Such a change can be viewed as a change in the internal selection environment of the firm. As a result, some organizational subunits may receive considerably more resources and expand their activities while others may find their level of activity curtailed or even eliminated.

Changes at the managerial or institutional level, however, need not be tightly linked to changes at the technical level and, in turn, performance outcomes. Indeed, conventional wisdom suggests that many changes at the managerial level are never manifested at the technical level. Thus, understanding the survival implications of organizational level changes requires that one be sensitive not only to different impetuses to change but to the interrelationship of change with the elements of the organizational structure.

Selection Environments: Natural and Artificial

In considering the survival of business enterprises, the selection environment tends to be either implicitly or explicitly defined as a competitive market in which less effective organizations are ultimately driven out of business. Organizations, however, operate in a variety of selection environments. Environments in which such fitness based selection occurs are termed here natural selection environments. Selection pressures, however, need not reflect efficiency or other traditional performance measures (Meyer and Zucker, 1988). Organizations may be buffered from such "natural" selection pressures by a variety of mechanisms. For instance, product markets may be shielded from competitive forces by government actions. Financial capital need not be allocated by pure market forces. Indeed, business units within large corporations only indirectly compete for capital on financial markets.

As Reich (1985:356) notes, large corporations are "centers of vast social and economic networks of suppliers, dealers, financial institutions, employees, and service industries. . . . [As a result,] how these companies respond to crisis is therefore intimately conditioned by, and profoundly affects, the way these social systems respond." In his cross-country analysis of cases of financial distress, Reich examines the extent to which firms redeploy resources internally, such as into new product lines, versus the extent to which resources are redeployed externally as a result of the contraction of the firm and the associated layoffs of employees and liquidation of physical and financial assets.

One important factor in determining whether resources are redeployed internally or externally is the nature of the relationships of financial institutions and the corporation. In particular, in settings in which an individual bank has a major financial commitment to the firm in terms of loans and its equity interest in the firm, the bank has both much more detailed information regarding the firm's competitive position and financial health and a much greater commitment to preserving the firm in some form. Thus, the relationship is less adversarial in that there is greater goal congruence between the two parties and, in addition, there is less information asymmetry between them. As a result of both of these attributes, it is more likely that rapid and effective intervention will take place to avert the collapse of the firm.

More generally, following the distinction made by Dosi (1990), capital markets can be characterized as being either competitive or institutional. In the former, capital is raised in competitive financial markets; in the latter, capital is obtained by direct institutional sources. Typically, this is a financial entity such as a bank, but it may in some instances be an industrial firm. With institutional sources of capital, firms are buffered from the selection pressures of capital markets. As a result, consistent with Meyer and Zucker's (1989) arguments regarding permanently failing organizations, a firm may be in an uncompetitive position in product markets but still survive for a considerable period.

More broadly, one can consider a firm's ties to its various constituent groups or stakeholders, such as labor, government, suppliers, and sources of capital, as a form of social capital (Coleman, 1988). This social capital, in turn, acts as a significant buffer from selection pressures. How a firm's social capital evolves over time is, however, to a great extent dependent on the particular institutional environment in which the firm operates. For instance, the degree of social capital with respect to suppliers is vastly less in a regime where supply relations are negotiated on a short-term basis and approximate classic market, arm's-length conditions. At the other extreme, if supply relations are deeply embedded, as in the case of the Japanese auto industry (Odaka, Ono, and Adachi, 1988), then a high level of social capital will emerge over time and, as a result, suppliers will be willing to relax repayment schedules and engage in other behaviors to help the corporation through a period of financial distress. Thus, the nature of a firm's institutional environment has important implications for the firm's ability to accumulate social capital. As a result, we should observe quite distinct patterns of organizational mortality in different institutional settings when an industry is subjected to major technological changes in its competitive environment.

Organizational Evolution: Problem Representation and Institutional Environments

As was suggested earlier different institutional environments may provide more or less opportunity for organizational level changes to occur to the extent that they vary in the extent to which organizations are buffered from selection pressures. The firm's institutional environment may also impinge on the motivation for change within the organization. This section considers such linkages and thereby bridges the earlier discussion of organizational evolution with the consideration of selection environments.

While it is standard practice in economic analysis to treat firms as serving a purely instrumental role of providing value through the transformation of inputs to outputs, there is a long tradition in the sociology of organizations (Gouldner, 1959; Selznick, 1957) that "organizations are more than instruments for attaining narrowly defined goals; they are, fundamentally, social groups attempting to adapt and survive in their particular circumstances" (Scott, 1987:52). Selznick (1957:17) uses the term "institutionalization" to refer to the process by which an organization becomes "infused with value beyond the technical requirements of the task at hand." In order

to eliminate confusion regarding the various uses of the term "institutional", referring both to the instilling of values as used previously and to the social environment
in which organizations operate, the term "biotic" is used here to refer to the first
meaning of institutional and the term "institutional" will be reserved for the second
meaning of the term.

Thus, not only do organizations face both task oriented and institutional selection pressures (Carroll and Huo, 1986), but they may orient themselves toward either
an instrumental goal of profit maximization or a biotic one of survival. Firms that
face both competitive capital markets and product markets are likely to have an
instrumental perspective. Such firms would not have an extraordinary commitment
to a particular product area and, in keeping with portfolio analysis of strategic management (Abel and Hammond, 1979), would be relatively quick and disciplined in
their reallocation of resources among divisions depending on their competitive position in the various markets in which they operate. A firm which is dependent on
competitive capital markets can only justify a continued commitment to a given
product domain if it can expect an attractive return from reinvestment in that
domain. Such reinvestment is likely to be attractive only if the firm is leveraging
some of its existing resources, such as marketing, distribution, or complementary
technologies. This discipline imposed by capital markets is attenuated for business
units that are part of larger corporate entities which have high levels of retained earnings from other lines of businesses. The investment decisions of such a firm may, to
a much greater extent, reflect the discretionary judgments and preferences of its management (Baumol, 1967; Marris, 1963).

It might seem that instrumental organizational forms would tend to dominate
institutionally oriented organizations. Consider, however, an ecology consisting of
both biotic and instrumental organizational forms competing in the same market
settings. Given the premise that the biotic form is concerned with survival in a particular product market domain, such organizations would tolerate more modest
financial returns and make greater strategic investments than instrumental firms.
Thus, such firms will exhibit superior capabilities and more aggressiveness in product
market competition. From an ecological perspective, such forms should tend, over
time, to dominate product markets in which they compete with instrumental organizations. Furthermore, not only will these firms have favorable survival prospects,
but during the process of market disequilibrium as they force the instrumental firms
out of the marketplace, they may be rather profitable as well.

While, as suggested, biotic organizations may exhibit extraordinary competitive
strengths in market settings, in other settings such organizations may exhibit quite
poor performance. If such a firm is confronted with highly competitive product markets, then it will be driven to develop extraordinary competitive capabilities in order
to enhance its chances of survival. Alternatively, in more sheltered product markets,
such firms may exhibit quite poor competitive capabilities given the absence of competitive forces from either financial markets or product markets. Such firms could be
termed X-inefficient, in reference to the work of Leibenstein (1966). Because such
firms are sheltered from product market competition, they may be profitable; however, because of the lack of competitive pressures from either financial markets or
product markets, such firms are likely to be inefficient and, in turn, not technologically progressive.

For instance, consider the radically different patterns of organizational and industry evolution across the United States, Japan, and Europe in the semiconductor industry. While all firms faced the same technological upheavals, the impacts of these changes on firm survival differed considerably across the three regions. From the perspective of features of the institutional environment that may buffer organizations from selection pressures, the European experience is particularly interesting. As Malerba (1985) documents, the European firms were relatively slow and not terribly effective in their response to the technological changes associated with the invention of the transistor and subsequently, the integrated circuit. Consistent with this lack of organizational level adaptation, these firms experienced significant decline in market share; however, there has been relatively little exit from product markets by these firms. In contrast, in the United States, the incumbent firms that manufactured vacuum tubes have exited the succeeding technological subfields in the electronic components business (Tilton, 1972).

The contrast between European and Japanese firms illustrates how the absence or presence of competition in product markets radically affects the implications of institutional sources of capital. Many European and Japanese firms could be viewed as having institutional sources of capital. However, there is considerable variation in the extent of product market competition that these firms have faced. While it is a caricature, suggesting a fair degree of inaccuracy but perhaps still capturing some element of truth, European firms have tended to face relatively less intense product market competition than Japanese firms in recent decades. In the case of the Japanese firms, this is largely the result of a commitment to an export-based industrial policy which, in turn, forced the Japanese firms to face competitive global product markets. In contrast, European firms have served relatively protected national markets and have exported, to a large extent, to less competitive markets of Eastern Europe. The domestic European markets were protected in the sense that there was some buffering from the pressure of imports and that these markets were, in many cases, not large enough to support multiple domestic producers.

The case of the transition in the electronics industry from transistors to semiconductors is interesting because it involves a common technological shock across three distinct institutional environments. The variation in industry evolution in the three settings is broadly consistent with the arguments developed here with respect to how the institutional environment of firms influences both the persistence of established firms and their degree of efficiency or technological progressiveness.

Adaptive Populations: Organizations, Institutions, and Markets

The question with which this chapter started was what forces influence the survival of established firms in the face of radical changes in their competitive environment. While this is, in some sense, a natural question to ask from the perspective of business strategy or organizational theory, from the perspective of economics it is somewhat peculiar. The question an economist is more likely to pose is, What is the most efficient means for a society to respond to changes in firms' technical environment? Is it more efficient for adaptation to occur at the level of individual organizations or via the decline and possible death of established firms and the birth and rise to dominance of new enterprises? From such a public policy perspective, one faces not only the question of firm survival, but the broader question of whether the internal reallocation of resources within firms is more effective or socially less disruptive than reallocation of human, financial, and physical resources externally, across organizations and markets.

This chapter has not touched on such important public policy questions but rather has addressed some of the basic forces associated with organizational survival in such environments. The question of firm survival in changing environments is a fundamental issue of business strategy and an intellectual challenge to our theories of organizational and industry evolution. In particular, to respond effectively to this challenge it is necessary to consider the interplay between forces of organizational change and survival. As suggested here, factors that may facilitate survival may impede change. Furthermore, one must look beyond the boundaries of the organization itself in order to understand fully the forces at work. Variation in institutional environments may account for much of the discrepancy in survival rates that we observe. As a result, developing multinational comparisons of the impact of technological change, as suggested by the discussion of the electronics industry, will help us understand the role of a firm's institutional environment in influencing both organizational evolution and organizational survival.

Notes

1. Related to the distinction made here, March and Shapira (1992) consider the effect on decision making of changing the focus of attention between a survival criterion, which as termed here is a stock variable, and the relationship between performance and the aspiration level, which is more dependent on current outcomes.

2. Furthermore, the notion of adaptation is often taken to mean changes that enhance an organization's survival prospects; however, it is more appropriate to consider adaptation as neutral with respect to the survival implication of such changes. For instance, as March (1982:567) notes, given the risk of reorganization, for some organizations, "efforts to survive will have speeded up the process of failure." In a similar vein, Hannan and Freeman's (1989) discussion of structural inertia reflects this dual nature of change processes in analyses of organizational mortality. They characterize adaptation as a process involving competing risks. Not only is there an impact of change on the likelihood of failure associated with a possible reduction of an organization's fit with its environment, but efforts to realign an organization with a changing environment pose a second risk, that of reorganization.

3. It is worth noting, however, that a concern with the internal power structure is not absent in the work of Cyert and March (1963) and Nelson and Winter (1982). Indeed, these authors discuss the inherent conflicts among organizational subunits or interest groups and argue that the need to prevent conflict among these groups will tend to be an additional force of inertia in organizations.

10

Mimetic Learning and the Evolution of Organizational Populations

STEPHEN J. MEZIAS AND THERESA K. LANT

The ecological (Hannan and Freeman, 1977) and institutional (Meyer and Rowan, 1977) perspectives have emerged as two dominant but distinct paradigms in organizational theory since their inceptions over a decade ago. Initially, one reason why these theories may have seemed irreconcilable, at least superficially, was the difference in the research questions that the original authors posed. Hannan and Freeman (1977) pointed to an apparent diversity of organizational forms and offered an ecological explanation for this multitude. Meyer and Rowan (1977) and especially DiMaggio and Powell (1983) stressed the lack of diversity of forms and proposed the mechanism of institutional isomorphism by which this diversity is eliminated. More recent work concerning populations of organizations has recognized the similarity of the interorganizational field (DiMaggio and Powell, 1983; Meyer and Scott, 1983) and the population (Hannan and Freeman, 1977, 1984; McKelvey and Aldrich, 1983) as units of analysis. For example, both institutional and ecological perspectives have been used in explaining the evolution of a population of Voluntary Social Service Organizations in the greater Toronto area (Singh, House, and Tucker, 1986; Singh, Tucker, and House, 1986; Singh, Tucker, and Meinhard, 1988; Tucker, Singh, and Meinhard, 1990). Singh and Lumsden (1990:182) argue that this convergence of the ecological and institutional paradigms "may be viewed as one of the more exciting research developments in organization theory."

In this study, we will focus on the role of organization level change in the evolution of organizational populations. Ecological theory has been dominated by Hannan and Freeman's (1984:150) argument that "in a world of high uncertainty, adaptive efforts . . . turn out to be essentially random with respect to future value." Given the assumptions of costly change and negative selection, the random value of change assumption guarantees that organizations that change their structures will suffer higher mortality rates than these that do not change. This study relaxes the assump-

The authors would like to thank Joel Baum, Charles Fombrun, John Freeman, Heather Haveman, Dan Levinthal, Jim March, Frances Milliken, Bill Starbuck, several anonymous reviewers, and participants at a Wharton School seminar and the conference on Evolutionary Approaches to Organization for comments. In the grand tradition of such acknowledgments, we hold ourselves responsible for all remaining errors, ramblings, and confusion.

tion of random change on the basis of two developments in the ecological literature: The first is the increasing amount of empirical evidence to suggest that the relation between organization level change and the evolution of organizational populations may be more complicated than current conceptualizations, which are dominated almost exclusively by the argument that change increases mortality (Singh and Lumsden, 1990:179–82). The second is the rapprochement of the institutional and selection perspectives, which suggests that organizational level change can be linked to selection perspectives by positing a role for institutional theory in guiding organizational change (Singh and Lumsden, 1990:182–84). As an alternative to the assumption of random change, we will describe organizational level change as the outcome of an experiential learning process guided by mimetic search.

We believe that this combination of the institutional and organizational learning perspectives offers three enhancements to current theory about the role of organization level change in the evolution of organizational populations: First, although we maintain the argument that successful adaption is made more difficult and costly under conditions of uncertainty (Hannan and Freeman, 1984), we recognize explicitly that in the face of uncertainty, organizations may substitute institutional rules for technical rules (Meyer, Scott, and Deal, 1983). For example, if mimetic search can overcome the random value of change under conditions of high uncertainty, then such institutional rules may mitigate the liability of organizational level change. Second, an organization learning perspective is used to model the change processes of individual organizations that make up the population; the elaboration of organizational level processes allows for a more complete analysis of the role of organization level change in the evolution of organizational populations. Third, we model firms as engaging in a mimetic search process without assuming the existence of a highly developed institutional order. A finding that organizations using mimetic search can survive without extensive institutional support is a conservative test of the argument that the use of these rules mitigates the liability of organizational change. It also provides a theoretical basis for understanding the rise of institutional environments. Using this model, we conduct a simulation study to determine the conditions under which some significant proportion of a population consists of firms that change their core features according to a mimetic search process. These conditions establish a baseline for the study of institutionally guided change as an engine of change in the characteristics of the population. At the end of the chapter implications for organizational theory and research are suggested; in particular, we speculate on the use of an institutionally informed ecology of learning as a tool to understand institutional effects on population dynamics.

An Ecology of Learning

This attempt to understand the role of organizational change in the evolution of organizational populations follows from a growing body of literature summarized by Fombrun (1988:224): "Indeed, the changing mix of characteristics in surviving organizations is increasingly regarded as a joint effect of both institutional and ecological influences." This chapter develops a model of an institutionally informed ecology of learning. Our use of ecology follows from the fact that the unit of our study is the population of organizations, and all of the results are reported at the population level. In addition, there is a selection of organizational characteristics through different death rates for organizations with different characteristics. It is an ecology of learning because we argue that organization level change is guided by a process of experiential learning (Levitt and March, 1988); thus, organizational learning may have a significant impact on the evolution of organizational populations. The ecology is institutionally informed because the model focuses on particular patterns of organizational learning and change that are based on the mimetic processes discussed in the institutional literature. The following sections specify our model by describing the characteristics of the individual organizations and the environment in which they learn.

Characteristics of Organizations

Organizations as Experiential Learning Systems. Organizations in this ecology learn from experience through a process that is "routine-based, history-dependent, and target oriented" (Levitt and March, 1988:319). The learning process has three basic components: First, unlike the typical actors of neoclassical economics that optimize in obtaining information (Varian, 1978:231–48), a learning model suggests that the acquisition of information by organizations takes place in a routinized, heuristic process of search (Cyert and March, 1963; Nelson and Winter, 1982). Second, organizations have a target level of performance or aspiration level to which they compare their actual performance. In each period, they determine whether they have performed above or below this aspiration level (Cyert and March, 1963; Payne, Laughunn, and Crum, 1980). Third, performance above or below aspiration level affects the likelihood of organizational change. Change to core features of the organization is more likely when performance is below aspiration level (March and Simon, 1958; Cyert and March, 1963; Levitt and March, 1988). In sum, an organizational learning model suggests that the principle impetus for organizational change and adaptation is performance below aspiration level; the content of change depends on the outcomes of an organizational search process.

The growth of an experiential learning system can be represented as follows:

$$R_{it} = R_{it-1} + P_{it} - c_1 n1_{it} - c_2 n2_{it} R_{it-1}. \tag{1}$$

We assume that there are I distinct firms observed over T time periods; thus, we have $i = 1, \ldots, I$ and $t = 1, \ldots, T$. R_{it} are the resources of firm i at time t. P_{it} is the realized performance of firm i at time t, c_1 is the cost of search, and $n1_{it}$ is the number of searches performed by firm i at time t. c_2 is the proportion of resources consumed in making one change to the core features of the organization, $n2_{it}$ is the number of changes to core features made by firm i at time t, and thus $c_2 n2_{it} R_{it-1}$ is the cost of change.

Organizations and Search Rules. The organizational search process consists of routine activities directed toward examining alternative modes of organizing and assessing their effectiveness. Two types of search are possible: The first type takes place at the beginning of the organizational life cycle to determine the characteristics of the organization to be founded. Following Hannan and Freeman (1987:911), this search is assumed to be directed in such a way that foundings have two main effects on the population of organizations: "Some foundings initiate an entirely new form and thus contribute qualitatively to the diversity of organizational forms in society. Most foundings replicate an existing form and contribute quantitatively to diversity." For this reason, founding search is modeled as an attempt to discover the relationship between firm type and performance rather than as an attempt to imitate. In this way, new firm types can be introduced to the population and existing types can be replicated.

The second type of search occurs after founding and follows rules derived from either the selection or the institutional perspective. The first search rule is derived from the assumptions of the selection perspective; after an initial founding period, firms experience a variety of inertial forces that make them structurally inflexible. These firms follow a fixed strategy and do not search or change at any time after founding. In terms of equation (1), this assumes that both $n1_{it}$ and $n2_{it}$ are zero for all fixed firms in all periods. The second search rule is derived from the institutional perspective. These firms follow a mimetic strategy; they search for information about what organizational characteristics are legitimated in their environmental niche. Fombrun (1988:227) emphasizes the centrality of a mimetic search process in crafting an institutionally informed ecology of organizations: "For organizations, this points to the importance of modeling the search processes through which managers acquire information about environments with which they then imitate competitors." In our model, we assume that legitimated characteristics are those that have been adopted by key firms or industry leaders (DiMaggio and Powell, 1983), which we define as the largest firm in the population. In periods subsequent to founding, there is a nonzero probability that mimetic firms will change their core features so as to become more similar to this industry leader. In terms of equation (1), this implies that both $n1_{it}$ and $n2_{it}$ may be greater than zero for any mimetic firm in any period.

Mimetic firms continue to engage in stochastic search behavior throughout their existence; the distribution of these searches depends on total resources and performance relative to aspiration level (Cyert and March, 1963; Levinthal and March, 1981). Each search involves examining one other firm type to determine whether it is the type of the largest firm in the population; for each such search conducted the firm incurs a cost equal to c_1 units of firm resources. Both problemistic and innovative search occur (Cyert and March, 1963; Levinthal and March, 1981; Mezias and Glynn, 1993); both types of search incur identical costs and are directed toward finding the type of the largest firm in the population. They differ, however, in two ways: First, problemistic search increases with the amount by which performance is below aspiration level. By contrast, innovative search increases as the focal firm becomes wealthy relative to other firms in the population. Second, they differ in terms of where organizational attention is allocated relative to the current firm type. In problemistic search, firms consider those changes that alter the status quo only slightly. Innovative search may be focused more widely and can lead to fundamental change.

Aspiration Levels and Change.   Since fixed firms never change after founding, aspiration levels are irrelevant for this portion of the population. Among mimetic firms, however, performance relative to aspiration level is the principal determinant of whether observable organizational change will result from postfounding search.

Mimetic organizations have a target level of performance or aspiration level that adapts over time according to a formula of the general form estimated in empirical studies of aspiration level adaptation (Lant and Montgomery, 1987; Glynn, Lant, and Mezias, 1991; Lant, 1992):

$$AL_{it} = A_0 + A_1 + AL_{it-1} + A_2 \times (P_{it} - AL_{it-1}), \tag{2}$$

where AL_{it} is the aspiration level of firm i at time t. A_0, A_1, and A_2 are parameters that govern the aspiration level updating process. In each period, firms determine whether they have performed above or below this aspiration level. The probability that a firm will change one or more characteristics depends on the difference between aspiration level and performance.[1] Consistent with research in this area, the distribution of the probability is discontinuous at the point where performance equals aspiration (Cyert and March, 1963; Mezias, 1988). For performance below aspiration level, the probability of change is an increasing function of the size of the discrepancy between actual performance and aspiration level. Although the probability of change is highest when performance is below aspiration level, there is a small probability that firms change even when performance is above aspiration level. Occasionally, as a direct result of search, firms discover good opportunities. In these situations, the probability of change depends on serendipity in the form of a conjunction between a good opportunity and a decision to act on it even in the absence of performance below aspiration level (Cyert and March, 1963; Levinthal and March, 1981). Each change to the core dimensions of the organization is assumed to be very costly (Hannan and Freeman, 1984); a proportion of the resources of the firm equal to c_2 in equation (1) is consumed by each change.

The Characteristics of the Environment

The environment in this ecology provides a mapping between organizational characteristics and performance. Both adaptive theories (Child, 1972; Galbraith, 1973; Tushman and Romanelli, 1985) and ecological theories (Carroll, 1984; Hannan and Freeman, 1977, 1984) argue that organizational performance is contingent on the fit between organizational characteristics and the environment. We assume that the relevant characteristics of organizations can be categorized into distinct firm types, designated $l = 1, \ldots, L$. Each firm type, l, has a base performance, BP_{it}, which may vary by type l and over time t. This number, BP_{it}, is a measure of the fit between firm type l and the environment at time t.

Fixed Characteristics of Environments. The environment is characterized by a level of carrying capacity that is fixed. As the level of carrying capacity increases, the environment can sustain more firms and competition among firms is less intense.[2] The population size is constrained by the carrying capacity via negative selection. A firm goes bankrupt when its resources fall to zero; if the number of firms is above the carrying capacity of the niche, then that firm is not replaced. If the number of firms is at the carrying capacity of the niche, the bankrupt firm is replaced. The search rule of the replacement firm is determined by a random draw from the surviving firms that had positive performance in the current period. For the sake of simplicity, this simulation focuses on established populations where competition is high (population size is at or near carrying capacity). Empirical study of the evolution of organizational populations has demonstrated that population size tends to increase until it reaches a peak (Carroll and Hannan, 1989:411): "Once the peak is reached, there is usually a sharp decline and sometimes stabilization." We simulate this period where the population moves back toward a size that the environment can sustain in the long term.

The second fixed characteristic of the environment is the level of ambiguity in the relationship between firm types and performance. In the real world of organizations, the true relationship between firm characteristics and performance is difficult to determine because of ambiguity (March and Olsen, 1976). The role of ambiguity is modeled here by assuming that firm performance consists of a systematic component based on firm type and a random component that differs for each firm in the population (March, 1988a; Lant and Mezias, 1990, 1992). This relationship is summarized by the following equation:

$$P_{it} = BP_{lt} + \mu_{it} \qquad (3)$$

μ_{it} is a random component that is added to the base performance of the firm's type in computing the actual performance of firm i at time t. These random components come from a distribution with a mean of zero; the level of ambiguity increases with the variance of the distribution of these random components. Defined in this way, ambiguity directly and differentially affects each firm in the population in determining actual performance in each period.

Ambiguity affects search at the time of founding as well. All firms in the population search at founding through the L firm types and examine the following relation for each of the l types:

$$FP_{ilt} = BP_{lt} + \mu_{ilt}. \qquad (4)$$

The decision rule is that firm i founded at time t becomes the type l that yielded the largest FP_{ilt} observation; more formally, organizations choose the firm type they will become, l, such that $\overset{max}{l} FP_{ilt}$ is satisfied.[3] Comparisons of different firm types to find a good type at the time of founding include both the actual base performance of type l and the random component μ_{ilt} that differs for each of L types. The distribution of μ_{ilt} is the same as the distribution of μ_{it}. Ambiguity in the founding search process creates a liability of founding search for both fixed and mimetic firms; the larger the level of ambiguity, the more likely it is that firms will experience an error during founding search. As a result, firms may adopt a type that does not have a high performance.

Characteristics of Environmental Change.   The frequency of change in the environment is captured by the probability that the relationship between firm type and base performance will change in any period of the simulation. The probability that this relationship will change in any of T periods is a Bernoulli random variable with a probability of 'success' or change given by $P(\Delta)$, $0 < P(\Delta) < 1$. The value of $P(\Delta)$ is a fixed characteristic of the environment.

The level of grain, or the magnitude of change, in the environment determines the size of the Bernoulli changes when they take place. Fine grained environments involve changes of relatively small magnitude, while coarse grained environments involve changes of relatively large magnitude (Freeman and Hannan, 1983; Hannan and Freeman, 1977). Given that a stochastic change in the environment has occurred, BP_{lt}, the base performance of type l at time t, will be a weighted combination of the previous base performance, BP_{lt-1}, and a new base performance, NBP_{lt}, drawn from the same distribution as that of the BP_{lt}. w_1 and $(1 - w_1)$, with $0 < w_1 < 1$, are the weights assigned to BP_{lt-1} and NBP_{lt}, respectively. Thus, the magnitude of an environmental change at time t is determined as follows:

$$BP_{lt} = w_1 BP_{lt-1} + (1 - w_1)NBP_{lt}. \tag{5}$$

A fine-grained environment will have a w_1 that is close to one, with a new base performance that is close to the old base performance.

Propositions

In order to derive the implications of organizational level change for the evolution of organizational populations, we examine the degree to which mimetic firms will survive in a population that consists of both fixed and mimetic firms. A finding that a significant proportion of firms in our simulated populations are mimetic would call into question the assumption that organizational level change does not impact population characteristics significantly. Our model of an institutionally informed ecology of learning suggests several theoretical proportions concerning the relative proportions of fixed and mimetic firms in the population. The propositions suggest several variables that might affect the proportion of mimetic firms in the population, denoted Y_{jt}, the proportion of mimetic firms in population j at time t. These variables, along with a description of the process by which parameter values were assigned, are discussed later.

Stable Survival of Mimetic Firms

In order to conclude that mimetic firms might be important to population dynamics from the observation of a finite sample of time periods, the proportion of mimetic firms in the population must be moving toward a stable level greater than zero. We must demonstrate that the system is approaching an equilibrium at the point where we measure the proportion of surviving mimetic firms. System stability implies that the rate of change in the proportions of fixed and mimetic firms should decrease over time, approaching zero. If mimetic firms survive in substantial numbers, and the proportion of fixed and mimetic firms is stable, then we will have demonstrated that mimetic firms will be a fairly permanent component of the population. The stable survival of mimetic firms suggests that institutional processes may be important in the evolution of organizational populations. Thus, in order to understand adequately how populations of organizations come to have certain characteristics, it may be necessary to consider organizational level change explicitly in models of population dynamics.

Fixed Characteristics of Environments

As described in the preceding section, certain features of the environment in our model are fixed for each population at the beginning of each run of the simulation and do not change. The effect of carrying capacity is explored by randomly assigning the number of firms that the niche can support, designated K. The values of K are draws from the uniform distribution of integers between 20 and 99. Since all populations are initialized with 100 firms, the value of K is a measure of the degree of downward pressure on the number of firms. This downward pressure on the size of the population constitutes the form of competition in this simulation and is operationalized via negative selection.[4] Thus, in our model, competition increases when carrying capacity decreases. Hannan and Freeman (1984) argue that selection pressures favor firms that do not change their structure. In general, the smaller the carrying capacity of a niche, the greater are selection pressures. Thus, mimetic firms will be at a disadvantage compared to fixed firms as a result of negative selection in niches with limited carrying capacity.

Proposition 1: The proportion of mimetic firms will increase as the carrying capacity of the niche increases.

The second fixed feature of the environment is the level of ambiguity in the relationship between firm characteristics and performance. The effect of ambiguity is explored by operationalizing μ_{it} in equation (3) and μ_{ilt} in equation (4) as random draws from the uniform distribution over the interval $-A$ to A. A is a random draw from the integers 0 to 25 that establishes the level of ambiguity at the start of each run of the simulation. In this ecology of learning ambiguity may impose two liabilities on firms: the liability of organizational change and the liability of founding search. As we explain later, the liability of change should decrease the proportion of mimetic firms as ambiguity increases; however, the liability of founding search should increase the proportion of mimetic firms as ambiguity increases. Thus, we test two opposing hypotheses about the effect of ambiguity.

The liability of organizational change was presented quite effectively by Hannan and Freeman (1984); they argued that high levels of ambiguity render attempts at adaptive change essentially random with respect to future value. Since change is costly but of random value, there is a significant liability of organizational change. Thus, the proportion of mimetic firms should decrease with the level of ambiguity.

Proposition 2A: The proportion of mimetic firms in the population will decrease as the level of ambiguity increases.

The liability of founding search is derived from applying this argument to understanding how firms become a certain type in the founding search process. The greater the ambiguity, the less effective is the founding search process at discovering the relationship between firm type and performance, producing a liability of founding search. Although mimetic and fixed firms will make mistakes during ambiguous founding search at approximately the same rate, the ability of mimetic firms to make adaptive changes after founding may help them to overcome this liability. Thus, the proportion of mimetic firms should increase with the level of ambiguity.

Proposition 2B: The proportion of mimetic firms in the population will increase as the level of ambiguity increases.

The final fixed parameters of the environment are the cost of search and the cost of change; these are invariant over time and identical for all search and change by all firms in the population for the entire length of the simulation. The cost of search, c_1 in equation (1), is expressed in the same units as organizational resources. This is the cost per search and determined by a random draw from the real numbers between 0 and 1. The cost of change to a core dimension of the firm, c_2 in equation (1), is expressed as a percentage of the total resources of the firm. Since change to core dimensions is very costly (Hannan and Freeman, 1984), the percentage of resources consumed by each change is determined by a random draw from the uniform distribution of real numbers between 0 and 0.5.[5] Hannan and Freeman (1984) suggest that spending resources to change the core dimensions of organizations will have detrimental effects on organizational survival. The organizational learning perspective highlights the costs of search. Thus, we propose that there will be both a liability of organizational change and a liability of organizational search.

Proposition 3: The proportion of mimetic firms in the population will decrease as the cost of search and the cost of change increase.

Characteristics of Environmental Change

Our final arguments concern the mediating effects of environmental change on the different liabilities faced by firms in the population. Two components of environmental change are considered important: the probability of environmental change and the magnitude of environmental change. The parameter $P(\Delta)$ governs the probability that the environment will change in any period; when the environment changes, the fit of a firm type, as measured by its base performance, changes as well. The greater is $P(\Delta)$, the more likely it is that the environment will change in any period. The magnitude of environmental change (Freeman and Hannan, 1983) is operationalized as the weight used in determining the new relationship between firm characteristics and performance at the time of an environmental change. The magnitude of environmental change decreases with the value of w_1 in equation (5). Both the values of w_1 and $P(\Delta)$ are assigned randomly from the uniform distribution of real numbers between 0 and 1 at the start of each run of the simulation.

Analysis based on the institutionally informed ecology of learning suggests two effects of environmental change. The first is an effect on the liability of founding search. In stable environments, the information about the relationship between firm type and performance gathered during founding search is more likely to remain valid since the relationship is unlikely to change. Similarly, lower performing types adopted as a result of errors committed in founding search remain lower performing. As a result, the liability of founding search may be a more serious problem for firms under conditions of environmental stability than under conditions of environmental change. The second effect of environmental change may be to produce a liability for firms resulting directly from the fact that the environment does change. Under conditions of environmental stability, firms that do not incur the costs of search and change have an advantage over firms that do, ceteris paribus. These firms do not search when there is nothing to find and, better yet, do not change when there is no advantage to gain. Under conditions of environmental change, however, there will be a liability of environmental change for firms that cannot adapt their structures to new environmental configurations. Thus, the expected effects of environmental change are captured by two predictions. First, in highly stable environments, mimetic firms will be helped by their ability to overcome the liability of founding search. Second, in changing environments, mimetic firms will be helped by their ability to overcome the liability of environmental change. If these predictions are correct, then the proportion of mimetic firms should be higher in environments characterized by very low or high levels of change. Propositions 4 and 5 predict that the effects of both the probability and magnitude of environmental change on the proportion of mimetic firms are U-shaped:

> Proposition 4: The proportion of mimetic firms will increase with very low or very high probabilities of environmental change.

Proposition 4 will be supported if the effect of the probability of environmental change is initially downward sloping from low rates of environmental change to intermediate rates of environmental change, and becomes upward sloping as the probability of environmental change reaches very high levels. To capture this U-shaped relation in a linear model, both the probability of environmental change, $P(\Delta)$, and its exponent are included in the analysis.

> Proposition 5: The proportion of mimetic firms will increase with a very low or a very high magnitude of environmental change.

Proposition 5 will be supported if the effect of the magnitude of environmental change is initially downward sloping from a high magnitude of environmental change to an intermediate magnitude of environmental change, and becomes upward sloping as the magnitude of environmental change reaches very low levels. To capture this U-shaped relation in a linear model, both the magnitude of environmental change, w_1, and its exponent are included in the analysis.

The Results of the Simulation

Operationalizing the Ecology

The model we develop assumes that organizations are distinguished by four core dimensions (Hannan and Freeman, 1984; Tushman and Romanelli, 1985); for the purposes of this simulation, the choice of labels for these dimensions is arbitrary. Distinct firm types are determined by different characteristics on these four core dimensions. For the sake of simplicity, we assume that firms have only two alternatives on each of these four dimensions; as a result, there are $2^4 = 16$ distinct firm types. Changes to core dimensions in this simulation involve movement from one of these sixteen firm types to another. At the start of the simulation, each of the sixteen firm types is assigned randomly a base performance level, $BP_{l0}, l = 1, \ldots, 16$ at time

$t = 0$. This base performance reflects the degree of fit of the *l*th firm type with the environment during the first time period. This base performance is stated as an integer that represents the increment to total resources that results from a given firm being a type *l* at this time. The range of possible values for performance has been restricted to the integers between -10 and 10. All sixteen types may be ranked from highest to lowest on this base performance.

A population is initialized with 100 firms, with 50 assigned to each of the mimetic and fixed search processes. The organization being founded becomes one of the sixteen firm types through the founding search process as per equation (4). The resources of all firms are set to an initial allocation of 30 units of resources at the time of founding. This level of resources imposes a significant liability of newness: firms of this initial small size are more likely to go bankrupt than larger firms because performance decrements in early periods can easily exhaust the initial allocation of resources. First, negative values of μ in equation (3) decrease performance, even leading to negative performance that can result in bankruptcy. Second, mistakes during founding search, affected by the size of μ in equation (4), may lead organizations to choose poor performing types as a result of founding search. Finally, the mimetic firms must bear the costs of search and change that can consume a considerable proportion of resources and can lead to bankruptcy; thus, mimetic firms face a greater liability of newness than fixed firms, ceteris paribus. In each period the performance of the firm, as defined in equation (3), is added to its resources. Subsequent to founding, fixed organizations get performance draws in each period but never search or change. By contrast, mimetic organizations get performance draws in each period, make search and change decisions, and update their aspiration levels.

To evaluate the propositions, a linear regression of the following form is estimated:

$$Y_j^{500} = \beta_0 + \beta_1 K + \beta_2 A + \beta_3 c_1 + \beta_4 c_2 + \beta_5 P(\Delta)$$
$$+ \beta_6 \exp(P(\Delta)) + \beta_7 w_1 + \beta_8 \exp(w_1) + e_{jt} \quad (6)$$

where K is carrying capacity, A is ambiguity, c_1 is the cost of search, c_2 is the cost of change, $P(\Delta)$ is the likelihood of environmental change, $\exp[P(\Delta)]$ is the exponent of the likelihood of environmental change, w_1 is the magnitude of environmental change, and $\exp(w_1)$ is the exponent of the magnitude of environmental change. We estimate this equation for 500 populations after 500 periods have elapsed; thus, $j = 1, \ldots, 500$. The results are used to obtain an estimate of the effect of each of the independent variables once the system has reached an equilibrium. Table 10.1 provides a summary of the variables and related research propositions.

Findings and Discussion

Our overall prediction was that some significant proportion of mimetic firms would survive in the long run. Figure 10.1 demonstrates that by period 500, approximately 20 percent of the firms are mimetic, compared with 80 percent that are fixed firms. Further, figure 10.1 also indicates that the rate of change in the proportion of firms of both types decreases over time. In particular, the slope of the lines tracking the proportion of fixed and mimetic firms in the population appears to be zero by period

TABLE 10.1   Predictions: The Effects of Organizational and
Environmental Characteristics on the Proportion of Mimetic
Firms in a Population

Equation (6):

$$Y_j^{500} = \beta_0 + \beta_1 K + \beta_2 A + \beta_3 c_1 + \beta_4 c_2 + \beta_5 P(\Delta)$$
$$+ \beta_6 \exp(P(\Delta)) + \beta_7 w_1 + \beta_8 \exp(w_1) + e_{jt}$$

Variable Name	Proposition	Predicted Effect
K (Carrying Capacity)	1	$\beta_1 > 0$
A (Ambiguity)	2	$\beta_2 < 0, \beta_2 > 0$
C_1 (Cost of Search)	3	$\beta_3 < 0$
C_2 (Cost of Change)	3	$\beta_4 < 0$
$P(\Delta)$ (Environmental Stability)	4	$\beta_5 < 0$
$\exp(P(\Delta))$	4	$\beta_6 > 0$
w_1 (Magnitude of Change)	5	$\beta_7 < 0$
$\exp(w_1)$	5	$\beta_8 > 0$

500. We take this as evidence that the proportion of fixed and mimetic firms in the population in period 500 is similar to what we would observe over an extended period: that is, approximately 20 percent of the population will consist of mimetic firms over the long run. Thus, figure 10.1 illustrates strong support for the proposition that some proportion of mimetic firms will will survive in the population even

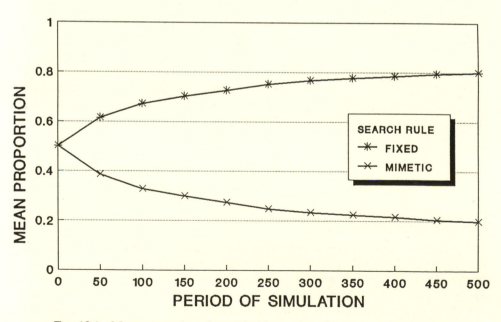

FIG. 10.1   Mean proportion of surviving firms of each type as a function of time

TABLE 10.2   Results: The Effects of Organizational and
Environmental Characteristics on the Proportion of Mimetic
Firms in a Population

Equation (6):

$$Y_j^{500} = \beta_0 + \beta_1 K + \beta_2 A + \beta_3 c_1 + \beta_4 c_2 + \beta_5 P(\Delta)$$
$$+ \beta_6 \exp(P(\Delta)) + \beta_r w_1 + \beta_8 \exp(w_1) + e_{jt}$$

Variable Name	Coefficient	T-statistics
Intercept	−.5994	−4.3930**
K (Carrying Capacity)	.0007	2.2333*
A (Ambiguity)	.0005	.4190
C_1 (Cost of Search)	−.1848	−6.9569**
C_2 (Cost of Change)	−.2540	−5.4825**
$P(\Delta)$ (Environmental Stability)	−.5785	−3.1076**
$\exp(P(\Delta))$	.4466	3.9939**
w_1 (Magnitude of Change)	−.7224	−3.6594**
$\exp(w_1)$	.4640	4.0064**

NOTE: T-statistics are presented for interested readers. They do not imply
that these are empirical results. Furthermore, T-statistics depend on sample
size, and sample size could be increased by conducting more simulation
runs; thus, such statistics should be interpreted with these caveats in mind.

*$p < .05$.

**$p < .01$.

after an arbitrarily long period. The results of testing propositions 1 through 5 are
presented in table 10.2, which reports the significance of estimated coefficients from
an ordinary least squares regression of the effects of carrying capacity, ambiguity, and
costs of search and change and the rate and magnitude of environmental change on
the proportion of mimetic firms in the population in period 500. The statistical
results are of interest in determining how the proportion of mimetic firms changes
along with changes in each independent variable. This question can be answered by
looking at the unstandardized coefficients in table 10.2.

The effect of carrying capacity on the proportion of mimetic firms is significant
and positive as predicted by proposition 1. Thus, as carrying capacity increased, the
proportion of mimetic firms that survived in the population also increased. This
result supports the argument that decreased selection pressures help mimetic firms.
An increase in carrying capacity equal to 10 percent of the variable's range results in
a 0.5 percent increase in the proportion of mimetic firms. The level of ambiguity in
the environment did not have a significant effect on the proportion of mimetic firms
in the population. A similar increase in ambiguity yields a 0.25 percent increase in
the proportion of mimetic firms. Thus, although the effect of ambiguity is in the same
direction as that of carrying capacity; its impact is only half as great, given the range
of values that we examined. An examination of the effect of ambiguity over time
revealed that the impact of ambiguity on mimetic firms oscillates over time. The
initial effect of ambiguity is positive, consistent with arguments about the liability of

founding search. Later on, the effect of ambiguity is negative, consistent with the arguments about the liability of organizational change. In period 500, the point at which we conduct the analysis, the effect of ambiguity is not significant. We do not know whether the effect would continue to oscillate if we continued the simulation beyond period 500, or whether the effect would eventually reach an equilibrium. We believe that ambiguity is an important variable that can potentially impact the survival of firms. More investigation is necessary in order to understand this impact. The effects of the cost of search and the cost of change are negative and significant, as predicted by proposition 3. The effects are somewhat larger than those for either carrying capacity or ambiguity. A similar 10 percent increase in the cost of search results in a 1.8 percent decrease in the proportion of mimetic firms; such an increase in the cost of change results in a 1.25 percent decrease in the proportion of mimetic firms. These results point to the significant liabilities of search and change: mimetic firms are at an increasing disadvantage compared to fixed firms as the cost of learning increases.

Proposition 4 predicted that the proportion of mimetic firms would increase in environments with either very low or very high probabilities of change. The results offer evidence of the predicted U-shaped relationship. The measure of the probability of environmental change, $P(\Delta)$, is negative and significant. This result indicates that the proportion of mimetic firms decreases as the probability of environmental change rises from a low to an intermediate level. The exponent of $P(\Delta)$ is significant and positive, indicating that the proportion of mimetic firms increases again as the probability of environmental change rises to a very high level. Figure 10.2 illustrates this curvilinear relationship. As the probability of change increases from 0 to 10 percent, the proportion of mimetic firms decreases by about 1.1 percent. As the probability of change increases from 10 to 20 percent, the proportion of mimetic firms decreases by only 0.6 percent. As the probability of change increases from 50 to 60 percent, the proportion of mimetic firms increases by about 2 percent; as the probability of change increases from 80 to 90 percent, the proportion of mimetic firms increases by about 5 percent. Thus, when the environment is stable, mimetic firms gain some benefit from being able to correct errors made during founding search. However, this benefit quickly disappears at low to moderate levels of environmental change; the costs of search and change incurred by mimetic firms soon outweigh any benefit they gain from correcting founding errors. As the probability of environmental change reaches 50 percent or more, mimetic firms begin to benefit from their ability to overcome the liability of environmental change.

Proposition 5 predicted that the proportion of mimetic firms would increase in environments with either a very low or a very high magnitude of change. The results offer evidence of the predicted U-shaped relationship. The measure of environmental grain, w_1, is significant and negative. This result indicates that the proportion of mimetic firms decreases as the magnitude of environmental change falls from a high level to an intermediate level. The exponent of w_1 is significant and positive, suggesting that the proportion of mimetic firms increases again as the magnitude of environmental change reaches a very small level. Figure 10.3 illustrates this curvilinear relationship. As the value of w_1 increases from 0 to 10 percent, the proportion of mimetic firms decreases by only 0.6 percent. As w_1 reaches values of 50 percent and higher, the proportion of mimetic firms increases. As w_1 increases from 70 to 80

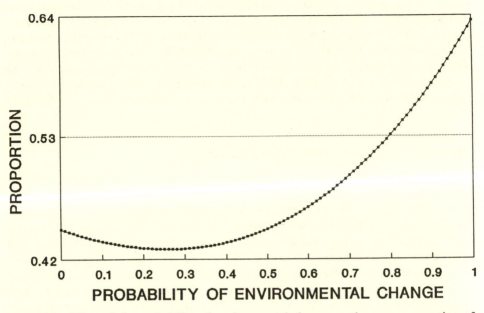

FIG. 10.2 Effect of the probability of environmental change on the mean proportion of mimetic firms

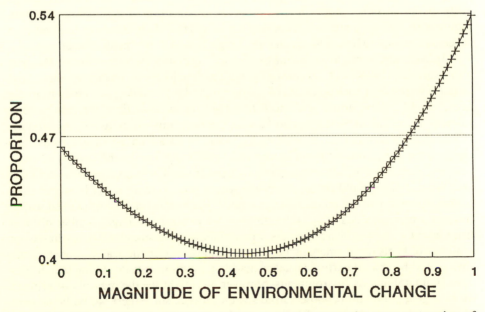

FIG. 10.3 Effect of the magnitude if environmental change on the mean proportion of mimetic firms

cent, the proportion of mimetic firms increases by about 2.6 percent; increases from 90 to 100 percent result in increases in the proportion of mimetic firms of almost 5 percent. These results suggest that when environmental changes are large, mimetic firms benefit from their ability to overcome the liability of environmental change. When environmental changes are small, mimetic firms benefit from their ability to overcome errors in founding search. At intermediate magnitudes of change, however, the costs that mimetic firms incur from searching and changing outweigh the benefits.

Limitations and Suggestions for Future Research

The generality of the results from the simulation may be limited by the particular choices we made in operationalizing this ecology of organizational learning. In this section, we suggest several dimensions on which the simulation could be expanded, and we discuss the possible implications of such changes. One possible limitation is that organizations in our ecology do not increase their competency at search and change activities as their age and experience increase. Allowing firms to increase their competence at search and change could give mimetic firms a better chance of survival if the cost of search and change decreased as competence increased. With respect to search, firms in our simulation do not improve on their ability to search by searching, and all firms in the population have identical costs of search (see Leventhal and March, 1981). Further, problemistic and innovative searches (Cyert and March, 1963) have the same cost. These simplifying assumptions to facilitate understanding the direct effect of the cost of search on the probability of survival of firms that search. With respect to change, we do not include an explicit term to measure the probability of successful change; for purposes of this simulation, a lower probability of successful change increases the expected number of change attempts required to achieve a successful completion of change. This increases the cost of a successful change: More difficult change is regarded as more costly change.

In addition, it might be useful to take into account the suggestion of Hannan and Freeman (1984) that organizations will be less likely to change as they grow larger. The result of such a pattern of change might be that older, successful mimetic firms would behave more and more like fixed firms over time. Presuming that mimetic firms had achieved a good fit with the environment, reducing the amount of resources devoted to search and change would be an advantage in stable environments. However, it would result in mimetic firms' experiencing the liability of environmental change typically experienced by fixed firms. These implications lead us to ask, What if firms could change from one search process to another? In stable environments, we might see an increasing number of mimetic firms adopt a fixed search process, whereas in changing environments, we might see a large number of fixed firms adopt a mimetic search process. In ambiguous environments, we might see the majority of firms in an emerging population choose a mimetic search process, since they would be able to correct mistakes made in an ambiguous founding search process. In unambiguous environments, however, we might see the majority of firms in an emerging population choose a fixed search process, since there would be no benefit to searching or changing after the initial founding search. These speculations suggest what might happen if we simulated organizational populations while they were emerging and growing as well as during the periods of peak and decline. In order to simulate this emergent period, we would also need to include an ongoing birth process, rather than just the replacement birth process operationalized in this model. We might also examine the effect of population density on the rate at which firms go bankrupt. That is, as competition increases (as the population gets closer to its carrying capacity), some firms will be forced out of the population before their resources fall to zero. We expect that the effect of such competition on mimetic firms would depend on the variables we examined in this simulation, such as the cost of search and change and the frequency and magnitude of environmental changes. All of these changes represent extensions to the institutionally informed ecology of learning that would further demonstrate its utility.

The Role of Mimetic Learning

The results of this simulation offer an interesting illustration of how different assumptions lead to different conclusions about the importance of organization level change in understanding population dynamics. Hannan and Freeman's (1984) contention that change is random with respect to future value implies that the study of inert firms replacing each other is all that is necessary in order to understand the evolution of organizational populations. This implies that organization level change is not an important focus for the study of the evolution of organizational populations. In this chapter, the assumption of random change has been relaxed on the basis of two developments in the ecological literature: The first is the increasing amount of empirical evidence suggesting that organization level change may play an important role in the evolution of organizational populations (Singh and Lumsden, 1990:179–82). The second is the rapprochement of the institutional and selection perspectives, which guided the choice of the type of organizational level change addressed explicitly in this study (Singh and Lumsden, 1990:182–84). We replaced the assumption of random change with the assumption that firms engage in institutionally guided mimetic search and change. Using this alternative assumption, we highlighted the liabilities of founding search and environmental change in addition to the liabilities of organizational change usually considered in ecological models (Hannan and Freeman, 1984; Carroll, 1984). A simulation methodology was used to assess the minimum conditions under which a significant proportion of mimetic firms would persist in the population. The survival of mimetic firms in our simulation did not depend on the existence of an elaborate institutional environment. Thus, we suggest that the operationalizations in our model provide the baseline conditions under which organizational level change guided by a mimetic process may be an important element in models of the evolution of organizational populations.

Our results suggest that understanding mimetic learning and organization level change will be more important in understanding the evolution of organizational populations under the following conditions: (1) Low levels of competition, as measured by higher carrying capacity, increase the proportion of mimetic firms. (2) Low costs of search and change increase the proportion of mimetic firms. Thus, mimetic firms do experience a liability of both search and change. (3) A relatively low or a relatively high magnitude of environmental change increases the proportion of mimetic firms relative to an intermediate magnitude of change. (4) A relatively low or a relatively high probability of environmental change increases the proportion of mimetic firms relative to an intermediate probability of change. The third and fourth points suggest that mimetic firms are helped not only by their ability to overcome the liability of environmental change, but also by their ability to overcome the liability of founding search under conditions of environmental stability.

Evolution and Organization Level Change

In general, the results of the simulation suggest that a significant proportion of mimetic firms can survive under a wide range of conditions. Our choice of ranges used in operationalizing the simulation are based on empirical measures or are consonant with theoretical treatments of the underlying concepts. These assumptions define some boundary conditions under which organizations that are capable of mimetic learning will survive over relatively long periods. These results are obtained by making relatively few assumptions about the institutional environment. The only institutional process operationalized in the simulation is mimetic: Mimetic firms in the population engaged in search that enabled them to imitate the largest firm in the population. There is no cooperation among the mimetic firms to pool or otherwise lower the costs of search and change. There is no transfer of resources from a centralized authority to those firms that follow the mimetic search process. There is no central coordination at the level of the institutional environment or diffusion of professionalized personnel to increase normative or coercive pressures to adopt certain characteristics (DiMaggio and Powell, 1983; Meyer and Scott, 1983). The ability of a significant proportion of mimetic firms to survive for long periods absent such additional support suggests how mimetic organization level change might evolve even in the absence of a well-developed institutional environment.

Imitation of the largest firm in the population, a search process based on institutional theory and the literature on organizational learning, is a robust strategy over time, even under conditions of competition, ambiguity, costly search and change, and environmental variability. This is illustrated by the fact that the average proportion of mimetic firms in the population is still above 20 percent even after 500 periods (figure 10.1). This result suggests that under a fairly general set of conditions, a significant proportion of organizations in a population that have the ability to change core features of their structure may survive. On the basis of this conclusion, we believe that models of the evolution of organizational populations have an obligation to take into account the potential effects of change at the level of individual organizations. We do not believe that dismissal of the possibility of organization level change is acceptable as a principle for the study of the evolution of populations of organizations. In addition, we believe that our results suggest an intriguing possibility: What if mimetic firms, recognizing their common interest, form a coalition to influence, strengthen, or even create the institutional environment?

Pursuing the implications of the formation of an institutional environment by a coalition or coalitions among firms that have the ability to change core features also may be an important area for future research. The institutional literature has suggested two phenomena that might be the result, and both may form interesting areas for future research. First, the institutional literature has suggested that there will be increases in the legitimate and coercive power of the nation-state. The findings of Barnett and Carroll (1992) regarding the effect of governmental action, the Kingsbury Commitment, on the evolution of populations of telephone companies provides evidence of how state action might affect the evolution of organizational populations. Second, the institutional literature has predicted the rise of professionalized sectors (Meyer and Rowan, 1977; Meyer and Scott, 1983; DiMaggio and Powell, 1983). The recent consolidation of the formerly Big Eight firms into the Big Six represents an obvious example of how these sectors change over time. The interrelationship of the evolution of populations of professional organizations and the evolution of the populations of organizations that they serve may be one way to link the rise of professional sectors explicitly with the evolution of populations of organizations. We believe the exploration of both of these phenomena forms an important and interesting agenda for future evolutionary research.

Appendix

The values of the parameters of the aspiration level formula, A_0, A_1, and A_2 in equation (2), were assigned randomly from the values of these parameters estimated by Lant (1992) in a study of aspiration level adaptation. The results reported here are not changed by effects from any combination of these values. When mimetic firms search, they attempt to discover the type of the largest firm in the population and adopt its characteristics; this is true for both problemistic and innovative search. Problemistic search occurs if and only if firm performance is below aspiration level and involves searching any of the four types that would require only one change to firm structure. For example, a firm type 1111 engaging in problemistic search might search types 1110, 1101, 1011, or 0111. Thus, no more than four problemistic searches will be conducted; the actual number conducted is binomial with $n = 4$ and π given as follows:

$$\pi = \frac{P_{it} - AL_{it-1}}{\min_{i} (P_{it} - AL_{it-1})} \tag{7}$$

Thus, the probability of one problemistic search is the ratio of the amount by which the focal firm fell below its aspiration level and the largest amount by which any firm in the population performed below its aspiration level. Innovative searches can be performed by any mimetic firm in any period; these can involve examination of any of the 15 firm types other than the current type of the focal firm. Thus, the number of innovative searches will be binomial with $n = 15$ and π given as follows:

$$\pi = \frac{R_{it}}{\max_{i} R_{it}} \tag{8}$$

Thus, the probability of one innovative search is the ratio of the focal firm's resources to the resouces of the largest firm in the population at time t. Problemistic searches are conducted first, and those firm types searched in the problemistic process are not considered in the innovative search process. Thus, no firm type will be searched twice in the same period.

For firms performing below aspiration level in a given period, the probability of change is binomial with $n = 4$ and π as given in equation (7) for problemistic search. For firms performing above aspiration level the probability of change is binomial with $n = 4$ and $\pi = 0.05$.

Notes

1. The size of the organization does not affect the likelihood of organizational change in this simulation; thus, the implications of the results are limited by this assumption.

2. Both fixed and mimetic firms draw on the same resources in the environment and thus are affected by the same carrying capacity.

3. All firms engage in founding search at the initialization of the simulation. After initialization, all firms that replace bankrupt firms also engage in founding search to determine which firm type they will become. As discussed previously, however, whether firms are fixed or mimetic is a property inherited from a firm randomly drawn from among all those with positive performance in the period of the replacement.

4. This negative selection process results in the birth of new firms only after another firm has exited the population. We do not include elements of mass or concentration in our operationalization of competition.

5. We have talked about organizational change in terms of core dimensions of the organization. Thus, the type of change we are interested in modeling results in significant changes to the characteristics of an organization. Some institutional theorists (Meyer and Rowan, 1977) have suggested that organizations change peripheral features while buffering their core characteristics. Under the assumption that core changes are more costly than peripheral changes, the continuum from core to peripheral changes can be represented by the distribution of the cost of change across populations in the simulation. Thus, the implications of this simulation are not necessarily limited to a discussion of changes to core dimensions.

COMMENTARY

Taking on Strategy, 1–2–3

CHARLES J. FOMBRUN

Ecology has long been chastised for its implication of managerial irrelevance: By stressing the importance of selection pressures in the dynamics of organizational populations, ecologists have often angered strategists who assert the importance of managerial initiatives in the process of corporate change.

The chapters in this section should appease the critics somewhat. That's because the authors ask a provocative question: How can an ecological perspective enlighten us about key strategic changes that managers initiate? In so doing, they turn our attention away from organizational ecology's more familiar interest in the process of selection and place the spotlight squarely on the more managerially relevant question of *variation.*

To call attention to variation, however, is also to step, however gingerly, onto the turf of business strategy, itself a wary intruder on the contested terrain of industrial economics. The chapters in this section do it in quite different ways: By dint of persuasion and simulation, through event-history analysis, and by analysis of sequences. In seeking to contribute to a theory of strategic change, their authors ask us to bear in mind that (1) organizational changes are contextual, (2) organizational changes are strategic, and (3) organizational changes are paradoxical. By trying to shed light on the forces that impel companies to alter their strategic positions, they open a potentially fruitful dialogue between disparate literatures in strategy and organization.

Changes Are Contextual

A clear and familiar contention of these chapters is that managers do not initiate change in a vacuum: Changes are heavily influenced by environmental conditions. Instead of the traditional emphasis on the external environment, however, the authors also call to our attention two more novel points.

First, changes are not propelled solely by the *external* environments of firms, but also by *internal* political and cultural conditions that impel managers to circumnavigate into and out of product/market domains. A rich literature on organizations supports the merit of incorporating into our evolutionary models features of firms' internal environments that might oblige managers to carry out changes. Inertial forces that derive from firms' internal configurations of features impede firms from changing. The chapters by Ginsberg and Baum and Levinthal both suggest how internal competency traps might spur managerial action. Haveman's study also relates internal predispositions (such as available slack resources) to observed rates of change.

Of course, we should also keep in mind that cognitive theorists dispute that any one-to-one correspondence obtains between managers' *perceptions* of internal and external environments and actual conditions. After all, it may not be the objective conditions that propel change, but rather the subjective interpretations of those environments by careerist top managers (Fombrun and Zajac, 1987). Were they readily available, cognitive data about environments could be easily substituted, allowing a juxtaposition and test of competing theories about evolutionary change within the shared methodological framework that the authors provide.

Second, even if we buy into an external point of view, we are also reminded that the environment itself may well be changing at a pace that closely matches that of the organization. Can we, then, legitimately establish "the environment" of a firm when that environment itself is changing as a consequence of the actions managers are continually taking? Some simplifying assumptions become necessary.

For instance, Heather Haveman (chapter 8) studied diversification by savings and loan associations in the United States between 1977 and 1987. A key problem she faced was that evolving deregulation actually thrust S&Ls into competition with established firms in neighboring populations, whether commercial banks, brokerage firms, credit unions, insurance companies, or even investment banks. So to specify the environment of S&Ls was no simple task: As Heather rightly acknowledges, the boundaries of the population are themselves shifting, making measures of density based solely on the number of S&Ls involved in a market difficult to trust as accurate estimates of rivalry in a particular market.

The problem of these converging industries could be partly addressed by raising the level of analysis to that of the corporate community: The density estimates would require defining the denominator as *all potential competitors,* a number that varies from year to year on the basis of regulatory impediments into and out of the different markets. Even so, that will not account for how the actions taken by firms affect the environment that other firms face. The efforts to model coevolution by Joel Baum and Jitendra Singh, chapter 18 in this volume, suggest, perhaps, how we might begin to address this problem.

Dan Levinthal also reminds us that firms are embedded in networks that shape how managers think, what environmental issues they see, and thus the actions they take. Whatever theory of competition we develop must therefore address itself to the institutional and cognitive context within which strategies are formed.

I fully agree (Fombrun, 1986). Take the case of the S&Ls. My reading of the sad history of S&Ls makes me want to infuse the bare bones of observed organizational changes with the meat of embeddedness. In his book *The S&L Debacle,* Larry White (1991) explained how the changes in domain S&Ls made were largely driven by the need to increase revenues in order to attract depositors. He and others point to the key role that Michael Milken's junk bonds played in enabling S&Ls to diversify out of their low-interest-rate mortgage portfolios. Moreover, mortgage-backed securities were invented by the broker Lew Ranieri at Salomon Brothers.

To refine our theory-building efforts, I suspect we will need increasingly to ask ourselves questions of marginal sensitivity: When does it make sense to study environments as external to firms, and at what point does it stop making sense? When is a population the relevant environmental context within which to study organizational change, and when does it make more sense to view the community as the appropriate context?

To address these questions requires a theory about the factors that drive competition. Incorporating into evolutionary analyses what are essentially complementary measures of density, mass, and linkage intensity offers an extremely useful starting point. Additional benefit might be gained from scrutinizing the work of industrial economists like Richard Caves and Michael Porter, who strive to define competitive conditions more carefully and whose work might help frame future studies of how organizations adapt to changing environments. For instance, defining competition in terms of the intensity of rivalry, and incorporating measures of the elasticity of substitution with neighboring product-market sectors, and of vertical interdependence (what Ron Burt called the industry's "structural autonomy") might help determine which industries to study, and to understand the factors that fueled their evolution.

Changes Are Strategic

Organization theory has often failed to differentiate mundane changes from more strategically minded mutations. Most of the changes described in this section encroach directly on the study of how firms respond strategically to changing environments by radically altering their internal resource profiles, and thereby effecting change in their competitive postures. The chapters in this section draw our attention beyond the mundane to changes that are more likely to alter firms' relative postures vis-à-vis rivals. We can anticipate some lively exchanges in the future with the growing literature of strategic management.

Among them is a probable urging by students of strategy to classify managers' initiatives more microscopically. They suggest, for instance, that managers make three types of strategic changes to adapt to environments:

1. *Business-level* initiatives that involve more aggressive investments in achieving differentiation through cost reduction or innovation within individual businesses (Porter, 1980);
2. *Corporate-level* initiatives that involve broadening the diversity of product/market sectors, businesses, or industries firms serve (Rumelt, 1974);
3. *Collective-level* initiatives that involve forming joint ventures, alliances, and other network ties with rivals, suppliers, and distribution (Astley and Fombrun, 1983).

Each of these strategic responses constitutes a coping mechanism for firms, a means of adapting to environmental turbulence (Bourgeois, 1980). In essence, then, these three types of initiatives constitute a strategic repertoire: Firms adjust their strategic positions by altering their *profile* across the business, corporate, and collective levels.

Strategists would contend that strategic initiatives actually trade off one against the other: When managers select strategies, they decide how best to allocate resources by considering *jointly* proposals at the business, corporate, and collective levels. A study of strategic change should therefore encompass all three types of responses.

Moreover, all investments, diversifications, and joint ventures are not equal: To discuss diversification efforts, for instance, requires that we appreciate the *ground zero* from which each firm's actions spring. A diversification initiative by a single business firm is doubtless more radical than by a firm whose portfolio is already quite broad, and for which an acquisition may simply constitute an incremental change.

This point came to mind when reading Ari Ginsberg and Joel Baum's chapter on patterns of diversification in a set of forty-two bank holding companies formed after 1956. I suspect the acquisitions meant quite different things to the particular banks: Some were aggressive investments, others defensive; some were propelled by efforts to explore latent synergies in seemingly related businesses, while others were simply efforts to "hedge" in a changing regulatory environment. To demonstrate momentum requires juxtaposing it against a rival explanation, one perhaps grounded in the different motives that might be propelling the diversification initiative.

Moreover, a single acquisition is only one element in a diversification strategy: We need to understand the strategy itself—its starting point and endpoint—before we can actually classify firms into similar diversification types. Often, strategies begin and end with a change in chief executive officer. Sometimes, they endure over multiple regimes. Do the cumulative results of multiple acquisitions produce a sensible pattern that we can discern in each of the banks under study?

Finally, what constitutes "relatedness" in and of itself is a matter of continuing debate in that industry and has changed somewhat since 1956, the starting point for the study. Activities deemed legitimate for banks to engage in have evolved as new technologies and new institutional rules have come to redefine the basic business of banking from service activities to risk management. I wonder, therefore, how comfortable we should feel about sequences that are generated from seemingly distinct categories that blur upon closer scrutiny. Again, as with all questions of boundary definition, the question comes down to sensitivity analysis: How robust are our categories?

The remedy is not obvious, but it seems to me important that we recognize the ambiguities that inhere in seemingly straightforward classifications of strategies themselves. When can we describe a *strategy*—rather than merely a strategic act— as related or unrelated? Is it appropriate to focus solely on acts of diversification in studying a sequence of strategic actions without also discussing parallel transformations at the business and collective levels that might also have modified firms' strategic postures? If strategic alliances are an alternative means of diversifying risk, is it not dangerous to omit them when observing patterns of diversification?

I ask these questions because I think it will prove key in future ecological studies of strategic change to clarify the dimensionality of the concept of "strategy" itself, much as in the previous section I suggested that future studies of evolutionary dynamics in organizational collectivities will also need a clearer concept of what constitutes suitable antecedants for defining "competition."

Changes Are Paradoxical

An exogenous stimulus-response logic has characterized most studies allied with an ecological framework—but not these. Ginsberg and Baum (chapter 7) ask how past acquisitions and divestments affect the likelihood of future acquisition behavior. Haveman (chapter 8) and Mezias and Lant (chapter 10) all recognize explicitly that the prior actions of firms aggregate into characteristics of environments: They include them as features to which firms subsequently respond, and I especially like the intriguing variable Haveman labels "market mass," perhaps a surrogate measure of industry-level inertia and momentum.

We are also reminded that social changes are replete with paradoxical processes and are animated by contradictions that develop over time: Actions beget reactions and are intertwined with outcomes like profitability and performance, which are themselves only loosely coupled with survival (Fombrun, 1988). Dan Levinthal rightly calls our attention to the fact that managers are quite skillful at designing systems and practices and at coopting powerful institutional elements that buffer firms from performance downturns and prevent them from failing. In a learning model, the systemic and contradictory properties of organizations are far more evident than in traditional exogenous worldviews.

In fact, a large part of organization theory describes how internal changes are provoked, not directly by environmental changes, but by the mediating influence of leadership changes or performance declines. In a study of failing firms, Don Hambrick and Richard d'Aveni (1988) found that strategic actions were not, in fact, isolated occurrences, but initiatives that were closely intertwined with objective conditions, social perceptions, and group dynamics within firms. They therefore point to forces for change that are also partly endogenous.

Recognizing a reciprocal chain of interdependencies, a combination of endogenous and exogenous forces propelling change, suggests the merit of looking more closely at the joint patterning of actions and outcomes in a collectivity: At how intensification of business-level activity compensates, perhaps, for increased riskiness in portfolio diversification; or how joint ventures increase or decrease in tandem with changes in business-level aggressiveness and corporate-level diversification. The sudden popularity of strategic alliances suggests there may be some merit to investigating these compensatory processes in a common framework.

Other systemic interactions, of course, are likely, and less straightforward to deal with: the likelihood that forging alliances, a strategy intended to help firms cope with increasing environmental turbulence, probably itself *increases* the macrolevel uncertainty firms actually experience; or that the attempt to diversify away risk through acquisitions itself overextends the knowledge of firms' managers and actually *increases* the firm's vulnerability; or that increased aggressiveness within a business unit is costly and may drain the firm of vital resources needed for long-run success (the familiar trade-off between advertising and R&D).

Although such paradoxical and compensatory processes are not addressed directly by the chapters presented in this section, they are not irrelevant. As their authors agree, to study strategic changes as if they were one-shot interventions uncoupled through time is to limit artifically the scope of our theorizing about how managers act and react to one another and to their environments. In their simulation, Steve Mezias and Theresa Lant call our attention to the fact that firms may formulate their strategies purely in an imitative manner, that is, without direct regard to environmental conditions—and that it may pay off. They ask us implicitly to incorporate assumptions about strategic interactions between firms as an important dimension for thinking about how firms and populations change.

In (Con)Quest of Strategy

The terrain of strategic management is likely to be increasingly contested as ecologists take on the study of variation, learning, and change and indicate their relevance for how organizations, populations, and industries evolve. The explorations presented herein suggest, however, some possible avenues of cooperation between students of strategy and students of evolutionary dynamics.

For one, strategy researchers have yet to develop a dynamic framework for studying how firms adapt. Ecologists have such a framework and back it up with the appropriate methodology to test longitudinal hypotheses. Ecologists, however, lack a conceptual theory for identifying either the nature of "competition" or the constituent components of "strategy." These are not in short supply in strategy research.

In recent years, strategy researchers have sought to develop a theory of strategic change (1) by incorporating stronger cognitive assumptions into their models and (2) by drawing heavily on game theory to formalize strategic interactions and network relationships into their models. These two domains also constitute important and necessary directions for ecologists to explore in coming years.

By drawing our attention to these points of tangency between the literatures of strategy and organization, the authors in this section signal the existence of potentially rewarding lines of inquiry in future studies of firms' evolutionary dynamics.

On Behalf of Naïveté

WILLIAM H. STARBUCK

Peering Into Mirrors

The phenomena we see reflect ourselves. When we report what we see, our reports tell much about ourselves—they may even tell more about us than about the phenomena we claim to be observing (Starbuck and Milliken, 1988).

In research, the phenomena we see reflect our analytic procedures. When we report research findings, our reports tell much about our analytic procedures. Our reports may tell more about our analytic procedures than about the phenomena we claim to be analyzing (Starbuck, 1981; Webster and Starbuck, 1988).

This chapter advocates changes in our theorizing and our testing of theories. These changes would help us to formulate more meaningful theories and to evaluate them more rigorously. Although the issues and prescriptions apply generally, the discussion emphasizes time series because these are central in studies of evolutionary dynamics. A time series is a sequence of observations collected over time—for example, annual counts of steel mills over 30 years.

This first section explains why time series so readily support multiple interpretations, including spurious or deceptive inferences. This ambiguity implies that we should use tough criteria to test theories about series. This section also points out that sustaining a null hypothesis is often more useful than rejecting one, but journals favor studies that do the opposite and they encourage scientists to lie. The subsequent section reviews six reasons organizational scientists should pay serious attention to null or naïve hypotheses that describe behaviors as having large random components. We are trying too hard to invent and show the superiority of causal theories, often complex ones; and we too quickly reject simple hypotheses that are more parsimonious. The third section points out how often social scientists test their theories against null hypotheses that they can always reject. Statistical tests would have more import if scientists would test their theories against null models or against naïve hypotheses.

Ambiguous Reflections of Time

> While the past entertains, ennobles, and expands quite readily, it enlightens only with delicate coaxing.
>
> B. FISCHHOFF

This commentary has benefited from the useful suggestions of Eric Abrahamson, Joel Baum, Jacques Delacroix, Charles Fombrun, Theresa Lant, Jim March, and John Mezias.

Those who analyze time series are especially likely to see what their methods dictate. Most time series have high autocorrelations, and autocorrelations foster spurious relations between series.

Ames and Reiter (1961) studied autocorrelations in actual socioeconomic series. They plucked one hundred series at random from *Historical Statistics for the United States*. Each series spanned the twenty-five years from 1929 to 1953.

Five sixths of the series had autocorrelations above .8 for a one-year lag, and the mean autocorrelation was .837 for a one-year lag. Even after Ames and Reiter removed linear trends from the series, the mean autocorrelation was .675 for a one-year lag.

Social scientists often calculate correlations between series—for example, the correlation between the number of operating steel mills and gross national product. But, high autocorrelations produce high correlations between series that have nothing to do with causal links between those series.

This explains why social scientists find it easy to discover high correlations between series even when series have no direct causal relations (Lovell, 1983; Peach and Webb, 1983). Ames and Reiter correlated randomly selected series. They found a mean (absolute value) correlation of .571 between two series. For 46 percent of the pairs, there existed a time lag of zero to five years that made the two series correlate at least .7.

Ames and Reiter simulated the widespread practice of searching for highly correlated pairs of series. They picked a target series at random and then compared this series with other series that they also picked randomly. On average, they needed only three trials to draw a second series that appeared to "explain" at least half the variance in a target series. Even after they corrected series for linear trends, they needed only five trials on average to draw a series that seemed to "explain" at least half the variance in a target series.

Ecologists often decompose series conceptually into repeated trials and then try to draw inferences about the processes that generate these series. However, series provide very treacherous grounds for such inferences.

A series that depends causally on its own past values amplifies and perpetuates random disturbances. The process that generates a self-dependent series does not forget random disturbances instantly. Instead, it reacts to random disturbances when generating future outcomes. Replications of such a process produce very different series that diverge erratically from their expected values. An implication is that observed series provide poor evidence about the processes that generated them. A single series or a few replications are very likely to suggest incorrect inferences (Pant and Starbuck, 1990). Gould (1989, 1991) has repeatedly argued that biologists have drawn erroneous inferences about evolution on the basis of improbable, nonrecurring, no-replicatable events.

Wold (1965) used computer simulations to show how far self-dependent series diverge from their expected values. He assumed three very simple models, generated series, and then tried to infer which model had generated the series. When he looked at a single instance of a series, inference was hopeless. He could, however, make fairly accurate estimates of central tendencies when he made 200 replications with 100 events in each series—20,000 observations.

Wold used very simple one-variable equations to generate series. Such simple processes are uncommon in socioeconomic analyses. To simulate the kinds of statistical inferences that social scientists usually try to draw from longitudinal data, I have extended Wold's work by generating autocorrelated series with the properties noted by Ames and Reiter: Each series included a linear time trend and was second-order autocorrelated with an autocorrelation coefficient above .6. Each series included 25 events, a length typical of published studies. Each analysis involved three series: Series Y depended causally on series X, but series W was causally independent of both X and Y.

Using accepted procedures for time series, I then estimated the coefficients of an equation that erroneously hypothesized that Y depended upon both X and W.

- The coefficient estimates *nearly always* showed a statistically significant correlation between Y and W—a reminder of the often ignored injunction that correlation does not equal causation.

- The modal coefficient estimates were reasonably accurate; most of the errors fell between 10 and 50 percent. But estimates of absolutely small coefficients had errors as high as 4 million percent.

Because Wold had shown that replications led to better estimates of central tendencies, I expected replications to allow better estimates of the coefficients. I wanted to find out how many replications one might need to distinguish causal dependence from independence with a misspecified model. To my surprise, replications proved harmful almost as often as helpful: Nearly 40 percent of the time, the very first series analyzed produced more-accurate-than-average coefficient estimates, and so replications made the average errors worse. Thus, replication often fostered confidence in the coefficient estimates without increasing the estimates' average accuracy.

These challenges imply that analysts of series should consider alternative theories and draw conservative inferences. Carroll and Delacroix set an excellent example in this respect when they analyzed newspapers' mortality. They considered several alternative explanations for the observed death rates—ecological, economic, political, and idiosyncratic. Then they (1982:191) warned readers: "On the one hand, our analysis clearly demonstrates that organizational mortality rates vary across a wide range of environmental dimensions, including industry age, economic developments, and political turbulence. On the other hand, as in many historical explorations, data often did not allow us to choose among alternative explanations of these findings."

Nearly all socioeconomic series look like artificial series that have three properties (Pant and Starbuck, 1990): First, each new value of a series is a weighted average of the series' previous value and an increment. Second, some series give past values little weight, but most series give past values much weight. Third, the increments are utterly random. Because autocorrelation makes it easy to discover high correlations between such series, it is especially important to use tough criteria for concluding that relations exist.

Then, should not every analysis take as a benchmark the hypothesis that observed events arise primarily from inertia and random perturbation? Should not scientists discard hypotheses that fit the data no better than this naïve one?

In this regard, *Administrative Science Quarterly* deserves praise for publishing an article in which Levinthal (1991a) showed that a type of random walk can generate data in which new organizations have higher failure rates than old ones. Such a random walk does not explain all aspects of organizational survival, but it makes a parsimonious benchmark. When espousing more complex theories, organizational scientists should prove them superior to a naïve model such as Levinthal's.

Warped Reflections in Print

Francis Bacon, Platt (1964), and Popper (1959) have argued persuasively that science makes progress mainly by showing that some hypotheses are incorrect, not by showing that other hypotheses might be correct. Observations may be consistent with many, many hypotheses, only a few of which have been stated. Showing a specific hypothesis to be consistent with the observations only indicates that it is one of the many plausible hypotheses. This should do little to reduce ambiguity, but it is likely to create a premature belief that the tested hypothesis is the best hypothesis.

More dependable progress comes from eliminating poor hypotheses than from sustaining plausible ones. For scientists, it is better to rule out what is not true than to find support for what might be true.

Translated to the domain of conventional statistical tests, this reasoning implies that rejecting a null hypothesis is a weak contribution. Indeed, rejecting a null hypothesis is often trivial, especially in studies with many observations (Webster and Starbuck, 1988). Further, in the social and economic sciences, theories are often so vague and open to so many interpretations that it may be impossible to identify implications of a rejected null hypothesis. A stronger contribution comes from *failing* to reject a null hypothesis insofar as this rules out some hypotheses.

Of course, in the social and economic sciences, journals show bias in the opposite direction. Journals regularly refuse to print studies that fail to reject null hypotheses, and there is reason to believe many published articles reject null hypotheses that are true (Blaug, 1980; Greenwald, 1975). The only effective way to expose such errors is by failing to replicate prior findings, but journals also decline to publish replications.

Even worse, editors and reviewers regularly urge authors to misrepresent their actual research processes by inventing "hypotheses" after-the-fact, and to portray these "hypotheses" falsely as having been invented beforehand. There is, of course, nothing wrong with inventing hypotheses a posteriori. There would be no point in conducting research if every scientist could formulate all possible true hypotheses a priori. What is wrong is the falsehood. For others to evaluate their work properly, scientists must speak honestly.

It is as if journals were striving to impede scientific progress.

I know a man who has made two studies that failed to reject null hypotheses. In both studies, he devoted much effort to formulating a priori theories about the phenomena. In the second case, this man revised his two a priori theories to accommodate critiques by many colleagues, so the stated hypotheses had rather general endorsement. In both studies, he felt strong commitments to his a priori theories, he tried very hard to confirm them, and he ended up rejecting them only after months of reanalysis.

In the first case, he also made reanalyses to "test" a posteriori hypotheses that journal reviewers proposed: The reviewers advised him to portray these hypotheses falsely as having been formulated a priori, and they told him to portray the null hypothesis falsely as an alternative a priori hypothesis.

Because his first study had met such resistance, he did not even attempt to describe the second study forthrightly as a test of two alternative theories against a null hypothesis: Instead, convinced that journals do not want honest reports, he wrote his report as if he had entertained three alternative theories from the outset.

The man has so far not succeeded in publishing either study, although one prominent journal asked for three sets of revisions before finally rejecting the manuscript. Reviewers have complained that the studies failed to reject the null hypotheses, not because the alternative hypotheses are wrong, but because the basic data are too noisy, because the researcher used poor measures, or because the stated hypotheses poorly represent valid general theories.

These complaints are not credible, however. In the first case, the researcher reprocessed the raw data several times, both to improve the accuracy of measures and to meet the objections of reviewers. He also tested, but did not confirm, hypotheses that the reviewers themselves had proposed. In the second case, before gathering data, the researcher had sought extensive input from colleagues so as to make his hypotheses as defensible as possible. Thus, the reviewers seem to be giving methodological reasons for rejecting manuscripts that contradict their substantive beliefs (Mahoney, 1977).

In both studies, after-the-fact reflection suggests that the null hypotheses make very significant statements about the phenomena. That is, after one accepts (albeit reluctantly) the idea that the null hypotheses describe the phenomena well, one sees the phenomena quite differently than past research has done, and one sees opportunities for innovative research in the future. Thus, the reviewers have rejected innovative works that have profound implications.

Willy-Nilly Moves

There are many reasons to expect organizations' behaviors to appear somewhat random. Hannan and Freeman (1984:150) remarked that organizational changes may be "random with respect to future value." Changes may also look random with respect to their nature. This section surveys reasons for this apparent randomness and thus reasons why null or naïve hypotheses often fit data well.

The Red Queen's Hypothesis

> Ultimately, evolutionary success for each competitor comes from acquiring tricks, skills, and strategies to evolve faster and more effectively than the competition.
>
> J. H. CAMPBELL

An organization has advantages only in comparison to other organizations. Communication and imitation destroy advantages. When an innovative property spreads throughout a population of organizations, none of the individual organizations has gained an advantage over the others, and no organization has a higher probability of survival. In fact, making organizations more alike would likely lower their survival probabilities by intensifying competition. Similarly, competitors' responses to innovation destroy advantages. When one type of organization adopts an innovative property, competing types adapt to this property so as to neutralize its advantages.

Van Valen (1973) labeled this aspect of biological evolution the Red Queen's hypothesis. In Lewis Carroll's *Alice Through the Looking Glass*, the Red Queen tells Alice that she should not expect to have gone anywhere even through she was running just as fast as she could. In Looking Glass Land, said the Red Queen, "you see, it takes all the running *you* can do, to keep in the same place. If you want to get somewhere else, you must run at least twice as fast as that!"

The analogy of Looking Glass Land applies even more aptly to organizations than to biology: The more visible a property's advantages, the more organizations that can perceive these advantages and the stronger their motivations to adopt similar properties. For instance, Mansfield (1963) found that more profitable innovations are adopted more quickly by more firms. Therefore, the clearer the advantages of an innovative property, the more rapidly it will attract imitators and the more rapidly it will cease offering advantages. The properties most likely to confer persistent advantages are those having highly debatable advantages. When choosing properties to imitate, organizations face trade-offs of risk versus expected return that resemble the trade-offs with financial investments.

Organizations may react to the Red Queen's hypothesis either by imitating other organizations or by trying to innovate. Both reactions make the behavior and performance differences among organizations look more random.

As Carroll (1984:72) observed: "Recent ecological theory . . . emphasizes the multilineal probabilistic nature of evolution. Thinking has shifted so much in this direction that, as with bioecology, evolution is no longer equated with progress, but simply with change over time." However, ecologists have been trying to achieve this reorientation by treating survival-neutral and survival-degrading changes as random errors (Carroll, 1984:72–73). Since survival-neutral and survival-degrading changes may themselves be systematic, ecologists' current approach confounds these changes with survival-enhancing ones.

It may prove helpful to classify changes as either systemic, temporary, or random. Besides adjusting to systematic, long-term opportunities and threats, organizations adapt to temporary fads, transient jolts, and accidental disturbances. For instance, Delacroix and Swaminathan (1991) concluded that nearly all organizational changes in the California wine industry are cosmetic, pointless, or speculative.

Organizations' members and environmental evaluators may be unable to distinguish fads and fashions from significant ideas and innovations: These, too, compete for adherents, and they originate and spread through much the same processes. Just as clothing buyers choose different colors and styles from year to year, so may organizations try new ideas or alter properties for the sake of change, and so may the evaluators of organizations pursue fleeting opportunities or espouse new myths about organizational effectiveness (Abrahamson, 1990).

Pursuing Illusory Opportunities

From the viewpoint of a single organization, the Red Queen's Hypothesis turns opportunities into transient illusions. The organization perceives an opportunity and moves to exploit it. If only one organization were to act alone, the opportunity might be real. However, communication and imitation convert the opportunity into an illusion, and the organizations that try to exploit the opportunity end up no better off—perhaps worse off.

Two theories of firm growth have emphasized illusory opportunities. Andrews (1949) pointed out that firms may expand to obtain short-run cost savings that never become real. From a short-run perspective, managers see some costs as "fixed," meaning that they will not increase if the amount of output goes up incrementally. These fixed costs seem to create opportunities to produce somewhat more output without incurring proportional costs, so managers expect the average cost per unit to decrease as output rises. Yet over the long run, all costs do vary with output. The long-run cost per unit might stay constant or increase as output does up. Thus, managers might endlessly expand output because they expect growth to decrease average cost, while growth is actually yielding the opposite result.

Penrose (1959:2) similarly contrasted short-run and long-run perspectives, but she argued, "There may be advantages in *moving* from one position to another quite apart from the advantages of *being* in a different position." She (1959:103) wrote: "The growth of firms may be consistent with the most efficient use of society's resources; the result of past growth—the size attained at any time—may have no corresponding advantages. Each successive step in its growth may be profitable to the firm and, if otherwise under-utilized resources are used, advantageous to society. But once any expansion is completed, the original justification for the expansion may fade into insignificance as new opportunities for growth develop and are acted upon."

Since organizations cannot foretell the distant future, a change that promises benefits today often proves damaging the day after tomorrow. Thus, a change today will likely stimulate still other changes to correct its unexpected results, but these may in turn produce more unexpected results (Pant and Starbuck, 1980).

Solving Unsolvable Problems

One interesting and prevalent type of change is an effort to solve an unsolvable problem. Unsolvable problems exist because societies espouse values that are mutually inconsistent. Since organizations embody societal values, they are trying perpetually to satisfy inconsistent demands. Organizational properties that uphold some values conflict with properties that uphold contrary values.

Hierarchical dominance affords an example. Western societies advocate democracy and equality, but they also advocate hierarchical control, unity, and efficiency. People in these societies expect organizations to adopt hierarchical structures, and to use these structures to coordinate their actions and to eliminate waste. But of course, hierarchical control is undemocratic and unequal. Everyone understands why subordinates do not do as their superiors dictate, and everyone also understands why organizations have to eliminate this inefficient disunity.

So, organizations try to solve the "problem" of resistance to hierarchical control—by making hierarchical control less visible or by aligning subordinates' goals with superiors' goals. In the late 1940s, the solution was for managers to manage "democratically." But after a while, most subordinates inferred that their superiors' democracy was insincere, and this solution failed. In the early 1950s, the solution was for managers to exhibit "consideration" while nevertheless controlling task activities. But after a while, most subordinates inferred that their superiors' consideration was insincere, and this solution failed. In the late 1950s, the solution was Management-by-Objectives, in which superiors and subordinates were to meet periodically and to formulate mutually agreed goals for the subordinates. But after a while, most subordinates inferred that their superiors were using these meetings to dictate goals, and this solution failed. In the 1960s, the solution was "participative management," in which workers' representatives were to participate in managerial boards that made diverse decisions about methods, investments, staffing, strategies, and so on. But after a while, most workers inferred (a) that managers were exerting great influence upon these boards' decisions and (b) that the worker's representatives were benefiting personally from their memberships in these boards, and this solution failed. In the early 1980s, the solution was "organizational culture," by which organizations were to produce unity of goals and methods. But after a while, most managers learned that general solidarity did not translate into operational goals and methods, and employees resisted homogenization, and this solution failed. In the late 1980s, the solution became "quality circles," which broadened into "total quality management." But after a while . . .

Thus, one fad has followed another. From a short-run perspective, many organizations adopted very similar "solutions" and from a long-run perspective, many organizations have adopted loosely similar "solutions." Although the various solutions have affected superior-subordinate relations, these effects have been negative as often as positive, and the fundamental "problem" persists. Long-run changes in the fundamental problem and in the various solutions seem to have arisen from economics, education, social structure, and technologies rather than from intraorganizational practices. So the fads' effects look weak and largely random. From a very-long-run perspective, organizations seem to have tried a series of unsuccessful practices.

Unsolvable problems also exist because organizations' overall goals encompass inconsistent subgoals: To achieve more general goals, organizations must pursue subgoals that call for conflicting actions.

An example is profit maximization. Firms try both to obtain as much revenue as possible and to keep costs as low as possible. To maximize revenues, the marketing personnel want their firms to produce customized products that are just what the customers want and to have these available whenever the customers want them. To minimize costs, the production personnel want to minimize inventories and machine downtime, so they want to deliver the same product to every customer, or at least to produce different products in optimal quantities on efficient schedules. One outcome is that the marketing personnel and the production personnel often disagree about what to do and when to do it. Conflicts are unpleasant, however, so firms attempt "conflict resolution." Conflict resolution can at best improve short-run symptoms because these conflicts are intrinsic to profit maximization.

Such intraorganizational conflicts tend to generate solutions over time that vary around long-run equilibria. Deviations from equilibrium occur as first one side and then the other scores a point. Should one side score repeatedly, pushing the joint solution well off center, higher management has to intervene and rebalance power. Although there is a need for long-run balance, the short-run moves around that balance point may look erratic and make no sense from a long-run perspective. Thus, a random walk might describe the short-run moves well. A random walk would be even more likely to describe the moves well if these were aggregated across several firms: Even if all the firms were dealing with the same technologies and selling in the same market, the intraorganizational conflicts in different firms would generate different solutions at each time.

Multiple Forces

A random walk may also accurately and efficiently describe moves produced by the interactions of multiple forces that act independently. Such moves resemble Brownian motion—the erratic moves of a dust particle in the air, which one can see in a sunbeam. Molecules of air collide with a dust particle constantly and from all sides: During an instant, unequal numbers of molecules hit the particle from different directions, and the dust particle responds by moving in one direction or another. The dust particle's moves are not literally random. One might, in principle, explain them with a complex model that accounts for a multitude of air molecules. It is more practical, however, to describe the moves as a random walk about a slowly drifting equilibrium. Randomness serves as a concise summary of complexity.

To generate moves that generally resemble a random walk, there need not be multitude forces. Fewer forces have the effect of many forces if each force varies in intensity from time to time. Moves in one dimension—say, higher or lower—might look random if just a few forces acted in each direction. Causal processes of this sort pervade the behavioral and social sciences.

Self-Dependent Iteration

Self-dependent, inertial causal processes propagate random perturbations and may even amplify them. A random event does not merely affect a single period, it becomes part of the foundation for future periods. The effects of random perturbations may accumulate over time until they dominate the behavior of a causal process. Thus, one random fleeting perturbation may instigate a persistent series of consequences that fabricate the appearance of a systematic pattern over a fairly long period. The more inertial a process the longer each random perturbation can affect its actions, and Ames and Reiter found that socieconomic series have a mean autocorrelation of .837.

Iterative processes can also produce the appearance of randomness even though no random events affect them. One property that can yield this result is nonlinear feedback. For example, computers use completely deterministic, simple calculations to generate pseudo-random numbers. These numbers are not actually random: each repetition of a calculation produces precisely the same pseudo-random numbers. Yet these imposters are what we use to create the appearance of randomness. Indeed, in nature, nonlinear deterministic processes may generate many of the phenomena that appear to be stochastic (Mandelbrot, 1983).

Action Generators

Many organizational actions do not reflect current, identified needs or goals. Although some actions arise from problem solving, others arise from action generating. Indeed, action generating is probably much more prevalent than problem solving. In their action generating mode, organizations follow programs thoughtlessly. The programs may be triggered by calendars, clocks, job assignments, or unimportant information (Starbuck, 1983).

For instance, strategic planning departments gather and distribute information, make forecasts, hold meetings, set goals, and discuss alternatives whether or not they face specific strategic problems, whether or not their current strategies seem to be succeeding or failing, whether or not strategic planning is likely to prove useful to them. They probably do these things according to an annual calendar that is independent of the timing or appearance of strategic issues. Although one might expect to observe relations between the efforts devoted to strategic planning and the contexts in which it occurs, such relations in the short run might be quite independent of such relations over the long run. That is, in the long run, firms might discard planning practices that appear useless or harmful, so practices might reflect properties of industries, markets, or technologies. Yet such selection would be quite noisy because of the long delays between strategic actions and their results, and because of the loose connections between planning practices and strategic actions. In the short run, firms might try ideas experimentally, so their practices would be influenced by interpersonal networks, consultants, or the press. Thus, short-run changes in planning practices ought to have insignificant long-run effects and to be independent of their long-run value.

Organizations regularly make changes that look partially random. In some cases, it is short-run changes that look random; in other instances, systematic short-run patterns seem to produce random long-run changes. In some cases, performance outcomes seem to be random; in other instances, it is behaviors that look random.

Because organizations' environments react in ways that counteract any gains one organization makes at the expense of others, organizations' behaviors ought to appear random when interpreted in frameworks that emphasize competitive advantages. Because organizations cannot forecast accurately far into the future, their behaviors ought to appear random when interpreted in frameworks that emphasize long-run goals. Because problem analyses assume illusory gains and because some problems have no solutions, organizations repeatedly take actions that have no long-run results. Because actions reflect multiple independent forces, short-run actions may look erratic and inexplicable. Because causal processes feed back into themselves, random events have long-lasting effects and nonrandom processes may produce the appearance of randomness. Because some actions arise from action generators, they have no bases in immediate problems or goals. Because organizations attend to different issues, see different environments, and act at different times, aggregating across several organizations makes behaviors look more random, at least when interpreted in frameworks that emphasize short-run causes or effects.

Thus, organizational scientists should take seriously null or naïve hypotheses that describe behaviors as having large random components. Such hypotheses do not imply that organizations see their actions as random. Hypotheses that emphasize randomness may be parsimonious even when complete, deterministic descriptions would be possible. If simple hypotheses can describe behaviors rather accurately, one must then decide whether the gains from complex, causal descriptions are worthwhile.

Scientists should also take seriously the possibility that complex and seemingly causal relations occur by accident. Because so few empirical "findings" are replicated successfully, scientists need to remain aware of the high probability that observed patterns result from idiosyncratic data. Null or naïve hypotheses that describe behaviors as having large random components provide insurance against idiosyncratic data because they make weak assumptions about statistical properties such as symmetry, independence, and uncorrelated residuals.

Why Play Croquet When You Can't Lose?

Very often social scientists "test" their theories against ritualistic null hypotheses (a) that the scientists can always reject by collecting sufficient data and (b) that the scientists would not believe no matter what data they collected and analyzed. As proofs of knowledge, such statistical significance tests look ridiculous. Such tests are not merely silly, however, because they turn research into a noise generator that fills journals, textbooks, and courses with substantively meaningless "findings."

Scientists can be certain of rejecting any point null hypothesis that defines an infinitesimal point on a continuum. The hypotheses that two sample means are exactly equal is a point hypothesis. Other examples include these null hypotheses:

correlation $= 0$
frequency $= 0$
rate $= 0$
regression coefficient $= 0$
variance$_1 =$ variance$_2$

All two-tailed hypotheses about continuous variables are tested against point null hypotheses.

The key property of a point hypothesis is that the probability of rejecting it goes to 1 as observations accumulate. If a point hypothesis has not already been rejected, the scientist has only to make more observations (or to make more simulation runs). Thus, passing a "hypothesis test" against such a null hypothesis tells little about the alternative hypothesis, but much about either the scientist's ability to formulate meaningful statements or the scientist's perseverance and effort.

Also, point null hypotheses usually look implausible if one treats them as genuine descriptions of phenomena (Gilpin and Diamond, 1984). For instance, some contingency theorists have assumed that randomly different organizational structures are the only alternative to structures that vary with environmental uncertainty. Do these contingency theorists really believe that *no* other factors—such as technology—influence organizational structures nonrandomly?

Ritualistic hypothesis tests resemble the croquet game in Wonderland: The Queen of Hearts, said Alice "is so extremely likely to win that it is hardly worthwhile finishing the game." If a theory can only win a ritualistic competition, it would be better to leave it unpublished.

A Proposal from Bioecology

Bioecologists have been debating whether to replace null hypotheses. Connor and Simberloff (1983, 1986) argued that interactions within ecological communities make statistical tests based upon simple null hypotheses too unrealistic. They proposed that bioecologists replace null hypotheses with "null models." Connor and Simberloff (1986:160) defined, "A null model is an attempt to generate the distribution of values for the variable of interest in the absence of a putative causal process." That is, one uses a "null model" to generate a statistical distribution, and then one asks whether the observed data have high or low probabilities according to this distribution.

For example, different islands in the Galapagos hold different numbers of species of land birds: These numbers might reflect competition among species, physical differences among the island, or vegetation differences. Using a "null model" that ignored competition among species, Connor and Simberloff (1983) estimated the statistical distributions of the numbers of species pairs on islands in the Galapagos: Their estimates assumed that each island held the number of species observed on it and that each species inhabited as many islands as observed, but that species were otherwise distributed randomly and independently. All the observed numbers of species pairs fell within two standard deviations of the means in the distributions implied by this null model, and most observations were close to the expected values. So, Connor and Simberloff inferred that competition among species had little effect on the numbers of species of Galapagos land birds.

Not suprisingly, some bioecologists have voiced strong reservations about null models (Harvey et al., 1983). Among several points of contention, Gilpin and Diamond (1984) argued (a) that null models are not truly null because they make implicit assumptions and (b) that they are difficult to reject because fitting coefficients to data removes randomness. Gilpin and Diamond do have a point, in that describing such models as "null" might create false expectations. Connor and Simberloff's null model, for instance, took as premises the observed numbers of species on each island and of islands inhabited by each species. These numbers allow for some physical and vegetation differences among the islands, and Gilpin and Diamond noted that these numbers might reflect competition among species as well. On the other hand, Connor and Simberloff (1986:161) pointed out that scientists can choose null models that virtually guarantee their own rejection: "For this null model, and for null models in general, if one is unwilling to make assumptions to account for structure in the data that can reasonably be attributed to causal processes not under investigation, then posing and rejecting null hypotheses will be trivially easy and uninteresting."

Computers play a key role in this debate. The distributions computed by Connor and Simberloff would have required superhuman effort before 1950. One of the original reasons for using point null hypotheses was algebraic feasibility. Because statisticians had to manipulate statistical distributions algebraically, they built analytic rationales around algebraically amenable distributions. Computers, however, give scientists means to generate statistical distributions that represent more complicated assumptions. It is no longer necessary to use the distributions published in textbooks.

Rather than compare the data with two-standard-deviation confidence limits, as Connor and Simberloff did, however, it is more sensible to compute a likelihood ratio of the kind described below. Although Connor and Simberloff's approach has the advantage of looking like a traditional hypothesis test, it entails the parallel disadvantage of treating truth as a binary variable. A model is either true or false. Likelihood ratios allow one to treat truth as a continuous variable—one model may be more true than another, and yet both of the compared models may be unlikely.

Naïve Hypotheses

An alternative and related proposal derives from forecasting. Because they regularly confront autocorrelated time series, forecasting researchers usually disdain null hypotheses and instead compare their forecasts with "naïve forecasts."

For example, a naïve person might advance either of two hypotheses about a series. One naïve hypothesis—the no-change hypothesis—says that the next value will be the same as the current value. This hypothesis makes no specific assertions about the causal processes that generate the series. It merely expresses the idea that most causal processes are inertial: What happens tomorrow will resemble what is happening today. The second naïve hypothesis—the linear-trend hypothesis—says the trend observed since yesterday will continue until tomorrow: The next value will differ from the current value by the same amount that the current value differs from the previous value. This hypothesis expresses the idea that most causal processes are inertial in trend as well as in state.

Neither of these naïve hypotheses says anything profound. Either could come from a young child who has no understanding of the causal processes that generate a series. So, one should expect more accurate predictions from a complicated forecasting technique—or from a scientific theory that supposedly does say something profound.

Comparing focal hypotheses with naïve hypotheses instead of null hypotheses gives the comparisons more credibility and more substantive significance. In this volume, Ginsberg and Baum (Chapter 7) compare their theory to the foregoing naïve hypotheses. Had they stopped after merely testing the null hypotheses that acquisition rates do not vary with diverse variables, we would know only that their theory is better than nothing. However, they also show that their theory fits the data distinctly better than naïve statements about inertia. I find this impressive.

Note that Ginsberg and Baum might have made an even more useful contribution if it had turned out that their theory was *no* more accurate than the naïve models. Such an outcome would have shown that a simple explanation—inertia—works very well. As it happens, of course, this is not the case. Inertia is not a powerful explanation for these data. But that is the main inference we ought to draw from the superiority of Ginsberg and Baum's theory. We should not infer that their theory is correct. Not only may their theory not be correct in detail, it may not even take account of the most important causal factors. There may be several other explanations that would be even more effective.

Also note that some naïve hypotheses, including the two just discussed, are point hypotheses. If one uses them as null hypotheses, conventional statistical tests too will inevitably disconfirm them. So instead one calculates the likelihood ratio (Jeffreys and Berger, 1992):

$$\frac{\text{Probability (Data if the focal hypotheses are true)}}{\text{Probability (Data if the naïve hypothesis is true)}}$$

If the focal hypotheses work better than the naïve hypothesis, the ratio will be substantially greater than one. One must then ask whether the ratio is large enough to justify the greater complexity associated with the focal hypotheses.

Such comparisons usually have more meaning if one states the likelihood ratios on a per-trial or per-period basis. For example,

$$\left[\frac{\text{Probability (Data if the focal hypotheses are true)}}{\text{Probability (Data if the naïve hypothesis is true)}}\right]^{1/n}$$

where n denotes the number of time periods.

Simple Competitors May Win in the Future

Ginsberg and Baum's comparisons with naïve hypotheses make their theory look impressive because improving on naïve hypotheses is difficult. Substantive theories often turn out to be no better than naïve hypotheses.

Ginsberg and Baum do not, however, test their theory with predictions. Naïve hypotheses generally look much better when used to make genuine predictions about the future than when used to rationalize the past (Pant and Starbuck, 1990; Starbuck 1983).

Since the 1950s, macroeconomists have invested enormous resources in trying to create complex, mathematical, statistically estimated theories that predict short-run phenomena well. The teams that developed these models included some of the world's most respected economists, and they spent hundreds of man-years. They used elegant statistical methods. They did not lack financial or computation resources, for the U.S. government has spent many millions of dollars for data gathering and research grants. Major industrial firms pay large sums for the predictions generated by these models. So, these models represent the very best in economic or social forecasting.

Elliott (1973) tested the predictive accuracies of four of the best-known macroeconomic models. Of course, all these models had been published originally with evidence of their predictive accuracies, but these demonstrations had involved postdicting the very data from which the models' coefficients had been estimated, and each model had been fitted against data from different periods. Elliott fitted all four models to data from the same period, then measured their accuracies in predicting subsequent events. Three models turned out to be as accurate as the no-change hypothesis. The simplest of the models, which was the most accurate, was as accurate as the linear-trend hypothesis.

The findings of Makridakis and colleagues (1979, 1982) resemble those of Elliott. They compared 24 statistical forecasting methods by forecasting 1,001 series. They found that no-change hypotheses beat others 38 to 64 percent of the time. Also, no-change hypotheses were less likely to make large errors than any other method. Yet, the most accurate forecasts came from exponential smoothing, which beat every other method at least 50 percent of the time. Exponential smoothing is a version of the linear-trend hypothesis; it assumes data include random noise and it filters this noise by averaging. The averaging usually gives more weight to newer data.

Metaphysico-Theologico-Cosmolo-Nigology

Research findings may tell more about analytic procedures than about the phenomena being studied. We need to state theories more meaningfully and to evaluate them more rigorously.

Series are central in studies of evolutionary dynamics, and we should use especially tough criteria to test theories about them. Observed series provide poor evidence about the processes that generated them, and they offer many opportunities for spurious or deceptive inferences. A self-dependent series does not forget random disturbances instantly; it reacts to random disturbances when generating future outcomes. Replications produce very different series that diverge erratically from their expected values.

Sustaining a null hypothesis is more useful than rejecting a null hypothesis. Rejecting a null hypothesis does little to reduce ambiguity, and it is often a trivial achievement. It does not prove the value of the alternative hypothesis. A stronger contribution comes from failing to reject a null hypothesis insofar as this rules out at least one ineffective alternative hypothesis. Yet, journals work in the opposite direction. They reject studies that do not reject null hypotheses, and they do not publish replications. Editors and reviewers urge authors to lie by portraying after-the-fact "hypotheses" as having been invented beforehand.

Null or naïve hypotheses often fit organizational data well because organizations make changes that have insignificant long-run effects. Organizations' behaviors should appear random with respect to competitive advantages because organizations' environments try to counteract the gains one organization makes at the expense of others. Organizations' behaviors should appear random with respect to long-run goals because organizations cannot forecast far into the future. Short-run actions may look erratic and inexplicable because actions reflect multiple independent forces. Random events may have long-lasting effects and nonrandom processes may produce apparent randomness because causal processes feed back into themselves. Organizations repeatedly take actions that have no long-run results because problem analyses seek illusory gains and because some problems have no solutions. Many actions have no bases in immediate problems or goals because they come from action generators. Aggregating across organizations makes behaviors look more random because organizations attend to different issues, see different environments, and act at different times.

Much too often social scientists "test" their theories against null hypotheses that the scientists can always reject by collecting enough data. Such tests turn research into a generator of substantively meaningless "findings."

Scientists who are willing to gather sufficient data can reject any null hypothesis that specifies an infinitesimal point on a continuum. The probability of rejecting a point hypothesis goes to 1 as the observations grow numerous. Also, most point null hypotheses look implausible if one treats them as genuine descriptions of phenomena.

One response to this situation is formulate "null models" that incorporate some simple assumptions about the data. One uses the null models to generate statistical distributions and compares the data with these distributions.

An alternative response is to compare focal hypotheses with naïve hypotheses. A naïve hypothesis represents one or two basic ideas of the sort that a naïve person might advance. Theories often turn out to be no better than naïve hypotheses—especially when both are used to predict future events. However, some naïve hypotheses are also point hypotheses. In such cases, rather than formulate the analysis as a significance test, scientists should use likelihood ratios to compare the alternative hypotheses.

Living in the Best of All Possible Worlds

We are trying too hard to show the superiority of complex causal theories, while too quickly rejecting simple null or naïve hypotheses that say behavior has large random components. We are, indeed, so eager to discern causality that we embrance a hollow statistical methodology, we spurn replication, and we refuse to publish articles that interpret events simply. Although social construction of reality is a pervasive phenomenon, it may not be a useful foundation for scientific research.

> Master Pangloss taught the metaphysico-theologico-cosmolo-nigology. He could prove to admiration that there is no effect without a cause; and, that in this best of all possible worlds, the Baron's castle was the most magnificent of all castles, and My Lady the best of all possible baronesses.
>
> It is demonstrable, said he, that things cannot be otherwise than they are; for as all things have been created to some end, they must necessarily be created for the best end. Observe, for instance, the nose is formed for spectacles, therefore we wear spectacles. The legs are visibly designed for stockings, accordingly we wear stockings. Stones were made to be hewn, and to construct castles, therefore My Lord has a magnificent castle; for the greatest baron in the province ought to be the best lodged. Swine were intended to be eaten, therefore we eat pork all the year round; and they, who assert that everything is right, do not express themselves correctly; they should say that everything is best.
>
> Candide listened attentively, and believed implicitly. . . . (Voltaire, chapter I, part I of *Candide; or the Optimist*)

IV

Population
Evolution

11

Minimalism, Mutualism, and Maturity: The Evolution of the American Trade Association Population in the 20th Century

HOWARD E. ALDRICH, CATHERINE R. ZIMMER, UDO H. STABER, AND JOHN J. BEGGS

American trade associations, as minimalist organizations, have grown into a mature population in an environment characterized by intrapopulation norms supporting mutualistic behavior, lack of significant interpopulation competition, and an institutional environment that was usually strongly supportive of capitalist structures. Research on two other evolving populations in the United States—state bar associations and national trade unions—illustrates two alternative fates that trade associations might have experienced. State bar associations, after decades of experimentation with alternatives, finally settled on an organizational form that gave them monopoly control over the admission of lawyers to the bar in all 50 states. The bar associations' stunning achievement was solidified because they successfully mobilized to win state support. Trade unions, by contrast, struggled to achieve legitimacy against a hostile business community and a state that was antagonistic or indifferent until the 1930s. Even after achieving national legal standing, trade unions (like trade associations) stood outside the formal structure of the state and (unlike trade associations) have gradually seen their gains eroded over the past three decades.

We bring together our research on the foundings, mergers, and transformations, and disbandings of American trade associations to tell the story of a population that escaped, at lease up to now, the unhappy fate of its companion population—trade unions—but that has never achieved the iron-clad legitimacy of another population with similar collective goals—state bar associations. As mimimalist organizations, these populations differ in some important respects from private, profit-oriented businesses that are the subject of most evolutionary analyses. As organizations with a political agenda, they also differ from many of the non-profit-oriented organizations that evolutionary researchers have studied.

Empirical research in population ecology has arrived at the point where much has been learned about the conditions driving change over time in founding and dissolution rates in particular organizational populations, considered one at a time.

Our tables and text were whipped into shape by Deborah Tilley.

The preliminary evidence suggests that fundamental processes, such as density-dependent dynamics, may be common to all kinds of populations. Such universal processes, however, are not sufficient to produce identical outcomes for different populations, or even similar populations, such as trade associations, trade unions, and state bar associations. Instead, investigators must examine the unique historical trajectory of each population to understand how and why it evolved.

After spelling out the features of trade associations as minimalist organizations, and outlining the pressures—unique to trade associations—which drive organizational and population change, we describe our study design, and then discuss the key factors affecting trade associations at the institutional/sociopolitical, interpopulation, and intrapopulation levels of analysis.

Minimalist Organizations: Logics of Membership and Influence

Trade associations are business interest organizations, and as *minimalist organizations* (Halliday, Powell, and Granfors, 1987) they can survive on very low overhead expenses and supportive services. In several important respects, they differ from

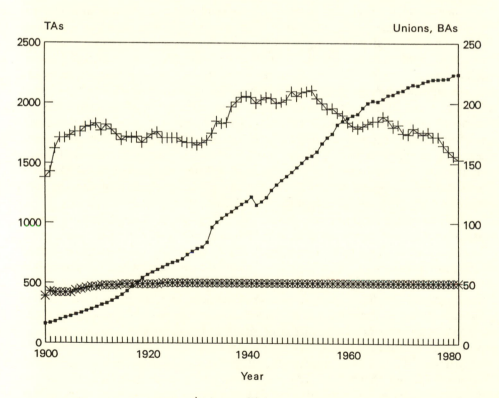

FIG. 11.1   Number of trade associations, unions, and state bar associations, 1900–1982

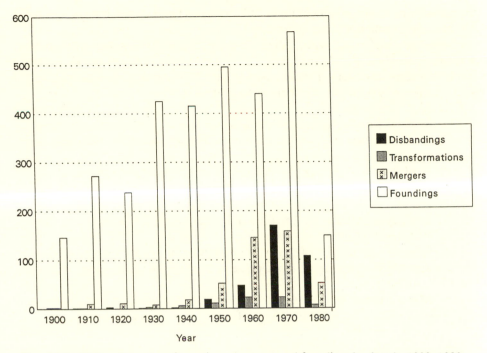

Fig. 11.2   Disbandings, transformations, mergers, and foundings by decade, 1900–1980

many previously studied populations of organizations: they are voluntary associations which depend upon the survival of their constituents for their own existence, they represent segments of the most politically privileged sector in capitalist countries, they strive for a monopoly position—or at least attempt to restrain competition—within their domain, and they restrict their prospects of changing domains by making substantial investments in their claimed domains. In these respects, they resemble most closely the state bar associations studied by Halliday, Powell, and Granfors (1987) and the trade unions studied by Hannan and Freeman (1987, 1988a).

However, there are significant differences in the growth patterns of the three populations over the course of this century, as shown in figure 11.1. State bar associations had achieved a monopoly position in all states by 1923, and thus their density did not subsequently change. None failed after 1923, and so no foundings occurred, either. Trade unions achieved their highest density in the 1950s, and then disbandings and mergers combined to reduce their number substantially. As a fraction of the private sector labor force, they now claim only about 12 percent of the work force and are continuing to decline. Trade associations have been very successful, as a population, although unlike their European counterparts, they have never achieved the monopoly position taken by state bar associations.

Growth in the density of the trade association population density appears smooth and unbroken in figure 11.1, but underlying the developing population were four distinctive types of events, as shown in figure 11.2: foundings, disbandings, mergers, and transformations. The changing balance between these events favored foundings, and so the population grew. Growth was rapid at first but slowed in the 1970s as the number of mergers increased.

The Industrial Fabrics Associations International (IFAI) is a typical association: it includes more than 2,500 members who make finished products out of industrial fabrics, ranging from custom-made awnings and boat covers to camping tents and soft luggage. Its services for members include the following:

1. Technical services (e.g., by working with organizations writing standards which affect the industry, such as the American Society for Testing and Material)
2. Marketing services (e.g., by defining, tracking and forecasting the end markets for industrial textiles, and offering such information via special reports)
3. Industry education (e.g., by funding a chair in industrial fabrics at the Philadelphia College of Textiles)
4. Government relations (e.g., by representing the industry's position to appropriate government agencies, departments, and congressional committees)
5. Manufacturing services (e.g., by improving plant productivity by allowing members access to the latest information on sewing equipment and attachments)

The Two Logics

In recruiting members and providing services, trade associaitons face two central pressures: a logic of membership and a logic of influence (Schmitter and Streeck, 1981). These logics affect associations' governance structures and the strategies their members pursue in deciding whether to form new associations and how to expand the membership of existing associations. How well association managers carry out their strategies affects whether the population will evolve via adaptation or the selective elimination of associations.

The *logic of membership* compels trade associations to minister to the needs of member firms, creating a governance structure to manage the diversity of members' interests. As interest associations, trade associations are subject to the collective rationality problem (Olson, 1965). They resemble labor unions in that their survival depends not only on how well they represent membership interests, but also on how effective they are in aggregating the parochial preferences of their members. Unlike bar associations, trade associations not only represent the political interests of members but also focus on stabilizing relations among members.

The more diversity within an association, the greater the problem of governance. At some point, adding another industrial sector may complicate governance so severely that potential members consider founding a new association instead of joining any existing one. Many trade associations straddle the boundaries of several industries, narrowly defined. For example, the American Butter Institute, founded in 1908, includes not only butter manufacturers but also packagers and distributors. The Metal Building Components Manufacturers' Association represents firms manufacturing and firms selling metal building components for architectural, commercial, industrial, and agricultural use.

The logic of membership suggests an inherent pressure within the association population toward the proliferation of associations over time. During their early years, many trade associations operate out of the offices of a member firm, with firms taking turns subsidizing much of the administrative overhead required to sustain the association. During their later years, successful associations often become part of a network of associations, connecting through shared memberships or joining forces on common issues.

The *logic of influence* compels association to manage competition with other associations and relations with the state to meet their substantive goals. For example, a primary focus of national trade associations is lobbying the federal government, responding to attempted regulation, or mitigating the negative effects of legislation. Dealing with external relations requires attention to domain definition and various forms of interorganizational relations. Thus, assocation foundings and growth are driven, in part, by state policies and economic events that might trigger firms' willingness to band together for collective action.

State policies can have general effects over the long term by reinforcing the political culture and structure within which organized business interests define their place, and specific public policies or political events in the short term can influence the necessity and feasibility of collective action. Economic events affect the distribution of resources and the terms on which they are available to businesses and thus shape the conditions for organized action. As the economy grows, more resources are available to potential association organizers, as new industries are created and existing ones expand.

Using hypotheses derived from considering the two logics—membership and influence—under which associations operate, we examined four vital events for the population: foundings, disbandings, mergers, and transformations. The evolutionary implications of focusing on minimalist organizations with low overhead costs and low rates of transforming or terminating events are several. First, foundings are probably less sensitive to intrapopulation conditions among minimalists than for other organizational forms. In some respects, minimalists resemble *r*-strategists in their ability to mobilize resources quickly, and so they are probably fairly sensitive to changing environmental conditions. Second, minimalists' survival is only loosely tied to changing environmental conditions, given a generally supportive normative environment. The size of their resource base and the effectiveness of their interorganizational networks are probably more important to their survival than external threats.

Study Design

Because we are mostly summarizing results from previous analyses, we forego the usual positivist hypothesis testing format and present our study design *before* discussing the key environmental variables that shaped the population's growth. Our discussion is informed by previous studies on other organizational populations—specifically trade unions and state bar associations—that have identified the key deter-

TABLE 11.1   Measurement of Variables

Dependent Variables

Foundings: A count of the number of trade associations founded in a given
                              year.

Disbandings: A dichotomous variable coded 1 (0.3%) in the year a disbanding
                              occurred, coded 0 otherwise.

Transformations: A dichotomous variable coded 1 (0.07%) in the year a
                              transformation occurred, coded 0 otherwise.

Mergers: A dichotomous variable coded 1 (0.4%) in the year a merger
                              occurred, coded 0 otherwise.

Independent Variables

$\ln(\text{GNP})(t-1)$:   The natural log of gross national product per capita from the
                              U.S. Statistical Yearbook, lagged 1 year. (mean = 7.84, sd =
                              0.40)

Republican administration: A dichotomous variable coded 1 for years when a Republican
                              president was in office (1901–12, 1921–32, 1953–60, 1969–
                              76, 1981–82), coded 0 otherwise.

World War I, II: Two dichotomous variables coded 1 for the years of World War
                              I (1916–18) and World War II (1941–45), coded 0 otherwise.

NIRA 1, 2, 3:   Three dichotomous variables coded 1 for the years the National
                              Industrial Recovery Act was in effect (1933–35), coded 0
                              otherwise.

Strikes: Annual number of strikes divided by 1,000 and lagged 1 year.
                              (mean = 3.87, sd = 1.33)

Union foundings: Annual number of unions founded, lagged 1 year. (mean =
                              3.68, sd = 3.51)

Union density: Annual number of active unions, lagged 1 year. (mean =
                              184.38, sd = 14.58)

Density, $N(t)$, $N^2(t)/1{,}000$: Number of trade associations active in a year and the quadratic
                              term divided by 1,000. (mean = 1,608.56, sd = 576.95)

Density at birth: Number of active trade associations in the year an association is
                              founded. (mean = 471.23, sd = 476.22)

ln (# competitors):   The number of trade associations active in the same year that
                              organize the same 4-digit SIC code as the focal association.
                              (mean = 1.10, sd = .90)

Predecessors: A function of the number of trade associations active prior to
                              the measurement year that organize the same 4-digit SIC
                              code, $1/(\text{age}+1)^2 \times \ln$ (number of predecessors + 1).
                              (mean = .05, sd = .25)

Previous disbandings $(t-1)$: Annual number of trade association disbandings, lagged 1 year.
                              (mean = 6.62, sd = 9.20)

Previous transformations   Annual number of trade association transformations, lagged 1
$(t-1)$:   year. (mean = 1.43, sd = 1.44)

Previous mergers $(t-1)$:   Annual number of trade association mergers, lagged 1 year.
                              (mean = 9.67, sd = 8.28)

Previous foundings $(t-1)$:   Annual number of trade association foundings, lagged 1 year.
                              (mean = 45.01, sd = 15.5)

Age, Age^2:   Number of years a trade association has been active and
                              quadratic term. (mean = 24.09, sd = 20.07)

(continued)

TABLE 11.1   (continued)

Vertical linkages:	A dichotomous variable coded 1 (30%) if the trade association includes firms from more than one link in the chain of production, coded 0 otherwise.
General-interest associations:	A dichotomous variable coded 1 (1.1%) if the trade association organizes across industry boundaries, coded 0 otherwise.
Division of an association:	A dichotomous variable coded 1 (2.8%) if the trade association was a division, institute, or committee under the umbrella of another association, coded 0 otherwise.
ln (# SIC codes):	The natural log of the number of 4-digit SIC codes organized by the association. (mean = 1.27, sd = 0.72)
Affiliated with an association:	A dichotomous variable coded 1 (7.0%) if the trade association had any one of the following interorganizational ties: being loosely affiliated in a coalition, working group, or other arm's-length relationship, or being a member of a peak association, coded 0 otherwise.
Peak association:	A dichotomous variable coded 1 (3.4%) if the trade association was a peak association, coded 0 otherwise.
Founding by merger, transformation, or spin-off:	Three dichotomous variables coded 1 if the trade association was founded by merger (3.1%), transformation (1.6%), or spin-off (0.7%), respectively, *de novo* foundings are coded 0 as the reference category.
ln (membership):	Natural log of the annual number of members of the trade association. (mean = 4.96, sd = 1.80)
ln (budget):	Natural log of the annual budget of the trade association. (mean = 4.82, sd = 1.58)
ln (staff):	Natural log of the annual staff of the trade association. (mean = 1.88, sd = 1.04)

minants of vital rates. To these key factors we add others, derived from the logics of membership and influence.

Descriptive information about associations was collected from directories of national trade associations, as well as various Department of Commerce publications, research monographs, business history journals, newsletters, and other historical sources. The details of information sources are discussed in Aldrich and Staber (1988) and Aldrich et al. (1990). Our sample is as close to a complete listing of all trade associations ever founded as is possible, given our sources. We focus on the period 1900–1982, as data on trade association life cycles improved considerably from the 19th to the 20th centuries. Table 11.1 shows all variables used in the analysis and their operationalizations (for details, see Aldrich et al., 1990).

We estimated models of trade association *foundings* using ordinary least squares regression. As a check on the reliability of our results, we also estimated our models using Poisson regression, as well as negative binomial regression. We found no substantively important differences among the results of the estimation techniques. Using several methods of detection (Gujarati, 1988), no significant autocorrelation was found, either.

We estimated models of trade association *disbandings, transformations,* and *mergers* using discrete time event history analysis (Allison, 1984). An association was coded as disbanding when it ceased active operations without merging, being acquired, or otherwise continuing to exist in any form. An association was coded as ending its existence in a merger if it joined with, or was acquired by, another association to form a new association. An association was coded as undergoing a transformation if it changed its goals or organizing domain in a fundamental way, such as enlarging substantially the industries that it represented.

The dependent quantity we modeled was the discrete-time hazard rate, $P(t)$, which is the probability that an event will occur at a particular time to a particular association, given that the association is at risk at the time. Because $P(t)$ is a probability, we chose the log-odds transformation, and used logistic regression to estimate the effects of explanatory variables. The event history data set has one record for each year an association was active, with associations added to the file when they were founded and dropped when they experienced a terminating event.

Trade Associations in an Evolving Environment

We focus on three sets of forces that, over the 20th century, affected trade association foundings, mergers and transformations, and disbandings: long-term growth and differentiation in the American economy, interpopulation competition between trade associations and trade unions, and intrapopulation dynamics. We consider organizational characteristics in a subsequent section. Figure 11.2 shows the distribution, by decade, of the four vital events analyzed in our chapter.

The disbanding rate of trade associations is extremely low, with the observed marginal odds of an association disbanding over the entire study period at about .0033 to 1. This rate is much lower than that for unions (Hannan and Freeman, 1988a) and is difficult to compare to the rate for bar associations because their rates are so contingent on historical period (Halliday, Powell, and Granfors, 1987:469). The observed marginal odds of an association's undergoing a transformation, per association year, are about .0007 to 1. The observed marginal odds of an association's completing a merger, per association year, are about .0044 to 1. The marginal odds are small primarily because most associations were active for a fairly long time, thus experiencing many years without a terminating event of any kind. We think this is a substantively important characteristic of minimalist organizations.

Long-Term Changes: Economic and Political Trends

Theories of niche width and competitive exclusion imply that the association population expanded with industrial growth. Increasing economic differentiation should have led to newly emerging industries creating their own trade associations, and trade associations to limiting themselves to industries where members are most easily recruited. On the assumption that resources (such as money, members, personnel, and legitimacy) for organizing interests are limited, resources can only be mobilized at the expense of other organizations, so association foundings will keep pace with the growth of new industries which may be organized.

As shown in table 11.2, economic growth had a major impact on foundings, as

TABLE 11.2   OLS Regressions of Trade
Association Foundings on Economic, Period,
Union, and Population Dynamics Variables
(1901–82)

Independent Variables	Unstandardized Coefficients
$\ln(\text{GNP})_{t-1}$	26.2124**
NIRA1	108.9935***
NIRA2	26.4617
NIRA3	14.0820
World War I	11.6771**
World War II	−0.0823
Republican Administration	2.1314
TA Density$_{t-1}$	0.0319**
TA Density$^2/1,000_{t-1}$	−0.0133**
$\ln(\text{TA Disbandings})_{t-1}$	3.8205
$\ln(\text{TA Disbandings})^2_{t-1}$	−1.0527
TA Foundings$_{t-1}$	−0.0018
TA Foundings$^2_{t-1}$	0.0000
Union Foundings$_{t-1}$	0.1838
Union Density$_{t-1}$	−0.0553
Strikes/1,000$_{t-1}$	2.8060**
Intercept	−178.2740**
R^2	.8627

*** $p < .01$.
** $p < .05$.

indicated by the strongly positive coefficient for ln(GNP), providing striking evidence that the carrying capacity of the associational environment was increasing over time. Forces of industrialization and market expansion led to an increasing division of labor in the production and distribution of goods and services, with consequences for the emergence of economic interests. Manufacturing and other sectors of economic activity not only produced a higher volume of differentiated outputs but created groups situated in different economic positions that became the carriers of different and potentially conflicting economic interests. Unfortunately, studies of labor union foundings (Hannan and Freeman, 1987) and state bar association foundings (Halliday, Powell, and Granfors, 1987) did not examine the influence of economic growth.

Economic growth increased association foundings, but it apparently also raised the odds of association's disbanding, as shown in table 11.3. We doubt that economic growth directly reduces the life chances of trade associations; rather it was associated with an unmeasured force that affected associations. One possibility is that technological obsolescence drove firms out of business, and thus ultimately doomed some industries' trade associations. Economic growth had no discernible effect on association transformations or mergers.

Trade associations in the United States developed under the skeptical eye of policymakers who were chiefly concerned with enforcing optimal competition. The

TABLE 11.3　Models of Trade Association Disbandings, Transformations, and Mergers

Independent Variable	1 Disbandings		2 Transformations		3 Mergers	
	Log-Odds	Odds	Log-Odds	Odds	Log-Odds	Odds
ln (GNP)$_{t-1}$	2.2684*	9.6639	0.2558	1.2915	0.0616	1.0635
Republican admin.	−0.3453**	0.7080	−0.1976	0.8207	0.1064	1.1123
World War I	1.0199	2.7729	a	a	−0.1773	0.8375
World War II	a	a	−0.0764	0.9264	−1.0386*	0.3539
NIRA1	2.4844**	11.9940	a	a	1.5031**	4.4956
NIRA2	a	a	a	a	a	a
NIRA3	a	a	2.2560**	9.5448	a	a
Strikes/1,000$_{t-1}$	1.0000	2.7183	0.4000	1.4918	−2.7100***	0.0665
Union foundings$_{t-1}$	0.0296	1.0300	−0.0041	0.9959	0.0090	1.0090
Union density$_{t-1}$	−0.0025	0.9975	0.0191	1.0193	0.0362***	1.0369
Density—$N(t)$	−0.0044*	0.9956	−0.0022	0.9978	−0.0041***	0.9959
$N^2(t)$/1,000	0.0020**	1.0020	0.0011	1.0011	0.0020***	1.0020
Density at birth	−0.0003**	0.9997	0.0006**	1.0006	0.0001	1.0001
log (# competitors)	−0.0884	0.9154	0.1568	1.1698	0.3027***	1.3535
Predecessors	−2.3958**	0.0911	2.3162	10.1371	−1.3377***	0.2624
Previous disbandings$_{t-1}$	−0.0215*	0.9787	—	—	—	—
Previous transformations$_{t-1}$	—	—	−0.0859	0.9177	—	—
Previous mergers$_{t-1}$	—	—	—	—	0.0229**	1.0232
Previous foundings$_{t-1}$	0.0179**	1.0181	−0.0142	0.9859	−0.0073	0.9928
Age	0.0159	1.0160	0.0190	1.0192	0.0040	1.0040
Age^2	−0.0004***	0.9996	−0.0002	0.9998	0.0000	1.0000
Vertical links	−0.6381***	0.5283	−0.7540**	0.4705	−0.5049***	0.6036
Gen. interest assn.	0.0187	1.0189	a	a	a	a
Division of an assn.	0.0775	1.0805	0.1629	1.1769	−0.0277	0.9727
ln (# SIC codes)	−0.1244	0.8830	−0.1575	0.8543	−0.0338	0.9668
Affiliated with an assn.	−0.6713**	0.5110	−1.1141	0.3282	0.0623	1.0643
Peak assn.	−0.6873*	0.5029	−1.0558	0.3479	−0.4896	0.6129
Founding by merger	−1.0139**	0.3628	0.0476	0.9535	0.1582	1.1714
Founding by transformation	−0.2222	0.8008	1.6279***	5.0932	−0.5904	0.5541
Founding by spin-off	−0.1645	0.8483	a	a	0.0784	1.0816
# Association-years	102,725		102,725		102,725	
# Events	311		76		450	
Model χ^2	475.99***		53.505***		274.96***	
Degrees of freedom	25		23		25	

NOTE: Coefficients are effects of independent variables on log-odds and odds that ending events will occur.—: These variables are not included in the model. a: These parameters could not be estimated because of zero cells.

*** p < .01.

** p < .05.

* p < .10.

absence of a corporatist mentality has been interrupted only three times, when the federal government sought the concerted cooperation of business in channeling productive and distributive efforts during times of national emergencies: World War I, World War II, and the NIRA. During World War I, trade associations became an instrument for mobilizing productive resources in each industry (Cuff, 1973). A similar effort was mounted during World War II. Carroll, Delacroix, and Goodstein (1990) argued that intensive state mobilization of societal resources during wartime has had a major impact on organizations and noted that state-induced organizational innovations were especially likely during long wars.

Our data indicate that the effects of government actions on vital rates in the trade association population were mixed. Increased governmental intervention in the economy apparently increased association foundings during World War I but not during World War II, net of other factors. Disbanding and transformation rates, already quite small during the decades of these wars, were not significantly changed during the war years. Merger rates, however, were reduced during both wars, although the effect was only statistically significant during World War II. These findings reinforce the view that government actions during the wartime years "froze" into place the preexisting economic structures (Marx, 1976).

During the National Recovery Administration period, from 1933 to 1935, an unprecedented increase in the formation of trade associations occurred (Himmelberg, 1976). By contrast, in their study of unions, Hannan and Freeman (1987) discovered that the founding rate for industrial unions did not change significantly with the passage of the Wagner Act in 1935, despite the extensive legal protection it gave to union organizing activities. The impact of the NIRA was most immediately felt in 1933, but the effects wore off quickly. The NIRA's failure to insulate new associations against disintegrative forces is clearly evident, as the disbanding rate jumped substantially in the first year that the act was in force. The NIRA also substantially raised the odds of associations merging in its first year, but not in subsequent years. Not until the third year after its passage did the NIRA have any effect on association transformations, substantially raising the odds of such events.

The Republican party has often been called the "party of business," and several Republican administrations in this century have certainly lived up to that label. We found an insignificant small increase in foundings of trade associations during Republican administrations, and a significant modest decrease in disbandings. During the years of Republican administrations, there was *no* significant change in association transformation or merger rates. Taken together, these results suggest that collective action by businesses has been only modestly affected by which political party is in power. Business has power in the United States not because of its ties to a particular political party, but because it is perceived as the fundamental force generating economic growth.

Our analysis of the long-term economic and institutional forces affecting the trade association population shows that economic growth was a key force, whereas political events played a more modest role. The dominant political event in association foundings was the NIRA, but its effect was short-lived and it did nothing to lengthen the lives of existing associations.

Interpopulation Competition: Organized Labor and Trade Associations

Organized labor is relatively weak in the United States, and thus business interest organizations have been relatively unconcerned with trade union activity in the 20th century. In contrast to the latter half of the 19th century, when numerous associations emerged to organize strike breaking, today very few national trade associations deal with any aspect of industrial relations. Even though we expected the population of unions to have little effect on the population of trade associations, we included data from Hannan and Freeman's (1987, 1988a) study because of interest in the potential relationship between these two important populations.

Neither union foundings nor union density had a significant effect on trade association foundings. When we disaggregated the union data into craft and industrial unions, we still found no effects. We also found no effects of union foundings or density on association disbandings. However, union density *did* have a slight effect on association merger rates, possibly reflecting association moves to create stronger associations to confront trade unions in the political arena. By contrast, union strike acitivity *did* affect foundings, although the effect was modest. This effect may reflect the extent to which business leaders treat strikes as a barometer of underlying political conditions and perhaps even as an early warning system. Strike activity had no significant effect on disbandings and had a substantively trivial effect in lowering association mergers.

Perhaps the lack of any direct effect of union foundings or density on trade association foundings is not surprising, given the highly decentralized nature of U.S. industrial relations. Unlike European unions, which are highly centralized and conduct nationwide bargaining with employers' associations, U.S. unions meet employers mostly at the local community level, except for a few heavy manufacturing industries and the public sector.

Intrapopulation Dynamics

The most consistent finding emerging from ecological studies of organizational foundings and disbandings has been that intrapopulation dynamics (density, foundings, disbandings) play a major role, although the precise effects may vary across organizational forms. Increasing density can increase the legitimacy of a population, and hence increase organizational foundings and decrease disbandings, in two ways (Ranger-Moore, Banaszak-Holl, and Hannan, 1991). First, increases in the size of a population can heighten the likelihood that people begin to take the form for granted. Early associations were managed by executives from member firms, on loan from their companies. As the management of associations evolved and became more professionalized, however, trade associations increasingly turned to people formally trained in management. The professionalization of public administration, and the evolution of college and university degree-granting programs, also generated a pool of people who were readily available to serve the now-taken-for-granted form. Second, new populations may benefit by gaining social approval or official endorsement, especially if they operate in politically charged environments, as trade associations do. The logic of influence implies that trade associations have a collective interest in mutualistic relations, as individual associations strive for recognition, or at least tolerance, by the public and the state.

The effect of density on *foundings* is curvilinear, with foundings initially *increasing* as density increases but then *decreasing* at higher densities, as shown in table 11.3 The pattern of density dependence we obtained is thus comparable to those of previous studies, but the substantive effects are smaller. Trade unions (Hannan and Freeman, 1987) experienced a much sharper rise in founding activity initially, and then a sharper drop in foundings, as density grew. Apparently, mutualistic effects within the trade association population were quite strong, even at high densities, so that the competitive effects which inhibited foundings in the union population were substantially muted.

Density has the expected quadratic effect also on association *disbanding*—the first-order term is negative and the second is positive, as shown in table 11.3. This finding is thus consistent with Hannan and Freeman's (1988) estimates for curvilinear density dependence in union mortality rates, although our effects are substantively smaller than theirs. Density's effect on the odds of *merger* almost exactly parallels its effect on the odds of disbanding, suggesting that, for many associations, merger may have been an alternative to disbanding. Weaker associations, facing the prospects of declining membership and lessened political power, may have chosen to merge with another association rather than disband. Density has no effect on the odds of transformation, suggesting that in addition to being much rarer events than disbandings or mergers, transformations also respond to different population dynamics.

We were particularly interested in the effects of direct competitors and predecessors on associations, especially in niches where the predecessors are still active and are thus potential competitors. The minimalist argument implies that direct competition between associations is minimized by norms of mutual tolerance or even support, unlike a more resource-driven ecological model, which implies that the negative effects of competition should raise disbandings. Because of population norms supporting mutualistic behavior, we expected that the level of direct competition between trade associations organizing firms in the same industry would be minimal, as Halliday, Powell, and Granfors (1987:457) argued for state bar associations. Staber (1982) found evidence for such norms during intensive interviews with the heads of 71 trade associations in New York and Washington. Association officers explicitly discounted the possibility of overt competition with other associations in the same industry, arguing instead that "mutual accommodation" was more likely.

For disbandings, the coefficient for the log of the number of competitors in table 11.3 is extremely small and statistically insignificant. Competitors also have no effect on the odds of an association's undergoing a transformation. In contrast to our results for disbandings, we found that the number of associations sharing the same 4-digit SIC domain increased the odds of mergers. Weaker associations, facing the prospect of declining membership and lessened political power, may turn themselves over to other associations in their domain, rather than disband.

Our results regarding the impact of predecessor associations *strongly* confirmed our expectations and indicate that the facilitative effects of predecessor associations on survival dissipate about eight years after an association's founding. Having predecessors also sharply reduces the odds of merging with other associations, although not as much as it reduces the likelihood of disbanding. We suspect that the antimerger effect results from a more careful choice of a niche, so as to minimize overlap of goals or organizing strategies with the predecessors. Transformations are not affected by having had predecessors in the same industry.

Our results strongly suggest that trade associations have been very effective at partitioning resources among themselves (Carroll, 1985). The effects of density are positive throughout the population's growth, although the positive effect declined somewhat as the population grew beyond 1,500 associations. Associations in the same narrowly defined 4-digit SIC industry affect each other's survival chances only to the extent of raising the odds of mergers, and having a predecessor in the same industry provides substantial protection against an early demise. Although Carroll wrote of resource partitioning between large and small organizations, the concept can also be extended to the normative consensus that inhibits organizations from directly threatening others' existence. Trade associations seem to have learned this strategy more thoroughly than trade unions.

Evolution in this population appears less driven by direct competition than in other populations, where efficiency is more of a concern. To the extent that organizations work out among themselves an implicit agreement over domain sharing, intrapopulation variation is suppressed and managers are under less pressure to achieve an optimal allocation of their resources.

Organizational Characteristics

For foundings, environmental forces are the entire story, as they set the context within which associations emerge. For mergers, transformations, and disbandings, however, internal organizational characteristics may make an association more or less vulnerable to environmental conditions. Even though they are minimalist organizations, able to operate on low overhead, trade associations still wrestle with serious governance problems. Interest diversity can make policy setting extremely difficult (Staber, 1987). We found, however, that internal association diversity, as measured by the number of SIC codes it represented, did not affect its odds of disbanding, transforming, or merging. Our results also showed that having vertical links to firms in other industries significantly *lowered* the odds of disbanding, transforming, and merging. Vertical linkages may be a form of domain defense and a way of achieving greater domain consensus. Vertical links among member firms are instrumental in information sharing and strategic pooling of resources. If such links are carefully chosen and fit in the overall strategy of firms, the governance problems associated with internal diversity can be reduced.

Trade associations can attempt to increase their influence by attaching themselves to larger associations at little or no cost to the host association. Forming ties to another association increases external sources of information and may give associations greater visibility for their activities. Our data show that affiliation with another association sharply lowers the odds of disbanding, although it has no effect on the odds of transformation or merger. Our results thus differ from those of Hannan and Freeman (1988a), who found that affiliation with a national federation was *not* effective in lowering trade unions' disbanding rates.

Founding conditions have a lasting influence on some types of vital events for trade associations. Associations founded via mergers have significantly lower odds of disbanding than those founded on their own. They can draw on the organizational experiences of members and administrators from their component associations to prevent the common mistakes that totally new foundings make. Merged associations are also larger than their predecessors, and this makes them more credible players of the logic of influence. Associations founded via transformations and spin-offs also have lower odds of disbanding, but the relationships are not statistically significant. Transformation is apparently an ongoing strategy for some associations, as associations founded via transformation are five times as likely to experience another transformation as are other associations.

As a check on whether our results might be biased by our failure to include measures of association size—a variable *not* included because it is available only for about half the associations—we reanalyzed the equations in table 11.3, although we did not reanalyze transformations because of a reduced sample size and a small number of events. We used three size measures, treated as time-varying independent variables lagged one year: membership, budget, and staff size. All three size measures substantially reduced the odds of disbanding. With membership included, vertical ties no longer significantly reduce disbandings, and with staff size included, founding by merger no longer reduces the odds of disbanding. Other relationships are unaffected. Of the three size measures, only budget has a significant impact on the odds of merger, with larger associations more likely to merge and the other relationships unaffected. However, this information is available for only about one fifth of the sample, and so we treat the result with caution. Our cautionary check thus shows that omitting association size has not biased the results reported.

We focused on three sets of environmental forces affecting the evolution of trade associations, using two models: a logic of membership and a logic of influence model. Each captures some aspects of the organizational and environmental conditions facing trade associations and member firms. First, the *logic of membership* suggests the need for associations to minimize internal diversity and thus for the association population to proliferate over time, as the industrial structure becomes more complex. We found that long-term growth in the American economy had a powerful effect on the association population. We also found that rising density somewhat facilitated association foundings during much of the 20th century, and that the competitive effects of a growing population size were extremely small, unlike results from other populations, such as labor unions.

Second, the *logic of influence* suggests the need for the business community to respond to state actions, as well as the actions of potential competitors such as unions, and thus for the association population to grow as a response to changes in public policies. We found that some state actions—during the depression and also during the First World War—enhanced association foundings, but that other actions—Republican administrations and the Second World War—did not.

Our results demonstrate the need to distinguish between events that temporarily change the environment for organizations and those which change it permanently. The National Industrial Recovery Act was a powerful institutional change, but its effects were short-lived, as it was not in effect long enough to create a new institutional framework for trade association foundings and survival. Similarly, the effects of favorable government treatment of trade associations during World War I were short term, disappearing immediately after the war was settled. The historical record thus shows how transitory apparent institutional change can be—once the structures the national government had put in place were removed, the more traditional adversarial relationship between business and government resumed. We are thus led to qualify Carroll, Delacroix, and Goodstein's (1990) proposition about the long-term effects of war on organizations, by positing that such effects persist in fragmented but centralized states (their classification of the United States) only if permanent institutional arrangements—such as government agencies or departments—are created to oversee them. In the United States, no formally organized route through which trade associations affect state policies exists; instead, policy outcomes are a matter for individual firms and associations that pursue negotiation and bargaining with the relevant agencies, departments, or committees.

We might also consider the possibility that the political environment of trade associations and other collective interest organizations is the outcome, rather than the cause, of associative action. This in itself would explain why otherwise similar organizational populations may suffer different fates, depending on their political effectiveness and internal governability. Unlike trade associations and state bar associations, trade unions must continually prove themselves as worthy participants in the political porcess. As political interest organizations, trade associations have been successful in getting the most out of formal ties with other associations, and they have successfully built upon the experience of their predecessors.

The historical record supports the argument that trade associations fought for legitimacy early in their history, but we must also consider the possibility that increasing density is a proxy for the spread of knowledge about effective forms. We found that being affiliated with other associations, as well as having a predecessor association in the same industry, very strongly reduced an association's likelihood of disbanding. We are inclined to agree with Ranger-Moore, Banaszak-Holl, and Hannan (1991:61–62) that "the effect of competition is stronger for the population defined at a local level than for a national population." As minimalist organizations, very concerned with symbolic legitimacy, trade associations have gone out of their way at the national level to avoid entangling themselves in disputes with other associations. Norms against overt competition with associations recruiting from the same domain facilitate internal governance and contribute to stability in the population of associations.

Over the course of the 20th century, trade associations (and business interest groups more generally) have attempted to create a rhetoric in which they were seen as legitimate influences on government. As minimalist organizations, their resources are mainly limited to what they can mobilize through member firms. Thus, at the population level, additional trade associations help extend the reach of all associations by mobilizing more firms. Associations have a vested interest in helping more associations start, rather than in competing with them.

Our data, although not as complete as we would like, show that trade associations rarely change their form, as measured by the rarity of name changes, structural transformations, and changes in the size of staffs, budgets, and membership (analyses not included in this chapter). The evolution of the population is driven primarily by foundings, dissolutions, and mergers. Thus the evolution of formal associative action in the U.S. trade association population is the outcome of changes in the size of the population, net of environmental constraints, rather than of changes in organizational form. The most significant evolutionary change that has occurred is interorganizational and institutional: the development of normative constraints supporting noncompetitive relations among associations.

12

Disruptive Selection and Population Segmentation: Interpopulation Competition as a Segregating Process

TERRY L. AMBURGEY, TINA DACIN, AND DAWN KELLY

"Why are there so many kinds of organizations?" Hannan and Freeman (1977:936) posed this question in their seminal article on population ecology. Essentially they are asking why we observe variability among organizations. At first, the answer to this question appears obvious: Organizations have different purposes, goals, building blocks, and so on. But this response is incomplete—it does not explain the causal mechanism underlying the process of organizational heterogeneity. To understand organizational heterogeneity fully, two additional components need to be introduced: the assertion of organizational evolution and the theory of natural selection.

We refer to organizational evolution as an assertion because it is essentially a descriptive statement about change at multiple levels. Organizations are assumed to come from a common "pool"; over time they "descend with modifications." Consequently, we see changes occur within populations of organizations (microevolution), or the emergence of different and distinct sub-groups of organizations (speciation), or the evolution of entire populations (macroevolution).[1] While evolutionary change is a useful framework, it does not address *how* the process occurs—for that we need the theory of natural selection.

Evolutionary theorists view natural selection to be the primary mechanism driving change in organizational populations. The selection process is characterized as proceeding through three stages (Aldrich, 1979; Campbell, 1969). The first stage is *variation*, the existence of variability is necessary for selection to occur. Aldrich (1979) claimed that organizational variations "provide the raw material from which selection can be made" (p. 28). The second stage is *selection*, organizations face selection pressures in the form of environmental constraints and internal criteria (Aldrich, 1979:29). Variations that fit with environmental and organizational requirements are selected. The third stage is *retention*; through retention, organizational modifications become part of the population. The retention stage includes processes that preserve,

This research was supported by a grant to the first and second authors from the Center of Credit Union Research, School of Business, University of Wisconsin–Madison.

duplicate, or reproduce the selected variations for future occasions or generations (Aldrich, 1979:34).

This chapter examines evolutionary development in the population of credit unions in the United States. Selection processes can generally be categorized into three patterns—stabilizing, directional, and disruptive (Grant, 1985). It is suggested that these different *patterns* of selection must be considered in order to account for the evolutionary changes observed within the credit union population.

The purpose of this chapter is to test empirically for the existence of size-localized disruptive (segregating) selection among credit unions. Such selection would help account for the emergence and maintenance of distinct strategic groups within the population of credit unions. The existence of distinct subgroups within a population of organizations implies a mechanism which produces clustering rather than smooth and continuous variation.[2]

The results of such an investigation would inform strategic management by empirically establishing the risks associated with movement between strategic groups. They would also inform ecological theory, which has systematically ignored disruptive selection in empirical studies.

This chapter is part of a larger study on credit unions. The analyses reported here focus on organizational factors such as size and field of membership, to account for increases or decreases in the risk of failures and mergers among credit unions.[3] Other analyses of patterns of founding and growth are also being conducted.

Patterns of Selection: Stabilizing, Directional, and Disruptive

Selection processes can be placed into three general patterns.[4] The first pattern, *stabilizing selection*, operates to reduce the variance of a population along some dimension. The dimension of size, for example might be subject to stabilizing selection—organizations close to some 'optimum' size are favored while larger and smaller organizations are systematically selected out of the population. The result is a size distribution with a smaller variance.

Directional selection operates to move the mean of a population along some dimension. For example, small organizations might face a higher intensity of selection than medium or large organizations. The results of this process would be a larger mean size and a positively skewed distribution.

Disruptive selection operates to remove members of the population from the interior of the distribution along some dimension. Using the dimension of size as our example, both large and small organizations might be favored while medium organizations are selectively removed from the population. The result of this process would be a multimodal size distribution.

Figure 12.1 provides a graphic representation of the three patterns of selection. The three distributions on the top represent a distribution 'prior to' selection. The three distributions on the bottom represent the distribution 'after' selection. The leftmost pair illustrates stabilizing selection, the central pair illustrates directional selection, and the rightmost pair illustrates disruptive selection.

It is important to note that actual populations are likely to experience a more complicated pattern of selection involving a mixture of the three processes. For

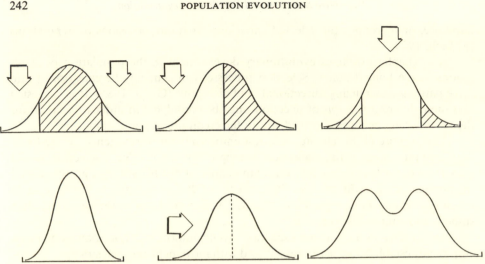

FIG. 12.1 Patterns of selection: stabilizing, directional, and disruptive

example, stabilizing processes may involve different intensities of selection on the ends of the distribution (adding a directional component), or disruptive processes may be mixed with directional or stabilizing processes. In a sample of day-care centers, Baum (1990a) observed that organizations may in fact be subject to differential selection on varying organizational dimensions.

Disruptive Selection and Size-Dependent Competition

One of the few models in organizational ecology to predict a pattern of disruptive selection is the size-dependent model of competition. Hannan and Freeman (1977:945–46) argued that organizations of different sizes draw upon different resources in the environment. Consequently, the intensity of competition among organizations in a population is a function of their relative position in the size distribution—organizations of similar size compete with one another more than organizations of very different sizes.

This model of intrapopulation competition implies a pattern of disruptive selection. Large organizations pose a competitive threat to medium sized organizations but not to small organizations in the same population. Similarly, small organizations threaten medium sized organizations but not large ones in the same population. Organizations in the interior of the size distribution end up 'between a rock and a hard place'—tactics which help fend off large organizations make them more vulnerable to small organizations, and vice versa.

Empirical studies have provided mixed support for size-localized models of intrapopulation competition. Hannan, Ranger-Moore, and Banaszak-Holl (1990) conducted exploratory analyses of banks and life insurance companies in New York. Their study found that the size distributions developed in a way consistent with size-localized competition although positions of the 'gaps' in the distributions were not correctly specified.

Baum and Mezias (1991) used a variety of measures of size-localized competition to analyze failure and growth among licensed day care centers. Their study found that size-localized competition reduced growth rates but did not affect failure rates. Furthermore, the size distribution of day care centers did not develop any gaps—it did not deviate significantly from a lognormal distribution.

The mixed support generated by the empirical studies may be due to idiosyncrasies of the populations that were examined. However, another possibility is that the exclusive focus of *intrapopulation* competition is masking the role of *interpopulation* competition.

There has been very little empirical research examining the interaction of different organizational populations (i.e., community ecology). However, at least two studies have examined the interactions of different organizational populations with overlapping niches and both found significant cross effects (see also part V, "Community Evolution").

Brittain and Wholey (1988) studied the competitive interaction of different populations of electronic component manufacturers. They found a competitive structure which they described as "an amalgam of symbiotic, predatory, and competitive relationships involving both strategic and technological competition" (Brittain and Wholey, 1988:215).

Hannan and Freeman (1989) examined the relationships between different populations of national labor unions. They found that the growth of the population of craft unions stimulated the founding rate of industrial unions, but the growth of industrial unions depressed the founding rates of craft unions (Hannan and Freeman, 1989:97).

We argue that size-dependent competition can produce disruptive selection even in the absence of intense intrapopulation competition. Size-dependent competition can arise because of differential levels of competition with other populations. If different sized organizations draw upon different resources, it is likely that a population member's exposure to competition from *other* populations will vary by size. Organizations in the interior of the size distribution may face a higher intensity of selection because their exposure to competition from other populations is greater than that of small organizations and their ability to defend themselves is less than that of larger organizations.

In this study we develop and test several hypotheses about size-dependent selection. The population used in the analyses consists of credit unions in the United States. Credit unions provide a rare opportunity to explore interpopulation competition because direct competition among credit unions is limited by administrative regulations.

Historical Background and Context

Credit unions are member-owned not-for-profit cooperatives that represent both borrower and saver interests. As cooperatives, credit unions arose for primarily economic reasons, but they operate with nonpecuniary principles in mind. These principles (espoused by the World Council of Credit Unions) include statements about democratic structure, service to members, and social goals of the credit union. The democratic structure of credit unions is reflected in a voluntary membership policy; membership is open to anyone within the credit union's *field of membership*.

Common Bond and Field of Membership

The term 'common bond' refers to the relationship among members of a group served by a credit union and often formed the basis for founding. A credit union's 'field of membership', on the other hand, legally defines the scope of its membership. The field of membership of early credit unions was quite broad. The use of common social bond, although encouraged as a basis for founding, was largely voluntary during the early stages of the credit union movement. However, by focusing on founding credit unions on the basis of common bond, the credit union industry began to flourish.

Common bond became the basis for bringing groups of individuals together to form new unions. It proved to be a viable mechanism with which to found new credit unions and easily diffuse credit union principles across the United States. Additionaly, the relational aspects of the common bond requirement enabled credit unions to achieve economic benefits such as loan safety as well as moral responsibility and loyalty toward the organization (Burger and Dacin, 1991:5).

The common bond could be based upon a number of ties. Some credit unions were organized along rural, community lines, whereas industrial credit unions were based on occupational groups. Industrial credit unions founded on the basis of occupational bonds and community credit unions based on associational ties flourished during the early part of the movement.

In order to further the diffusion of credit unions across the United States, the concept of common bond was formally incorporated in the Model Credit Union Act by the Credit Union National Extension Bureau. This act described the common bond as pertaining to both large and small groups bound by occupation, or association, or membership in groups within a well-defined neighborhood, community, or rural district.

Aside from its potential for instilling a spirit of cohesiveness and trust, the notion of common bond has some definite economic/efficiency benefits associated with it. A significant advantage in the early years was that the common bond feature of credit unions served to lower administrative costs. This was especially so for credit unions organized along occupational lines because it was easier to obtain reliable information about the creditworthiness of its prospective borrowers.

The common bond was also argued to be a practice which instilled a sense of moral responsibility in members, making them less likely to default on loans. In turn, lower default rates allowed credit unions to charge lower loan rates. The common bond also enhanced loyalty to the credit union, thereby making members less sensitive to fluctuations in deposit interest rates. Relational aspects of common bond also served to retain the cooperative spirit within the movement (Burger and Dacin, 1991:4–8).

Legislation and Regulation

The Federal Credit Union Act was passed by Congress in 1934. This act was patterned after the Model Credit Union Act but was more restrictive in several ways. First, the notion of common bond was formalized and narrowly defined. Second, the services and privileges of credit unions were restricted. The Federal Act of 1934 provides a definition of common bond which has often been rigidly interpreted. That law states that "membership shall be limited to groups having a common bond of occupation or association, or to groups within a well-defined neighborhood, community or rural district." Thus credit unions that were federally chartered and those chartered by state laws based on the Federal Credit Union Act were restricted in their common bond requirements.

The enabling legislation also placed financial restrictions on credit unions. Credit unions could not maintain deposits with or borrow money from Federal Reserve banks. The maximum amount of unsecured personal loans was set at $50 and the maximum maturity was set at 2 years.

In the late 1960s and early 1970s, federal regulatory requirements dropped the requirement that members needed to have extensive associational ties. The definition of common bond was also relaxed to include members who had retired or who had left the company or organization. This change came to be known as the "once a member, always a member" policy.

The early 1980s witnessed continued liberalization of the National Credit Union Administration's (NCUAs) policies on mergers and field of membership. In 1982, NCUA revised its policies with regard to credit union chartering, charter amendments, and mergers. The changes in merger policy had a profound impact on the concepts of common bond and field of membership. Credit unions were now able to exist with multiple group fields of membership and provide broader services to credit union consumers.

This was accomplished by reinterpreting section 109 of the Federal Credit Union Act, which stated a federally chartered credit union's field of membership is limited to groups within a well-defined neighborhood, community, or rural district. NCUA reinterpreted this to mean that multiple groups, each with its own distinct common bond, can coexist within the scope of a particular credit union's field of membership. NCUA determined that as long as it required each group to maintain its own common bond, its policies were in compliance with the Federal Credit Union Act. Therefore, federally chartered credit unions could now include "select employment groups" with unlike common bonds within their field of membership.

Liberalization of NCUA policies opened up new avenues for credit union growth and expansion. For the first time in the history of the credit union movement, disparate groups, each with its own common bond, could belong under the umbrella of the same credit union. The relaxation of field of membership policies allowed the benefits of credit union service to be made available to many small groups unable or unwilling to charter their own credit union.

However, the relaxation of field of membership policies also dilutes the common social bond which was the foundation of the early credit unions. Growth in size through the addition of multiple groups has the potential for dissipating the economic and social advantages associated with a strong common bond.

Changes in technology also stimulated a trend toward a more diverse membership. The advent of automated teller machines and electronic funds transfer capabilities made it possible for credit unions to enhance their service and access and serve a much broader and more diverse membership. This increased sophistication in computer technology made it possible to access new members and do so in a feasible manner. Payroll deductions or direct deposits could now be made much more efficiently and, if desired, from a number of different employers.

The growth in membership was frequently accompanied by the addition of a broader profile of services. In the earlier years, credit unions specialized in share (savings) accounts and small personal loans. During the eighties there was a proliferation of service offerings, especially by larger credit unions.

For example, the Credit Union National Association tracks eight "key" services—share drafts, certificates of deposit, first mortgages, direct deposit of federal recurring payments, credit cards, ATM cards, and traveler's checks. The percentage of small credit unions offering two or fewer of these services dropped by 10 percent during the decade, from 88 to 78 percent. Large credit unions, on the other hand, have seen a dramatic increase in service offerings. In 1980 only 9 percent of large credit unions offered seven or eight of the key services, but by 1989 *76 percent* offered seven or eight of the key services and a wide variety of other services as well (Credit Union National Association, 1989).

One consequence of the changes in credit unions was a shift in the dynamics of competition. However, much of the increase in competition was a result of increased competition with other financial service organizations: diversified credit unions were more prone to heavy competition from banks.

Credit Unions and Competition

In the early stages of the movement, the founding of credit unions within field of membership boundaries virtually eliminated the presence or desire for competition among credit unions. In essence, each credit union operated within its difinitive field of membership. Direct competition was virtually nonexistent within the credit union population.

A desire to prevent direct competition was originally an idealogical component of the cooperative movement. However, this desire was transformed into a chartering requirement for credit unions. Beginning in 1936, the policy of credit union regulators has been to charter only new credit unions which do not conflict with existing credit unions (Burger and Dacin, 1991:15).

The current policy of the National Credit Union Administration is that overlapping fields of membership is to be avoided as a general rule and to the extent possible—only credit unions which "will not materially affect the interests of other credit unions or the credit union system" will be chartered except in unusual circumstances (*Federal Register*, 1989:31168).

Although intrapopulation competition is relatively weak, the expansion of credit union services has resulted in increased interpopulation competition. The American Bankers Association (Lowrie, 1989) stated its views on credit unions and banks in the following ways:

The separateness and distinctiveness of the two forms of institutions have eroded in recent years to the extent that at least some of the larger credit unions are now in direct and near total competition with their commercial bank neighbors. Credit unions now offer trust services, certificates of deposit, credit cards, mortgage and electronic funds transfer services. Since October 1974, increasing numbers of credit unions have been offering their members share draft services which compete in a direct way with commercial bank checking accounts.

Size and Failure

We argue that credit unions now face a mix of directional and disruptive selection. The result of these selection pressures is an increase in the size of smaller credit unions and the segmentation of the population into two strategic groups. One group consists of small to medium sized credit unions with relatively narrow service profiles. This group emphasizes the social solidarity of a common bond and competes only indirectly with other financial service organizations. The other group consists of very large full service credit unions which directly compete with other financial service organizations.

A wide variety of studies have demonstrated that rates of organizational failure generally decline with increased size (Baum and Oliver, 1991; Barnett, 1990; Delacroix et al., 1989; Singh et al., 1986; Freeman, Carroll, and Hannan, 1983). We expect the same pattern among credit unions. Very small credit unions should face a high risk of failure, not because of competitive pressures but because of administrative inefficiencies. For example, many small credit unions do not have even a single full time employee and utilize manual share accounting. Thus, the risk of failure should decline with increased size.

Very large credit unions should face a very low risk of failure. Their asset base allows the use of sophisticated technology and the employment of a skilled staff. They will be able to compete effectively with other financial service organizations and may have a competitive advantage because of their tax-exempt status, lower operating overhead, and lower cost of capital (American Bankers Association, 1989:177–79).

However, we argue that the risk of failure will not decline monotonically with size. There should be an area in the interior of the size distribution where the risk of failure rises. Medium to large credit unions will face a situation where they are too large and diverse to maintain the advantages of a strong common bond but not large enough to compete effectively with the other financial service organizations offering similar services.

These arguments suggest the following hypothesis:

Hypotheses 1: The rate of failure is a cubic function of size. The linear component of the function is negative, the quadratic component is positive, and the cubic component is negative.

The most frequent method for a credit union to exit the population is through revocation of its charter and liquidation of its assets. In recent years, however, an increasing number of credit unions are existing through merger. In most instances, there are reasons to treat failures and mergers as analytically distinct—firms which are performing well can be more attractive candidates for a merger than firms performing poorly. However, the nature of credit unions is such that aggressive acquisition programs are not a viable strategy for credit union growth. Consequently we expect the same pattern of size dependence among mergers as among failures.

Hypotheses 2: The rate of merger is a cubic function of size. The linear component of the function is negative, the quadratic component is positive, and the cubic component is negative.

Data and Methods

Two sources of data were used in the analyses reported here. First, annual statistical reports filed with NCUA between 1980 and 1989 are used as the source of information on credit union attributes. Second, the NCUA roster of liquidations and mergers was used to indicate which credit unions failed or exited through merger.

The NCUA annual reports contain comprehensive, time-varying information on key financial characteristics of federally chartered or state chartered/federally insured credit unions. Information on the date of founding and the field of membership is also included in the call reports. The NCUA data cover 20,248 credit unions during 1980–89.

The NCUA statistical reports were combined with the list of credit union liquidations, assisted mergers, and mergers compiled by NCUA. This list covered the period 1980–89. In the analyses reported here, liquidations and assisted mergers were considered failures and analyzed together. Unassisted mergers were not considered failures and were analyzed separately. The consolidation resulted in 611 liquidations or assisted mergers and 224 mergers available for statistical analysis.

These data were used to construct an event history for each credit union in the form of a sequence of annual time periods or 'spells'. Each credit union's first spell began in 1980 or at the time its founding.[5] If the first spell was survived, the organization's second spell began on January 1 of the following year. This pattern continued until the credit union no longer existed or until the end of the sample period, in which case spells were coded as right censored. Thus, time-varying covariates were updated throughout the data annually.

Variables

The variables used in the analysis fall into three groups. The first consists of variables used to gauge the effect of size. The second is a set of variables used to evaluate the effect of field of membership. The last is a set of control variables such as age, financial characteristics, and the number of credit unions in the local market.

The primary focus of these analyses is the existence of disruptive selection which separates the population into two distinct subgroups. If disruptive selection is occurring among credit unions there will be an increase in the rate of failures and mergers in the interior of the size distribution. One way to test for disruptive selection is to include a cubic function of assets in the models (e.g., assets, assets squared, and assets cubed). If there is a significant positive squared term, then disruptive selection is occurring in the midrange of the distribution. Alternatively, discrete categories of asset size can be constructed and entered as a set of dummy variables.

Both approaches were used in these analyses. A cubic function of assets (in units of $10 million), assets squared, and assets cubed was constructed. Assets cubed was divided by 1,000 for the purposes of rescaling. A set of dummy variables was constructed with the following asset categories: under $2 million, $2 to 5 million, $5 to 50 million, $50 to 250 million, $250 to 750 million, and over $750 million. The under $2 million category was excluded from the model and used as the reference category.

The field of membership information on the NCUA reports was used to construct a set of categorical dummy variables: occupational, associational, residential, and other. The 'other' category consists of low income credit unions, corporate central credit unions, and credit unions that have a nonstandard field of membership because of prior mergers.

The financial control variables consist of total expenses, net income, and loans more than 6 months delinquent (all in units of $1 million), the capital/asset ratio, and the loan/deposit ratio. The remaining control variables were age (in days) and local density, represented by the number of other credit unions in the same county at the beginning of the observation period.

Models and Estimation

The hypotheses were tested by parametric models of credit union failure and merger. The analyses were conducted with a multivariate point process approach, with the chances of failure and merger considered as competing risks (Amburgey, 1986). Operationally, the basic model of each type of event was specified in terms of the instantaneous transition rate:

$$\lambda_j(\tau) = \lim [Pr_j(\tau, \tau + \Delta\tau)/\Delta\tau],$$

where Pr_j is the discrete probability of credit union j experiencing failure of merger between τ and $(\tau + \Delta\tau)$, conditional on being at risk for the event at time τ. The rates of failure and merger were specified as a loglinear function of the covariates so that

$$\lambda_j(\tau) = \exp(\beta x_{jr})$$

A loglinear specification was used in order to preclude negative predicted rates.

The parameters of the model were estimated by using the method of maximum likelihood with Tuma's (1982) RATE program, which reduces the bias that would otherwise result from the presence of right-censored cases (Tuma and Hannan, 1984). Significance levels were evaluated by examining F ratios for each of the coefficients. Statistical improvement for hierarchically nested models was evaluated by using the χ^2 likelihood ratio test.

Results

Table 12.1 presents the estimated coefficients when a cubic function of asset size is used to model the rates of failure and merger. All three components of the cubic function are statistically significant. The negative linear term (assets) indicates that small credit unions have the highest rate of failure and merger and the rate declines as size increases. The positive quadratic term (assets squared) indicates, however, that after a certain size is reached, further increases in size increase the rate of failure and merger. The negative cubic term indicates that after this 'danger zone' of size is passed, further increases in size again decrease the rate of failure and merger so that very large credit unions exhibit the lowest risk of exiting the population.

All three of the field of membership (FOM) variables have positive and significant coefficients in the failure model. Thus, compared to an occupational field of membership, all other types exhibit a significantly higher risk of failure. The associ-

TABLE 12.1   The Effects of Credit Union Characteristics on
Failure and Merger Rates: Cubic Model

	Failures	*Mergers*
Age	.0001*	.0001†
	(.000)	(.000)
Assets	−1.309*	−1.020*
	(.225)	(.289)
Assets squared	.057*	.061*
	(.014)	(.015)
Assets cubed/1,000	−.881*	−.936*
	(.372)	(.292)
Associational FOM	.490*	.131
	(.102)	(.178)
Residential FOM	1.477*	.231
	(.116)	(.289)
Other FOM	1.443*	.722†
	(.189)	(.417)
Delinquent loans	.510*	.433*
	(.043)	(.084)
Capital/assets	−1.889*	−2.004*
	(.205)	(.171)
Loans/deposits	.002	−.621*
	(.004)	(.280)
Net income	.051	−.307
	(.118)	(.232)
Total expenses	.704*	.202
	(.185)	(.270)
Density	.0003	.0007*
	(.0002)	(.0003)
χ^2	558.30	120.12
Degrees of freedom	13	13
Number of events	611	224

* significant at $p < .05$, † significant at $p < .10$. Standard errors are given in parentheses. FOM, field of membership.

ational form has a moderately higher risk of failure; the residential and 'other' categories have *substantially* higher risks of failure.

Field of membership does not, however, substantially affect the rate of merger. Associational and residential credit unions do not significantly differ from occupational credit unions in the likelihood of merger. There is a positive coefficient for the 'other' category, but it is only marginally significant.

The effects of the control variables are generally not surprising, but there are differences in their effects on failures and mergers. The effects of delinquent loans and the capital/asset ratio are consistent; higher levels of delinquent loans increase the risks of both failure and merger, while a higher capital/asset ratio decreases the risks of both failure and merger. Similarly, older credit unions are less likely both to fail and to exit through merger.

One the other hand, a high loan/deposit ratio decreases the risk of exit through merger but has no effect on the risk of failure. Similarly, a higher number of other credit unions in the same county increases the risk of merger but not the risk of failure. Finally, higher levels of total expenses increase the risk of failure but have no significant effect on the risk of merger.

Table 12.2 contains the estimated coefficients for models of failure and merger which use discrete asset size categories rather than a cubic function. The categorical variables provide a less precise estimate of the effects of size, and the extremely small number of credit unions in the larger categories effectively precludes statistically significant estimates for those categories. Nonetheless, the categorical variables are informative since they indicate where the disruptive selection is occurring in the population of credit unions.

A comparison of the five largest size classes to the smallest (less than $2 M) suggests that the disruptive selection is occurring among credit unions in the $250–750 M range. The estimated effects are increasingly negative up to $250 M. The coefficient for the $250–750 M size class is more positive than that of either of the adjacent size classes.

The effects of the other variables are essentially the same as in table 12.1. An increase in the number of explanatory variables decreases the statistical power of the analyses, so there are some variations in the numerical values of the estimates. These variations are, however, inconsequential.

The analyses reported here focus on organizational factors which increase or decrease the risk of failure and merger among credit unions, particularly size and field of membership. There are several patterns in the evolutionary development of credit unions which deserve attention. The first is the significant evidence that the population is becoming separated into two different size classes. The findings summarized in table 12.1 indicate that small credit unions clearly suffer the *highest* risk of failure or merger. But a larger size does not uniformly enhance the viability of a credit union. There is a "danger zone" wherein medium sized credit unions face a higher risk than other credit unions which are both smaller and larger in size. Figure 12.2 provides a graphic representation of the relationship between size and the risk of failure.

A comparison of the coefficients of the different terms of the cubic function indicates that the disruptive selection is not extremely large. The analysis which uses categorical size variables also suggests that the disruption is not extremely large. This means that the separation of credit unions into two subgroups is proceeding at a relatively slow pace rather than being a rapid process. Nonetheless, if the same pattern continues in the future, there will be an increasing separation of credit unions into two distinct size classes.

The second pattern is the substantial difference in the risks of failure and merger between credit unions with an occupational field of membership and all other credit unions. The fates of credit unions in the 'other' category are hard to gauge since it is such a diverse group. The effect of having either an associational or residential field of membership is unambiguous; the associational form exhibits a higher risk of failure or merger, and the residential form suffers a *much* higher risk of such outcomes.

TABLE 12.2   The Effects of Credit Union Characteristics on
Failure and Merger Rates: Dummy Variable Model

	Failures	*Mergers*
Age	.0001*	.00003†
	(.000)	(.000)
$2–5 million	−.701*	−.567*
	(.153)	(.217)
$5–50 Million	−.817*	−.722*
	(.192)	(.266)
$50–250 Million	−1.261†	−1.988
	(.685)	(1.457)
$250–750 Million	−.561	2.097
	(1.938)	(1.582)
$750 Million or greater	−12.430	−9.967
	(14.190)	(49.730)
Associational FOM	.473*	.115
	(.102)	(.178)
Residential FOM	1.474*	.221
	(.116)	(.289)
Other FOM	1.439*	.682
	(.189)	(.420)
Delinquent loans	.412*	.368*
	(.049)	(.097)
Capital/assets	−1.893*	−2.009*
	(.126)	(.170)
Loans/deposits	.002	−.609*
	(.004)	(.279)
Net income	−.375*	−.567*
	(.105)	(.166)
Total expenses	−.012	−.147
	(.078)	(.098)
Density	.0003	.0007*
	(.0002)	(.0003)
χ^2	583.44	117.71
Degrees of freedom	15	15
Number of events	611	224

* Significant at $p < .05$, † significant at $p < .10$. Standard errors are given in parentheses. FOM, field of membership.

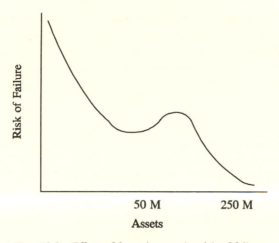

FIG. 12.2   Effect of firm size on the risk of failure

We believe that the implications of this research for ecological theory are substantial. Ecological views of disruptive selection have focused entirely on competition *within* the population. Our results suggest that ecological models of selection need to be revised to incorporate competition among populations. The development of size-localized models of competition was an important refinement, but they will remain incomplete as long as they are based solely on competition among members of the same population.

The results of this study also emphasize the importance of allowing for mixed selection processes. Most ecological research has emphasized a single pattern of selection. We argue that ecology must start incorporating mixed patterns—credit unions are unlikely to be alone in experiencing a complicated set of selection pressures.

Finally, this research highlights the complexity of segregating and blending processes. Hannan and Freeman (1989) forcefully argued that the question of organizational forms should be approached from the perspective of boundaries and the processes that maintain or erode them. We see the development of credit unions as a dramatic example of how the erosion of one organizational boundary can create a new boundary.

Institutional rules segregated credit unions from other financial service organizations, specified the allowable organizing principles, limited the allowable services,and effectively suppressed direct competition, In fact, credit unions were a single population in a community of populations where

> each financial institution had its own role to play. The services it could offer and the geographic area over which it could offer these services were defined, competition among the various types of financial institutions was restricted, and the Federal government assumed a major role in controlling the activities of financial institutions. (Burger and Dacin, 1991:11).

The relaxation of the institutional rules segregating the different populations has not, however, resulted in a simple blending of the different forms. Among the population of credit unions, an institutionally based boundary separating it from other populations has been replaced by a competition based boundary separating credit unions of different sizes.

Notes

1. These terms are borrowed from Grant (1985).

2. The strategy literature refers to such mechanisms as mobility barriers, barriers which deter firms from shifting between strategic groups. The ecological literature refers to such mechanisms as segregating processes, processes which create sharp discontinuities and boundaries between different organizational forms (Hannan and Freeman, 1989:54–55).

3. The term 'field of membership' is specific to the credit union movement and basically defines the scope of a credit union's membership.

4. The following discussion relies on Grant (1985).

5. Consequently, except for those credit unions founded after 1980, the data are left-censored.

13

Externalities and Ecological Theory: Unbundling Density Dependence

JACQUES DELACROIX AND HAYAGREEVA RAO

The ecological-evolutionary perspective asks how the organizational panorama changes over time and why there are so many different kinds of organizations. The general answer it provides is that organizations disband and are rapidly replaced by new ones somewhat different from them, and that environmental discontinuities create new niches wherein new kinds of organizations may arise (Brittain, chapter 17, this volume). This formulation distinguishes carefully between the emergence of a new organizational form, on the one hand, and the founding of instances of an existing organizational form, on the other. Its guiding paradigm is environmental selection, in contrast with the voluntaristic, individual organizational adaptation view prevailing elsewhere in the study of organizations (Hannan and Freeman, 1977; Aldrich, 1979; McKelvey, 1982).

Influential scholars working within this perspective have proposed that a great deal of selection, and the propensity to found new organizations are density-dependent (Hannan and Freeman, 1989; Carroll and Hannan, 1989b; Hannan and Carroll, 1992). They propose specifically that changing "density" (organizational population size, or the total number of organizations of a particular form in existence at one time), affects both foundings and disbandings differentially according to the age of an organizational form. In the early history of the form, population growth is accompanied by a high incidence of foundings and by a low rate of disbandings. At some point, different for each organizational population but always unpredicted, the effects of density on the incidence of foundings and on the rate of disbandings reverse themselves, becoming negative for the one and positive for the other. Over the whole history of the organizational form the relationship between population density and the incidence of foundings is represented by a convex curve, that between density and the disbanding rate, by a more or less symmetrical concave curve.

Density dependence theorists account for the right branches of both curves in terms of conventional competition: when many like organizations compete for lim-

We thank Howard Aldrich and Mark Seabright for useful comments on a very early draft of this paper and Paul DiMaggio and Bill McKelvey for the same kind of help on a late draft. We are also grateful to Jitendra Singh for his tenacious effort to keep us on the right path, whether he succeeded or not.

ited sustenance resources (such as readership for newspapers, members for labor unions, customers for semiconductor firms), the results are a lowered frequency of foundings and a heightened rate of disbandings (Hannan and Freeman, 1988a, 1988b; Amburgey, Dacin, and Kelly, chapter 12, this volume.) They explain the left branches of both curves, where population growth improves the viability of the form, with a radical departure from classical evolutionary theory. They contend that in the early history of an organizational form (such as labor unions and newspapers in the 19th century, or semiconductor firms in the mid-20th century), the primary environmental resource, determining both organizational survival and organizational founding, is social legitimacy: Recent organizational forms, by virtue of their newness, appear unfamiliar and lack the legitimacy of established forms. This lack of legitimacy in turn hinders the ability of instances of the form to acquire other resources directly necessary for their sustenance. Correspondingly, disbanding rates tend to be high and founding frequencies low in populations of new organizational forms. As a form multiplies nevertheless, its legitimacy increases and conventional within-population competition ultimately sets in. The radical departure in this formulation resides in the idea that legitimacy, unlike other resources, is not consumed but created by population growth (see Baum and Singh, Chapter 18, this volume). Proponents of this view claim that it possesses a high degree of generality applying to all organizational forms, past, future, and present (Hannan and Freeman, 1989; Carroll and Hannan, 1989b; Hannan and Carroll, 1992).

In this chapter, we argue, in two steps, that the density-dependence formulation cannot possess a high degree of generality. In the first step, we argue that the legitimacy-based explanation of the positive effect of density on foundings and of the negative effect of density on disbandings is theoretically unjustified. In the second step, we show that density dependence, deprived of the artificial unitariness that the legitimacy explanation imparts to it, involves three different processes. Borrowing the concept of externality, we discuss how these processes, which respond to different organizational logics, may link density with foundings and with disbandings in ways not necessarily compatible with the original density dependence formulation. We also sketch out measurement possibilities that would allow for direct investigation of these three processes within the technical and other strictures commonly encountered by organizational ecologists.

Density Dependence Reviewed

The density dependence formulation engenders empirical research at a fast clip. Accordingly, what follows is a progress report valid only up to the date of this writing, in early 1993. This review includes both published and unpublished studies.

Relationships between density and the incidence of foundings of the predicted form have been found for populations of 19th and 20th century American labor unions and urban newspapers (Hannan and Freeman, 1989), for American brewing firms observed between 1634 and1988 (Carroll and Swaminathan, 1991), for German brewing firms from 1900 to 1988 (Carroll et al., 1989), for six populations of urban American newspapers (Carroll and Hannan, 1989b), for Manhattan banks from 1792 to 1980, and for life insurance companies from 1792 to 1937 (Ranger-Moore, Banaszak-Holl, and Hannan, 1991). Findings in support of this thesis are also reported with respect to ethnic newspapers in the United States from 1877 to 1914 (Olzak and West, 1991), for Italian cooperatives, 1963–1987 (Lomi and Freeman, 1990), and for Saskatchewan purchasing cooperatives, 1906–1988 (McLaughlin, 1991). Studies of entry into the medical imaging industry (Mitchell, 1987), into the health maintenance field (Wholey, Christianson, and Sanchez, 1990), and into sectors of the savings and loan industry (Haveman, chapter 8, this volume) also give it indirect support.

Studies of voluntary social service organizations in Toronto (Singh, Tucker, and Meinhard, 1991), of semiconductor firms (Hannan and Freeman, 1989), of three newpaper populations (Carroll and Hannan, 1989b), and of Pennsylvania telephone companies (Barnett and Amburgey, 1990) sought and failed to find the predicted convex relationship between density and the incidence of foundings. Baum and Oliver, studying day-care centers, report (1992) that the effect of density on foundings is simply monotonic and negative (i.e., competitive) when relational density (the number of links between members of the focal population and government and community organizations in the population's environment) is controlled for. As they note, however, this finding might be interpreted as giving refined support to the legitimacy-based thesis.

Support for the predicted concave relationship between density and disbanding rates has been found with respect to American labor unions and one population of urban newspapers (Hannan and Freeman, 1989), three other city newspaper populations (Carroll and Hannan, 1989b), trade associations (Aldrich et al., 1990) semiconductor firms (Hannan and Freeman, 1989), American brewing firms (Carroll and Swaminathan, 1991), and Manhattan bank and life insurance companies (Banaszak-Holl, Ranger-Moore, and Hannan, 1990). Baum and Singh's studies (1992, 1993) of day-care centers give converging findings.

A number of studies of the same general kind have tested the density-disbandings thesis and reported nonconforming findings pertaining to voluntary social organizations (Singh, Tucker, and Meinhard, 1991), Atlantic Canada worker cooperatives (Staber, 1989), California wineries (Delacroix, Swaminathan, and Solt, 1989), German breweries (Carroll et al., 1989), Bavarian breweries (Swaminathan and Wiedenmayer, 1989), Pennsylvania telephone companies (Barnett and Amburgey, 1990), as well as Iowa and Pennsylvania telephone companies (Barnett, 1990). Baum and Oliver (1992) reported a monotonic positive relationship between density and the rate of failure (in keeping with conventional competition conceptualizations) controlling for relational density. Rao and Reddy (1992) also reported a monotonic, positive relationship between density and mortality in a population of American automobile manufacturers observed from the inception of the industry to 1941. They argued that density-dependent disbandings are not likely in a technologically heterogenous population.

Peterson and Koput (1991a) assail part of the density dependence formulation on methodological grounds. They claim, on the basis of a large-scale simulation, that the negative relationship between population size and the disbanding rate in the early history of an organizational form is an artificial product of unobserved heterogeneity within the population. In a rejoinder, Hannan, Barron, and Carroll (1991:411) report that when age is controlled for, unobserved heterogeneity produces spurious negative density dependence in only 3 of 10 replications. Several scholars have also pointed out that it makes little sense to compute population "density" in a manner which gives equal weights to all organizations, irrespective of size (Winter, 1990; Barnett and Amburgey, 1990).

Beyond this, Singh and Lumsden (1990) comment that it is difficult theoretically to reconcile the empirical findings of relatively strong support for density dependence in foundings and relatively weak support for density dependence in disbandings. Finally, Zucker (1989) has taken the whole density dependence thesis to task on theoretical grounds, criticizing Hannan and Freeman for imposing the concept of legitimacy expost facto and without direct measurement on empiricist findings that would otherwise remain unexplained.

Proponents of the density dependence findings have responded with their own methodological criticism of nonconforming studies. They claim that findings fail to support their formulation because they are based on histories of organizational forms that are truncated on the left (Carroll and Hannan, 1989b; Hannan and Carroll, 1992). However, they overlook responses to this anticipated argument as presented in Delacroix, Swaminathan, and Solt (1989), ignore the nonconforming findings in studies covering the whole history of the organizational form, including their own (e.g., Carroll et al., 1989) and even treat as supportive findings resolutely contradicting the density dependence thesis (Carroll and Hannan, 1989b:578, on Delacroix et al., 1989). Sometimes they are insensitive to substantive implausibilities in their own demonstration. Thus, the support for the density dependence thesis in Carroll and Swaminathan's study of American breweries (1991) rests on the implicit argument that breweries in early colonial America were illegitimate because they were strange, not taken for granted. This, in turn, entails the belief that English settlers did not bring the brewery organizational form with them to American shores. In the next section of the chapter we take up again Zucker's criticism through a search of the literature on legitimacy.

When Do Organizations Lack Legitimacy?

For "legitimacy" to be used as a genuine higher order concept, it must be capable of operationalization along a finite number of dimensions. The concept of legitimacy is found in two broad streams of sociological literature. The first, meticulously reviewed and discussed by Zelditch and Walker (1984), addresses authority relations within organizations and small groups. It does not appear to have direct relevance to the ecological use of the term except in one respect: they remark that "propriety does not directly determine impropriety" (1984:20) and that a structure will persist even without substantive support providing the opposition is inactive, a thesis pursued by Rao and Delacroix (1988), in the context of the density dependence formulation and with respect to business organizations specifically.

The second stream, traceable to Weber, is concerned with macroprocesses akin to those of organizational ecology. Weber (1947) viewed organizations as a combination of powers and emphasized the social validity of powers as the source of legitimacy. In this context, the core source of "legitimacy" is the fact of being in accordance with the law. By extension, other sources are the fact of being taken for granted (Stinchcombe, 1968) and moral approval, without reference to the narrowly defined legality of the actions, institutions, or organizations being considered (Smelser, 1963; Berger and Luckman, 1966; Zucker, 1987).

Stinchcombe (1968:158–66) states that organizations are social mechanisms for deciding how authority and other resources are to be used. He describes the legitimacy of organizations as hinging on their ability to rely on law, government, and public opinion "as reserves in case of need." In Stinchcombe's view (1968:188–98), the initial organizational act is a proposal endorsed and actively backed by entrepreneurial coalitions which aim to obtain a distinct combination of powers. A new organization comes into existence when a "legal personalty" is acquired, that is, "a set of powers—money, land, legal power, licenses and so forth—committed to a single decision-making apparatus with a relatively narrow purpose" (Stinchcombe, 1968:194).

This emphasis on the authorization of organizational structure and taken-for-grantedness (Scott, 1987a) has been adopted by Dowling and Pfeffer (1975) and by institutional theorists (DiMaggio and Powell, 1983; Meyer and Rowan, 1977), and through them, by some organizational ecologists (Singh, Tucker, and House, 1986; Carroll and Huo, 1986; Hannan and Freeman, 1989). Accordingly, legitimacy is a central concept in models that treat the "environment as institution" (Zucker 1987:444; DiMaggio and Powell, 1983; DiMaggio, 1988; Thomas and Meyer, 1984). At the heart of this institutional perspective is the idea that isomorphism with the state-dominated normative order facilitiates organizations' access to resources and therefore raises their survival chances (Meyer and Rowan, 1977). To the extent that the state normative order either reflects or generates the dominant social values, conformity with the latter is also a source of legitimacy. Also, to the extent that submission to scrutiny is a habitual condition of state approval, submission to scrutiny in general may constitute yet another source of legitimacy (Etzioni, 1987). Thus, conceptualizations of legitimacy, past and present, coalesce around a diffuse but nevertheless clear construction of legitimacy as a successfully passed political and moral test where the examiners are civil authorities and public opinion in varying proportions. It is difficult to maintain a strict distinction between the two categories of examiners in modern democratic societies where citizens tend to have a good opinion of the law and where opinions readily become law.

This general view of organizational legitimacy implies fairly forthrightly the conditions under which lack of legitimacy will imperil new organizational forms. This particular brand of "liability of newness" (the tendency of young organizations to have high rates of mortality) will arise when organizational formation entails the conquest of existing combinations of values and powers, or the conversion of existing combinations of values and powers, or, especially, when organizational formation involves the creation of new powers and values. It follows from this established usage that new organizational forms should not be equally vulnerable to the withholding of legitimacy. Organizational forms resting on innovative configurations of powers and values must be particularly vulnerable. Conversely, new organizational forms which are mere versions of existing forms must encounter minimal difficulties in this respect. Moreover, given the implicit centrality of the state in the original conceptualizations of legitimacy, organizational forms which derive a large proportion of resources from the state (such as semiconductor firms in their beginnings) must be especially vulnerable.

Although Hannan and Freeman's original findings (1987, 1988a, 1989) have since been joined by other conforming and nonconforming findings (see Singh and Lumsden [1990] and Hannan and Carroll [1992] for reviews other than our own), the strength of the density dependence thesis still relies largely on findings relative to labor unions and newspapers (Hannan and Freeman, 1989), and perhaps breweries (Carroll and Swaminathan, 1991). The two relevant studies are the only ones which both lend support to density dependence in foundings and disbandings on the one hand and satisfy the condition of observation from the origin of the form on the other (Hannan and Carroll, 1992). We will argue that these organizational forms should be regarded as uncommonly vulnerable to the withholding of legitimacy as defined.

Labor unions would, in the 19th century, appear extremely illegitimate because they created a dramatic new power: the power to strike (Beard, 1939; Perlman, 1937; Stinchcombe, 1968). Newspapers, according to Carroll himself (1987:13), were essentially "a political tool" that disrupted the existing social order through their ability to mobilize public opinion on a historically unprecedented scale. In the religious context of the 19th century, alcohol-dispensing organizations such as breweries were also perceived, at times, as disruptive of the social order, as indicated by the voluminous prohibitionist propaganda culminating in the 1920–34 national Prohibition in the United States. Hence, it is possible to believe that for newspapers, labor unions, and breweries, growing numbers played an important part in the overcoming of environmental hostility. It does not follow from these examples that all new organizational forms must face environmental hostility which can only be overcome by sheer weight of numbers.

Labor unions, newspapers, and other such organizations that are clearly disruptive of the prevailing social order may be comparatively rare. Yet, it is possible to broaden the class of organizations to which the state pays active attention to include such disparate forms as day-care centers and money-lending organizations of every ilk (see Amburgey, Dacin, and Kelly, chapter 12; Ginsberg and Baum, chapter 7; and Haveman, chapter 8, this volume). Much support for the density dependence formulation thus comes from the study of abnormally regulated organizations because such organizations are also the most likely to yield the long and detailed records organizational ecologists require. Even broader categories of organizational forms, however, especially those involved in business but also nonprofit organizations, are both granted fairly automatic state approval and are thence less likely to encounter shortage of legitimacy and less prone to leave records exploitable by organizational ecologists.

As Smelser (1963:25) notes, "one of the apparent paradoxes of free enterprise is that it has been the basis for legitimizing many types of economic arrangements." Wiley and Zald (1968) state that certification and inspection of novel organizational forms are routine and standardized and do not present problems in modern industrial societies. Explicit and well-understood property and contract law, tax incentives, and support for broad-based training of individuals for business careers (as in M.B.A. programs) are some of the concrete ways in which capitalist societies recognize the legitimacy of business organizations, including those of new forms (Etzioni, 1987).

More importantly, such societies make provisions for explicit and universalistic tests of certification uniform for all organizations, past, present, and future.

This discussion suggests that the legitimacy explanation does not ensure the generalizability of the density dependence formulation as stated. Such general character must be obtained, if at all, from another source. Next we unbundle the phenomenon on density dependence in a search for subprocesses which may possess the generality claimed for the overall process.

Unbundling Density Dependence

Taking apart the mechanisms by which growing density may reduce disbanding rates while raising the incidence of foundings, we find a causal assumption and three unrelated substantive propositions. The causal assumption is that some organizations derive benefits from belonging to a population which are beyond what their own contribution would explain. These benefits include a heightened ability to survive (for existing organizations) or an enhanced likelihood of being founded. As far as both survival and birth are concerned, latter instances of the form do not have to overcome all the difficulties encountered by early instances, or not to the same degree. Considered in this manner, the mechanisms by which some organizations benefit from the contributions of others seem familiar; they constitute simply a collection of externalities. An "externality" exists when there is an inequality between private costs and benefits on the one hand and collective costs and benefits on the other (Arrow, 1970; Baumol and Oates, 1975). Externalities may be positive or negative (Mansfield, 1977:427–29), an important fact not explicitly taken into account by the density dependence formulation.

Recasting density dependence arguments in these terms leads to the recognition of three main categories of externalities which appear to underlie the concept of legitimacy as used by density dependence advocates.[1] First, early entrants into an industry incur the cost of developing the *reputation* of the organizational form in question. Thus, early entrants into the industry may create user awareness of new products and habituate civil authorities and potential recruits to the new organizations providing them. Early entrants may also assist in developing a track record which makes it possible for financial institutions to assess the credit worthiness of new instances of a new organizational form. Second, late entrants may be able *vicariously to learn* at low cost from the conduct of early entrants. Third, early entrants assume the costs of establishing an *infrastructure* which later entrants can use at lesser expense and risk. In particular, early entrants may set up personnel and supply and distribution networks. They may also support the costs of developing technical standards in cooperation with suppliers and buyers. Finally, early entrants may set up trade associations to further their collective interests or engage in activities which facilitate the subsequent establishment of a trade association. All of these actions of early entrants contribute to the creation of a community of functionally specialized populations. This means that later entrants are free riders on the investment made by others into government and community relations (Baum and Oliver, 1992).

Some of the positive externalities stemming from the activities of early entrants may be amplified by population growth. The more widespread an organizational form, the easier it is for risk-averse actors to assess it, as employees, financiers, and founders. Similarly, the more widespread an organizational form, the greater are the opportunities for learning about it. Moreover, as an organizational form diffuses, the cost of supporting its infrastructure is shared among an increasing number of units and across a larger organizational mass. Nevertheless, using population growth as the only surrogate for exernalities has two undesirable consequences. First, this practice jumbles together three distinct processes which may not, in fact, move in unison. Second, this practice obfuscates the possibility that externalities, including those accompanying rising density, may be negative.

The clarity of an organizational form's reputation and the opportunity for vicarious learning about the form both seem to hinge on the visibility of existing and predecessor instances of the form. Visibility, in turn, may be largely a function of raw numbers. Nevertheless, it is necessary to separate the relationship between density and reputation from that between density and vicarious learning for two reasons. First, reputation, the generic concept most closely associated with the particular concept of legitimacy, gives rise to negative as well as to positive externalities. By an accident of language, this is not the case for legitimacy. Second, the positive externality of vicarious learning must be subject to the law of diminishing returns, which need not be the case for the positive reputational externality. In addition, the confusion between infrastructural and other processes inherent in the legitimacy explanation also conceals a useful link between the population level and the community level of organizational analysis.

Even reliance on density as a surrogate only for positive externalities creates three problems already remedied, if not always explicitly noted by other researchers. For one, using population size as a measure of positive externalities presumes that all existing organizations contribute equally to the reputation of the form, to vicarious learning, and to the creation of infrastructure. In doing so, researchers using density-based measures of externality overlook the possibility that larger organizations have stronger effects than smaller organizations. Population mass, or the sum of the sizes of all existing organizations, has been found to reduce the failure rate and to increase the founding rate even when the effects of simple population size are controlled for. This suggests that larger organizations improve the viability of other organizations to a greater extent than do smaller organizations (Barnett, 1990; Barnett and Amburgey, 1990). Second, in using density as a measure of positive externalities researchers fail to consider whether older organizations contribute more of everything than do younger organizations. Older organizations, by the very fact of their longevity, are likely to have contributed more to the reputation of the form as well as to the construction of the infrastructure than younger organizations. Moreover, the opportunities to learn vicariously from older organizations are greater than the chances to learn vicariously from younger organizations. Conversely, this practice ignores the possibility that older organizations may have erected barriers to the entry of new organizations, a fact which is contrary to the logic of legitimacy but may run concurrently with it. Third, relying on population size to measure all positive externalities forces the researcher to make inferences about unobserved social processes: the growth of reputation, the incidence of vicarious learning, and the development of an infrastructure, which may not unfold at the same pace nor indeed in the same direction. We discuss next how independent, measurement-oriented conceptualizations of reputation, of vicarious learning, and of infrastructure development could be constructed.

Reputational Externalities

The reputation of an organizational form no doubt influences its ability to obtain financial and personnel resources over and beyond the ease of its access to civil authorities and their benevolence toward the form. The willingness of other social actors, such as potential suppliers and distributors, to commit to instances of the form is also affected by its reputation. Reputation, in turn, depends on several factors.

First, the absence of a track record is an absolute obstacle to the establishment of a reputation. Hence, we would expect some measures of population size to be positively associated with reputation. Each independent instance of the population provides a data point. Consequently, the number of units must be important. But the overall visibility of the form must depend on how much social space it occupies relative to the other populations vying for the attention of observers. This social space must also be approximately commensurate with the duration of organizations, or with the time that observers have had to assess the corresponding form. Therefore, reputation must also be a function of the cumulative age of the units in the population. All the organizations of the same form cannot contribute equally to the reputation of the form. *Ceteris paribus* we should expect larger and older organizations to contribute more than smaller and newer ones. Larger organizations should contribute more first, because of their superior visibility. In addition, the objective importance of their performance to the health of the communities to which they belong ensures that they are the object of systematic observation.

Older organizations should contribute disproportionately because of the length of their individual track records. Again, *ceteris paribus,* credit analysts are probably more comfortable passing judgment on long records than on short ones. Beyond this, perceptually, it is easier to assess a few large and old organizations than a large number of small and new ones although the total mass of the former may be equal to the total mass of the latter. Consequently, the reading of the track record of the whole population will be facilitated by the existence in its midst of large and of old organizations.

The idea of a reputational externality makes little sense if the possibility of a bad reputation is not allowed. It is not enough for an organizational form to possess a track record, however clear and easy to read, to gain the automatic approval of relevant observers. In most situations, a bad record is worse than no record at all. It would be difficult to argue, for example, that the population of savings and loans associations, which was still quite large in 1992, after the crisis, was viewed more favorably by investors than it was in 1942, when it was smaller and its form more novel. The possiblity that acceptance diminishes as density grows is not considered by the legitimacy explanation because "legitimacy" is a term not capable of denoting negative values. In general, observers must be alert to negative evidence. Well-publicized events such as bankruptcies and lay-offs must, as well as a high incidence of foundings ("fertility"), figure prominently in the ongoing evaluation of the form and must be taken as reputational signals. Consequently, any estimation of the effects of density on disbandings and foundings through reputation should hypothesize explicitly on the direction of such signals.

The visibility of negative reputational events, their accessibility to relevant observers, must be a complex function of the mass of the failed organizations, of the physical proximity of the failure events, and of their recency. This, because we assume here that observers are likely to scan most effectively their proximate environment and because we suppose that they have finite memories. Old events contribute less to reputation (including negative reputation) for two reasons. First, records dissipate (are lost) with time. Second, observers may decide consciously that old information is less pertinent than new information. This assumption calls for a weighting of failure events negatively to reflect remoteness in time, perhaps through a form of distributed lag, as used by Russell and Hanneman (1991), for example.

Finally, although all social observers potentially contribute to building the reputation of a form, they probably do not contribute equally. There are specialized actors whose main function is to monitor and to assess. Accordingly, we believe that Hannan and Freeman's emphasis on financial organizations is well placed. In general, we expect the monitoring function to be the better performed, the more independent professional evaluators on the scene. However, it is not possible to specify the strength or the direction of the indirect association between the former variable on the one hand and the disbanding rate and incidence of foundings on the other. The more effectively the monitoring function is performed, the greater may be the costs of justifying a new founding or of promoting the survival of a poorly performing organization. The efficacy of monitoring, in turn, depends upon a redundancy of observation, which implies multiple observers, and on the resources at their disposal. Such observers are often themselves organizations. Hence, this discussion of population processes merges into the consideration of community processes.

The logic of reputational processes leads to counterintuitive predictions not usually contemplated by density dependence arguments. Thus, one might argue that the degree of confidence that specialized monitors such as banks and other financial institutions have in an organizational form is adequately summarized by its degree of indebtedness. A high debt intensity of an organizational population can only be the result of conscious action by financiers. To argue otherwise is to denounce the evaluation performed by financiers and all statements affirming benefits based on the judgment of evaluators and, by implication, much of the logic of density dependence. Therefore, the higher the indebtedness of population, the more confident are financiers of the prospects of the organizational form. The underlying appraisal process may affect foundings and disbandings differentially: a high level of population indebtedness should constitute at once an incentive to support existing forms *and* to restrict the birth of new instances.

Vicarious Learning as an Externality

To learn vicariously is to learn through the experience of others by imitating or by avoiding what others do.[2] Organizational ecology is predicated on the existence of vicarious organizational learning. Although the state mandates organizational forms to an extent, its specifications are not detailed enough to account for the fact that organizational ecologists are able to reach a fair degree of agreement as to what constitutes an organizational population. That organizations founded a century apart are sufficiently alike to justify the concept of organizational "form" implies a high incidence of imitation (DiMaggio and Powell, 1983; Aldrich et al., chapter 11, this volume). The opportunity to imitate must be a function of the number of instances of the form, as envisaged by the density dependence formulation, but it cannot be an exclusive function of this number. Instead the sum total of relevant information available to imitators comprises all actions of all existing organizations of the same kind, all failures of instances of the form that are accessible to the observer, and probably also all observable founding events. The record of past organizations of the form (distinct from the specific event of their disbanding) should also be included. We will ignore this last point for the sake of brevity, but it should be incorporated in any measurement pertaining to learning.

The relationships between the number of organizations in simultaneous existence, vicarious learning, and the disbanding rate, on the one hand, and between those and the incidence of foundings on the other are substantially different. Learning can only affect the failing rate through policy change or structural transformation. However, the sign of the causal relationship between change/transformation and the disbanding rate is largely undetermined and leaves open the possibilities of both inertia and attempted adaptation. The more organizations there are, the greater the opportunities to learn (through mimicry, see Mezias and Lant, chapter 10, this volume) and the more frequently existing organizations must attempt transformation. But, from an ecological viewpoint, attempts to transform organizational structures re-create liabilities of newness and jeopardize the survival of organizations (Hannan and Freeman, 1989; Amburgey, Kelly, and Barnett, 1993). From an adaptationist viewpoint, some changes may enhance the survival of organizations (Singh, Tucker, and House, 1986). Hence the direction of the relationship between the sum total of information available and the disbanding rate is also theoretically undetermined. Insofar as foundings are concerned, the greater the number of organizations, the greater the potential to learn, the more likely are potential founders to start new organizations on the basis of vicarious learning. This is as specified by the density dependence formulation. Thus, the larger the population, the greater the opportunity to learn, the more frequent attempts at transformations, the higher the failing rate, and the higher the founding rate, or alternatively, the lower the failing rate and the higher the founding rate.

While the sum of the population's experience contributes to vicarious learning, the ability of focal organizations to access experience must recede with time. Consequently, each informational item used to express the possibility that vicarious learning has taken place must be weighted by the inverse of its age. Obviously, any a priori weight assignment is arbitrary and researchers must experiment with different formulas according to the kind of organization studied.

To the extent that all population information aids both survival and foundings, organizational failures and other forms of disbandings, which are more dramatic, and therefore more visible events than most everyday organizational actions, ought to promote both survival (as found by Delacroix, Swaminathan, and Solt, 1989) and foundings. From the standpoint of vicarious learning, density, although it is systematically related in the long run to the frequency of disbandings, must be a poor proxy for this variable. Cumulatively, one cannot say whether a high frequency of prior disbandings should constitute a negative or a positive externality. Whether it worsens the life chances in the population through a reputational path or whether it promotes survival by serving as an object lesson about conduct to be avoided remains an empirical question. The answer to this question cannot be uniform across populations because some organizational forms are easier to observe than others, and this favors the second path. Hence, one should not expect a generic positive association between prior disbandings on the one hand and the subsequent failure rate on the other. Uniformity of findings in this connection is, in and of itself, suspicious.

Infrastructural Externalities

Infrastructural expansion is the third and indirect process through which rising density may increase the incidence of foundings and depress the disbanding rate. This is an indirect process because an increasing population does nothing to improve the chances of its own survival or the incidence of foundings, in an infrastructural sense. The relevant assumption of the density dependence formulation is that a growing population somehow induces whatever infrastructural development it needs. Taking this functionalist argument at face value, we argue that density is a poor and unnecessary proxy for infrastructural development because the infrastructure pertaining to a given focal population itself comprises other organizations. These can be identified and enumerated. Therefore, the study of the causes and effects of infrastructural development can, in principle, be approached with conventional methods of organizational ecology. On the one side, it is possible to test empirically the commonsense notion that a growing focal population necessarily implies an expanded infrastructure. On the other side, the fact that the infrastructure is largely composed of other organizations allows for the straightforward testing of hypotheses pertaining to its association with disbanding rates and with the incidence of foundings. Such hypotheses would be shaped by the following rationale:

The infrastructure consists of resources and relationships created by the organizations in the existing population and by organizations now disbanded. Largely a community of functionally related and specialized organizational populations (see Barnett, chapter 16, this volume), the infrastructure enables existing organizations in the focal population, and new start-ups, to embed themselves at low cost into supplier and distributor networks and personnel recruitment milieus, and to benefit by the existence of trade associations. The relationship between infrastructural development and the disbanding rate ought to be direct: as suppliers, distributors, and sources of personnel expand, focal organizations are increasingly assured of access to raw materials, markets, and personnel. Similarly, the existence of trade associations enables focal population members to extract protection and other artificial benefits from legislatures and regulatory agencies and even to overcome the consequences of a bad reputation of the form.

The connection between infrastructural development and foundings is less direct for two reasons. First, it relies on a heightened *perception* of reduced costs and risks of organizing. Second, although focal population growth may be enhanced by infrastructural development, the latter may also be associated with barriers to entry established by early entrants. Here again, we discover a theoretical indeterminacy not noted by the legitimacy explanation of density dependence. While it is easy to accept that more infrastructure can only lower the disbanding rate (or at least, the failing rate, narrowly defined), its effects on foundings need not be symmetrical. The larger the population, the more developed its infrastructure but also, *ceteris paribus*, the older the population and the more likely are early entrants to have established barriers to entry. To the extent that population age and size overlap, it is not theoretically clear which effect should prevail. We note in passing that an important element of infrastructure, trade associations, may have the raising of such barriers as one of their primary purposes.

Unlike reputational and vicarious learning processes, infrastructural expansion should have only ephemeral effects on disbandings and on foundings, except for the possibility of brief erroneous delayed perception in relation to the latter. For a given focal organization at time t only the state of the infrastructure at time t matters. The infrastructure as it was five years before is irrelevant (except in the very indirect sense that it contributed to the survival and founding of population members still in existence at time t). Hence, the measurement of infrastructure should be entirely concerned with the present and with the very recent past, unlike reputational and vicarious learning measurements.

Puccia and Levins (1985) propose that most modeling strategies cannot at once maximize generality, realism, and precision. The thesis of density dependence of organizational foundings and disbandings seems to sacrifice precision and, to a lesser extent, realism to generality. However, ongoing empirical research has produced less than a consensus about its validity. We questioned, following Zucker (1989), the use of the concept of legitimacy as an umbrella explanation for these empirical findings which do conform. We argued in this chapter that "density dependence" encompasses at lease three categories of externalities, only one of which is related (imperfectly) to legitimacy processes, strictly defined. We pointed out that these three categories of externality should not in principle produce identical outcomes and that some lead to counterintuitive outcomes. When density dependence is unbundled into the externality processes that it comprises and the empirical research conducted on its components, we may find that density dependent phenomena are either more or less general than claimed.

Notes

1. Our analysis of legitimacy as an externality differs from current discussion of "network externalities" in the technological innovation literature. First, students of "network externalities" refer to "positive consumption" or the benefits flowing to producers from the increased use and adoption of a technology or a standard (Katz and Shapiro, 1985; Arthur, 1989). By contrast, we believe that legitimacy as used by ecological theorists refers more to what may be called "positive supply externalities," that is, the increased benefits flowing from the activities of early entrants and the existence of large numbers of the same form. Second, ecological theorists, unlike economists, treat "positive supply externalities" (such as taken-for-

grantedness, trained talent, and collective action) as bounded, because they argue that the competitive effects of density overwhelm in the end the legitimation effects of density.

2. Vicarious learning has been widely discussed under the rubric of imitation in the technological innovation literature and under the label of mimetic isomorphism in the institutional literature (see DiMaggio and Powell, 1983). Both literatures emphasize how organizations adopt ideas, structures, and technologies but overlook how organizations *avoid* ideas, structures, and technologies. We use the term vicarious learning to denote both adoption and avoidance of ideas, structure, and technologies.

14

Resource Partitioning and Foundings of Banking Cooperatives In Italy

JOHN FREEMAN AND ALESSANDRO LOMI

This study of the founding of Italian Rural Cooperative Banks is intended to contribute to the integration of ecological and institutional theories of organization. Specifically, we propose a model according to which institutional practices and expectations related to abstract principles and moral (or noneconomic) values materialize in concrete features of the organizational structure. These constrain the competitive behavior of the organizations assuming that form. These behavioral constraints produce immediate ecological consequences at the industry level in terms of niche width and resource partitioning, which have implications for the persistence (or change) of the original institutionalized practices.

Following the law and economics literature (Jensen and Meckling, 1976a, 1979; Williamson, 1985; Hansmann, 1990) organizational forms, and hence organizational diversity, are conceptualized here in terms of alternative property rights arrangements chosen by organizational members to coordinate activities, mediate their personal interests, and resolve potential conflicts. As we explain in detail later, doing so has the advantage of defining the "unobservable blueprint" underlying the notion of organizational form (Hannan and Freeman, 1977) in terms of observable organizational characteristics.

In studying credit organizations we derive the empirical implications of Powell's contention that "[i]nstitutional and technical factors are not dichotomous, but rather dimensions along which environments vary. Both types of environments place pressures on organizations to which they must be responsive in order to survive" (1990:186; see also Scott, 1991:168). As Scott and Meyer (1983) pointed out, credit institutions are among the best examples of organizations that are *simultaneously* subjected to strong *competitive pressures* originating from the structure of the financial sector, and to strict *procedural requirements* imposed by credit authorities (typically the central banks) and by national states (typically through economic policy). We expect a study of credit organization to clarify the technical and institutional nature of many other important societal sectors.

In this paper we try to develop arguments about how technical and institutional

This research was supported by N.A.T.O.—C.N.R grant number 215.24/10 (Division of Economic, Sociological and Statistical Disciplines).

pressures jointly shape the dynamics of organizational populations in the context of processes of organizational founding. During the last 55 years, national governments and central credit authorities have regulated the dynamics of competition in the Italian banking industry by prescribing specific organizational prerequisites that new entrants had to meet in order to operate legitimately as "banks." After the enactment of the 1936 Banking Law, only credit institutions formally incorporated as (limited liability) cooperatives were de facto granted access to the banking industry. In this way institutionalized norms and expectations defining the identity of cooperative organizations became encoded in the organizational form necessarily assumed by the new entrants. This institutionally prescribed organizational form has represented a major set of constraints on the competitive and market behavior of new banking organizations. In the banking organizations under study, this means that the market in which they operate, the services they provide, the competitive strategies that are feasible, and the relationships between organizational members and clients are all constrained and, in a fundamental way, defined by specific dimensions of the organizational form.

The institutionalized practices encoded in the organizational form provide the assurance that organizations can function reliably, and that they will be operating tomorrow after receiving resources today (Hannan and Freeman, 1984). That is, the reason individuals trust organizations such as banks is that they believe that the organizations will perform as advertised. Such beliefs are stimulated and supported by specific features of the organizational form. In other words, we see these beliefs of trust as institutionalized in the sense that they are founded in widespread experience with frequently replicated procedures through which organizations come into existence and operate.

Norms related to the abstract notion of cooperation produced direct and con-

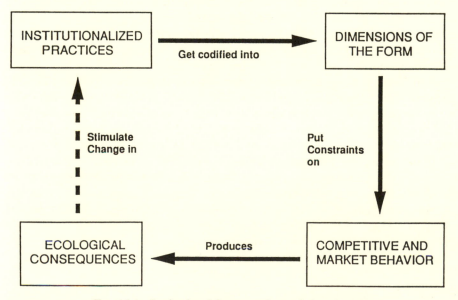

FIG. 14.1   Institutional factors and population dynamics

crete ecological consequences through the definition of the organizational form which new banks were forced to assume in order to operate legitimately. Specifically, we show how institutional constraints imposed on the organizational form induced processes of niche segregation and resource partitioning at the industry level (Carroll, 1985). Small unit banks successfully established themselves at the fringes of the market and exploited peripheral resource spaces opened by competition among the large core banks competing to occupy the center of that market.

Finally, the consequences of these ecological processes in terms of industry structure, behavior, and performance create the conditions for persistence (or disruption) of the original institutional practices. In the Italian banking industry, such practices have been extremely persistent and have survived virtually unchanged during the last 55 years. Our argument about the ecological consequences of institutionalized practices is summarized in Figure 14.1.

Institutional Processes and Banking Cooperatives

We begin a more detailed analysis of the institutional underpinnings of cooperative organization by noting two streams of logic running through the literature on institutional approaches to organizational research. The first of these might be called the *bureaucratic imperative argument.* According to this line of reasoning, organizations operate in a world of constraints imposed by the state. Bureaucratic regulations are, of course, formalized norms. So the use of the state's authority, political power, and even the threat of violence shapes organizations according to those normative prescriptions and proscriptions.[1] To the degree that these regulations have consistent effects over an organizational field, such action by the state produces "coercive isomorphism" among the organizations affected (DiMaggio and Powell, 1983). By elaborating laws through "guidelines" and other policies, the administrative bureaucracy of the state both manufactures and enforces norms to which individual organizations conform.

This isomorphism underlies the concept of organizational form developed by population ecologists. It should be noted, however, that it can also generate diversity by introducing segregating mechanisms (Hannan and Freeman, 1986a, 1989). This is precisely how savings and loans (S&Ls) were distinguished from banks in the United States. And the erosion of this regulatory distinction led to the disappearance of the S&L form.[2] Put simply, the bureaucratic imperative argument is that organizations are set up the way they are because some superordinate organization imposes a set of practices and structures on them. Applied to banking cooperatives in Italy, the bureaucratic imperative has operated through the efforts of the developing nation state to organize the banking sector.

The second stream of reasoning might be called the *cultural imperative argument.* According to this argument, organizations adopt a set of practices because the people being organized have accepted a culture that has organizational implications. The view of culture institutional theorists have most often found useful focuses on the set of typifications, ends, and means that actors take for granted. As DiMaggio and Powell (1991:28) put it: "Cultural frames thus establish approved means and define desired outcomes, leading business people to pursue profits, bureaucrats to seek budgetary growth, and scholars to strive for publication." These cultural frames transcend particular organizations but often emanate from organizations. In the empirical situation under study here, the Catholic Church overtly supported cooperative organization. It is this support and the norms of community responsibility and ethical behavior that answer the question of trust.

Cooperation

The origins of Italian cooperative banking are often interpreted by historians of the labor movement as an outcome of the attempt by the ruling class to prevent the spread of socialist ideals among rural populations, rather than the result of a genuine "social movement" (Earle, 1986). This "paternalistic" component in the origins of cooperative organizations was apparent in the attempts of the north Italian liberal politicians to channel social discontent into organized economic action.

Like cooperation in agriculture and construction, credit cooperation in Italy has its origins in the northeastern regions, and the earliest organizations were introduced in Italy by liberal Italian politicians copying existing German organizations. The first Italian cooperative organization, established in 1853, was the Workers' Selfhelp Society of Turin (Piedmont). Ten years later, the first cooperative bank (the Banca Popolare di Lodi) was founded, and it still exists today. These two organizations were the vanguard of two forms of cooperative credit organizations which can still be found virtually unchanged in the Italian banking industry: popular cooperative banks (PCBs) and rural cooperative banks (RCBs). A key characteristic of these cooperative forms is their way of defining interests of owners, that is, property rights.

Property Rights

Organizational change can be conceptualized as a process whereby actors select alternative organizational forms in ways that are institutionally constrained (Nelson and Winter, 1982; Campbell and Lindberg, 1990). The structure of property rights affects this selection process (Robbins, 1987; Lazerson, 1988), and hence organizational diversity.

The 1936 Banking Act established the kinds of organizational actors that can legitimately operate in banking. That is, this act defined banks in Italy. According to this act (Art. 1), there are eight admissible kinds of banks in Italy:

1. Public Law Banks
2. Banks of National Interest
3. Saving and Loans banks
4. Pawn Institutions
5. Private Stock Banks
6. Agencies of foreign banks
7. Popular Cooperative Banks (PCBs)
8. Rural and Cooperative Banks (RCBs)

These legal categories identified and distinguished the organizational actors on the basis of form of ownership or control (state, private, mixed, collective), size (large, small), scope of operations (national, local), and strategy in terms of financial services rendered and customers served. These strategies also differ on specialism/generalism. The state owned Public Law Banks and state controlled Banks of National Interest are providers of the whole array of financial services found in banking, while the others specialize.

The crucial assumption underlying the notion of organizational form is that it is possible to identify relatively invariant organizational characteristics that make for stability over time, committing the organization to a recognizable set of environmental dependencies and to a limited range of plausible behaviors. In Italy, financial innovation, technological and institutional change, and the globalization of financial services have been in continuous development during the last fifty years. They have progressively eroded the differences in strategy and, in some circumstances, size and scope of organizations. Similar processes occurred in the United States for commercial and mutual banks (Ranger-Moore, Banaszak-Holl, and Hannan, 1991; Haveman, 1992). In spite of these powerful blending processes (Hannan and Freeman, 1986a:60), the fundamental distinction among different organizational forms based on ownership structure has remained.

The value of concentrating on alternative property rights arrangements to define the organizational form is that it allows the definition of invariant and observable characteristics of the organizational forms that commit the correspondent organizations to a limited range of possible actions and to specific resource constraints. The relation between organizational structure and alternative contractual arrangements that the organizational members may choose is important not only for its substantial consequences in terms of efficiency, effectiveness, and profitability at the level of single organizations (Jensen and Meckling, 1976a; Jones, 1983; Williamson, 1985), but also for its theoretical standing as one of the central problems of organizational theory. In describing the "problem of organization," Coleman (1974:39) notes the fact that

> to gain the benefits of organization, they (the organizational members) must give over the use of certain rights, resources or power to the corporate body. Only in this way can the corporate actor have the necessary power to carry out the purposes for which they created it. But each person, in turning over these rights, thereby loses a large measure of control over them.

Thus, the structure of property rights defines the institutional basis of power relations among individuals in the production process within the organization and in exchange between organizations, and not just relationships between agents and property (Bowels, 1984). So the system of property rights encoded in the organizational structure plays an important role in motivating and monitoring self-interested individuals, and in generating collective behavior (Simon, 1947, 1951; Crozier and Friedberg, 1977; Kulik, 1989); it is in this sense that structure of property rights can be considered as a concrete, observable, and stable set of instructions to generate, organize, and terminate collective action.

Specifically, for the case in point, the early 1932 law (No. 656) defined Rural Cooperative Banks as "cooperative associations whose main goal is to exercise rural and agricultural credit." Thus, with their first institutional recognition RCBs were established as specialized credit institutions. The scope of operation of RCBs was progressively expanded in the following years. At the present time, RCBs can be understood as

1. *Cooperative organizations.* As such, they give preference in activating loans and other financial operations to members (Law 1937:1206, 15), and operations with nonmembers cannot exceed 25 percent of the total deposits.
2. *Credit institutions.* As such, they are subjected to the general norms regulating competition and organization in the banking industry.
3. *Specialized lenders* to agricultural and craft organizations. As such, they are restricted by the law to a very specific functional and geographical specialization in terms of the professional activity of their clients, and of the kinds of financial services that they can offer.

The Cooperative Movement in Italy

Among all the Western economies, Italy has the largest and fastest growing system of producer, construction, agricultural, and consumer cooperatives in existence. At the end of 1989, for example, there were 21,199 producer and 45,784 construction cooperative organizations. During the decade 1980–90 the *minimum* number of producer cooperatives founded per year was 2,015 in 1983. Producer cooperatives constitute about the 20 percent of the overall Italian "cooperative movement." (All data from *Ministero del Lavoro e della Previdenza Sociale: Statistiche della Cooperazione,* various years).

Roots of Contemporary Organizational Forms. Popular Cooperative Banks (PCBs) were adapted from the Shultze–Delitzsch model of "people's bank" established in Germany where members could buy shares for a small investments and could take loans in proportion to their shareholding, but their responsibility was limited to their holding. The first PCB was founded in Lodi near Milan March 28, 1864. Since the early years of their existence, PCBs displayed the tendency to behave like ordinary investor owned banks lending to outside customers and discounting bills of exchange.

Like PCBs, Rural Cooperative Banks (RCBs) were imported into Italy from Germany. They were modeled on the Raiffeisen system of "rural credit unions," or "country saving banks," established in Germany in 1848. Leone Wollemburg established the first RCB on June 20, 1883, in Loreggia, a village near Padua-Venetia. The original objective of the "Wollemburg banks," as RCBs were sometimes called, was to provide basic financial services and modest credit to rural populations and to fight usury, which contributed to the progressive pauperization of agricultural workers and to the massive exodus from rural areas that ensued (Agostini, 1985:18). RCBs spread rapidly in areas characterized by high agricultural intensity and by a diffuse system of small craft businesses. In general, they tended to retain those distinct traits of collective organizations that soon vanished in PCBs.

The Role of the Catholic Church. The "Catholicization" of Rural Cooperative Banks can be understood in a broader context of two campaigns conducted by parishes in rural areas. The first resisted the spread of socialist ideas among agricultural populations (Degli Innocenti, 1977). The second was an attempt by the clergy to reduce the exodus of peasants to cities and, most of all, abroad (Agostini, 1985). The diffusion of socialist ideas and the migration of rural populations tended, respectively, to break the ideological monopoly of the Church in rural areas and to shrink its most important resource base. RCBs were set up and operated with the explicit goal of improving the "moral and material" conditions of the members, and hence to contrast these potentially disastrous macrolevel changes in the distribution of environmental resources. The following excerpt from the February 1895 issue of *La Cooperazione Popolare* (p. 27) illustrates the self-conscious role of the Church in the diffusion of RCBs (emphasis and translation ours):

> A particularly important role in the diffusion of this movement [of credit cooperatives] has been played by clergymen in the countryside, who saw their own people die or escape to America, while liberals were trying to steal country people from the perishes to dechristianize them [*scristianizzarli*], and make them slaves [*asservirli*] of socialism. Under our flag—liberals say—you will reach on earth that happiness that priests only promise you in heaven. While liberals and socialists made noise, parish priests worked for the promotion and diffusion of these economic associations [i.e., RCBs] in rural areas . . . which became, as the Pope wishes, sources of wealth, and of legitimate, strong Catholic action.

At a general level, the emergence and diffusion of Catholic RCBs were the effects of a conscious organizational effort of the Church to expand Catholic presence and influence over many aspects of Italian social and economic life. In 1891, new Catholic social and political involvement received a decisive stimulus from Pope Leo XII's encyclical *Rerum Novarum* on the "conditions of the working classes," which for the first time recognized the right of workers to organize themselves and to set up self-managed institutions, thus marking the beginning of the organizational involvement of the Church in the public and economic life of the recently born Italian nation state.

One year after the encyclical, on April 5, 1892, the priest Don Luigi Cerutti founded the first officially Catholic RCB in a village near Venice. Exploiting the diffused network of parishes, Catholic RCBs spread rapidly to other northern regions with a strong Catholic agrarian population. Although the direct involvement of the clergy in the management of RCBs was considerable even before 1892, after the founding of the first officially Catholic RCB it became predominant.

With the exception of few "ad hoc" administrative rules, RCBs, like PCBs, remained virtually unregulated during the first 50 years of their existence (Costi, 1986). This reflected the ambiguity of the central government's attitude toward cooperation in general, which has swung over the years from neutral to negative, with the enactment of occasional laws that recognized the existence and status of cooperative organizations as corporate bodies. The first attempts to give comprehensive regulation to cooperative banks coincides with the financial crises of the 1920s and 1930s, and with the rationalization of the banking sectors in virtually all the industrialized economies (Costi, 1986). The bureaucratic imperative assumes prominence in the period between the two wars. Because of endemic urban "overbanking" (a technical term referring to oversupply of banking services and an excessive number of banks), the banking laws of 1926 and 1927, and finally, the Banking Act of 1936 were enacted to simplify and regulate the Italian banking industry.

The situation reversed, however, when Mussolini took power in 1922. The fascists' hostility to cooperative socialism fed the trend toward restriction of this mode of organizing. This "deinstitutionalization" ultimately led to banning of both RCBs and PCBs.

In this historical account, we can see the Italian state striving to organize banking activities with the focus of attention on urban centers and the economic activity that would make Italy a modern, industrialized society. But we also see the Catholic Church fostering cooperative banking in the hinterlands. In this period, the Church provides the fabric of time honored institutionalized practices that encourage participation and trust. If small farmers trust anyone not kin to them, that person is likely to be the local priest. If they have faith in the stability of any institution, it is likely to be the Church. Catholic theology and social philosophy provide the basis in belief that underscores trust. But these institutional effects do not develop as an impersonal, generalized trust. Rather, they come packaged in organizational forms that make concrete a set of expectations and practices that make the cooperative organization practical.

Organizational Form

The empirical analysis that follows focuses on the Rural Cooperative Banks. We chose to study this form because it has maintained its cooperative nature throughout its history. This was less true of the PCBs.

In today's RCBs, dividends cannot exceed the legal interest rate, and the statutory charter of RCBs usually contains a proviso of mutual aid according to which residual capital will be donated for the development and diffusion of mutual and cooperative activities in case of bankruptcy. There is a limit to the share of capital that a single member may own in a Rural Cooperative Bank. In 1981 this limit was set at approximately $1,600. The Central Bank establishes the minimum capital requirements that have to be met to obtain authorization for entry and operation. RCBs are required to have at least 30 members. Their members can only be physical persons, farmers or craftsmen who are permanent residents (or run their business) in the same geographical area where the bank is located. The members of an RCB can in theory be held liable without limit for the contractual obligations of the bank. Limited financial returns to members, mutual aid provisions and mutualistic orientation, limited ownership, limits on the extent of business with nonmembers, and the fact that the members are by and large the patrons and the beneficiaries of the bank's activity make the RCBs close to ideal cooperative forms of organizations.

The scope of activity of RCBs is strictly limited to the geographical area (the city or the village) in which the bank has its headquarters and they are, in general, legally barred from growing by branching. This norm sets RCBs aside from all other organizations in the Italian banking system. Also, the kind of loans and financial services that RCBs can provide is strictly established by law. RCBs are allowed to lend money beyond the short term (finance of capital and machinery of agricultural firms) and to negotiate medium to long term loans with customers and members.

These concrete institutional elements, embedded in the organizational structure of Rural Cooperative Banks, strongly limit their ability to change over time. These elements also reduce the intrapopulation heterogeneity, giving unitary character to the population of RCBs. Consequently, as social and economic conditions in Italy evolve, their effects on banking organizations should be revealed in the dynamics of vital events such as foundings.

Ecological Consequences

Founding Processes

After 1948, when cooperative banking was legalized, the population of RCBs surged as a result of waves of foundings (see Figure 14.2). To understand such dynamics, we need to consider both the competitive processes at work and the dynamics of resource supplies that characterize the organizational forms in question.

Following previous ecological research (Marrett, 1980; Delacroix and Carroll, 1983; Carroll and Huo, 1986; Hannan and Freeman, 1987), organizational founding is conceptualized here as an arrival process whose rate is affected (i.e., accelerated or decelerated) by institutional constraints related to regulation, by economic processes related to the differential size and market power of a few large organizations in the industry, and, finally, by ecological forces related to (intra)population density,

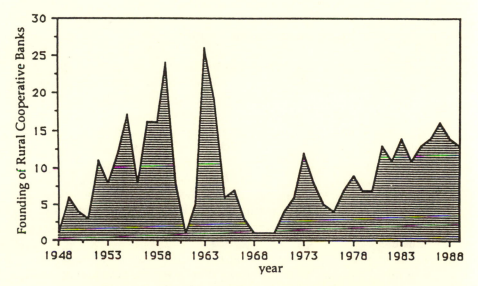

FIG. 14.2   Foundings of rural cooperative banks (RCBs)

changes in the level of resource availability, and community level interactions between organizational subpopulations.

Resource Partitioning

In his analysis of newspaper industries, Carroll (1985, 1987) has proposed the hypothesis that competition among large generalist organizations to occupy the center of the market will free resources at the periphery of the system that are most likely to be absorbed by specialist organizations. Such a hypothesis implies that, in concentrated markets with few large generalists, specialist organizations may be able to exploit resources without (or, at least, before) engaging in direct competition with larger generalist organizations. Carroll calls the process generating such an outcome *resource partitioning*. It yields the hypothesis that rates of founding of local specialist organizations will rise in the fringe habitats as oligopolistic concentration increases among large generalist organizations in the center. A parallel set of predictions follows for mortality.

Economic theories of industrial structure have emphasized the relation between firm size, market power, or concentration and profitability. Market power leads to entry prevention through economies of scale advantages, absolute cost advantages, and, possibly, advantages due to product differentiation and to capital availability (Bain, 1956). It is usually predicted that large organizations will use their market power to reduce the entry rate of new organizations and protect the profitability of the industry. This suggests the following question: *Does growth of large generalist organizations deter specialist firm entry, or does it stimulate entry?* Before moving on to test the resource partitioning hypothesis, it is important to recognize the conditions under which resource partitioning is to be expected in a given industry and to verify that the population at hand actually conforms to the assumptions of the theoretical model. Among the seven conditions indicated by Carroll (1987:211) as crucial to the applicability of the resource partitioning model, the following four assume particular importance in the Italian banking industry:

1. *Once chosen, structures and strategies commit the organization to a limited range of plausible behavior and to a set of relatively stable environmental dependencies.* This is certainly the case for Rural Cooperative Banks, which cannot either change organizational form or be acquired by organizations other than cooperative banks. Normative and organizational elements severely constrain the range of strategic behavior available to RCBs.
2. *Positive economies of scale characterize the production function.* Theory and empirical evidence indicate that such economies do characterize banking, and this has far reaching implications for the competitive strength and advantage of larger core banks and for the overall industry structure.
3. *Environmental resources are heterogeneously distributed.* This condition is again satisfied in the sample under study given the strong heterogeneity in social and economic conditions across Italian regions.

4. *Price competition is limited.* As a direct consequence of the previous point, heterogeneity in the location and quality of demand, in resource availability, and in local market conditions introduces necessary elements of strategic differentiation and nonprice competition among banking organizations.

We test the resource partitioning hypothesis of a positive effect of concentration and size of the largest generalist organizations (core state-owned or state-controlled national banks) on the founding rate of local specialist unit banks (RCBs). Similarly the resource partitioning hypothesis maps onto the prediction of a positive relation between the appearance of new local specialist cooperative banks and the growth (and progressive despecialization) of incumbent cooperative banks through merger with and acquisition of other cooperative banks (i.e., through the only growth strategy available to them given that RCBs are legally barred from growing through branching).

The resource partitioning hypothesis is expected to hold at the national level but may not work the same way at the local level. They can be expected to grow to fill available resource spaces in these local regions. In doing so, however, they create opportunities for specialists in regions not dominated by core banks. So some regions should show the effects of resource partitioning while other should not; there should be interaction effects across regions. In particular, the regions where core banks are strongest (largely in the north) should show weaker resource partitioning effects.

Attention to concentration and to market share controlled by the larger organizations makes it possible to introduce market power considerations explicitly into the ecological analysis of organizational founding, to add an important dimension to ecological theories of organizations.

Models

Following recent research in organizational ecology (see Hannan and Carroll, 1992 for a review), the empirical analysis is based on processes whose rates have the following general regression structure

$$\lambda(t) = \exp(\theta x_t), \tag{1}$$

where λ is a column vector containing the values assumed by the response variable (the yearly count of organizational foundings), x_t is a vector of exogenous factors, and θ is a vector of unknown parameters to be estimated. In the models discussed here the vector x_t typically contains information on (a) intrapopulation vital events and density; (b) demographic structure and processes in other interdependent (sub)populations of banking organization, including information about size, market share, and productive capacity of the largest core banks; and (c) general environmental characteristics such as availability of crucial organizational resources and exogenous effect of regulation.

National Level of Analysis

In the national level analysis of the founding rates of cooperative banks, the generic model (1) is specified as

$$\lambda_t = \exp\left(\beta_1 N_t + \beta_2 N_t^2 + \gamma P2 + \xi S_t + \sum_{k=1}^{K} \theta_k x_k\right). \tag{2}$$

In (2) N_t describes population density. The usual expectation is that the first order effects of density should be positive, indicating rising legitimacy and, therefore, higher founding rates. The effects of N^2 should be negative, indicating the approach of the carrying capacity as the population density grows. (Hypothesis: $\beta_1 > 0$, $\beta_2 < 0$.) Although there are several reasons why these data are not appropriate for a rigorous test of the density dependence model, we report the estimates to make our work comparable to other studies of foundings.

$P2$ is the period effect during which central credit authorities imposed a virtually absolute block to new entries in the Italian banking industry. (Hypothesis: $\gamma < 0$.) This represents a suspension of many otherwise legitimate practices but differs from the period of fascist rule in that cooperative organization was banned outright during the political upheaval before and during World War II.

S_t is the size of the core national banks. According to the resource partitioning hypothesis, the effects of size on the founding rate should be positive. (Hypothesis: $\xi > 0$.) In the following section, we describe three alternative operationalization of S_t.

The term $\sum_{k=1}^{K} \theta_k x_k$ represents the control factors used in the empirical estimation. Because they are less central to our theoretical interest, we group them together. However, we do make specific predictions about their effects on founding rates. The density of Savings and Loan banks (Hypothesis: $\theta_1 \neq 0$) is studied as a possible competitive population.

Births of Popular Cooperative Banks (PCBs), the second (sub)population of cooperative banks existing in Italy, was included to control statistically for the plausible conjecture of a positive association between births in the two (sub)populations due to the common standing of these two organizational forms with respect to regulation and environmental variation. (Hypothesis: $\theta_2 \neq 0$.) Following Delacroix and Carroll (1983) and Hannan and Freeman (1989), failure of Rural Cooperative Banks (RCBs) was also introduced as a regressor. The chain reactions normally triggered by bank failures at the level of the entire economy pose especially difficult regulatory challenges because of the high degree of liquidity characterizing banks' assets and liabilities. The Bank of Italy has effectively reached the objective of industry stabilization by carefully screening entrants (only local specialist cooperative banks allowed) and by strictly controlling exits, making failures virtually impossible by organizing "rescue operations" of organizations in crisis and by favoring, sometimes even mandating, their acquisition by other banks. As a consequence, organizational disbanding is not expected to have long-lasting consequences on founding of Rural Cooperative Banks. Rather, we expect it is a signal of transient uncertainty that may negatively affect the decision of the Bank of Italy to authorize new entries in the short run. (Hypothesis: $\theta_3 < 0$.)

In the analysis conducted at the national level, heterogeneity in the distribution of resources is conceptualized as the coefficient of variation in banks' loans across Italy's twenty geographical regions. When the object of study are organizations that can neither diversify their activity geographically (RCBs cannot branch out) nor rely on a wide resource base (they are credit institutions specialized in agricultural credit), local resource munificence or scarcity assumes paramount importance. Heterogeneity in resource distribution makes it difficult for organizations operating on a national level, trading on economies of scale, to exploit the multitude of local habitats efficiently. So the founding rate of RCBs should be positively correlated with heterogeneity, regional imbalance in this analysis. (Hypothesis: $\theta_4 > 0$.)

The organizational form most likely to compete directly with RCBs are Agrarian Private Stock Banks, which perform many of the same functions as RCBs and operate in the same localized rural areas. The difference, of course, is that they are not cooperative organizations. Following a now extensive literature in organizational ecology (see, for example, Hannan and Freeman, 1986b, 1987), the competitive effect of private stock banks is modeled by introducing its density to equation (2). The larger the population of Private Stock Banks, the lower the birth rate of RCBs should be. (Hypothesis: $\theta_5 < 0$.)

As the main resource utilized by banking organizations, the amount of deposits collected by the entire banking system was used as a basic indicator of the environmental carrying capacity and is expected to affect the founding of RCBs positively. This follows the literature on banking, in which deposits are often conceptualized as a proxy for demand of banking services (Conigliani, 1983). (Hypothesis: $\theta_6 > 0$.)

On the basis of the indications provided by the resource partitioning hypothesis, the number of intrapopulation mergers among RCBs is included to control for organizational growth of RCBs, since external growth is the only growth strategy legally available to RCBs. (Hypothesis: $\theta_7 > 0$.)

Measuring Size. One potential problem in the empirical test of the resource partitioning hypothesis is the definition of an unambiguous measure of organizational size, a construct far more ambiguous and ill defined than population density. If the differential burden imposed on the carrying capacity by larger organizations (and therefore the intensity of competition generated by them) is to be included in the model of population dynamics, mass is probably better represented by some measure of the total productive capacity, or output, not unlike plant size or productive capacity in the case of industrial organizations. Unfortunately, for organizations in service businesses the notion of output or plant size often proves elusive, and it is difficult to identify exactly the sources of economies of scale. In banking, as in most other service activities where the "output" cannot be stored (restaurants, hotels, travel agencies, professional services, and the like), growth cannot be effectively obtained by simply increasing "plant size" but only by geographical expansion and diffusion, or, in general, by moving the service closer to the origin of demand. For banking organizations the number of branches controlled is proposed as an appropriate proxy for the concept of "productive capacity installed," which, according to Winter (1990), is the quantity that captures the differential burden placed by large organizations on the environmental carrying capacity, and hence better represents the intensity of competition in an industry.

The resource partitioning hypothesis of a positive relation between size of the larger core national banks and the founding rate of local specialist cooperative unit banks is also tested by looking at the effects of relative size or market share, measured in terms of the fraction of total loans, deposits, and number of agencies (i.e., the fraction of the total productive capacity of the industry) controlled by the larger core banks. The interest in market share, rather than absolute size, is justified by the fact that in many industries market share is associated with profitability (Schmalensee, 1985), and that market share is often interpreted as a proxy for competitive strength, and of the ability of the largest organizations to mobilize resources collectively and improve their market position (Ravenscraft, 1983). Finally, a third operationalization of size (S_t), used to test for the effect of competitive strength of larger organizations on the birth rate, is the proportion of productive capacity jointly commanded by the large core banks, measured as the number of branches (agencies) controlled by PLI and BNI over the total.

Regional Level of Analysis

The processes by which social institutions regularize organizational practices and the processes by which they compete are both important for organizational ecology. In fact, each is best understood in the context of the other. However, a fundamental problem is that they may not occur at the same level or pertain to the same unit of analysis. So while competition may be localized and resource availability may display considerable heterogeneity across microunits, cultural factors may be societal. This problem is particularly severe for the density dependence model as it specifies the relationship between the two as a ratio.

We know that in Italy the rate of economic and social change was quite different in various regions of the country. Even today, the north has an economy that competes successfully with the rest of Europe while the south looks in many respects more like a third world country. The risk of being misled by unobserved heterogeneity manifested across regions is, therefore, particularly serious in this study. So the national level analysis must be accompanied by a further analysis at the regional level.

The bureaucratic imperative can be seen in the efforts of policymakers to regulate the provision of financial services so as to redress economic differences across the country while preserving the ability of large generalists urban banks to compete in international financial markets. After the 1936 Banking Act was passed, policymakers and central credit authorities chose cooperative banks to organize and diffuse banking and financial services in a country characterized both by strong regional differences in industrial activities and by a complex texture of small and craftlike business firms. The diffusion of cooperative banks was a direct consequence of policy efforts to control concentration in industry and to diffuse banking in market areas in which private stock and large core banks could not operate profitably and were, therefore, unwilling to establish new branches. So we would not expect to see resource partitioning in the northern areas because of close proximity to the urban areas in which the core banks dominate. Instead, it should operate most clearly in the remote south and the islands.

Regional variations include cultural and political differences as well as differences in economic base. The Catholic Church has played a more central role in northern political processes, and its efforts to organize banking cooperatives were more aggressive there as well. The result was a rapid growth of cooperative banking in the 19th and early 20th centuries. In the southern regions, cooperative banking lagged. So in more recent times, the areas less well served are in the south, and we would expect to see both a higher rate of founding and stronger effects of resource partitioning.

In the regional analysis the generic model (1) is specified as

$$\lambda_{it} = \exp\left(a_i^* + \beta_1 N_{it} + \beta_2 N_{it^2} + \gamma P2 + \xi S_t + \pi Q_{it} + \sum_{k=1}^{K} \theta_k x_{kit}\right) \tag{3}$$

where $i = 1, 2, \ldots, N$, indexes the regions in the sample; $t = 1, 2, \ldots, T$, identifies the time periods for which data at the regional level were available (1964–88); λ_{it} is the founding rate in the region i in time period t; and a_i^* is a (1×1) scalar constant representing the effects of those variables specific to the ith region in more or less the same fashion over time. In other words, a_i^* represents the time-invariant region-specific effects introduced to take into account heterogeneity in local social and economic conditions across geographical regions, or "regional imbalance" as it was labeled in the national level analysis.

All the variables appearing in equation (3) are the same as those discussed in the previous subsection. The main difference is that they are measured at the level of the regions. The models are specified slightly differently, because some of the variables are constant (or close to it) in some of the regions. This group includes density of savings and loans. Births of PCBs and deaths of RCBs are left out either because there was little variance or because (unreported) analyses show no effects. In their place are agencies of PCB. Two variables are introduced in the term $\sum_{k=1}^{K} \theta_k x_k$ to control for observable and measurable local differences that are believed to affect the founding rate of cooperative banks significantly at the regional level. Both variables can be seen as part of an attempt to specify as explicitly as possible the specialized resource base supporting the organizational form under investigation. The first variable is regional agricultural employment used as a proxy for agricultural intensity of the region. Given that RCBs specialize in financing agricultural and small craft businesses, it is expected that high levels of agricultural intensity will contribute to creating an environment supportive for this specialist form. (Hypothesis: $\theta_8 > 0$.) The second variable introduced in the regional analysis is the total number of cooperative organizations (producer, consumer, construction, transportation, and agricultural cooperatives) present in the four standard geographical areas in which Italy can be partitioned (north, center, south, and islands). This variable is interpreted as the "force of the cooperative movement" and is supposed to operate beyond the strictly regional scope. That is, it is assumed that its effect will operate similarly in different regions within the four standard areas. (Hypothesis: $\theta_9 > 0$.)

These hypotheses are summarized in table 14.1.

TABLE 14.1   Summary of Hypotheses

Parameter	Variable	Hypothesis
	National Level (Equation 2)	
β_1, β_2	Density	$\beta_1 > 0, \beta_2 < 0$
γ	Regulation (1968–71)	$\gamma < 0$
ξ	Size core banks	$\xi > 0$
θ_1	S & L density	$\theta_1 \neq 0$
θ_2	PCB births	$\theta_2 \neq 0$
θ_3	RCB deaths	$\theta_3 < 0$
θ_4	Regional imbalance	$\theta_4 > 0$
θ_5	Agencies of private stock banks	$\theta_5 < 0$
θ_6	Deposits	$\theta_6 > 0$
θ_7	RCB mergers	$\theta_7 > 0$
	Regional Level (Equation 3)	
β_1, β_2	Regional density	$\beta_1 > 0, \beta_2 < 0$
γ	Regulation (1968–71)	$\gamma < 0$
ξ	Regional size core banks	$\xi > 0$ (but with regional interaction effect)
θ_2	PCB agencies	$\theta_2 \neq 0$
θ_5	Deposits in region	$\theta_5 > 0$
θ_6	RCB mergers in region	$\theta_6 > 0$
θ_8	Agricultural employment in region	$\theta_8 > 0$
θ_9	Cooperative organizations in region	$\theta_9 > 0$

Estimation

Much organizational research on founding has addressed the entry of organizations in populations using conventional time series methods based on ordinary least squares and its variations (Pennings, 1982; Delacroix and Carroll, 1983; Tucker et al., 1988; Tucker et al., 1990). Following recent methodological developments in organizational ecology research, estimation in this study is based on maximum likelihood methods that conveniently allow us to take into account the discrete nature of the process of organizational founding (Hannan and Freeman, 1989; Hannan, 1991). The statistical analysis of sequences of discrete random events can be seen as a specific instance of the study of a noncategorical limited dependent variable; the dependent variable is limited because it is defined on an integer state space. It is noncategorical because the state space is conceptually infinite, two characteristics shared by many kinds of event recurrences (Maddala, 1989).

Specifically, let Y_t be an event counter taking only nonnegative integer values representing the number of occurrences of the event of interest (organizational births in the present case), and let x_t' be a vector of exogenous variables. Assume that the values recorded by the counter $y_1, y_2, \ldots, y_n$, are independent and follow a Poisson distribution with parameters $\lambda_1, \lambda_2, \ldots, \lambda_n$, respectively; then the problem is to estimate $P(Y_t = y_t \mid x_t)$ (i.e., the probability of observing a given number of organizational foundings in a given period conditional on the sample value of the covariates included in the model). Let the cumulative number of foundings in a population by time t be represented by the random variable $Y(t)$. The arrival rate of the process $Y(t)|t \leq 0$ can be defined as

$$\lambda_y(t) = \lim_{\Delta t \to 0} \frac{\Pr[Y(t) + \Delta(t) = 1 | Y(t) = y]}{\Delta t}$$

The present research, where information on the arrival process has the structure of aggregate counts of events within yearly periods, starts with the assumption that the flow of arrivals follows a Poisson process according to which, conditional on the vector of observed characteristics x_t, the probability of y_t arrivals in a given time interval is

$$\Pr(Y_t = y_t | x_t) = \frac{\exp(-\exp(\theta x_t'))(\exp(\theta x_t'))^{y_t}}{y_t!} \tag{4}$$

The present study analyzes the pooled cross section time series data on organizational foundings available at the level of thirteen Italian regions in an analysis of a covariance/panel data analysis statistical framework (Hausman, Hall, and Griliches, 1984; Hsiao, 1986).

Data

Archival sources officially compiled by Italian monetary and credit authorities, the Bank of Italy, and the Italian Central Institute of Statistics (ISTAT) provided the data analyzed in this study. For the data drawn from the period 1948 through 1974, a valuable and consistent data source has been the first volume of a never completed three volume series edited by the Bank of Italy in 1977 on the demographic and financial structure of the Italian banking system from 1936 to 1974 (*Banca d'Italia,* 1977). From 1974 to 1988, the data on the dependent variable of the study (both at the national and the regional level), and on the demographic structure and change in the (sub)populations of banking organizations, were provided by the periodic statistics bulletin of the Bank of Italy *(Bollettino Statistico)* and by the annual report of the control activity on the banking system *(Bollettino di Vigilanza).* This information was cross-checked with that contained in the *Annual Report of the Governor of the Bank of Italy,* and with that in the *Annual General Meeting of the Shareholders.*

The data on agricultural employment were found in the *Annuario Statistico Italiano* (ISTAT, several years), while the data on the number of cooperative organizations and their geographical distribution were found in the *Statistiche della Cooperazione,* a yearly statistical bulletin published by the Italian Ministry of Labor and Social Security, which is the political body in charge (legally and administratively) of Italian cooperative organizations.

With few notable exceptions (e.g., Hannan and Freeman, 1987, 1988b), most available data on organizational foundings over time, including the present, are available in the form of counts aggregated over some time unit (usually the year). To estimate the models presented, data on founding activity at the national and regional levels are required. At the national level, the time series of the aggregate counts of

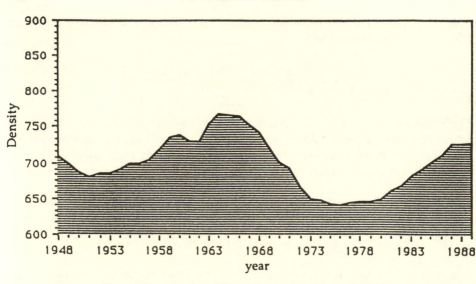

FIG. 14.3a   Density of Rural Cooperative Banks (RCBs)

organizations founded each year from 1948 to 1988 in the two (sub)populations of cooperative banking organizations simply consists of a column vector of 41 observations.

The study concentrates on this period to learn more about organizational founding rates during subperiods of the overall population history characterized by structural and competitive conditions believed to be favorable to larger organizations. The first ten years after the Banking Act are excluded from the analysis because of the

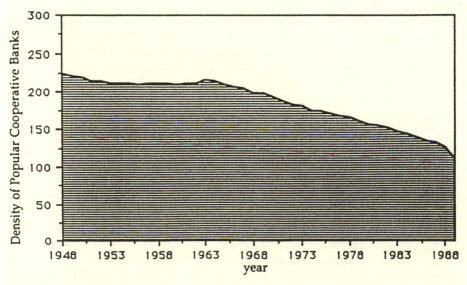

FIG. 14.3b   Density of Popular Cooperative Banks (PCBs).

structural diversity in environmental conditions characterizing the war years, and because of the institutional discontinuity represented by the transition from the fascist regime to the new constitutional Italian republic in 1948.

The two times series of cooperative banking organization foundings are quite different (see figures 14.3a and 14.3b). While the RCB population rises and falls repeatedly over time, ending about where it starts, the population of PCB declines secularly. Both populations had been declining during the 1930s and 1940s, but some still existed when World War II ended. Consequently, the data are left-censored and analysis of mortality is likely to be misleading. In addition, these design difficulties make density dependence results misleading, so we do not purport to test the density dependence model.

Each of the 41 records corresponding to the annual count of organizations founded is associated with an array of exogenous characteristics providing information on population demographics (e.g., intrapopulation density), community structure (e.g., density and vital events of other subpopulations), size, market share, productive capacity of the core national banks, and environmental resources related to the carrying capacity (e.g., deposits). The time series showing the foundings of RCBs shows the usual waves of foundings. In addition, however, it shows that RCB foundings increased over most of the seventies and eighties.

Table 14.2 reports the descriptive statistics of the variables contained in the data set analyzed at the national level and used to estimate the model of community level interaction between RCBs and PCBs. At the regional level, yearly data on foundings are available only from 1964. The analysis is based on the data set obtained from pooling over time the cross sectional data on the 13 regions selected for the study. Among these regions, four are located in the north (Lombardia, Veneto, Trentino Alto Adige, and Friuli Venezia Giulia), three in the center (Emilia-Romagna, Marche, and Lazio), five in the south (Campania, Abruzzi and Molise, Basilicata, Puglia, and Calabria), and one is an island region (Sicilia). The result of "stacking" the data contained in the 13 "panels" for the 25 years covered by the study was the

TABLE 14.2   Descriptive Statistics

	Mean	SD	Minimum	Maximum
Agencies of BPC	134.3	144.1	9	703
Private banks (agencies)	175.3	224.6	7	1,082
Agricultural employment (millions)	20	13	2.7	57
Cooperative enterprises	19,743	8,819	4,729	35,483
S & L density	3.82	4.20	0	16
Deposits (billions of lire)	10	15	.51	91
Market share of national banks	.21	.14	.03	.56
Density of national bank agencies	127.3	106.9	13	397
P2 (1968–71)	.16	.367	0	1
PCB births	.06	.24	0	2
RCB births	.62	1.01	0	5
RCB density	48.5	47.0	6	207
RCB failures	.15	.49	0	4
RCB mergers	.54	1.49	0	14

pooled cross section/time series data set of 325 observations used to perform the analysis at the regional level.

Results

We begin with the national level of analysis. Our longer time series at this level enables us to examine the historical process more completely, but we do so at the risk of being misled by unobserved regional heterogeneity.

National Level Results

The national level results are presented in table 14.3. They show a positive linear effect of RCB density on the rate of founding. The quadratic specification failed to show the intrapopulation competition effects generally thought to be associated with a carrying capacity cap on the population. This is particularly interesting, we think, because the variable introduced to measure that carrying capacity, total bank depos-

TABLE 14.3   National Level Analysis of Founding Rates (1948–88)

	1		2		3		4	
Constant	−15.216	(11.166)	−13.936	(9.925)	−49.421*	(16.296)	−42.924*	(13.850)
RCB Density	.007*	(.002)	.008*	(.002)	.005*	(.002)	.005*	(.002)
P2 (1968–71)	−1.688*	(.398)	−1.702*	(.399)	−1.637*	(.399)	−1.651*	(.398)
Market share deposits	−.030	(4.500)						
Market share loans			−2.386	(3.853)				
Market share agencies					35.094*	(13.275)		
Size (number of agencies)							.003*	(.001)
S&L density	.184*	(.102)	.191*	(.103)	.418*	(.137)	.451*	(.140)
PCB births	.100*	(.038)	.108*	(.039)	.090*	(.037)	.091*	(.037)
RCB deaths	−.103*	(.027	−.102*	(.027)	−.091*	(.027)	−.085*	(.028)
Private banks agencies	−.0010	(.0007)	−.0012*	(.0005)	−.0001	(.0006)	−.003*	(.001)
Deposits	.003*	(.001)	.002*	(.001)	.003*	(.001)	.003*	(.001)
RCB mergers	.018	(.136)	.019	(.014)	.010	(.012)	.007	(.012)
Regional imbalance	.004	(.028)	−.004	(.026)	.047*	(.029)	.045	(.028)
x^2	62.8		61.9		58.8		57.1	
Log likelihood	−109.8		−109.6		−106.4		−105.7	
Degrees of freedom	11		11		11		11	
Cases	41		41		41		41	

NOTE: $p < .05$.

its (DEPOSITS), has the expected positive effect on the RCB birth rate. On the other hand, the left-censoring clearly evident in figure 14.3a precludes strong inferences about density dependence. However, we do need to control the effects of overall density on the founding process in order to make inferences about the other effects, particularly those involving resource partitioning. The heightened regulations of the 1968–71 period have the expected depressing effect on the rate of birth. This suspension of legitimate independence seems to have been effective in stifling cooperative banking organization.

The resource partitioning hypothesis is supported when size is measured in organizational terms rather than market share terms. When measured by either deposits or loans, size of core banks does not have a significant effect on RCB birth rates. But core bank share of agencies (branches) and absolute number of agencies both have a powerful *positive* effect, as predicted. It is especially interesting that the resource partitioning argument is supported when counts of organizations are used to measure the size of core banks but that their market shares of loans and deposits have no statistically significant effect. It seems that capacity rather than demand concentration is the relevant characteristic.

The density of private savings and loans shows a mutualistic effect on the RCB birth rate. This positive effect persists regardless of the operationalization used for core bank size. Similarly, the birth rate of the other form of cooperative bank, PCB, has a positive effect on RCB births. The failure rate of RCBs has a negative effect. While these effects might reflect genuine mutualism, they are also consistent with spurious effects produced by unobserved conditions in the environment. The lagged mortality rate of RCBs has the predicted negative effect on the birth rate of RCBs. Again, the effect persists when different core bank size operationalizations are tried. So these results replicate the findings of others of an apparent signaling effect of waves of failures.

The size of private stock banks, measured by their numbers of agencies, has an inconsistent effect on RCB birth rates. We expected to see competition here, and do so when core bank size is measured by total number of agencies, and also by market share measured in loans, but not using the other two measures of core bank size. The hypothesis that total deposits would have a positive effect on RCB foundings is supported. We view this as simply a control for the scale of economic activity and of the overall market for banks in Italy. So its importance is to provide such controls for analysis of the other effects. The number of RCB mergers has no apparent effect on the rate of RCB founding. This is consistent with other research showing that merger rates operate quite differently than and often independently of other vital rates.

Regional imbalance, measured as the coefficient of variation in total bank lending activity across regions, has a positive effect on the RCB birth rate only in the third model, where the effects of central bank dominance in agencies are controlled. This is an attempt to consider regional effects at the national level of analysis, but it assumes that these effects are independent of the other terms in the Poisson regression. Since both the bureaucratic and cultural imperative arguments lead to differences in how this organizational form will be treated across regions, the regional imbalance measure may not capture all the complexity of interest. We turn to a more detailed examination of these regional differences next.

Regional Analysis

In studying RCB founding rates at the level of the 13 regions, in table 14.4, the number of observations rises so statistical significance is "easier" to achieve. Also, of course, direct comparisons with the results reported in table 14.3 are hazardous because the specifications are different. The price paid for more detailed data at the regional level is fewer years of data and a more restricted set of regressors.

Right away we see an important difference. Density dependence has the expected nonmonotonic effect on the founding rate (model 3), not the positive linear effect, as in table 14.3. The difference between model 1 and model 3 is statistically significant at the .05 level using the likelihood ratio test. When region is considered, density dependence becomes nonsignificant. This seems to result from regional interaction, discussed later. The resource partitioning effect is present in models 1, 2, and

TABLE 14.4 Regional Analysis of Founding Rates of Rural Cooperative Banks (1964–88)

	1		2		3		4	
Constant	−2.260*	(.384)	−2.240*	(.391)	−2.254*	(.417)		
Density			.001	(.002)	.027*	(.012)	.014	(.021)
Density^2 (000)					−.130*	(.060)	.002	(.001)
P2 (1968–71)	−1.930*	(.459)	−1.940*	(.459)	−2.020*	(.461)	−1.730*	(.470)
Market share national bank agencies	3.200*	(.670)	3.150*	(.684)	3.570*	(.701)	−1.250	(4.320)
Density of national bank agencies (00)	.044	(.060)	.046	(.030)	−.090	(.080)	.650*	(.330)
Deposits (00,000)	.006	(.006)	.006	(.006)	.003	(.006)	.002*	(.001)
RCB mergers	.236*	(.036)	.244*	(.035)	.251*	(.036)	.340*	(.043)
Agricultural employment (000)	.010	(.008)	.010	(.008)	.003	(.009)	.100*	(.020)
Cooperatives (000)	.030*	(.013)	.030*	(.010)	.020*	(.010)	.080*	(.002)
North: 1							−5.070*	(1.120)
North: 2							−15.130*	(2.890)
North: 3							−9.010*	(1.960)
North: 4							−11.650*	(2.790)
Central: 1							−8.710*	(1.640)
Central: 2							−5.680*	(1.720)
Central: 3							−5.170*	(1.000)
South: 1							−4.000*	(1.400)
South: 2							−2.820*	(1.270)
South: 3							−3.610*	(1.630)
South: 4							−5.200*	(2.720)
South: 5							−7.580*	(2.110)
Islands							−7.010*	(2.350)
x^2	392.9		393.2		386.0		−289.1	
Log likelihood	−311.0		−310.9		−308.3		−271.3	
Degrees of freedom	8		9		10		22	
Cases	325		325		325		325	

NOTE: *$p < .05$.

TABLE 14.5   Regional Analysis of Founding Rates of Rural Cooperative Banks (1964–88)

	North and Center		South and Islands		All	
Constant	−1.980*	(1.040)	−3.670*	(.830)	−2.170*	(.415)
Density	.003	(.029)	.048	(.047)	.037*	(.013)
Density^2 (000)	−.001	(.013)	−.034	(.082)	−.002*	(.001)
P2 (1968–71)	−1.080*	(.489)	−2.760*	(1.020)	−1.810*	(.424)
Market share national bank agencies	1.120	(2.680)	5.090*	(1.870)	2.260*	(.715)
Density of national bank agencies (00)	−.030	(.180)	.183	(.401)	−.220*	(.120)
Deposits (000,000)	.002*	(.001)	.008*	(.004)	.016*	(.007)
RCB mergers	.257*	(.040)	.426*	(.257)	.255*	(.040)
Agricultural employment (000)	.002	(.002)	.003	(.002)	.000	(.001)
Cooperatives (000)	−.009	(.032)	.078*	(.035)	.009	(.014)
Central	.0006	(.0006)			−.974*	(.241)
South & Islands					.487*	(.120)
Islands Only			−817	(1.370)		
x^2	216.9		161.7		403.6	
Degrees of freedom	11		11		13	
Cases	175		150		325	

NOTE: *$p < .05$.

3, but when region is controlled, its sign changes (to −1.250) and it becomes non-significant. Deposits, the carrying capacity measure, has consistently positive effects, as before. Agricultural employment also has a positive effect at the regional level.

It seems clear that there are major differences in founding rates across regions. The coefficients of the dummies for the south and islands do appear to be more negative than in the north. But table 14.4 treats these regional differences additively. We really expect that both economic and institutional factors operate differently in the south and the north. Resource partitioning should also differ in that the rural areas in the north are geographically close to the urban areas where the core banks are dominant.

Table 14.5 presents analyses that aggregate the 13 regions into broader geographical regions. We do this to permit comparison of models in a way that is intended to resemble analysis of covariance. Within each of the two mega-regions, we include a dummy variable to adjust for the additive effect of being in one or the other part of the mega-region. So in the first column, where north and center are aggregated, we estimate the effects of being in either the north or the central area. These dummies do not produce statistically significant effects. This suggests that the important differences are between north and south, not within mega-regions.

The period dummy for the effect of stringent regulation continues to have a strong negative effect. But most other regressors seem to have negligible effects in the north and center (first column). Only total deposits and mergers continue to have effects. Most importantly, market share of national core bank agencies has no effect. There does not seem to be resource partitioning in the northern and central regions. This is consistent with an interpretation that this effect largely reflects a division of labor between the rural periphery and the industrial center. Competition within the industrial center does not matter so much. The core banks' dominance is too strong there.

Looking at the south and islands analysis, we can see generally strong effects of most variables. Most of the effects are coming from the south and islands market share of core banks, measured in agencies, a particularly interesting finding. As we expected, the resource partitioning effect is powerful in the south and islands but weak in the north and center. As the core national banks increase their share of capacity (measured by number of agencies), the birth rate of the RCB in the rural south and islands regions grows.

In both super-regions, density dependence is not statistically significant in this analysis. It is only at the national level that such effects are significant. However, the signs of the coefficients are in the usually predicted direction and the magnitudes are quite stable across mega-regions. The standard errors are much larger, as one would expect with the smaller number of observations in the first two models reported in table 14.5.

We started by presenting a descriptive model of how institutionalized practices rooted in abstract administrative principles are codified into concrete dimensions of organizational forms and produce ecological consequences at the industry level by limiting the range of possible competitive behaviors. Then we explored the empirical implications of this model in the context of the founding of Italian rural cooperative banks, an organizational population whose evolutionary dynamics has been influenced by both technical (or competitive) as well as institutional (or procedural) pressures. In fact, the banking sector conforms to Scott and Meyer's definition of technical sector in the sense that banking organizations "[a]re rewarded for effective and efficient control of the work process" (Scott and Meyer, 1983:140), but it is also true that state regulation and the status of banking as a service of "public interest" have produced a set of "[r]ules and requirements to which individual organizations must conform if they are to receive support from the environment" (Scott and Meyer, 1983:140).

The overall pattern of results across different levels of analysis supported the hypotheses of the joint effects of institutional norms and ecological processes in organizational founding. Our conclusion that institutional environmental elements strongly affect organizational founding rates is in basic agreement with earlier attempts to explore the ecological consequences of institutional practices (Carroll, Goodstein, and Gyenes, 1988; Carroll and Huo, 1986).

The research provides strong support for the resource partitioning hypothesis. Under conditions of positive economies of scale and heterogeneously distributed resources, and in the presence of few large oligopolistic organizations competing at the national and international levels, small specialist cooperative unit banks were able to draw on the resource base freed at the periphery of the system without engaging in direct competition with the larger generalist core banks. Size and market share of the larger organizations have a positive effect on the founding rate of rural cooperative banks.

The research extends the theory underlying the resource partitioning hypothesis by examining ways in which institutional practices channel organizational founding in ways that reflect the opportunities and constraints imposed by the social and political system. Specifically, the southern and islands locales show much stronger effects of the period dummy that shows successful regulation by the state—an instance of the bureaucratic imperative. Resource partitioning as estimated by the share of agencies operated by the core national banks, positively affects the birth rate of RCBs and this effect is much stronger in the south and islands.

What we have called the cultural imperative works primarily to produce earlier organizing in the northern part of the country. This is not to say that such cultural factors have no effect on the data analysis by region. In fact, if knowledge of how to operate such organizations and acceptance of them as legitimate ways of providing secure banking services diffuse through the human population, then liabilities of newness, experienced in the north, pay off for subsequent organizing attempts in the south.

The intricate interdependence of social structure and the competition and mutualism that underlie the ecological approach to organizations are underscored here. This interdependence is what distinguishes organizational ecology from economics and offers the greatest promise for analysis of institutional practices that so often pose insoluble problems of measurement for the study of social structure and organizations.

Notes

1. This literature is large and this theme is so pervasive that one can do little more than cite a few representative examples. See Meyer (1970, 1980), Meyer, Scott, and Deal (1981), and Fligstein (1992).

2. See Heather Haveman's argument, chapter 8, this volume.

15

The Evolution of Socially Contingent Rational Action: Effects of Labor Strikes on Change in Union Founding in the 1880s

LYNNE G. ZUCKER AND ITA G. G. KREFT

> Economics is all about how people make choices; sociology is all about how they don't have any choices to make.
>
> —J. DUESENBERRY

Sometimes social context constrains or alters choices, sometimes not. Clearly, models in economics that are predicated on autonomous, rational action by individuals generally predict very well. Sociologists cannot afford to ignore the large body of empirical support. But there is also evidence that institutional pressures, and the social relations resulting from them, alter action (from an institutional perspective, Tolbert, 1985; Zucker, 1987; Dobbin et al., 1988; from a population ecology perspective, Singh, Tucker, and Meinhard, 1991; Baum and Oliver, 1992).

Social scientists too often treat social process as if it is just there, a by-product of human activity, as if no human agency is required to produce it. Even in the most recent treatments, social activity is as ubiquitous as air and just as costless (Granovetter, 1985). Economic activity is empirically as ubiquitous, but its production is seen as highly variable; when the incentives are not strong, as in the command economies, economic action will be depressed and economic structure will be poorly developed. We need to rethink institutional structure and social action in these terms. Institu-

Support of the research in this chapter was provided by grants to Lynne G. Zucker from the National Science Foundation (86-07657) and from the Institute of Industrial Relations, UCLA. We appreciate the technical support from Zhong Deng and Kam-bor Yip. The strike data set was constructed under these grants and is archived at the Data Archives Library, ISSR, UCLA. The Knight of Labor data set was provided by the Inter-University Consortium for Political and Social Research (ICPSR), through the ISSR Data Archives Library. We have added month of founding to these data, relying on other archival records. We have benefited greatly from comments at the Conference on Evolutionary Dynamics of Organizations, organized by Joel Baum and Jitendra Singh, and especially from points made by Jim March on cultural embeddedness. Comments from Joel Baum, Michael Darby, John Padgett, and Kaz Yamaguchi improved the quality significantly.

tional structure is a product that requires time, attention, resources, and human action to produce. Deciding to produce a given structure draws resources away from other activities, and it is unlikely that such resource flow will occur in the absence of identified demand.[1]

When demand for institutions is high, there is likely to be no single "best solution." Multiple optima form, primarily because of conflict among interested parties, conflict related to differing self-interest and interpretations of worldviews. These optima are bracketed by social context, that is, socially significant groupings of persons (e.g., native vs. foreign born), organizations (e.g., firms, industries), or social institutions (e.g., geographic regions as a proxy). Action becomes contingent on social variations.

Under these conditions, based on social conflict rather than on social consensus, institutional evolution is divergent, creating multiple social orders, not *the* social order. Action becomes legitimated gradually as solutions are evaluated across different contexts. This is strikingly different from most neoinstitutional theory that assumes institutional evolution is both sudden and convergent, terminating in institutional isomorphism (DiMaggio and Powell, 1983; Dobbin et al., 1988; Powell and DiMaggio, 1991).

Evolution of Labor Union Institutions: Knights of Labor

The institutional structure we are examining is the formation of labor union locals by the Knights of Labor (Garlock, 1973). They were produced in response to divergent self-interest between workers and employers, increasingly a problem as the percentage of wage and salary workers grew from 12 percent in 1800 to 55 percent in 1880 (Zucker, 1983: table 4). As one observer remarked (Ely, 1888:94), "Where one laborer rises to the position of a wealthy man, ten small producers have lost their independent positions and fallen into the rank of wage receivers."

Conflict between employers and workers increased sharply in the 1880s. On the one side, employers complained about workers shirking, wanting fewer hours of work at higher wages, to the point where employers would rather invest in mechanization than deal with an increasingly antagonistic work force (especially in coal mines). On the other side, workers complained of exploitation by more powerful employers and their associations (Powderly, 1890:22): "Employers' object was to make profit from the sale of their product, and to secure from other men as much labor as possible, at the lowest rate of compensation." Conflict over wages, hours of work, working conditions, and treatment of individual workers led to protracted battles: Workers would withdraw their labor, often in a strike, while employers would lock workers out, bring in strikebreakers, and fire workers.

There had been so few strikes prior to 1880 that no tabulations were kept by the Bureau of Labor; in 1880 the first preliminary report was prepared, and a retrospective and more complete report was produced by a compilation of newspaper and labor paper reports, coupled with individual interviews conducted with strikers and employers (Bureau of Labor, 1888). Figure 15.1 presents the overall pattern of strike frequency between January 1881 and December 1886, as recoded from the original Bureau of Labor data. These strikes are all coded at the firm level, providing firm-level data on such variables as size of firm, number of workers out on strike, and number of workers fired by the employer. Seasonal fluctuation is marked, and a trend over the period to increasing strike activity can be seen. The increase in strike activity in March–June 1886 occurred as part of a general movement to form unions, especially by organizations other than the Knights of Labor (e.g., American Federation of Labor 1888).

While too complex to represent graphically, the differences in strike activity across industries and between regions of the county are increasing over time. Some industries are increasingly "strike prone," as are some regions, while others are increasingly "strike resistant." However, these trends are quite small; most are non-significant. While evolution of the context is slight, we predict that how the context alters action *does* evolve: Linkage early in the process is slight, but context increasingly alters the rate of development of institutional structure, the founding of union locals, Local Assemblies (LAs), over time.

To examine changes in the rate of founding Knights of Labor LAs as a consequence of a strike in the same county, we subtract the number of union locals founded six months *before* the strike begins from the number founded within the six months *after* the strike ends: if it is a positive number, then more union locals are founded after the strike (a higher founding rate), while if it is a negative number, then more locals are founded in the six month period prior to the strike. Over a third of all strikes in the 1881–83 period are associated with increases in the founding rate, while over half of all strikes in the 1884–86 period are associated with increases in the rate.[2] The observed response to strikes follows the wisdom of the time (Ely, 1886):

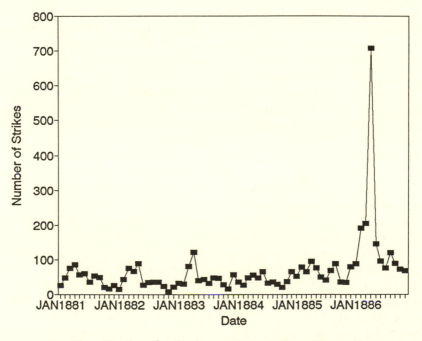

FIG. 15.1   Number of strikes by month (excluding wildcat strikes)

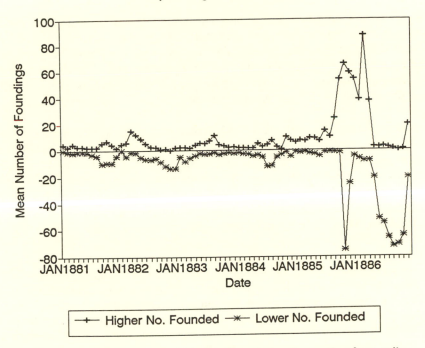

FIG. 15.2   Mean number of LA foundings during six months after a strike

"Trade-unions have, as a rule, grown up out of coalitions formed during a strike." Generally, few union foundings occurred during a strike, since worker attention and resources were focused on the strike itself.[3] Figure 15.2 illustrates the mean number of Local Assemblies founded, where a plus sign (+) indicates a higher number is founded after the strike and an asterisk (*) indicates a higher number prior to the strike.

Socially Contingent Rational Action

To theorize globally about "embeddedness" of economic activity makes social relations relevant but allows them to remain largely unmeasured (as in Granovetter, 1985). We must specify more precisely *what* actions are occasioned by institutions and the *form* the institutional intervention is likely to take to enter the debate over neoclassical theories of the firm. The major purpose for studying the formation of Local Assemblies (or LAs, as the Knights of Labor called them) is to define the conditions under which rational action is socially contingent and to identify when it is not.

Social contingency is not predefined for each action. To argue that it is would be similar to arguing that some social structure, such as family, is inherently more institutional than other structure (see Zucker, 1977 for a more complete discussion of this point). Instead, the dependence of that action on social context is a variable; thus, we can examine its evolution. The extent of evolution depends on how contested the terrain is, or how ambiguous, and how successful institutional formation has been at resolving the conflict or ambiguity. At one point in time, an action may not be conditioned by social context. Later, it may be so conditioned. We assume no necessary directionality: Social context may become increasingly relevant, as it does in the case of LAs here, or it may become less relevant. There is also no inherent reason for *any* evolution: some actions may be static at a given level of social contingency.

Social contingency, and institutional processes in general, arise as efficient solutions to information problems that develop from economic activity. Some of these information problems take the form of a social dilemma, where self-interest yields nonoptimal outcomes for the group, while other information problems take the form of uncertainty, replacing imperfect or missing information with socially derived predictions to serve as a basis for action. In general, institutions arise to solve information problems. These information problems take three distinctive forms:

> *Marxian or Agency Problems*: Self-interest diverges and alters behavior sufficiently that there is no common solution for joint action and thus suboptimal outcomes are produced. As interests become increasingly polarized, it is more likely that "bad faith" interpretations are made of each other's actions: workers "shirking" (the agency problem) or employers "exploiting" (the Marxist problem). In the 1880s, employers complain that workers demand both lower hours and higher wages (shirking); workers complain that employers do not pay a living wage and use company housing and stores to rob them of the value of their labor (exploiting). Both sides express frustation with their low ability to alter the other's actions, workers using exit and employers using firing as last resorts.[4]

> *Indeterminacy Problem*: Action is not clearly and certainly related to outcome, so that each actor has insufficient basis for a rational calculus that might produce independent but convergent action.[5] For example, creating a new Local Assembly may or may not tend to produce better working conditions; new structures are often difficult to evaluate or assess. In contrast, workers' actions during a strike have direct effects on the likelihood of success of that strike. Thus, within the same arena it is possible to have some actions that are perceived as strongly related to outcome, while other action is not so clearly related and is therefore more likely to be socially conditioned.

> *Trust Problem*: Joint action is required, but there is not enough information available for each actor to predict the likely action of the others. One solution is to use information available about the action taken by other members of that group. For example, group-level differences in the rates of given actions such as strikebreaking by employers in different industries and regions of the country are often the best predictor of whether or not one's own employer may engage in strikebreaking in the strike that is planned next week. The expected costs and benefits, then, are socially conditioned on the average response of the group rather than on the action of the specific other.[6]

Demand for Institutional Action and Structure

The three information problems, separately and jointly, produce *demand* for institutional action and structure. As long as the demand is not completely met, institutional elaboration will continue, making action increasingly socially contingent. We examine a case, employment relations in the 1880s, where demand was increasing and therefore expect to find the formation of LAs to be increasingly socially contingent. Evolution in institutional context was increasing and positive, and rested on the first two of three general processes: (1) New domains of action are generated in which prior institutional solutions do not operate (employment relations emerge in the mid-1800s); (2) information problems become more severe (both recognition of divergent self-interest and growth in the average size of firms, creating nonowner managers with a new set of interests); and (3) prior institutional solutions gradually decline or collapse (not operative in our period; occurs much later in trade union decline beginning in the mid-1900s).[7]

Demand resulting from the three information problems can produce two very different kinds of institutional structure, one that leads to convergent action, the other that produces institutional differentiation and divergent action. Institutional evolution has two distinct regimes that differ both in process and in outcome.

> *Institutional Convergence*: When interest polarization, uncertainty, and demands for joint action are relatively low, the institutional structure produced is uniform, even rulelike, creating a "level playing field." Action often becomes ceremonial, decoupled from direct sanctions, resting on tradition and taken-for-granted patterns of action (Meyer and Rowan, 1977; DiMaggio and Powell, 1983). Institutional isomorphism is the outcome of convergent institutional evolution, and except during the evolutionary process itself is very difficult to study empirically because there is little variance to be explained (DiMaggio and Powell, 1983; Granovetter, 1985). Under conditions of static institutional isomorphism, rational action models both are tractable empirically and provide more interesting explanations.[8] Generally, institutional structure can be treated as a fixed cost included in a rational calculus, except when institutionalization affecting the same action varies from high to low.

> *Institutional Differentiation*: When uncertainty and demand for joint action are relatively high, the relevance of any single institutional solution is less clear. In general, the higher the conflict-based demand for institutional structure, the more likely is differentiation. *The* social order is replaced by *many* social orders, many local optima that permit exchange to continue: choice is conditioned on social context differences, so that it may be rational to found another Knights of Labor LA in industries and regions of the United States where employers typically are less conciliatory, for example, less likely to settle grievances without a strike and more likely to fire workers and bring in strikebreakers, but not rational to do so in other industries and regions. This process frames action differently across social contexts (Goffman, 1967, 1974), providing context-dependent "vocabularies of motives" (Mills, 1940).

This variance on the institutional level—both during the evolutionary process and after its completion—makes empirical research more practical and more interesting. Here, variance begets variance: except at the origin of the evolutionary process, divergent evolution is more transparent to the actors than convergent. Differentiation makes it clear that there *are* choices, alternative paths of action.

Thus, divergent evolution tends to continue as alternative lines of action open up possibilities or even directly impinge on local optima, without new demand. But convergent evolution, absent new demand, tends to become static and resistant to change (depending on degree of institutionalization; see Zucker, 1977).

Linking Levels: Institutional Structure and Action

As Giddens (1979) has pointed out, structure that has no effect on action is not properly "social" structure. It may be an artifact of prior social process, but not a living, evolving part of a social system. Just because contextual social variables are significant in a model does not explain how they alter action on the microlevel. In order to understand the effect of institutional structure on activity that occurs roughly within its boundaries, we need to examine three aspects that have received little prior attention.

First, variables that describe the expected aspects of institutional structure that will affect action, here the founding of Knights LAs, must be identified. Normally, variables that describe action occuring at the time and place or variables describing characteristics that are "local" in nature are entered into the equation, but institutional structure is characterized by a dummy variable such as industry that provides no information on the characteristics of industry that are supposed to alter action. We pose a more specific question: what differences between industry A and industry B might be expected to produce the observed differences in action?

Average values for each industry are entered into the equations, within each of four geographic regions, since we expect social institutions to vary by region also. Here, for example, we predict that two major characteristics of industries by region will affect the change in union local founding rates, pre to post strike (six months before the strike begins compared to six months after the strike ends), controlling for characteristics of that particular strike: (1) total number of strikes in each industry/region and (2) proportion of strikes in each industry/region that are broken by the employer.

Second, we need to construct an explanation of how those differences in context (the macrolevel) alter action at the microlevel. Some of the strike and firm characteristics that are significant predictors will actually alter in impact—magnitude and even direction of effect—across the different social contexts of action. For example, in some industries and regions the proportion of workers discharged by the employer may *decrease* the founding rate of LAs (pre/post strike), while in others it may strongly increase it. We believe this is due to social context: there are conditions under which workers may be mobilized by attempts to "break the strike," while under others they will be demoralized by these same kinds of attempts by employers. Charisma of strike leaders, state of the overall labor market (alternative job possibilities), even motives attributed to employers, may all modify the effect of proportion of workers discharged.

Third, among those coefficients that vary significantly across institutional context, we expect that the actual "path" along which influence travels from social context (here, industry/region) to the microlevel (here, strike and firm) can be identified. Significant interaction terms between the variables that describe the social context, such as number of stirkes, and variables that describe the strike or firm, such as duration of strike, indicate a direct path of influence between structure and action.

So far we have been using our substative study as illustrative material in order to develop more general theory. Now we turn in more detail to the role of strikes in changing the rate of founding Local Assemblies in the 1880s.

Demand, Social Contingency, and Action in Founding Knights of Labor Local Assemblies

Strikes are the key event occasioning founding of new Knights of Labor Local Assemblies. Most strikes are *not* organized by unions at the beginning of the 1880s; over half are by 1886. Strikes are the "at risk" unit, on the county level, much as the number of women of childbearing age would be the at risk unit for births (Zucker, 1989a; Zucker, Yip, and Kalmijn, 1992:60). Since we are explicitly modeling the strike as the "at risk" unit, we define the expected effect on founding as the difference between founding rates six months after the strike ends minus the rates six months before it begins in the same county, comparing region and industry.

Characteristics of strikes, as well as of existing union locals and of the firms that are struck, should directly affect the likelihood of founding a new Knights LA in that county. If a consensus or resource mobilization model applies, so that it is unity, "solidarity," among workers that counts, we expect that on the local county level the proportion striking and involved would be a key explanatory variable. If LAs are formed mainly in response to employer action, primarily reactive, then we expect that characteristics associated with increased levels of conflict in the strike would be positively related to founding. We also expect that the power of unions (to organize and fund the strike) and the power of workers (offensive strike, rather than a defensive strike against wage reduction) would increase founding rates.

To the extent that new institutional structure, here LAs, reflects *consensus* we would expect very little variation among contexts (industry and region): There is a clear "best solution" and most action lines up on that basis. *Conflict*, however, implies different views about how to resolve problems and more commonly produces structure contingent on social variables, local optima that alter the LA formation rate. Our central predictions are based on specifying conditions that underlie these two models of institutional structure and resulting action.

> I. *Conflict-Based Institution Formation*: When conflict based on divergent self-interest and worldviews yields different solutions to problems of coordinated or joint action, then degree of conflict predicts the formation rate of new institutional structure. If employers fire workers and bring in strikebreakers, then the poststrike founding rate of union locals will increase. If industries and regions are characteristically high in number of strikes, in workers fired, or in strikes broken, then the poststrike founding rate of union locals will increase.

> II. *Demand for Institutions*: When demand for institutional structure is high, then under conditions of ambiguity action will be altered by social contingency. If the level of conflict is significantly higher in some social contexts than in others (e.g., regions and industries), then it will increase the poststrike founding rate in those relative to the others. Institutional structure is characterized by fragmented legitimation.

III. *Institutional Evolution*: When demand for institutions is high, then social contingency gradually increases differentiation, yielding divergent evolution with local optima. Context effects (here regional, industrial) are not expected to be significant at time 1, but are at time 2, in predicting increased formation rate of LAs post strike.

IV. *Action Without Institution*:When demand for institutional structure is low, social contingency does not alter action. If action and outcome can be directly related (as in strike characteristics and strike success), then the optimum solution will be implemented in each instance, without significant social context (here regional, industrial) variation.

V. *Socially Contingent Rational Choice*: If there is divergent institutional evolution, that is, fragmented legitimation with different local optima, then covariate effects on institutional formation will be context-dependent. In some social contexts (e.g., Southern textile), the covariate may increase institutional formation after a strike, while in other contexts (e.g., Northeastern steel) that same covariate may decrease formation.

Data and Variables

Our data set has been pieced together from a number of sources: government reports (notably Bureau of Labor 1888), historic records from the period (especially *Journal of United Labor 1880–1889* and data collected by Garlock, 1973), and geographic atlases covering the 1880s (Paullin, 1932). We have also added information from major economic histories of that period (Easterlin, 1960; Kuznets, Thomas, and Lee, 1957; Kuznets, Miller, and Easterlin, 1960). Further, we have coded and matched industry categories in use in the 1880s across the strike and Knights of Labor data sets.

The data set contains detailed county-level data that allow us to conduct a much more precise test of causal ordering than has been possible in earlier work that has had to rely on aggregate data. We have information at the firm level on strikes, including, for example, what proportion of the work force was actually out on strike (Zucker, 1989b; Zucker, Crabbe, and Wu, 1988); we also have information at the Local Assembly level for the Knights of Labor. Further we know the details of timing at the level of the month for union founding (by adding month to the data provided by Garlock to ICPSR; Garlock, 1973). We have data at the level of the day for strikes (Bureau of Labor, 1888). Thus, we can specify with a high degree of precision which specific union formations occurred before, during, or after particular strikes in the same county.

The variables are defined in table 15.1, grouped into four main categories. First, the two institutional-level variables are defined; each has forty categories, crossing ten industries with four regions (industries are mining, metals, tobacco, textile, brick/stone quarry, leather goods, building trades, machines/glass, other1—primarily ship and railroad car building and other2; regions are West, North Central, North East, and South).

Second, two variables are drawn from the Garlock data set (1973), with the addition by us of month of founding of each LA. Third, we define a series of strike characteristics, each at the level of the individual firm involved in the strike. Since most

TABLE 15.1   Variable Definitions*

Mean	SD	Industry/Region Context	
−.000	.065	BREAKP	Proportion of strikes broken by the employer by region/industry
−.001	1.000	NSTRIKES	Number of strikes by region/industry
Knight LAs			
.000	1.000	EXIST	Number of local assemblies that exist on the first day of the strike in the county in which the strike took place
3.258	43.348	FOUND-CHRATE	Number of local assemblies that are founded in the six months *after* the strike ends minus the number of local assemblies founded in the six months *before* the strike begins
Strike Characteristics			
.824	.29	PSTRIKE	Proportion of work force that is striking
.120	.324	HOURS1†	Change in hours first cause of strike
.075	.264	RULES1†	Change in work rules first cause of strike
−.000	.437	OFFENSE†	Offensive (i.e., for wage gain) or defensive (against wage decrease proposed by employer) strike
−.000	1.200	LDURAT	Log of the number of striking days eliminating all strikes one day or less ("wildcat")
−.000	.343	STBREAK†	Strike breakers brought in from other places by the employer
−.000	.488	OUNION†	Ordered by a union or not
−.001	.500	SUCCESS†	Strike success (1 = succeed and partially succeed)
.151	.262	RFIRED	Number fired as a proportion of all employees prior to the strike
Firm Characteristics			
.000	.999	ZSIZE	Number of employees, Z score
.898	.288	PFEMALE	Proportion of women employees in the firm

NOTES: N = 4,726 strikes, 681 strikes omitted: 597 wildcat (one day or less) strikes and 84 strikes with missing data on one or more variables. All independent variables are centered; see text.

† 1 = YES, 0 = NO.

strikes during this period involved only a single firm, most variables simultaneously describe both. Finally, we define two firm characteristics, size and proportion female.

Because of skewed distributions, duration of strike is converted to a log, while size of firm is computed as a Z score (subtracting from the mean, dividing by the standard deviation) to make the scale of the variable more comparable to that of other variables. Since we have special interest in interactions between levels of analysis (context effects), as discussed previously, we had special concern about colinearity. Interaction terms tend to be highly correlated with the variables that compose them. Recent proof that eliminating high correlation in these terms creates more stable models (Aiken and West, 1991) provided strong incentive for us to experiment. We transformed all of the independent variables by centering, creating deviation scores (each value minus its mean). Since centering is a relatively novel technique (introduced in Aiken and West, 1991), we checked the effect on results by running equations with and without converting to deviation scores. Except for the interaction terms, all coefficients were identical or highly similar; all had the same level of significance. There was a substantial reduction in significance for most interaction terms.

Analysis: Hierarchically Nested Data

For the most part, the research on both strike activity and Knights of Labor activity in the 1880s has pooled all data in a national model, not considering the effects of social context at all (e.g., using aggregate data on strikes as in Snyder, 1974, 1977; Edwards, 1978, 1981; Kaufman, 1982; Skeels, 1982; and/or using aggregate data on unions as in Carroll and Huo, 1985, 1988). Industry has at best been entered as a dummy variable, and studies that have been more sensitive to context have focused on one locality or state.

Procedures for the analysis of data from clustered samples recognize such groupings or clustering and a large literature exists which shows how to obtain valid inferences from such data. Most of this literature discusses simple statistics, such as means, and rarely more complex models, such as regression. Since clustering induces dependency between units in the same cluster, statistical models based on independence assumptions become invalid. What matters here is the structure of the population which is represented in the sample. Even if we draw a simple random sample from a clustered population, the dependency of the observations remains and affects many inferences based on statistical models that assume independency of observations. Since in nonexperimental situations groups have already been developed, perhaps in group settings that have no relation to the groups now being composed for purposes of analysis, we talk about post hoc grouping. The data might be grouped in a number of arbitrary ways, with the assumption that group members are more alike than members of different groups.

Historically the problem of clustered data has been posed as a need to choose an appropriate unit of analysis. But the choice of unity may be the wrong question. The real need may be for statistical models that explicitly represent the multiple organizational levels typically encountered in sociological research. The mismatch between the hierarchical character of most sociological data and traditional statistical techniques leads to many spurious inferences. With the recent development of a statistical theory of random coefficient models, the basis for a more appropriate approach is available. This approach is variance decomposition.

The variance decomposition approach offers a comprehensive framework for description and analysis of data with hierarchical structure (see Longford, 1986: VARCL-interactive software for Variance Component Analysis Applications). Variance components models can be viewed as a generalization of the ordinary regression models. If the world under study is plainly not governed by change mechanisms, then stochastic modelers need to think explicitly about which uncertainty they are describing and under what conditions. We will develop our model explicitly in the discussion that follows. The decomposition of this uncertainty or error in different parts is clear in variance component models (e.g., beginning in Model 3, and elaborated in the models that follow Model 3).

The linear model contains mostly only one error term, denoted by e_i (in Model 1) or e_{ij} (in Model 2), which captures the chance mechanism or the personal measure of uncertainty. Error has that precise meaning in our discussion of the hierarchical linear model, continuing after discussion of Models 1 and 2 (see Model 3 later). The simple linear regression model has only subscript i for the individual, without respect for any group membership.

$$Y_i = a + bX_i + e_i \qquad (1)$$

The estimation method is ordinary least squares (OLS), which does not explicitly allow for any hierarchy. OLS estimates are consistent, but their standard errors tend to underestimate the true standard errors if grouping (or the design) was accounted for. The design effect is the quotient by which the OLS standard error should be inflated (Longford, 1986).

By introducing another index j to identify groups, we generalize the regression model to include group membership of individual i in group j.

$$Y_{ij} = a + bX_{ij} + e_{ij} \qquad (2)$$

Extending the model even further with an error term associated with groups we get a simple variance component model.

$$Y_{ij} = a_j + bX_{ij} + \delta_j + e_{ij} \qquad (3)$$

where δ_j (the group or industry region level disturbance) and e_{ij} (the individual or strike level disturbance) are mutually independent. X is a strike level variable and Y is the predicted score: the difference in the rate of birth of unions is pre and post strike. The dependent variable is measured at the lowest level, which is the level of the individual strikes.

Strikes in the same region and industry share a common δ_j, have a variance of σ^2 and have an intraclass correlation, ρ. ρ is a measure of homogeneity. Absence of homogeneity corresponds to ρ equal to zero.

Model 3 is no longer a standard regression or any ordinary generalized linear model, since it contains two residuals rather than a single random residual. The term *multilevel* refers to the random part in the model, which is defined as varying between units at different levels of the hierarchy. Thus, Model 3 is a two-level model because there is a random variation between strikes (level 1) and between industries and regions (level 2).

Efficient estimates, for example, maximum likelihood or generalized least squares estimates, can be obtained by using one of a number of recently developed algorithms and corresponding software. The present analyses are carried out by using a software system for two-level analysis, VARCL, which is based on an empirical Bayesian (EB) estimation method. The advantage of applying a model-based approach to our hierarchical nested data is that these models provide more efficient estimates than the traditional approaches, while they also allow us to explore interesting group variations between industries and regions. We explicitly explore the effects that certain characteristics of strikes and firms have on the birth of new unions, while allowing different models for different industries and regions.

Interaction Effects

By adding a second level variable to the model, for instance, the industry level variable Z_j for proportion of strikes broken by the employer, we obtain interaction effects. Z_j is the proportion of broken strikes in the past for each industry and predicts the variation in the intercepts (a_j) and variation in the slopes of X (b_j) over industries.

The EB estimation method employed here depends critically on the validity of the assumption of exchangeability (that is, our region/industry data could be replaced by other region/industry divisions without altering the effects) among the parameter estimates in Model 4.

$$Y_{ij} = a_j + b_j X_{ij} + e_{ij} \tag{4}$$

where

$$a_j = \gamma_{00} + \gamma_{01} Z_j + \delta_{0j} \tag{4a}$$

and

$$b_j = \gamma_{10} + \gamma_{11} Z_j + \delta_{1j} \tag{4(b)}$$

In equation (4) a_j and b_j are defined as varying over contexts j, to interact with a context level variable Z_j and have error terms defined as δ_j's. The second level error terms are assumed to covary, and have a normal distribution, with mean 0 and variance/covariance matrix Σ: $N(0, \Sigma)$. A priori, we assume that the regression coefficients a_j and b_j are differing randomly over industries, meaning that we assume they are independently sampled: the assumption of independence or exchangeability. But the conception underlying Model 4 is that the regression coefficients for industries depend in some systematic way on the proportion of broken strikes (Z_j) in the past.

Modeling exchangeability as in Model 4 depends on the extent of our knowledge about the units of analysis and the kinds of measurements available. Departure from exchangeability can be modeled if we have reasons to suspect that the size of the regression coefficients for one industry is different from that of another and depends in some way on regional and industrial history. In our example we assume that the history of industries differs in respect to the proportion of strikes in the past that were broken and/or the number of strikes in the past. Model 4 implies exchangeability only for industries with the same Z_j values. The adequacy of Model 4 compared to Model 3 can be tested with a goodness of fit test. The difference in deviance between the two models follows a χ^2 distribution. The differences between Model 3 and 4 are partly in the fixed effects, since the context variable Z_j and the interaction of Z_i with X_{ij} are added to the model, and partly in the random effects, since the slope coefficient for X is fitted as a random coefficient instead of a fixed one. Note that $Z_j X_{ij}$ is a cross level interaction of strike level variable X_{ij} with industry level Z_j, as is clear in Models 5 and 6, obtained by substituting equations (4a) and (4b) in Model 4.

$$Y_{ij} = (\gamma_{00} + \gamma_{01}Z_j + \delta_{0j}) + (\gamma_{10} + \gamma_{11}Z_j + \delta_{1j})X_{ij} + e_{ij}. \tag{5}$$

Multiplying and rearranging Model 5 results in Model 6:

$$Y_{ij} = \gamma_{00} + \gamma_{01}Z_j + \gamma_{10}X_{ij} + \gamma_{11}Z_jX_{ij} + (\delta_{1j}X_{ij} + \delta_{0j} + e_{ij}). \tag{6}$$

Note the complicated error term between parentheses. The value of the error term connected with the random slope of X changes with values of X. The correlation between X_{ij} and the error term is the reason that application of OLS to Model 6 leads to biased estimates.

Findings: Multilevel Analysis of Founding and of Strike Success

We present our main findings in several ways. Briefly summarizing our analysis, we first consider changes in Local Assembly founding rates, breaking our analysis into Period 1 and Period 2, each a three year time block (table 15.2). Table 15.2 presents both first-level results, examining local strike effects on union local founding, and second-level results, examining effects on industrial and regional differences in conflict (number of strikes and proportion of strikes broken) on founding rates. We then examine whether second-level (industry/region) variables are as important in predicting a more tightly related outcome, strike success (table 15.3), and test whether the structure evolves with time. Finally, we explore the variation across regions and industries of our random coefficients: hours as the first cause of the strike, duration of the strike, size of the firm, and proportion of workers fired by the employer.

I. *Conflict-Based Institution Formation*: When conflict based on divergent self-interest and worldviews yields different solutions to problems of coordinated or joint action, then degree of conflict predicts the formation rate of new institutional structure.

In table 15.2, we do not find support for a conflict model of union local formation on the first level: the number of strikebreakers and proportion of workers fired, the "conflict" indicators, are not significant. There is also no support for a consensus model on the first level: the proportion of workers out on strike (PSTRIKE) is not significant.

On the second level, there is much stronger support for the conflict model, but the nature of the support is different across the time periods. The proportion of strikes broken increases the founding rate slightly in the first period, but there are no first-level variables that vary significantly across the region/industry contexts. Inexplicably, we do, however, find a significant interaction: proportion broken (second-level) with proportion fired (first-level). The second-level effects are much stronger in

TABLE 15.2 Multilevel Comparison of 1881–83 to 1884–86: Predicting Change in Union Local Assembly Founding Rates

Variables	Period 1 1881–83 (N = 1,564)			Period 2 1884–86 (N = 3,162)		
	Est.	SE	T-score	Est.	SE	T-score
	Effects of First-Level Characteristics					
GRAND MEAN	.182			−.216		
HOURS1	−.450**	.161	2.80	−.008	.063	.13
RULES1	−.077	.092	.84	−.161**	.060	2.68
SUCCESS	.004	.053	.08	.065*	.035	1.86
OUNION	.099	.055	1.80	.227***	.037	6.14
STBREAK	.111	.074	1.50	−.103*	.053	1.94
OFFENSE	.108*	.057	1.90	.152***	.038	4.00
EXIST	−.402***	.088	4.57	−.446***	.016	27.88
LDURAT	−.026	.024	1.08	−.072***	.021	3.43
ZSIZE	.040	.034	1.18	.036	.025	1.44
PFEMALE	−.055	.105	.52	.173**	.072	2.40
RFIRED	.087	.121	.72	−.095	.091	1.04
PSTRIKE	−.087	.101	.86	−.044	.070	.63
	Est.	SE	T-score	Est.	SE	T-score
	Effect of Second-Level Context					
BREAKP	1.650**	.595	2.77	−.528	.433	1.22
NSTRIKE	−.036	.074	.49	.096**	.039	2.46
	Sigma	SE	T-score	Sigma	SE	T-score
	Random Effects: Covariates[a]					
GRAND MEAN	.380***	.067	5.67	.182***	.026	7.00
HOURS1	.104	.128	.81	.145***	.060	2.42
LDURAT	.039	.024	1.63	.060**	.020	3.00
ZSIZE	.056	.038	1.47	.067***	.019	3.00
RFIRED	.170	.152	1.12	.244**	.089	2.74
	Est.	SE	T-score	Est.	SE	T-score
	Interaction Effects					
BREAKP						
X HOURS1	3.255	2.118	1.54	.132	.770	.17
X LDURAT	.454	.349	1.30	.337	.254	1.33
X ZSIZE	−.978	.595	1.64	−.424	.350	1.21
X RFIRED	−3.172**	1.465	2.17	1.008	1.066	.95
NSTRIKE						
X HOURS1	.171	.151	.11	−.032	.056	.55
X LDURAT	.027	.024	1.13	−.018	.018	1.00
X ZSIZE	.018	.040	.45	.001	.024	.04
X RFIRED	.157	.106	1.48	−.057	.077	.74

NOTE: *p < .05. **p < .01. ***p < .0001.

[a] First-level variables that vary across context.

TABLE 15.3 A Multilevel Analysis of Strike Success: Comparison of 1881–83 to 1884–86

Variables	Period 1 1881–83 (N = 1,564)			Period 2 1884–86 (N = 3,162)		
	Est.	SE	T-score	Est.	SE	T-score
Effects of First-Level Characteristics						
GRAND MEAN	.489			.419		
HOURS1	−.188*	.091	2.07	−.068	.062	1.10
RULES1	−.049	.043	1.14	.006	.030	.20
OUNION	.201***	.025	8.04	.095***	.019	5.00
STBREAK	−.130***	.035	3.71	−.137***	.027	5.07
OFFENSE	.094***	.027	3.48	.019	.019	1.00
EXIST	.034	.041	.83	−.033***	.008	4.13
LDURAT	−.041***	.013	3.15	−.038***	.012	3.17
ZSIZE	−.052***	.013	4.00	−.001	.010	.10
PFEMALE	−.003	.049	.06	.018	.037	.49
RFIRED	−.667***	.055	12.13	−.593***	.036	16.47
PSTRIKE	.189***	.047	4.02	.230***	.036	6.39
	Est.	SE	T-score	Est.	SE	T-score
Effect of Second-Level Context						
BREAKP	.034	.190	1.79	−.599*	.218	2.75
NSTRIKE	−.004	.019	.21	−.028	.020	1.40
	Sigma	SE	T-score	Sigma	SE	T-score
Random Effects: Covariates[a]						
GRAND MEAN	.072***	.015	4.50	.091***	.015	6.06
HOURS1	.129	.107	1.21	.207***	.047	4.40
LDURAT	.034*	.015	2.27	.038*	.011	3.46
ZSIZE	.003	.014	.21	.009	.013	.69
RFIRED	.097	.056	1.73	.051	.043	1.19
	Est.	SE	T-score	Est.	SE	T-score
Interaction Effects						
BREAKP						
X HOURS1	−.078	1.299	.06	.866	.640	1.35
X LDURAT	−.019	.179	.11	.094	.137	.69
X ZSIZE	−.007	.253	.03	−.061	.129	.47
X RFIRED	−1.462*	.650	2.25	1.211*	.451	2.69
NSTRIKE						
X HOURS1	−.037	.083	.45	−.012	.049	.25
X LDURAT	−.004	.013	.31	−.007	.010	.70
X ZSIZE	.028	.016	1.75	−.002	.010	.20
X RFIRED	.055	.049	1.12	.027	.031	.87

NOTES: *$p < .05$. **$p < .01$. ***$p < .0001$.

[a] First-level variables that vary across context.

the second period. Here, the number of strikes by region/industry becomes significant, and all first-level variables tested vary significantly by the context (hours as cause, duration of strike, firm size, and proportion fired). No interactions are significant, contrary to our expectations. The significant second-level effects support our prediction that action will be altered by social context differences (industry, region) when the outcome is ambiguous, as it is in the effects of founding new Knights of Labor Local Assemblies.

II. *Demand for Institutions*: When demand for institutional structure is high, then under conditions of ambiguity action will be altered by social contingency.

Because the institution-building process was so new at the beginning of the time period, we expected to be able to observe a very disorganized, not socially contingent founding process early (1881–83) and a much more organized and socially contingent founding process later (1884–86). In fact, we see a very different explanation of strike effects on founding in the two periods. On the first level, variables generally increase in predictive value across the time periods: ordered by union is nonsignificant in the first period but increases founding after a strike significantly and strongly in the second period. Further, number of strikebreakers becomes significant and negative, duration becomes strongly significant and negative, while the proportion female becomes significant and positive. The number of LAs that exist when the strike begins increases its negative effect fivefold. While hours as the first cause of the strike is negative in the first period, its effect is replaced by rules in the second period.

III. *Institutional Evolution:* When demand for institutions is high, then social contingency gradually increases differentiation, yielding divergent evolution with local optima.

Overall, there are strong time effects on the first-level variables and on covariates across contexts. However, the second-level differentiation appears about equally strong over time, just involving different variables. Conflict engenders development of institutional structure in a socially contingent mode.

IV. *Action Without Institution:* When demand for institutional structure is low, social contingency does not alter action.

Predicting strike success generates very different models than predicting LA founding (see table 15.3). As expected, there is little effect of second-level context; first-level models are generally consistent over time and very strong. The strongest predictor on the first level in both time periods is the proportion fired, which reduces the likelihood of success. Two other variables that are highly significant across both time periods, increasing the likelihood of success, are strike ordered by union and proportion who are striking and involved. Differences in the models are offensive strikes increasing success in the first period only; number of LAs that exist at the beginning of the strike decreasing success in the second time period; and size of firm decreasing success in the first time period. It is interesting to note that the important variables in explaining founding rate changes in relation to strikes are not the same

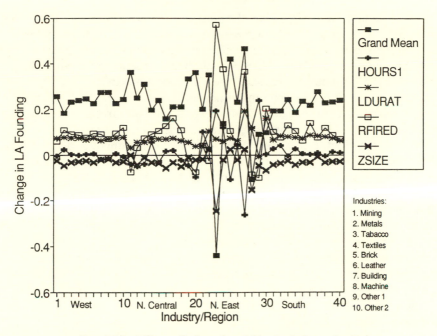

FIG. 15.3 Effects of selected variables by industry/region

as those explaining success: founding rate cannot be considered just another form of successful outcome. On the second level, both the overall lack of effect and the marginal negative effect on success of conflict (proportion of strikes broken by region/industry) also highlight the rational choice process operative when action and outcomes can be directly related.

V. *Socially Contingent Rational Choice:* If there is divergent institutional evolution, that is, fragmented legitimation with different local optima, then covariate effects on institutional formation will be context-dependent.

As figure 15.3 illustrates, the same variable may have very different effects on the founding rate change pre/post strike in different regions and industries. Look, for example, at the proportion of workers fired. In some regions and industries, it has a positive effect on the founding rate, while in others it has a negative effect. The amount of variance is striking and strongly supports our proposition.

Implications of Our Argument and Results

Institutions form in response to demand, and social conflict is one form of demand. Social conflict may, in fact, be an especially strong form of demand because it highlights divergence in self-interest among the relevant parties. Our findings of significant second-level (industry/region) effects on both number of strikes and proportion of strikes broken on founding rates of union locals pre/post strike provide strong empirical support.

These findings also suggest an elaboration of the idea that social structure is actualized, is real, only as it is expressed in social action (Giddens, 1979): social action creates social structure; here, conflict between employees and employers generates new union locals. Maintenance of institutional structure may require little further social action, supporting the static view of institutions that is so prevalent (but only accurate for the most highly institutionalized; see Zucker, 1977). But elaboration in size and function or growth in how widespread the structure is does require further social action. Institutional structure, then, is often dynamic.

A second distinct, but related implication of our argument and results is that institutional development and institutional isomorphism are **not** the same concepts. The creation of new institutional structure may increase homogeneity within a culture, or it may actually increase the variance through structural differentiation. That is, the conditions under which the same institutional structure forms may be quite variable, and these conditions may strongly alter the founding rate. Our findings provide very strong support for this argument.

Not only do different contexts alter formation rates of LAs pre/post strikes, the industrial/regional context alters the effects of specific independent variables, such as the number of workers fired, on the Local Assembly formation rate. That is, the conditions under which the same institutional structure forms may be quite variable: Local optima determine whether institutions form, the amount or number, and the kinds of institutions. Across regions and industries, the same variables have very different impacts on formation. The implications of these results are profound: Independent variables may be present, but not "expressed," that is, have no effect on the dependent variable in one social context, in another have a marked positive effect, and in still another have a marked negative effect. Theories of socially contingent rational choice, then, must specify the conditions under which choice is expected to vary by social context more precisely than in our present work. For example, selection of random variables must be explicitly theory-driven, embedded in a causal comparative framework (Zelditch, 1971).

Finally, legitimacy evolves: it seldom develops suddenly, especially in contested terrain. We found evidence of its evolution, changing the relationship between the social context of action and the formation rate of institutional structure. Indeed, as the rate of institutional formation increased, so did its differentiation by industry and region. Since it was in the context of the strike that unions evolved, we examined the strike as the unit at risk for a "birth" of a new Local Assembly (Zucker, 1989a), generally after the end of the strike activity. Legitimation is most likely when the relationship between process and outcome is ambiguous. We have presented the results of predicting strike success over time, a less ambiguous means-end relation, and demonstrated that there were few context effects and little evolution, at least over the six years we studied intensively here. We argue, then that legitimacy evolves slowly under most conditions, gradually emerging from social process.

In conclusion, we take a strong position that institutional structure does not just "happen." Human agency is required to form it, and resources are required to maintain it. We have stated the problem from a neofunctionalist standpoint: there must be measurable demand for institutional structure or it will not be formed. We argue that this demand will often vary as a function of social context. When it does, possibly more often in conflict-based processes, then the result is fragmented legitimation, where the same structure is institutionalized in one context, but not institutionalized in another, producing cultural differentiation.

Notes

1. Demand for institutional structure is a new concept in the social science literature. But the idea that some resources are necessary for new social structure has been explicitly recognized in social movements research, conceptualized as "resource mobilization" (classic statement in McCarthy and Zald, 1977). In fact, interest groups often form explicitly to stimulate demand for institutions of a particular sort. In doing so, individuals and groups commonly disguise self-interested reasons by recasting them in terms of the common good, thus stimulating demand for new structure and action through fraud and misrepresentation.

2. After the May Day 1886 Haymarket riots, the public reaction to strike activity was so negative that the founding rate of new LAs was actually *depressed* after strikes. While we keep this period in the multivariate analysis, we exclude it here because the averages for the last six months are so atypical.

3. Unions founded during a strike as a direct consequence of strike activity were limited to strikes whose cause was "union representation" and to very long (more than one month) strikes. These constitute under 2 percent of all cases. Slightly over 20 percent of all strikes showed no change in founding rate either before or after the strike.

4. Workers, lower in power, create conflict-based institutions (strikes, union locals); employers, higher in power, create incentive-based institutions (wage payment schemes, performance evaluation protocols, a middle management who monitors, evaluates, and differentially rewards).

5. At the level of the task itself, outcome may be clearly determined by the process (action); if you do the work correctly, the outcome is success. These tasks are inert, and rational action provides the best explanation of their performance. Other tasks, however, have much less certain links between action and outcome: the surgery was performed perfectly, but the patient died. These *active* tasks are much more likely to be conditioned by social variables. See Dornbusch and Scott (1975) for further discussion. DiMaggio and Powell (1983) provide a discussion of professional action as institutionalized that implicitly extends the Scott/Dornbusch model.

6. If action of the other is uncertain, as uncertainty increases so does the likelihood that exchange will fragment. It will fragment in ways that increase predictability, increase trust: subgroups or subcultures of exchange form (e.g., mixed assemblies of the Knights fail and are replaced by single trade locals, limited to one occupation usually in one industry; Korean banking institutions form in the United States to serve the Korean community), and firms remove dependence on an external exchange mechanism, fragmenting production/marketing by moving it inside the firm, causing the firm to grow. Thus, group size may grow (the firm), shrink (subcultures), or stay the same, just becoming more homogeneous (the trade union local); exchange in each case fragments.

7. If there is no change in demand, then the evolutionary process should reach an equilibrium point and then stop. Institutional context will be static, and social contingency constant over time. If information problems actually decline, then demand for institutional structure should decrease; social contingency should erode and eventually disappear.

8. Static convergent institutional structures and actions are best studied comparatively across societal sectors or between societies where degree of institutionalization and/or content differ significantly (Zelditch, 1971).

COMMENTARY

Evolution and Organizational Science

BILL MCKELVEY

My topic concerns the state of evolutionary thinking about organizational populations. While I do not refer specifically to any particular chapter in this book, you
safely may assume that the papers presented at the conference contributed substantially to the thrust of my remarks about the general state of evolutionary
thinking.

After pointing out the diverse definitions of the term *evolution*, I have chosen
to emphasize the following points: (*1*) The relevance of evolutionary thinking to the
study of organizations, with particular reference to natural selection theory and the
role of managers in organization change, and (*2*) the need for a closer link between
population ecology and evolutionary theory in organizational research.

Evolutionary Variations

Absent an explicit definition of how an author uses the term *evolution* the reader
might assume one of a wide range of possibilities. There could be a definition of the
term for every author, so diverse are the views. Consider those listed in the *Oxford
English Dictionary* (Simpson and Weiner, 1989):

1. Process of opening out or unfolding.
2. Process of emergence or protrusion.
3. Process of disengaging or giving off.
4. The unfolding or straightening of a curve.
5. Process of working out in detail.
6a. Process of developing from a rudimentary to a mature or complete
    state.
6b. The idea that embryos are developed or expanded from a preexisting
    form.
6c. The origination of the species.

My thanks to Joel Baum for many helpful suggestions.

7. The development of growth, according to inherent tendencies, of anything that may be compared to a living organism.
8. The formation of heavenly bodies from cosmic matter.
9. The development of human societies.

I could add that for many people evolution is:

10. Any kind of slow change, as opposed to revolution.
11. Any change so gradual that it is imperceptible.
12. Advancement, in the sense that the organism or social entity gets more
    complex, more flexible, more efficient, more capable, smarter, prettier,
    nearer to God, or whatever value one might attach to being more
    advanced.
13. The same as development, in the sense that a single organization
    evolve as it ages, though in biology a distinction is made between the
    development of an organism and the evolution of a species or popu-
    lation.

The Importance of Natural Selection Theory

Evolutionary Epistemology

In his classic paper "Evolutionary Epistemology," Don Campbell (1974b) gives Karl
Popper most of the credit for the existence of an evolutionary epistemology today.
Central to this view, the key tenets believed by followers of a particular paradigm
(Kuhn, 1970), or scientific domain (Shapere, 1977), are viewed as the result of variations that are subsequently accepted or rejected by the relevant scientific community. Within this perspective, the various paradigms (in the best sense of Kuhn's
usage) now present in organization theory are seen as variations, each subject to
eventual acceptance or rejection as the reigning explanation of organizational form
(structure, function, process) over time. The most extended presentation of this perspective is given in Toulmin (1972).

Campbell (1974b) also cites Popper for originating the idea of a nested hierarchy
of the selective elimination process of weeding out poor variations. Following this,
we see that there are many variations of the evolutionary concept (Level 1) nested
within the evolutionary paradigm (Level 2) within organizational science (Level 3).
My question is, How can organizational scientists at Level 3 elevate the evolutionary
paradigm (Level 2) to the position of primary importance when evolutionists at Level
2 are not making any progress in selectively eliminating poor evolutionary concepts
at Level 1?

Basic Elements of an Evolutionary Theory of Organizations

To reduce confusion, and possibly speed up the process of narrowing the number of
evolutionary variants at Level 1, I propose the following elements of an organizational evolutionary theory. Space precludes more than a minimal presentation. Most
of the relevant arguments already have been made in the many works cited in this

commentary and have been covered in McKelvey (1982) along with a more comprehensive discussion of a total of 24 basic principles. I give a simplified overview here.

1. The information an organization needs for survival competence is held, or interpreted from written material, by its members in the form of "blueprints" (Hannan and Freeman, 1977), "routines" (Nelson and Winter, 1982), or "comps" (McKelvey, 1982). Organizational form is defined as the visible structural/behavioral result of the set of comps held by an organization.

2. Darwinian (1859) evolution only takes place when all four principles of natural selection are in effect:
   a. There are variations in comps.
   b. Environmental forces selectively discriminate against some variations and favor others.
   c. Favored variations are retained and diffused throughout the organization or population.
   d. Competitive context is such that organizations holding a larger proportion of favored comps deprive organizations holding fewer favored comps of required resources, leading to the eventual failure of the latter (Lewontin, 1978).

3. A population is a polythetic grouping of organizations competing to survive within the resource constraints of a particular niche, in which each viable member holds many but not all favored comps, each favored comp is held by several members, but no single favored comp is necessarily held by all members.

4. Evolutionary change is defined as change in the total pool of comps held by the viable members of a population.

5. Because of the rapid pace of organizational evolution, at any given time an organizational population will contain members holding viable and nonviable sets of comps (compools).

6. Changes in a population of organizations occurs through both Darwinian and Lamarckian processes.
   a. Via the Darwinian process, an organizational population changes as new members holding more favored comps compete into failure members holding less favored comps.
   b. Via the Lamarckian[1] process, an organizational population changes as existing members adapt to environmental pressures by replacing less favored comps with more favored comps.

7. Whether Darwinian or Lamarckian population level change, changes in comps within organizations are primarily the result of the Darwinian process under conditions of uncertainty, but may be Lamarckian under conditions of certainty or predictability.

8. Both organizational and population level stases are punctuated with infrequent periods of very rapid adaptive change, with the possibility of gradualistic adaptation in between.

The Advantages of Natural Selection Theory

I have a number of reasons for preferring natural selection theory to the more traditional explanations of organizational change, which focus on the so-called visible hand (Chandler, 1977):

1. The theory of competition elaborated by evolutionary ecologists, such as Pianka (1988) and Roughgarden (1979b), is much less ideological than that posed by economists and does not rest on so many assumptions about human behavior and rationality.
2. As I will argue, natural selection theory, combined with learning theory, offers a much more objective base of organizational analysis since the data are drawn from visible environmental resources and constraints and visible organization structural/behavioral attributes.
3. Biological natural selection and ecological theories offer organizational scientists a conceptual depth and breadth for individual organizational level and population level analysis not readily available elsewhere.
4. Natural selection and ecological theories stress the competitive behavior of members of populations within specific niches or resource pools. There are a number of implications:
   a. A local population in a specific niche is the only basic unit for scientific generalization that we have. I might add that only with a sound general classification of populations can we expect to have any basis of generalizing beyond the basic populations.
   b. Given the incredible variability of human intentionality and behavior in organizations, the only basis of reasonably expecting patterned organizational behavior worthy of explanation and generalization occurs when we track changes in organizational form in the context of competition for scarce niche resources. Absent attention to finite niche resources, absent attention to competition, and absent objective measures I see no science of organizations. Why would there be any pattern to identify and generalize if there are no reasons for any variation to fail? They would all exist!
   c. We get out from under the pre-Copernican specter of a science centered around managers. As long as our field focuses on the visible hand, we seem to have a science only for managers. Also, cognitive intentionality and motivational drives are not directly measurable. They are subject to misguided positive attributions (Jabes, 1978), retrospective logic and wishful thinking (Weick, 1979) and gaming (Rasmussen, 1989).
   d. We will move toward a clearer understanding of the relation between population regulation and growth in the short term and population evolution over the long term.
   e. We will move toward a clearer identification of the "evolutionarily significant" comps in a population that offer competitive advantage in a given niche, and the "evolutionarily significant" niche attributes or forces driving the changes in the population. Neither of these can

be identified independent of the other, nor without tracking their interrelationship over time in a competitive context in a specific niche. To use Sommerhoff's (1950) term from long ago, they are "directively correlated" in this sense.

Occam's Razor

Scientists usually prefer the simplest possible explanation. The law of parsimony dates back to William of Occam (A.D. 1349): "For purposes of explanation things not known to exist should not, unless it is absolutely necessary, be postulated as existing" (Simpson and Weiner, 1989: vol. 13, p. 245). Occam's razor cuts to the heart of the matter. Ever since Simon (1947), Maslow (1954), and March and Simon (1958), the study of organizational behavior has been dominated by mentalistic concepts (such as perception, rationality, intentionality, need based motivation, and phenomenological interpretation), despite the longtime complaints of the behaviorists (Skinner, 1953) that such concepts are unobservable and hence not suitable material for science. With the emergence of the culture and transaction cost based theories, the razor seems to be getting duller, not sharper.

Natural selection theory offers an alternative much more to Occam's liking. Consider explaining how the "hub" routing approach now used by many airline companies came to dominate the population. We have the visible and invisible hand explanations, the latter being natural selection.

Let's assume an uncertain opaque environment and no knowledge of the hub concept or its advantage. Under the invisible hand of natural selection four statements are needed by way of explanation:

1. The hub idea was one of a number of blind variations identified retrospectively, that was inadvertently, explicitly, or possibly experimentally tried at Delta Airlines. We do not need to know how the variations came to be, only that they existed some years ago.
2. Some time along the way someone at Delta discovered that if aircraft on feeder routes arrived and left Atlanta in a certain time relationship with the arrivals and departures of aircraft on trunk routes, the filled-to-empty seat ratios for both kinds of routes improved.
3. The idea found favor at Delta, was favorably received by other airlines, and thus was retained and diffused throughout the population. (The visible hand could apply here, but we do not need to know whether it was visible or not, only that the idea persisted and spread.)
4. While not the only important element in the survival of airlines, the hub concept certainly had a hand in the emergence of Delta as a dominant competitor and in the failure of some others.

It is possible that this explanation is false in the Delta case or with respect to explaining survival in the airline population. I am not here to argue this one way or the other. My point is that only four statements are needed for a complete explanation and all important data points can be objectively measured. No auxiliary statements or further assumptions are needed.

Consider the number of statements required for the visible hand explanation:

1. Someone (could be a group) decided that information about the airline environment was necessary and arranged for its collection.
2. Someone decided the information deserved a response.
3. Someone decided that the information suggested an environmentally posed problem—possibly tougher competition, changed costs, changed consumer habits, and so on—calling for a new approach.
4. Someone conceived of the basic hub idea—no small order—that the benefits of bringing feeder aircraft into Atlanta at the same time, some period of time before the trunk aircraft left, and vice versa, would outweigh the hazards of gate congestion, the uncertain effects of changing all the schedules, problems with the weather, crew scheduling problems, fueling backups, baggage congestion, and on and on.
5. The person was listened to by a champion.
6. The idea was channeled up to the appropriate decision-making level without being massaged into oblivion.
7. It survived the test against further information, alternative ideas, devil's advocates, and so forth.
8. The people in the dominant coalition agreed with all of the previous steps—all had more or less the same biases, perceptions of the environment, interpretations of the data, level of confidence in the hub idea, commitment to overcoming the resistance to change typically encountered, and so forth.
9. The dominant coalition did not get into turf battles, did not see careers and empires at stake, was willing to take a significant risk, did not "garbage can" the problem to death—I hope Cohen, March, and Olsen (1972) will forgive me for turning their wonderful concept into a verb.
10. The appropriate organization change program was implemented.
11. An organizational culture was in place that fostered innovation and ameliorated resistance to change and interdepartmental lack of cooperation.

Additional assumptions (auxiliary statements) are necessary:

12. All the relevant information was properly collected.
13. The person (group) was unbiased and perceptually accurate enough to see or, as Weick (1979) would put it, "enact," the correct view of the environment.
14. The person drew the correct conclusions about the portending problems.
15. A champion existed.
16. The idea actually got to the right decision making level and was not impacted somewhere along the line.

You can see that many more statements (my list is only approximate) are necessary for the explanation to hold. What is the joint probability that all of these will occur at the right time at Delta for the visible hand theory to have worked? I would say about zero! Worse, some of the statements clearly involve subjective notions—bias, perception, politics, power, motivation, and so forth—making a test of the theory much more difficult. And, relative to other organizational form novelties, such as whether a new cultural solution is good, whether an M or H form might be preferred, whether the M form divisions should be highly or only partly related, and so forth, the hub innovation strikes me as relatively straightforward and easily amenable to analysis. In other words, I picked a relatively simple example for my comparison.

Strategic Choice and Evolution

Do managers have rational choice and do they control, or at least influence, the strategic direction of firms? The simple answer is yes, of course. Managers can almost do anything they want, leaving aside whether their thoughts are smart or stupid, seat-of-the-pants or carefully thought through. Managers clearly can control the future of their firm. They can sell the firm totally; they can sell divisions and add others; they can sell their products at a loss; they can make poor quality products; they can make too many products; they can make products no one wants to buy; they can fire everyone or selected groups: they can create cashflow crises, and so on. But under conditions of uncertainty can they prepensively conceive and successfully implement a novel adaptive change that enhances survival in the face of intense competition?

This is the point in my MBA class where I introduce my "ice-cream cone" model of industry evolution. First picture a cone (see below) with a nice large scoop of ice cream on it. At the top part of the cone are the dominant "centroid" firms in the industry, firms that would be thought of as current exemplars. These firms typically form the centroid in a taxonomic cluster. Straggling down the lower part of the cone are "lagging" members of the industry. These are the firms that are asleep; can't figure out what to do to get better; are locked into obsolete plant and equipment; have personnel who are poorly trained, unwilling to learn, try new behaviors, work

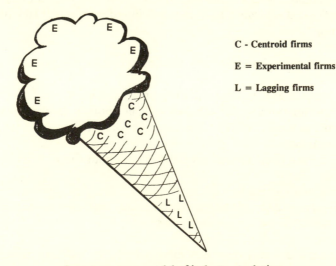

C - Centroid firms

E = Experimental firms

L = Lagging firms

Ice-cream cone model of industry evolution

harder, and so forth. They could be firms that, say, in electronics, were at the top of the vacuum tube business but lost out in the switch over to semiconductors, or GM in the present auto business. Scattered around the curved edge of the ice cream are the "experimentals." These are the peripheral small custom product firms that look for new niches, try new products, try new technology. Many of them fail, but every once and a while one succeeds. It becomes the Xerox, the Texas Instruments, the American Telephone and Telegraph (a long time ago), the IBM, and so forth, of the next evolutionary direction in an existing industry or the first mover in a new industry.

Two fundamentally different decision processes apply here. When one may identify the existing trend of the industry, mimetic (DiMaggio and Powell, 1983), or copying, behavior is appropriate. Managers in the lagging firms at least ought to be able to find out, evaluate, and implement strategies and behaviors copied from more successful firms. The Japanese have always done this rather successfully. These managers do not face true uncertainty in the sense that something has not yet happened, but rather self-imposed uncertainty about things that have happened elsewhere but of which they are ignorant. They do not make decisions under uncertainty. Rather, they make decisions in the fog of poor intelligence gathering. When successful behaviors are already known to be favored, or when industry trends are identifiable, managers can carry out strategic choice within the context of discovering and copying successes elsewhere, or forecast, anticipate, plan, and implement policies in the context of predictable trends. This approach works well during periods of convergent evolution in unpunctuated environments.

But when the strategic context is truly uncertain in the sense that the next punctuation is unpredictable, or the next trend in consumer taste is unknown, or the next technological breakthrough is unknown, or the predatory strategies of competitors are unknown, or the next new product wrinkle introduced by a competitor is unknown, and so forth, forecasting and planning are useless. In fact they can give a false sense of security as many companies, such as Shell Oil (noted for long range planning and scenario development), have discovered in times of environmental punctuation. Under conditions of true uncertainty, the odds of making a correct strategic choice and successfully implementing it are about zero, as I indicated in the previous section.

Darwinian variations are best seen as behavioral trials, some of which prove out positively and some of which fail. Unless you believe that policy manuals stand up and get things done all by themselves, you are not going to have much trouble accepting the idea that variations are in fact human behaviors. Some might be consciously planned; others might just happen; some might happen as a result of other planned events. These unintended consequences could appear consciously motivated by those making them but could appear irresponsible and unmindful or blind by those taking broader perspectives.

Once variations are interpreted as trial-and-error learning events, you can see that people are in the thick of Darwinian evolutionary theory. Managers can increase or decrease the number of variations in their firm. They can work to increase the quality of variations or trials. Trial behaviors may be blind as to whether they will prove truly successful in an uncertain world. But they do not have to be totally stupid. And they don't have to be outright mistakes. If a study were done, my guess is that most managers take their organization out of the competitive game by initiating stupid mistakes much more often than they win the game with any kind of favored trial. An analogy here is the Super Bowl in professional football—American style. It is generally believed that the winning team is the one that makes fewer mistakes rather than the one that has the flashier offense. As in football, usually, a few low risk successful trials coupled with an absence of stupid mistakes will put a firm in a strong competitive position.

In organizations the natural selection process works hierarchically. Trials and retention and diffusion work at a given level, but selection depends on acceptance of the trial at the next higher or outer level. A new product trial or variation, for example, could be favored or rejected by a superior or by the external market.[2] In many organizations managers are so "selective" that new trials dry up—they are unrewarded activities. Most organizations have great difficulty rewarding risky behaviors that most of the time are going to be errors or failures. The motivation of new behavioral trials and the skills associated with knowing when to stop a particular trial before it gets out of hand, like the Ford Edsel, the Convair 990, or the ill fated billion dollar Exxon venture into office equipment, are critically important managerial behaviors.

Critics tend to think of selective discrimination as something that happens "out there" in the market or via some other inanimate process, as in "The environment selects." Let's face it: Most selection is done by superiors—inside, I repeat, inside organizations. Most new product ideas are selected out long before they get to market. I am not arguing at this point whether this is good or bad, only that the trials, if there are any, are reviewed and quashed by managers inside the organization, not by some inanimate nonhuman process in the environment. But let's talk about the external market, or resource environment, too. Ultimately it is the prime determinant of survival. Remember the famous Peters and Waterman (1982) dictum "Stay close to your customer." Customers are alive. They talk. They complain. Good managers can call them up and hear their tale of woe, or congratulations. What is inanimate about this?

Paying close attention to the implications of the four natural selection principles produces managerial behavior much more suitable to the experimental firms in an industry, or to centroid firms that are considering taking experimental positions, ideally with innovative divisions or product groups. How to increase the number of trials in a firm? How to prevent poor trials from costing a firm too much? In other words, how to foster "inexpensive experimentation"? How to prevent frustrated employees from walking out the door with promising trials in their heads? How to get successful trials in one part of a large firm to be tried elsewhere? How to get a firm to learn vicariously and quickly from the successful trials by competitors?

Managers and academic strategy professors who think that they can select and control the destiny of their firm under conditions of uncertainty suffer from delusions of grandeur. What they can do is pay close attention to the principles of natural selection. As you can see, managers can be intensely involved in every element of the natural selection process. They just cannot determine in advance which trial is going to be successful. I find that the Darwinian framework does not take managers out of responsibility and control for organizational success. It does, however, point their thinking in a more constructive direction for many circumstances.

Population Ecology and Evolution

Darwin Versus Lamarck

Organizational population ecologists, like their biological counterparts, take a strictly Darwinian view of evolution, as best I can determine. Hannan and Freeman say, "Our work approximates a Malthusian-Darwinian position on the nature of change in organizational populations over time. We think that the current diversity of organizational forms reflects the cumulative effect of a long history of variation and selection" (1989:20). Noting that Nelson and Winter (1982:11) say, "Our theory is unabashedly Lamarckian," Hannan and Freeman add, "Thus it may be useful in analyzing patterns of long-term change in organizational forms to employ models that incorporate Darwinian mechanisms rather than Lamarckian ones" (1989:23). It is clear from the subject matter of their book that Hannan and Freeman focused on niche and density dependent effects on organizational foundings and failures—the DD-FF framework. Evolutionary theory figures only on 7 of the 341 pages of their book. They admit, "We do not have anything resembling a fully developed evolutionary theory of organizational change" (p. 20).

Biological population ecologists study the regulation and growth of species, almost all of which have not evolved significantly in the Darwinian sense for millions of years (Stanley, 1989). These ecologists have put considerable attention into the intersection of ecology and evolutionary processes recently. Some six books appeared in the late 1970s with the words *ecology* and *evolution* in their titles (the ones best known to organizational ecologists are Pianka [1988] and Roughgarden [1979b]. Quite a number of recent microevolutionary biological studies are reported by Travis and Mueller (1989). Stanley (1989), the noted punctuationist, mentions more macroevolutionary ones. Roughgarden (1979b) offers the best insights into the modeling implications of the intersection. Feldman (1989) points out, however, that the research record is not robust enough to support some claims by various advocates.

Since the pace of evolution of organizational populations is, I believe, very much faster than for biological species (I trust I do not need a citation here), ecological and evolutionary dynamics much more closely intertwine. Population ecologists have been slow to pick up the scent. Their models typically do not include selection effects on organizational forms as dependent variables, a point also made in a review by Singh and Lumsden (1990).

Its seems to me that we have seen enough basic tests of the DD-FF framework. The field could benefit from some movement into new topic areas. The debates between Darwinians and Lamarckians and between gradualists and punctuationists seem especially relevant for organizational scholars. Here are some possibilities:

Unpunctuated Environments

From the Darwinian perspective, the most interesting case occurs when environment and niche conditions remain unpunctuated over a long period, what Tushman and Romanelli (1985) term convergent evolution. Only under these conditions can we test for the effects of gradualistic change on selection. Fortunately there are industries and populations that remain unpunctuated for decades, such as steam boiler making, sand casting, iron smelting, and horse racing. Some, like glass and locomotives, are essentially stable except for, say, one punctuation. Unpunctuated populations soon are regulated by k conditions (Hannan and Freeman, 1989). Hannan and Freeman (1984) argue for no organizational adaptation—just death and replacement; Tushman and Romanelli (1985) argue for convergent organizational change, that is, gradual change between framebreaking environmental shocks; Miller and Friesen (1984) argue for only punctuated organizational change after a long buildup of pressure—three different hypotheses of change under unpunctuated circumstances. It is time for Stinchcombe's (1968) "crucial experiment."

Punctuated Environments—the r to k Shock

According to punctuationists, such as Eldredge and Gould (1972) and Stanley (1979), population changes occur as spikes or punctuations separated by long periods of stasis. In this view the best test of the ecological determinants of selection occurs when rapid changes in population size occur.

Accompanying most r to k transitions (shakeouts), a rapid die-off of r types is followed by a buildup of k types, the latter starting from a very small number. A basic principle of biological punctuation is that the gene pool is so severely narrowed in a very small population that the prevailing niche conditions, coupled with selection pressures, can push the population's evolutionarily significant characteristics in a novel direction very quickly (Stanley, 1979). If the same basic process also prevails in organizations, then most selection effects of population regulation occur in the early stages of a population's growth, when the shakeout occurs. This was Stinchcombe's (1965) conclusion, though he did not state it quite this way. The implications of this are that the r to k transition becomes one of the most important times in the life histories of populations (and individual member organizations, since most of them fail at this time) in which to study selective discrimination and consequent population change. Yet I have found not a single study of this important event by population ecologists. The dissertation by Randle (1990) is an exception.

Punctuated Environments—the k to r Shock

Tushman and Romanelli (1985) and Anderson (1986) focus our attention on "framebreaking" change that follows on the heels of "competence destroying" technological change after a long period of "convergent evolution" in a population (their key terms in quotes). In the ecologists' terms this is a k to r shock—the viability of a population in which k types have come to dominate after an extended unpunctuated period is destroyed by an external technological shock beyond the adaptive capability of most, if not all, the k types. Examples of k to r technological shocks abound: steam to diesel locomotives, slide rules to hand calculators, analog to digital watches, mechanical typewriters to electronic word processors, reciprocating to jet commercial aircraft engines. Tushman and Anderson mention a number of others. These punctuations greatly reduce the size of a population such that the few remaining k types or first postshock entering r types hold a vastly reduced and usually significantly different compool. This kind of selective discrimination gives a jump-start to a new direction in the evolution of the population.

There are other kinds of *k* to *r* shocks. A severe recession can rapidly reduce the size of a population and concurrently impose such a different set of conditions and resources that the punctuation sets the population rapidly off in a new evolutionary direction. Government deregulation in the 1990s, such as in banks, airlines, and trucking, had the effect of significantly reducing the population, thereby providing a punctuated start in a new direction. In the telecommunication industry the breakup of the AT&T monopoly gave rise to several new small populations that rapidly grew in new evolutionary directions.

The dynamics in adjacent industries can also set up *k* to *r* punctuations. The emergence of the frozen food population provided a down-sizing punctuation and resultant new evolutionary dynamics in the canning population. Competition from other financial services populations brought about the near-collapse of the savings and loan population. It has down-sized nearly to extinction. The firms left will certainly have a significant effect on the evolution of the population as it rebounds, if it rebounds. The selective directions taken by the few remaining savings and loan institutions should be interesting to study, and surely the timing is ideal.

The major points of this commentary are the following: We need better definition of organizational evolutionary theory. Specifically we need enough of what I have called "level 1" discussion so that nonevolutionists know what the paradigm stands for. Some consensus here would not hurt. But, if there have to be alternative definitions, we need an elucidation of the pros and cons associated with each view. Without this kind of basic work why should our nonevolutionist colleagues take the paradigm seriously?

Second, we need to present the scientific reasons why evolutionary theory makes an important contribution to the study of organizational change more effectively. The nesting idea is critical. Evolutionary principles apply at various levels of organization. Selection of trials or variations always imposes itself from the next-most outer ring of the nesting. If selection is brought within a particular nested set, the theory does not make sense. The law of parsimony makes a strong argument for evolutionary theory, acording to my analysis.

Third, evolutionary theory does not mean environmental determinism, loss of managerial prerogatives, loss of human choice, or dehumanization of organizations. There is a natural affinity between trial-and-error-learning and natural selection theories. Much managerial behavior is embedded in the processes underlying the four natural selection principles.

Fourth, there remains an exciting research agenda for population ecologists and evolutionists. Consider the following causal chain:

Niche dynamics → Population dynamics → Selective discrimination

Population ecologists have worked mostly on the middle element. I think more telling research will come from links to the left and right elements. This research falls into two broad venues: Unpunctuated environments and punctuated environments. There are a host of interesting questions calling for study in each of these venues. Surely the time has come to move beyond the basic DD-FF framework. This work cannot sensibly proceed without attention to taxonomy and classification in order to decompose populations into their separate and frequently countervailing subpopulations. More explicitly, organizational science could be accelerated if we:

1. Moved on to the host of evolutionarily more relevant studies.
2. Paid more attention to the ecological aftermath of natural environmental shocks.
3. Refined the basic hypotheses by highlighting the conditions that qualify the hypotheses as they apply in different contexts. Implicit in this is the question of taxonomy and classification.
4. Moved toward a crucial experiment (Stinchcombe, 1968) where ecological and Darwinian explanations are pitted directly against competing theories.
5. Weaned ourselves from the frequently weak proxy measures and archival data based on what many observers believe are trivial populations, such as rural telephone companies, Argentine newspapers, ancient New York insurance companies, rural Italian cooperative banks, minimalist trade associations. No doubt, these provided a good start. But what does population ecology have to say about important populations today? And what would happen if strong operational measures were substituted for weak proxies?

Having made the last comment, let me hasten to add that from the narrow perspective of what is good for scientific progress, pertinent and sound deductive tests of the theory on trivial populations are better than weak tests on populations the lay community may consider more important. Thus, biological ecologists and evolutionists spend much more time studying fruit flies (*Drosophila*) than vanishing bristlecone pines, rain forests, cheetahs, elephants, apes, and whales. Also, ecologists tend to study phenomena that have short life cycles. Who wants to wait around for three generations of bristlecone pine trees to die? It could take 12,000 years. What assistant professor can wait through three generations of automobile companies—even if it is only a century—and beat the tenure clock? Nevertheless, I suppose colleagues have a right to wonder whether it all works on anything important.

Notes

1. Lamarck (1809) published the first truly scientific theory of natural selection. The key elements of his theory are that acquired characteristics are heritable and variations arise in response to adaptive needs, not by chance.

2. For Darwinian evolutionists (organizational or biological) external agents cause selection. For organizations these agents are superiors, markets, competitors, institutional structures, governments, and the like. Choice of one trial over others by members within a group or subentity is part of the process leading to a particular variation being tried, not environmental selection.

Progress and Problems
in Population Ecology

DAVID J. TUCKER

The purpose of this commentary is to comment on the preceding chapters, somehow to consider how and what they contribute to knowledge about organizations, and what the implications are for future research programs. But, how to do this in a reflective and rational manner? One way is to start with the observation that over the past dozen or so years population ecology has been a very fruitful enterprise, with research studies proliferating and demonstrating ever-increasing levels of methodological sophistication. Following from this is the question of whether these chapters define and help solve important puzzles in population ecology that have not yet been addressed, and whether they do so in a scientifically rigorous manner. If the answers are yes on both counts, and they are, then it is clear that these chapters are part of the cumulative knowledge process that is helping to refine and affirm the ecological analysis of organizational populations as an important subfield in organization theory. This of course is the safe conclusion and means we are all on the right road (more or less) and can continue.

A second, and ostensibly more informative approach is to start by asking a broader question: Is organizational ecology contributing to progress in the theory of organizational evolution and organization science? If so, in what way, and how do these particular chapters fit into this schema? In this regard, social scientists, it seems, never tire of invoking the idea of a paradigm shift to characterize a fundamental change in the theoretical orientation of a discipline or profession. Organization scientists are no exception. The emergence of population ecology in organization theory has been warmly greeted by numerous scholars as an important paradigm shift, representing among other things the disposition of contingency theory from its hegemonic position. What has not been acknowledged in this discourse, however, are the implications of a paradigm shift for understanding scientific progress. Paradigms, it will be recalled, are conceptual frameworks scientists use to give intelligibility to phenomena (Kuhn, 1962). Once a group of scientists agree on a paradigm (or framework), they set about testing hypotheses drawn from it and attempt to explain the world by means of it. A scientific revolution occurs when one paradigm is rejected for another. However, because such choices result from political and propandistic forces, and not from rational discourse, an important implication is that gains in knowledge may well be accompanied by losses. This questions the view expressed in the preceding paragraph that progress in science results from some form of linear cumulative advance. To be specific, what is the calculus for determining that the gains achieved by embracing population ecology compensate for the losses sustained by rejecting contingency theory?

How then to think about ecological analysis of organizational populations and what its emergence represents by way of progress in organizational theory? How are we to evaluate statements that it represents a minirevolution in organization science, and that it has deposed contingency theory? Is it the case, as implied by the Kuhnian view, that winning a paradigm battle is its own justification, and that we should be satisfied to judge the accomplishments of population ecology on essentially an ahistoric basis, using rules of success laid down by its practitioners? And what are the implications of how these questions are answered for appraising the contributions of individual pieces of research as reflected in the preceding chapters? Larry Laudan's (1984) work on a theory of scientific progress offers an approach for dealing with these and similar questions.

Elements of a Model of Scientific Progress

To begin, Laudan notes that the question of what progress is must be kept separate from observations that we may make about what is morally and cognitively desirable. The term *progress* is not being used to refer to improvements in the social, material, or spiritual conditions of life. Instead, the emphasis is on "cognitive progress," which is defined in terms of processes that further the intellectual aspirations of science (Laudan, 1984:7). Following from this, Laudan proposes that to derive a framework to guide analysis of cognitive progress, it is necessary to "go back to basics," to begin with an understanding of the essential purpose of science. Here Laudan argues that most would agree that the fundamental aim of science is the solution of problems. However, very little attention has been given to exploring this perspective in detail. What are the different types of problems? What makes one problem more important than another? What are the criteria used for judging something an adequate solution to a problem? To deal with these and other related questions, Laudan defines a model of scientific progress. The core assumptions of this model are twofold: one, the solved problem is the basic unit of progress; two, the aim of science is to maximize the scope of solved problems, while minimizing the scope of unsolved and anomalous problems. A full explication of this model is beyond the scope of this commentary. I shall confine myself to a brief description of a central feature which is most relevant to our discussion here, namely, a taxonomy of problems.

According to Laudan, there are two different kinds of problems that scientific theories must solve—empirical problems and conceptual problems. Empirical problems are "substantive questions about the objects that constitute the domain of any given science" (Laudan, 1984:15). They are divided into three types—solved and unsolved problems, and anomalous problems, with the latter referring to empirical problems which a particular theory has not solved but which has been solved by a competitor. An example of an empirical problem generally considered important to population ecology is the question of why older organizations show a lower propensity to disband than newer organizations (Stinchcombe, 1965; Carroll and Delacroix,

1982; Freeman, Carroll, and Hannan, 1983; Singh, Tucker, and House, 1986). Although this problem cannot be declared as clearly solved (Bruderl and Schussler, 1990; Bruderl, Preisendorfer, and Ziegler, 1991; Fichman and Levinthal, 1991), it is not anomalous in the sense that it has not been solved by a competitor.

Conceptual problems are higher order problems. They are questions about the well-foundedness of the theories that have been devised to solve empirical problems and may have internal or external sources. Internal conceptual problems arise when a theory is found to be logically inconsistent or when central concepts are chronically ambiguous. While examples of internal logical inconsistency are not easily located in population ecology, that is not the case with conceptual ambiguity. Here I point to the various discussions and exchanges in the literature centered on questions about the meaning of such central concepts as population, form, strategy, founding, disbanding, and legitimacy (e.g., Hannan and Freeman, 1977; McKelvey, 1982; McKelvey and Aldrich, 1983; Carroll, 1984; Astley, 1985; Young, 1988; Freeman and Hannan, 1989; Singh and Lumsden, 1991). To be fair, this problem is not unique to population ecology but seems endemic to the social sciences. By the same token, its persistence may be telling us something about the pace of our own scientific progress.

External conceptual problems are generated for a theory when it is in conflict with another theory or doctrine which generally is accepted as well founded. One source of such problems is when a new theory makes assumptions about substantive aspects of its domain that are incompatible with the assumptions made by another generally well regarded theory. A fairly obvious example here is the structural inertia assumption in population ecology (Hannan and Freeman, 1977; 1984), which in proposing that organizations resist change as a result of various internal and external constraints, challenged the dominant adaptation view of organizations as changing continuously, with determinants of change assumed to be mainly internal.

Another frequent source of conceptual problems involves normative difficulties which occur when the methodological rules followed in theory appraisal are considered to be not well founded. An example here can be found in exchanges in the literature regarding the appropriateness of investigating the relationships among legitimation, the density of organizational populations, and mortality by inferring legitimation from a model as opposed to measuring it directly (Carroll and Hannan, 1989c; Zucker, 1989; Petersen and Koput, 1991a; Hannan, Barron, and Carroll, 1991; Baum and Oliver, 1992). Finally, conceptual problems arise when the central thrust of a particular theory is seen to be incompatible with, or as not offering mutual reinforcement for, broader extrascientific beliefs, or certain social or political ideologies. An example of the latter was identified earlier by Aldrich (1979:32) when he raised the notion that evolutionary models of organization might be associated with social Darwinism and, thus, conservative political ideology. An example of the former is implicit in Perrow's (1985) critique that Langton (1984), in using the ecological theory of bureaucracy to explain the transformation of the British pottery industry, obscures what really occurred because Langton ignores the role of power and human intentionality. Underlying the difference between Langton and Perrow's views is disagreement over the broader metaphysical question of whether explanations of social phenomena must inevitably be based on teleological forms of thinking (Warriner, 1978).

In the remainder of the commentary, I use this taxonomy of problems to form observations about how the contributions of the preceding chapters contribute to progress in the ecological analysis of organizational populations. After that I broaden Laudan's concept of progress by arguing that it is time for population ecology to address questions about organizational performance.

The Practice of Solving Scientific Problems

A cursory overview of the evolution of population ecology starts with Hannan and Freeman's (1977) article "The Population Ecology of Organizations," which defined the phenomenon of organizational diversity as an important unsolved problem in organization theory. Subsequently, studies dealing with dynamic change processes in organizational populations proliferated (see Carroll, 1984; and Singh and Lumsden, 1990 for reviews). Reflection on the nature of these numerous studies, taking account of Laudan's taxonomy of problems, reveals that the primary focus of population ecology has been on developing theoretical arguments to solve specific empirical problems. For example, Singh and Lumsden (1990), in their review of the literature, identify six different themes in how ecologists have approached the empirical problem of accounting for patterns of organizational mortality. Secondary attention has been given to conceptual problems, with the main focus on one type of problem, namely, methodological well-foundedness of appraisals of specific theoretical arguments. Examples are the exchanges mentioned about the measurement of legitimation, as well as observations concerning the propriety of appraising density dependence arguments in population ecology without the benefit of data that describe the full history of foundings and disbandings in an organizational population (Carroll and Hannan, 1989).

The studies reported in the five preceding chapters conform with this pattern. Four are aimed at illuminating empirical problems and one at illuminating a normative difficulty. On the empirical side are the chapters by Aldrich, Zimmer, Staber, and Beggs; Amburgey, Dacin, and Kelly; Freeman and Lomi; and Zucker and Kreft that deal with various facets of the ecological analysis of organizational populations. On the conceptual side is the chapter by Delacroix and Rao, which presents what amounts to an explication (Hempel, 1952) of the controversial legitimacy concept.

This brings us to the heart of this commentary—how we understand the contributions of these studies to progress in the ecological analysis of organizational populations. Recall here that progress is defined in terms of a theory's capacity to accumulate solved problems while minimizing the number and scope of unsolved problems. The more numerous and weighty the problems that a theory can adequately solve, the better it is. By the same token, it counts against a theory if it generates anomalous and conceptual problems.

Overall it does not appear that the results of the preceding studies produce new empirical problems that are anomalous in the sense that they have been solved by competitors but not by population ecologists. Neither do the results of these studies appear to add to the stock of existing conceptual problems. This suggests that at least the scope of the ecological analysis of organizational populations is not being deflated. But, do these studies add positive value? That is to say, do they contribute to progress and, if so, in what way? Answering these questions requires focusing more specifically on the kind of problem each study addresses. I start with the four chapters that focused on empirical problems.

The chapter by Aldrich et al. investigates a number of questions about the foundings, mergers and transformations, and disbandings of American trade associations. Understanding this study's contribution requires reference to Halliday, Powell, and Granfors' (1987) earlier study of vital events in a national population of state bar associations. In that study, they differentiate between minimalist and nonminimalist organizations, thereby establishing the problem of why different forms of organization may not always exhibit the same patterns of foundings and failures as solvable within an ecological theory of organization. In Laudan's terms (1984:31), this means that Halliday and colleagues took what initially seemed an anomalous problem for population ecology and turned it into a positive instance of it. Aldrich and associates' study affirms the significance of the distinction drawn by Halliday, Powell, and Granfors (1987), thereby engendering increased confidence among ecologists that they are coming to understand more clearly the nature of dynamic change processes in organizational populations.

The chapter by Amburgey, Dacin, and Kelly uses data on credit unions to investigate a problem first identified by Hannan and Freeman (1977) of the effect of size dependent competition on the operation of disruptive selection pressures in organizational populations. What is significant about their analysis is that it moves a problem from the realm of the "unsolved" to the realm of the "solved." By demonstrating an empirical effect of position in the size distribution on risk of failure, it affirms the problem of disruptive selection as genuine. This not only makes this particular problem amenable to future study, but also enhances the credibility of population ecology and expands its domain.

The contributions of the studies by Freeman and Lomi (chapter 14) and by Zucker and Kreft (chapter 15) are essentially of the same type as that made by Amburgey et. In each study, empirical analyses demonstrate conjectured problems as actual, and as amenable to solution within an ecological framework. Specifically, Freeman and Lomi show the problem of understanding the evolution of resource partitioning as genuine through their analysis of data on banking cooperative in Italy, and Zucker and Kreft show the problem of the embeddedness of activity as genuine through an analysis of the formation of labor unions by Knights of Labor that succeeds in linking social structure to action.

Delacroix and Rao's chapter is unique in the sense that it deals with an internal conceptual problem—the ambiguity and confusion associated with the meaning and usage of the term 'legitimacy'. They deal with this problem through a process of explication (Hempel, 1952; Dumont and Wilson, 1967). They provide a meaning analysis of legitimacy in the sense that they identify the various assumptions inherent in the meanings that have been given to it. They provide an empirical analysis of legitimacy in the sense that they show how their arguments about the meaning of legitimacy can be used to construct testable hypotheses. The contribution of this study lies in its emphasis on adding conceptual clarity to population ecology; this emphasis, among other things, has implications for enhancing the comprehensibility and persuasiveness of research findings.

Before concluding, a brief word on the weighting of problems is in order. Thus far, the implication has been that the various problems introduced by the different authors are on the same footing. I do not propose to change this as far as the empirical problems are concerned. One reason is limited space, associated perhaps with limited intestinal fortitude. Another is the comparative newness of the ecological analysis of organizational populations as a domain of scientific inquiry. This limits the reasons for singling out one or more of the problems identified as more significant than the others. By the same token, the increasing pace of ecological research suggests that future commentaries will be more severely constrained to deal with the issue of how and why certain problems are more crucial than others.

On the question of the relative importance of the conceptual problem of legitimacy, Laudan (1984:64–66) argues that, generally speaking, resolving conceptual problems is more important than resolving empirical ones. Further, one of the determinants of the importance of a conceptual problems is its age. The longer a theory is known to have a particular conceptual problem, the greater importance that problem assumes in debates about the acceptability of the theory that has generated it. Suffice it to say here that the legitimacy problem continues to age, and debates concerning it show no sign of abating.

The Issue of Organizational Performance

Of the numerous unanswered questions that might be identified as central to advancing the ecological analysis of organizational populations (see Singh and Lumsden, 1990; Tucker, Baum, and Singh, 1992), only one will be discussed here—connecting ecological analysis to issues with direct implications for improving the social conditions of life. As is clear from the preceding analysis, contending with a social science in terms of its contribution to cognitive progress does not necessarily entail consideration of its contribution to social progress. However, neither is it disconnected from it (e.g., Ross, 1991). To paraphrase Louis Pasteur, satisfaction in science comes not only from discovery but also from practical application (Beyer, 1982:588). "There are not two sciences. There is only one science and its application, and these two activities are linked as the fruit is to the tree."

McKelvey and Aldrich (1983), writing in a special issue of *Administrative Science Quarterly* on the utilization of organization research, observed that because students of organization typically have focused their investigations on the internal operations of organizations, they frequently have been criticized for producing knowledge relevant only to the concerns that managers and/or owners have about improving the efficiency and effectiveness of specific organizations. However, because population ecology is aimed at population-level phenomena, it carries with it the implication of generating knowledge useful to policymakers. Policymakers, McKelvey and Aldrich (1983:120) argue, are oriented to populations of organizations rather than to particular organizations. Their questions are about trends, changes, and effects in different functional sectors of society, as opposed to issues of organization design or strategy.

Others beside McKelvey and Aldrich have raised the issue of associating the ecological analysis of organizational populations with policy-making (e.g., Rundall and McLain, 1982; Hilgartner and Bosk, 1987; Sutton, 1991; Burstein, 1991; Tucker,

Singh, and House, 1992; Tucker and Hurl, 1992). Generally, however, the emphasis has been on invoking ecological reasoning to illuminate the origin and nature of particular policy problems or policy structures. There has been much less emphasis on using such a perspective to deal with the application-oriented problem of evaluating policy effects. Despite the apparent strength of our analytic machinery, we do not yet have studies examining how dynamic change processes in populations of organizations affect the macroquality aspects of organization performance in areas like homelessness, family violence, mental illness, poverty, discrimination, unemployment, and child care.[1]

Conventionally, organization science, similarly to most other aspects of social science, presents itself as having a twofold justification. On the one hand is the idea of pursuing knowledge for its own sake. On the other is the frequently presented view that it has much to contribute in improving the social conditions of life. I have tried to show in this commentary that adopting a problem-solving approach in assessing social science research does not necessarily lead to a rejection of either or both branches of this argument. Accepting that how we organize ourselves reflects the essence of what we are (Scott, 1991), the implication is that working to solve an intellectual problem may be as fundamental to the human condition as working to solve a material problem (Laudan, 1984:225). What we have to be mindful of is that we are not devoting our scarce resources to problems that "are as cognitively trivial as they are socially irrelevant" (Laudan; 1984:225). The history of ecological research, as well as the contributions of the chapters examined in this commentary, show we have done well on the cognitive side. The challenge now is whether we can do as well on the social side.

Note

1. Macroquality refers to the performance of a functional sector as whole in delivering services to a population as a whole. In contrast, microquality refers to performance in the more conventional sense as concerning how well, or how poorly, a particular organization provides services to the individual recipients of its service. See Uwe (1973) and Scott (1991:358).

V

COMMUNITY
EVOLUTION

16

The Liability of Collective Action: Growth and Change Among Early American Telephone Companies

WILLIAM P. BARNETT

Contemporary organization theories generally accept a basic premise of community ecology—that by operating collectively organizations share common fates (Hannan and Freeman, 1977; Carroll, 1984; Barnett and Carroll, 1987). Resource dependence and network researchers find that organizations often build cooperative ties that then mutually affect their performance (Pfeffer and Salancik, 1978; Burt, 1983; Powell, 1990). Institutional theories depict organizations as operating within "fields" or "sectors" of shared purposes and expectations (DiMaggio and Powell, 1983; Scott, 1987), where collective action is conditioned by broader social institutions (Streeck, 1985). Even organizational economists now allow for "hybrid" forms characterized by extramarket linkages among organizations (Williamson, 1991).

Although our theories can accommodate the fact of collective action, our attention has been limited to the ways in which such action benefits organizations—such as resolving inadequacies of the market (Baker, 1990), increasing chances of organizational survival (Baum and Oliver, 1991), and protecting organizations from the hazards associated with change (Miner, Amburgey, and Stearns, 1990). However, in the spirit of Selznick (1949), we should allow for the fact that collective action by organizations is a two-edged sword. Just as alliances enhance organizations' strategic capabilities, they also open organizations to inadequacies beyond their immediate control—so that colletive action has the potential to deteriorate into mutual demise.

This chapter argues that a liability of collective action results when an organizational community lacks cohesion. Fragmented, uncoordinated organizational communities fare poorly compared to better-organized communities, and member organizations suffer as a result. For example, the "industrial order" among German machine tool manufacturers gives them advantages not shared by their American counterparts (Herrigel, 1992). Furthermore, organizational inertia theory implies

This research was supported partly by the AT&T Fellowship in Telephone History, and by the Chancellor's Patent Fund of the University of California, Berkeley. I thank Joel Baum, Glenn Carroll, Paul DiMaggio, Michael Hannan, and Joel Podolny for their thoughtful reviews. Several people helped me to locate and collect the data, especially Gerry Barrett of the Telephony Publishing Corporation and Robert Lewis, Robert Garnet, and Mildred Ettlinger of the AT&T Historical Archives.

that attempts to remedy this problem by rationalizing community structure are likely to be resisted, and may even cause organizations to fail.

In this chapter I demonstrate these processes in analyses of organizational growth and failure among early American telephone companies. Elsewhere it was shown that geographically based structures developed among networks of independent (non-Bell) telephone companies, and these were fruitfully analyzed from a community ecology perspective (Barnett and Carroll, 1987, 1993; Barnett, 1990). Yet to be explained, however, is why the independent telephone movement suddenly stopped growing in market size after enjoying an early heyday.

Two explanations are investigated. One is that competition from the Bell System debilitated the independent telephone movement. Another looks at the structure of the independent movement itself, attributing its demise to community fragmentation. Next, I place these scenarios in their historical setting.

The Early Growth of Independent Telephony

After Phillip Reis invented the first electronic telephone in Germany in 1861, knowledge and applications of telephone technology spread among budding electricity hobbyists and engineers (DuMoncel, 1879; MacLaren, 1943). This diffusion increased rapidly after Elisha Gray and Alexander Bell separately developed commercially viable liquid transmitters in 1875 (MacMeal, 1934). Although Bell's innovations were patented and suppressed widespread entry into the American industry until 1894, some audacious entrepreneurs started companies anyway. This occurred especially in Pennsylvania, the sample site for this study, where the independent telephone movement began with a considerable lead in market share as show in table 16.1.

The number of independent telephone companies nationwide increased rapidly during the first decade of this century, and table 16.1 shows that Pennsylvania was no exception. In rural areas mutual companies appeared, organized by local residents and farmers, while commercial companies were formed in towns and cities (Fischer, 1992). Independent companies extended their service regions mainly by connecting with neighboring companies in contiguous areas. Consequently, symbiosis was important to organizational survival in the industry, especially between small single-switchboard companies that provided access to local areas and large companies oper-

TABLE 16.1   The Growth and Decline of Independent Telephony in Pennsylvania

Year	Total Companies	Magneto Companies	Common-battery Companies	Independent Telephones	Total Telephones	Independent Market Share
1885	11	11	0	9,858	12,163	.81
1890	14	14	0	23,717	37,313	.63
1895	23	23	0	59,372	100,908	.59
1900	110	98	12	95,503	164,578	.58
1905	177	152	25	258,998	379,244	.68
1910	423	392	31	377,806	584,146	.65
1915	489	445	44	421,772	747,731	.56
1920	395	332	63	419,462	983,551	.43
1925	367	295	72	408,980	1,271,503	.32

ating multiple exchanges that linked entire regions (Barnett, 1990). Over time, these organizations developed a loosely coordinated community structure, although service quality was harmed by the system's many gaps and overlaps (Barnett and Carroll, 1987, 1993).

Concern grew among the general public, policymakers, and independent telephone entrepreneurs that the independent movement should be unified in order to maintain a viable alternative to the Bell System (Brooks, 1976). In 1912 the U.S. Department of Justice and the Bell System agreed to the "Kingsbury Commitment," which until 1922 limited Bell's ability to acquire competing companies and forced Bell to allow access to its long-distance network (Barnett and Carroll, 1993). In 1913, the State of Pennsylvania required neighboring telephone companies to connect their systems (FCC, 1939:137). And, by 1915, telephone equipment manufacturers and independent telephone companies had each formed unified national trade associations (MacMeal, 1934). Taken together, these developments suggest that the independent telephone movement was prepared to expand faster than ever after about 1910. As table 16.1 shows, however, independent telephony in Pennsylvania suddenly stopped growing during this period and never recovered. Why did this occur?

Competition from Bell

Many analysts contend that the stagnation of independent telephony was caused by competition from the Bell System (FCC, 1939; Danielian, 1939). Intriguingly, the Kingsbury Commitment may have inadvertently stimulated growth-based competition, since it effectively made rapid growth Bell's only allowable strategy. Such growth could come either by taking subscribers away from independent companies or by expanding into unserved markets, but either way it would limit the potential size of the independent companies. The patterns in table 16.1 are consistent with this scenario. Just as the independent movement stagnated, the Bell System grew explosively:

> Hypothesis 1: Competition from the Bell System stunted the growth of the independent telephone movement.

Community Fragmentation

Another answer applies the ideas developed by Barnett (1990). On the basis of Hawley's (1950) theory of community ecology, I predicted that a community structure worked well for telephone companies that were both compatible and complementary, but that incompatible organizations harmed all companies by fragmenting the system. These hypotheses were supported in analyses of failure rates in data that included this sample (Barnett, 1990). The incompatibility problems were due to the proliferation of companies using "magneto" instruments, which were notorious since the power level of each instrument could not be centrally controlled (Homans, 1904). Later and more gradually, some independent companies adopted the centrally operated, standardized "common battery" to supply transmission power—facilitating the coordination of networks (Jewett, 1928). This opened the way for some companies to adopt "loaded lines," extending their transmission ranges and making possible the multiple-exchange companies that stood in symbiotic relation to single-switchboard organizations.

Just as technical compatibility and fragmentation affected survival among independent telephone companies, so might they account for the stagnation of the independent movement. As table 16.1 shows, the number of magneto companies skyrocketed just as the independent movement stopped growing—while companies with common-battery systems remained relatively few. I propose:

Hypothesis 2A: The operation of companies using magneto systems lowered growth rates throughout the independent system.

Hypothesis 2B: The operation of companies using common-battery systems increased growth rates throughout the independent system.

Organizational Change and Community Adaptation

Since technical compatibility and complementarity were important to the independent movement, it is curious that technical change was not more widespread. Such diffusion would have opened the way to better coordination and, according to hypothesis 2, the independent telephone movement would have continued to grow. This possibility raises a more general issue. If, as I argue, poor coordination among organizations reduces their viability, then one might expect organizations to change so that coordination is improved—making the liability of collective action merely a transitory problem.

However, organizational ecology theory predicts that major organizational change is hazardous, because it is resisted by existing organizational processes and because new roles and capabilities take time to develop (Hannan and Freeman, 1984). Consequently, organizations are unlikely to adopt major changes, and organizations that do are more likely to fail. For organizations that survive change, this increased hazard should fall over time, as new organizational processes and roles are institutionalized (Hannan and Freeman, 1984). By this thinking, new technologies diffused slowly in the early telephone industry because organizations were resistant to change, and because organizations attempting to change failed when doing so. This suggests the hypothesis initially proposed by Hannan and Freeman (1984), and supported empirically in studies of other organizational populations (Freeman and Hannan, 1989; Amburgey, Kelly, and Barnett, 1992):

Hypothesis 3: Organizations that changed technology initially suffered an increased failure rate, with this hazard then falling over time.

With the liability of collective action in mind, hypothesis 3 raises the problem of organizational inertia to the community level. Organizational communities are not easily rationalized, since resistance to change among constituent organizations retards their attempts to adapt to one another's requirements. Fragmented organizational communities thus are unlikely to improve their collective structure quickly, and so the liability of collective action is likely to persist over time. Next, I operationalize these hypothese in models of organizational growth and failure.

Baseline Growth Model

Following a large literature I base the growth model on "Gibrat's law" of proportionate effect, which states that proportionate growth is random and independent of current size: $S_{it2} = S^u_{it1}w_{it2}$, where S represents the size of organization i at a given calendar time t, w allows for random size changes for each organization i, and $E[\mu] = 1$.[1] This is a good baseline model because, without elaborate explanations, it can produce skewed size distributions similar to the pattern that developed in the Pennsylvania data, illustrated in figure 16.1. (This pattern is typical of many populations of business firms; see Ijiri and Simon, 1977.) Also, a power function of this sort worked well in Fischer and Carroll's (1987) study of aggregate telephone diffusion.

Gibrat's law implies that organizations per se do not matter to the growth process; any arbitrary division of aggregate size into parts that grow proportionately would give the same result. We know, however, that growth rates vary according to qualitative differences among organizations. Indiosyncrasies, such as unique strategic capabilities, are likely to generate organization-specific differences in growth. More systematic variation is likely to result from structural differences between organizational forms, and differences that develop as organizations age (Starbuck, 1965, 1968; Eisenhardt and Schoonhoven, 1990). The baseline model is easily generalized to include such organizational heterogeneity:

$$S_{it2} = S^u_{it1}\exp{[r_i + \gamma\tau_i + \zeta'X_{it1}]w_{it2},} \tag{1}$$

where r is an organization-specific growth rate, τ measures the age of organization i, and X includes variables describing differences between organizational forms (which are allowed to vary over time as organizations change).[2] For the telephone companies, forms were distinguished according to whether a company was mutual or commercial, used common-battery or magneto technology, and operated a single switchboard or multiple exchanges (Barnett, 1990).

Organizational ecology theory extends this model, postulating that organizational growth is limited by the environment's "carrying capacity" for a given form of organization (Freeman and Hannan, 1975). Growth rates fall as a population of organizations collectively expands to fill this capacity. This effect can be incorporated in the model by including L_{t1}, which represents the degree of latency in a niche—or the amount of additional growth that a niche can support. In this study, L measures the size of the human population less the number of telephones—an approximation of the number of unserved potential telephone subscribers.

A considerable amount of work also predicts that growth rates are affected by competition at the population level (Freeman and Hannan, 1975; Hannan and Freeman, 1978; Carroll, 1981; Hannan and Ranger-Moore, 1990; Hannan, Ranger-Moore, and Banaszak-Holl, 1990). Growth is limited by competition among organizations in the same niche. Operationally, this assertion can be tested by using the

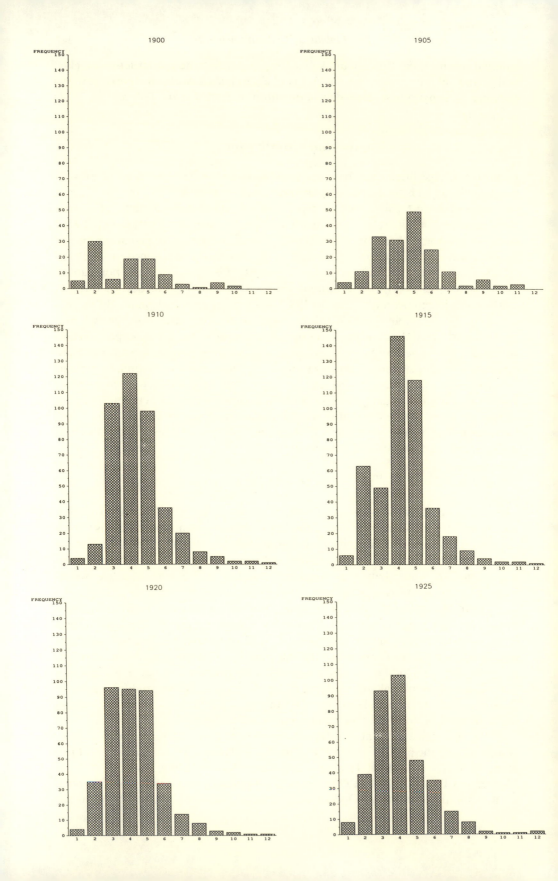

so-called density dependence (Hannan and Freeman, 1989) model, in which the fates of organizations of a given form depend on D, the density (number) of such organizations. If growth rates fall as D increases, there is evidence of competition. An interesting variation on this approach is used in a work-in-progress by Barron and West, who apply Hannan's legitimacy-competition model (Hannan, 1986; Hannan and Carroll, 1992) to organizational growth. They use a quadratic specification of density to find support for the hypothesis that increasing numbers initially increase growth rates as the population gains legitimacy, but eventually dampen growth through competition as the population becomes very dense.

Finally, organizational ecology theory also emphasizes the importance of population dynamics (Delacroix and Carroll, 1983). In particular, as organizations fail they free up resources that can be used by other organizations. This so-called renewal process can be operationalized by including F, a lagged measure of the number of organizational failures. Incorporating L, D, and F, into the model yields

$$S_{it2} = S_{it1}^{\mu}\exp\left[r_i + \gamma\tau_i + \zeta'X_{it1} + \pi L_{t1} + sF_{t1} + \alpha D_{t1}\right]w_{it2}, \qquad (2)$$

in which μ, r, γ, and ζ parameterize organization-level effects, the "niche parameter" π captures the effect of resource availability, s allows for a renewal process, and α is the so-called competition coefficient.

Modeling Community Structure

A major deficiency of equation (2) is that it constrains all organizations in D to affect one another's growth rates similarly. If, in fact, subpopulations of organizations have different effects, then D should be disaggregated appropriately and these effects should be modeled separately. Estimates of the "community matrix" of competition coefficients can then be used to test hypotheses about community structure (May, 1974).

I use this approach to test hypothesis 2. Disaggregating density into separate counts for companies with magneto systems, D_m, and companies with common-battery systems, D_c, permits each to have its own separate effect on growth rates. However, these density measures also reflect size differences—with common-battery companies considerably larger than magneto companies on average. If the competitive force generated by an organization depends on its size, this fact could bias the effects of D_m and D_c. Consequently, the model should also include a density term that weighs organizations according to their sizes. This variable, M_i, is the "mass," or collective size, of all independent companies less the size of organization i (Barnett and Amburgey, 1990). Including D_c, D_m, and M_i in the model results in

$$S_{it2} = S_{it1}^{\mu}\exp\left[r_i + \gamma\tau_i + \zeta'X_{it1} + \pi L_{t1} + sF_{t1} + \psi M_{It1} + \alpha_m D_{mt1} + \alpha_c D_{ct1}\right]w_{it2}. \qquad (3)$$

FIG. 16.1 Log-size distributions of independent telephone companies in Pennsylvania

In these terms, hypothesis 2A predicts $\alpha_m < 0$ —where companies using magneto technology decreased the growth rates of all independent companies. Hypothesis 2B predicts the opposite effect from companies with common-battery systems: $\alpha_c > 0$.

Modeling Competition from Bell

To test Hypothesis 1, the growth model must allow for the possibility that competition from Bell was responsible for the decline of the independents. This could have occurred through three distinct competitive processes: (1) direct competition between Bell and individual independent companies; (2) diffuse competition where Bell's growth reduced the size of the latent market L, which in turn reduced independent company growth rates; or (3) community-level competition, where the independent movement collectively lost to Bell—so that a given independent company declined simply because it was part of a larger system that failed as a whole.

The first process, direct competition from Bell, is easily modeled by extending equation (3) to include $\psi_B M_B$, the effect of Bell's size (some subscripts are omitted for clarity):

$$S_{it2} = S_{it1}^* \exp [r_i + \gamma\tau_i + \zeta'X_i + sF + \alpha_m D_m$$
$$+ \alpha_c D_c + \psi_I M_I + \psi_B M_B + \pi L]w_i. \quad (4)$$

If $\psi_B < 0$, then there is evidence of direct competition—so that as Bell became more predominant in the market, independent companies declined in size as a result. Meanwhile, the possibility that Bell generated diffuse competition is already reflected in the effect of L, the size of the latent market. If $\pi > 0$, then growth of the independents was slower as the latent market L decreased in size. Since Bell's growth reduced L, a positive estimate of π implies diffuse competition from Bell as it occupied the untapped market.

Finally, the model needs to reflect the possibility that the stagnation of individual telephone companies resulted from their collective defeat by the Bell System. In general, organization researchers are unprepared to study collective competition of this sort. We tend to model the fates of organizations under the assumption that the relevant causes act upon organizations rather than upon the collectivities of which they are members. Yet an organization may succeed or fail simply because it is a member of a community that succeeds or fails in competition at a collective level. This has occurred, for example, among U.S. baseball teams when entire leagues have failed as a result of competition from other leagues (Land, Davis, and Blau, 1992). Similarly, manufacturing organizations typically must choose to conform to some technical standards rather than others—a vital decision since the ultimate success or failure of a venture can depend on whether it conforms to the prevailing standard. How can the effects of such collective success or failure be modeled at the organization level?

My approach to modeling this sort of competition requires two assumptions. First I assume that community-level competition is "contact-dependent." This means that, given two collectivities, the strength of their competition with one another depends on the likelihood that both attempt to exploit the same resource. For example, Christianity and Islam would be assumed to compete more strongly as they increasingly proselytize the same potential members. Second, I assume that the frequency of such attempts is proportionate to the size of a given collectivity, consistent with Gibrat's law of proportionate effect. As I show in the Appendix, these assumptions generate a useful result: *Community-level expansion and competition can be modeled at the organization level as size-dependent interactions with the latent market and the mass of the competing community.* Thus, to model the organization-level consequences of the fate of independent telephony as a whole, the model should include the effects of $S_i L$ and $S_i M_B$:

$$S_{it2} = S_{it1}^{\kappa} \exp\left[r_i + \gamma\tau_i + \zeta'X_i + sF + \alpha_m D_m + \alpha_c D_c \right.$$
$$\left. + \psi_I M_I + \psi_B M_B + \pi L + \beta S_i L + \delta S_i M_B\right]w_i. \quad (5)$$

This allows a complete test of hypothesis 1, since if $\delta < 0$ then there is evidence that the independent companies were collectively harmed by the Bell System.

Modeling the Consequences of Change

Hypothesis 3 is modeled in terms of the instantaneous rate of failure, defined as $r_i(t) = \lim([q_i(t,t + \Delta t)/\Delta t]$, where t is the age of organization i, q is the probability i will fail between t and $t + \Delta t$, and the rate r is explicitly modeled as a function of t (Tuma and Hannan, 1984). The hypothesis predicts a sawtoothed pattern, where $r_i(t)$ increased immediately when an organization changed its technology, and then declined gradually over time.

This prediction is tested using the approach developed in Amburgey, Kelly, and Barnett (1993), which distinguishes two distinct consequences of change. On the one hand, one must allow for the fact that change alters an organization's form—and therefore its position in the larger ecology of organizations—which in turn affects its survival chances. For example, change can increase an organization's viability by giving it the benefits of more advanced technologies, while also decreasing its viability by moving it into a more competitive—and so more hazardous—niche (Barnett, 1990). These can be thought of as the "content effects" of change. Only after controlling for the content of change is it possible to model the consequences of change per se distinctly, as in the specification

$$r(t) = \exp\left[\theta'X + a(\ln t) + b(\ln t)^2 + c\Delta Z + g\tau_{\Delta z}\right],$$

where t is organizational age, X are the other covariates in the model (including variables describing the organizational and niche characteristics being changed), ΔZ is set equal to 0 before an organization changes its technology and equal to 1 afterward, and $\tau_{\Delta z}$ is the backward recurrence time since the most recent technological change for each organization. $\tau_{\Delta z}$ is set equal to 0 for each organization until it changes its technology for the first time. Given these definitions, hypothesis 3 predicts $c > 0$ and $g < 0$—where change immediately increased the failure rate, which then gradually decreased.

To specify the variables in X, I use as a baseline the best model from Barnett (1990), where failure rates among these companies were studied exhaustively. This includes variables at the organization level—especially controls for technological form (common-battery versus magneto and single- versus multiexchange), exogenous environmental factors, and variables that describe the organizational population. This last set of variables includes density terms and interactions to capture the effects of technological complementarity and compatibility. The model was then extended to include additional effects. A dummy variable for the period of Bell's patent was included, since the hazard of failure during that period likely was high because of Bell's aggressive legal policy. Also, the model includes "density delay"— the density of the population at the time each organization was founded—a variable expected to reflect the frailty of organizations founded under conditions of resource scarcity (Carroll and Hannan, 1989a).

Data and Methods

The data include the life histories of all 707 telephone companies that operated in the State of Pennsylvania at any time from the invention of the telephone until the onset of effective federal regulation in 1934. Data were recorded for each organization for each year over the sample period. Size in terms of the number of telephones, ownership form (mutual or commercial), and technology form (common battery versus magneto and single versus multiple exchange) were measured for each organization for each year. (See Barnett, 1990 for a complete description of the data and sources.)

The failure models were estimated by the method of maximum likelihood available in the software RATE (Tuma, 1979). This program allows covariates to be updated from year to year throughout an organization's lifetime. Also, RATE reduces the bias that would otherwise result from the fact that 276 of the 707 organizations in the sample do not fail during the study period by modeling the cumulative survival time of these "right-censored" cases (Tuma and Hannan, 1984).

The growth model is of the form $Y = W^n exp[bV]$. Transforming each side of the equation to its natural logarithm results in the linear equation $\log(Y) = a(\log(W)) + bV$, which can be estimated by least-squares techniques. However, ordinary least-squares estimates from these data may be biased because 431 organizations fail over the study period. As they fail, organizations pass out of the sample without their final size changes represented in the data—a potential source of sample-selection bias.[3] In an attempt to correct for this bias, I used Lee's (1983) generalization of Heckman's (1979) two-stage sample selection estimation procedure. This entailed using the estimates of the failure model to calculate $F(t)$, the cumulative hazard function, which was then used to calculate $\lambda = [\phi(\Phi^{-1}[F(t)])/[1 - F(t)]$, where ϕ and Φ are the standard normal density and distribution functions, respectively. λ was included as a regressor in the growth model to yield an estimate of selectivity bias and improve the consistency of the other estimated parameters.[4]

It is likely that the model's residuals will be autocorrelated, because the data contain repeated observations from the same organizations, and heteroscedastic, because of the wide size distribution of these organizations. It is well known that these problems will render ordinary least-squares estimates inefficient, and for the model of interest (with lagged size as a regressor) autocorrelation generates bias. Consequently, the model was estimated using generalized least-squares, assuming heteroscedasticity and first-order autoregression. This was done in stages. Ordinary least-squares estimates produced residuals ϵ, which were then used to estimate an autocorrelation coefficient ρ for each organization using $\epsilon_{t2} = \rho\epsilon_{t1} + v$. The vector of estimated ρ was then used to transform the data by first-differencing according to $X_{t2}' = X_{t2} - (\rho X_{t1})$. Ordinary least-squares estimates were then obtained from the transformed data, and the residual variance estimates for each organization were used to obtain weighted least-squares estimates (Judge et al., 1980).

With the organization-year as the unit of analysis, the 707 organizations yield 11,842 observations. Growth model estimates were obtained with only 11,309 observations on 659 organizations, however, because of missing data and because Bell Telephone of Pennsylvania was excluded from the analysis. Also excluded were companies that lived for only one or two years, since at least three observation-years was needed for the transformed data to include the minimum-required two panels for a given organization. Consequently, the estimate of age dependence and other parameters in the growth models may be biased by the exclusion of extremely short-lived organizations.

Results

Table 16.2 reports the parameter estimates for the growth models (other than the organization-specific fixed effects). The three models differ according to their specification of density dependence. The first two models include aggregate density, with the quadratic specification in model 2 statistically significant in both terms. However, the directions of the effects do not support the legitimation-competition hypothesis. Density dependence was strictly competitive and increased at an increasing rate.

Model 3, which includes disaggregated density effects, tests hypotheses 2A and 2B. As predicted, magneto density reduced growth rates while common-battery density increased growth. Substantively these effects were powerful. In 1915, for example, the existence of 445 magneto companies reduced sizes—in a single year—by nearly 10 percent compared to what they would have been otherwise.[5] Hypothesis 2B also is supported, with common-battery companies increasing the growth rates of other companies. The small number of common battery companies limited the impact of this effect, although it was not trivial. In 1925, for example, the fact that 72 companies had adopted the standardized common-battery technology increased sizes by 3 percent over what they would have been otherwise—again in a single year. In any case, the mutualism generated by common-battery companies was never sufficient to offset the negative effect of the magneto companies. Overall, these results support my claim that fragmentation stunted the growth of the independent movement.

These disaggregated density effects shed light on the strange pattern found for the quadratic density specification in model 2. The initial increase in the aggregate population may well have increased the legitimacy of the form, but these earliest companies nearly all used magneto technology—fragmenting the system and slowing

TABLE 16.2   GLS Estimates of Organizational Growth Models

Independent Variables	Models		
	(1)	(2)	(3)
$\ln(\text{size})_{t1}$	.9056*	.9050*	.9066*
	(.0028)	(.0028)	(.0029)
Organizational age	−.0146*	−.0142*	−.0141*
	(.0011)	(.0012)	(.0013)
Common-battery	−.0044	−.0032	−.0064
	(.0037)	(.0036)	(.0035)
Multiple exchange	−.0016	−.0010	−.0024
	(.0012)	(.0012)	(.0059)
Common-battery $\times$ multiple exchange	.0103*	.0095*	.0120*
	(.0043)	(.0043)	(.0042)
Latent market ($/10^6$)	.1788*	.1750*	.1664*
	(.0117)	(.0118)	(.0127)
Bell subscribers ($/10^6$)	.1395*	.1370*	.1341*
	(.0134)	(.0134)	(.0143)
Other independent subscribers ($/10^6$)	.1508*	.1460*	.1448*
	(.0095)	(.0097)	(.0101)
Size($/1,000$) $\times$ latent market($/10^6$)	.0001*	.0001*	.0001*
	(.00004)	(.00004)	(.00005)
Size($/1,000$) $\times$ bell subscribers($/10^6$)	−.0006	−.0007*	−.0007
	(.00033)	(.00033)	(.0004)
Lagged organizational deaths	.0001*	.0001*	.0001*
	(.00002)	(.00002)	(.00003)
Density	−.0002*	−.0002*	
	(.0001)	(.0001)	
Density^2 ($/100$)		−.0001*	
		(.00005)	
Common-battery density			.0004*
			(.0001)
Magneto density			−.0002*
			(.00001)
λ	.0030	.0029	−.0035*
	(.0016)	(.0017)	(.0018)
F value of ΔR^2 compared to a model with only the fixed effects	630.99†	533.42†	553.75†
Organizations	659	659	659
Organization-years	11,309	11,309	11,309

NOTES: *$p < .05$. Standard errors appear in parentheses.

† The model improves over one containing only the fixed effects, $p < .05$.

growth rates as a result. This would account for the negative first-order density effect in model 2. The later wave of additional magneto companies likely exacerbated this fragmentation, increasing the negative density effect at an increasing rate.

Turning to hypothesis 1, there is evidence that the net effect of Bell was to slow the growth of the independent companies, but this conclusion would have eluded detection by simpler models. In fact, looking only at Bell's direct effect at the organization level would lead to the opposite conclusion. The main effect of Bell's size on growth rates is positive and significant in all models, suggesting mutualism between Bell and the independents; as Bell grew, the independents benefited with higher growth rates—probably because of their connections to the Bell System. This tells only part of the story, however, since diffuse competition from Bell was strong. The positive effect of the size of the latent market in all models—both the main effect and the interaction with size—shows that as the market became saturated growth rates among the independents slowed, both individually and collectively. Table 16.1 shows that Bell's growth was largely responsible for this saturation. Overall the results indicate that as Bell expanded the independents benefited, since they were allowed to connect to the Bell System, but this benefit was more than offset by diffuse competition from Bell for new subscribers.

Bell also generated direct competition, but at the community level. The interaction between Bell's market and size, which captures the organization-level effects of community-level competition, was negative and significant (or very nearly significant) in all models. This indicates that as Bell grew, the independent movement collectively stagnated.

The effects of other variables also warrant discussion. The mass of the independent telephone movement positively and significantly affected growth rates. Also, all models show a renewal process where lagged organizational failures significantly increased growth rates. Among the organization-level effects, size and age are each negatively related to growth, while the most technically advanced companies—those with common-battery power and multiple exchanges—grew fastest. Finally, selectivity bias was negative when significant, as expected.

Finally, hypothesis 3 is addressed by the estimates of the failure model in table 16.3. As predicted, technical change among these organizations immediately increased their failure rates, with the negative effect of 'time since change' indicating that the organizations gradually recovered from this effect over time ($p < .10$). In particular, the estimates predict that an organization took about 16 years to recover from the increased hazard of failure due to technological change. It is no wonder, then, that technological improvements diffused so slowly through the independent telephone movement, and that the organizational community consequently remained plagued by technological fragmentation.

Other results from table 16.3 are noteworthy. Most of the results remain as reported in Barnett (1990). However, density delay—which was not included in the earlier study—is negative and statistically significant, the opposite of what has been found in other studies (Hannan and Carroll, 1992). Also, age dependence had been positive in the earlier study. However, when modeled as a log-quadratic, the age effect is positive only for 4 or 5 years and then turns strongly negative—a pattern consistent with some other studies (See Brüderl and Schüssler, 1990; Fichman and Levinthal, 1991).

TABLE 16.3   Maximum-Likelihood Estimates of the Organizational
Failure Rate

Independent Variables	Estimates
Constant	5.828
	(3.574)
Organizational size/1,000	−.0004
	(.0010)
ln(Organizational age)	.7991*
	(.2726)
$(ln(Organizational age))^2$	−.2278*
	(.0789)
Commercial	−.4266*
	(.1151)
Common-battery	−.1747
	(1.150)
Multiple exchange	−.4642*
	(.1332)
Common battery $\times$ multiple exchange	−6.433*
	(2.361)
Technological change	.7232*
	(.2383)
Time since technological change	−.0432
	(.0230)
Calendar year	−.2089
	(.1169)
Patent period	.3315
	(.2140)
Number of farms	.0087
	(.0060)
Number of manufacturing establishments	−.0003*
	(.0001)
Number of electrical equipment manufacturers	.0517*
	(.0167)
Market share variance	−.8691
	(1.721)
ln (Mass)	−.2824*
	(.1419)
Density delay	−.0030*
	(.0006)
Magneto density	.0038*
	(.0014)
Common-battery density	.0275*
	(.0124)
(Magneto density) $\times$ (common battery)	.0049
	(.0029)
(Common-battery density) $\times$ (common battery)	.1131*
Among firms with the same transmission technology	(.0378)
Among firms with complementary transmission technologies	−.0712*
	(.0280)
χ^2	133.05
Df	22
Dissolutions	431
Censored cases	276
Organization-years	11,842

NOTE: *$p < .05$. Standard errors appear in parentheses.

I began by noting that various organization theorists see the importance of collective organizational action, but with an eye on its beneficial consequences to organizations. These findings demonstrate, however, that a liability of collective action can plague members of poorly coordinated organizational communities. Worse yet, this problem is not easily solved, since organizational inertia makes it hazardous for organizations to change in order to increase community cohesion. Consequently, the liability of collective action is likely to endure in any given community, making it more pervasive than our neglect of the phenomenon would imply.

For community ecology theory, the liability of collective action can be seen as a corollary to Hawley's (1950) theorem that the development of community structure lessens vulnerability to the exogenous environment. His theorem suggests that dependence on the exogenous environment is replaced by dependence among symbiotic organizational forms as community structure develops. If that structure is poorly coordinated, however, the fitness of the entire community is reduced. Consequently, although collective action makes organizations less vulnerable to the exogenous environment, it also makes them more susceptible to the liabilities that result from poor coordination with their allies.

It should be noted that these ideas are not new to organization theory. An entire generation of research was devoted to the problem of coordination within organizations. My aim is to raise our sights to see how coordination is important also at the community level. This echoes Parsons' (1956:80) challenge that we confront the problem of "system integration" by studying "the compatibility of the institutional patterns under which the organization operates with those of other organizations and social units, as related to the integrative exigencies of the society as a whole (or of subsystems wider than the organization in question)."

Community ecology theory is well suited to take on Parsons' challenge. However, as DiMaggio observes in his commentary to part V, our attempts may expand the scope of inquiry beyond the comfortable boundaries of "populations" as we now think of them. This is only a problem, however, if we define community ecology so broadly that it amounts to the study of any and all forms of "coevolution." So defined, community-level research could easily degenerate into overly broad descriptions of economy and society, and our conceptual tools— "networks," "communities," and the like—would amount to little more than competing metaphors.

If, instead, theory guides our efforts, then our work can remain bounded—allowing the formulation and testing of middle-range hypotheses. Theory should define (1) the scope of inquiry and (2) the integrative processes that shape community dynamics. In terms of scope, we should strictly maintain the definition of "organizational community" to mean collectivities of organizations united through the bonds of commensalism or symbiosis (Barnett and Carroll, 1987). Although still very broad, this definition limits our attention to organizational collectivities based on a division of labor in the Durkheimian sense—where forms work together, and so share a common fate, because of either complementary differences or supplementary similarities (Hawley, 1950). By this definition, not every network is a community.

In terms of the integrative processes in question, theory directs us to the "segregating and blending processes" that define boundaries within social systems (Hannan and Freeman, 1986a). Propositions about community integration in general can be tested in terms of the segregating and blending processes relevant to a given setting. For the telephone industry, technological factors were key to community integration, so the liability of collective action was generated there by technological fragmentation. In other settings, system integration—and so the liability of collective action—would hinge on different sorts of factors. For example, incompatible ideologies among churches or social movement organizations, language differences among newspaper organizations, and technological mismatches or conflicting labor policies among various forms of manufacturing organizations would impair collective organizational action—and consequently harm the viability of such organizations should they pursue collective strategies.

Looking ahead, I see promise in developing the strategic implications of community ecology. As we come to understand community-level regularities, such as the liability of collective action, we increase our ability to manage such action in order to attain organizational goals. With or without such an understanding, managers of organizations will engage in collective action. However, as long as the consequences of such behavior are shaped by symbiosis and commensalism, collective action uniformed by community ecology is at risk of generating unanticipated consequences.

Appendix: Organization-Level Consequences of Community-Level Competition

In order to model collective competition, I assume that (1) competition between two given collectivities is "contact dependent," so that the strength of competition depends on the likelihood that both collectivities attempt to control the same resources, and (2) each collectivity's frequency of attempts to control resources is proportionate to its size—consistent with Gibrat's law of proportionate effect.

From these assumptions, it is easy to express the likelihood of competition between two collectivities. First, let r_{kI} represent the rate at which a given resource k is sought by a given collectivity I. The proportionality assumption (Gibrat's law) implies $r_{kI} = v_I M_I$, $v_I \geq 0$, where M_I denotes the aggregate size of collectivity I, and the coefficient v_I allows for proportionality. Similarly, the rate at which resource k is sought by a second collectivity B can be expressed as $r_{kB} = v_B M_B$, $v_B \geq 0$. In these terms, the likelihood of both collectivities attempting to control resource k is $r_{kI} r_{kB} = (v_I v_B) M_I M_B$, $v_I v_B \geq 0$. This is a useful result. It shows that *if competition is defined as occurring when two collectivities attempt to control the same resource, Gibrat's law implies that the strength of competition varies according to the interaction of the sizes of the two collectivities.*

On the basis of this result, competition between collectivities is well represented by Bartholomew's (1982) model of competing diffusion processes:

$$dM_I/dt = \sigma_I + \beta_I M_I L + \delta_I M_I M_B + \mu_I M_I, \qquad \mu_I < 0, \qquad \text{(A1)}$$

$$dM_B/dt = \sigma_B + \beta_B M_B L + \delta_B M_I M_B + \mu_B M_B, \qquad \mu_B < 0. \qquad \text{(A2)}$$

Allowing the two collectivities to represent the independent telephone movement and Bell, the masses M_I and M_B denote the number of telephones in each system at a given point in time. Each system can expand to fill a maximum capacity N, which denotes the potential number of telephone subscribers in a given year in Pennsylvania. L, which measures the size of the latent market, is thus defined as $L = N - M_I - M_B$. Given these definitions, the first term in each equation depicts growth generated by the system's "source," the interaction terms in each reflect the contact-dependent spread of each system into either L or the other system, and the loss rate (μ) allows for attrition unrelated to competition.

What this model means to individual organizations depends on the "aggregation relations" that translate the aggregate variables into organization-level terms (Hannan, 1991). I assume that each organization shares in the collective process to a degree proportionate to its size. Consequently, additive aggregation is used, so that equation (A1) represents the sum of D organization-level processes. In particular, setting $\sigma_I = \Sigma_i r_i$ and $M_i = \Sigma_i S_i$—where i ranges from 1 to D, r_i is the organization-specific baseline growth rate, and S_i is the size of organization i—equation A1 can be additively disaggregated:

$$
\begin{aligned}
dM_I/dt &= \sigma_I + \mu M_I + \beta M_I L + \delta M_I M_B \\
&= \Sigma_i dS_i/dt = \Sigma_i r_i + \mu \Sigma_i S_i + \beta L \Sigma_i S_i + \delta M_B \Sigma_i S_i \qquad \text{(A3)} \\
&= \Sigma_i r_i + \Sigma_i \mu S_i + \Sigma_i \beta S_i L + \Sigma_i \delta S_i M_B.
\end{aligned}
$$

Equation (A3) shows that equation A1 is the aggregation of D organization-level growth equations of the form

$$
dS_i/dt = r_i + \mu S_i + \beta S_i L + \delta S_i M_B, \qquad \mu < 0. \qquad \text{(A4)}
$$

This result shows that *contact-dependent processes at the aggregate level are manifested as size-dependent processes at the organization level.* $\beta S_i L$ captures size-dependent growth because of the extent of the latent market. Intuitively, this term allows organization i to grow faster into the latent market L as either S_i or L is larger, since under those conditions there will be greater contact between organization i and the latent market. Meanwhile, $\delta S_i M_B$ depicts size-dependent competition with Bell. Again, this term reflects contact dependence. As either organization i or Bell is larger, competition from Bell is expected to be greater since they increasingly vie for the same subscribers. In this way, *community-level competition can be modeled at the organization level as a size-dependent interaction with the mass of the competing community.*

Note that these results easily generalize beyond the case at hand. For example, the "systems" could represent competing technologies among manufacturing organizations, competing ideologies among social movement organizations, or competing patterns of worker organization— such as by craft versus by industry—for labor unions. In any of these cases, one could model the organizational consequences of competition at the collective level by using this approach.

Also, note that—contrary to DiMaggio's commentary—organizations do not have to lie entirely within one or another grouping to use this approach. An organization's fate can be partially related to the fates of each of several competing collectivities. In this case S_i in the model is replaced by separate terms representing the size of the organization's commitment to each of the competing groupings, such as the size of investment in each of two competing technological standards. Multiple competitive processes are thus allowed to act on a single organization.

Notes

1. Empirical tests of Gibrat's law find $\mu < 1$ (e.g., Evans, 1986; Hall, 1986), indicating that smaller firms have disproportionately high growth rates. Such results have encouraged speculation that smaller firms have higher growth rates for structural (Birch and MacCracken, 1982) or strategic (Lazerson, 1988) reasons. However, Leonard (1986) shows that negative size dependence in organizational growth rates can simply be the result of regression to the mean.

2. There is evidence that an organization's growth rate depends on its industry's stage of development (Starbuck, 1965; Eisenhardt and Schoonhoven, 1990). This suggests that the effects of historical (calendar) time t should also be included in the model. However, historical time adds no information to a model with organization-specific fixed effects (r_i) and organizational age (τ_i), because the fixed effects act as cohort dummies and calendar year is a linear function of cohort and age.

3. Sample selection bias would not be an issue if the data were updated every time an organization changed size all the way up to the time of failure. These data, however, are measured in annual panels, so size changes over the year in which an organization fails are not known. Note that the amount of missing information in this terminal period, and so the potential severity of this problem, is greater the longer the interval between panels.

4. In Heckman's model it is assumed that $F(t)$ is normally distributed. This allows λ to be estimated by the inverse mills ratio from a probit model (see Maddala, 1983). However, Goldberger (1983) shows that this approach is sensitive to violations of the normality assumption. Lee's approach, used here, requires no such restrictions on the distribution of $F(t)$.

5. From table 16.3, the multiplier due to 445 magneto companies is exp $[-.0002 \times 445]$, or .91.

17

Density-Independent Selection and Community Evolution

JACK BRITTAIN

As originally conceived, organizational ecology explicitly addressed the interpopulation dynamics that account for the evolution of organizational communities (Hannan and Freeman, 1977:942–46). A number of early ecological studies examined community development (Brittain and Freeman, 1980; Freeman and Hannan, 1983; Carroll, 1985), but the focus of recent ecological research has shifted to population analyses. And in particular, recent research has placed great emphasis on the role of density in population growth and decline (Hannan and Freeman, 1989; Carroll and Hannan, 1989b).

The legitimacy-competition density formulation (Hannan and Freeman, 1989) was a significant contribution to ecological theory and has motivated considerable empirical research. But it has been at the cost of irrelevance to the broader concerns of organization theory. The legitimacy-competition density model is an endogenous, autocorrelated process specification, and as such, it focuses on specification issues that are of little interest to other organization theorists. In addition, the density-dependent formulation contributes little to our understanding of community development and the emergence of social structures, issues central to the original formulation.

While organizational ecology has drifted into a preoccupation with density, other organization theorists have followed ecology's lead and focused on community development, producing significant contributions linking the evolution of social structure to technological discontinuities (Tushman and Anderson, 1986; Anderson and Tushman, 1990), entrepreneurship (Schoonhoven, Eisenhardt, and Lyman, 1990), institutional developments (Scott, 1987), and historical change (Delacroix and Swaminathan, 1991). In the original density-dependent argument (Brittain and Freeman, 1980), considerable weight was given to technological change, institutional structures, entrepreneurship, and historical events in explaining community development. These *density-independent* factors are central to the argument presented

The author gratefully acknowledges the insightful and helpful comments of Glenn Carroll, Paul DiMaggio, John Freeman, Joel Baum, Rong-Xin Chen, Bryant Hudson, David Loree, Steve Mueller, Yuwei Shi, Jon Thornberry, and Diane VanMaele. Each helped make this a better chapter.

here. Understanding how they operate to impact population growth and community evolution is vital if organizational ecology is once more to play a role in research on organizational communities.

The density-independent argument developed in this chapter is illustrated with a study of the firm populations manufacturing electronic components from 1947 to 1981. The community of firms in this industry is organizationally and strategically diverse. This diversity emerged from a population of homogeneous receiving tube firms operating in an oligopolistic industry structure (Webbink, 1977). Technological change was central to the development of this industry and is an important feature in the model of community evolution presented in this chapter.

Density-Independent Selection

The ecological model developed in this study distinguishes between two general processes that together explain the growth and decline of organizational populations and, as a result, the evolution of organizational communities. The first is competitive density, which includes direct market competition, strategic competition from firms in the same market, and indirect competition that impacts firms through supply shortages that drive up costs, substitutable goods that drive down market prices, and competition for skilled labor and other knowledge resources (Wholey and Brittain, 1986). Ecological competition models also incorporate mutualistic and cooperative relationships at the community level, including symbiotic technological interdependencies (Barnett and Carroll, 1988) and agglomeration economies (Arthur, 1989). In addition, the ecological density specification can account for asymmetries in interpopulation relationships, a feature of the model that helps explain the social dynamics characterizing innovator and imitator populations, parasitic marketing efforts, and the persistence of second-source populations in industries with a dominant producer (Brittain and Wholey, 1988).

The second ecological process that accounts for population growth and decline is the density-independent influence of historical events (Brittain and Freeman, 1980). Density independence, as defined by the ecological framework, encompasses all variables that are not linked to population size, including environmental dislocations due to variations in the business cycle, changes in government policy, technical change (Anderson and Tushman, 1990), political disruptions (Carroll and Huo, 1986), and any other fundamental environmental change, whether institutional or economic, that impacts the rate of organization entries and exits. It is possible to trivialize this characterization of the environment, but to do so misses the fundamental, path-dependent insight provided by the ecological model: *density-independent events happen to, and their implications are shaped by, the organizational social structure of the time.* It is this insight that explains why the community of firms manufacturing electronic components would not look the same if the transistor was discovered in 1907 instead of 1947. Because in the intervening 40 years—an instant in the span of human social history—the radio industry emerged as an oligopoly, AT&T became a monopoly, the government launched an effort to dismember AT&T, and a defense industry was created in the aftermath of two world wars, features of the organizational community of 1947 that fundamentally shaped the evolution of the components manufacturing industry (Brittain and Freeman, 1980).

Ecological Model

Organizational ecologists capture the dynamics of population growth and decline with the Lotka–Volterra model (Hannan and Freeman, 1977). The basic model for J populations is

$$\frac{dN_i}{dt} = r_i N_i \left(\frac{K_i - N_i - \sum_{j \neq i}^{J} \alpha_{ij} N_j}{K_i} \right), \qquad (1)$$

where N_i = number of firms in population i, K_i = environmental carrying capacity for population i, r_i = growth response parameter for population i, α_{ij} = the effect of population j on i. This specification describes the *growth rate* of an organizaitonal population, where growth is influenced by population size relative to the environmental carrying capacity for the population and the expansion and contraction of populations of firms pursuing competitive and mutualistic business strategies (Barnett and Carroll, 1988; Brittain and Wholey, 1988).

The reason organizational ecologists have focused on density dependence is apparent after multiplying equation (2) through by N_i and simplifying the coefficients:

$$\frac{dN_i}{dt} = r_i \left[N_i - N_i^2 K_i^{-1} - \sum_{j \neq i}^{J} c_{ij} N_j \right], \qquad (2)$$

where

$$c_{ij} = \alpha_{ij} \frac{N_i}{K_i} = \text{effect of population } j \text{ on } i.$$

The bracketed portion of the equation indicates that growth varies with population size (N_i), is limited by environmental carrying capacity (K_i), and is influenced by other populations in the community ($c_{ij} N_j$). This specification is illustrated in figure 17.1 ($r_i = 0.2, c_{ij} = 0$).

Although this model incorporates the environment, it is as a fixed constraint. This characterization of carrying capacity is appropriate in some instances, but it misrepresents community development where environmental discontinuities affect environmental munificence, which is the difference between population size and carrying capacity in the Lotka–Volterra model. In the latter case, changes in relative population sizes reflect differences in population responses to environmental discontinuities rather than population densities, a distinction between *density-independent* and *density-dependent* evolution (Brittain and Freeman, 1980). The model introduced in this chapter suggests that this pattern of development can be modeled by allowing the carrying capacity to vary over time.

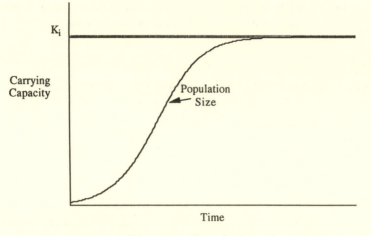

FIG. 17.1   Population growth with a fixed carrying capacity

Carrying Capacity Specification

All organizations depend on environmental resources to some degree, whether these are insured patients in a hospital, government funding for a social service agency, manufacturing workers for an industrial union, or customer purchases for a business. When the resource base supporting a population of organizations expands significantly, the number of organizations is expected to increase as well, *ceteris paribus.* Accounting for the impact of such environmental shifts means redefining the carrying capacity in equation (2) as:

$$K_i = K_i(t), \tag{3}$$

where $K_i(t)$ characterizes environmental variation over time. An expanding carrying capacity operates as a growth accelerator in equation (2) by decreasing the dampening effect of density squared. Similarly, a decrease in $K_i(t)$ decreases the growth rate by increasing the impact of competitive density (N_i^2), which acts to lower the growth rate associated with current population size (N_i). This pattern of response is illustrated in figure 17.2, which shows how a hypothetical time varying carrying capacity (3 percent random disturbance) affects two organizational populations.

Figure 17.2 illustrates two important theoretical points. First, carrying capacity can shift with little apparent impact on a population. For instance, the left hump in figure 17.2 reflects the pattern one might observe with a new government funding program that is cancelled because of budget cutbacks before the population of organizations has grown to anticipated levels (e.g., Singh, Tucker, and Meinhard, 1991). When this occurs, the consequences are not necessarily disastrous for existing organizational populations, a point illustrated by the population represented by the solid line (population s, $r_s = 0.2$, $c_{sj} = 0$). The results are detrimental for the population represented by the dashed line (population d, $r_d = 0.4$, $c_{dj} = 0$), but this is because it responds rapidly to environmental changes, not because its environment is different (Brittain and Freeman, 1980).

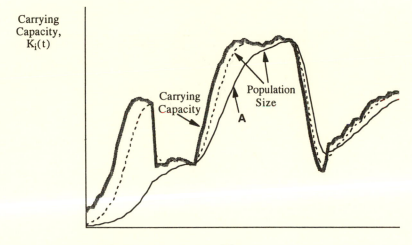

FIG. 17.2   Population growth with a time varying carrying capacity

Recent work in organizational ecology treats *population size and density as synonymous* constructs, a conceptualization that makes sense if carrying capacity is fixed (see figure 17.1). But if the reality of carrying capacity is more like that depicted in figure 17.2, it becomes apparent that density is defined by the relationship between population size and the carrying capacity (Brittain and Freeman, 1980; Delaroix and Swaminathan, 1991), which in turn means density is also time varying. So, although the size of population *s* is greater at point A than it is on the right side of the graph, population density at A is lower than at any point on the far right side of the graph.

The second point illustrated by figure 17.2 involves community evolution. If carrying capacity is fixed, then community evolution is a matter of relative densities and timing of entry, a characterization that is virtually identical to that of evolutionary economics (Nelson and Winter, 1982; Winter, 1990). But in some instances, community evolution reflects exogenous events that impact population carrying capacity and has little relation to current population size.

This point is demonstrated for two competing populations in figure 17.3. Population *s* (solid line) is by definition the stronger competitor ($\alpha_{ds} = 0.4 > \alpha_{sd} = 0.1$), while population *d* (dashed line) trades on rapid response to environmental changes ($r_d = 0.8 > r_s = 0.2$), a distinction capturing what are termed, respectively, *K* and *r* population strategies (Brittain and Freeman, 1980). These population characteristics are identical in figures 17.3a and 17.3b, but the evolution of the communities is quite different. In the fixed carrying capacity case, *d* initially dominates the industry, but this dominance is eroded as *s* grows and interpopulation competition swings the balance of competition in favor of *s*. In figure 17.3b, the variation in the carrying capacity over time results in a rough parity between the populations, a result that reflects the values of the population response parameters, the pattern of carrying capacity variation, and the timing of environmental discontinuities relative to community development.

It is obvious, given figure 17.3, that many patterns of community evolution are

(a)

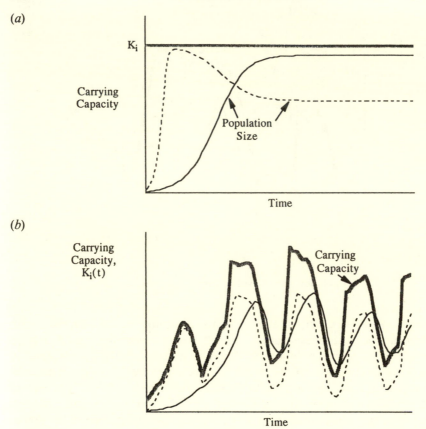

(b)

FIG. 17.3 Population growth for competing populations (a) fixed carrying capacity; (b) time varying carrying capacity.

possible given different histories of carrying capacity variation and different population characteristics. And this in turn means the ecological model needs to account for changing carrying capacities if it is going to explain community evolution.

Environmental Variation over Time. Characterizing carrying capacity variation over time is a descriptive problem, but it is a problem at a different level of analysis than most organization–environment research. At the population and community levels of analysis, carrying capacity variation reflects institutional changes that redefine the feasibility of alternative modes of organizing (Scott, 1987), the impact of patterned variation in resource environments (Wholey and Brittain, 1989; Brittain and Wholey, 1990), and environmental discontinuities that reinforce, and sometimes undermine, existing organizational competencies (Tushman and Anderson, 1986).

  Organization theory has—all things considered—a comprehensive understanding of the cross-sectional variation in organizational environments (Pfeffer and Salancik, 1978; Scott, 1992). Organization theory's treatment of time series variation within and across organizational environments, on the other hand, has not evolved a great deal beyond Thompson's (1967) distinction between environmental con-

straints and contingencies. Much of the institutional literature and research on technological discontinuities focuses on changes in Thompson's constraints, a construct
linked to environmental features that extend beyond the life histories of individual
organizations, while contingency theory and organizational ecology examine the
impact of more immediate fluctuations in resources and competition on organizational structures and demographics.

The distinction between constraints and contingencies suggests two distinct
dynamics of change are operating at the community level, one that is associated with
the creation of population niches and a second that drives population size. On the
basis of this distinction, the following carrying capacity specification is proposed:

$$K_i(t) = f(\theta_i(t), \pi_i Z(t)), \tag{4}$$

where $Z(t)$ is a vector of time varying independent variables that influence population size and $\theta_i(t)$ is a set of time varying constraints that define the population niche.

The Theoretical distinction between $\theta_i(t)$ and $Z(t)$ is a distinction between the
social processes of institutionalization and those processes governing an organizational form's growth and decline. The distinction between $\theta_i(t)$ and $Z(t)$ is also a distinction between public and private goods (Olson, 1965).[1] Organizational niches are
by definition organizing opportunities. They are social products arising out of the
social division of labor (Durkheim, 1893) created in the course of knowledge development (Schumpeter, 1934; Tushman and Anderson, 1986) and facilitated by
socially defined governance structures (Carroll, Goodstein, and Geynes, 1988). The
opportunities defined by these social proesses are not restricted, but social provisions
governing private goods are equally important factors in population proliferation.

As Stinchcombe (1965) so astutely observed, opportunities alone cannot explain
the proliferation of organizations. The resources marshaled by the people running
organizations are as necessary to the growth of an organizational population as transportation systems that make it feasible to transfer goods, a financial system to facilitate exchanges, and the knowledge that makes production feasible. The private
goods respresented by $Z(t)$ are not unique to any particular population, but each
population is expected to have a unique pattern of resource utilization captured by
the π_i vector in equation (4). This in turn means that each population in a community will have a different carrying capacity, even if all rely on the same resources.

Carrying Capacity Model. Most organizations, and commercial enterprises in particular, operate within a range of production capabilities and personnel competencies. Organizational researchers have identified a number of structural mechanisms
that are used to extend this operating range, including staffing critical personnel categories excessively (Freeman and Hannan, 1975), professionalizing the labor force
(Hage and Aiken, 1970), creating a flexible division of labor to foster organizational
learning (Burns and Stalker, 1961), and rigidly structuring production activities to
minimize training expenses and facilitate periodic layoffs (Brittain and Wholey,
1990). What this work suggests is something that seems obvious: organizations do
not operate at capacity at all times.

Because organizations have a range of operating capabilities, existing organizational populations are going to capture some carrying capacity fluctuations, even if

capacity is limited for any particular organization. What this means substantively is that the population of established organizations is going to have some capacity to capture market growth and deal with environmental variations, either because of underutilized capacity or as a result of capacity growth (Mueller, 1992). From the standpoint of equation (2), this capacity absorption will not influence demographic processes when the number of organizations in the population (N_i) is well below the environmental carrying capacity (K_i), a situation in which resources are abundant relative to population size and intrapopulation competition is correspondingly low. But the impact of excess capacity is going to add to resource competition as N_i approaches K_i, which means capacity absorption operates as a function of N^2 (i.e., that as carrying capacity approaches its upper limits, excess capacity contributes to the suppression of further population growth).

This argument suggests the following volume absorption function, $\nu(N_i)$

$$\nu(N_i) = \nu_i N_i^2, \tag{5}$$

where ν_i is the capacity adjustment parameter for population i ($\nu_i > 0$). A simple interpretation of this function is that direct competitors are "bigger" when a population is in the vicinity of, or over, its carrying capacity, and as a result, the population growth rate decreases. It is important to note that ν_i is a population, not a firm, characteristic. This parameter is expected to vary with the technological and capability development of organizational populations, features that have implications for population size and the distribution of firm sizes within the population (Nelson and Winter, 1982).

For a given resource Q, an increase in resource availability will only lead to a net increase in population size where $Q_t + \Delta Q > \nu_i N_i^2(t)$ or

$$\frac{Q_t + \Delta Q}{\nu_i N_i^2(t)} > 1. \tag{6}$$

Equation (6) indicates that resource growth has a net impact on population growth only if the increase in resources is greater than the population's available excess capacity.

Not all resources are subject to capacity absorption. Public goods such as social legitimacy, for instance, are critical resources that established firms cannot prevent potential entrants from accessing (DiMaggio and Powell, 1983; Scott, 1987). For example, increased legitimacy has increased the environmental carrying capacity for health maintenance organizations by causing states to remove restrictive regulations that made it impossible for HMOs to operate. But once restrictive regulations were removed, not-for-profit HMOs were not able to capture the newly created carrying capacity and keep for-profit HMOs out of the health delivery community (Wholey and Burns, 1989). So in the model developed here, changes in public goods—as represented by $\theta_i(t)$—are not subject to capacity absorption.

The factors in equation (4) are independent with respect to the total carrying capacity in any instance, which suggests an additive model. Taking this additivity into account and applying the volume absorption function (equation [6]) to $Z(t)$ as discussed leads to the following specification for the carrying capacity component of equation (2):

$$K_i^{-1}(t) = \theta_i(t) + \pi_i \frac{Z(t)}{vN_i^2}, \tag{7}$$

which indicates that the carrying capacity for population i varies as a step function with changes in the availability of public goods and continuously with fluctuations in the resource environment (to the degree that these variations are not absorbed by existing firms).

Substituting equation (7) into equation (2) produces the following population expansion rate specification:

$$\frac{dN_i}{dt} = r_i N_i - r_i \theta_i(t) N_i^2 + \kappa_i Z(t) + \sum_{j \neq i}^{J} s_{ij} N_j \tag{8}$$

$$\kappa_i = \frac{r_i \pi_i}{v_i}$$

$$s_{ij} = -r_i c_{ij},$$

indicating that the rate of population growth is characterized by non–linear density dependence, with expansion increasing at a decreasing rate where carrying capacity is constant and varying with carrying capacity when it changes over time. Strategic competitor density (N_j) decreases the growth rate when s_{ij} is negative, but s_{ij} can also be positive, reflecting the variants of mutualism identified in the empirical literature (Barnett and Carroll, 1988; Brittain and Wholey, 1988).[2]

Implications for Models of Community Development

The effects of population size as a generator of population growth and constraint on expansion, the core contributions of the density-dependent perspective, are preserved in equation (8). The model still presumes that organizational entrepreneurs are a product of organizing experiences (Stinchcombe, 1965; Freeman and Brittain, 1986), that organizing successes attract mimicry (DiMaggio and Powell, 1983), and that organizational communities are based on complex webs of competitive, mutualistic, and asymmetric population interactions (Barnett and Carroll, 1988; Brittain and Wholey, 1988). But equation (8) does *not* presume an absolute maximum population size that governs intrapopulation competition. Instead, population growth is constrained by bounded public goods that define the population niche and is sustained by resource expansion influenced by institutional and ecological processes. And it is the differential availability of resources over time and the time specific characteristics of social niches that determine the evolutionary history of organizational populations.

The r_i and v_i parameters and s_{ij} coefficients defined in equation (8) do not vary with time. they reflect observable population characteristics, capturing the ease with which organizations in a given community are created, the capacities defined by the mode of organizing, and the strategic vulnerabilities of the population. In a stable environment, these parameters are sufficient to characterize community structure. But few organizational environments are stable indefinitely. The theoretical argument advanced here is that it is environmental variation—in conjunction with historical processes that define organizing options—that is the engine driving community evolution. And it is periods of instability, during which populations are created and densities develop, that define the social structure of organizational communities.

The processes generating community structure within this framework are demographic. Community structure emerges out of relative rates of entry and exit, rates that change independently with changes in the institutional, resource, and technical environments in which the community is embedded. It is at the level of these demographic processes that it is possible to demonstrate the value of the model presented here. In this chapter an empirical analysis of the historical development of the semiconductor components manufacturing industry is used to show how the density-independent perspective accounts for community evolution.

Community Evolution in Semiconductor Manufacturing

The industrial community composed of firms manufacturing electronic components changed in a fundamental way after the transistor was discovered in December 1946. Prior to this technological breakthrough, the industry was an oligopoly dominated by some of the giants of the industrial age. RCA, General Electric, Westinghouse, and Sylvania together controlled close to 90 percent of the components market and were the technology leaders of their day. In less than twenty years, these firms were second tier players in an industry where products could become obsolete before they went to market, slivers of silicon were running computers, and firms seemingly materialized overnight to dominate huge product markets that had not existed a year before (Brittain and Freeman, 1980). Along with these changes, the character of this industrial community changed as the components market expanded exponentially, technologies defined new opportunities, and organizing options and financing became better understood.

In the thirty-five years following the discovery of the transistor, 2,550 firm entries and exits took place and 1,380 separate decisions were made to invest in a manufacturing facility, hire employees, develop products, arrange licensing agreements, and obtain government operating permits regulating everything from sewer hookups to parking spaces, and market electronic components. And 1,170 separate decisions were made to abandon the components market to competitors, in some cases abrogating leases, defaulting on debts, and throwing dedicated workers into unemployment. The community of firms that defines the electronic components manufacturing industry is a product of these two demographic processes operating in conjunction over time.

Strategic Populations

Figure 17.4 shows how worldwide sales of active electronic components (receiving tubes plus semiconductors) and the number of firms, both foreign and domestic, selling electronic components in the United States have grown over time. The growth in both firms and component sales since 1953 is largely due to the expansion of demand for semiconductor components. The exponential sales growth that has char-

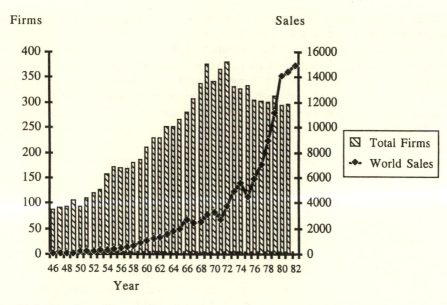

Fıg. 17.4   Number of firms selling electronic components in the United States and worldwide component sales, 1946–82 (sales in millions of constant dollars, 1967 = 100)

acterized the semiconductor market would seemingly guarantee success for any firm that can get a product to market, but the growth in the number of firms producing electronic components belies the industry's historically high failure rate (Tilton, 1971; Webbink, 1977; Wilson, Ashton, and Egan, 1980). This combination of rapid growth and high failure rates may seem anomalous, since it is generally assumed that growth is one key to strategic success. In this case, however, the conditions that are driving growth—decreasing prices and ongoing innovation—also drive firms out of the industry at an astonishing pace.

A distinctive strategic consequence of rapidly evolving components technologies is "first-mover" advantages. These arise for several strategic reasons beyond production learning economies. First, the version of a product that is introduced earliest and most widely adopted becomes the technical standard to which all subsequent devices must conform. This forces firms with different versions of the same product to pay for costly redesign work to make their devices compatible and results in further learning curve advantages for the initial entrants. Second, because components buyers have historically refused to adopt components without an assured second source, first-movers are in a position to negotiate favorable reciprocal technology licensing agreements in exchange for lucrative second source licenses. Finally, first-movers can reap significant windfall profits from their initial learning economy advantages, profits that can be used to invest in additional R&D and production capacity.

Opportunities exist for firms pursuing follower strategies, but they are in the efficient production of established devices, not on the frontiers of innovation. Even when leading-edge technologies are developing rapidly, the greatest share of the market is in the wake of the most recent breakthrough. This market reflects the prior purchasing decisions of systems firms that have developed products around certain components and will stick with those designs until new technologies meet the cost criteria specific to their needs. These secondary adopters will not support the margins that are available in military electronics and electronic instruments, but they will buy washing machine control chips in volume and with the certainty of long-term supply contracts. Firms marketing to such users must accept much lower margins and greater competition, but they avoid the risks and costs of knowledge investments.

The distinction between first-mover and follower strategies matches the advantages that the ecological model associates with r and K population strategies.[3] As illustrated in figure 17.2, populations with high population response values (r_i) compete within an organizational community on the basis of their ability to exploit newly created pools of resources rapidly, while populations that grow through competitive advantage tend to expand more slowly, but gain ground on other populations as density increases. Previous work indicates first-mover and follower populations in semiconductor manufacturing have the population parameters expected of r and K strategies (Brittain and Wholey, 1988), suggesting this designation captures important population-level features of the firms operating in this industry.

Firms can pursue first-mover or follower advantages as either technical specialists or generalists. Specialists are very common in the industry, especially among followers. Generalists are also found in large numbers, especially where production efficiencies can be achieved by operating in multiple technical arenas (e.g., within integrated circuits). As in earlier studies of the industry (Brittain and Freeman, 1980; Brittain and Wholey, 1988), this study uses four strategies to characterize firm populations: r-specialists, r-generalists, K-specialists, and K-generalists. These categories capture the specialism–generalism distinction used in earlier ecological work (Hannan and Freeman, 1977; Carroll and Delacroix, 1982; Hannan and Freeman, 1989) and incorporate the order of entry aspects of strategy that are a central feature of high-technology industries.

Data

The firm participation data used to estimate the models in this paper were drawn from the *Electronics Buyers' Guide*. This source was published as a supplement to *Electronics* from 1941 until 1962, when it became a separate annual publication. Firm listings in the *Buyers' Guide* are free, although advertising space is also available. The *Buyers' Guide* is structured in the same way as the telephone *Yellow Pages*, with all firms receiving a single line listing and some purchasing additional advertising space ranging from small boxed displays to multipage layouts. The volumes are organized by products, with firms included under all relevant categories. The *Buyers' Guide* is a reference volume used mainly by engineers, purchasing agents, and sales-personnel for information on device availability. Inclusion is advantageous because the *Buyers' Guide* is used as a centralized source for purchasing information.[4]

Data were gathered for 1946–81 for all producers of 87 "active" electronic components distributed across the 12 product categories listed in table 17.1. This period was selected for two reasons. First, for theoretical reasons it is important that the observational framework capture the initiation, proliferation, and stabilization of firm participation in the industry. As can be seen in figure 17.4, the number of firms

TABLE 17.1   Electronic Component Product Groups

Receiving tubes
  • Diodes/rectifiers
  • Triode/multiple grid
  • Microwave receiving tubes
Discrete semiconductor components
  • Diodes and rectifiers
  • Transistors and thyristors
Integrated circuits
  • Digital integrated circuits
  • Analog/linear integrated circuits
  • Signal converting integrated circuits
Custom and semicustom devices
  • Custom integrated circuits
  • Hybrid circuits
Optoelectronic Devices
  • Light-emitting devices
  • Photosensitive devices

in the industry peaked in the early 1970s, even though sales increased sharply in subsequent years. Second, the observation period ends in 1981 because international government intervention in the components market began to influence what could be sold where after this time (Borrus, Millstein, and Zysman, 1982). The 1946–81 frame captures the period prior to the discovery of the transistor, includes all the major design innovations that have defined the industry, and brackets the years when the community structure of the industry was established.

A total of 1,461 firms and 445 distinct corporate divisions were identified as components manufacturers. The number of years in components production averaged 6.5 for the sample as a whole, with a range of 1 to 60 years.[5] Within the time frame of the study, the maximum number of firms in the industry never exceeded 350, and the mean number of manufacturers per year was 220 firms.

Firm Strategic Classification

Because the specialism/generalism characterization is defined as market focus, it is operationalized at the product group level. Although it is possible to construct a categorization that ranges from one to twelve, the theoretically meaningful distinction is between single product group firms and multiple product group firms. The distribution of the number of product groups per firm has a mean of 2.1 and is skewed toward 1, which is not surprising. The relative percentage of specialist and generalist firms varies historically, with specialists accounting for between 40 and 54 percent of all firms in the industry at different points in time.

The second strategic dimension used in this paper distinguishes between *r* and *K* population strategies. This distinction involves the relationship between order of entry and the level of competition firms face in a particular product market. The early entrant avoids competition by virtue of the market growth early in the product life cycle (Moore and Tushman, 1982), while later entrants must develop operating efficiencies to compete with other firms in order to be successful. This dimension is operationalized with the disaggregate information on product offerings coded from the *Electronics Buyers' Guide* and supplemental materials from various sources that report on industry history. An earlier study found that the dramatic price declines indicating emerging competition did not develop in any semiconductor market within the first three years after product introduction (U.S. Department of Commerce, 1979), which suggests that firms entering in the first three years achieve returns that can fund other developments. On the basis of this finding, r-strategists were defined as firms entering a product category in the three calendar years following a new product introduction ($t, t + 1, t + 2$).

Firm Characteristics. Table 17.2 presents the descriptive statistics for the four populations used in this study. The data in the table are averages for all firms in each strategic population (standard deviations in parentheses). Unless otherwise specified, these are means for each firm's last observation.[6] One point worth noting is that the r-strategy firms generally have more products and greater sales than their K-strategy counterparts. But the variable standard deviations are generally so large that it is impossible to identify any consistent firm-level differences across these populations.

Figure 17.5 shows the distribution of firms by strategy group over time. K-specialists are the dominant strategic form in the industry, accounting for as much as 80 percent of total firm participation during some periods, but as little as 55 percent at other times. The other strategic populations grew as the market for components expanded, but the patterns differ from that of the K-specialist population. The K-generalist population remained relatively stable through most of the 1950s, dipped sharply during the 1960 recession, then steadily increased to a new plateau in the 1960s. The r-generalist population, on the other hand, grew steadily until the mid-sixties, remained relatively stable for more than a decade, then began a gradual decline. Finally, the r-specialist population had waves of growth in the late fifties and early seventies with no apparent plateau.

TABLE 17.2   Firm Characteristic Means by Strategy (standard deviation in parentheses)

Variables	r-Specialist	K-Specialist	r-Generalist	K-Generalist
Products	3.42	1.87	13.09	6.57
	(3.70)	(1.62)	(10.83)	(7.08)
Sales > $1 million—first	.50	.30	.63	.42
	(0.50)	(0.46)	(0.49)	(0.49)
Sales > $10 million—first	.13	.07	.24	.16
	(0.34)	(0.26)	(0.43)	(0.37)
Sales > $1 million—last	.58	.38	.84	.56
	(0.50)	(0.49)	(0.37)	(0.50)
Sales > $10 million—last	.12	.09	.47	.22
	(0.33)	(0.29)	(0.50)	(0.41)
Foreign firm dummy	.03	.05	.12	.14
	(0.16)	(0.22)	(0.33)	(0.34)
Divisionalized	.11	.13	.38	.23
	(0.31)	(0.34)	(0.49)	(0.42)
Time in industry	3.67	4.35	11.28	6.73
	(3.76)	(6.56)	(12.13)	(8.93)
Number of firms	76	1031	74	280

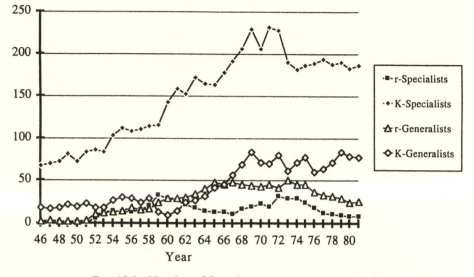

FIG. 17.5   Number of firms by strategy category, 1946–81

Carrying Capacity Variables

The carrying capacity for the four strategic populations in the semiconductor industry is defined by four sets of variables. The measures used are listed in Table 17.3. All dollar figures are in constant dollars (1967 = 100, based on the industrial commodities producer price index for manufactured goods, U.S. Bureau of the Census, 1975; U.S. Bureau of Labor Statistics, 1984).

The variables used in this study capture the environmental features that industry observers have identified as key determinants of the industry's growth (Tilton, 1971; Webbink, 1977; Braun and MacDonald, 1978; Wilson, Ashton, and Egan, 1980; Levin, 1982; Freeman, 1982, 1986). The expansion of sales levels, which reflect repeat purchases, without doubt explains a great deal about the expansion of the populations producing components. New sales, foreign sales, and industry level revenue growth are also used in the models estimated in this chapter to capture the changing nature of sales over time. The revenue growth measure, in particular, needs explanation. This measure is included to capture two variables that cannot be independently assessed, the costs of production and variations due to business cycles. It is assumed that the slope of the sales-per-firm time series trend provides a rough estimate of escalating production costs associated with new generations of technology, while the deviation in actual sales from this trend is due to the ups and downs of the economy as they impact the components industry.

The finanacial indicators used in this study capture the breadth of capital markets and the time series variation in key sources of capital for the industry. Real interest rates and aggregate investment rates capture the cost and availability of capital in general, a resource that is vital for starting companies and maintaining the growth rates that characterize firms in this industry. In addition, the growth of venture capital has been crucial to firms entering this industry, just as firms in this industry have considerably enriched venture capitalists (Freeman, 1986).

TABLE 17.3   Carrying Capacity Measures

Variable	Source
Technological regime (θ)	
Transistor era (dummy variable, 1947–59 = 1)	
Integrated circuit era (dummy variable, 1960–70 = 1)	
Microprocessor era (dummy variable, 1971–81 = 1)	
Market resources (Z_1)	
Total worldwide sales (millions of constant dollars, 1967 = 100)	Tilton, 1971; Webbink, 1977; U.S. Department of Commerce, 1979; U.S. Department of Commerce, 1982; Dataquest, 1984
Change in worldwide sales (change in sales from previous year)	Computed with worldwide sales
Revenue (deviation from predicted sales per firm trend)	Computed with worldwide sales
Worldwide sales in foreign markets (percentage of total worldwide sales)	1947–67: Tilton, 1971; 1967–1976: U.S. Department of Commerce, 1979; 1976–81: Dataquest, 1984
Worldwide sales by foreign firms (percentage of worldwide sales)	1947–67: Tilton, 1971; 1967–76: U.S. Department of Commerce, 1979; 1976–81: Dataquest, 1984
Financial resources (Z_2)	
Venture capital funds (millions of dollars, 1967 = 100)	Rubel, 1982; Bigler Investment Management, 1983; Venture Economics, 1984
Aggregate investment (total nonresidential, fixed investment component of GNP)	U.S. Bureau of the Census, 1975, 1984
Real interest (effective interest rate on long-term corporate bonds)	Leuthold, 1981
Innovation measures (Z_3)	
Design innovations (as identified by panels of industry experts)	Tilton, 1971; Webbink, 1977; U.S. Department of Commerce, 1979; Wilson, et al., 1980; *Electronics*
Process innovations (as identified by panels of industry experts)	Tilton, 1971; Webbink, 1977; U.S. Department of Commerce, 1979; Wilson et al., 1980; *Electronics*
Patent activity (filings by dominant firms)	Webbink, 1977; Wilson et al., 1980; Levin, 1982; U.S. Department of Commerce, 1983

The models estimated in this chapter also include three different measures of technological change. The design and process innovation indicators capture the frequency and magnitude of changes in product design and process technologies, while the patent indicator traces the proliferation of routine innovation in the later years of the industry's history.

Finally, dummy variables are used to capture the historical variation in technology definitions, changes that have had important consequences for social definitions of electronic products, the breadth of components markets, and the perceived value of solid state technologies. Three eras are identified, each defined by the dominance of a single type of device. The first is the transistor era, which forever changed the nature of electronics and launched the switch to solid state circuitry. The second is the integrated circuit era, which was characterized by the rapid diffusion of solid state electronics into military and industrial systems. The third era is that of the microprocessor, which brought affordable computing to applications as mundane as washing machines and as sophisticated as engineering desktops.

The mean values for the independent variables are listed in table 17.4. The real dollar average sales level has a maximum of approximately $5 billion. The average yearly growth in sales for the industry is $130 million dollars, with a maximum gain of $807 million (1971–72) and loss of $982 million (1974–75, constant dollars: 1967 = 100). These are relative to a real dollar sales average of approximately $3 billion.

Model Estimates

The expansion in the total number of components producers from 92 in 1947 to 298 in 1981 occurred because entries into semiconductor manufacturing were greater than exits from the industry. The components market was twenty-nine times larger in 1981 than in 1947, which is more than enough to account for this threefold growth in total firm participation. The market growth argument is quite simple: the number of firms operating in the industry has increased because the market has grown.

TABLE 17.4   Environment/Carrying Capacity Measures: Means and Standard Deviations

Variables	Mean	Standard Deviation	Minimum	Maximum
Market resources				
Total worldwide sales	2,008.02	1,534.24	156.07	5,149.20
Change in worldwide sales	130.03	370.33	−982.45	807.62
Revenue	0.07	1.27	−3.67	2.95
Percentage foreign sales	26.19	19.02	0.00	48.39
Foreign firm market share	17.57	15.71	0.00	44.84
Financial resources				
Venture capital funds	200.15	150.45	6.64	460.37
Aggregate investment	71.22	30.13	32.48	122.62
Real interest	1.16	2.26	−7.63	3.95
Innovation indicators				
Design innovations	1.31	1.32	0.00	5.00
Process innovations	1.14	1.06	0.00	4.00
Total patent activity	251.20	141.04	1.00	488.00
Number of observations: 35				

This explanation suggests a relatively uniform pattern of demographic events across the strategic populations operating in the industry. The actual incidence of entries and exits over the industry's history indicates this is not the case (figure 17.6). This variation is not surprising, however, if one considers the effects of competition and density-independent selection. The complex pattern of fluctuations observed in figure 17.6 is undoubtedly the product of environmental variations involving market resources, rising foreign competition, instabilities in financial markets, and fits and spurts in the development of product and process innovations. The model estimates presented here capture these relationships.

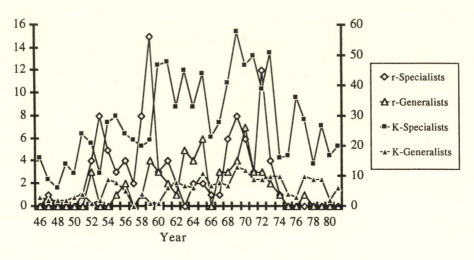

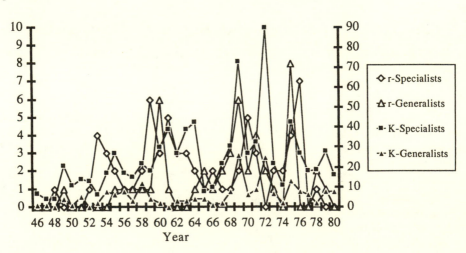

FIG. 17.6 Longitudinal distribution of entries and exits: (a) number of entries by strategy group; (b) number of exits by strategy group.

Empirical Model

Hannan and Freeman (1988b) have developed an empirical specification for the ecological model based on a Yule process. The specification they use is

$$\lambda(t) = N_t^a e^{\gamma N^2_t + \mu Q_t}, \tag{9}$$

where a is the speed of adjustment parameter, γ is the extreme density parameter, μ is the vector of coeficients capturing the independent variable effects, and $\lambda(t)$ is the rate of event occurrence. This directly parallels the model represented by equation (8), although the interpretation of the N^2 term is different in the specification developed in this chapter.

Equation (9) is estimated by using the proportional hazards procedure in SAS (SAS Institute Inc., 1983) with data on the waiting time between entries and exits for each of the strategic populations discussed earlier. This procedure produces partial likelihood estimates for the natural logarithm of the hazard. The partial likelihood method allows the estimation of independent effects without specifying an explicit time function (Tuma and Hannan, 1984), which is useful for the across population comparisons that are of interest here.

Since newly established component firms suffer from a "liability of newness" (Freeman, Carroll, and Hannan, 1983) and are therefore likely to accelerate exit rates, this study controls for possible age heterogeneity by distinguishing between firms that have been in the industry one year or less (n_i) and established firms (e_i). Thus, population size N for population i is defined as $N_i = e_i + n_i$. Since this is an additive function, it needs to be transformed into a product to distinguish the demographic effects within the logarithmic transformation required for estimation (this product is then a sum). Accordingly, the population size variable in equation (9) is transformed into

$$N = ey, \tag{10}$$

where y is the number of new plus established firms divided by the number of established firms. The multiplier y varies between 1 and 2 for the populations studied here and captures the percentage of the population that is new entrants.

The ideal data for testing a waiting time model have the exact date of event occurrence. But it is almost impossible as a practical matter to obtain such data for any representative sample of an organizational community over any meaningful history. Only the year in which an event took place is known, but it is clear that the events occurring in a given year are scattered over the entire year. As Brittain (1989) has shown, the mean waiting time for the year is an unbiased estimate for the true waiting time in this situation, which makes it feasible to order the waiting times within a year randomly around the mean waiting time, a procedure utilized here.

The model estimates are presented in tables 17.5 and 17.6. All the models are tested relative to models with a typical density specification, which in this case includes all the variables listed under population size. In every case, accounting for carrying capacity variations associated with the Z vector in equation (8) significantly improves model fit. Similar tests not reported here were performed comparing the

TABLE 17.5   Partial Likelihood Estimates of Entry Rate Models by Strategy Groups

	r-Specialists	K-Specialists	r-Generalists	K-Generalists
Population size				
Log number est. firms ($t - 1$)	11.1122*	6.3149*	8.4123*	8.8923*
Log new firm indicator ($t - 1$)	7.9562*	4.8102*	−6.7553	−1.2400
Transistor regime ($t - 1$)	1.2741*	−0.0696*	0.0470	−1.0811*
Integrated circuit regime ($t - 1$)	0.3266	0.0130*	0.3251	−0.1134*
Microprocessor regime ($t - 1$)	1.9149*	−0.0013	0.4068*	−0.1848*
Competitive relations				
r-Specialists ($t - 1$)	—	0.5481*	0.1373*	0.2369*
K-Specialists ($t - 1$)	0.2508*	—	−0.0512	0.0676*
r-Generalists ($t - 1$)	−0.6432	−0.5514*	—	0.0610
K-Generalists ($t - 1$)	0.9006*	0.2686*	0.5583*	—
Market resources				
Revenue ($t - 1$)	17.4389*	4.6134*	9.4277*	1.7078*
Total sales ($t - 2$)	−0.0144*	−0.0120*	−0.0203*	0.0007
Change in market size ($t - 1$)	−0.0452*	−0.0191*	−0.0171*	0.0009
Change in market size (t)	0.0167*	0.0030*	0.0044*	0.0037*
Percentage foreign sales ($t - 1$)	−0.3916*	0.1523	−0.5135*	−0.3080*
Foreign firm market share ($t - 1$)	−0.3862	0.1899*	2.5149*	0.3711*
Financial resources				
Venture capital funds ($t - 1$)	0.0156*	−0.0246*	0.0592*	0.0029
Aggregate investment ($t - 1$)	0.1366	0.4786*	−0.6965*	−0.1460*
Real interest ($t - 1$)	−2.7861*	1.9526*	1.1954*	0.5783*
Innovation patterns				
Design innovations ($t - 2$)	1.9512*	−0.3560*	−0.2499	−0.4100*
Process innovations ($t - 2$)	1.3948*	−1.4562*	0.4332*	−0.0618
Total patent activity ($t - 1$)	−0.0333*	−0.0164*	−0.0387*	−0.0312*
Number of events	106	1006	59	210
Number of observations	117	1006	74	210
Degrees of freedom	15	15	15	15
Model chi-square	197.62	2066.31	131.08	299.20
Log likelihood ratio	.441	.436	.485	.399
Model significance	$p < .0001$	$p < .0001$	$p < .0001$	$p < .0001$

NOTE: *$p < .05$.

full model with models containing only density indicators, and again, the results overwhelmingly indicated that the model developed here significantly improves on the fit obtained with a simple density specification.[7]

Entry and Exit Results

Perhaps the most important finding of this study is that the distribution of these events is not random, a distinct possibility when dealing with large numbers of independent events. Prior empirical studies of entry and exit processes have mainly concerned themselves with the effects of density, prior demographic events, and historical periods. Such studies have greatly informed organization theory's understanding of competition's role in shaping organizational populations, but the independent variables used in these models are proxies for environmental effects that the findings

TABLE 17.6   Partial Likelihood Estimates of Exit Rate Models by Strategy Group

	r-Specialist	K-Specialist	r-Generalist	K-Generalist
Population size				
Log number est. firms (t)	0.7746	27.1004*	−0.6328	0.8117
Log new firm indicator (t)	8.0581*	23.3963*	13.6620*	1.3322
Transistor regime(t)	1.6364*	−0.0879*	0.0917	1.0102*
Integrated circuit regime (t)	1.3572*	−0.0634*	0.0955	0.3806*
Microprocessor regime (t)	−0.9639*	−0.0436*	0.0491	0.4973*
Competitive relations				
r-Specialists (t)	—	0.1083*	0.0915*	−0.0590*
K-Specialists (t)	−0.0935*	—	−0.0311	0.0330*
r-Generalists (t)	0.5899*	−0.0377	—	0.4410*
K-Generalists (t)	−0.0455	0.3437*	−0.0372	—
Market resources				
Revenue (t)	−0.8416	0.9476*	−3.7214*	1.1218*
Total sales (t − 2)	0.0065	−0.0086*	0.0051	−0.0079*
Change in market size (t − 1)	−0.0044*	−0.0072*	−0.0032*	−0.0041*
Change in market size (t)	0.0074	−0.0051*	−0.0041*	0.0024
Percentage foreign sales (t)	−0.4964*	0.3092*	0.1040	−0.1707*
Foreign firm market share (t)	0.6827*	0.2481*	−0.5219	0.9796*
Financial resources				
Venture capital (t)	−0.0035	0.0032	0.0059	0.0269
Aggregate investment (t)	−0.2712*	−0.2187*	−0.0766	−0.5511*
Real interest (t)	−0.9568	0.4601*	−0.0231	0.5129*
Innovation patterns				
Design innovations (t − 2)	1.9057*	−0.5899	−0.5585*	−0.3899
Process innovations (t − 2)	1.1740*	−0.5854	−0.9172*	0.0340
Total patent activity (t)	−0.0215*	−0.0296*	0.0125*	0.0087*
Number of events	68	848	50	204
Number of observations	77	848	61	204
Degrees of freedom	15	15	15	15
Model chi-square	124.82	1365.89	59.50	327.85
Log likelihood ratio	.483	.420	.367	.458
Model significance	$p < .0001$	$p < .0001$	$p < .001$	$p < .0001$

NOTE: $*p < .05$.

presented here indicate are independent of density and historical period. Theoretically, this means that community development cannot be understood without information about the environmental carrying capacity's role in population growth.

The coefficients for the technological era indicators vary a great deal across eras and across populations. In general, the entry rate effect of the N^2 term increases across eras for all populations and the exit rate effect decreases, a pattern that should occur whenever an industry is becoming "established." There are a couple of minor inconsistencies in this result, so caution is in order in interpreting the finding. But given the primitive operationalization used here, any pattern is encouraging.

Financial resource availability is an important factor in firm entry and has implications for the survival of K-strategists. The availability of speculative venture funds is particularly important in explaining r-strategy entry, while aggregate investment and the cost of capital are important for the K-strategy populations (reduce exit rates). The effect of real interest rates on entries is somewhat puzzling, although interest rates are going to be high when increasing investment activity is putting a strain on capital availability. This was not an anticipated effect, but it is a reasonable explanation for this otherwise anomalous result.

All the strategic populations manufacturing semiconductors have grown as a function of market growth. Increasing revenue and new sales have accelerated entry rates, while exit rates have fallen with sales growth, revenue, and the volume of repeat sales. This generalization is qualified, however, by the negative effects of sales and lagged change in sales on entry rates. But once the importance of organizations as entrepreneur generators is recognized, it becomes apparent that part of the explanation is entrepreneurial activities during industry downturns. It is during such downturns that potential entrepreneurs are most likely to begin looking into other career options (Freeman and Brittain, 1986). The significance of this effect does not contradict the basic market resource finding but merely indicates that entry is influenced by competition at other levels.

Although the effects of innovation are not as general as those of the market, they are as important. The population strategies used to categorize firms capture the bets firms are making on how the environment is going to vary over time. A critical component of this gamble is management's guess about when innovations are going to take place and what form they are going to take. This choice process produces variation in entry patterns, while the insight supporting the strategic bet results in variable exit rates. The results also indicate that patent efforts by established firms created knowledge barriers to entry for all strategic populations, while decreasing the exit rates for specialist firms. Since specialists' product portfolios are much narrower than are those of generalists, it is not surprising that they benefit from the order that well-defined patent positions bring to a market.

The environmental turbulence that characterizes components manufacturing is a function of the unpredictability of market variations, competition, and technical change. The evolution of the community of firms producing electronic devices is linked to this turbulence in a way that reflects the strategic options defined by the environment and the competitive densities in the existing community. The result is a demography determined by selection, but there is a lot of human energy and creativity implicit in this process. The community of firms operating at any point in time may be a product of entry and exit processes, but entry and exit are manifestations of human actions. Arguing that selection processes govern industrial community evolution does not diminish this human role—it merely describes the structure within which human initiative operates.

The demographic volatility that characterizes electronic components manufacturing is not surprising given the volatility of semiconductor markets. The business uncertainties associated with this variation are difficult to manage, a task made even more arduous by the problem of anticipating the twists and turns that industry sales are prone to take when customers are actively double and triple ordering across several suppliers to ensure timely deliveries during shortages. These sources of uncertaintly exist because firms need resources controlled by environmental forces. Resource shortages can arise because competition makes it difficult to get timely deliveries, increases costs where supply is slow to react to demand, causes labor shortages for skilled employees, and allows customers to switch readily to other suppliers. Such market effects are the realization of increasing competitive densities, which make it more difficult both for new firms to enter and for marginal firms to do business. As competitive densities increase, these problems are exacerbated and population growth slows, because either entry is diminished or failures become more frequent.

Entry opportunities and exit rates are also influenced by density-independent events such as technical innovation, governmental regulatory changes, or historical occurrences such as wars, natural disasters, and territorial expansion. Density-independent selection may also change the nature of competition, but this change is brought about as a result of shifts in the environmental carrying capacity. The effect may be positive as well as negative, or may be disastrous for an established population while encouraging entry among innovating firms. While competitive density is expected to produce a decrease in the entry rate and an increase in the exit rate, density-independent selection is expected to result in *increased entries and increased exits*. And it is this impact on entries that determines the course of subsequent community evolution (Astley, 1985).

In semiconductors, major technological changes have precipitated periods of density-independent selection that have had a major impact on the industry, producing a large number of failures and significant entry opportunities. Firms operating in the industry share a reliance on knowledge, market, and financial resources, but firms in each strategic group are affected differently by environmental events. In addition, the impacts of environmental dislocations are not symmetric for entry and exit processes. For instance, the same process innovations that encourage entry by r-specialists also undermine the position of existing r-specialist producers, while playing to the strengths of the r-generalist population. Organization theorists and ecological researchers know little about how such interdependent effects shape community evolution. On the basis of the findings presented here, it is clear that such an understanding must build on empirical research on the relationship between carrying capacity dislocations and community evolution.

The firms participating in an industrial community at any time are the survivors in a social history of environmental dislocations, evolving technologies, redefined social norms, and changing institutional regulations (Tushman and Romanelli, 1985). The history of every industry includes firms that have failed (Freeman, 1982; Carroll, 1983), exploited new opportunities (Winter, 1971), been founded in response to conditions that no longer exist (Stinchcombe, 1965; Delacroix and Carroll, 1983), and retreated into market niches protected from competition (Carroll, 1985). Such histories are not the product of a time series of density responses. They are defined by organizations' entering and exiting in a context of environmental change. These demographic processes are not independent of the environment but rather reflect individual and organizational responses to changing business and community conditions.

This study raises questions about the relationship between ecological and institutional arguments. One interpretation of the finding presented here is that they document the institutional structure of the semiconductor industry, the role of evolving definitions of capital and institutionalized rules for sharing knowledge on community development, and the history-dependent processes that define the industry's role in society. It is certainly true that institutional insights played a key role in the arguments about carrying capacity variation presented in this chapter. But to see the argument presented here as an integration of institutional and ecological arguments is to misunderstand the power of the ecological model's simple characterization of organization populations and communities.

The intention here is not integration. Rather, the point of the model developed in this chapter and the empirical study is to show that ecological explanations can subsume institutional arguments. The tension between institutional and ecological theorists that has done so much to advance organizational research would be ill served by any other position.

Notes

1. This interpretation was suggested by Paul DiMaggio. The author gratefully acknowledges the insight.

2. The careful reader will note that c_{ij} is an inverse function of K_i, indicating that strength of competition varies with environmental munificence. However, c_{ij} also includes N_i, which, when multiplied with the carrying capacity specification developed here, results in a ratio of population size to resource levels. Since these covary with time, their net impact is 1, and the specification reduces to equation (8). It may be theoretically fruitful to examine potential time varying properties of s_{ij}, but it is an issue beyond the scope of this chapter.

3. The term "strategy" is used here to refer to characteristic population-level parameters and should not be interpreted as a property of firms.

4. *Electronics* and the *Buyers' Guide* are published by McGraw-Hill. The company has a full-time staff person whose job is to keep the *Buyers' Guide* listings current, as well as sales people who service advertising accounts. Each firm in the guide is contacted yearly and any new information is added to the forthcoming volume. The McGraw-Hill staffers involved need to maintain the currency of the listings because these are critical to their job of selling advertising. Furthermore, it is in their interest to produce a comprehensive listing in order to maintain the publication's appeal as a purchasing source. The *Buyers' Guide* was the primary source for information on the dates of firm participation in the industry. These data were checked against directories of manufacturers for the New England states, California, Arizona, and Texas, which accounted for 67 percent of all semiconductor firms in 1972 (Webbink, 1977). This check indicated that the *Buyers' Guide* coverae of the industry is 95.9 percent, and most of the firms that were not included were very small. The unincluded firms identified during the directory search were added to the data base.

5. Actual year of entry into tube production (Tyne, 1977) is included for firms that predated the *Buyers' Guide*.

6. The first and final observations correspond with entry and exit in most cases but are the 1947 observations for firms founded prior to that year and the 1981 observations for firms with no terminal event.

7. Since the model developed in this chapter partials the N^2 term across technological eras, it is not possible to construct a hierarchical model test of this specification relative to the typical density specification. The model estimated here does significantly improve on the density specification, however, regardless of what permutation is used to conduct a hierachical model test.

18

Organization-Environment Coevolution

JOEL A. C. BAUM AND JITENDRA V. SINGH

In his influential treatment of organizational theory, Scott (1987) distinguishes among organizations as natural, rational, and open systems. This last view of organizations as open systems, which emerged over roughly the last three decades as a counterpoint to earlier closed systems thinking, has been a dominant theme in theories of organization. Thus, structural contingency theory (Lawrence and Lorsch, 1967), strategic contingency theory (Hickson et al., 1971), institutionalization theory (Meyer and Rowan, 1977; Meyer and Scott, 1983), resource dependence theory (Pfeffer and Salancik, 1978), and population ecology theory (Hannan and Freeman, 1977, 1989) have all emphasized the relationships between organizations and their external environments, although specific treatments differ by theory. In most approaches organizations tend to become isomorphic with their environments through processes of either adaptation or selection (or combination of the two). In large part, most theories have studied organizational change in relation to exogenous environmental change.[1]

Examined less frequently is how organizations (and populations) systematically influence their environments, and how organizational environments, fundamentally comprised of other organizations and populations (DiMaggio and Powell, 1983), in turn influence those organizations. The essence of feedback is a circle of interactions; the patterns of behavior of any two variables in a feedback loop are linked, each influencing the other and in turn being influenced by the behavior of the other. The concept of feedback is intimately linked with the concepts of interdependence and mutual or circular causality (Richardson, 1991). In a feedback perspective, the unidirectional view of cause-and-effect relationships gives way to a circular, looplike view of mutual causality.

In this chapter we attempt to study the simultaneous evolution, or *coevolution,* of organizations and their environments. The chapters by Rosenkopf and Tushman and Van de Ven and Garud in this volume also adopt broadly similar coevolutionary approaches. Whereas Rosenkopf and Tushman study the coevolution of organiza-

This research was supported, in part, by a grant from the Office of Research Administration, University of Toronto. We are grateful to Charles Lumsden for helpful discussions on coevolution and Paul DiMaggio, Daniel Levinthal, Joe Porac, Raaj Sah, and Larry Van Horn for comments on an earlier draft. For assistance with data collection and coding we also thank Debbie Freeman, Brian Gaon, Gayle Greenbaum, and Sonja Saksida.

tions and technology in the early evolution of radio systems, Van de Ven and Garud examine the roles of technical and institutional events in the emergence of a biomedical innovation, cochlear implants. The study of coevolution fundamentally is a feedback approach to the study of organization-environment relations. As a result, it forces a different view of organization-environment relations than is usually adopted. A coevolutionary approach assumes that changes may occur in *all* interacting populations or organizations, permitting change to be driven by both direct interactions and feedback from the rest of the system.

What Is Organization-Environment Coevolution?

Central to the concept of organization-environment coevolution are the interactions between organizations and their environments and the consequences of these interactions for the dynamics of the organization-environment systems. A coevolutionary approach requires that sets of coacting organizations and their environments be the object of study and changes in *all* interacting organizations be allowed to result not only from the direct interactions between pairs of organizations but also by indirect feedback through the rest of the system (Roughgarden, 1983). This feedback is seen as the structure underlying dynamic system behavior and is viewed as responsible for the behavior of organization-environment systems. For coevolutionary ideas to apply in a particular system, the variables composing the system (organizations or environmental resources, for example) must interact. The distinctive feature of coevolution is that an organization that stimulates the evolution of another organization is, in turn, itself responsive to that evolution, and the response is predictable. Coevolution can be direct or diffuse. In *direct coevolution,* one population evolves in response to another population, which has itself evolved in response to the first population (Janzen, 1980). In *diffuse coevolution,* one or more populations evolve in response to several other populations in a broader ecological community (Futuyama and Slatkin, 1983).

The goal of coevolutionary inquiry is understanding how the structure of direct interactions and feedback within organization-environment systems gives rise to their dynamic behavior. Coevolutionary inquiry attempts to predict how variables in the system respond to changes in other system variables or in changes to the structure of the system itself. In some cases a coevolutionary equilibrium may be established. In such cases, the conventional approach of treating the environment as exogenous may be quite appropriate. In others, there may be no coevolutionary equilibrium and organizational evolution may continue over long periods. The properties of coevolutionary systems are often not obvious. Coevolution implies nonlinear feedback among interacting populations, and such nonlinearities can substantially complicate attempts to understand evolutionary change (Levins, 1983).

Why Study Coevolution?

The usual approach to studying organizations, which involves modeling relations between independent and dependent variables, is likely to be quite appropriate in simple systems of relationships that do not involve complex feedback processes. However, as one moves to phenomena which are moderately complex, the system properties (such as feedback) become more important. In such systems of relationships among variables, it is less meaningful to separate dependent from independent variables. Changes in any one variable are caused endogenously by changes in others. Such systems of relationships are instances where a coevolutionary approach can add the most value. The key issue is that as a result of higher order feedback processes, the effects of changes in one variable frequently belay intuitions based on simple cause-effect logic of linear relations between independent and dependent variables. Although the specific example of a coevolutionary process we discuss later is in the domain of community ecology, we think coevolutionary thinking has much greater generality (for example, see Rosenkopf and Tushman, chapter 19, and Van de Ven, chapter 20, this volume).

An Application to Coevolution in Ecological Communities

Although the applicability of coevolutionary thinking has broader scope, we think a useful starting point is the study of community ecology, an important theme in recent organizational ecology research (Singh and Lumsden, 1990). The evolutionary significance of the interactions among organizational populations is widely recognized in the population and community ecology literatures (Astley, 1985; Brittain and Wholey, 1988; Carroll, 1984; Fombrun, 1986, 1988; Hannan and Freeman, 1989). Interactions between organizations create organizational communities, networks of organizations that exist with unit properties of their own (Barnett and Carroll, 1987; Hawley, 1986). Community ecology investigates the evolution of patterns of structure represented in the interactions among populations and considers the system-level consequences of these interactions for the dynamics of coacting sets of populations (Astley, 1985; Hannan and Freeman, 1989). Community-level interactions moderate population dynamics by altering the selection pressures that organizations face, making it difficult to account for population dynamics by referring only to the focal population (Fombrun, 1988). Recently, studies of the evolution of community-level interactions between organizational populations have appeared, and the consequences of the interactions among populations for the structure and dynamics of ecological communities are now emerging as an important area of inquiry (Barnett, 1990; Barnett and Carroll, 1987; Brittain and Wholey, 1988).

While such studies clearly illustrate how ecological interactions can influence the dynamics of differentiated populations of organizations, most have not formally examined the implications of feedback in the network of ecological interactions for the coevolutionary dynamics of the systems in their entirety.[2]

There are four main sections of this chapter. In the first section we illustrate several key properties of coevolutionary systems. In the second we introduce the technical aspects of the qualitative approach called *loop analysis* (Puccia and Levins, 1985), we employ to model coevolution. In the third section, we derive and test qualitative predictions about coevolution in the child care system of Metropolitan Toronto based on several models we advance. Finally, we discuss some of the implications of a coevolutionary approach for the study of evolution in ecological communities of organizations and, more generally, the study of organization-environment relations.

Coevolution in Ecological Communities

In the social sciences, feedback systems are frequently captured in terms of differential equations. The nonlinear feedback idea underlying the structure of coevolutionary systems is present in the differential and difference equations used to represent dynamic phenomena in the natural and social sciences. For example, the Lotka-Volterra or density-dependent model of population growth provides an instance of feedback embedded in differential equations:

$$\frac{dN}{dt} = rN\left(1 - \frac{N}{K}\right),\qquad\qquad (1a)$$

where dN/dt is the growth rate of the population over time dt, N is the size of the population, K is the carrying capacity of the population, and r is the intrinsic growth rate of the population. In the Lotka-Volterra model the growth rate depends on how far the population is from its carrying capacity. When the carrying capacity K is large relative to the number of population members N, $(1 - N/K)$ approaches unity and the growth rate responds to rN, which represents the tendency of the population to grow at an exponential rate when N is low. However, as N approaches K, $(1 - N/K)$ approaches zero and the growth rate is slowed by competition as the population uses up available resources. Eventually $(1 - N/K)$ dominates, bringing the population's growth to an end. Should N exceed K, $(1 - N/K)$ becomes negative and the growth rate becomes a rate of decline. The result is an S-shaped logistic growth curve.[3] Thus, over time, the population changes its own growth tendencies. In feedback terms, the system displays a shift in *loop dominance* (Richardson, 1991). When N is low, the positive effect of r dominates and increasingly rapid growth occurs. When N gets high, the damping effect of $(1 - N/K)$ begins to dominate and the growth rate begins to decelerate, becoming zero when N reaches K.

Equation (1a) models the density-dependent selection acting on the growth of a solitary population but does not consider interactions with other populations. However, it is difficult to understand the dynamics of a single population of organizations in isolation because the dynamics of populations are commonly linked with one another (Fombrun, 1988; Hannan and Freeman, 1989). When an evolving population interacts with other populations its growth depends on the nature and strength of *all* its ecological interactions with other populations. Consider, for example, the simple case of two competing populations. Competition can be incorporated by modifying equation (1a) to reflect the effect of the size of one population on the growth rate of another:

$$\frac{dN_A}{dt} = rN_A\left(1 - \frac{N_A}{K_A} - \alpha_{AB}\frac{N_B}{K_A}\right)$$
$$\frac{dN_B}{dt} = rN_B\left(1 - \frac{N_B}{K_B} - \alpha_{BA}\frac{N_A}{K_B}\right). \qquad (1b)$$

As the second equation in (1b) shows, the system is now composed of two populations A and B, which affect each other's growth rates through competition. The second equation is the mirror of the first. The terms α_{AB} and α_{BA} are competition coefficients between populations A and B. These coefficients represent the proportional effect each member in one population has on the carrying capacity of the other. Thus, the presence of a member of population A (B) reduces by the fraction α_{AB} (α_{BA}) the resources available for population B (A).

Since the concept of a feedback loop is fundamentally visual, we will use visual terms to help describe the loop concept underlying feedback and mutual causality. Figure 18.1 shows the *loop structure* and *qualitative predictions* for this competitive system.[4] In the figure, following standard visual notation (Puccia and Levins, 1985), a line with an arrowhead is a *positive link* (+), which signifies an enhancing effect. A line with a circlehead (i.e., small circle enclosing a dash) is a *negative link* (−) and represents a decreasing effect. The links connect the *variables* (represented by the large circles) that make up the system being studied. The competitive system in figure 18.1 is composed of two variables A and B, the size of population N_A and the size of population N_B, respectively. A link from A to B means that A *causally influences* B. Thus, if A influences B, and B in turn influences A, the pair of links connecting A and B form a loop of mutual causality or feedback. Each feedback loop has a *polarity*. The polarity of a loop reflects the loop's tendency either to reinforce or to dampen a change in any one of its elements. A loop that tends to reinforce or amplify a change is a *positive* feedback loop. A loop that tends to diminish a change is a *negative* feedback loop. In a positive feedback loop, an increase (decrease) in A feeds around the loop, causing A to increase (decrease) still further. A negative loop has the opposite effect. The concept of loop polarity is at the heart of the analytic and explanatory power of loop analysis.

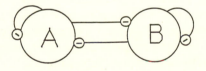

	A	B			A	B
INCREASE A	−	+		INCREASE A	+	−
INCREASE B	+	−		INCREASE B	−	+

*Assumes competition dominates

*Assumes self-effects dominate

FIG. 18.1   Competition model

Links that connect a variable to itself are *self-effect* links. Self-effects result from other variables in the system. For example, self-effect links are used to show that the growth rate of the variable depends on its own level (i.e., a population dampens its own growth rate by using up resources). If these variables are included in the model, the self-effect links are omitted, but if the variable is not in the model, then the self-effect would be necessary. However, introducing more variables into the models in order to encompass complexity makes computations increasingly unwieldy. Therefore, these self-effects are frequently used to model the self-damping effects of variables on their own growth (Puccia and Levins, 1985:79). This simplification does not alter any other properties of the system of interest. The table of predictions shows how the level of each variable will change (increase, decrease) or remain unchanged in response to a change in its own value, or that of any other variable in the system.[5]

The competitive system model in equation (1b) has several noteworthy properties. In contrast to the logistic growth trajectory represented by the single-population model in equation (1a), the competitive system is potentially unstable.[6] If the positive feedback loop formed by the competitive interactions between populations A and B is weaker than the product of the self-effect links the system is stable, leaving the size of each population at some equilibrium level. But if the competitive interactions are stronger than the self-effects the system is unstable, and a change in the size of either population initiates a vicious circle (e.g., an increase in A lowers A, which lowers B, which in turn lowers B, lowering A, . . .). This graphically illustrates the general result that coexistence of competitors requires that the effects of competition within populations must be stronger than the competitive effects between populations (Hannan and Freeman, 1989:101–2). This result can also be derived from the equations in (1b). Setting the equations in (1b) equal to zero and solving for the nonzero equilibrium values of N_A and N_B shows that stable coexistence requires that $1/\alpha_{BA} < K_B/K_A < \alpha_{AB}$. Therefore, populations whose competition coefficients approach unity can coexist only under a particular K_A/K_B ratio. Any disturbance is likely to move the system away from the conditions that support coexistence, and the system will not tend to restore itself (Hannan and Freeman, 1989:101). The competitive system also helps to illustrate the counterintuitive effects of indirect feedback on system dynamics. Even though all direct links in this competitive system are negative, as a result of higher-level feedback in the system, half the qualitative predictions are positive.

There are many other possible interactions among populations. For example, the equations in (1c) show a model of a predator-prey system:

$$\frac{dN_A}{dt} = rN_A\left(1 - \frac{N_A}{K_A}\right) - cN_AN_B$$

$$\frac{dN_B}{dt} = cN_BN_A - rN_B\left(1 - \frac{N_B}{K_B}\right),$$

(1c)

where A is the prey population and B is the predator population. This system assumes that (1) in the absence of predators (i.e., $N_B = 0$), prey exhibit logistic

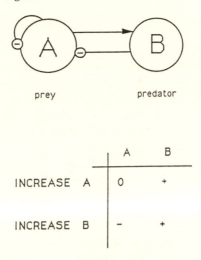

prey   predator

	A	B
INCREASE A	0	+
INCREASE B	–	+

FIG. 18.2 Predator-prey model

growth; (2) in the absence of prey (i.e., $cN_A = 0$), predators die out; (3) the growth rates of prey and predators are proportioned to the numbers in each population (i.e., $-cN_AN_B$ and cN_BN_A). Figure 18.2 illustrates the loop structure and presents the table of predictions for this predator-prey system. The self-effect link for the predator population (B) is omitted since its resource, the self-damped prey population (A), is included in the model. The difference in the loop diagrams for the competitive and predator-prey systems is the positive link from A to B. This change is sufficient to stabilize the system. The predator-prey system again illustrates the effects of higher-level feedback in the system. As the table of predictions shows, although the predator population has no self-effect, increases in the size of the predator population increase its own abundance. This model also shows that a variable may be linked to itself and to other variables, may change other variables but not change itself. For example, while an increase in the size of the prey population is predicted to increase the size of the predator population, and even though the prey population is self-damping, it has no effect on itself.

These simple models help to show how the dynamics of evolving populations depend fundamentally on the nature and strength of *all* their ecological interactions. The different patterns of interaction defining the competitive and predator-prey systems substantively influence the growth of the populations in these systems and the properties of the systems (e.g., their stability) reflected in the configuration of qualitative predictions. The nonobvious predictions for several of the direct links demonstrate the complicating effects of higher-order feedback. In addition, the model of the competitive system illustrates the potentially critical role of the relative intensity of interactions between populations for the dynamics of systems and their evolution. These examples also demonstrate how loop models can be used to describe the mathematical models created to represent and study the dynamic behavior of complex systems. In the next section, we provide a more detailed description of loop modeling methods.

Qualitative Modeling of Coevolutionary Systems

The loop modeling methods we employ in this paper focus on qualitative understanding rather than numerical prediction—knowing whether variables increase, decrease, or remain unchanged, rather than specifying by precisely how much. Loop analysis is most powerful when the systems under study are of an intermediate level of complexity. In highly interconnected systems, some predictions will be ambiguous because relative strengths of interactions will determine the sign of a prediction. In cases where reciprocal interactions are absent loop analysis does not add very much to our understanding. In the domain of complex social systems, this approach has several advantages. It permits the inclusion of variables which are difficult or impossible to measure, as long as the direction of the effect of one variable on another is known. When the structure of the system is unknown, alternatives can be modeled to uncover important differences among them. Thus an important strength of loop analysis is its independence from quantification. We now introduce several terms and attributes of loop models that add to the basic terms defined earlier. Our discussion of loop analysis techniques draws on Puccia and Levins (1985, chapters 2–4), which is the basic reference to the analytical approach described here. For purposes of comparability, we adopt the standard notation used in Puccia and Levins (1985).

Loop Models: Terms, Properties, and Predictions

Paths and Path Lengths. Consider the three-variable system illustrated in figure 18.3. In the figure, a *path* is a series of links starting at one variable and ending on another, without crossing a variable twice. For example, the path from P to H is $-a_{HP}$ and the path from P to N is $(-a_{HP})(-a_{NH})$, or more simply, $a_{HP}a_{NH}$. The number of links in a path determines its *path length*. Path length is also equal to 1 less than the number of variables along the path. For example, the length of the path from P to N, $a_{HP}a_{NH}$, is 2 since the path contains two links and three variables. Clearly, there can be more than one path between two variables. For example, the path from P to N is either $a_{HP}a_{NH}$ or the single link a_{NP}. The symbol for paths from variable i to variable j of length $k-1$, where k is the number of variables along the path, is $p_{ji}^{(k)}$. For each path there is a *complementary subsystem:* the subsystem of variables and their interconnections which are not included in the path. The complementary subsystem has $n-k$ variables, where n is the number of variables in the total system and k is the number of variables in the path. The symbol denoting the complementary subsystem is $F_{n-k}^{(comp)}$.

Loops and Loop Lengths. A *loop* is a path that returns to its starting point without crossing any variable twice. In figure 18.3, going from P to N, N to H, and H to P is a loop which can be written $(a_{NP}a_{HN}a_{PH})$ or [PNH]. Unlike a path length, a *loop length* has the same number of links as variables. The loop [PNH] has a length of three. Figure 18.3 contains the loops given in table 18.1.

Loops are either *conjunct* or *disjunct*. Conjunct loops have at least one common variable. Disjunct loops have no common variables. For example, in figure 18.3, the loops of length 2, $[-HN]$ and $[-HP]$, are conjunct loops because each includes the variable H. In contrast, the loops of length 1, $[-N]$ and $[-H]$, are disjunct loops

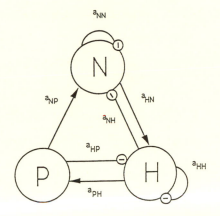

	P	N	H
INCREASE P	+	+	−
INCREASE N	+	+	0
INCREASE H	+	+	0

Fɪɢ. 18.3   Three variable example model

because they have no variables in common. The conjunct and disjunct loops in figure 18.3 are given in table 18.2.

Feedback and Feedback Levels. The term *feedback* signifies that an action or activity initiated by someone or something sets in motion activities or responses by others which then affect the original source of the activity (Puccia and Levins, 1983:17). As described previously, feedback can be either positive or negative. *Positive feedback* occurs when an increase (decrease) in one variable causes other variables to change in ways that increase (decrease) the initial variable further. Conversely, *negative feedback* occurs when an increase (decrease) in a variable results in changes in other variables that lead to a decrease (increase) in the initial variable.

The *feedback level* is the number of variables in the feedback loop. The feedback levels in any system can range from 1 to the total number of variables in the system. Feedback at any level k, where k is the number of variables in the feedback loop, is denoted as F_k. Feedback at level k is found by determining all loops of length k or products of *disjunct* loops that have a combined length of k, and then adding them together. More formally,

$$F_k = \sum_{m=1}^{k} (-1)^{m+1} L(m,k), \tag{2a}$$

TABLE 18.1   Loops and Loop Lengths for Figure 18.3

Loops of Length 1	*Loops of Length 2*	*Loops of Length 3*
(i) $(-a_{NN})$ or $[-N]$	(i) $(-a_{HN}a_{NH})$ or $[-NH]$	(i) $(a_{NP}a_{HN}a_{PH})$ or $[PNH]$
(ii) $(-a_{HH})$ or $[-H]$	(ii) $(-a_{HP}a_{PH})$ or $[-PH]$	

TABLE 18.2   Conjunct and Disjunct Loops for Figure 18.3

Conjunct Loops	*Disjunct Loops*
$[-N]$ and $[-HN]$	$[-N]$ and $[-H]$
$[-N]$ and $[NPH]$	$[-N]$ and $[-HP]$
$[-H]$ and $[-HN]$	
$[-H]$ and $[-HP]$	
$[-H]$ and $[NPH]$	
$[-HN]$ and $[-HP]$	
$[-HN]$ and $[NPH]$	
$[-HP]$ and $[NPH]$	

TABLE 18.3   Feedback Calculations for Figure 18.3

Level $(k =)$	*Feedback*	$\Sigma\,(-1)^{m+1}L(m, k)$
0	$F_0 \equiv -1$	
1	$F_1 = [-N] + [-H]$	$(-1)^{1+1}L(1, 1) + (-1)^{1+1}L(1, 1)$
2	$F_2 = [-NH] + [-HP] + (-1)[-N][-H]$	$(-1)^{1+1}L(1, 2) + (-1)^{1+1}L(1, 2)$ $+ (-1)^{2+1}L(2, 2)$
3	$F_3 = [NPH] + (-1)[-N][-HP]$	$(-1)^{1+1}L(1, 3) + (-1)^{2+1}L(2, 3)$

NOTE: Feedback at level 0 is defined for all systems as -1. See Puccia and Levins (1985; chapter 6).

where $L(m, k)$ has the meaning m disjunct loops of length k. For example, $L(1, 2)$ signifies one disjunct loop of length 2; there are two variables in a single loop. L (2, 3) signifies a combination of two disjunct loops whose total length is 3. The feedback calculations for figure 18.3 at each level k are presented in table 18.3.

System Stability. What are the properties that determine the stability of a system? That is, if the variables in the system are at some levels (density, volume, mass, rate, for example), and then something happens to the system, what determines what happens to these values? In a stable system the variables might return to their original levels when changed. In an unstable system, when changed, the variables may increase, decrease, or oscillate forever. There are two criteria for stability in loop models. First, feedback at all levels greater than 0 (i.e., F_0) must be negative. That is, $F_k < 0$, for all k. Second, negative feedback in high level loops cannot be too strong compared to negative feedback in lower level loops. The second criterion only applies when there are more than two variables in the system. For systems of three or four variables the second criterion for stability is $F_1F_2 + F_3 > 0$.[7] Thus, a combination of both negative feedback (criterion one) and positive feedback (criterion two) contributes to the system stability (Puccia and Levins, 1985:28). Using the feedback calculations shown, the stability criteria for figure 18.3 are given in table 18.4. Thus the system in figure 18.3 is stable as long as the assumption about the relative strengths of short and long loops holds.

Predicting Change. For any loop model, a table of predictions can be constructed to show how the level of each variable in the system will change (increase, decrease, remain unchanged) in response to a change in its own value or that of any other variable.[8] To predict the direction of change in the equilibrium value of variable X_j due to a parameter change in the growth rate of variable i we use the following equation:

$$\frac{\partial X_j^*}{\partial c} = \frac{\sum_{i,k} \left(\frac{\partial f_i}{\partial c}\right) (p_{ji}^{(k)})(F_{n-k}^{(comp)})}{F_n}. \tag{2b}$$

The equation reads, take all functions that include the parameter being changed ($\partial f_i/\partial c$, where f_i is the function for the growth rate of the variable X_i, and c is a parameter that determines that growth rate of variable i), outline each possible path ($p_{ji}^{(k)}$) from variable i to the jth variable (X_j) whose equilibrium value is being calculated, multiply each path by the feedback of the appropriate complementary subsystem ($F_{n-k}^{(comp)}$).[9] Sum over all functions and paths, and divide by the overall system feedback (F_n) (Puccia and Levins, 1985:41). For example, the predicted effect of a parameter change in P on the equilibrium value of the variable N is calculated as follows:

1. Let the parameter change ($\partial f_p/\partial c$) for the variable P be positive (+). The prediction for a negative parameter change in N is obtained by reversing the sign of the final prediction.
2. There are two paths from P to N, one of length 2, [PN], or $p_{NP}^{(2)}$, which has a positive (+) value, and one of length 3, [PHN], or p_{NP}^3, which also has a positive (+) value.

TABLE 18.4 Stability Calculations for Figure 18.3

Stability condition 1: $F_1 < 0$, for $i = 1-3$

Level (k =)	Feedback	Feedback Value
1	$F_1 = [-H] + [-N]$	$F_1 < 0$, negative (−) feedback
2	$F_2 = [-NH] + [-HP] - [N][H]$	$F_2 < 0$, negative (−) feedback
3	$F_3 = [NPH] - [N][HP]$	$F_3 < 0$ if $|[N][HP]| > |[NPH]|$ (i.e., short loops are stronger than long loops)

Stability condition 2: $F_1F_2 + F_3 > 0$

$$= \{[-H] + [-N])\} \{[-HP] + [-HN] + [-H][-N])\} + \{[NPH] - [N][HP]\}$$
$$= \{[-H] + [-N])\} \{[-HP] + [-HN] + [-H][-N])\}$$
$$= [-H][-HP] + [-H][-HN] + [-H][-H][-N] + [-N][-HP] + [-N][-HN]$$
$$+ [-N][-H][-N]$$
$$= [H][HP] + [H][HN] + [H][H][N] + [N][HP] + [N][HN] + [N][N][H]$$
$$= > 0, \text{ positive (+) feedback}$$

3. The complementary subsystem to [PN] is [H]. The complementary feedback is $F_{n-k}^{(comp)}$, where n is the total number of variables in the system, and k *is* the number of variables along the path [PN]) $= F_{3-2}^{(comp)} = F_1^{(comp)} = [-H]$, which has a negative $(-)$ value. There is no complementary subsystem to [PHN]. Therefore, $F_{3-3}^{(comp)} = F_0^{(comp)}$, which by definition has the value of -1.

4. The overall system feedback F_n, is F_3, which, as shown in earlier calculations, is negative $(-)$ if the assumption that short loops are stronger than long loops holds.

5. Thus, $(\partial f_p/\partial c) = (+), \Sigma p_{NP}^{(k)} = (+), \Sigma F_{n-k}^{(comp)} = (-), F_3 = (-)$. Therefore, $\Sigma(\partial f_p/\partial c)(p_{NP}^{(k)})(F_{n-k}^{(comp)})/F_3 = (+)(+)(-)/(-) = (+)$. In other words, an increase in the growth rate of P is predicted to increase in the equilibrium abundance of N.

The remaining calculations for constructing a table of predictions for figure 18.3 are presented in table 18.5. We calculate the effects of a parameter change in each variable i sequentially. The calculations are based on a positive parameter change, that is, the change in $\partial f_i/\partial c$ is positive $(+)$. As noted, the predictions for a negative parameter change (i.e., the changes in parameters that result from growth rate decline) are obtained by reversing the signs for the effects. Also, recall that the overall system feedback (F_n) in figure 18.3 F_3 is negative $(-)$ if short loops are stronger than long loops. This holds true for all calculations.

The predicted effects derived in table 18.5 are summarized in the table of predictions in figure 18.3. These calculations help illustrate how nonobvious responses

TABLE 18.5   Qualitative Prediction Calculations for Figure 18.3

X_i	$\partial f_i/\partial c$	X_j	$p_{ji}^{(k)}$	Path Value	Complementary Subsystem	$F_{3-k}^{(comp)}$	$\Sigma(\partial f_i/\partial c)(p_{ji}^{(k)})(F_{n-k}^{(comp)})/F_n$
P	(+)	P	$p_{PP}^{(1)}$	(1)	[NH]		
						$[-NH] - [H][N] = (-)$	$(+)(1)(-)/(-) = (+)$
		N	$p_{NP}^{(2)}$	(+)	[H]	$[-H] = (-)$	$(+)(+)(-)/(-) = (+)$
		N	$p_{NP}^{(3)}$	(+)	[∅]	$F_0^{(comp)} = -1$	$(+)(+)(-)/(-) = (+)$
		H	$p_{HP}^{(3)}$	(−)	[∅]	$F_0^{(comp)} = -1$	$(+)(-)(-1)/(-) = (-)$
N	(+)	N	$p_{NN}^{(1)}$	(1)	[HP]		
		H	$p_{HN}^{(2)}$	(+)	[P]	$[-HP] = (-)$	$(+)(1)(-)/(-) = (+)$
		P	$p_{PN}^{(3)}$	(+)	[∅]	$F_1^{(comp)} = 0$	$(+)(+)(0)/(-) = (0)$
H	(+)	H	$p_{HH}^{(1)}$	(1)	[PN]	$F_0^{(comp)} = -1$	$(+)(+)(-1)/(-) = (+)$
						$F_2^{(comp)} = 0$	$(+)(1)(0)/(-) = (0)$
		P	$p_{PH}^{(2)}$	(+)	[N]	$[-N] = (-)$	$(+)(+)(-)/(-) = (+)$
		N	$p_{NH}^{(2)}$	(−)	[P]	$F_1^{(comp)} = 0$	$(+)(-)(0)/(-) = (0)$
		N	$p_{NH}^{(3)}$	(+)	[∅]	$F_0^{(comp)} = -1$	$(+)(+)(-1)/(-) = (+)$

NOTE: The value of the path from a variable to itself is defined as unity: $p_{ii}^{(k)} \equiv p_{ii}^{(1)} \equiv p_{ii}^{(0)} \equiv 1$ (Puccia and Levins, 1985:36)

of variables to parameter changes in other system variables occur because the responses of variables depend not only on the direct relations of the variables themselves but also on feedback in the rest of the system. A variable may change in a direction opposite from what common sense would lead us to predict. For example, while N is directly self-damping, the predicted effect of a parameter increase in N on the equilibrium level of N is positive ($+$). This is a result of the combined effects of the negative feedback in the complementary subsystem for the path [N] and the overall system. A variable may be linked to other variables, may change other variables, but may not change itself. For example, while parameter changes in the variable H are predicted to affect both P and N (although the effect on N is ambiguous, as discussed later), it has no effect on itself. This occurs because the complementary feedback for the self-effect link [$-$N] is zero. The direct effect of a variable may not be observed at the point of contact, but only in a variable several steps away. For example, while N has a direct link to H but not to P, parameter changes in N affect P but not N. This occurs because the complementary feedback for the path [NH] is zero. The calculations also show how ambiguity can arise in feedback systems. In this case, the ambiguity in the effect of a parameter change in H on the equilibrium abundance of N results from the different values of the two possible paths from H to N (i.e., [$-$HN] and [HPN]).

This completes the discussion of the technical aspects of loop models and loop analysis. The use of loop models, however, only begins with these mechanics. Using these modeling techniques we now derive and test qualitative predictions about the child care system of Metropolitan Toronto from several loop models we advance in order to show some of the kinds of coevolutionary thinking that loop modeling permits.

Coevolution in a Child Care System

Qualitative models are built to answer questions about an event or activity to understand or explain better a set of observations. Variables of interest are partially decided by the reasons for building the model and partially by the system structure. Here we build several models representing the child care system in Metropolitan Toronto during the period 1971–89. We begin the process of model building with a brief description of the basic variables in the system: sizes of organizational populations, demand for services, and government subsidization.[10] We use this information to postulate models of the system. We build several alternative models of the system and compare the predictions derived from the different models. These differences become the focus of study as the different tables of predictions are matched to observed correlations among the system variables during the 1971–89 period.

Child Care System Variables

Child Care Organization Populations. Since the Day Nurseries Act was established in 1946, child care organizations in Ontario have been required to obtain an annual operating license from the Ontario Ministry of Community and Social Services. Among other things, the minimum standards for licensing include program director and staff qualifications, staff/child ratios, program content, and wide-ranging facility requirements. The Day Nurseries Act distinguishes two types of child care organizations: day care centers and nursery schools. *Day care centers* are licensed to provide full-time (more than six consecutive hours) collective care to five or more children from birth up to and including nine years of age. They continue to provide day-long care to children from low-income and single-parent households and, increasingly, dual-income households. In contrast, *nursery schools* are licensed to provide part-time (less than six consecutive hours) educational programs to five or more children aged two and one-half up to and including five years. Nurseries provide preschool-aged children with an enriching educational environment for a few hours each day. The part-time and educational nature of the services provided by nurseries limits their client to relatively high-income households who value enrichment experiences for their children but do not require full-time care for them.

As a result of the differences in their services, day cares and nursery schools also possess distinct configurations of human and capital assets (Baum, 1989). In part, these differences arise from staff and facility requirements specified in the Day Nurseries Act for different ages of children and program length. The staffs of these two kinds of child care organizations also tend to differ in their educational backgrounds. Consistent with the educational orientation of nurseries, their staffs tend to have university degrees in early childhood or primary-level education or certification in a particular theory or approach to early-childhood education (e.g., Montessori and Adlerian). By comparison, the staff at day cares tend to have community college diplomas in child care work or early-childhood education.

In recognition of their relatively distinct services, client niches, and configurations of human and capital resources, we treat day care centers (DCCs) and nursery schools as distinct populations (McKelvey, 1982). Therefore, we define population size separately for day care and nursery as the number of each of these types of child care organizations in Metropolitan Toronto at the start of each year. These data were compiled by using two sources. The Community Information Center of Metropolitan Toronto's annual *Directory of Day Cares and Nursery Schools in Metropolitan Toronto,* which began publication in 1971, provided detailed information on all child care organizations in Metropolitan Toronto. The Ministry of Community and Social Services maintains annual licensing records of all day cares and nurseries in Ontario, starting in January 1979, in its *Day Nurseries Information System.* These archives provided additional information on these organizations and cross-reference to the *Directory.*

Demand for Day Care. The demand for day care is largely a function of the number of children and the nature of the family. For example, Rose-Ackerman (1988) found that the number of children in single-parent households and the percentage of women in the work force significantly influenced the demand for DCC services in the United States. Additionally, Baum and Oliver (1991, 1992) found that increases in the percentage of women in the work force lowered the mortality rate and increased the founding rate of day care. Therefore, following Baum and Singh (1992,

1993), we measured the demand for day care in each year with the following equation:

$$DCC\ demand = ED + \%WW(NC - ED - EN)$$
$$+ \%SP[(NC - ED - EN)(1 - \%WW)], \quad (3)$$

where *ED* and *EN* are, respectively, the number of children enrolled in DCCs and nurseries, *NC* is the number of children from birth to 10 years of age, *%WW* is the percentage of women in the work force on a full-time basis, and *%SP* is the percentage of households with children from birth to 10 years of age that are single-parent. In equation (3) the demand for day care comprises three additive components. The first is the number of children who are currently enrolled. The second is an estimate of the number of children with working mothers who are not enrolled. The third is an estimate of the number of single-parent children who are not enrolled. The third factor is calculated after subtracting the estimated number of children with working mothers not enrolled, since the majority of single parents in Metropolitan Toronto are women (Social Planning Council of Metropolitan Toronto, 1981; City of Toronto Planning and Development Department, 1983). Notably, as described earlier, the demand for nursery schools is likely to be distinct from the demand for day cares as defined in equation (3).[11]

Government Subsidization of Child Care. During the twenty years between the end of World War II and 1966 the Day Nurseries Act remained unchanged and government involvement in child care was minimal. In 1966, the Canadian federal government renewed its financial support of day care with the Canada Assistance Plan. In this plan, the federal government agreed to share with the provinces 50 percent of day care costs for families considered to be "in need." The Day Nurseries Act was also amended in 1966. The revised act provided a major impetus for the creation of new day care centers by increasing from 50 to 80 percent the provincial share of operating costs incurred by municipal centers. Additionally, for the first time, financing was made available for the purchase of child care services from privately operated day care centers (both nonprofit and for profit) by municipalities for the children of families in need using funds made available by federal, provincial, and municipal agencies.

The Children's Services Division (CSD) was created to implement this program in Metropolitan Toronto. This municipal agency establishes purchase of service agreements (POSAs) with privately operated nonprofit and for-profit day care centers. The CSD does not establish purchase of service agreements with nursery schools. Through these agreements the CSD provides subsidized care for the children of city residents who qualify for financial assistance. A day care with a purchase of service agreement is eligible to enroll the children of parents whose fees are subsidized by the CSD. Parents who are receiving the division's assistance are free to purchase services from any DCD with a POSA. We measured government subsidization of the day care population with the value (in constant dollars) of the CSD annual budget. This budget amount measures the level of government resources provided to parents-in-need for purchasing services from DCCs with POSAs.

Models of the Child Care System

We will describe a series of four models for the child care system. Although these models are neither exhaustive nor definitive, they illustrate the use of loop models. The variables in the models (figures 18.4a–4d) are DCC population size (D), nursery population size (N), DCC demand (K), and CSD budget amount (B). Each model includes an identical baseline specification for interactions of the DCC population, DCC demand, and CSD budget that is based on the foregoing description of the child care environment in Metropolitan Toronto and findings from earlier studies of child care in Metropolitan Toronto (Baum, 1989; Baum and Oliver, 1991, 1992; Baum and Singh, 1992, 1993). The baseline specification consists of (1) positive links from DCC demand (K) to the DCC population size (D) and to the CSD budget (B), (2) a positive link from the CSD budget (B) to the DCC population size (D), and (3) a positive link from the DCC population size (D) to DCC demand (K). Following Puccia and Levins (1985:13) both resources in the system are treated as self-damped. For example, the CSD budget is self-damped because it is set by provincial and federal legislation and bounded by bureaucratic inertia. There is no self-effect link for the day care population since its self-damped resources are included in the model.

    We vary the signs for the links between the DCC and nursery populations within each model in order to explore the implications of the nature of the interaction between these populations for the dynamics of the child care system as a whole.[12] Model 1 (figure 18.4a) includes symmetric negative (i.e., competitive) interactions between the DCC and nursery populations. Model 2 (figure 18.4b) includes symmetric positive (i.e., mutualistic) interactions. Models 3 and 4 (figures 18.4c and 18.4d) include asymmetric interactions (i.e., one positive and one negative link). For reasons of simplicity and parsimony, the nursery demand is not included directly in the models. Instead, the effects of the nursery population's use of available resources are captured by a negative self-effect link.

    For each model a table of predictions is given for the change in the equilibrium levels of the system variables due to changes in any one of them. The stability characteristics of these models are sometimes ambiguous and require additional assumptions about the relative strengths of feedback loops. These details would complicate the presentation; therefore, the tables of preductions should be taken as given.[13]

    Model 1 (figure 18.4a) includes a symmetric competitive interaction between the DCC and nursery populations. As illustrated in the table of predictions, this model contains several notable, nonobvious predictions. For example, while the signs of all paths connecting the DCC population size (D), DCC demand (K), and CSD budget (B) are positive, a positive change in one of these variables is frequently predicted to lower the equilibrium levels of the others. Notably, increases in DCC demand and CSD budget are predicted to lower the equilibrium size of the DCC population, while increases in the DCC population size are predicted to lower the equilibrium demand for DCCs and the CSD budget amount. At the same time, while the paths from the nursery population size to all other system variable are negative, increases in the nursery population size are predicted to increase equilibrium levels of DCC demand and the CSD budget; and vice versa. Even more striking, although the model specifies a symmetric competitive interaction between the DCC and nursery populations, a positive change in either population's size is predicted to increase

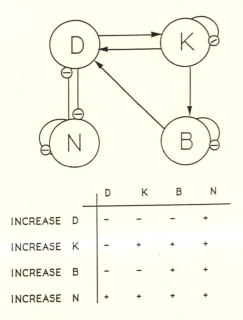

	D	K	B	N
INCREASE D	-	-	-	+
INCREASE K	-	+	+	+
INCREASE B	-	-	+	+
INCREASE N	+	+	+	+

FIG. 18.4a   Child care model 1. D, day care population size; K, demand for day care; B, children's service division budget; N, nursery population size

	D	K	B	N
INCREASE D	-	-	-	-
INCREASE K	-	+	+	-
INCREASE B	-	-	+	-
INCREASE N	-	-	-	+

FIG. 18.4b   Child care model 2. D, day care population size; K, demand for day care; B, children's service division budget; N, nursery population size

	D	K	B	N
INCREASE D	+	+	+	-
INCREASE K	+	+	+	-
INCREASE B	+	+	(+)	-
INCREASE N	+	+	+	-

FIG. 18.4c   Child care model 3. Predictions in parentheses assume that complementary feedback is negative. D, day care population size; K, demand for day care; B, children's service division budget; N, nursery population size

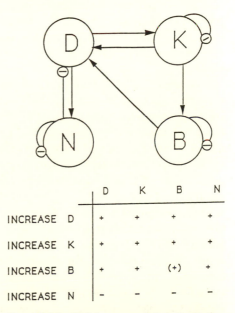

	D	K	B	N
INCREASE D	+	+	+	+
INCREASE K	+	+	+	+
INCREASE B	+	+	(+)	+
INCREASE N	-	-	-	-

FIG. 18.4d   Child care model 4. Predictions in parentheses assume that complementary feedback is negative. D, day care population size; K, demand for day care: B, children's service division budget; N, nursery population size

the equilibrium abundance of the other. Thus, the effects of the direct competitive interaction between day care and nursery are not observed at the point of contact, but in variables several steps away (i.e., increases in the nursery population size are predicted to raise the equilibrium levels of DCC demand and the CSD budget, which are in turn predicted to lower the equilibrium size of the DCC population). These counterintuitive predictions and system properties, which result from higher-level feedback in the system, help to reinforce two related points discussed earlier: (1) the impact of a change to the structure of a system can be felt at places removed from the change, and (2) the patterns of correlations among variables depend not only on the relations of those variables themselves, but also on interactions in the rest of the system.

Model 2 (figure 18.4b) includes a mutualistic interaction between day care and nursery. As the table of predictions shows, with the exception of the predicted self-effect, all predictions for the nursery population (i.e., in column 4 and row 4 of the table of predictions) are the reverse of those in model 1. Increases in the nursery population size are now predicted to lower the equilibrium levels of DCC demand and the CSD budget, and vice versa. In addition, although a mutualistic interaction is specified for the DCC and nursery populations, as a result of higher-level feedback, increases in either population's size are predicted to lower the equilibrium abundance of the other. However, all predictions for the relations among the DCC population, DCC demand, and CSD budget remain unchanged. Thus, as is the case in model 1, the system-level predictions for the interaction between day care and nursery are counterintuitive and the direct mutualistic interaction between the DCC and nursery populations represented in the model is observed only in variables several steps away (i.e., increases in the nursery population size lowers the equilibrium levels of DCC demand and the CSD budget, which in turn raise the equilibrium size of the DCC population).

Models 3 and 4 (figures 18.4c and 18.4d) include asymmetric interactions between day care and nursery. The specification in model 3 is that the DCC population competitively influences the nursery population, while the nursery population has a mutualistic effect on the DCC population. This specification is reversed in model 4. As the tables of predictions for these models illustrate, when these asymmetric specifications are included, all predictions for the relations among the DCC population, DCC demand, and the CSD budget become positive.[14] These changes result from the effects of the negative feedback in the asymmetric DCC-nursery interactions on higher-level feedback and feedback in complementary subsystems. While the two asymmetric relationships lead to the same predictions for the relations among the DCC population, DCC demand, and the CSD budget, they result in different predictions for the nursery population size (i.e., in column 4 and row 4 of the tables of predictions). When the competitive link in the asymmetric specification is from the DCC population to the nursery population (i.e., model 3), increases in all system variables, including the nursery population size, are predicted to lower the equilibrium size of the nursery population, while increases the nursery population size are predicted to increase the equilibrium levels of all other variables. These predictions are reversed in model 4.

Table 18.6 summarizes the predictions of the child care system models (figures 18.4a–d) and gives the proportion of models with the same predicted sign in each

TABLE 18.6   Prediction Summary for Child Care Models and Proportion of Models with Same Predicted Sign

Model	D/D	D/K	D/B	D/N	K/D	K/K	K/B	K/N	B/D	B/K	B/B	B/N	N/D	N/K	N/B	N/N
1	−	−	−	+	−	+	+	+	−	−	+	+	+	+	+	+
2	−	−	−	−	−	+	+	−	−	−	+	−	−	−	−	+
3	+	+	+	−	+	+	+	−	+	+	(+)	−	+	+	+	−
4	+	+	+	+	+	+	+	+	+	+	(+)	+	−	−	−	−
+	2/4	2/4	2/4	2/4	2/4	4/4	4/4	2/4	2/4	2/4	4/4	2/4	2/4	2/4	2/4	2/4
−	2/4	2/4	2/4	2/4	2/4	0/4	0/4	2/4	2/4	2/4	0/4	2/4	2/4	2/4	2/4	2/4

column. For example, the predicted self-effects for increases in the size of the DCC population are listed in the first column, which is labeled 'D/D'. Models 1 and 2 predict a negative (−), self-damping effect; models 3 and 4 predict a positive (+), self-enhancing effect. All the child care models predict a positive correlation of the DCC demand and CSD budget (i.e., K/B). All models also predict self-enhancing effects for DCC demand and CSD budget (i.e., K/K and B/B). These are robust predictions because they are independent of the different assumptions underlying the models. Should empirical data indicate negative correlations for these relations, then the foregoing model of the child care system becomes suspect. The incompatability of observations with *all* models may indicate the existence of unidentified variables that were not included in the models. Alternatively, it may suggest the need to modify the relationships among variables already included in the models.

Discussion of Results

A set of alternative models such as those in figures 18.4a–18.4d and the corresponding tables of predictions can be used in several ways. The most direct use is to compare observed patterns of correlation among the variables with the model predictions. This provides a basis on which to differentiate the models and choose among them. Table 18.7 presents observed correlation patterns for the annual growth rates (i.e., dX/dt) of each variable at time t given a change in all system variables at times $t − 1$, $t − 2$, and $t − 3$.[15] Table 18.8 summarizes the proportion of predictions matching the observed correlations for each model and gives binomial probability for each match. Overall, the predictions of the child care system models strongly parallel the

TABLE 18.7   Observed Correlation Patterns and Proportion of Models Predicting Observed Correlation

Time	D/D	D/K	D/B	D/N	K/D	K/K	K/B	K/N	B/D	B/K	B/B	B/N	N/D	N/K	N/B	N/N
$t − 1$	+	−	+		+	+	+		+	−	+		−	−		
correct	2/4	2/4	2/4		2/4	4/4	4/4		2/4	2/4	4/4		2/4	2/4		
$t − 2$	+	+	+	−	+	+	+	−	+	+		−	−	+	+	−
correct	2/4	2/4	2/4	2/4	2/4	4/4	4/4	2/4	2/4	2/4		2/4	2/4	2/4	2/4	2/4
$t − 3$	+	−	+	−	−		−	−	+	−	+	−	−	+		+
correct	2/4	2/4	2/4	2/4	2/4		0/4	2/4	2/4	2/4	4/4	2/4	2/4	2/4		2/4

NOTE: Correlations of zero are omitted for simplicity. Given the small sample size, $n \leq 18$, we used $p < .15$ as the criterion for determining correlations substantively different from zero.

TABLE 18.8   Proportion of Predictions Matching Observed Correlations for Each Child Care
Model

	Proportion of Predictions Matching Observed Correlations			
Model	Correlation t − 1	Correlation t − 2	Correlation t − 3	Total
1	5/16 (.55)	4/16 (.75)	6/16 (.34)	15/48
2	7/16 (.18)	6/16 (.34)	9/16 (.03)	22/48
3	7/16 (.18)	14/16 (.00)	8/16 (.07)	27/48
4	9/16 (.03)	10/16 (.01)	4/16 (.75)	21/48
All models	26/64	34/64	25/64	85/192

NOTE: Binomial probabilities, assuming $\theta = .30$, are in parentheses.

observed pattern of correlations among the variables, with the highest proportion of predictions matching the observed correlations at time $t − 2$. Among the different models of the child care system, model 3 (figure 18.4c) has the highest proportion of predictions matching the observed correlations (87.5 percent for time $t − 2$, 56.3 percent overall).

When empirical observations are not readily available, the pattern of summary predictions can help in planning research. Since it is often not possible to measure, influence, or sometimes even observe all system variables, the best way to gain maximum information is to obtain data that will help distinguish among different models. When there is considerable consistency within the rows of alternative models, research focused on the differences between particular models will be the most informative. Examining the predictions from sets of models may indicate that studying or creating a change in one system variable will be sufficient to decide among alternatives. However, when there are major differences between rows in the tables of predictions, more information can be obtained from a broader research focus.

Another use of the set of graphs is designing system interventions to bring about desired changes in particular system variables. If the Children's Services Division were given a mandate to increase the abundance of nursery schools while maintaining the size of the day care population, its policy planners could study the effects of increasing or decreasing the growth rate of its budget. The best fitting model of the child care system, model 3 (figure 18.4c), indicates that a decrease in the CSD budget would have the desired effect of increasing the equilibrium size of the nursery population; however, it would also lower the equilibrium size of the DCC population. Alternatively, its planners could investigate the implications of making different modifications (i.e., adding or removing a variable; adding, removing, or changing a link) to the previous models of the child care system to aid in designing potential interventions. For example, the different implications of permitting nursery schools to establish Purchase of Service Agreements and compete directly with day cares for the children of subsidized parents-in-need versus the creation of a separate funding program dedicated to the nursery population could be examined.

Implications

As we have tried to demonstrate in this chapter, one of the more important consequences of taking a coevolutionary approach is that one can begin to understand the relationships between a set of organizational and environmental variables as a *system*. At the level of the system of relationships, as a consequence of feedback in the system, changes in one variable can produce quite counterintuitive changes in another variable. In complex systems of relationships, dependent-independent variable distinctions become less meaningful since changes in any one variable are caused endogenously by changes in others. It is in such systems of relationships that a coevolutionary approach can add the most value. We think this view has some important implications for organizational researchers and practitioners.

A coevolutionary view can potentially add value to organizational problems that share the stylized structure in which an organization (or a group of organizations) responds to elements in its environment (or other organization) and the environment, in turn, changes in response to the focal organization's actions. Such patterns may exist in the domains of public policy and regulation, technological innovation, and mutual competition, to name but a few.

An important concern of public policy decision makers is the impact that a specific program or policy may have on an organizational population. On the other hand, organizations targeted by a specific regulatory policy are interested in enactment of favorable regulations. Public policy is intended to, and does, shape organizational actions but is, in turn, shaped by the lobbying efforts of organizations and their agents. Coevolutionary thinking can inform the efforts of both organizational and public policy decision makers and suggest actions quite different from linear cause-effect thinking. An example illustrates how a well-intentioned policy can sometimes have surprising consequences when feedback relationships exist.

Some earlier research on the dynamics of a population of voluntary social service organizations in Metropolitan Toronto during the period 1970–82 had examined the impact of changes in the institutional environment of this population on the dynamics of entry and exit (Tucker et al., 1988:148–49; Singh, Tucker, and Meinhard, 1991:411). In 1971, the Canadian government created a program called Opportunities for Youth with the aim of increasing citizen participation in solving social problems. This program constituted a major institutional change for the population of voluntrary social service organizations and influenced both the founding and mortality patterns. However, research results showed that the program appeared to have been so successful in facilitating organizational founding that it pushed the population size above the carrying capacity, reducing founding and increasing the mortality rate. These effects, which were contrary to the spirit of the government program, seem difficult to understand in a worldview in which more funding translates into more organizations. But it seems eminently sensible if, beyond a certain point, population growth is seen as a self-damping process.

In addition to informing the thinking of public policy makers, the preceding discussion also has a bearing on how organizations might approach advocacy or lobbying activity. This is simply the other side to the coin of public policy. Just as employing a coevolutionary approach has the potential to alert decision makers to unintended consequences of public policy choices, so too can organizations become better informed about what kinds of choices favor or are inimical to their interests. For example, as our earlier discussion of model 1 (figure 18.4a) for the child care system in Metropolitan Toronto made clear, even though day care centers and nurseries are assumed to exert direct competitive influences on each other, an increase in the population size of either nurseries or day care centers has the effect of increasing the population size of the other. If this model is a valid representation of the system of relationships, an implication is that it may be in the best interests of the day care center and nursery populations to promote each other's welfare, even though they are competitors. Of course, the presence of feedback processes is at the heart of this phenomenon.

Related in intimate ways to technological innovation is the phenomenon of mutual competition, which can sometimes lead to competitive *arms races* (Dawkins, 1982). Indeed, a coevolutionary view of technological evolution is an example of competitive dynamics. The simplest case of mutual competition is that of two organizations, each of which responds to, and influences, the action of the other. Clearly the environment to which each organization adapts is largely endogenous, and a coevolutionary view seems appropriate. Related in fundamental ways is the Red Queen's Hypothesis (Van Valen, 1973), which suggests that the environment of a species deteriorates continually because other coevolving species continue to evolve. Consequently, much like the Red Queen in Lewis Carroll's *Through the Looking Glass,* each species has to evolve faster even to hold its own against the others. Clemons (1991) has explored the implications of the Red Queen Hypothesis in the context of technology driven competitive applications. As the technological applications diffuse to other competitors, the competitive advantage requires continuous improvement to be sustainable.

Generally consistent with such thinking about mutual competition is the view that, in specific circumstances, it is sensible for an organization to encourage the development of competitors. This may be especially true in the early stages of a population's growth when the legitimacy of the population itself is being established. In a related vein, Conner (1991) has demonstrated how it can be advantageous for a software firm to encourage cloning by other firms. A larger installed base makes it more likely that the firm's software will survive the early period in which product standards are still being decided. The positive feedback loop embedded in this argument has a broadly coevolutionary spirit.

Notes

1. Some exceptions are Forrester's (1958, 1968) approach to modeling industrial dynamics that is explicitly built on the feedback concept; Weick's (1969, 1979) approach to organizing in which the environment is actively enacted by organizational actors, giving it a more endogenous character; and the work on organizational learning by March and his colleagues, particularly questions of mutual learning (Levitt and March, 1988; March, 1991, personal communication).

2. An exception is Carroll's (1981) dynamic analysis of national systems of education that explicitly discusses the implications of feedback for community dynamics and stability.

3. The logistic growth model is one example of a more basic loop structure. Many nonlinear systems consisting of a positive and a negative loop generate S-shaped behavior over time (Richardson, 1991).

4. In this section we present only the basic information required to reach the loop models. The technical aspects are described in the next section of the chapter. Readers interested in developing an understanding the technical details of loop modeling first may read the next section before proceeding.

5. The predictions in the tables are calculated on the basis of the assumption of a positive (+) change (i.e., increase in the level of a variable). The predictions for a negative (−) change are obtained by reversing the signs for the predictions.

6. For interested readers, the feedback, stability, and qualitative prediction calculations for the competitive and predator-prey systems described in this section are given in the appendix. These calculations are described in detail in the next section of the chapter.

7. For five variables the second criterion is $F_1F_4 + F_1F_5 - F_1F_2F_3 - F_3 > 0$. For more variables it is more complicated. See Puccia and Levins (1985, chapter 6).

8. Predictions about changes in transition rates are also possible. See Puccia and Levins (1985:53–59).

9. The feedback of the complementary subsystem is identical to the feedback at the level $n - k$ for the entire system as defined in equation (1). For example, in figure 18.3, the path [HP] of length 2, p_{PH}^2, has the complementary subsystem [N], which has complementary feedback, $F_{3-2}^{(comp)} = F_1^{(comp)} = [-N]$, which is negative (−). Note that like F_0, $F_0^{(comp)} \equiv -1$ (Puccia and Levins, 1985:38).

10. For additional details on the ecology of child care in Metropolitan Toronto see Baum (1989) and Baum and Oliver (1991, 1992).

11. As described later, for reason of parsimony and simplicity the effect of the demand for nursery are not modeled directly but, instead, accounted for through a damping self-effect link for the nursery population.

12. While we build and examine the implications of a variety of different models, any matrix of interaction coefficients, including empirically derived matrices such as those in Carroll (1981) and Boeker (1991), can be given a loop model representation and evaluated by using loop analysis techniques. For an example, see Baum and Korn (1993).

13. For interested readers, the detailed feedback, stability, and qualitative prediction calculations for each model of the child care system are available from the authors.

14. A prediction in parentheses means the result is ambiguous and requires additional assumptions. In this case, the assumptions are about the relative strengths of complementary feedback loops. The predictions given in the tables that are in parentheses require the assumption that complementary feedback is negative.

15. $(dX/dt)_{t-n}$ is defined as $(X_{t-n} - X_{t-n-l})/X_{t-n-l}$. We use these correlation patterns as surrogate estimates for the effects of changes in each variable on the equilibrium levels of each variable. This approach requires the assumption that lagged changes in growth rates are positively correlated with equilibrium abundance. We report correlations for multiple time lags because the speed of these dynamic community-level interactions is unknown.

APPENDIX TABLE   Calculations for the Competitive and Predator-Prey System Models in
Figures 18.1 and 18.2
Feedback and Stability Calculations (stability condition: $F_i < 0$,   for $i = 1$–2)

Competitive Model		
Level (k =)	*Feedback*	*Feedback Value*
1	$F_1 = [-A] + [-B]$	$F_1 < 0$, negative $(-)$ feedback
	$F_2 = [AB] - [-A][-B]$	$F_2 < 0$, if $|[A][B]| > |[AB]|$
		(i.e., short loops are stronger
2		than long loops)

Predator-Prey Model		
Level (k =)	*Feedback*	*Feedback value*
1	$F_1 = [-A]$	$F_1 < 0$, negative $(-)$ feedback
2	$F_2 = [-AB]$	$F_2 < 0$, negative $(-)$ feedback

Qualitative Prediction Calculations

Competitive System Model						
X_i $\partial f_i/\partial c$ X_j	$p_\mu^{(s)}$	*Path value*	*Complementary subsystem*	$F_{2-k}^{(comp)}$	$\Sigma(\partial f_i/\partial c)(p_\mu^{(k)})(F_{n-k}^{(comp)})/F_n$	
A (+) A	$p_{AA}^{(1)}$	(1)	[B]	$F_1^{(comp)} = [-B] = (-)$	$(+)(1)(-)/(-) = (+)$	
B	$p_{BA}^{(2)}$	(−)	[∅]	$F_0^{(comp)} = -1$	$(+)(-)(-1)/(-) =$ $(-)$	
B (+) A	$p_{AB}^{(2)}$	(−)	[∅]	$F_0^{(comp)} = -;1$	$(+)(-)(-1)/(-) =$ $(-)$	
B	$p_{BB}^{(1)}$	(1)	[A]	$F_1^{(comp)} = [-A] = (-)$	$(+)(1)(-)/(-) = (+)$	

Predator-Prey System Model						
X_i $\partial f_i/\partial c$ X_j	$p_\mu^{(k)}$	*Path value*	*Complementary subsystem*	$F_{2-k}^{(comp)}$	$\Sigma(\partial f_i/\partial c)(p_\mu^{(k)})(F_{n-k}^{(comp)})/F_n$	
A (+) A	$p_{AA}^{(1)}$	(1)	[B]	$F_1^{(comp)} = 0$	$(+)(1)(0)/(-) = (0)$	
B	$p_{BA}^{(2)}$	(+)	[∅]	$F_0^{(comp)} = -1$	$(+)(+)(-1)/(-) =$ $(+)$	
B (+) A	$p_{AB}^{(2)}$	(−)	[∅]	$F_0^{(comp)} = -1$	$(+)(-)(-1)/(-) =$ $(-)$	
B	$p_{BB}^{(1)}$	(1)	[A]	$F_1^{(comp)} = [-A] = (-)$	$(+)(1)(-)/(-) = (+)$	

NOTE: Predictions for the competition model assume $F_2 < 0$, which requires that damping self-effects are stronger
than competition. See discussion in text.

19

The Coevolution of
Technology and Organization

LORI ROSENKOPF AND MICHAEL L. TUSHMAN

Consider three examples of technological competition and selection:

Machine tooling technology. During World War II, two distinct technologies for automated machine tooling emerged. Numerically controlled (NC) machines replaced the series of shop-floor worker movements with mathematical equations developed by engineers, while record-playback (RP) machines recorded the movements of the shop-floor worker on paper tapes. NC machines were much more technology-intensive and cost-intensive than RP machines, but the academic-military-industrial complex of MIT, GE, and the Air Force propelled NC technology to completely dominate RP technology. (Noble, 1984)

Electrical supply systems. During the late nineteenth century, both alternating current and direct current electrical supply systems served to deliver electricity to consumers. Each had different advantages: AC systems were able to span greater geographic distances, whereas DC systems were more cost-efficient in densely populated areas. In different countries, electrical supply systems took different forms due to the political ideologies and their attendant regulation (Hughes, 1983). In the U.S., the victory of AC systems over DC systems resulted more from Edison's decision to pull financial support from his DC technology development than from any inherent weaknesses in the technology. (David, 1987)

Typewriter keyboards. During World War II, the U.S. Navy found that typists using a Dvorak keyboard could improve their typing speeds by 40% after only a two-week retraining period. Nonetheless, this technical advantage did not generate the power for the Dvorak keyboard to overcome its well-known QWERTY counterpart. The embedded base of equipment and skilled typists led to the retention of the QWERTY keyboard and the loss of these potential productivity advances. (David, 1985)

This chapter has benefited from the careful reviews of Paul DiMaggio, Don Hambrick, Donald Nagle, Richard Nelson, Ron Burt, and Jitendra Singh. We also appreciate the comments of the participants of the conference on Evolutionary Dynamics of Organizations at the Stern School of Business.

These three examples of technological competition and selection demonstrate the many instances where choices between competing technologies are not obvious. In all three cases, the technologies that dominated were not better in a technical sense; instead, the dominant technological outcomes were socially constructed and determined by organizational coalitions. Furthermore, the emergence of these dominant technologies, though socially constructed, served to shape and constrain subsequent organizational action and interaction.

In this chapter, we explore organization and interorganization evolution in the context of technological evolution. Traditional studies in organization theory speak of "technological determinism," positioning technological change as the exogenous event that spurs organization and interorganization evolution. In contrast, economic and social histories of technological change speak of "social construction of technology," stressing the primary role of community organization in determining the nature of technological evolution. We argue that technology and organization coevolve, and that this process of coevolution is characterized by periods of social construction and periods of technological determinism.

We examine organization dynamics and their influence on technological evolution in the context of the technology cycle, arguing that the impact of community organization on technological change is greatest after technological discontinuities and during the process of convergence on a dominant design. Before the dominant design emerges, technological communities are characterized by extensive flux in actors, linkages, and power. This community-level evolution slows during the era of incremental technological change, when the dominant design constrains the nature of community dynamics. During this period, technological evolution determines the nature of community evolution.

With our focus on the evolution of systemic technologies and their associated communities, we show that community organization dynamics are more pronounced for complex technologies. For simple technologies, competing designs may be compared on straightforward measures such as price/performance ratios. Selection of a dominant design is based on these technical considerations, and the influence of sociopolitical factors is minimal. For complex technologies, the direction of technological change is more uncertain, as there are many ways to measure the performance of competing technologies. Thus, there are many trade-offs between competing technologies that cannot be adjudicated through simple comparisons of price/performance ratios. Social, political, and organizational factors are brought to bear on the process of technological selection; the influence of these nontechnical factors is accentuated because a greater variety of organizations are involved in the evolution of complex technologies. This community of organizations evolves as new organizations introduce technological discontinuities, as coalitions form around technological substitutes, as incumbent organizations resist these efforts at substitution, and as interorganizational processes of compromise and accommodation affect a dominant design.

We view community organization evolution and technological evolution as two dynamic, interlinked processes. Various scholars suggest that social or economic systems of organizations are the necessary unit of analysis for the study of technological change (DeBresson and Clark, 1991; Nelson, 1990; Van de Ven and Garud, 1989). We define the organizational community as the set of organizations that are stakeholders for a particular technology (Tushman and Rosenkopf, 1992). Depending on the technology, this set of organizations can include suppliers, manufactuers, user groups, governmental agencies, standards bodies, and professional associations. This definition of "community" is broader than that of most community ecologists; in addition to the standard set of interdependent organizational populations (suppliers, manufacturers, and users), our focus on technological evolution requires the inclusion of unique actors such as governmental agencies, standards bodies, and professional societies. The ties between organizations in the community and the distribution of power among these organizations vary with the technology. For example, the role of cooperative action between firms for patent pooling is common for systemic products like radio systems, but much less so for nonsystemic products like contact lenses.

We illustrate our theory with examples from many industries, but focus on the evolution of continuous wave radio technology in the early 20th century. Using radio as an exploratory case study, we can observe several concurrent areas of technological evolution. The most central component of a radio system is the transmitter. We call this component a "core subsystem" because all other radio technologies depend on the transmitting technology. Alternator, arc, and vacuum tube transmitters competed to become the dominant continuous wave transmitter, spurring development of complementary receivers and new methods of frequency allocation. At the same time, continuous wave radio systems were met with resistance by incumbent spark-gap systems. Organizational coalitions around these competing technological regimes were further altered by the changing markets for radio system technology: while the original point-to-point continuous wave radio systems were developed for wireless telegraphy and telephony, the rise of broadcasting expanded the market for continuous wave systems.

The chapter has two major sections. In the first, we detail a perspective on technology cycles, focusing on changing technical characteristics of products and processes. This process of technological evolution provides the context for community organization evolution, which we examine in the second section. The dynamics of community organization evolution are intimately linked with technological evolution: while technical change can spur community evolution, interorganizational change within the technological community simultaneously shapes the nature of technological evolution. We offer some testable hypotheses about differences in community-level evolution between the two stages of the technology cycle.

Systemic Technological Evolution: Interlinked Technology Cycles

Our study of the coevolution of technology and organization begins by focusing on technological evolution. In this section, we examine the Anderson and Tushman (1990) technology cycle model and then extend it to systemic technologies. We begin with a brief summary of the technology cycle model; more detailed descriptions of the model are available in Anderson and Tushman (1990) and Tushman and Rosenkopf (1992).

The Technology Cycle

Drawing from work in sociology, history, economics, and industrial engineering, Anderson and Tushman (1990) argue that technological change can be characterized by sociocultural evolutionary processes of variation, selection, and retention (D. T. Campbell, 1969). Variation is driven by stochastic technological breakthroughs. These technological discontinuities initiate substantial technological rivalry between alternative technological regimes, as the introduction of continuous-wave radio components led to competition among alternator, arc, and vacuum-tube transmitters (Aitken, 1985). Since technical rivalry is often not settled by technical logic, social and organizational dynamics select from among technological opportunities, single industry standards, or dominant designs (Tushman and Rosenkopf, 1992). Positively selected variants then evolve through retention periods marked by incremental technical change, increased interdependence, and enhanced competence within and between communities of practitioners: as the aeronautical community grew with the dominance of the turbojet engine, for example, its subcommunity of gas turbine practitioners also designed gas turbines for ships and offshore oil production platforms (Constant, 1987). These periods of incremental technical change may be interrupted by subsequent technological breakthroughs: in the American photographic industry, for example, eras of incremental change ended with the introductions of collodion plates, gelatin plates, and roll film (Jenkins, 1975).

Thus, the technology cycle has four components: technological discontinuities, eras of ferment, dominant designs, and eras of incremental change. Technological discontinuities and dominant designs are events that mark the transitions between eras of ferment and eras of incremental change, as illustrated in figure 19.1a. Technological advance is, then, driven by the combination of chance events (variation), direct social and political action of organizations in selecting between rival technical regimes (artificial selection), and incremental, competence-enhancing, puzzle-solving action of many organizations learning by doing (retention). This retention stage provides a context for the subsequent technological discontinuity.

Using the technology cycle model, figure 19.1b shows the evolution of radio transmitters in the early 20th century in greater detail. Prior to 1900, all radio transmitters were of the spark-gap variety. These transmitters were capable of sending dots and dashes (radiotelegraphy), but not the human voice (radiotelephony). Recognizing this need, scientists and engineers developed devices that could transmit continuous waves and therefore carry the human voice. Three distinct types of continuous wave variants emerged: alternator, arc, and vacuum-tube transmitters. Each type of transmitter found certain applications, and each type had different advantages and disadvantages. Through a series of political, organizational, and economic processes, vacuum tube transmitters came to dominate the market during the 1920s. Subsequent technological developments refined the vacuum tube transmitter until the invention of transistor-based components during World War II.

The technology cycle model is a useful frame for examining the development of simpler components or subsystems of larger products or technologies. For example, Anderson and Tushman (1990) describe the technological development of cement manufacture by focusing solely on cement kiln throughput, and the technological development of minicomputers by focusing solely on central processing unit speed.

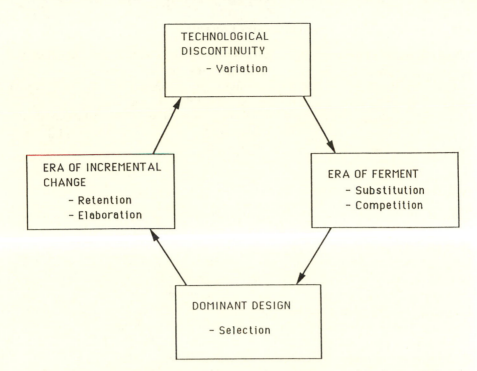

FIG. 19.1a   The technology cycle. (adapted from Anderson and Tushman, 1990)

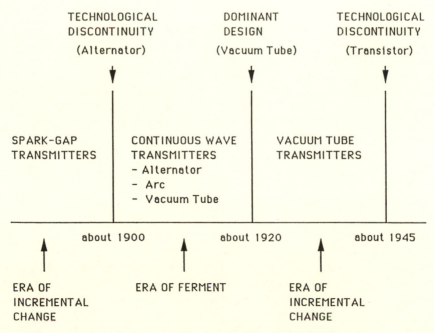

FIG. 19.1b   Technological evolution of radio transmitters

While it is useful to focus on one core subsystem of the process or product, this focus ignores technological developments in other subsystems. For example, minicomputer evolution should also take into account improvements in input/output transfer and their interplay with central processing units. Likewise, radio transmitters do not evolve independently; their development is intertwined with the evolution of radio receivers and transmission management technologies. How can we extend the technology cycle model to accommodate this complexity?

A Systems View of Products

This interpretation of the radio system as a collection of interdependent components can enhance the use of the technology cycle model. Tushman and Rosenkopf (1992) view products as systems of components, linkages, and interfaces. Any product or process can be modeled as a collection of these three types of interdependent subsystems: components (transmitters, receivers) provide basic functionality, linkages (in this case, just air) physically connect components, and interfaces (frequency allocation) allow communication between components. The reader is referred to Tushman and Rosenkopf (1992) for more extensive discussion of these concepts.

Products vary in their levels of technological complexity. This range can be defined by the numbers and types of subsystems in the product, the level of interdependence between these subsystems, and the boundaries of the product. Nonassembled products, such as cement and glass, have no separable components, while simple assembled products, such as guns and skis, are constructed from components that are fit together in an assembly process. More complex products are systemic in nature. Closed assembled systems, such as automobiles and watches, require linkage technology between components for assembly, while open assembled systems, such as phone systems and electricity distribution systems, contain complicated interface technologies to connect their closed, assembled systems. Closed assembled systems are contained in some sort of casing, while open assembled systems do not have a clear-cut boundary. Figure 19.2 illustrates how drivers of technological progress, bases of design dominance, arbiters of dominant designs, and the influence of social, political, and organizational dynamics become more complicated as technological complexity increases. In this chapter, we focus primarily on systemic technologies, because these more complex technologies are influenced much more heavily by social, organizational, and political processes (Tushman and Rosenkopf, 1992). For less complex technologies, we expect similar, but truncated, processes of sociopolitical influence.

For complex systems, technological evolution occurs through the interdependent evolution of subsystems. Figure 19.3 shows how radio systems are composed of multiple, interdependent components, each of which has its own technology cycle. For early radio systems, both transmitter and receiver technologies evolved from spark-gap to continuous wave components, while transmission management technology evolved from "shouting the loudest" to frequency allocation. For most technologies, certain core subsystems spur complementary innovation in other peripheral subsystems. With watch technology, for example, the transition from springs to batteries as the core technology of the energy component allowed the transition from mechanical escapements to quartz crystals in the oscillation component as well as

Technological Complexity	Driver of Technological Progress	Basis of Design Dominance	Arbiter of Dominant Design	Influence of Social, Political, and Organizational Dynamics
Non-assembled and Simple Assembled Products	- Subprocess replacement or elimination - Materials substitution - Product substitution	Technical superiority of easily measured dimensions of merit	Single or focused practitioner community	Minimal
Closed Assembled Systems	- Subsystem substitution or dominant design - Core subsystem evolution - Linkage technology	Competition among alternative designs with diverse dimensions of merit	Heterogeneous professional and organizational communities	High
Open Assembled Systems	- Core subsystem substitution or dominant design - Linkage or interface technology	Competition among alternative subsystem designs with diverse dimensions of merit	Multiple and diverse organizational, professional, and governmental communities	Pervasive

FIG. 19.2   Role of technological complexity. (adapted from Tushman and Rosenkopf, 1992)

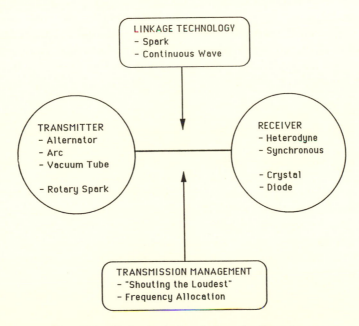

FIG. 19.3   Technological evolution of radio systems

the development of digital display faces. Likewise, for electricity supply systems, innovations in the power generation components (AC, DC, or polyphase) spurred compatible innovations in peripheral subsystems (e.g., for transformation, control, and utilization) that constrained system performance (Hughes, 1983).

Therefore, to examine systemic technological evolution, we can consider the evolution of core subsystems and this evolution's effects on interdependent subsystems within the product. At the subsystem level, we model technological evolution with Anderson and Tushman's (1990) technology cycle. At the system level, then, technological evolution may then be considered as a collection of interlinked technology cycles: while a technology cycle may be identified for each subsystem, much of the force that spurs technological evolution of any particular subsystem is generated by the technological evolution of the remainder of the system.

Summary

In this section, we have described the technology cycle, where technological discontinuities and dominant designs are the events that demark eras of ferment and eras of incremental change (Anderson and Tushman, 1990). This model of technological evolution is best applied at the subsystem level of analysis. To understand the nature of systemic change, technological evolution of systems should be viewed as the interdependent evolution of subsystems, driven by the technology cycles of core subsystems.

In the next section, we examine evolution within the network of organizations that compose the technological community. This community-level evolution simultaneously shapes and is shaped by evolution in the technical domain. Furthermore, like technological evolution of systems, evolutionary dynamics of communities may be identified for the entire system, or they may be limited to subcommunities that correspond to particular subsystems.

Evolutionary Dynamics of Community Organization

What is the nature of the coevolution of technology and organization? While organizations introduce technological innovations they are at the same time constrained by the current technological state of the art. Especially for systemic technologies, organizations can only innovate fruitfully by integrating their technology development with existing systems. Technological innovations at the subsystem level must be compatible with the existing embedded base; otherwise, converters must be developed or entirely new systems must be built. Interorganizational activity can facilitate or hinder system-level innovation.

Technological Communities: Actors, Linkages, and Power

To understand the dynamics by which technology and organization coevolve, we employ the community as our unit of analysis. Usage of the community level of analysis has been rather limited within organization theory and strategy, but there are several precedents. The term "community" has generally been taken to include multiple, diverse, and interdependent populations of organizations (Astley and Fombrun, 1983); Astley, 1985). Since our specific interest is in how particular product classes evolve, we define the "technological community" as the set of organizations that are stakeholders for a specific product class (Tushman and Rosenkopf, 1992).[1]

Actors. While such a community includes interdependent populations of firms (suppliers, manufacturers, and users), it will also include unique actors such as research labs, patent agencies, regulatory bodies, professional societies, trade associations, consortia, and other types, depending on technological and political contexts (Nelson, 1990). It is this broader collection of organizations that act and interact, spurring the evolution of a technological system.

Nelson (1990) calls this set of organizations and their activity the "capitalist engine," as community organization in a capitalist system drives technological variation, selection, and retention. DeBresson and Clark (1991) suggest that a "network of innovators" is the interorganizational form that spurs technological evolution. Likewise, Van de Ven and Garud (1989) argue that development of new technology is driven by the parallel evolution of a "social system".

Linkages. The actors in a technological community are interdependent; they are connected by a variety of interorganizational linkages. As pictured in figure 19.4, the actors in the technological community (depicted by circles) forge interorganizational linkages in a variety of ways. Solid lines between actors represent joint activity

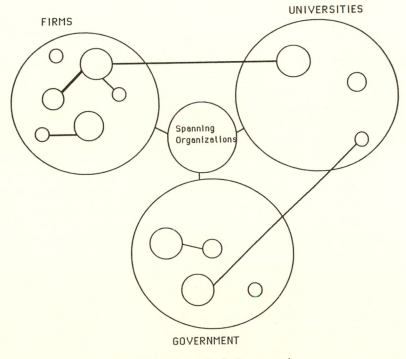

FIG. 19.4   Technological community

between the actors, such as patent pooling between organizations to form systems; joint development efforts between academia, government, and firms; or military contracting that specifies the character of technological innovation. In addition, innovating firms can be linked to regulatory bodies, as the nature of new innovations can be controlled by these bodies. In other cases organizations such as standards bodies, trade associations, professional societies, and consortia are composed of representatives from multiple organizations. While these organizations are actors in themselves, they create a series of institutionalized linkages among many actors in the community. These "organization-spanning actors" are shown as overlapping the various organizational domains in figure 19.4.

Power. The actors in the technological community differ in their abilities to shape and influence the paths of technological change, as suggested by the various sizes of the circles in figure 19.4. There are several possible bases for this power differential. An organization's ability to influence technological change can be examined from a resource dependence perspective. Firms with technology strength or market strength control resources that other organizations need, and power accrues to these firms as others need access to new technology or to the market. Likewise, powerful users, such as military bodies that contract for specific innovations, can control technological developments because they are funding the innovation. In addition, other organizations can strongly influence technological progress because of social or political status within the community, such as regulatory bodies, standards bodies, or other associations. The power of any actor to construct technological change socially can grow or diminish over time.

The Evolution of Technological Communities

Community organization evolution, therefore, is the changing character of these actors, linkages, and power as the technological community develops products and processes. We argue that the evolution of a technological community runs parallel to the evolution of the technology itself; just as processes of technological evolution are fundamentally different between the era of ferment and the era of incremental change, community-level evolutionary processes also fundamentally differ during these two stages of the technology cycle. At the community level of analysis, we can observe structural changes in actors, linkages, and power that drive and are driven by technological evolution. In this section, we describe these organizational dynamics in the context of the technology cycle, stressing differences across levels of technological complexity.

We argue that the emergence of a dominant design is a result of community organization dynamics; while the community undergoes extensive evolution during the era of ferment, the dominant design signals a stabilization of community structure as inter-organizational agreements are reinforced. We posit that technological discontinuities initiate a period of community reorientation, while dominant designs initiate a period of community convergence, where these periods of reorientation and convergence are the community analogues of Tushman and Romanelli's (1985) theory of organization reorientation and convergence.

The emergence of technological discontinuities and dominant designs occurs through organizational and interorganizational activity during the eras of ferment and incremental change. While organizational activity during the era of ferment centers around developing technological variants, establishing dimensions of merit, and building systems around these variants, organization activity during the era of incremental change focuses on the standardization and elaboration of the dominant design. Since the different stages of the technology cycle are characterized by these very different activities, we argue that the power of actors in the technological community and the interorganizational linkages created vary with the community activities that attend each stage of the technology cycle.

In the following sections, we examine the nature of community organization evolution before and after the emergence of a dominant design. Each section begins with examples from the radio industry.

Technological Discontinuities and Eras of Ferment

Before 1900, the Marconi Company's spark-gap systems dominated the market for point-to-point radio telegraphy. Continuous wave radio systems, based on competence-destroying technology, grew out of the desire to transmit the human voice via radio telephony, which spark-gap systems were unable to do. Three types of continuous wave transmitters emerged; for each, its entrepreneurial inventor formed a firm to market his technology.

Reginald Fessenden formed the National Electric Signaling Company (NESCO) to build alternator-based systems, working closely with General Electric on alternator development. John Elwell formed the Poulsen Wireless Company (soon to become the Federal Telegraph Company) to build arc-based systems, purchasing U.S. patent rights from Vladimir Poulsen in Denmark. Lee DeForest formed the American DeForest Wireless Telegraph Company (ADWTC) to build audion-based (vacuum-tube) systems, often negotiating with AT&T for potential sale of his patents. With the technology in its infant stages, Fessenden and DeForest utilized spark-based components in their systems. The Marconi Company, with a near monopoly on the world's spark gap systems, chose to ignore this competitive threat, not only refusing to interconnect their systems with those of competitors, but also choosing not to research or develop any continuous wave technology.

Each of the three continuous-wave innovators attempted to build systems that would provide radio service to guarantee a market for their components as well as generate service revenue. They made heavy use of patents and litigation to protect their inventions, but the process of system-building was so time-consuming and money intensive that these firms generally verged on the brink of bankruptcy. Firms faced these problems by selling patents, recapitalizing, or selling out. NESCO eventually entered receivership and its patents passed to GE, where Alexanderson had developed much of the alternator technology at Fessenden's request. ADWTC recapitalized several times but was eventually stripped of its assets due to convictions for stock fraud and patent infringement; their patents passed to American Marconi. DeForest, however, retained the audion patent, which he sold to AT&T. The Navy purchased all Poulsen (Federal) patents in 1918. Finally, Westinghouse entered the fray by purchasing the Armstrong patents by 1920. Thus, control of the technology passed from small, entrepreneurial firms to large, institutionalized corporations.

The radio community grew not only from the entry of new firms and associations, but also from the emergence and active participation of military, legislative, and regulatory bodies. As the U.S. Navy became a very large user of radio technology, it spurred technological development along particular trajectories by contracting for ever more powerful transmitters and complementary receivers. The Navy also lobbied for legislation that would prioritize their needs, such as patent moratoriums and frequency allocation, during World War I (Aitken, 1985).

The rise of continuous wave radio technology stimulated tremendous growth in radio traffic, resulting in jammed airwaves and subsequent attempts at regulation. Organizations of smaller users became visible in the community: associations of radio amateurs lobbied for frequency allocation, staging cross-country transmission demonstrations to gain publicity. Likewise, as radio broadcasting grew, the Radio Broadcasting Society represented the hundreds of independent broadcasters, attempting to protect their interests against those of the corporate-sponsored stations (and later networks).

Thus, the emergence of continuous wave radio transmitters, a competence-destroying technological discontinuity, enabled new actors to join the radio community and new inter-organizational linkages to form. Continuous wave firms entered the market, interacting with regulatory, legislative, military, and amateur organizations to shape the nature of technological evolution.

Just as technological discontinuities serve as variation mechanisms during technological evolution, they also initiate patterns of community organization evolution. As the technological community breeds new variants and builds technological systems around these variants, we argue, new actors and new interorganizational linkages emerge within the community. Competence-destroying technological discontinuities are typically introduced by new entrants to the community (Anderson and Tushman, 1990). For example, in the American photographic industry, three competence-destroying film-processing innovations (introduction of collodion plates in 1855, gelatin plates in 1880, and roll film in 1895) were introduced by firms outside the existing photographic community (Jenkins, 1975). Likewise, new firms entered the technological community with competence-destroying innovations in the cement, minicomputer, and flat glass industries (Anderson and Tushman, 1990).

The birth of new actors in the technological community is not limited to firms. Subsequent to the technological discontinuity, other types of actors organize and grow to influence technological evolution. In the chemical processing and aircraft industries, the rise of chemical and aerospace engineering as disciplines served as a locus of research as well as a training ground for future engineers (Rosenberg and Nelson, 1991). Similarly, the rise of professional associations serves as a medium for information sharing and socialization (Layton, 1986; Hughes, 1983). Large, powerful users of a technology, such as military bodies, shape technological evolution via contracting, as in the machine tool and aircraft industries (Noble, 1984; Mowery and Rosenberg, 1981). Smaller users may organize to lobby for their needs via user groups and trade associations. Finally, regulatory or legislative bodies may exert control over technological development in the interest of safety or public property rights (Hughes, 1983; Aitken, 1985).

As technological discontinuities interrupt predictable patterns of technological evolution to begin the era of ferment, dimensions of merit and their measurement become unclear; this increased technological uncertainty characterizes competition between and among technological regimes. For example, in the medical diagnostic imaging industry, doctors found it difficult to judge between competing technologies (X-ray, nuclear, ultrasound, and CT scanner) because they were unsure whether to base their decisions on properties of resolution or scan time (Yoxen, 1987). Likewise, the competition between single- and multichannel cochlear implant devices took several years to resolve because of the difficulty of measuring a device's ability to discriminate speech (Van de Ven and Garud, chapter 20, this volume). Producers, doctors, and users could not decide whether to rely on the FDA-approved single-channel device or to heed reports from users that multichannel devices seemed to be more effective. In general, proponents of particular technological variants at the subsystem level seek to cooperate with other firms so that complementary subsystems will support the technology through the creation of an entire system, as seen in today's battles between DOS and UNIX consortia. Thus, competing systems are supported by clusters of firms which try to coopt other organizations in the technological community.

Organizational and interorganizational activity during the era of ferment focuses on developing markets and matching technology to these markets, as technology stakeholders attempt to influence the outcome of technological competition in their favor. During the era of ferment, organizations must develop not only technical competence, but also interorganizational network skills to forge alliances in order to shape critical dimensions of merit and critical industry problems (Astley and Fombrun, 1983; MacKenzie, 1987). This interorganizational action buttresses technological competition and defines selection outcomes. For example, Remington's development of the touch-typing method and its free training courses enabled the typewriter manufacturer to build a coalition of QWERTY keyboard users that ensured the keyboard's emergence as a de facto standard (David, 1985).

Thus, accompanying the emergence of new variants and new actors in the community is the development of a social system comprising these actors (Van de Ven and Garud, 1989). This network of organizations and interorganizational relations will have a structure similar to that of the technology itself: subcommunities that parallel the subsystems of the technology may be identified. Within and among subcommunities, supporters of the discontinuity, whether new entrants to the community or incumbents, will adjust patterns and practices within organizations and reconstruct interorganizational patterns of competition and cooperation between themselves and with incumbent organizations. Such a pattern is currently evolving around the six competing high-definition television standards. Thus, during the era of ferment, community organization evolves such that organizational clusters form around competing technological variants (Clark and DeBresson, 1990). Discontinuous technological change spurs the evolution of organizational forms, interorganizational relationships, and affiliations that span industry boundaries (Meyer, Brooks, and Goes, 1990). In the machine tool industry, for example, MIT, GE, and the Air Force cooperated to develop numerically controlled machine tools, while smaller firms worked together to develop record-playback technology (Noble, 1984). Likewise, in the electric supply industry, an Edison-led coalition supported direct current technology as it competed with the Westinghouse-led alternating current coalition (Hughes, 1983).

Figure 19.5a offers a stylized example of the network character of the technological community, subsequent to technological discontinuity, during the era of ferment. Figure 19.5a is a much more fragmented network than that of figure 19.4.

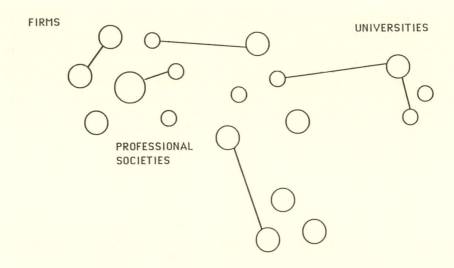

FIRMS

UNIVERSITIES

PROFESSIONAL
SOCIETIES

GOVERNMENT

FIG. 19.5a   Technological community, era of ferment

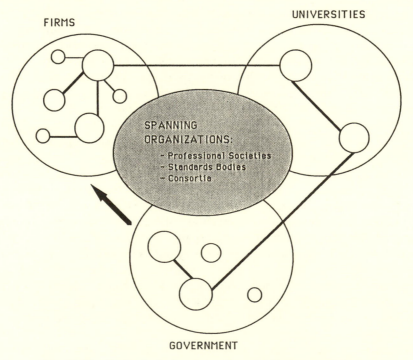

FIRMS

UNIVERSITIES

SPANNING
ORGANIZATIONS:
- Professional Societies
- Standards Bodies
- Consortia

GOVERNMENT

FIG. 19.5b   Technological community, era of incremental change

With new firms entering the community, few linkages exist among rival firms or between firms and other types of actors. Spanning organizations, such as professional societies and standards bodies, are not institutionalized: only a few of the organizations in the community have representatives in these bodies, so they are not yet influential. As the era of ferment continues, the new firms will have created linkages among themselves, with existing firms, and with nonfirm bodies, suggesting network clusters around competing variants. Linkages between incumbent members of the community will also be redefined, so that the community network begins to approximate that of figure 19.4.

Dominant Designs and Eras of Incremental Change

The standardization of continuous wave radio systems involved many different actors. Much of the determination of dimensions of merit and measurement of variants along these dimensions was performed by governments and military bodies within countries. In the United States, responsibility for the development of the radio system for point-to-point military transmission rested with the Navy. In the course of building this system, the Navy developed specifications for ever more effective components, thereby spurring and directing technological innovation by their supplier firms. The Navy also conducted experiments to select the best components from the field of technological competitors. Similar dynamics occurred with Telefunken, the German state radio organization, except that Telefunken's ownership of the industry reduced conflict and eliminated the need for contracting between government and private industry, as in the U.S. In addition, during World War I, the Navy declared a patent moratorium to speed systems integration during the state of military emergency.

Voluntary cooperative efforts and legislation together enforced transmitting rights. The International Wireless Conferences of 1903 and 1906 discussed the issue of interconnection between rival point-to-point wireless systems, because the Marconi company refused to handle other traffic. Later conferences addressed the issue of radiofrequency spectrum allocation among competing amateur, corporate, and military users; attendees took the proposed solutions home to their governments for approval. Within the U.S., Congress took up the issue of allocating radiofrequency spectrum wavelengths to transmitters and broadcasters to adjudicate the interference between and among amateur, corporate, and military users.

To facilitate the growth of a national radio system, the U.S. Navy subsumed American Marconi and guided the formation of RCA via funding and cross-licensing between General Electric, AT&T, Westinghouse, and several other service providers and manufacturers. Since the World War I patent moratoriums had expired, the cross-licensing of patents between these firms allowed higher-quality, more ubiquitous systems to develop. Furthermore, by consenting to build a single joint radio system instead of competing, the organizations of the Radio Group and the Telephone Group could focus on their basic competencies: manufacturing of components for General Electric and Westinghouse; service provision for RCA and AT&T.

The selection of a dominant design settles technological competition, drawing the era of ferment to a close. This selection occurs through the determination of appropriate dimensions of merit for the product and the measurement of technological variants along these dimensions. After the dominant design emerges, further refinement and elaboration of this design occur during the era of incremental change. During the emergence of the dominant design, the primary function of the community is standardization; during the era of incremental change, the primary function of the community is the elaboration of the standard. During these phases of the technology cycle, community organization evolution is convergent in nature: the social system that supports the dominant design remains powerful and builds systematic interdependencies that retain the technology, while other coalitions either joint the mainstream or vanish from the community.

Standardization. Closure of the critical dimensions of merit is shaped by a process of compromise and accommodation involving suppliers, vendors, customers, and governments (Constant, 1989). For example, David (1985) and Frost and Egri (1990) describe the collusion, compromise, accommodation, and coalitions of divergent interest groups in the competition between QWERTY and Dvorak typewriter keyboards. Similarly, Noble (1984) and Hughes (1983) describe activities of champions, networks of coalitions and interest groups, and the use of language and negotiations tactics to shape standards in the machine tool and power system industries. While dominant designs are characterized by a package of technological features, they are achieved via consensus-building at the community level. Standardization may be driven by organizations explicitly designated for this purpose, but it may also occur via the actions of various actors in the community, as we will describe later.

The function of standardization may be explicitly designated to a voluntary industry committee, such as for computer communications protocols (Farrell and Saloner, 1988) and operating systems (Gabel, 1987). The activities of standards bodies have become especially prevalent in communications technologies, where representatives of major firms and governmental bodies attempt to define technological trajectories in a proactive manner. While standards bodies prioritize dimensions of merit and their measurement, they have neither the money to contract for specific innovations nor the legislative power to enforce particular designs. Yet they represent a voluntary effort by multiple constituencies to reach consensus on a dominant design, allowing the development of technological systems.

Legislation also shapes the course of technological evolution, particularly for systemic technologies where constituents share linkage facilities. Government regulation drives the adoption of television broadcasting standards (Pelkmans and Beuter, 1987). Regulatory policy shaped the vastly different electrical supply systems of the United States, United Kingdom, and Germany (Hughes, 1983); it also caused differences in availability, efficacy, and safety of pharmaceuticals between the United States and Europe (Bodewitz, Buurma, and deVries, 1987).

Other technologies become de facto standards via indirect action. The market power of a dominant producer may swing enough weight behind a particular design to make it a standard, as in the case of the IBM 370 series mainframe and the IBM personal computer (DeLamarter, 1986), or AT&T's Touchtone standard (Brock, 1981). A powerful user may mandate a standard, as the U.S. Air Force imposed numerical control on the programmable machine tool industry (Noble, 1984). A group of firms may form an alliance around a standard, as in the case of shared bank card systems (Phillips, 1987). Thus, while many technological variants can emerge subsequent to a technological discontinuity, *one* variant is selected as the dominant design via social, political, and organizational processes.

Dominant designs, then, emerge not from technical logic, but from a negotiated logic enlivened by actors with interests in competing technical regimes. Social logic drives technical progress as suppliers, customers, or governments react to the uncertainty and inefficiencies associated with eras of ferment. Where technological discontinuities may be driven by random events or strokes of genius, such as Fessenden's discovery of the alternator for continuous wave radio transmission, dominant designs are driven by the visible hand of organizations interacting with other organizations and practitioner communities to shape dimensions of merit and industry standards to maximize local needs (Noble, 1984; Abernathy, 1978; Aitken, 1985). Actions of individuals, organizations, and networks of organizations shape dominant designs which, in turn, close the era of ferment. These socially driven outcomes directly affect the time path of technical change until the next technological discontinuity.

Elaboration. After dominant designs emerge, technical uncertainty decreases and the nature of technical change shifts from variation to incremental change. Technical clarity and convergence on a set of technical parameters permit firms to design standardized and interchangeable parts and to optimize organizational processes for volume and efficiency (Hounshell, 1984). Practitioner communities develop industry-wide procedures, traditions, and problem-solving modes that permit focused, incremental technical puzzle solving (Constant, 1987). Dominant designs permit more stable and reliable relations with suppliers, vendors, and customers. From customers' perspectives, dominant designs reduce product class confusion and promise dramatic decreases in product cost. Finally, if the product is part of a larger system, industry standards permit systemwide compatibility and integration (David, 1988; Farrell and Saloner, 1985).

While the organizational evolution of the technological community drives technological change during the era of ferment, it is this very process of organizational convergence on a dominant technology that retards organizational evolution after a dominant design emerges. The dominant design embodies the set of technological compromises and organizational agreements that remain stable throughout the era of incremental change; technological and organizational change during this era focuses on process-based improvements that reduce cost and uncertainty (Abernathy [1978] and Hollander [1965] detail such process-based improvements for automobile and rayon manufacture, respectively). Thus, both technological and organizational evolution during this period are characterized by processes that serve to retain the dominant design.

Community organization evolution during the era of incremental change allows incremental elaboration of the dominant design. Community evolution consists of convergent behavior, as organizations develop interlinked competencies and nonconformists vanish. Cost-based competition leads competitors to establish and elaborate interorganizational agreements that reduce transaction costs and buffer their technical cores (Thompson, 1967). The high costs of radio show production, for example, spurred the rise of more cost-efficient national radio broadcasting networks at the expense of transcription syndicates and regional networks (Leblebici et al.,

1991). Shakeouts occur: firms that cannot compete on cost drop out, as do firms that did not adopt the dominant design. For example, in the snowmobile industry, the number of manufacturers dropped from over a hundred to one dozen after the adoption of safety and noise standards in 1965: the industry evolved from conditions of perfect competition to oligopoly (DeBresson and Clark, 1991). These phenomena lead the technological community to converge to a set of ever-more interlinked organizations; the multiple sets of organizational clusters around technological variants converge to a singular, interdependent cluster.

Within technical communities, organizations which reinforce this period of incremental, order-creating, technical change become prominent. Critical problems are defined, legitimate procedures are established, and community norms and values emerge from interaction among interdependent actors (Van de Ven and Garud, 1989). During periods of incremental change, informal know-how trading occurs among competitors (von Hipple, 1987). Both standards bodies and professional societies are institutions which facilitate focused technical problem solving and know-how trading. Technical journals expand, providing another forum for this sort of knowledge dissemination (Nelson and Rosenberg, 1991). Universities develop curricula that train engineers in practice traditions; Hughes (1983) has shown the convergence of electrical engineering curricula at various institutions. These traditions cross traditional disciplinary boundaries: for example, Constant (1980) describes the evolution of practice traditions in the turbojet industry as the result of knowledge sharing among combustion, mechanical, aerospace, and metallurgical engineers.

Figure 19.5b (p. 416) depicts the network characteristics of the technological community, subsequent to the emergence of a dominant design, in the era of incremental change. Compared with figure 19.5a (pre-dominant design), figure 19.5b illustrates a singular cluster of firms around a dominant technology; all other firms have dropped from the community. Furthermore, this cluster is well connected with government and academic institutions, and the activities of professional societies and standards bodies have become highly interdependent with the innovative activity of firms.

Over time, periods of normal technology development build ever-more interlinked competencies among technological communities and related suppliers, vendors, and customers. As competencies are deepened about given technical premises and as routinized problem-solving modes become institutionalized, technological mind-sets and momentum build in a product class (Jenkins, 1975; Hughes, 1983). While technical progress may be substantial, the community of practitioners look more and more inward, as problem solving becomes more routinized and rigid as the era of incremental change unfolds (Myers and Marquis, 1969; Dutton and Thomas, 1985). These interlocked and rigid processes are located within the community of practitioners and competing organizations (see, for example, Constant's [1980] description of the evolution of practice traditions among technologists and engineers in the turbojet community). Where dominant designs are established by the visible hand of a few powerful organizations competing for dominance, in the era of incremental change, technological progress is driven by the invisible hand of a multitude of organizations competing within sharp technical, social, and normative constraints (Van de Ven and Garud, 1989).

The response of veteran firms and communities to external threat is increased commitment to the status quo (Cooper and Schendel, 1976; Foster, 1986). Since technology has social and community effects, threatened technical communities resist technological change both by increased persistence in the prior technical regime and by increased political action (see Frost and Egri [1990] for a thorough discussion of these political processes). For example, in the watch, steel, and power industries, new technologies, such as quartz, turbojet, and SST, were resisted by enhanced technical efforts in the soon-to-be obsolete technology and by increased political efforts (Landes, 1983; Constant, 1989; Horwitch, 1982). In the early electric light bulb industry, GE purchased patents (or entire firms) for competing technological variants and then suppressed them, maintaining support for its own bulbs and systems (Bright, 1949).

Given the technical momentum generated by normal technological progress, existing technical communities and/or organizations virtually never give birth to radically new, competence-destroying technologies. The locus of technological discontinuity occurs from outside the existing technical community and from outside veteran organizations (Tushman and Anderson, 1986; Cooper and Schendel, 1976). In the 20th century U.S. radio broadcasting industry, for example, changes in transaction technology (the move from general broadcasting to sponsored programs, then from sponsored programs to advertising time, and from advertising time to listener exposure) were introduced by fringe players and initially resisted by the dominant players. The success of these radical innovations empowered the innovators and led the dominant players eventually to adopt these same practices because of competitive threat (Leblebici et al., 1991). During eras of incremental change, then, community and organizational norms and processes drive incremental, normal technical progress but discourage variation required for breakthrough technical advances within the community.

Summary

The nature of community organization evolution varies with the stage of the technology cycle. From the emergence of a technological discontinuity to the selection of a dominant design, community organization evolution drives technological competition and selection. In contrast, during the era of incremental change, the nature of the dominant design and its associated community organization constrain further community evolution. Figures 19.5a and 19.5b summarize community activity and evolutionary dynamics in the context of the technology cycle. Before the emergence of a dominant design, the structure of the technological community is chaotic; after the dominant design is established, community structure is ordered. After a technological discontinuity, an era of ferment ensues. New organizations enter the community, redefining the interactions of community members; a period of community reorientation parallels the era of technological ferment as social and technical systems are built around competing technological variants. The emergence of new actors and new linkages during this period leads to a redistribution of power among these players. In contrast, the emergence of a dominant design begins a period of community convergence: nonsupporters of the dominant technology reorient or vanish, and interorganizational agreements around the dominant systems are strengthened and elaborated. This period also brings the prominence of institutions that elaborate and retain the technology, such as standards bodies, educational curricula, and professional societies. While power accrues to the dominant coalition, actors and linkages which do not reinforce this coalition will drop out of the community.

The images in figures 19.5a and 19.5b suggest some testable propositions about the differences in community evolution before and after the emergence of a dominant design. To wit:

Proposition 1A: Entry rates of firms increase during the era of ferment and decrease during the era of incremental change.

Proposition 1B: Exit rates of firms decrease during the era of ferment and increase during the era of incremental change.

Proposition 2: The rate of change in the membership of spanning organizations increases more during the era of ferment and decreases during the era of incremental change.

Proposition 3: The distribution of power becomes less concentrated during the era of ferment and more concentrated during the era of incremental change.

Proposition 4: Rates of linkage formation and dissolution increase during the era of ferment and decrease during the era of incremental change.

These propositions have been derived from the study of systemic technologies. We suggest that these differences in evolutionary dynamics will be lessened for non-systemic technologies because of the lower levels of technological uncertainty and the more homogeneous technological communities. The more complex the product, the greater the variety of organizations involved in selection of a dominant design. Open systems, spanning geographic distances, require governmental regulation or legislation. These systems, such as telephone or electrical supply, evolve through additions to an embedded base, requiring cooperation between service providers and component manufacturers. The more variegated the technological community, the more intricate the network of interorganizational linkages developed to select a dominant design. Where selection among less complex technological variants may be accomplished solely by professional societies or voluntary standards bodies, for more complex technologies, legislative and regulatory bodies are involved in the process of technological selection.

We also expect that these differences in evolutionary dynamics will be accentuated during competence-destroying technological change and lessened for competence-enhancing technological change. Competence-destroying technological discontinuities set the context for extensive community organization evolution, as new firms enter the industry and new linkages form. Competence-enhancing technological discontinuities require less community organization evolution, as they are typically introduced by industry incumbents (Anderson and Tushman, 1990). Building on existing competence and know-how, competence-enhancing technological discontinuities can emerge without radical change in community organization. That is, the existing community structure can accommodate competence-enhancing technological discontinuities; however, changes in scale, scope, or technical performance associated with the adoption of the discontinuity can lead to community evolution as first-movers gain power through competitive advantage and laggards lose power.

Finally, these differences in evolutionary dynamics should also be accentuated for technological change in core subsystems and lessened for technological change in peripheral subsystems. Discontinuities in core subsystems involve larger subsets of the technological community than discontinuities in peripheral subsystems, because the multiple interdependencies between core subsystems and other product subsystems require organizational coordination of change in the core subsystem with the other subsystems. In contrast, discontinuities in peripheral subsystems may emerge and be reconciled with only the involvement of the subcommunities holding stake in the peripheral subsystem and its few interdependent subsystems.

In this chapter, we have examined the coevolution of technology and organization. Technologies evolve through cycles, where technological discontinuities and dominant designs demark eras of ferment and eras of incremental change. A parallel process of community organization evolution simultaneously drives and is driven by cyclic technological progress. Changes in actors, linkages, and power shape technological competition and selection during the era of ferment, from the emergence of a technological discontinuity until convergence on a dominant design. This period of community reorientation culminates with the development of a social system that supports incremental technical progress. Community organization evolution throughout the era of incremental change is characterized by elaboration of linkages and strengthening of institutional roles, without major change in powerful actors or interorganizational linkages.

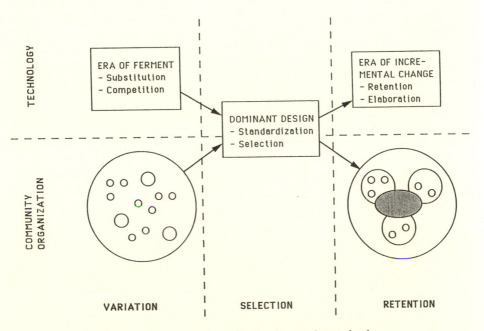

FIG. 19.6 Coevolution of technology and organization

The emergence of a dominant design is the conceptual anchor of the coevolutionary dynamics of technology and organization (see figure 19.6). Prior to the ascending of the dominant design, technical variation is paralleled by community variation. Convergence on a set of technical attributes for a dominant design is matched by interorganizational convergence of the technological community. While technologies are socially constructed before the emergence of a dominant design and organizational communities are technologically determined after the emergence of a dominant design, the reciprocal influences of technology and organization are the greatest during the window of convergence on a dominant design.

In this chapter, we have focused on systemic technologies. These technologies, with their complicated networks of components, linkages, and interfaces, give rise to an extensive variety of actors, roles, and patterns of interaction that illustrates the dynamics of community organization evolution. For less complex products, the functions required of the technological community are the same, but the dynamics of evolution are less complex as fewer actors are involved in the process.

The implications of this theory for research and practice are extensive. The propositions developed in this study need to be validated through empirical examination at the community level of analysis. Detailed, longitudinal studies of technological change and community organization dynamics must be compared across various levels of technological complexity to understand the coevolution of technology and community organization.

Much of the organization-based literature on managing innovation has focused on encouraging innovative behavior within the firm. Yet by focusing on the community as the level of analysis, firm-specific innovation must be viewed in the context of larger technological and organizational systems; interdependence between technological subsystems and their associated communities must be managed via strategic interorganizational activity. Future research must examine the performance and policy implications of such community-level actions.

Note

1. Such a definition merits comparison with related chapters in this book. Baum and Singh, chapter 18, this volume, distinguish between organizational and environmental actors, in the tradition of Litwak and Hylton (1962) and DiMaggio and Powell (1983). They examine the interdependence between day care and nursery populations (the organizational field) in the environmental context of changing budgets and demand, where governmental agencies determine budgets and the population of child care users requires a certain level of service. Our view of community, parallel to that of Van de Ven and Garud, chapter 20, this volume, treats technology as environmental context while including traditional environmental actors such as governmental associations, professional societies, and user groups with the organizational field. We do so because the actions of these unique organizations so strongly influence and are influenced by the course of technological evolution.

20

The Coevolution of Technical and Institutional Events in the Development of an Innovation

ANDREW H. VAN DE VEN AND RAGHU GARUD

How and *why* are technological innovations developed and commercialized? Answers to these how and why questions have significant practical implications for public policymakers, entrepreneurs, investors, and managers engaged in the highly uncertain and novel development of innovations. The how question requires a process description of the temporal sequence of events that occur to create and transform basic scientific knowledge into commercially viable products or services. Based on an intensive longitudinal field study, this chapter provides such a process description by narrating the events that were observed to occur over a 35-year period to develop and commercialize the cochlear implant, a new-to-the-world biomedical technology that provides hearing to profoundly deaf people. The why question calls for a theory of change that explains this observed process. This chapter examines the utility of a social evolutionary theory of change for explaining the development and commercialization of cochlear implants.

A growing interest in biological analogies of evolution throughout the social sciences (Hannan and Freeman, 1989) led a growing number of scholars in the 1980s and 1990s to explain the dynamics that govern technical and institutional change as a social evolutionary process of variation, selection, and retention. Variation is the creation of a novel technical or institutional form within a population under investigation. Selection occurs principally through competition among the alternative novel forms that exist, and actors in the environment select those forms which optimize or are best suited to the resource base of an environmental niche (Hannan and Freeman, 1977:939). Retention involves the forces (including inertia and persistence) that perpetuate and maintain certain technical and institutional forms that were selected in the past (Aldrich, 1979).

We gratefully appreciate useful suggestions from Graham Astley, Joel Baum, Robert Burgelman, William Barnett, Joseph Galaskiewicz, Richard Nelson, Elaine Romanelli, Richard Rosenbloom, Vernon Ruttan, Jitendra Singh, and Michael Tushman on earlier versions of this chapter. Support for this research has been provided (in part) by a grant to the Strategic Management Research Center at the University of Minnesota from the Program on Organization Effectiveness, Office of Naval Research, under contract No. N00014-84-K-0016.

Organizational scholars view the temporal relations among variation, selection, and retention either as a continuous and gradual process (McKelvey, 1982; Nelson and Winter, 1982; Hannan and Freeman, 1989) or as a punctuated equilibrium (Utterback and Abernathy, 1975; Tushman and Romanelli, 1985; Lumsden and Singh, 1990). The latter, and currently more popular view, is exemplified by Anderson and Tushman's (1990) cyclical model of technological change illustrated in figure 20.1. This model posits that technological breakthroughs are variations which trigger a discontinuous but relatively short period of ferment and competition between alternative technological regimes. This era of ferment closes when social and political dynamics select a dominant product design from among competing alternatives. The selected dominant design subsequently evolves through a relatively long retention period of incremental process improvements, which, in turn, is interrupted by the next technological discontinuity or round of product innovation (Utterback and Abernathy, 1975).

Whether change is viewed as a gradual or punctuated process, most organizational models of evolution[1] do not adequately examine the origins of novelty itself to explain how a new organizational form or technological discontinuity emerges, and how the era of ferment unfolds to produce a dominant design that diffuses and becomes recognized into a population or a market (Romanelli, 1991a). Indeed, the origins of variation or technological discontinuity are not explained; they are assumed to be rare discrete events produced by random or "blind" chance (Campbell, 1974; McKelvey, 1982) or by individual genius (Anderson and Tushman, 1990:605). This exploratory research was undertaken to examine directly the origin of novelty itself, by which a new-to-the-world biomedical innovation and industry emerge. We argue that the origination of innovations has a dynamic history of its own which requires systematic study and explanation.

Study of the origins of novelty requires a more fine-grained model of the process of social evolution than has been adopted in the past. The process of variation, selection, and retention has typically been treated as a simple linear sequence of three discrete events: (1) a random event occurs in which a novel variation is created, followed by (2) a selection event in which an environmental agent chooses the variation over competing alternatives, and (3) the selected variation is then progressively reinformed through retention processes of incremental improvements and diffusion. As figure 20.1 illustrates, this sequence is not repeated until another major technological discontinuity arises. To describe and explain how innovations emerge we argue that

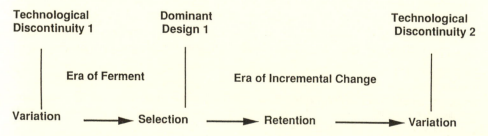

FIG. 20.1   Illustration of technology cycle in punctuated equilibrium model (adapted from Anderson and Tushman, 1990)

social evolutionary processes are better viewed as a cumulative progression of numerous interrelated acts of variation, selection, and retention over an extended period of time.

Several detailed historical studies of technological innovation support our argument. Usher (1954:60) demonstrated that the history of mechanical invention is *not* the history of single inventors, nor of random chance events. Gilfillan (1935:5) observed "a perpetual accretion of little details. . . probably having neither beginning, completion nor definable limits" in the gradual evolution of shipbuilding. Constant (1980) found that advances in aircraft propulsion emerged not from flashes of disembodied inspiration but from many individually small changes and recombinations of existing technology, which add up to what might be called a technological revolution. Moreover, many complementary innovations in technical and institutional arrangements are usually required and serve as "bottlenecks" that interrupt the innovation development journey (Binswanger and Ruttan, 1978; Hughes, 1983). Research reviews by Mowery (1985), Thirtle and Ruttan (1986), Freeman (1986), and Dosi (1988) show that the commercial success or failure of a technological innovation is, in great measure, a reflection of many other institutional innovations which embody the social, economic, and political infrastructure that any community needs to sustain its members. Thus, as Rosenberg (1983:49) states, "What is really involved is a process of cumulative accretion of useful knowledge, to which many people make essential contributions, even though the prizes and recognition are usually accorded to the one actor who happens to have been on the stage at a critical moment."

Discontinuities are inherent to the numerous technical and institutional events performed by many actors over an extended period to develop and commercialize an innovation. Individual events are often not made known to others, and various "acts of insights" pertaining to technical and institutional capabilities are often required to overcome bottlenecks. These acts of insights accumulate probabilistically; they do not proceed deterministically under the stress of necessity or "progress" (Rosenberg, 1983). They are possible for only a limited number of individuals and organizations who, by virtue of their different roles and functions, become exposed to conditions which bring both awareness of problems and elements of solutions within their frames of reference. As Usher (1954:67) stated, "emergent novelty becomes truly significant only through accumulation" of many individual acts of technical and institutional change undertaken by numerous actors over time.

These historical studies suggest that a better understanding of the process of novelty can be obtained when the evolutionary concepts of variation, selection, and retention are defined as micro-events or individual events, rather than as macrostages of evolution. Some of the events that are observed to occur in the development of an innovation (here cochlear implants) represent changes in the technology, here defined as cochlear implant artifacts (devices and equipment) and the body of knowledge embodied in the design or architecture of these artifacts (Layton, 1986). Among technical events, some represent novel variations or unprecedented advances, while most are incremental activities undertaken either to expand upon, modify, or adapt an ongoing technical course of action. Other events may pertain to institutions, commonly defined as the administrative rules, routines, or programs used to evaluate artifacts and to coordinate organizational actions and expectations (Ruttan, 1978; Powell and DiMaggio, 1991). Among institutional events, some deal with creating

**Variation Process
-- Novel Technical
  Advances**

**Selection Process
-- Institution Rule-
  Making Events**

**Retention Process
-- Institution Rule-
  Following Events**

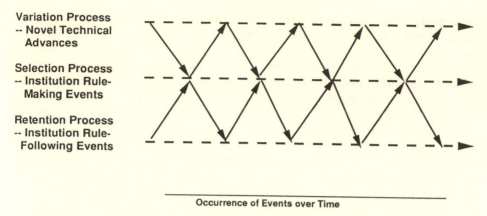

Occurrence of Events over Time

FIG. 20.2   Illustration of research design for examining technological evolution

or modifying rules, and thereby represent institutional selection mechanisms. Some others are programmed by previously established institutional rules or routines, and the process of rule following indicates a retention of those rules.

Figure 20.2 illustrates a research design for examining the temporal relationships at work during the course of these events. By focusing on events, one can gain a more detailed microanalytical description of not only how variation, selection, and retention processes unfold over time, but also how these events are temporally related and thereby facilitate and constrain the development and commercialization of an innovation. In other words, instead of preordaining the process of innovation development as a simple linear progression of variation, selection, and retention stages (as figure 20.1 illustrates), focusing on events opens up the inquiry to greater empirical possibilities. Specifically, this exploratory study was guided by the proposition that *numerous novel technical (variation) events, institutional rule-making (selection) events, and institutional rule-following (retention) events occurred and coevolved over time to facilitate and constrain the development and commercialization of cochlear implants.*

Methodology

A longitudinal real-time study of the emergence of the cochlear implant technology and supporting industry was undertaken from 1983 to 1989. It began by collecting baseline data through interviews and archival information on the prior history of cochlear implants and writing a case history on the development of the innovation prior to 1983 (see Garud and Van de Ven, 1989, 1990). Real-time data were collected with multiple methods and from multiple sources on the major events in the development of the innovation and industry over time. These sources included direct field observations and attendance at trade conferences where numerous interviews were conducted with actors from different organizations involved in different functions of cochlear implant development, reviews of trade literature, monthly observations of day-long management meetings of one of the firms involved in this innovation, as well as the administration of standardized questionnaires and interviews with key actors involved in the innovation every six to twelve months.

Following procedures discussed by Van de Ven and Poole (1990), the multiple data sources were content analyzed to develop a chronological list of events in the development of cochlear implants. Events were defined as critical incidents when actions occurred to develop the major functions related to the development of the cochlear implant technology and industrial system. Van de Ven and Garud's (1989) systems framework was adopted to identify and track nine technical and institutional functions that need to be developed or put in place to commercialize a new-to-the-world innovation. These functions include: the development of institutional legitimation, regulations, and standards; resource endowments of basic scientific research; financing arrangements; and educational competence and proprietary firm activities of applied R&D, clinical trials, manufacturing, and marketing.

Over the seven years of real-time tracking plus historical baseline data, 771 events were recorded in the database. Of course, these events do not represent the population of occurrences in the development of cochlear implants. Thus, as is well established in classical test theory of item sampling (Lord and Novick, 1968), the events represent a sample of indicators describing what happened over time. However, the events do not represent a random sample. Although the researchers gained unprecedented access to many of the key actors and firms engaged in cochlear implant development over the years, this degree of access was not uniform across all actors. Moreover, during intensive periods of activity it was impossible for the research team directly to observe simultaneous events going on in multiple sites in Austria, Australia, and the United States. We compensated for these limitations by conducting interviews and obtaining relevant documents from the actors involved in the events as soon after they occurred as possible.

To enhance the validity of tabulating events, the entry of events from raw data sources into the data file was performed by two researchers (who were also engaged in real-time field observations). Consensus was required between these researchers on a consistent interpretation of the decision rules used to identify events. In addition, the resulting list of events was reviewed by selected informants who were engaged in different functions of cochlear implant development.

In order to analyze temporal patterns in this chronological list of qualitative events, each event was coded in terms of the following dichotomous indicators of variation, selection, and retention processes of social evolution:

1. Rule-Making Events—A selection process was evident if the event had the effect of creating or modifying institutional rules or routines.
2. Rule-Following Events—A retention process was indicated if the event was programmed or governed by existing institutional routines or rules.
3. Novel Technical Events—A variation process was evident if the event represented a precedent to any that occurred before, and at the time of occurrence did not represent the making or following of institutional rules.

In addition to these key indicators of evolution processes, each event was coded in terms of the actors involved and the functional topic or subject matter addressed.

See Van de Ven and Garud (1992) for these coding decision rules. Two researchers independently coded each events, and they agreed on 93 percent of all codes. Differences were resolved through mutual consensus.

Historical Narration of Cochlear Implant Creation

Of the total 771 events that were observed to occur in the development and commercialization of cochlear implants from 1955 to 1989, 265 events (or 35 percent) were identified as indicators of our three evolutionary processes: 63 novel technical variation events, 107 institutional rule-making (selection) events, and 95 institutional rule-following (retention) events. The rest were events in which neither variation, selection, nor retention processes (as defined by our coding decision rules) were evident. Figures 20.3 and 20.4 plot the number and cumulative frequency (respectively) of these events during cochlear implants' development from 1955 to 1989. To maximize visual clarity, the horizontal axis of the dates when these events occurred shifts from a yearly scale (for 1956–77) to a semiannual scale (for 1978—89) in the figures, because during the latter years a steep increase in the number of events occurred.

Three qualitatively different periods in the historical development of cochlear implants are noted at the bottom of figures 20.3 and 20.4. The first, an Initiation period, began about 1955 and consisted primarily of advances in basic scientific knowledge which led to the creation of prototype devices of cochlear implants by universities and basic research institutes. This period culminated in the efforts by private firms beginning in 1977 to obtain access to prototypal cochlear implant devices for developing proprietary products by entering into relationships with basic research institutes and by initiating applied R&D, manufacturing, clinical trials, and marketing functions. Once these relationships and proprietary functions were established, a second Expansion period is shown in which a rapid growth occurred in the number of events from 1983 to 1986 to develop and commercialize cochlear implants. This expansion period was followed by a Stabilization period during which a dominant design for cochlear implant products emerged, and the very structures created in prior periods for industry growth began to constrain further development.

Over the three periods of cochlear implant's development, figures 20.3 and 20.4 show that novel technical advances produced by basic research prior to 1978 continued to exceed the number of institutional rule-making and rule-following events until 1983 but were surpassed and exceeded by the latter during the industry expansion and stabilization periods. Furthermore, a few rule-following events (consisting of following institutional rules to obtain patent rights) preceded the first establishment of institutional rules unique to cochlear implants in 1972, and both appeared to grow in an oscillatory fashion during the industry expansion period (1983–86). The graphs show that by 1989, no more institutional rule-making events occurred while rule-following events continued to occur, and will presumably exceed the number of rule-making events if the industry Stabilization Period continues.

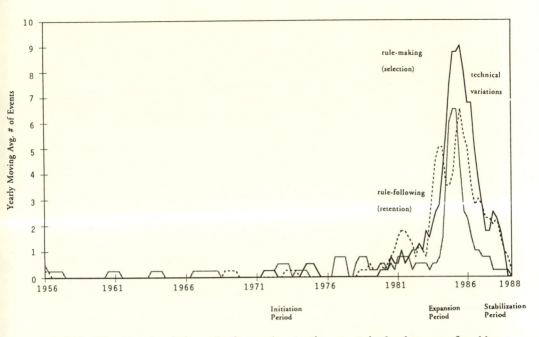

FIG. 20.3   Number of variation, selection, and rentention events in development of cochlear implants

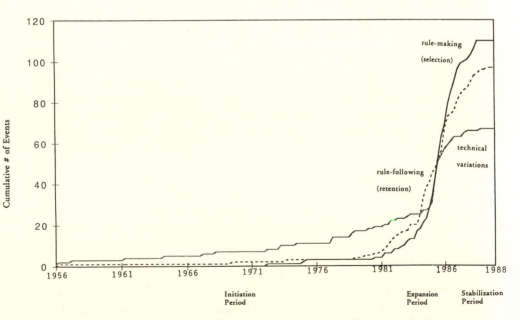

FIG. 20.4   Cumulative number of variation, selection, and retention events in development of cochlear implants

The Initiation Period

Basic research and technology advances by academic research units predated by more than 22 years any commercial activities of what came to be a cochlear implant industry. These technical advances were supported by research contracts and grants from public research foundations and philanthropists (which present institutional selection events), and by a few institutional legitimation events by otological professional associations. Several earlier technical variation events set the stage for this institutional support. The concept of using electricity to bring hearing to the deaf goes back almost 200 years, when an Italian scientist, Volta, first observed the effects of electrical stimulation of the ear (ASHA, 1985). More recently, experiments involving such stimulations were conducted by French researchers in 1957. The first cochlear implant in the United States was performed in 1961 by a clinical physician, William House, founder of the Walt Disney Hearing Center (now named the House Ear Institute) in Los Angeles. After many trials and disappointments with attempts to develop more sophisticated multiple-channel devices, House and his colleague, Jack Urban, pursued a strategy of beginning with the simplest single-channel device for restoring hearing to the profoundly deaf by using an experimental trial-and-error approach to guide their research.

In contrast, other researchers at this time were pursuing more theoretical technical approaches. These researchers argued that the cochlea was a complex organ which could only be replicated by the insertion of a cochlear device that had multiple electrodes, each electrode allowing the transmission of different frequencies at different locations of the cochlea. During the 1970s, cochlear implant research programs were under way at the universities of Stanford, Utah, California—San Francisco, Melbourne in Australia, and Innsbrook in Vienna, Austria. Researchers at these universities disseminated the results of their work in typical academic ways: through journal publications, professional conferences, student education, patent applications, and research proposals.

As one should expect with a new technological paradigm (Dosi, 1982; Rappa, 1989), the institutional legitimacy of basic research in cochlear implants has historically been a contested terrain. Several early institutional rule-making attempts to select a technical direction were unsuccessful. For example, one controversy occurred in the mid-1970s when Dr. House was censured by colleagues in his professional association for continued development of a single-channel device. Many otologists believed that once a single-channel device was implanted, the ear would be unsuitable for a multiple-channel system, which some thought was technically superior to a single-channel system. This delayed proprietary appropriation of cochlear implants by private firms occurred because those developing multiple-channel devices were purported to be on the verge of a major breakthrough, which did not materialize until several years later.

The contested legitimacy of cochlear implants spilled over into institutional research funding decisions. These decisions in turn were influenced both by chance events in an unrelated area and by technological preferences that channeled future basic research in particular directions. For example, in the early 1960s researchers at Stanford University submitted a research proposal to NIH. This proposal included plans for human implantation of a cochlear implant device when developed. After a site visit by an NIH review panel, the researchers received a favorable scientific recommendation but were not awarded a research contract on moral grounds. NIH later reversed this decision. This change in attitude was triggered by some unrelated experiments in England on human cortical stimulation in blind persons. This work was published in 1967 and generated much interest in the United States. It stimulated NIH to establish its own new neural control laboratory with the mission to underwrite contracts for research in electrical stimulation. The main targets for these contracts were vision and cerebral stimulation; hearing was "an afterthought" (Simmons, 1985).

From 1970 to 1987 the NIH provided various universities a total of $29 million in grants and contracts for cochlear implant research. However, little of this institutional funding was directed to developing single-channel designs. A resource allocation officer of NIH attended the first international conference related to cochlear implants in 1973, became impressed with the scientific rationale for multichannel implants, and concluded that NIH should support basic research on multichannel designs as a way of encouraging alternatives to the controversial single-channel devices that House was implanting in increasing numbers of patients.

This 1973 international conference represented the first major institutional event to recognize and legitimize the cochlear implant technology. Several other actions occurred years later, involving two most influential professional associations to legitimize cochlear implants. The first was an official endorsement of cochlear implants by the American Medical Association in 1983. The second was the creation of a special ad hoc committee on cochlear implants by the American Speech Language and Hearing Association (ASHA) in 1984. In May 1985, ASHA published a widely read survey of firms in the cochlear implant industry. In 1985, the American Academy of Otolaryngology–Head and Neck Surgery endorsed the cochlear implant device to the the Office of Health Technology Assessment (OHTA). On the basis of this endorsement, OHTA published a health technology assessment report (1986) endorsing the safety/efficacy of cochlear implants, a step essential for receiving Medicare coverage for the implants (discussed in the next period).

By the late 1970s seven leading research units worldwide had developed prototype cochlear implant devices for human implantations. But human implantation required following institutional rules on review and approval of biomedical devices for the FDA in the United States and similar regulatory agencies in other countries. Obtaining such approval was a costly and extended process, which often exceeded the resource endowments of the academic research units. This set the stage for establishing relationships among basic research units and private firms. Basic research units needed additional resources and competencies that private firms could provide to conduct clinical trials, manufacture, and market their prototype devices. Some private firms, in turn, were following basic research advances in otology and awaited the development of concrete prototype devices, because abstract theories that were available in the public domain and published in technical journals were very difficult to appropriate for commercial applications.

Between 1979 and 1982 five private firms (3M, Storz, Symbion, Nucleus, and Biostem) initiated proprietary cochlear implant activities. In order to acquire the basic scientific knowledge for proprietary use, these firms commonly negotiated and entered into interorganizational relationships with different universities and teaching clinics who were undertaking basic research during the first period.

Industry Expansion Period

Figures 20.3 and 20.4 show that from 1983 to 1986 a dramatic increase occurred in the number of events related to development of the cochlear implant industry. This rapid industry expansion period will be described in terms of the major developmental patterns that occurred in parallel and coevolved over time to construct the emerging industry system.

Proprietary Activities. Private firms undertook R&D, manufacturing, clinical trials and regulatory processes, and marketing activities. These activities began sequentially from 1979 to 1981, and all grew at rapid but differentiated rates during the expansion period. While technical variation events through applied R&D were dominant at the beginning of this period, the number of institutional rule-following events to conduct clinical trials and obtain regulatory approvals for devices surpassed that of all other functions at the end of this expansion period. As discussed later, institutional regulations of the FDA largely expla. the sequential development of these proprietary functions.

However, instances of opportunistic "leapfrogging" of institutional rules were also observed. For example, a firm submitted an informal application to the FDA for a premarket approval (PMA) for its cochlear implant device before the necessary preceding research and clinical trials were truly completed. It was reported that the application was submitted in order to identify FDA's standard of the number of clinical trials necessary to obtain regulatory approval. The FDA declined the informal application.

Institutional Regulation. All medical products, including cochlear devices, are subject to review and approval by the FDA in the United States. The essential rules in the approval process have been summarized by Yin and Segerson (1986). In order to conduct clinical tests on humans, an "investigational device exemption" (IDE) based on clinical tests of the device on animals must be obtained from the FDA. Next, each of the clinical sites is required to obtain an "Institutional review board" clearance to certify its capability to conduct clinical tests on humans. After test results indicate that a minimum level of safety and effectiveness has been achieved, the device must be submitted to the FDA panel for a premarket approval (PMA). If the FDA finds that the device is safe and effective, it grants its approval for commercial sale after having approved the prevalence of "good manufacturing practices." This entire procedure of obtaining FDA approval from the initiation of clinical trials on animals can take anywhere from three to five years and cost millions of dollars (Grabowski and Vernon, 1983).

New operational rules were needed to apply this institutional regulatory structure for new-to-the-world biomedical innovations. In 1981, 3M undertook the institutional rule-following event of applying to the FDA for an IDE for its first cochlear implant device. This institutional rule-following event led to a series of institutional rule-making events. It was reported that FDA personnel and panel members did not possess the necessary knowledge to evaluate the application. As a result, 3M was requested to prepare additional documents and information in order to educate FDA personnel and scientific review panels about the nature of cochlear implants and the safety of electrical stimulation of the cochlea. In November 1984, the FDA awarded the 3M-House device its first PMA approval for the commercial release of a cochlear implant product in the U.S. Noting the historic nature of his approval, the FDA announced, "This is the first time that one of the five human senses has been replaced by an electronic device."

At the same time, the FDA undertook a contradictory institutional selection event by circulating a status report stating that the multichannel device was potentially superior to the single-channel technology it had just approved. Resonating with the FDA report and initiated by competing firms, other testimonials began to appear in the news media urging customers to wait for the superior multichannel implant.

In response, researchers associated with the single-channel technology claimed that there was no evidence to suggest that multichannel devices were superior to single-channel devices. In reaction, physicians who were implanting multichannel devices argued that it was unethical to implant a single-channel device when a multichannel device would be available soon. The net effects of these claims and counterclaims were that 3M's window of market opportunity as producer of the only commercially available device was limited and the second-mover, Nucleus, achieved the institutional legitimation of an "FDA approved" status for its multichannel device even though formal approval was not granted until July 1985.

Parallel with its efforts to increase sales of the 3M/House device, 3M initiated efforts to protect its window of opportunity by requesting the FDA to apply to other firms' devices the same rigorous rules to which they had been subject. This appeal was made in response to a request from the FDA to manufacturers seeking their inputs for crafting guidelines for PMA applications. 3M argued the FDA rules should specify that a minimum of 100 patients be required before a device be approved by the FDA. To support these arguments, 3M researchers organized a technical seminar for FDA staff in January 1985 in Washington, D.C. Nucleus also provided its inputs in making these institutional FDA rules by using technical rationales to justify its political institutional ends. Since Nucleus had data on only 43 patients at the time of its premarket approval application to the FDA, imposing a minimum of 100 patients to demonstrate clinical safety as proposed by 3M, could significantly delay Nucleus's device approval by the FDA. Thus, audiologists from Nucleus argued that the sample size required in clinical trials should be a function of the claims made about each device, the statistical approach adopted to support such claims, and the actual performance of each device. After some deliberations, the FDA agreed with Nucleus's arguments. In June 1985 the FDA circulated draft guidelines stating that it would not specify the number of patients required for a PMA application; rather, it would leave sample size requirements flexible.

Health Insurance. While private firms were simultaneously following FDA regulations to develop their devices and competing to influence the construction of these institutional regulations to benefit their proprietary purposes, they also cooperated with one another, and with other public-sector actors, to obtain financial reimbursement for patients from health insurance carriers for cochlear implantations. Health insurance coverage was considered critical to market success because the cost of a cochlear implant and associated surgical expenses averages $20,000 per patient. Radcliffe (1984) reported that this cost would severely restrict adoption of commercially available cochlear implants.

3M and Symbion in 1983 were the first to initiate efforts to convince third party insurance payors to extend coverage to cochlear implants. Other firms also sought coverage for their cochlear devices. In 1983, 3M was successful in obtaining coverage for its experimental single-channel House device. However, the health insurance coverage applied only to a very small population of the deaf. In December 1985, a Cochlear Implant Industry Council, consisting of representatives from 3M, Nucleus, Storz, and Symbion, was formed under the auspices of the Hearing Industries Manufacturers' Association. The purpose of this institutional innovation was to create a united proposal to the Prospective Payment Assessment Committee of the Public Health System to obtain broader Medicare coverage for cochlear implants. The council provided a united front to reconcile the previously different individual self-interest appeals of rival firms. In December 1986, the council was successful in obtaining wider coverage for cochlear implants from third party payors as well as from Medicare. As noted earlier, the willingness of health care insurance carriers to include cochlear implants in their medical payment reimbursement systems was also influenced by cochlear implant endorsements of prestigious medical associations, as well as FDA regulatory approvals of several cochlear implant devices.

Having successfully completed negotiations for Medicare coverage, the council began to address other issues for joint action that would benefit the growth of the industry. For instance, they developed and submitted their recommendations to the FDA to change its rules by simplifying clinical testing requirements in order to reduce the costs involved. The council also disseminated public service announcements about cochlear implants in order to increase public awareness and legitimacy. In addition, the American Association of Otolaryngology initiated a committee of representatives from industry, clinics, audiology, psychoacoustics, and other disciplines to study and recommend technical standards for this industry.

Industry Standards. Throughout this industry expansion period technological and market uncertainties remained high, and the absence of common criteria for testing and comparing alternative cochlear implant devices made it difficult to evaluate the safety and efficacy of competing technologies (Health Technology Assessment Report, 1986). Because each device embodied different technical features, testing and reporting standards during the initial part of the industry expansion period served more to legitimate particular paths than to act as selection mechanisms for the technologically superior paths (Garud, 1990). Firms developed and used standards to signal to the scientific and clinical communities the legitimacy of their particular claims. But, at the same time, these testing and reporting standards reflected each firm's proprietary product attributes. As Constant (1980) observed with the jet aircraft engine, testing and reporting standards almost became tautological with the products they were supposed to test, with the two forming a self-reinforcing cycle. As a result, technical changes were reflected in multiple institutional standards, each confirming the expectations of different researchers, while not yet possessing the power to act as selection mechanisms.

This, unlike prior periods where few institutional standards existed, the industry expansion period witnessed the proliferation of standards. While claims earlier had been perceived as noise and hyperbole, now they were ambiguous, possessing relevant cues only to those who understood or employed particular standards while being vague to others employing a different set of standards. There were frequent reports of exaggerated claims made by rival firms of the superiority of their devices (Windmill et al., 1987). But given the lack of commonly accepted testing and reporting standards, it was not clear which firm was exaggerating.

Other independent researchers began forming, each with a different frame of reference and the power to develop industrywide standards on testing comparisons and reporting. For example, results of comparative tests conducted by the University of Iowa began appearing in clinical journals in 1985. The results suggested that multichannel devices were superior to single-channel devices. Over time, other articles continued referencing the University of Iowa results, thereby increasing their visibility. These technical reports and articles accumulated and began shaping the selection of institutional rule-making events. According to one informant, the multichannel technology earned greater legitimacy as a result of the theoretical rationale justifying its design, which the House single-channel design lacked to the same degree. The early results of independent testing units, which appeared to confirm the initial announcements by the NIH, the FDA, and some health insurance carriers, also contributed to the favorable reputation of the multichannel technology.

As institutional testing procedures and standards congruent with the multichannel technology became more widely accepted over time, the testimonials of various researchers and firms began to be less ambiguous. Key technology evaluators began to employ standards associated with the multichannel device, which now possessed the power to select other trajectories. These standards began to be commonly accepted (becoming a potent institutional selection mechanism) and, in turn, triggered other selection mechanisms. For example, audiologists interfacing with the ultimate customer began to provide media testimonials that caused patients to await availability of more sophisticated products, even though the 3M/House single-channel device had received regulatory approval and was commercially available. Thus, despite regulatory approval, the 3M/House device became prematurely obsolete.

Industry Stabilization Period

By 1986, as figures 20.3 and 20.4 illustrate, a leveling off occurred in the number of events in the development of cochlear implants. The technical and institutional infrastructure for industry takeoff had become largely established. Another institutional selection mechanism, the market, could finally begin operating to determine the commercial viability of cochlear implants. Institutional selection mechanisms developed in prior periods played out to select the multichannel technology, as embodied in the Nucleus 22-channel device, as the dominant design for the industry. Furthermore, the very institutional mechanisms and resource endowments created to facilitate industry emergence became inertial forces that hindered subsequent technological development and adaptation by individual firms.

Market Selection Mechanism. By mid-1985 the FDA had approved two devices for large scale commercial sale to customers. However, diffusion and adoption among potential beneficiaries were slow and sales of cochlear implants from 1986 to the present are far below expectations. Contrary to a strongly held assumption, many profoundly deaf patients were not adopting cochlear implant devices even though several proven devices were commercially available. This assumption could not be seriously tested until cochlear implant devices were commercially available and used to create a new market. Prior to that time, firms reported no difficulties finding enough patients for clinical trials of experimental devices. As noted previously, 3M and Nucleus conducted extensive marketing studies and training programs from 1984 to 1986 with leading otological clinics throughout the United States. They received numerous public accolades and endorsements from otologists and patients alike applauding the arrival of cochlear implants. But clinical trials of experimental devices among carefully selected patients, as required by the FDA regulatory process, do not substitute for the "acid test" of attempting to penetrate and create a new market with commercially aprpoved devices.

Institutional Selection of a Dominant Design. The interactions of institutional and technological events of prior periods resulted in a changing set of criteria for evaluating alternative cochlear implant designs over time. Initially, FDA evaluators felt more comfortable in granting regulatory approval to a single-channel device because its simplicity facilitated the FDA evaluation process. It also possessed the best potential device to demonstrate safety, particularly when the effects of electrical stimulation were unclear. However, the demonstration of device safety, while necessary to legitimate the new technology, was not sufficient to offer sustained legitimacy to the particular product. Efficacy (or the ability to provide speech discrimination) was required for a particular technological path to gain legitimacy. Thus, those who pursued the single-channel route performed a yeoman's service for other, more complex designs that followed by establishing the institutional legitimacy of the new class of technologies.

The importance of establishing this safety for the entire industry was reflected in an incident when some of the FDA-approved House single-channel devices failed in the market in 1985, prompting a voluntary recall of the device by 3M. At 3M's initiative, representatives from all companies agreed not to engage in adverse publicity on this event, since this could irreparably tarnish the image of the entire new industry.

In 1987, comparative tests carried out by independent institutions surfaced results that were not congruent with the growing theory that single-channel devices were too simple to provide speech discrimination. These results were obtained from studies by the University of Iowa on the Hochmiar single-channel device, and by the Central Institute for the Deaf in St. Louis, on the House single-channel device for children. The lead investigators of these studies, both previously strong critics of the single-channel technology, stated the need to reexamine assumptions as a consequence of the strong performance of the single-channel devices. These results led an audiologist at the House Ear Institute to make a plea to the technical and institutional communities to "be more open to possibilities and less tied to theory of the full potential of the single-channel device."

But these study results and appeal came too late. In 1988, the NIH and the FDA jointly sponsored a "consensus development conference" for the purpose of selecting future directions for NIH funding and regulatory approvals. At the conference, House stated that results documented by the University of Iowa and the Central Institute for the Deaf clearly suggested the need to reexamine old theoretical biases. Instead, the institutional selection event of a consensus statement emerged among the conference participants that multichannel devices were superior to the single-channel devices—at least in adults. In explaining the consensus conference statement, Berliner stated that otologists were "converging on the multi-channel device in order to reduce cognitive dissonace of the most appropriate device that they should implant."

Institutional Lock-in to Technological Paths. Ironically, the very institutional structures that emerged to facilitate and provide momentum to the emergence of the cochlear implant industry became inertial forces that constrained the flexibility of private firms to adapt to the changing circumstances in the stabilization period. Indeed, the market and institutional selection pressures mentioned previously prompted several firms with the nonwinning design to take steps that were thwarted by the very institutional structures they earlier worked hard to develop.

For example, in 1986, 3M decided to discontinue any further major investments in the development of the House single-channel device, and to shift development efforts to its second-generation Hochmiar device, as well as a new multichannel device. This prompted the FDA to send a directive to 3M requiring that it maintain its field service and support activities for the 3M/House single-channel device—a directive that 3M management had already issued internally.

In mid-1986, 3M undertook a concerted in-house effort to develop a multi-channel device with a new technological route that was believed to be superior to the Nucleus 22-channel device. After several years of R&D, 3M obtained approval from the FDA to commence clinical trials of the new device by human implantation. However, two related difficulties were encountered in obtaining a sufficient number of patients for clinical trials. First, health insurance carriers changed their rules by dropping coverage for experimental devices, choosing instead to reimburse patients for only those devices that had now been approved for commercial release by the FDA. Second, often on the selection advice of their otologists, patients expressed a preference for commercially approved cochlear implants that were proved to be safe and efficacious over experimental devices. Recognizing its mounting developmental costs and the new institutional and market hurdles to be surmounted to create a credible challenge to the new supremacy of the Nucleus device, 3M discontinued further development of its experimental multichannel device in 1988.

The commercial viability of cochlear implants as a profitable industry had become unpredictable and was questioned by industry analysts. Market demand for cochlear implants was reported to be insufficient to support more than two or three firms profitably. As a consequence, an industry shake out began to occur as firms deselected themselves from cochlear implant activities. Several pioneering firms exited from the new industry, some by selling their cochlear implant products, patents, and rights to the new industry leader, Nucleus, thereby solidifying its dominant position. In late 1985, Nucleus acquired Biostem's single-channel technology. Storz and Symbion announced plans to reduce their financial commitments to their cochlear implant programs, reportedly because they did not perceive the cochlear implant market to be growing at a fast enough pace. In 1986, Storz approached 3M for a possible collaborative relationship. Before negotiations could be completed, Storz was acquired by American Cynamide. Storz was reported to believe that the market for cochlear implants was growing at a much slower pace than anticipated. Symbion sought other partners in June 1986 for similar reasons. In October 1986, 3M, too, decided to shift its focus from cochlear implants to the development of advanced hearing aids in the short term. In August 1989, after nine months of negotiations, 3M divested from cochlear implants by selling its cochlear implant patents, products, and services to Nucleus. Nine months of multilateral negotiations were required to overcome numerous hurdles for 3M to exit from the cochlear implant industry. The principal challenges involved concerns expressed by 3M's basic research coventurers, the Hochmairs and House, that the transfer of joint rights to cochlear implant products and patents from 3M to Nucleus would not be in their interest. A consensus was achieved that was satisfactory to all parties involved.

Analysis of Cochlear Implant Evolution

Description and explanation of any emergent change process require a theoretical model with a set of concepts that are sufficiently operational to identify "what" activities and phenomena to observe and "where" to look for them. This exploratory study adopted a social evolutionary theory to examine the development and commercialization of cochlear implants. To make this theory operationally useful for understanding the process of novelty, we adopted a more fine-grained view of social evolution than has been used in the past by defining the concepts of variation, selection, and retention as micro- or individual events rather than as macrostages of evolution. Variation events were defined as instances when novel technical advances occurred, selection events as instances when institutional rules were created or modified, and retention events as instances when the actions of actors were observed to follow institutional rules. As with any definitions, some further subjective judgments were involved in identifying these events. As a consequence, further decision rules and standard evaluation procedures were adopted to tabulate and classify events in an operationally consistent manner. The net descriptive result of this microanalytical view of evolution events is shown in the previous section. We found it useful to organize and report in rich detail the sequence of events that occurred in the development and commercialization of cochlear implants.

But theory and data are reflexive. Just as a microview of social evolution was useful to describe the cochlear implant's development, the historical data suggest two important areas for refining and extending social evolutionary theory. First, we directly examined the evolution of novelty, or the punctuation process itself, by which a new-to-the-world biomedical innovation and its supporting industrial infrastructure emerged. The historical data provide little evidence to support the widely held assumption that novelty is produced by a discrete exogenous event of random chance or blind variation. Instead, figures 20.3 and 20.4 show that cochlear implants emerged through an accretion of numerous variation, selection, and retention events over a 35-year period. An important implication of this finding is that the generative process in which novelty emerges is not instantaneous; instead it entails numerous events involving many public and private sector actors over a long duration of time. This generative process has a dynamic history that itself is important to study systematically if one is to understand how true novelty emerges and how its path-dependent processes produce dominant technological designs and organizational imprinting.

Since variation or punctuation has been defined in various ways, one might question this conclusion. Can it still not be said that one or two random technical events triggered or directed this entire sequence of events? For example, some might isolate one event—such as the 1961 implant by House—as the critical variation or punctuating event by arguing that up until then the cochlear implant was just an idea being tossed around, and after that the process unfolds as described. However, the historical narrative shows that no single event and no single process was sufficient in itself to adequately explain cochlear implant development or industry emergence. An accretion of many technical variations and institutional rule-making and rule-following events involving numerous actors occurred over many years to create the cochlear implant technology known today. To isolate any one of these events as "the punctuation event" is not only arbitrary but inconsistent with the historical evidence.

Second, we noted in the beginning of the chapter that most organizational models of social evolution view the process as consisting of a simple linear sequence of variation, selection, and retention stages over time. From a macroperspective of the aggregate occurrences of events, figure 20.4 indicates support for this simple sequential ordering of cumulative events in the development of cochlear implants. The trajectories of the cumulative frequencies of technical, rule-making, and rule-following events reflect logistic curves, each with two inflection points that are typical of diffusion processes. The three curves reach their respective asymptotes at different points in time. Technical variation events peak in 1986–87, institutional rule-making (selection) events in 1988–89, and rule-following (retention) events some time later (actually, no asymptote for rule-following events is shown in figure 20.4). The temporal progression of cumulative events appears to go from technical variations to rule-making (selection) to rule-following (retention) events over time.

However, this aggregate temporal sequence does not indicate causality (i.e., that technical variations trigger subsequent events of institutional selection and retention). Indeed, a microanalysis of the order and sequence of individual events in the cochlear implant's development provides strong support for the proposition that variation, selection, and retention events coproduced each other over time, than for the alternative proposition that a simple linear causal sequence of stages among these events occured. By coproduction we mean that technical variation, rule-making (selection), and rule-following (retention) events influenced each other in a variety of temporal sequences.

The standard variation → selection → retention sequence is illustrated by experiments in England on human cortical stimulation that triggered the NIH's selection of research contracts in electrical stimulation in 1985, which, in turn, retained and funneled $29 million to cochlear implant researchers from 1970 to 1987. The opposite triggering sequence of retention → selection → variation is exemplified by the 3M/House device application in compliance with FDA rules, which triggered the FDA to become knowledgeable about and establish evaluation rules for cochlear implants, which, in turn, led to further technical advances in examining the effects of electrical stimulation of the cochlea. A third sequence of selection → retention → variation is illustrated by the consensus conference selection of multichannel devices as the dominant design, which is currently reinforcing Nucleus' market position and constraining further technical advances on single-channel devices.

Of course, what one chooses as the triggering and triggered events in these alternative sequences is arbitrary. Indeed, these and many other kinds of triggering sequences could be strung together to explain temporal influences between the 63 technical variation events, 107 rule-making selection events, and 95 rule-following retention events observed during the development and commercialization of cochlear implants. But the purpose of illustrating these alternative triggering sequences is not to tease out the statistical relationships between observed events; that is the subject of another paper (Van de Ven and Garud, 1992).

Instead, our purpose is to point out that in the historical development of cochlear implants, many instances were identified where variation, selection, and retention events interacted and coproduced each other through a variety of causal sequences. Moreover, the nature of the temporal influences on these evolutionary events changed over time. As the historical narrative described, the very technical advancements and institutional rules initially created to facilitate industry emergence subsequently became inertial forces that hindered subsequent technical developments.

While distinct, our meaning of coproduction among variation, selection, and retention events complements the concept of coevolution as used by Baum and Singh, chapter 18, this volume, and Rosenkopf and Tushman, chapter 19, this volume. Coevolution, as Baum and Singh define it, refers to the way changes in two or more interdependent populations interact over time. Thus, whereas we examine interactions between events in the historical development of a single system, Baum and Singh examine interactions between populations. In particular, they examine the interactions between developmental patterns of day care centers and nurseries, two subpopulations that comprise the child care system.

Rosenkopf and Tushman propose a conceptual scheme for examining stages in the coevolution of organizational and technological forms. They employ a punctuated equilibrium model to examine stages in the coevolution of organizations and technologies. Technological change, as Rosenkopf and Tushman state, is driven by the combination of chance events (variations) and direct social and political action of organizations in selecting among rival technical regimens (artificial selection), as well as by incremental competence enhancing activities of learning-by-doing and puzzle solving (retention). The punctuated equilibrium model provides a useful template for examining overall stages of coevolution, particularly across successive generations of technological growth. Rosenkopf and Tushman's examination of macrostages of coevolution is entirely consistent with our more microscopic focus on individual events, particularly within the punctuation stage of evolution.

This chapter has examined the creation of a new-to-the-world biomedical innovation from the microperspective of recording the occurrence of individual variation, selection, and retention events. We believe the exploratory findings extend organizational applications of social evolutionary theory in two ways. First, they question the widely held view that novelty originates as a rare discrete variation that emerges by random chance. The generative process in which novelty emerges is not instantaneous: it has a dynamic history of numerous events over an extended period that deserves systematic description and explanation. Second, at the macrolevel, the cumulative frequency of events appeared to progress in a simple linear sequence of variation, selection, and retention stages over time. However, this temporal sequence does not imply causality. At the microlevel, individual technical variation, rule-making selection, and rule-following retention events were observed to be highly related throughout the cochlear implant's development. The historical narrative shows that the very technical advancements and institutional rules initially created to facilitate industry emergence subsequently became inertial forces that hindered later technical developments.

Of course, these findings are currently limited to the emergence of the cochlear implant industry. Longitudinal studies of other technological and institutional innovations are sorely needed to generalize the findings and identify the conditions in which they apply and do not apply.

Note

1. Throughout this paper, when we make statements about organizational models of evolution we are referring to the writings of the following social psychologists (Gersick, 1990; Weick, 1979), organization theorists (Astley, 1985; Burgelman, 1991; Hannan and Freeman, 1977, 1989; McKelvey, 1982; Singh, 1990; Tushman and Romanelli, 1985), institutional economists (Dosi, 1982; Freeman, 1986; Nelson and Winter, 1982; Ruttan and Hayami, 1984), and sociologists (Aldrich, 1979; Boyd and Richerson, 1985; Campbell, 1969; Hull, 1988). These authors have proposed various formulations of evolutionary theory in terms of subject matter, level of analysis, and gradual versus saltational rates of change, and whether characteristics can be inherited within versus between generations of a population. In this chapter we view these formulations as variations on the same basic theory of social evolution, as opposed to different theories. Useful reviews of organizational evolutionary models are provided by Gersick (1990) and Romanelli (1991a). In addition, Van de Ven and Poole (1992) provide an interdisciplinary literature review which distinguishes evolution from other theories of change, such as life cycle, teleology, and dialectical theories.

The Challenge
of Community Evolution

PAUL DIMAGGIO

The chapters in the section on community evolution are at once stimulating and sobering. They are stimulating because they stretch the frontiers of organizational ecology. They are sobering because taking communities seriously creates not just major opportunities but also vexing challenges to the ecological paradigm. The reason, I shall argue, is that careful attention to the community level frustrates our best efforts to render the world simple enough to analyze. In the spirit of devil's advocacy, let me suggest the following proposition:

> Proposition: *The virtue of organizational ecology has been its use of simplifying assumptions to cast light on complex processes. To advance to the community level is to open up a Pandora's box of complexity.*

Specifically, the study of community evolution challenges three kinds of simplifying assumptions that have served ecologists well: that models can be properly specified without taking into account a broad range of interpopulation cross-effects; that the population is the correct level of analysis (and that we know when we have a population and when we have something else); and that it is sufficient to be concerned with *organizational* populations, rather than collecting and incorporating into our models information about populations of other kinds. Let us consider each of these questions in turn.

How Complex Must a Model Be?

The first issue can be raised, although not disposed of, most quickly. If, as Baum and Singh, chapter 18, this volume, argue (correctly, I believe), "coevolution" is ubiquitous and inevitable, on how many populations must we have data in order to specify a model properly? If we are committed to exploring not just direct cross-effects—competition or mutualism—but also more subtle indirect effects, do we not need

Valuable comments from both editors on earlier drafts are gratefully acknowledged.

data on many more populations than the number from which we ordinarily collect data, or can hope to collect them? Can we really model the vital rates of breweries, for example, without population data on wineries, liquor stores, taverns, supermarkets, and barrel makers?

Note that this problem is not unique to organizational ecology. Almost any attempt at statistical explanation faces the possibility that some key causal force, indicators of which are correlated with variables already in one's models, remains unmeasured and unaccounted. The dilemma is more conspicuous in organizational ecology, however, because ecologists have a theoretical framework that brings into focus the extent to which vital processes in many populations are mutually consequential. The challenge is to devise explicit criteria that enable one to decide when one can stop collecting data and trust results based on a finite number of populations.

Is the Population the Right Unit of Analysis?

The question of whether the population is the most applicable unit of analysis has three facets: one has to do with population boundaries, one with the role of very small populations (including populations of one) in community evolution, and one with the extent to which analysis should focus on populations or networks.

Boundaries. Ecologists have been sensitive to the difficulties of defining the boundaries of a population, and to the fact that those boundaries often change over the period of observation (see, e.g., Hannan and Freeman, 1989, chapter 3; Romanelli, 1991a). The problem of population heterogeneity is obdurate, though, and no one has come up with a solution.

As ubiquitous as boundary definition problems are, thinking about communities makes them worse. For one thing, it points to ambiguity—much remarked upon but unresolved—in what we mean when we talk about an "organizational form" (and therefore a "population"). Lots of "population" studies have been to some extent community studies, or at least can be interpreted that way. If a researcher equates a population with an industry, notes that the industry consists of generalists and spcialists, and investigates the cross-effects of each upon the other, is he or she not really operating at the community level? (Brittain [chapter 17] is unusually clear, and I think correct, in answering this question affirmatively.) If we aggregate up from such analyses to investigate the cross-effects of industries upon one another, do we retain the "subspecies" (generalists and specialists) as analytically distinct, or do we operate only at the "species" level? What is gained, and what is lost, by each procedure? Once again, there is a need for explicit criteria: under what conditions and for what purposes does it makes sense to define the "population" at a finer or grosser level of aggregation?

Moreover, much community-level evolution occurs not just by speciation, but through the effacement of boundaries between competing populations. Communications companies become computer companies, and vice versa; banks become retailers and retailers become banks; Walmart competes with supermarkets, and supermarkets stock videotape and stationery. In the nonprofit sector, schools expand to provide late-afternoon activities for poor kids, and YMCAs become yuppie health clubs. How do we accommodate this kind of change, which may ocur over relatively short period, in our units of analysis, and in the communities to which our populations belong? We are beginning to see valuable progress on aspects of the boundary issue in empirical studies of overlap in the niches of firms within a population (Baum and Singh, 1992; McPherson, 1983). But it remains easier to raise such questions than to answer them.

Tiny Populations and Path Dependent Evolution. A second way that the study of community evolution makes us question the primacy of populations as units of analysis is by calling attention to other forms of strategic interaction than the competition and mutualism that organizational ecology excels at modeling. This is part of what Brittain (chapter 17, this volume) means when he argues that the study of community evolution requires us to attend to "density-*independent*" development.

Several papers focus on discrete actions of such unique actors as government agencies, monopoly corporations, or major innovators. Van de Ven and Garud's story (chapter 20) would have been difficult to tell without concrete detail on the Food and Drug Administration, the National Institutes of Health, and the Walt Disney Hearing Center. If, as in the case of Barnett (chapter 16) one's concern is with how government actions affect vital or growth rates in an industry sector, it may suffice to treat powerful organizations as part of the environment. But if one is interested in *why* the "environment" acts as it does, and especially if one believes in path-dependent evolution, it may be necessary to rely more on narrative analysis of the behavior of significant organizations.

There are really two issues here. The first is that explaining many things about the coevolution of populations in a community requires narrative history as a complement to statistical analysis. The reason for this is that evolution often depends upon one-time actions by organizations that occupy structurally unique positions that shape the context for subsequent development and therefore require explanation in their own right. The second, related issue is that many communities consist of populations with relatively few members, making statistical population analysis impractical. (Conventional population methods would be appropriate in analyzing competition in the auto industry before the Depression, but less useful in understanding competition among GM, Ford, Chrysler, AM, and Studebaker in the 1950s. If one is only interested in automobiles, this is not much of a problem: one can stop, or shift to narrative history, in 1940. But that is a less satisfactory solution if one is interested in the effects of the auto industry on, e.g., the electric rail industry, throughout the century.)

Networks. Population models are better at capturing the effects of mass action—competitive or mutualistic—than the consequences of collective action, such as campaigns by trade associations or informal efforts by firms to influence the market or the state. Ordinary ecological models do not lend themselves to the analysis of collective action of this kind, except inferentially. One reason for this is that organizational ecologists rarely collect systematic data on relations among organizations in the populations they study.

Even so, it is natural to portray the community as a kind of network, as the chapters in this section do; indeed, network imagery and methods have a distinguished tradition in evolutionary biology (e.g., Lambert and Williams' [1962] pioneering use of structural equivalence analysis). A focus on networks undermines an emphasis on organizational populations as units of analysis because many networks rend populations asunder, by placing organizations in the same industry in different camps. Compare, for example, the U.S. notion of "industry" with the Japanese concept of *kigyo shudan*, or company group. The former resonates with the language of population ecology; it is no accident that U.S. scholars find it so natural to identify populations with industries. By contrast, Japanese company groups maintain the "one-set" rule: no more than one company in any given industry is a member of a given company group (Gerlach, 1992). To understand the fate of Japanese firms, one would want to take a community perspective, to be sure. But it is far from clear what, in the Japanese context, should be the population (if, by that, one means a set of organizations characterized by a "shared fate with respect to environmental variation"): the industry or the company group? Or do the complex relations among company groups, industries, and firms mean that the network, rather than the population, is the appropriate metaphor for thinking about such matters?

The Japanese example may be comfortably exotic to the Western reader, but similar alliances can be found close to home, in the small-firm networks of Europe, the international biotechnology field, and elsewhere (Perrow, 1992; Sabel, 1991). If these become the norm, we shall have to ask whether the conceptual artillery of organizational ecology remains serviceable at the community level. It is as if, in the biological sphere, a world of interspecies competition and symbiosis were supplanted by one in which various Arks, each containing pairs of animals of each species, struggle against one another for survival.

There are, of course, several ways in which network analysis and organizational ecology can be combined to their mutual advantage. Baum and Oliver (1991, 1992; see also Miner, Amburgey, and Stearns, 1990), for example, have looked at the effects on organization and survival of funding and sanctioning relations between government agencies and day care centers. Other ecological studies have collected data on cooperative interfirm networks in several settings (e.g., Freeman and Lomi, chapter 14, this volume; Powell and Brantley, 1993). A promising possibility, which to my knowledge has not been tried, would be to apply population models not to organizations, but to relations among organizations in different populations or networks. One could, for example, use ecological models to explain the creation and disbanding of alliances between biotech and pharmaceutical companies, as a way of tracking and explaining evolutionary forces in those fields.

Are Formal Organizations Enough?

The third challenge that the study of community evolution poses to organizational ecology is related to the kinds of animals that we acknowledge are living in the jungle. There are two facets to this issue: First, can we afford to look only at *formal* organizations? Second, can we afford not to take account of populations that are *not* organizational at all?

Why just formal organizations? If we are interested in the cross-effects of different kinds of organizations on one another, must we not account for *informal* as well as formal organizations? Do we honestly believe that formal organizations are the only kind of human group that constitute populations, or that only formal organizations influence one another's vital rates, or that rates for formal organizations are uncorrelated with rates for informal groups, so that omitting the latter does not bias estimates of the effects of the former? For example, if we were to study factors affecting birth rates of toy stores, could we afford to leave nuclear families out of the model simply because they are not formal organizations? (Actually they *are* formal organizations, chartered and regulated by the state, just as corporations are. But we exclude them from organization theory because of their distinctive purposes and cultural standing.) Presumably, increases in the birth rates of new "families" (by the filing of marriage rather than corporation papers) would be a good lagged predictor of demand for toys. Failing to control for the effects of families would probably lead to false conclusions: for example, we might "learn" that increases in birth rates of public schools "cause" increases in birth rates of toy stores (because both populations grow in response to increases in the number of procreative families).

Why not a population ecology of technologies? Indeed, why stop at organizations? In our focus on organizations (formal or otherwise), we are a little like flatlanders inching across a tabletop, never dreaming that length and breadth could be conjoined with depth. As Rosenkopf and Tushman (chapter 19, this volume; Levinthal, chapter 9, this volume) make strikingly clear, processes of organizational evolution go on in tandem with, and are influenced by, processes of technological evolution. If one is able to define organizational form on the basis of technology, as Barnett, chapter 16, does with his magneto companies, this issue can be finessed, but it is rare that a single technology alone is definitive. Usually, organizational populations and technologies are more loosely coupled, with one type of organization employing several technologies to varying degrees, and the same technology in use by several kinds of organization.

In other words, in the real world we have two evolutionary processes going on at once: competition among organizational populations, which make differential use of different technologies, and competition among technologies, which are used to varying degrees by different kinds of organizations. In some cases, a technology's fate makes or breaks an organization: as horses gave way to automobiles, blacksmith shops bit the dust. In others, the life chances of different technologies (e.g., the longtime advantage of AM over FM broadcasting) will be shaped decisively by the power or vitality of the organizations that have invested in them. In still other cases, marginal organizational choices will sustain a technology—and the organizations most dependent on this technology—that would not survive on purely technical grounds alone. (Thus Microsoft prospered along with DOS because lots of organizations in many populations adopted IBM and clone computers that used DOS, even though most hackers preferred UNIX.)

If one takes this argument seriously, one must conclude that many ecological models are misspecified because they fail to include cross-effects of measures of the fortunes of key technologies (when such measures are correlated with other exogenous variables) on indicators of the vital rates of organizational forms that rely on them. Similarly, organizational densities should be exogenous variables in models predicting the relative success of competing technologies.

Or a population ecology of occupations? Just as organizational and technological forms shape one another's fates, so do organizational forms and occupations. The most comprehensive recent analysis of the professions, Andrew Abbott's *The System of the Professions* (1988), takes an explicitly ecological perspective. Although Abbott does not employ formal models, one could easily use standard population models to analyze the competition among different professions at the core of his theory and case studies. Lots of organizations employ lawyers, for example, but few would be affected negatively if the legal profession suffered a downturn. On the other hand, if corporations cut their law departments in half, or turned over much of what lawyers do to human resources professionals, this might devastate the legal profession (and increase the "birth rate" of human resources professionals). Change in the status of homeopaths has extensive effects on the fate of homeopathic hospitals, and the life chances of engineering subprofessions and organizational populations that live by engineering innovation are intertwined. As in the case of technology, we note two interdependent, ongoing games, organized at different levels of analysis.

Again, if we take this argument seriously, we must question whether many ecological analyses are properly specified. Because we have reasonably good figures on the number of persons in many occupational categories over fairly long stretches of time, we can look at the cross-effects of occupational density on the vital rates of organizational forms. And, conversely, data on the density of relevant organizational forms should be useful in explaining the ebb and flow of many professions and occupations.

This way of thinking about technological and occupational evolution entails a decided shift in perspective. Rather than view the "community" as a level of analysis in the study of organizational evolution, perhaps we should treat the development of organizational communities as but one facet of the evolution of human communities. From this standpoint, studying the evolution of communities of organizations in isolation from the technologies and occupations that crosscut them is a little like trying to understand ecosystems by looking only at animals while ignoring plants.

If these arguments, all of which were suggested by reading the chapters in this section, have any merit, the study of community evolution is a subversive pursuit that pokes and prods at every chink in organizational ecology's armor. To summarize, if we pursue the insights in these chapters to their obvious conclusions, we are fated:

1. To be never happy with our models and to admit that we will never have enough data to specify them properly;
2. To be even more vexed by the unwillingness of population boundaries to hold still, and to be tempted constantly to forsake population analysis for narrative accounts in which history is driven by great organizations; or, conversely, analysis of networks of complementary organizations rather than populations of similar ones; and
3. To abandon our one-sided focus on formal organizations in favor of a more catholic application of evolutionary models to combinations of formal organizations, families, occupations, and technologies.

Does this mean that we would be better off if the genie of community evolution remained in the bottle? In the short run, it should be evident from the quality of the chapters in this section that this could not be further from the case. Moreover, in the long run, it is not at all evident that the fate I have described is such a bad one.

Satisfaction with one's models is probably the first step on the road to intellectual torpor. As the chapters in this section themselves demonstrate, there is much complementarity between statistical and narrative approaches and between the insights of ecology and network analysis. And the recognition that organizational evolution is inseparable from the evolution of technologies and occupations opens more possibilites for progress in the latter fields than it closes in the former. Scientific progress invariably generates puzzles and, if some puzzles indicate the exhaustion of a paradigm, others are signs of sustained vitality. I believe that the puzzles to which work on community evolution alerts us are of the latter variety.

On the Concept of "Organizational Community"

JOSEPH PORAC

Since I am not an expert on interorganizational research, it is difficult for me to evaluate the specific merits and sins of each chapter in the session on community evolution. Instead, I would like to use my position as a naïve outsider to make a few general comments about how organizational communities are conceptualized and studied. Even to a nonexpert, it is clear that the five chapters in the session cover a very wide range of community-level phenomena with a diverse array of analytical tools. This diversity suggests that interesting tensions exist below the theoretical surface, tugging and pushing researchers to move along different conceptual trajectories in their efforts to understand how organizational communities develop over time. In this brief commentary, I want to explore one of these underlying tensions and show how it can be used to make sense of the choices made in these chapters.

Searching for a Useful Level of Abstraction

In their book *The Explanation of Social Behavior*, Harré and Secord (1973) noted that social science must juxtapose two different levels of knowledge and discourse. First-order knowledge consists of the "lived experience" of actors in social settings. It is perceptual, unreflective, immediate, and shaped by the real time demands of the moment. First-order knowledge is the raw material of human social life, what many would say is the order of phenomena that social science must explain. In contrast, second-order knowledge consists of the concepts, propositions, and cognitive frameworks that are built up to describe and account for lived experience. Second-order knowledge is reflective on, rather than embedded within, social situations, and its purpose is to explain human experience post hoc. Second-order knowledge is often specifically linked to concrete settings. In such cases, second-order constructs are probably no different from a "layperson's knowledge" or "personal beliefs" about the situation. On the other hand, second-order knowledge is sometimes very abstract and applicable to many different settings. In such cases, we might view this as a "scientific theory" of the social world. Clearly, all sorts of gradations in abstraction are possible between these two extremes, but a choice is always at hand whether to remain close to the first-order experiential detail of human life or to generalize to a more abstract (and simplifying) description of social reality.

I bring up Harré and Secord because the distinction between first- and second-order social knowledge seems useful in understanding many of the differences among these chapters. At the heart of the matter is the meaning of the term "community." According to Webster's preferred definition, a community is a group of interacting people who usually share the perception of some common goal or trait. This everyday definition, while simple, captures several important psychosocial elements of community dynamics. The notion of an interacting group suggests that a community is a web of transactions through which members are actively exchanging ideas, resources, and affective commitments. That a community involves a perception of commonality in goals and traits suggests that communities are produced as much by the mind as they are by any intrinsic properties of the transactions themselves. Communal relationships require shared languages and cognitive structures that allow for communication and interpersonal coordination. This means that communities are enacted by people who are involved in multidimensional relationships and who work within the psychological framework of those relationships to create a unique social life.

It is this active social reality that must be captured by any system of second-order constructs. Here social scientists face the inevitable choice. Like Webster's definition, second-order constructs can remain close to specific community experiences and attempt to describe the social psychological reality of the interacting group with a nomenclature not far removed from the language of laypersons. One might inquire, for example, about cognitive and affective ties among community members, and how perceived commonalities create a sense of shared purpose and identity. Community "evolution" might be defined as changes in these cognitive and affective patterns over time. The downside of this choice, however, is that although it would preserve much of the rich interpersonal detail of community life, a microlanguage would suffer from the particularistic biases intrinsic to a focus on unique situational processes. To counteract these biases, social scientists might choose a more generic construct system that describes abstract properties of communities distilled to their purest form. Here, one might be interested in such global variables as community size, growth rate, membership variance, and geographic scope. Community evolution would be defined as changes in size, variance, growth rate, and so on, over time. The countervailing trade-off, however, is that while an abstract construct system of this sort conquers particularism, it does so by washing away much of the human detail that makes a community a viable social phenomenon.

Although the five chapters on community evolution are concerned with "organizational" rather than interpersonal communities, the issues surrounding the choice of second-order construct system are much the same. Should the organizational scientist capture the rich cognitive, affective, political, and economic details of life within organizational communities, or should he/she build a generic system of constructs that distills the essence of organizational communities down to a few index variables such that a reduced matrix of relationships can be isolated and measured. These chapters clearly illustrate the entire spectrum of choices available. Van de Ven and Garud take the most microscopic approach to the problem of organizational communities by mapping the string of events that emerged as scientists, managers, and government officials created a technological system around cochlear implant devices. For Van de Ven and Garud, the focal organizational community is a system of communicative relationships among organizational representatives who are actively vying for power, prestige, and profits. It is not surprising, then, that Van de Ven and Garud's analytical tools are engineered to embed the researcher within the complex social reality of the cochlear implant community, and to portray this reality at least partly from the viewpoint of the community members themselves. The quantitative and narrative data presented by these authors clearly reveal just how complex life really is at the center of an interorganizational network, and how exhausting it will be to isolate a coherent and plausible explanatory model of community dynamics. One almost wonders whether such molecular data are too rich in detail and too complex to comprehend fully. How far can we take such grounded inductive research before we need to make stronger simplifying assumptions?

Contrast this approach with that of Baum and Singh, the most macroscopic of the community researchers, who seek to develop an abstract nomenclature for describing the interactive relationships between Toronto day care centers and nurseries. To accomplish this objective, Baum and Singh adopt an "outsider looking in" analytical stance that takes them very far from the experiences of the typical child care entrepreneur bound by economic, personal, and political relationships with other organizations in the Toronto metro area. This detached viewpoint allows Baum and Singh many simplifications, the most important of which is a reduction of the complex ties among day care centers and nurseries to a single variable whose logical value denotes whether the size of one group facilitates, detracts from, or has no effect upon the size of the other. Baum and Singh make good use of this radical simplification. By applying a generic method for mapping causal simultaneity, these authors raise interesting and nonobvious questions about population interdependence within the child care community. It is important to note, however, that there is nothing about Baum and Singh's abstract method that is particularly unique to the study of organizational communities. The same method could be used to measure causal interdependence in any complex system, from washing machines to the human body. This abstraction allows Baum and Singh to rise above the din of life in the child care network, but inevitably leads to suspicions about the relevance of the questions that are being asked and the data that are eventually reported.

The sharp differences between Van de Ven and Garud's very particularistic methods and Baum and Singh's abstract causal nomenclature bring into relief the more moderate choices made in the other three chapters. Rosenkopf and Tushman remain close to the ebb and flow of events within organizational communities by mapping the social dynamics of technological innovation. These authors cogently point out that technological development is paced by the actions and standards of various stakeholders within the relevant community. They then set out to show how such social relationships have shaped technological evolution in a variety of technical domains. One can appreciate Rosenkopf and Tushman's analytical recipe: namely, use a variety of cases to derive inductively a generic model of the stages of technological evolution. However, when viewed next to Van de Ven and Garud's more molecular results, the trade-off involved in this recipe is clear: A stage model of technological development is unlikely to prove universally applicable to the minute details of all technological trajectories, and any effort to impose such a model strongly will likely lead researchers astray. For example, it is not entirely clear how Rosenkopf and Tushman's stage approach helps to make sense of the complex sequence of interrelated events shaping the development of cochlear implants. To their credit, Rosenkopf and Tushman are aware of these limits, but still, such limits do complicate the simple applicability of their second-order construct system.

Brittain's research is focused upon entry and exit rates in the semiconductor industry. When compared to the chapters by Van de Ven and Garud and Rosenkopf and Tushman, Brittain's study is clearly a step or two up the abstraction hierarchy. At the same time, Brittain's detailed conceptualization of the semiconductor community allows him to frame his research questions with a much richer set of contextual variables than is present in Baum and Singh's child care study. This detail counteracts any skepticism one might have about the meaning and relevance of his analytical approach. Brittain cultivates an interesting middle ground between a microscopic and a macroscopic point of view. In doing so, he moves beyond the study of density dependence and takes on the more intractable problem of modeling environmental resource availability directly. One advantage of this strategy is that it provides a grounded realism that often seems missing from other ecological studies. There are rich data to be explored here, and it is not unreasonable to believe that Brittain's expanded agenda contains the seeds of a possible synthesis merging community ecology, resource dependence theory, and perhaps even the comparative industry literature of industrial economics. One suspects, though, that the relatively narrow analytical strategies and dogmatic biological metaphors of organizational ecology will have to be loosened for such a synthesis to come to fruition. Even in Brittain's research, the limitations of such dogmatism are very evident. For example, Brittain's choice to use the "specialist" versus "generalist" distinction to describe intraindustry stratification seems artificial and unrelated to any intrinsic properties of the semiconductor business. When compared to state-of-the-art empirical classification efforts by, say, strategic group researchers, the specialist/generalist distinction is quite restrictive. A top down adherence to an abstract ecological construct system, without the benefit of more bottom up inductive data, is potentially dysfunctional for community level research.

A similar issue can be raised with Barnett's study of the early telephone industry in Pennsylvania. Barnett's abstract modeling of population interdependence allows him to tease apart statistical relationships that would be very difficult to untangle by more interpretive or molecular research methods. In this sense, Barnett's analysis is scientifically emancipating in its ability to isolate subtle regularities in the data. At the same time, however, Barnett's ecological frame of reference constrains his interpretation of the obtained results. Barnett accounts for the stagnation of independent telephone companies by suggesting that magneto coordination problems and incompatibility with common-battery companies reduced the "fitness" of the entire population of independent firms. While this explanation is very consistent with Barnett's abstract ecological lens, it is also a radical simplification of the social dynamics driving the development of large technological systems. Hughes (1987), for example, argues that technological domains such as electric utilities and telephone networks must be viewed as large spheres of problem solving in which system builders (e.g., engineers) attempt to satisfy user requirements within the constraints imposed by important financial, technological, and governmental stakeholders. The result is a socially constructed order in which technical, political, and financial considerations are fused. For instance, according to Hughes, the measurement of a system's "load factor" in electric utilities was motivated by the financial community's desire for a return on capital investment in power generation. System load eventually became a major efficiency criterion in the design and regulation of large power networks. In Hughes' view, this merging of financial and technical problem solving was a major force behind network consolidation and investments in large capital intensive electric utilities in the United States. Through international comparisons of London, Paris, Berlin, and Chicago, Hughes further shows how community characteristics are contingent upon a variety of psychosocial circumstances that become interwoven with system design. For example, in 1920 Berlin possessed 6 large power plants while London had more than 50 smaller ones. According to Hughes, Londoners designed their electric grid to protect the influence of local municipalities, while Germans were enhancing centralized authority by giving technological control to the Berlin city government.

Viewing technological systems as spheres of problem-solving activity contrasts with Barnett's ecological approach in that it suggests that a goal-directed dynamic is controlling the choices made by system builders. To understand the choice space facing telephone pioneers in turn-of-the-century Pennsylvania, we would need to know the cost structures of magneto, common-battery, and Bell System operations. We would need to understand the financial community's investment objectives, and the connection between technological choices and such objectives over time. We would, of necessity, need to understand the technological options available to system engineers, and the financial and social constraints forcing local communities to choose and retain a magneto technology over a common-battery system. Why couldn't magneto firms attract the necessary capital to make the transition to the more modern common-battery technology quickly enough to survive? Knowing these details would allow us to map very precisely the strategic choices made by system designers, financiers, and government officials. In the end, we may conclude that something like "fitness" was an issue, but it would be very clear that an ecological analysis is an abstract overlay on a complex psychosocial reality.

Weick (1979) suggests that any theory of organization must balance three scientific objectives: generality, simplicity, and accuracy. The five chapters on community evolution, all rigorous in their own right, demonstrate clearly that a satisfactory balance is very difficult to achieve. Microscopic research remaining close to the first-order reality of interorganizational networks will be rich in detail, but detail that is difficult to untangle and systematize in any simple and generalizable way. Macroscopic research linking community phenomena to social processes across a variety of domains, and employing highly abstract construct systems, will simplify and generalize, but only at the expense of rich first-order nuances. Such trade-offs strike at the very heart of the research endeavor. At stake are the researcher's definition of "community," the metaphors used to explain community dynamics, the meaning and importance of community "evolution," and the analytical strategies that are used to articulate empirically the researcher's point of view.

In making such trade-offs, the temptation to take an extreme stand is very strong. The choices are clear. If one believes in the viability and usefulness of general laws of nature, one will build abstract construct systems, perhaps importing them from other areas of scientific inquiry (e.g., evolutionary theory, population ecology), and attempt to apply them to organizational communities. If one is a humanist who wishes to remain close to the details of social life, such generalized theoretical overlays will always be inadequate descriptions of the uniquely human properties of organizational existence. Each of these extreme positions is viable in pure form but is likely to lead to rigid dogmatism and unproductive debates with the opposing camp. It seems more fruitful to take a middle ground, recognizing that interorganizational networks are uniquely human (and thus symbolic, purposive, and political) domains, but also recognizing that abstractions, even imported abstractions, are often useful heuristics that raise interesting questions that more particularistic frameworks overlook. Such a middle ground may not be radical enough to generate scholarly controversy, nor pure enough to lead to the tribelike behavior upon which academic reputations are often built. On the other hand, it is probably where the best balance among generality, simplicity, and accuracy will be found.

References

Abbott, A. 1988. *The System of Professions: An Essay on the Division of Expert Labor.* Chicago: University of Chicago Press.

Abbott, A. 1990. "A primer on sequence methods." *Organization Science* 1:375–92.

Abbott, A., and J. Forrest. 1986. "Optimal matching for historical sequences." *Journal of Interdisciplinary History* 16:471–94.

Abbott, A., and A. Hrycak. 1990. "Measuring resemblance in sequence data: An optimal matching analysis of musicians' careers." *American Journal of Sociology* 96:144–85.

Abel, D. K., and J. S. Hammond. 1979. *Strategic Market Planning.* Englewood Cliffs, NJ: Prentice-Hall.

Abernathy, W. J., and K. B. Clark. 1985. "Innovation: Mapping the winds of creative destruction." *Research Policy* 14:3–22. Elsevier.

Abernathy, W. 1978. *The Productivity Dilema.* Baltimore, MD: Johns Hopkins University Press.

Abrahamson, E. 1990. "Fads and fashions in administrative technologies." Ph.D. diss., Stern School of Business, New York University.

Abrahamson, E. 1991. "Managerial fads and fashions: The diffusion and rejection of innovations." *Academy of Management Review* 16:586–612.

Adler, P. S. 1993. "The 'learning bureaucracy': New United Motor Manufacturing, Inc." *Research in Organizational Behavior.*

Agostini, F. 1985. "Leone Wollemburg poiniere del credito agrario."In G. Zalin (ed.), *Un Secolo di Coopearzione di crdeito nel Veneto. Le casse rurali ed artigiane, 1883–1893,* Rome: Signum.

Aitken, H. 1985. *The Continuous Wave.* Princeton, NJ: Princeton University Press.

Aiken, L. S., and S. G. West. 1991. *Multiple Regression: Testing and Interpreting Interactions.* Newberry Park, CA: Sage.

Alchian, A. A., and H. Demsetz. 1972. "Production, information costs and economic organization." *American Economic Review* 62:777–95.

Aldag, R. J., and T. M. Stearns. 1991. *Management.* Cincinnati, OH: South-Western.

Aldrich, H. E. 1979. *Organizations and Environments.* Englewood Cliffs, NJ: Prentice-Hall.

Aldrich, H. E., and C. M. Fiol. 1992. "Fools rush in: Conditions affecting entrepreneurial strategies in new organizational populations."Unpublished manuscript, Sociology Department, University of North Carolina, Chapel Hill.

Aldrich, H. E., and U. H. Staber. 1988. "Organizing business interests: Patterns of trade association foundings, transformations, and deaths." In G. R. Carroll (ed.) *Ecological Models of Organizations.* 111–26. Cambridge, MA: Ballinger.

Aldrich, H. E., U. H. Staber, C. R. Zimmer, and J. J. Beggs. 1990."Minimalism and organizational mortality: Patterns of disbandings among U.S. trade association, 1900–1983." In *Organizational Evolution,* 21–52, Newbury Park, CA: Sage.

Alinsky, S. D. 1971. *Rules for Radicals: A Practical Primer for Realistic Radicals.* New York: Random House.

Allison, G. T. 1971. *The Essence of Decision.* Boston, MA: Little, Brown.

Allison, P. 1984. *Event History Analysis.* Beverly Hills, CA: Sage.

Amburgey, T. L. 1986. "Multivariate point processes in social research." *Social Science Research* 15:190–207.

Amburgey, T. L., and D. Kelly. 1985. "Adaptation and selection in organizational populations: A competing risks model." Paper presented at the Academy of Management Meetings, San Diego, CA.

Amburgey, T. L., D. Kelly, and W. P. Barnett. 1993. "Resetting the clock: The dynamics of organizational change and failure." Administrative Science Quarterly, 38:51–73.

Amburgey, T. L., and A. S. Miner. 1992. "Strategic momentum: The effects of repetitive, positional, and contextual momentum on merger activity." *Strategic Managment Journal* 13:335–48.

American Bankers Association. 1989. *The Credit Union Industry:Trends, Structure, and Competitiveness.* Washington DC: American Bankers Association.

American Federation of Labor. 1888. *Report of Proceedings of the Third Annual Convention of the American Federation of Labor.* St. Louis, MO, December 1-15. Reprinted in 1905, Bloomington, IL: Panatagraph Printing and Stationery Company.

American Speech Hearing Association 1985. "Cochlear Implant: Five companies respond to ASHA survey (1985)." Pp. 27–34.

Ames, E., and S. Reiter. 1961. "Distributions of correlation coefficients in economic time series." *Journal of the American Statistical Association* 56:637–56.

Anderson, P., and M. L. Tushman, 1990. "Technological discontinuities and dominant designs: A cyclical model of technological change." *Administrative Science Quarterly* 35:604–33.

Andrews, K. R. 1980. *The Concept of Corporate Strategy.*Homewood, IL: Richard Irwin.

Andrews, P. W. S. 1949. "A reconsideration of the theory of the individual business." *Oxford Economics Papers* 1:54–89.

Annuario Statistico Italiano. Various years. Rome: ISTAT.

Anthony, R. N., J. Dearden, and N. M. Bedford 1984. *Management Control Systems,* 5th ed. Homewood, IL: Irwin.

Arrow, K. J. 1970. "Political and Economic Evaluation of Social Effects and Externalities." In *The Analysis of Public Output.* New York: Columbia University Press.

Arthur, B. 1989. "Competing technologies." In G. Dosi et al. (eds.),*Technical Change and Economic Theory.* London: Pinter.

Arthur, B. 1989. "Competing technologies, increasing returns, and lock-in by historical events: The dynamics of allocation under increasing returns." *Economic Journal* 99:116–31.

Arthur, B. 1990. "Positive feedbacks in the economy."*Scientific American* 262:92–99.

Astley, W. G. 1985. "The two ecologies: Population and community perspectives on organizational evolution." *Administrative Science Quarterly* 30:224–41.

Astley, W. G., and C. J. Fombrun 1983a. "Collective strategy: The social ecology of organizational environments" *Academy of Management Review* 8:576–87.

Astley, W. G., and C. J. Fombrun. 1983b. "Technological innovation and industrial structure." *Advances in Strategic Management* 1:205–29.

Astley, W. G., and A. H. Van De Ven. 1983. "Central perspectives and debates in organizational theory." *Administrative Science Quarterly* 28:245–73.

Averill, M., and W. D. Kelton. 1982. *Simulation Modeling and Analysis.* New York: McGraw-Hill.

Axelrod, R. 1984. *The Evolution of Cooperation.* New York: Basic Books.

Bain, J. S. 1956. *Barriers to New Competition.* Cambridge, MA: Harvard University Press.

Baker, W. E. 1990. "Market networks and corporate behavior."*American Journal of Sociology* 96:589–625.

Banaszak-Holl J. J., Ranger-Moore, and M. T. Hannan. 1990. "Density dependence in the mortality processes of financial institutions: American life insurance companies and Manhattan banks." Technical Report 90-1,Department of Psychology, Cornell University.

Banca d'Italia. 1977. *Struttura Funzionale e Territoriale del Sistema Bancario Italiano.* Rome: Banca d'Italia.

Banca d'Italia. 1990. *Ordinary General Meeting of Shareholders.* Abridged report for the year 1989. Rome: Banca d'Italia.

Banca d'Italia. Various years. *Bollettino Statistico Della Banca d'Italia.* Rome: Banca d'Italia.

Banca d'Italia. Various years. *Bollettino di Vigilanza Sulle Aziende di Credito.* Rome: Banca d'Italia.

Bandura, A. 1977. *Social Learning Theory.* Englewood Cliffs,NJ: Prentice-Hall.

Banz, R. 1982. "The relationship between return and market value of common stocks." *Journal of Financial and Quantitative Analysis* 14:421–41.

Barley, S. R. 1988. "Actions, institutions and technical change: Toward a role-based theory of technology and the social organization of work." Unpublished manuscript, Cornell University.

Barnett, W. P. 1990. "The organizational ecology of a technological system." *Administrative Science Quarterly* 35:31–60.

Barnett, W. P., and T. L. Amburgey. 1990. "Do larger organizations generate stronger competition?" In J. V. Singh (ed.), *Organizational Evolution: New Directions,* 78–102. Newbury Park, CA: Sage.

Barnett, W. P., and G. R. Carroll. 1987. "Competition and mutualism among early telephone companies." *Administrative Science Quarterly* 32:400–421.

Barnett, W. P., and G. R. Carroll. 1993. "How institutional constraints affect the organization of early American telephony."*Journal of Law Economics and Organization.* Forthcoming.

Baron, D. 1973. "Limit pricing potential entry and barriers to entry." *American Economic Review* 63:666–77.

Bartholomew, D. J. 1982. *Stochastic Models for Social Processes,* 3d ed. New York: John Wiley and Sons.

Bateman, T. S., and C. P. Zeithaml. 1989. "The psychological context of strategic decision: A model and convergent findings." *Strategic Management Journal* 10:59–74.

Baum, J. A. C. 1988. "Ecological aggregates and heritable units: Towards an evolutionary perspective on organizations." Paper presented atthe Academy of Management national meetings, Anaheim, CA.

Baum, J. A. C. 1989. "A population perspective on organizations: A study of diversity and transformation in child care service organizations." Ph. D. diss., Faculty of Management, University of Toronto.

Baum, J. A. C. 1990a. "Why are there so many (few) kinds of organizations? A study of organizational diversity." *Proceedings of the Administrative Sciences Association of Canada* 11(5):1–10.

Baum, J. A. C. 1990b. "Inertial and adaptive patterns in organizational change." In *Academy of Management Best Papers Proceedings,* 165–69. San Francisco, CA: Academy of Management.

Baum, J. A. C., and H. J. Korn. 1993. "The community ecology of large Canadian companies, 1984–1991. *Canadian Journal of Administrative Sciences.* Forthcoming.

Baum, J. A. C., and S. Mezias. 1991. "Size-localized competition and organizational survival and growth." Unpublished manuscript, Stern School of Business, New York University.

Baum, J. A. C., and S. J. Mezias. 1992. "Localized competition and organizational failure in the Manhattan hotel industry, 1898–1990."*Administrative Science Quarterly,* 37:580–604.

Baum, J. A. C., and C. Oliver. 1991. "Institutional linkages and organizational mortality." *Administrative Science Quarterly* 36:187–218.

Baum, J. A. C., and C. Oliver. 1992. "Institutional embeddedness and the dynamics of organizational populations." *American Sociological Review* 57:540–59.

Baum, J. A. C., and J. V. Singh. 1992. "Organizational niches and competitive dynamics." Paper presented at the Academy of Management national meetings, Las Vegas, NV.

Baum, J. A. C., and J. V. Singh. 1993. "Organizational niches and the dynamics of organizational founding." *Organization Science,* forthcoming.

Baumol, W. J. 1967. *Business Behavior, Value and Growth.* NewYork: Harcourt, Brace and World.

Baumol, W. J., and W. E. Oates. 1975. *The Theory of Environmental Policy: Externalities, Public Outlays and the Quality of Life.* Englewood Cliffs, NJ: Prentice-Hall.

Baumol, W. J., J. C. Panzar, and R. D. Willig. 1982. *Contestable Markets and the Theory of Industry Structure.* New York: Harcourt Brace Jovanovich.

Beard, M. R. 1939. *The American Labor Movement.* New York: MacMillan.

Berger, P. L., and T. Luckman. 1966. *The Social Construction of Reality.* New York: Anchor Books.

Berger, P. L., and T. Luckman. 1967. *The Social Construction of Reality.* New York: Doubleday.

Beyer, J. 1982. "Introduction." *Administrative Science Quarterly* 27:588–90.

Bigler Investment Management. 1983. *Venture Captial: A Perspective.* San Francisco, CA: Bigler Investment Management.

Binswanger, H. P., and V. W. Ruttan. 1978. *Induced Innovation.* Baltimore: Johns Hopkins University Press.

Birch, D. L., and S. MacCracken. 1982. *The Small Business Share of Job Creation -- Lessons Learned from the Use of a Longitudinal File.*Washington, DC: Small Business Administration.

Blau, P. M. 1963. *The Dynamics of Bureaucracy.* Chicago: University of Chicago Press.

Blau, P. M. 1977. *Inequality and Heterogeneity.* New York: Free Press.

Blaug, M. 1980. *The Methodology of Economics: Or How Economists Explain.* Cambridge, England: Cambridge University Press.

Blute, M. 1979. "Sociocultural evolutionism: An untried theory."*Behavioral Science* 24:46–59.

Bodewitz, H., H. Buurma, and G. de Vries. 1987. "Regulatory science and the social management of trust in medicine," In *The Social construction of Technological Systems.* Cambridge, MA: MIT Press.

Boehm, C. 1978. "Rational pre-selection from hamadryas to homosapiens: The place of decisions in adaptive process." *American Anthropologist* 80:265–96.

Boehm, C. 1982. "The evolutionary development of morality as an effect of dominance behavior and conflict interference." *Journal of Social and Biological Structures* 5:413–21.

Boeker, W. 1989. "Strategic change: The effects of founding and history." *Academy of Management Journal* 32:489–515.

Boeker, W. 1991. "Organizational strategy: An ecological perspective." *Academy of Management Journal* 34:613–35.

Boorman, S. A., and P. R. Levitt, 1980. *The Genetics ofAltruism.* New York: Academic Press.

Borrus, M., J. Millstein, and J. Zysman. 1982. *International Competition in Advanced Industrial Sectors: Trade and Development in the Semiconductor Industry.* Berkeley, CA: Institute of International Studies.

Bourgeois, L. J., 1980 "Strategy and environment: A conceptual integration," *Academy of Management Review* 8:576–87.

Bourgeois, L. J. and K. M. Eisenhardt. 1988. "Strategic decision processes in high velocity environments: Four cases in the microcomputer industry." *Management Science* 34:816–35.

Bowels, R. 1984. "Property rights and the legal system." In E. Dwhynes (ed.), *What is Political Economy,* 187–208. New York: Basil Blackwell

Bower, J. 1970. *Managing the Resource Allocation Process.* Boston, MA: Harvard Business School Press.

Bowman, E. H. 1982. "Risk-taking by troubled firms." *Sloan Management Review* 23:33–42

Box, G. E. P., W. G. Hunter, and J. S. Hunter. 1978. *Statistics for Experimenters.* New York: Wiley.

Boyd, R., and P. J. Richerson. 1985. *Culture and the Evolutionary Process.* Chicago: University of Chicago Press.

Bradley, D. W., and R. A. Bradley. 1983. "Application of sequence comparison to the study of bird songs." In David Sankoff and Joseph B.Kruskal (eds.), *Time Warps, String Effects, and Macromolecules,*189–209. Reading, MA: Addison-Wesley.

Braun, E., and S. MacDonald. 1978. *Revolution in Miniature.*Cambridge, England: Cambridge University Press.

Brewer, M. B. 1981. "Ethnocentrism and its role in interpersonal trust." In M. B. Brewer and B. E. Collins (eds.), *Scientific Inquiry and the Social Sciences,* 345–60. San Francisco: Jossey-Bass.

Bright, J. 1949. *The Electric-Lamp Industry.* New York: Macmillan.

Brittain, J. W. 1989. "Environmental change and organization selection in semiconductor manufacturing." Ph.D. diss., University of California, Berkeley.

Brittain, J. W., and J. H. Freeman. 1980. "Organizational proliferation and density dependent selection." In J. Kimberly and R. H. Miles (eds.), *The Organizational Life Cycle.* San Francisco: Jossey-Bass.

Brittain, J. W., and D. R. Wholey. 1988. "Competition and coexistence in organizational communities: Population dynamics in electronics components manufacturing." In G. R. Carroll (ed.),*Ecological Models of Organizations,* 195–222. Cambridge, MA: Ballinger.

Brittain, J. W., and D. R. Wholey. 1990. "Structure as an environmental property: Industry demographics and labor market practices." In R. Breiger (ed.), *Social Mobility and Social Structure.* Cambridge, England: Cambridge University Press.

Brock, G. 1981. *The Telecommunications Industry.* Cambridge, MA: Harvard University Press.

Bromiley, Phillip. 1991. "Testing a Causal Model of Corporate Risk-Taking and Performance." *Academy of Management Journal* 34:37–59.

Brooks, J. 1976. *Telephone: The First Hundred Years.* New York: Harper and Row.

Brown, J. S., and P. Duguid. 1991. "Organizational learning and communities-of-practice: Toward a unified view of working, learning and innovation." *Organization Science,* 2:40–57

Brüderl, J., and R. Schüssler. 1990. "Organizational mortality: The liabilities of newness and adolescence." *Administrative Science Quarterly* 35:530–47.

Bureau of Labor, United States. 1888. *Third Annual Report, 1887: Strikes and Lockouts.* Issued by Commisioner of Labor.

Burgelman, R. A. 1983a. "A model of the interaction of strategic behavior, corporate context, and the concept of strategy." *Academy of Management Review* 8:61–70.

Burgelman, R. A. 1983b. "A process model of internal corporate venturing in the diversified major firm." *Administrative Science Quarterly* 28:223–44.

Burgelman, R. A. 1988. "Strategy-making as a social learning process: The case of internal corporate venturing." *Interfaces*18:74–85.

Burgelman, R. A. 1990. "Strategy-making in organizational ecology: A conceptual integration." In J. V. Singh (ed.), *Organizational Evolution: New Directions,* 164–81. Newbury Park, CA: Sage.

Burgelman, R. A. 1991. "Intraorganizational ecology of strategy-making and organizational adaptation: Theory and field research." *Organization Science* 2:239–62.

Burgelman, R. A., and B. S. Mittman. 1990. "CORPSTRAT: A computer simulation model of strategy-making in diversified firms." Unpublished Manuscript, Graduate School of Business, Stanford University.

Burgelman, R. A., and J. V. Singh. 1987. "Strategy and organization: An evolutionary approach." Paper presented at the Academy of Management Meetings, New Orleans, LA.

Burger, A. E., and T. Dacin. 1991. "Field of Membership: An Evolving Concept. " Madison, WI: Filene Research Institute.

Burns, T., and G.M. Stalker. 1961. *The Management of Innovation.* London: Travistock.

Burnstein, P. 1991. "Policy domains: Organization, culture, and policy outcomes." *Annual Review of Sociology* 17:327–50.

Burt, R. S. 1983. *Corporate Profits and Cooperation.* New York:Academic Press.

Business Week, August 4, 1986.

Business Week, October 25, 1991. *The Quality Imperitive* (special issue).

Campbell, D. T. 1958. "Common fate, similarity, and other indices of the status of aggregates of persons as social entities." *Behavioral Science* 3:14–25.

Campbell, D. T. 1959. "Methodological suggestions from a comparative psychology of knowledge processes." *Inquiry* 2:152–82.

Campbell, D. T. 1960. "Blind variation and selective retention in creative thought as in other knowledge processes." *Psychological Review* 67:380–400.

Campbell, D. T. 1965a. "Ethnocentrism and other altruistic motives." In D. Levine (ed.), *The Nebraska Symposium on Motivation* 13:283–311. Lincoln: University of Nebraska Press.

Campbell, D. T. 1965b. "Variation and selective retention in socio-cultural evolution." In H. R. Barringer, G. I. Blanksten, and R. W. Mack (eds.), *Social Change in Developing Areas: A Reinterpretation of Evolutionary Theory;* 19–48. Cambridge, MA: Schenkman.

Campbell, D. T. 1969. "Variation and selective retention insocio-cultural evolution." *General Systems* 16:69–85.

Campbell, D. T. 1974a. "Downward causation in hierarchically organized biological systems." In F. Ayala and T. Dobzhansky (eds.), *Studies in the Philosophy of Biology;* 179–86. Berkeley, CA: University of California Press.

Campbell, D. T. 1974b. "Evolutionary epistemology." In P. A. Schilpp (ed.), *The Philosophy of Karl R. Popper;* 413–63. LaSalle, IL: Open Court Publishing.

Campbell, D. T. 1975. "On the conflicts between biological and social evolution and between psychology and moral tradition."*American Psychologist* 30:1103–26.

Campbell, D. T. 1979. "Comments on the sociobiology of ethics and moralizing." *Behavioral Science* 24:37–45.

Campbell, D. T. 1982. "Legal and primary-group social controls."*Journal of Social and Biological Structures* 5:431–38.

Campbell, D. T. 1983. "The two distinct routes beyond kin selection to ultra-sociality: Implications for the humanities and social sciences."In D. L. Bridgeman (ed.), *The Nature of Prosocial Development: Interdisciplinary Theories and Strategies;* 11–41. New York: Academic Press.

Campbell, D. T. 1986. "Rationality and utility from the standpoint of evolutionary biology." *Journal of Business* 59:S355–S364.

Campbell, D. T. 1990a. "Levels of organization, downward causation,and the selection-theory approach to evolutionary epistemology." In G.Greenberg and E. Tobach (eds.), *Theories of the Evolution of Knowing* (The T. C. Schneirla Conference Series, Volume 4); 1–17. Hillsdale, NJ: Lawrence Erlbaum Associates.

Campbell, D. T. 1990b. "Epistemological roles for selection theory." In N. Rescher (ed.), *Evolution, Cognition, and Realism: Studies in Evolutionary Epistemology;* 1–19. Lanham, MD: University Press of America.

Campbell, D. T. 1991. "A naturalistic theory of archaic moral orders." *Zygon* 26:91–114.

Campbell, J. H. 1985. "An organizational interpretation of evolution." In D. J. Depew and B. H. Weber (eds.), *Evolution at a Crossroads: The New Biology and the New Philosphy of Science*, 133–68. Cambridge, MA: MIT Press.

Campbell, J., and L. Linndberg. 1990. "Property and organization of economic activity by the state." *American Sociological Review* 55:634–47.

Carroll, G. R. 1981. "Dynamics of organizational expansion in national systems of education." *American Sociological Review* 46:585–99.

Carroll, G. R. 1984. "Organizational ecology." *Annual Review of Sociology* 10:71–93.

Carroll, G. R. 1985. "Concentration and specialization: Dynamics of niche width in populations of organizations." *American Journal of Sociology,* 90:1262–83.

Carroll, G. R. 1987. *Publish and Perish: The Organizational Ecology of Newspaper Industries* Greenwich, CT: JAI Press.

Carroll, G. R. 1988. *Ecological Models of Organizations.* Cambridge, MA: Ballinger.

Carroll, G. R., and J. Delacroix. 1982. "Organizational mortality in the newspaper industries of Argentina and Ireland: An ecological approach." *Administrative Science Quarterly* 27:169–98.

Carroll, G. R., J. Delacroix, and J. Goodstein. 1990. "The political environment of organizations: An ecological view." *The Evolution and Adaptation of Organizations;* 67–100. Greenwich, CT: JAI Press.

Carroll, G. R., J. Goodstein, and A. Geynes. 1988. "Organizations and the State: Effects of the institutional environment on agricultural cooperatives in Hungary." *Administrative Science Quarterly* 33:233–56.

Carroll, G. R., and M. T. Hannan. 1989a. "Density delay in the evolution of organizational populations: A model and five empirical tests." *Administrative Science Quarterly* 34:411–30.

Carroll, G. R., and M. T. Hannan. 1989b. "Density dependence in the evolution of newspaper organizations." *American Sociological Review* 54:524–41.

Carroll, G. R., and M. T. Hannan. 1989c. "On using institutional theory in studying organizational populations." *American Sociological Review* 54:545–48.

Carroll, G. R., and Y. P. Huo. 1986. "Organizational task and institutional environments in ecological perspective: Findings from the local newspaper industry." *American Journal of Sociology* 91:838–73.

Carroll, G. R., and Y. P. Huo. 1988. "Organizational and electoral paradoxes of the knights of labor." In G. Carroll (ed.), *Ecological Models of Organizations;* 175–93. Cambridge, MA: Ballinger Press.

Carroll, G. R., P. Presendorfer, A. Swaminathan and A. G.Wiedenmayer. 1989. "Brewery and braurei: The comparative organizational ecology of American and German brewing industries." Working paper OBIR-34, Center of Research Management, University of California, Berkeley.

Carroll, G. R., and A. Swaminathan. 1991. "Density dependent organizational evolution in the American brewing industry from 1633 to1988." *Acta Sociologica* 34:155–75.

Cash, J. J., F. W. McFarlan, J. L. McKenney, and M. R. Vitale. 1988. *Corporate Information Systems Management.* Homewood, IL: Irwin.

Cavalli-Sforza, L. L., and M. W. Feldman. 1981. *Cultural Transmission and Evolution: A Quantitative Approach.* Princeton, NJ: Princeton University Press.

Caves, R. E., and M. E. Porter. 1977. "From entry barriers to mobility barriers." *Quarterly Journal of Economics* 90:241–61.

Chandler, A. D., Jr. 1962. *Strategy and Structure: Chapters in the History of the American Industrial Enterprise.* Cambridge, MA: MITPress.

Chandler, Alfred. 1977. *The Visible Hand.* Cambridge, MA: Belknap.

Cherns, A. 1976. "Principles of sociotechnical design." *Human Relations* 29:783–92.

Cherns, A. 1987. "Principles of sociotechnical design revisited."*Human Relations* 40:153–62.

Child, J. 1972. "Organizational structure, environment, and performance: The role of strategic choice." *Sociology* 6:2–22.

City of Toronto Planning and Development Department. 1983. *Social change in Toronto: A context for human services planning.* Toronto,Ontario: City of Toronto Planning and Development Department.

Clark, P.A. 1987. *Anglo-American Innovation.* New York: deGruyter.

Clemons, E. K. 1991. "Corporate strategies for information technology: A resource-based approach." *IEEE Computer* November: 23–32.

Cohen, K. J., and R. M. Cyert. 1965. "Simulation of organizational behavior." In J. G. March (ed.), *Handbook of Organizations;* 305–34. Chicago, IL: Rand McNally.

Cohen, L. E., and R. Machalek. 1988. "A general theory of expropriative crime: An evolutionary ecological approach." *American Journal of Sociology* 94:465–501.

Cohen, M. D., and R. Axelrod. 1984. "Coping with complexity: The adaptive value of changing utility." *The American Economic Review* 74:30–42.

Cohen, M. D., J. G. March, and J. P. Olsen. 1972. "A garbage can model of organizational choice." *Administrative Science Quarterly* 17:1–25.

Cohen, W. M., and R. Levin. 1989. "Empirical studies of innovation and market structure." In R. Schmalensee and D. Willig (eds.), *Handbook of Industrial Organization* 2:1060–1107. Elsevier.

Cohen, W. M., and D. A. Levinthal. 1989. "Innovation and learning: The two faces of R & D." *Economic Journal* 99:569–96.

Cohen, W. M., and D. A. Levinthal. 1990. "Absorptive capacity: A new perspective on learning and innovation." *Administrative Science Quarterly* 35:128–152.

Coleman, J. S. 1974. *Power and the Structure of Society.* NewYork: Norton Press.

Coleman, J. S. 1988. "Social capital in the creation of human capital." *American Journal of Sociology* 94:S95–S120.

Community Information Center of Metropolitan Toronto. 1971–89. *Directory of Day Care Centers and Nursery Schools in Metropolitan Toronto.* Toronto, Ontario: Community Information Center of MetropolitanToronto.

Conigliani, C. 1983. "Dimensioni aziendali, costi ed efficienza nel sistema bancario italiano." *Contributi alla Riceria Economica, No.21. Servizio Studi Della Banca d'Italia.*

Connor, E. F., and D. Simberloff. 1983. "Interspecific competition and species co-occurrence patterns on islands: Null models and the evaluation of evidence." *Oikos* 41:455–65.

Connor, E. F., and D. Simberloff. 1986. "Competition, scientific method, and null models in ecology." *American Scientist* 74:155–62.

Conner, K. R. 1991. "Strategic implications of high-technology competition in a network externality environment." Unpublished manuscript 91-07, Jones Center for Management Policy, Strategy and Organization, The Wharton School, University of Pennsylvania.

Constant, E. 1980. *The Origins of the Turbojet Revolution.* Baltimore, MD: The Johns Hopkins University Press.

Constant, E. 1987. "The social locus of technological practice: Community, system or organization." In W. Bijker et al. (eds.), *The Social Construction of Technological Systems.* Cambridge, MA: MITPress.

Constant, E. 1989. "Cause or consequence: Science, technology and regulatory change in the oil industry." *Journal of Business History* 426–55.

Cooper, A. C., and D. Schendel. 1976. "Strategic responses to technological threats." *Business Horizons.* February 19:61–69.

Costi R. 1986. *L'ordinamento bancario.* Bologna, Italy:Mulino.

Crecine, J. P. 1967. "A computer simulation model of municipal budgeting." *Management Science* 13:786–815.

Credit Union National Association. 1989. *Credit Union Services Profile.* Credit Union National Association.

Crosier, M., and E. Friedberg. 1977. *L'Acteur et le Système.* Paris: Soleil.

Csányi, V. 1989. *Evolutionary Systems and Society: A General Theory.* Durham, NC: Duke University Press.

Cuff, R. D. 1973. *The War Industries Board: Business-Government Relations During World War I.* Baltimore, MD: Johns Hopkins.

Cyert, R. M., and J. G. March. 1963. *A Behavioral Theory of the Firm.* Englewood Cliffs, NJ: Prentice-Hall.

Daft, R. L., and K. E. Weick. 1984. "Toward a model of organizations as interpretation systems." *Academy of Management Review* 9:284–95.

Danielian, N. R. 1939. *AT&T: The Story of Industrial Conquest.* New York: Vanguard.

Darwin, Charles. 1859. *On the Origin of Species by Means of Natural Selection.* London: Murray. (A Facsimile of the First Edition with an Introduction by Ernst Mayr {Cambridge, MA: Harvard University Press, 1964})

Dataquest. 1984a. "Consumption and factory shipments." In *Internal Report.* Santa Clara, CA: Dataquest.

Dataquest. 1984b. "Preliminary market share estimates." In *Internal Report.* Santa Clara, CA: Dataquest.

David, P. 1985. "Clio and the economics of QWERTY." *Economic History* 75:227–332.

David, P., and J. Bunn. 1988. "The economics of gateway technologies and network evolution." *Information Economics and Policy* 3:165–202.

Davis-Blake, A., and J. Pfeffer. 1989. "Just a mirage: The search for dispositional effects in organizational research." *Academy of Management Review* 14:385–400.

Dawkins, R. 1986. *The Blind Watchmaker.* Harlow, England: Longman Scientific and Technical.

Dawes, R., and R. Thaler. 1988. "Competition." *Journal of Economic Perspective* 2:187–97.

DeBresson, C., and P. Clark. 1991. "Strategic acts, networks and sector transformation." Unpublished manuscript.

Degli Innocenti, M. 1977. *Storia della cooperazione in Italia.* Rome: Editori Riuniti.

Delacroix, J., and G. R. Carroll. 1983. "Organizational foundings: An ecological study of the newspaper industries of Argentina and Ireland." *Administrative Science Quarterly* 28:274–91.

Delacroix, J., and A. Swaminathan. 1991. "Cosmetic, speculative, and adaptive organizational change in the wine industry: A longitudinal study." *Administrative Science Quarterly* 36:631–61.

Delacroix, J., A Swaminathan, and M. E. Solt. 1989. "Density dependence versus population dynamics: An ecological study of failings in the California wine industry." *American Sociological Review* 54:245–62.

DeLamarter, R. 1986. *Big Blue: IBM's Use and Abuse of Power.* New York, NY: Dodd, Mead.

Deming, W. E. 1981. "Improvement of quality and productivity through action by management." *National Productivity Review* 1:12–22.

Deming, W. E. 1986. *Out of the Crisis.* Cambridge, MA: MIT Center for Advanced Engineering Study.

DiMaggio, P. J. 1988. "Interest and agency in institutional theory." In L. G. Zucker (ed.), *Institutional Patterns and Organizations: Culture and Environment,* 3–22. Cambridge, MA: Ballinger.

DiMaggio, P. J., and W. W. Powell. 1983. "The iron cage revisited: Institutional isomorphism and collective rationality in organizational fields." *American Sociological Review* 48:147–60.

Dobbin, F. R., L. Edelman, J. W. Meyer, W. R. Scott, and A. Swindler. 1988. "The expansion of due process in organizations." In L. G. Zucker (ed.), *Institutional Patterns and Organizations,* 71–98. Cambridge, MA: Ballinger.

Dobyns, L., and C. Crawford-Mason. 1991. *Quality of Else: The Revolution in World Business.* Boston: Houghton Mifflin.

Donaldson, G., and J. W. Lorsch. 1983. *Decision Making at the Top.* New York: Basic Books.

Dornbusch, S. M., and W. R. Scott. 1975. *Evaluation and the Exercise of Authority.* San Francisco: Josey-Bass.

Dosi, G. 1982. "Technological paradigms and technological trajectories." *Research Policy* 11:147–62.

Dosi, G. 1988. "Sources, procedures, and microeconomic effects of innovation." *Journal of Economic Literature* 26:1120–71.

Dosi, G. 1990. "Finance, innovation and industrial change." *Journal of Economic Behavior and Organizations* 13:299–319.

Doti, L. P. "Bank Holding Company Act of 1956." In Larry Schweikart (ed.), *Encyclopedia of American Business History and Biography: Banking and Finance,* 1913–1989, 17–18. New York: Facts on File.

Dougherty, D. 1992. "Interpretive barriers to successful product innovation in large firms." *Organization Science* 3:179–203.

Dowling, J., and J. Pfeffer. 1975. "Organizational legitimacy, social values and organizational behavior." *Pacific Sociological Review* 18:122–36.

Downey, H. K., D. Hellriegel, and J. W. Slocum. 1975. "Environmental uncertainty: The construct and first application." *Administrative Science Quarterly* 20:613–29.

Downey, H. K., and J. W. Slocum. 1975. "Uncertainty: Measures, research, and sources of variation." *Academy of Management Journal* 18:562–78.

Downs, G., and L. B. Mohr. 1976. "Conceptual issues in the study of innovation." *Administrative Science Quarterly* 21:700–14.

Duesenberry, J. 1960. "An economic analysis of fertility." In University-National Bureau Committee for Economic Research, (ed.), *Demographic and Economic Change in Developed Countries.* Princeton, NJ: Princeton University Press.

DuMoncel, T. A. L. 1879 (1974 tr.). *The Telephone, Microphone and the Phonograph.* New York: Arno Press.

Dumont, R. G., and W. J. Wilson. 1967. "Aspects of concept formation, explication, and theory construction in sociology." *American Sociological Review* 32:985–95.

Dunham, R. and J. Pierce. 1989. *Management.* Glenview, IL: Scott Foresman.

Dunne, T., M. J. Roberts, and L. Samuelson. 1988. "Patterns of firm entry and exit in U. S. manufacturing industires." *RAND Journal of Economics* 19:495–515.

Durkheim, E. 1893 (1933 tr.). *The Division of Labor in Society.* Glencoe, IL: Free Press.

Dutton, J. E. 1993. "The making of organizational opportunities: An interpretive pathway to organizational change." In B. M. Staw and L. L. Cummings (eds.), *Research in Organizational Behavior,* 15. Greenwich,CT: JAI Press.

Dutton, J. E., and R. D. Freedman. 1985. "External environment and internal strategies: Calculating, experimenting and imitating in organizations." In R. Lamb and P. Shrivastava (eds.), *Advances in Strategic Management,* 3. Greenwich, CT: JAI Press.

Dutton, W., and A. Thomas. 1985. "Relating technological change and learning by doing." In R. Rosenbloom (ed.), *Research on Technological Innovation,* 187–224. Greenwich, CT: JAI Press.

Earle, J. 1986. *The Italian Cooperative Movement.* London: Allen and Unwin.

Easterlin, R. A. 1960. "Interregional differences in per capita income, population, and total income, 1840 to 1950." *Trends in the American Economy in the Nineteenth Century,* 24:73–140. Princeton,NJ: Princeton University Press National Bureau of Economic Research.

Eccles, R., and N. Nohria. 1992. *Beyond the Hype: Rediscovering the Essence of Management.* Boston: Harvard Business School Press.

Edwards, C. D. 1955. "Conglomerate Bigness as a Source of Power."In *NBER, Business Concentration and Public Power.* Princeton, NJ: Princeton University Press.

Edwards, P. K. 1978. "Time series regression models of strike activity: A reconsideration with American data." *British Journal of Industrial Relations:* 41:320–34.

Edwards, P. K. 1981. *Strikes in the United States* 1881–1974. Oxford: Basil Blackwell.

Edwards, R. C. 1979. *Contested Terrain: The Transformation of the Workplace in the Twentieth Century.* New York: Basic Books.

Eichler, N. 1989. *The Thrift Debacle.* Berkeley, CA: University of California Press.

Eiscnhardt, K. M., and C. B. Schoonhoven. 1990. "Organizational growth: Linking founding team, strategy, environment, and growth among U.S. semiconductor ventures, 1978–1988." *Administrative Science Quarterly:* 35:504–29.

Eldredge, N. 1985. *Unfinished Synthesis: Biological Hierarchies and modern evolutionary thought.* New York: Oxford University Press.

Eldredge, N. 1989. *Macroevolutionary Dynamics: Species, Niches, and Adaptive Peaks.* New York: McGraw-Hill.

Eldredge, N., and S. J. Gould. 1972. "Punctuated equilibria: An alternative to phyletic gradualism." In T. J. M. Schopf (ed.), *Models in Paliobiology,* 82–115. San Francisco: Freeman Cooper.

Eldredge, N., and S. N. Salthe. 1984. "Hierarchy and evolution." In R. Dawkins and M. Ridley (eds.), *Oxford Surveys in Evolutionary Biology* 1:182–206. New York: Oxford University Press.

Elliott, J. W. 1973. "A direct comparison of short-run GNP forecasting models." *Journal of Business* 46:33–60.

Ellsberg, D. 1961. "Risk, ambiguity and the savage axioms."*Journal of Economic Perspective* 2:187–97.

Ely, R. T. 1890. *The Labor Movement in America.* 3d ed. NewYork: Thomas Y. Crowell.

Emery, F. E., and E. L. Trist. 1965. "The causal texture of organizational environments." *Human Relations* 18:21–32.

Encyclopedia of Banking and Finance. G. G. Munn (ed.). Boston: Bankers Publishing Company.

Etzioni, A. 1987. "Entrepreneurship, adaption and legitimization."*Journal of Economic Behavior and Organization* 8:175–89.

Evans, D. S. 1986. "Gibrat's law, firm growth, and the fortune 500." Working Paper, Fordham University.

Fama, E. 1970. "Efficiency capital markets: A review of theory and empirical work." *Journal of Finance* 39:242–55.

Farrell, J., and G. Saloner. 1985. "Standardization, compatibility,and innovation." *Rand Journal of Economics* 16:71–83.

Farrell, J., and G. Saloner. 1988. "Coordination through committees and markets." *Rand Journal of Economics* 19:235–52.

Federal Communications Commission. 1939. *Investigation of the Telephone Industry in the United States.* Washington, DC: U.S.Government Printing Office.

Federal Register. 1989. Washington DC: Office of the Federal Register.

Feigenbaum, A. V. 1991. *Total Quality Control,* 3d ed. NewYork: McGraw-Hill.

Feldman, M. W. 1989. "Discussion: Ecology and evolution." In J. Roughgarden, R. M. May, and S. A. Levin, (eds.), *Perspectives in Ecological Theory,* 135–39. Princeton, NJ: Princeton University Press.

Fichman, M. 1989. "Attendance makes the heart grow fonder: A hazard rate approach to modeling attendance." *Journal of Applied Psychology* 74:325–35.

Filly, A. C. and R. J. Aldag. 1982. "Organization growth and types: Lessons from small institutions." In B. Staw and L. L. Cummings, (eds.),*Research in Organizational Behavior,* 9:559–75. Greenwich, CT: JAI Press.

Fiol, C. M., and M. A. Lyles. 1985. "Organizational learning."*Academy of Management Review* 10:803–10.

Fischer, C. S. 1992. *America Calling: A Social History of the Telephone to 1940.* Berkeley, CA: University of California Press.

Fischer, C. S., and G. R. Carroll. 1988. "Telephone and automobile diffusion in the United States, 1902–1937." *American Journal of Sociology* 93:1153–78.

Fischhoff, B. 1980. "For those condemned to study the past: Heuristics and biases in hindsight." In D. Kahneman, P. Slovic, and A.Tversky (eds.), *Judgment Under Uncertainty: Heuristics and Biases,*335–51. Cambridge, England: Cambridge University Press.

Fligstein, N. 1992. *The Transformation of Corporate Contol.* Cambridge, MA: Harvard University Press.

Fombrun, C. J. 1986. "Structural dynamics within and between organizations." *Administrative Science Quarterly* 31:403–21.

Fombrun, C. J. 1988. "Crafting and institutionally informed ecology of organizations." In Glenn R. Carroll, (ed.) *Ecological Models of Organizations;* 223–39. Cambridge, MA: Ballinger.

Fombrun, C. J., and E. J. Zajac. 1987. "Structural and perceptual influences on intraindustry stratification." *Academy of Management Journal* 30:33–50.

Forrester, J. W. 1958. "Industrial dynamics: A major breakthrough for decision makers." *Harvard Business Review* 36:37–66.

Forrester, J. W. 1968. *Principles of Systems.* Cambridge, MA: MIT Press.

Foster, R. 1986. *Innovation.* New York: Summit Books.

Freeman, C. 1982. *The Economics of Industrial Innovation.* Cambridge, MA: MIT Press.

Freeman, J. H. 1982. "Organizational life cycles and natural selection processes." In B. M. Staw and L. L. Cummings, (eds.), *Research in Organizational Behavior,* 4:1–32. Greenwich, CT: JAI Press.

Freeman, J. H. 1986. "Entrepreneurs as organizational products: Semiconductor firms and venture capital firms." In G. Libecap, (ed.), *Advances in the Study of Entrepreneurship, Innovation and Economic Growth.* Greenwich, CT: JAI Press.

Freeman, J., and J. Brittain. 1986. "Births of U. S. semiconductor firms." Paper presented at the Annual Meeting of the Academy of Management, Chicago, IL, August.

Freeman, J., G. R. Carroll, and M. T. Hannan. 1983. "The liability of Newness: Age dependence in organizational death rates." *American Sociological Review* 48:692–710.

Freeman, J., and M. T. Hannan. 1975. "Growth and decline processes in organizations." *American Sociological Review* 40:215–28.

Freeman, J., and M. T. Hannan. 1983. "Niche width and the dynamics of organizational populations." *American Journal of Sociology* 88:1116–45.

Freeman, J., and M. T. Hannan. 1989a. "Technical innovation, inertia, and organizational failure." Working paper, Department of Sociology, Cornell University.

Freeman, J., and M. T. Hannan. 1989b. "Setting the record straight on organizational ecology: Rebuttal to Young." *American Journal of Sociology* 95:425–39.

Freud, S. 1930. *Civilization and Its Discontents.* London:Hogarth.

Friedman, M. 1953. "The methodology of positive economics." In *Essays in Positive Economics.* Chicago: University of Chicago Press.

Frisch, K. von. 1950. *Bees, their Vision, Chemical Sense, and Language.* Ithaca, NY: Cornell University Press.

Frost, P., and C. Egri. 1990. "The political process of innovation." In L. Cummings and B. Staw (eds.), *Research in Organizational Behavior,* 13:229–95. Greenwich, CT: JAI Press.

Futuyama, D. J., and M. Slatkin. 1983. *Coevolution.* Sunderland, MA: Sinauer Associates Publishers.

Gabel, H. 1987. "Open standards in the European computer industry: The case of X/OPEN." *Product Standardization and Competitive Strategy.* Amsterdam: North Holland.

Galbraith, J. R. 1973. *Designing Complex Organizations.* Reading MA: Addison-Wesley.

Garlock, J. E. 1973. *Knights of Labor Data Bank.* Machine readable data file. Ann Arbor, MI: ICPSR.

Garud, R. 1989. "The emergence of the cochlear implant industry." Ph. D. diss. University of Minnesota, Carlson School of Management.

Garud, R., and A. H. Van de Ven. 1989. "Innovation and the emergence of industries." In A. H. Van de Ven, H. Angle, and M. S. Poole, (eds.),*Research On the Management of Innovation,* 409–532. New York: Harper Collins, Ballinger Division.

Garud, R., and A. H. Van de Ven. 1990. "Development of the cochlear implant program at 3M Corporation." Working paper, Strategic Management Research Center, University of Minnesota.

Gerlach, M. 1992. *Alliance Capitalism: The Social Organization of Japanese Business.* Berkeley, CA: University of California Press.

Gersick, C. J. G. 1988. "Time and transition in work teams: Toward a new model of group development." *Academy of Management Journal* 31:9–41.

Gersick, C. J. G. 1989. "Marking time: Predictable transitions in task groups." *Academy of Management Journal* 32:274–309.

Gersick, C. J. G. 1991. "Revolutionary change theories: A multilevel exploration of the punctated equilibrium paradigm." *Academy of Management Review* 16:10–36.

Giddens, A. 1979. *Central Problems in Social Theory: Action, Structure, and Contradiction in Social Analysis.* Berkeley, CA: University of California Press.

Gilfillan, S. G. 1935. *The Sociology of Invention.* Cambridge, MA: MIT Press.

Gilpin, M. E., and J. M. Diamond. 1984. "Are serious co-occurrences on islands non-random, and are null hypotheses useful in community ecology?" In D. R. Strong et al., (eds.), *Ecological Communities: Conceptual Issues and the Evidence,* 297–315 Princeton, NJ; Princeton University Press.

Ginsberg, A. 1988. "Measuring and modeling changes in strategy: Theoretical foundations and empirical directions." *Strategic Management Journal* 9:559–75.

Ginsberg, A. 1990. "Connecting diversification to performance: A sociocognitive approach." *Academy of Management Review* 15:514–35.

Ginsberg, A., and A. Buchholtz. 1990. "Converting to for-profit status: Corporate responsiveness to radical change." *Academy of Management Journal* 33:447–77.

Ginsberg, M. 1944. *Moral Progress.* Glasgow: Jackson.

Ginsberg, P. E. 1984. "The dysfunctional side effects of quantitive indicator production: Illustrations from mental health care (a message from Chicken Little)." *Evaluation and Program Planning* 7:1–12.

Glynn, M. A., T. K. Lant, and S. J. Mezias. 1991. "Incrementalism, learning, and ambiguity: An experimental study of aspriation level updating." *Academy of Management Best Papers Proceedings* 384–88. Miami, FL: Academy of Management.

Goffman, E. 1967. *Interaction Ritual.* Garden City, NY: Anchor.

Goffman, E. 1974. *Frame Analysis.* Cambridge, MA: Harvard University Press.

Goldberger, A. S. 1983. "Abnormal selection bias." In S. Karlin, T.Amemiya, and L. A. Goodman, (eds.), *Studies in Econometrics, Time Series, and Multivariate Statistics,* 67–84. New York: Academic Press.

Goodall, J. 1982. "Order without law." *Journal of Social and Biological Structures* 5:353–60.

Gould, S. J. 1980. *The Panda's Thumb.* New York: Norton.

Gould, S. J., and Lewontin, R. 1984. "The spandrels of San Marco and the Panglossian paradigm: A critique of the adaptationist program." In E. Sober (ed.), *Conceptual Issues in Evolutionary Biology,* 252–70.Cambridge, MA: MIT Press.

Gould, S. J. 1988. "The Panda's thumb of technology." In M. L. Tushman and W. L. Moore (eds.), *Readings in the Management of Technology,* 37–44. Cambridge, MA: Ballinger.

Gould, S. J. 1989. *Wonderful Life: The Burgess Shale and the Nature of History.* New York: Norton.

Gould, S. J. 1991. *Bully for Brontosaurus: Reflections on Natural History.* New York: Norton.

Grabowski, H. G. and J. M. Vernon. 1983. *The Regulation of Pharmaceuticals: Balancing the Benefits and Risks.* Washington, DC: American Enterprise Institute.

Granovetter, M. 1985. "Economic action and social structure: The problem of embeddedness." *American Journal of Sociology* 91:481–510.

Grant, V. 1985. *The Evolutionary Process: A Critical Review of Evolutionary Theory.* New York: Columbia University Press.

Greenwald, A. G. 1975. "Consequences of prejudice against the null hypothesis." *Psychological Bulletin* 82:1–20.

Gruter, M. 1982. "Biologically based behavioral research and the facts of law." *Journal of Social and Biological Structures* 5:315–23.

Gujarati, D. N. 1988. *Basic Econometrics.* New York: Hopkins.

Gup, B. E. 1984. *Management of Financial Institutions.* NewYork: Houghton Mifflin.

Haldane, J. B. S. 1932. *The Causes of Evolution.* London: Longmans Green.

Hall, B. H. 1986. "The relationship between firm size and firm growth in the U.S. manufacturing sector." NBER Working paper #1965.

Hall, R. I. 1976. "A system pathology of an organization: The rise and fall of the old Saturday Evening Post." *Administrative Science Quarterly* 21:185–211.

Hall, R. I., and W. B. Menzies. 1983. "A corporate system model of a sports club: Using simulation as an aid to policy making in a crisis."*Management Science* 29:52–64.

Halliday, T., M. Powell, and M. Granfors. 1987. "Minimalist organizations: Vital events in state bar associations, 1870–1930."*American Sociological Review* 52:456–71.

Hambrick, D. C., and R. A. D'Aveni. 1988. "Large Corporate Failures as Downward Spirals," *Administrative Science Quarterly* 33:1–23.

Hamilton, W. D. 1964. "The genetical evolution of social behavior."*Journal of Theoretical Biology* 7:1–52. Reprinted 1971. In G. C.Williams, (ed.), *Group Selection:* 23–87. Chicago: Aldine.

Hannan, M. T. 1986. "Competitive and institutional processes in organizational ecology." Technical report 86-13, Department of Sociology, Cornell University.

Hannan, M. T. 1991. *Aggregation and Disaggregation in the Social Sciences.* Rev. ed. Lexington, MA: Lexington.

Hannan, M.T., and G. R. Carroll. 1992. *Dynamics of Organizational Populations: Density, competition, and legitimation.* New York: Oxford University Press.

Hannan, M. T., G. R. Carroll, and D. Barron, 1991. "On the interpretation of density dependence in rates of organizational mortality: A reply to Peterson and Koput." *American Sociology Review* 56:410–15.

Hannan, M. T., and J. Freeman. 1977. "The population ecology of organizations." *American Journal of Sociology* 83:929–84.

Hannan, M. T., and J. H. Freeman. 1978. "Internal politics of growth and decline." In M. Meyer et al, (eds.), *Environments and Organizations.* San Francisco: Jossey-Bass.

Hannan, M. T. and J. H. Freeman. 1983. "Niche width and the dynamics of organizational populations." *American Journal of Sociology* 88:1116–45.

Hannan, M. T., and J. H. Freeman. 1984. "Structural inertia and organizational change." *American Sociological Review* 49:149–64.

Hannan, M. T., and J. Freeman. 1986a. "Where do organizational forms come from?" *Sociological Forum* 1:50–72.

Hannan, M. T., and J. Freeman. 1986b. "Disbanding rates of national labor unions, 1836–1985: Density dependence and age dependence."Technical Report: 86-6. Department of Sociology, Cornell University.

Hannan, M. T., and J. H. Freeman. 1987. "The ecology of organizational founding: American labor unions: 1836–1985."*American Journal of Sociology* 92:910–43.

Hannan, M. T., and J. H. Freeman. 1988a. "The ecology of organizational mortality: American labor unions, 1836–1985."*American Journal of Sociology* 94:25–52.

Hannan, M. T., and J. H. Freeman. 1988b. "Density dependence in the growth of organizational populations." In *Ecological Models of Organizations.* Cambridge, MA: Ballinger.

Hannan, M. T., and J. Freeman. 1989. *Organizational Ecology.* Cambridge, MA: Harvard University Press.

Hannan, M. T., J. Ranger-Moore, and J. Banaszak-Holl. 1990."Competition and the evolution of organizational size distributions." In J. V. Singh (ed.), *Organizational Evolution: New Directions,*246–68. Newbury Park, CA: Sage.

Hannan, M. T., and J. Ranger-Moore. 1990. "The ecology of organizational size distributions: A microsimulation approach."*Journal of Mathematical Sociology* 15:67–89.

Hansmann, H. 1988. "Ownership of the firm." *Journal of Law,Economics and Organization* 4:267–303.

Harré, R., and P. F. Secord. 1973. *The Explanation of Social Behavior.* Totowa, NJ: Littlefield, Adams.

Hartman, W., H. Matthes, and A. Proeme. 1968. *Management Information Systems Handbook.* New York: McGraw-Hill.

Harvey, P. H., R. K. Colwell, J. W. Silvertown, and R. M. May. 1983."Null models in ecology." *Annual Review of Ecology and Systematics* 14:189–211.

Hausman, J., B. Hall, and Z. Griliches. 1984. "Econometric models for count data with an application to the patents and R&D relationships."*Econometrica* 52:909–37.

Haveman, H. A. 1990. "Structural inertia revisited: Diversification and performance in the California savings and loan industry." Ph. D. diss., University of California, Berkeley.

Haveman, H. A. 1992. "Between a rock and a hard place: Organizational change and performance under conditions of fundamental environmental transformation." *Administrative Science Quarterly* 37:48–75.

Haveman, H. A. 1993. "Organizational size and change: Diversification in the savings and loan industry after deregulation." *Administrative Science Quarterly* 38:20–50.

Hawley, A. H. 1950. *Human Ecology: A Theory of Community Structure.* New York: Ronald.

Hawley, A. H. 1986. *Human Ecology: A Theoretical Essay.* Chicago: University of Chicago Press.

Hawley, A. H. 1988. Foreword to G. Carroll (ed.), *Ecological Models of Organizations.* Cambridge, MA: Ballinger Publishing.

Health Technology Assessment Reports. 1986. *Cochlear Implant Devices for the Profoundly Hearing Impaired.* National Center for Health Services Research and Health Care Technology Assessment.

Heckman, J. J. 1979. "Sample selection bias as a specification error." *Econometrica* 47:153–61.

Hedberg, B., P. C. Nystrom, and W. H. Starbuck. 1976. "Camping on seesaws: Prescriptions for a self-designing organization."*Administrative Science Quarterly* 21:41–65.

Heide, J. B., and A. S. Miner. 1992. "The shadow of the future: The effects of anticipated interaction and frequency of contact on buyer-seller cooperation." *Academy of Management Journal* 35:265–91.

Hempel, C. G. 1952. *Fundamentals of Concept Formation in Empirical Science.* Chicago, IL: University of Chicago Press.

Herrigel, G. 1992. "Industrial order in the machine tool industry: A comparison of the United States and Germany." In W. Streeck and J. R. Hollingsworth, (eds.), *Comparing Capitalist Economies: Variations in the Governance of Sectors.*

Herriott, S. R., D. Levinthal, and J. G. March. 1985. "Learning from experience in organizations." *American Economic Review* 75:298–302.

Herrmann-Pillath, C. 1991. "A Darwinian framework for the economic analysis of institutional change in history." *Journal of Social and Biological Structures* 14:127–48.

Hickson, D. J., C. R. Hinings, C. A. Lee, R. E. Schneck, and J. M. Pennings. 1971. "A strategic contingencies theory of intraorganizational power." *Administrative Science Quarterly* 16:216–29.

Hilgartner, S., and C. L. Bosk. 1988. "The rise and fall of social problems: A public arnas model." *American Journal of Sociology* 94:53–78.

Himmelberg, R. F. 1976. *The Origins of the National Recovery Administration: Business, Government, and the Trade Association Issue,1921–1933.* New York: Fordham University.

Hodgson, G. M. 1991. "Hayek's theory of cultural evolution: An evaluation in the light of Vanberg's critique." *Economics and Philosophy* 7:67–82.

Hodgson, G. M. 1992. "Optimization and evolution: Winter's critique of Friedman revisited." Report Nr. 11/92 of the Research Group on Biological Foundations of Human Culture at the Center of Interdisciplinary Research (1991/92), University of Bielefeld, D-4800 Bielefeld FRG.

Hodgson, G. M. 1993. *Economics and Evolution: Bringing Life Back into Economics.* Cambridge: Polity Press.

Hofstader, D. R. 1979. *Gödel, Escher, Bach: An Eternal Golden Braid.* New York: Basic Books.

Holland, J. H. 1975. *Adaptation in Natural and Artificial Systems.* Ann Arbor, MI: University of Michigan Press.

Hollander, S. 1965. *Sources of Efficiency.* Cambridge, MA: MIT Press.

Homans, J.E. 1904. *ABC of the Telephone.* 2d ed. New York: Theo. Audel and Company.

Honeycutt, R.L. 1992. "Naked mole-rats." *American Scientist* 80:43–53.

Hounshell, D. 1984. *From the American System to Mass Production.* Baltimore, MD: Johns Hopkins Press.

Horwitch, M. 1982. *Clipped Wings.* Cambridge, MA: MIT Press.

Hsiao, C. 1986. "Analysis of panel data." *Econometric Society.* Monograph No. 11. Cambridge: Cambridge University Press.

Hughes, T. P. 1983. *Networks of Power: Electrification in Western Society*, 1880–1930. Baltimore, MD: Johns Hopkins University Press.

Hughes, T. P. 1987. "The evolution of large technological systems."In W. E. Bijker, T. P. Hughes, and T. Pinch, (eds.), *The Social Construction of Technological Systems*, 51–82. Cambridge, MA: MIT Press.

Hull, D. L. 1980. "Individuality and selection." *Annual Review of Ecological Systems* 11:311–32.

Hull, D. L. 1988. *Science as a Process: An Evolutionary Account of the Social and Conceptual Development of Science*. Chicago: University of Chicago Press.

Hutchins, E. 1991. "Organizing work by adaptation."*Organization Science* 2:14–39.

Ijiri, Y., and H. A. Simon. 1977. *Skew Distributions and the Sizes of Business Firms*. New York: North Holland.

Imai, K., I. Nonaka, and H. Takeuchi. 1985. "Managing the new product development process: How Japanese companies learn and unlearn."In K. B. Clark, R. H. Hayes, and C. Lorenz, (eds.), *The Uneasy Alliance*. Cambridge, MA: Harvard Press.

Itani, J. 1982. "Intraspecific killing among nonhuman primates."*Journal of Social and Biological Structures* 5:361–68.

Jabes, J. 1978. *Individual Processes in Organizational Behavior*. Arlington Heights, IL: AHM.

Janzen, D. H. 1980. "When is it coevolution?" *Evolution* 34:611–12.

Jeffreys, W. H., and J. O. Berger. 1992. "Ockham's razor and Bayesian analysis." *American Scientist* 80:64–72.

Jenkins, R. 1975. *Images and Enterprise*. Baltimore, MD: Johns Hopkins Press.

Jensen, M. C. 1988. "Takeovers: Their causes and consequences."*Journal of Economic Perspectives* 2:21–48.

Jensen, M., and W. Meckling. 1976a. "Theories of the firm: Managerial behavior, agency costs, and ownership structure." *Journal of Financial Economics* 3:305–60.

Jensen, M., and W. Meckling. 1976b. "Rights and production functions: An application to labor-managed firms and codetermination." *Journal of Business* 52:469–506.

Jewett, F. B. 1977. "The telephone switchboard: Fifty years of history." In George Shiers (ed.), *The Telephone: An Historical Anthology*. New York: Arno Press.

Jones, G. 1983. "Transaction costs, property rights, and organizational culture: an exchange perspective." *Administrative Science Quarterly* 28:454–67.

Judge, G. G., W. Griffiths, C. R. Hill, and T. C. Lee. 1980. *The Theory and Practics of Econometrics*. New York: John Wiley and Sons.

Juran, J. M. 1989. *Juran on Leadership for Quality: An Executive Handbook*. New York: The Free Press.

Kahn, R. L., and D. Katz, 1962. "Leadership practices in relation to productivity and morale." In D. Cartwright and A. Zander, (eds.), *Group Dynamics: Research and Theory*, 554–70. Evanston, IL: Row, Peterson.

Kahneman, D., and A. Tversky. 1979. "Prospect theory: An analysis of decision under risk." *Econometrica* 47:263–91.

Kahneman, D., and A. Tversky. 1984. "Choices, values, and frames."*American Psychologist* 39:341–50.

Katz, D., N. Maccoby, and N. C. Morse. 1951. *Productivity, Supervision, and Morale in an Office Situation*. Ann Arbor, MI: Survey Research Center, University of Michigan.

Katz, M., and C. Shipiro. 1985. "Network externalities, competition and compatibility." *American Economic Review* 75:424–40.

Kaufman, B. E. 1982. "The determinants of strikes in the United States, 1900-1977." *Industrial and Labor Relations Review* 35:473–90.

Kazanjian, R. K., and R. Drazin. 1987. "Implementing internal diversification: Contingency factors for organization design choices."*Academy of Management Review* 12:342–54.

Kelly, D., and T. L. Amburgey. 1991. "Organizational inertia and momentum: A dynamic model of strategic change." *Academy of Management Journal* 34:591–612.

Kimberly, J. 1979. "Issues in the creation of organizations: Initiation, innovation and institutionalization." *Academy of Management Journal* 22:437–57.

Knights of Labor. 1880–1889. *Journal of United Labor.* Marblehead, Pittsburg, and Philadelphia, PA: Knights of Labor.

Kochan, T., J. Cutcher-Gershenfeld, and J. P. MacDuffie, 1992."Employee participation, work redesign and new technology: Implications for manufacturing and engineering practices." In G. Salvendy (ed.), *Handbook of Industrial Engineering.* New York: John Wiley and Sons.

Kulik, C. 1989. "The effects of job categorization on judgements of the motivating potential of jobs." *Administrative Science Quarterly* 34:68–90.

Kuhn, T. S. 1962/1970. *The Structure of Scientific Revolutions.* Chicago, IL: University of Chicago Press.

Kuznets, S., D. S. Thomas, and E. S. Lee. 1957. *Population Redistribution and Economic Growth: United States, 1870–1950.* Philadelphia: American Philosophical Society.

Kuznets, S. A. R. Miller, and R. A. Easterlin. 1960. *Population Redistribution and Economic Growth: United States, 1870–1950. II: Analyses of Economic Change.* Philadelphia: American Philosophical Society.

Lamarck, Jean Baptiste. 1809. *Zoological Philosophy.* Trans. H. Elliot. New York: Hafner, 1963.

Lambert, J. M., and W. T. Williams. 1962. "Multivariate methods in plant ecology. IV. Nodal analysis." *Journal of Ecology* 40:775–802.

Land, K. C., W. R. Davis, and J. Blau. 1992. "Organizing the boys of summer: density dependence and population dynamics in the evolution of U.S. Minor League Baseball Teams, 1883–1990." Working paper, Department of Sociology, Duke University.

Landi, A. 1989. *Dimensioni Costi e Profitti Nelle Banche Italiane.* Bologna, Italy: Il Mulino.

Langton, J. 1979. "Darwinism and the behavioral theory of sociocultural evolution: An analysis." *American Journal of Sociology* 85:288–309.

Langton, J. 1984. "The ecological theory of bureaucracy: The case of Josiah Wedgwood and the British pottery industry." *Administrative Science Quarterly* 29:330–54.

Langton, J. 1985. "Reply to Perrow." *Administrative Science Quarterly* 30:284–88.

Lant, T. K. 1992. "Aspiration level adaption: An empirical exploration." *Management Science* 38:623–44

Lant, T. K., and S. J. Mezias. 1990. "Managing discontinuous change: A simulation study of organizational learning and entrepreneurship." *Strategic Management Journal* 11:147–79.

Lant, T. K., and S. J. Mezias. 1992. "An organizational learning model of convergence and reorientation." *Organization Science* 3:47–71.

Lant, T. K., and D. B. Montgomery. 1987. "Learning from strategic success and failure." *Journal of Business Research* 15:503–18.

Laudan, L. 1984. *Progress and Its Problems.* Berkeley: University of California Press.

Laudon, K. C., and J. P. Laudon. 1988. *Management Information Systems: A Contemporary Perspective.* New York: Macmillan.

Lawrence, P. R., and J. W. Lorsch. 1967. *Organizations and Environments: Managing Differentiation and Integration.* Boston: Harvard Business School Press.

Layton, E. 1986. *The Revolt of the Engineers.* Baltimore, MD: Johns Hopkins Press.

Layton, E. T., Jr. 1986. "Technology as knowledge." In R. Landau and N. Rosenberg, (eds.), *The Positive Sum Strategy,* 31–41.Washington, DC: National Academy Press.

Lazerson, M. 1988. "Small firm growth: an outcome of markets and hierarchies." *American Sociological Review* 53:330–432.

Leblebici, H., G. Salanik, A. Copay, and T. King. 1991."Institutional change and the transformation of interorganizational fields: An organizational history of the U.S. radio broadcasting industry." *Administrative Science Quarterly* 36:333–63.

Lederberg, J. 1988. "Pandemic as a natural evolutionary phenomenon." *Social Science* 55:343–59.

Lee, L. F. 1983. "Generalized economic models with selectivity."*Econometrica* 51:507–12.

Leibenstein, H. 1966. "Allocative efficiency vs X-efficiency."*American Economic Review* 56:392–415.

Leonard, J. S. 1986. "On the size distribution of employment and establishments." NBER Working paper # 1951.

Leonard-Barton, D. 1990. "Mutual adaptation as a contributor to user satisfaction in internal technology transfer." Unpublished manuscript 91-029, Harvard Business School.

Leonard-Barton, D. 1991. "Core capabilities and core rigidities in new product development." Unpublished manuscript 92-005. Harvard Business School.

Leuthold, S. C. 1981. "Interest rates, inflation, and deflation."*Financial Analysis Journal* 37:28–41.

Levin, D. P. 1992. "Detroit slow to learn from Japan." *The New York Times,* May 5, D8.

Levin, R. C. 1982. "The semiconductor industry." In R. R. Nelson, (ed.), *Government and Technical Progress: A Cross-Industry Analysis.* New Haven, CT: Pergamon Press.

LeVine, R. A., and D. T. Campbell. 1972. *Ethnocentrism: Theories of Conflict, Ethnic Attitudes and Group Behavior.* New York: Wiley.

Levins, S. A. 1983. "Some approaches to the modeling of coevolutionary interactions." In Matthew H. Nitecki (ed.),*Coevolution,* 21–65. Chicago: University of Chicago Press.

Levinthal, D. 1990. "Organizational adaption, environmental selection, and random walks." *Organizational Evolution: NewDirections.* Newbury Park, CA: Sage.

Levinthal, D. A. 1991a. "Random walks and organizational mortality." *Administrative Science Quarterly* 36:397–420.

Levinthal, D. A. 1991b. "Organizational adaptation and environmental selection—interrelated processes of change." *Organization Science* 2:140–45.

Levinthal, Daniel. 1992. "Surviving Schumpeterian environments: an evolutionary perspective." *Industrial and Corporate Change* 1:427–43.

Levinthal, D. A., and J. March. 1981. "A model of adaptive organizational search." *Journal of Economic Behavior* 2:307–33.

Levitt, B., and J. G. March. 1988. "Organizational learning."*Annual Review of Sociology* 14:319–40.

Levitt, B., and C. Nass. 1989. "The lid on the garbage can: Institutional constraints on decision making in the technical core of college-text publishers." *Administrative Science Quarterly* 34:190–207.

Lewontin, R. C. 1978. "Adaptation." *Scientific American* 239:212–30.

Lindbloom, Charles. 1959. "The science of muddling through." *Public Administration Review* 19:79–88.

Litwak, E., and L. Hylton. 1962. "Interorganizational analysis: A hypothesis on coordinating agencies." *Administrative Science Quarterly* 6:395–420.

Lomi, A., and J. H. Freeman. 1990. "An ecological study of founding of cooperative organizations in Italy from 1963 to 1987: Some preliminary results." Working Paper 90-06, Johnson Graduate School of Management, Cornell University.

Longford, N. T. 1986. *Statistical Modeling of Data from Hierarchical Structures Using Variance Component Analysis: VARCL.* A Program developed at the Center for Applied Statistics. Lancaster University, UK.

Lord, F. M., and M. R. Novick. 1968. *Statistical Theories of Mental Test Scores.* Reading, MA: Addison-Wesley.

Lovell, M. C. 1983. "Data mining." *Review of Economics and Statistics* 65:1–12.

Lowrie, G. M. 1979. *Comments of the American Bankers Association on the Proposed Revisions to the Chartering and Charter Amendment Policies of National Credit Union Administration.* Correspondence.

Lumsden, C. J. 1989. "Review of *Organizational Ecology.*"(Hannan and Freeman, 1989). *Contemporary Sociology 18:549–51.*

Lumsden, C. J., and J. V. Singh. 1990. "The dynamics of organizational speciation." In J. V. Singh, (ed.), *Organizational Evolution: New Directions,* 145–63. Newbury Park, CA: Sage.

Lumsden, C. J., and E. O. Wilson. 1981. *Genes, Mind and Culture: The Coevolutionary Process.* Cambridge, MA: Harvard University Press.

MacKenzie, D. 1987. "Missile accuracy: A case study in the social processes of technological change." In W. Bijker et al., (eds.), *The Social Construction of Technological Systems.* Cambridge, MA: MIT Press.

MacLaren, M. 1943. *The Rise of the Electrical Industry During the Nineteenth Century.* Princeton, NJ: Princeton University Press.

MacMeal, H. B. 1934. *The Story of Independent Telephony.* Chicago: Independent Pioneer Telephone Association.

Maddala, G. S. 1983. *Limited-Dependent and Qualitive Variables in Economics.* Cambridge, England: Cambridge University Press.

Maddala, G. 1989. *Qualitative and Limited Dependent Variables in Econometrics.* Econometric Society Monograph Number 3 Cambridge England: Cambridge University Press.

Mahoney, M. J. 1977. "Publication prejudices: An experimental study of confirmatory bias in the peer review system." *Cognitive Therapy and Research* 1:161–75.

Maidique, M. A. 1980. "Entrepreneurs, champions and technological innovation." *Sloan Management Review,* Winter 20:59–76.

Majumdar, B. A. 1982. *Innovations, Product Developments and Technology Transfers: An Empirical Study of Dynamic Competitive Advantage: The Case of Electronic Calculators.* Lanham, MD: University Press ofAmerica.

Makridakis, S., et al. 1982. "The accuracy of extrapolation (time series) methods: Results of a forecasting competition." *Journal of Forecasting* 1:111–53. (Reprinted in Makridakis, S., et al. (eds.), *The Forecasting Accuracy of Major Time Series Methods,* 103–65. Chichester, England: Wiley, 1984.)

Makridakis, S., and M. Hibon. 1979. "Accuracy of forecasting: An empirical investigation." *Journal of the Royal Statistical Society, Series A* 142:97–145. (Reprinted in S. Makridakis, et al., (eds.), *The Forecasting Accuracy of Major Time Series Methods,* 35–101. Chichester, England: Wiley, 1984.)

Malerba, F. 1985. *The Semiconductor Business.* Madison: University of Wisconsin Press.

Mandelbrot, B. B. 1983. *The Fractile Geometry of Nature.* New York: W. H. Freeman.

Mansfield, E. 1963. "The speed of response of firms to new techniques." *Quarterly Journal of Economics* 77:290–311.

Mansfield, E. 1970. *Microeconomics: Theory Aplications.* New York: Norton.

March, J. C., and J. G. March 1977. "Almost random careers: The Wisconsin school superintendency, 1940–1972." *Administrative Science Quarterly* 22:377–409.

March, J. G. 1981. "Footnotes to organizational change."*Administrative Science Quarterly* 26:563–77.

March, J. G. 1988a. "Variable risk preferences and adaptive aspirations." *Journal of Economic Behavior and Organization* 9:5–24.

March, J. G. 1988b. "Wild ideas: The catechism of heresy."*Stanford Magazine,* Spring.

March, J. G. 1991. "Exploration and exploitation in organizational learning." *Organization Science* 2:71–87.

March, J. G., and J. P. Olsen. 1976. *Ambiguity and Choice in Organizations.* Bergen, Norway: Universitetsforlaget.

March, J. G., and J. P. Olsen. 1989. *The Organizational Basis of Politics.* New York: Macmillan.

March, J. G., and Z. Shapira. 1982. "Behavioral decision theory and organizational decision theory." In G. Ungson and D. N. Braunstein (eds.), *Decision Making: An Interdisciplinary Inquiry,* 92–115 Boston: Kent.

March, J. G., and Z. Shapira. 1987. "Managerial perspectives on risk and risk taking." *Management Science, 33:1404–1418.*

March, J. G., and Z. Shapira. 1992. "Variable risk preferences and the focus of attention." *Psychological Review* 99:172–83.

March, J. G., and H. A. Simon. 1958. *Organizations.* New York: Wiley.

Margulis, L. 1981. *Symbiosis in Cell Evolution.* San Francisco: Freeman.

Marrett, C. 1980. "Influences on the rise of new organizations: The formation of women's medical societies." *Administrative Sciences Quarterly* 25:185–99.

Marris, R. 1963. "A model of the 'managerial' enterprise."*Quarterly Journal of Economics* 77:185–209.

Marx, T. 1976. "Technological change and the theory of the firm: The American locomotive industry, 1920–1955." *Business History Review* 50:1-24.

Maslow, A. H. 1954. *Motivation and Personality.* New York: Harper.

Masters, R. D. 1982. "Evolutionary biology, political theory, and the orgin of state." *Journal of Social and Biological Structures* 5:439–50.

Matthews, D. Q. 1981. *The Design of the Management Information System.* New York: Moffat.

May, R. M. 1974. *Stability and Complexity in Model Ecosystems.* 2d ed. Princeton, NJ: Princeton University Press.

Maynard, F. B. 1985. *The Child Care Crisis.* Toronto: Viking.

Mayr, E. 1982. *The Growth of Biological Thought: Diversity, Evolution, and Inheritance.* Cambridge, MA: The Belknap Press of Harvard University.

McCarthy, J. D., and M. N. Zald. 1977. "Resource mobilization and social movement: a partial theory." *American Journal of Sociology* 82:1212–41.

McKelvey, B. 1982. *Organizational Systematics: Taxonomy, Classification, Evolution.* Berkeley, CA: University of California Press.

McKelvey, B., and H. E. Aldrich. 1983. "Populations, natural selection, and applied organizational science." *Administrative Science Quarterly* 28:101–28.

McLaughlin, P. 1991. "The organizational ecology of cooperative purchasing associations in Sasketchewan, Canada." Ph.D. diss., Cornell University.

McLeod, R. 1986. *Management Information Systems.* Chicago: Science Research Associates.

McPherson, J. M. 1983. "An ecology of affiliation." *American Sociological Review* 48:519–32.

McPherson, J. M. 1990. "Evolution in communities of voluntary organizations." In J. V. Singh (ed.), *Organizational Evolution: New Directions,* 224–45. Newbury Park, CA: Sage.

Mechanic, D. 1989. *Mental Health and Social Policy.* 3d ed. Englewood Cliffs, NJ: Prentice-Hall.

Mechanic, D., and D. A. Rochefort. 1990. "Deinstitutionalization: An appraisal of reform." *Annual Review of Sociology* 16:301–27.

Metropolitan Toronto Day Care Planning Task Force. 1986. *Blueprint for Childcare Services: Realistic Responses to the Need.* Toronto: Metropolitan Toronto Day Care Planning Task Force.

Meyer, A., G. Brooks, and J. Goes. 1990. "Environmental jolts and industry revolutions: Organizational responses to discontinuous change."*Strategic Management Journal* 11:93–110.

Meyer, J. W. 1970. "The charter: Conditions of diffuse socialization in schools." In W. R. Scott (ed.), *Social Processes and Social Structures*. New York: Holt Rinehart and Winston.

Meyer, J. W. 1980. "The world polity and the authority of the nation state." In A. J. Bergeson, (ed.), *Studies of the Modern World System*. New York: Academic Press.

Meyer, J. W., and B. Rowan. 1977. "Institutionalized organizations: Formal structure as myth and ceremony." *American Journal of Sociology* 83:340–363.

Meyer, J. W. and W. R. Scott, 1983. *Organizational Environments: Ritual and Rationality.* Beverly Hills, CA: Sage.

Meyer, J. W., W. R. Scott, and T. E. Deal. 1981. "Institutional and technical sources of organizational structure: Explaining the structure of educational organizations." In H. Stein (ed.), *Organization and the Human Services: Cross-Disciplinary Reflections*. Philadelphia: Temple University Press.

Meyer, M., and L. G. Zucker. 1989. *Permanently Failing Organizations*. Newbury Park, CA: Sage Publications.

Mezias, S. J. 1988. "Aspiration level effects: An empirical study." *Journal of Economic Behavior and Organization* 10:389–400.

Mezias, S. J., and M. A. Glynn. 1993. "The three faces of corporate renewal: Institution, revolution, and evolution." *Strategic Management Journal* 14:77–101.

Miles, R., and W. Randolph. 1980. "Influence of organizational learning styles on early development." In R. Kimberly and R. Miles, (eds.), *The Organizational Life Cycle,* 44–82. San Francisco: Jossey-Bass.

Miller, D., and P. H. Friesen. 1980a. "Archetypes of organizational transition." *Administrative Science Quarterly* 25:268–99.

Miller, D., and P. H. Friesen. 1980b. "Momentum and revolution in organizational adaptation." *Academy of Management Journal* 22:591–614.

Miller, J., and P. H. Friesen. 1984. *Organizations: A Quantum View.* Englewood Cliffs, NJ: Prentice.

Miller, R. E., and D. Sawers. 1968. *The Technical Development of Modern Aviation.* London: Routeledge and Kegan Paul.

Milliken, F. J., and T. K. Lant. 1991. "The effects of an organization's recent performance history on strategic persistence and change: The role of managerial interpretations." *Advances in Strategic Management* 7:129–56.

Mills, C. W. 1940 "Situated actions and vocabularies of motive." *American Sociological Review* 5:904–13.

Miner, A. S. 1987. "Idiosyncratic jobs in formalized organizations." *Administrative Science Quarterly* 32:327–52.

Miner, A. S. 1990. "Structural evolution through idiosyncratic jobs: The potential for unplanned learning." *Organization Science* 1:195–210.

Miner, A. S. 1991. "Organizational evolution and the social ecology of jobs." *American Sociological Review* 56:772–85.

Miner, A. S., T. L. Amburgey, and T. M. Sterns. 1990 "Interorganizational linkages and population dynamics: Buffering and transformational shields." *Administrative Science Quarterly* 35:689–713.

Ministero del Lavoro e della Previdenza Sociale: Statistiche della Cooperazione (various years).

Mintzberg, H. 1973. "Strategy-making in three modes." *California Management Review* 2:45–53.

Mintzberg, H. 1978. "Patterns in strategy formation." *Management Science* 24:934–48.

Mintzberg, H. 1979. *The Structuring of Organizations.* Englewood Cliffs, NJ: Prentice Hall.

Mintzberg, H. 1988. "Generic strategies: Toward a comprehensive framework." In R. Lamb and P. Shrivastava, (eds.), *Advances in Strategic Management* 5:1–67. Greenwich, CT: JAI Press.

Mintzberg, H. 1990. "The design school: Reconsidering the basic premises of strategic management." *Strategic Management Journal* 11:171–95.

Mintzberg, H., and A. McHugh. 1985. "Strategy formation in an adhocracy." *Administrative Science Quarterly* 30:160–97.

Mintzberg, H., and J. A. Waters. 1982. "Tracking strategy in an entrepreneurial firm." *Academy of Management Journal 25:465–99.*

Mitchell, W. 1987. "Dynamic tension: Theoretical and empirical analyses of entry into emerging industries." Paper presented at the Stanford Asilomar Conference on Organizations, Stanford, CA.

Mitchell, W. 1989. "Whether and when? Probability and timing of incumbents' entry into emerging industrial submarkets."*Administrative Science Quarterly* 34:208–30.

Mittman, B. S., and R. A. Burgelman. 1991. "CORPSTRAT, a computer simulation model of strategy-making in diversified firms: Technical description and user's guide." Unpublished manuscript.

Modigliani, F. 1958. "New developments on the oligopoly front."*Journal of Political Economy* 66:215–32.

Moody's Bank & Finance Manual. 1988. New York: Moody's Investors Service.

Morse, N. C., and E. Reimer. 1956. "The experimental change of a major organizational variable." *Journal of Abnormal Social Psychology* 52:120–29.

Mowery, D. C. 1985. "Market structure and innovation: A criticalsurvey." Paper presented at the conference on New Technology as Organizational Innovation. Netherlands Institute for Advanced Studies in Humanities, Wassenaar, May.

Mowery, D., and N. Rosenberg. 1981. "Technical change in the commercial aircraft industry, 1925–1975." *Technological Forecasting and Social Change* 20:347–58.

Muller, S. L. 1992. "Mass dependence in organizational founding rates: An ecological study of the American brewing industry from 1863 to1988." Working paper, University of Texas at Dallas.

Myers, S., and D. Marquis. 1969. *Successful Industrial Innovations.* Washington, DC: National Science Foundation.

National Credit Union Administration. 1989. "Interpretive Ruling and Policy Statement." *Federal Register* 54:31165–81.

Nelson, R. R. 1990. "Capitalism as an engine of progress."*Research Policy* 19:193–214.

Nelson R. R., and S.G. Winter. 1982. *An Evolutionary Theory of Economic Change.* Cambridge, MA: Harvard University Press.

Neter, J., and W. Wasserman. 1974. *Applied Linear Statistical Models.* Homewood, IL: Irwin.

Noble, D. 1984. *Forces of Production.* New York: Alfred A.Knopf.

Nonaka, I. 1988. "Creating organizational order out of chaos: Self-renewal in Japanese firms." *California Management Review,* Spring 30:57–72.

Normann, R. 1977. *Management for growth.* New York: Wiley.

Nystrom, P. C., and W. H. Starbuck. 1984. "To avoid organizational crisis, unlearn." *Organizational Dynamics,* Spring: 12:53–65.

Odaka, K., O. Keinosuke, and F. Adachi. 1988. *The Automobile Industry in Japan.* Oxford, England: Oxford University Press.

Olson, M. 1965. *The Logic of Collective Action.* Cambridge, MA: Harvard University Press.

Olson, M. 1968. *The Logic of Collective Action.* New York:Schocken.

Olzak, S., and E. West. 1991. "Ethnic conflicts and the rise and fall of ethnic newspapers." *American Sociological Review* 56:458–74.

Pant, P. N., and W. H. Starbuck. 1990. "Innocents in the forrest: Forcasting and research methods." *Journal of Management* 16:433–60.

Pantzar, M., and V. Csányi. 1991. "A replicative model of the evolution of the business organization." *Journal of Social and Biological Structures* 14:149–63.

Papa, M. J. 1990. "Communication network patterns and employee performance with new technology." *Communication Research* 17:344–68.

Parsons, Talcott. 1956. "Suggestions for a sociological approach to the theory of organizations." *Administrative Science Quarterly* 1:63–85.

Paullin, C. O. 1932. *Atlas of the Historical Georgraphy of United States.* Washington, DC: Carnegie Institution.

Pavitt, K. 1990. "What we know about the strategic management of technology." *California Management Review* 3:17–26.

Payne, J. W., D. J. Laughhunn, and R. Crum, 1980. "Translation of gambles and aspiration level effects on risky choice behavior." *Management Science* 26:1039–60.

Peach, J. T., and J. L. Webb. 1983. "Randomly specified macroeconomic models: Some implications for model selection." *Journal of Economic Issues* 17:697–720.

Pelkmans, J., and R. Beuter. 1987. "Standardization and competitiveness: Private and public strategies in the E.C. color TV industry." In H. Gabel, (ed.), *Product Standardization and CompetitiveStrategy,* 29–46. Amsterdam: North-Holland.

Pennings, J. 1982. "Organizational birth frequencies: An empirical investigation." *Administrative Science Quarterly.* 27:120–44.

Penrose, E. T. 1959. *The Theory of the Growth of the Firm.* NewYork: Wiley.

Perlman, S. 1937. *A History of Trade Unionism in the United States.* New York: MacMillan.

Perrow, C. 1985. "Comments on Langton's ecological theory of bureaucracy." *Administrative Science Quarterly* 30:278–83.

Perrow, Charles. 1986. *Complex Organizations: A Critical Essay* 3d ed. New York: Random House.

Perrow, C. 1992. "A society of organizations." *Theory and Society* 20:725–62.

Peters, T. 1990. "Get innovative or get dead." *California Management Review* 1:9–26.

Peters, T. 1991. "TQM is yet another trend that ignores management problems." *Baltimore Sun,* September 9.

Peters, T. J., and R. H. Waterman. 1982. *In Search of Excellence.* New York: Harper & Row.

Peterson, T., and K. Koput. 1991a. "Density dependence in organizational morality: Legitimacy or unobserved heterogeneity?" *American Review of Sociology* 56:399–409.

Peterson, T., and K. Koput. 1991b. "Unobserved heterogeneity or legitimacy in density dependence: A rejoinder to Hannan, Barron and Carroll." *American Review of Sociology* 56:416.

Pfeffer, J. 1981a. "Management as symbolic action: The creation and maintenance of organizational paradigms." In L. L. Cummings and B. M. Staw, (eds.), *Research in Organizational Behavior,* 3:1–52.Greenwich, CT: JAI Press.

Pfeffer, J. 1981b. *Power in Organizations.* Marshfield, MA:Pittman.

Pfeffer, J. 1982. *Organizations and Organization Theory.* Marshfield, MA: Pitman.

Pfeffer, J., and G. R. Salancik. 1978. *The External Control of Organizations.* New York: Harper & Row.

Phillips, A. 1987. "The role of standardization in shared bank card systems." In H. Gabel, (ed.), *Product Standardization and Competitive Strategy,* 263–82. Amsterdam: North Holland.

Pianka, E. R. 1988. *Evolutionary Ecology.* 4th ed. New York: Harper & Row.

Pimm, S. L. 1991. *The Balance of Nature? Ecological Issues in the Conservation of Species and Communities.* Chicago: University of Chicago Press.

Pimm, S. L., J. H. Lawton, and J. E. Cohen. 1991. "Food web patterns and their consequences." *Nature* 350:669–74.

Platt, J. R. 1964. "Strong inference." *Science* 146:347–53.

Popper, K. R. 1959. *The Logic of Scientific Discovery.* New York: Basic Books.

Porter, M. E. 1980. *Competitive Strategy: Techniques for Analyzing Industries and Competitors.* New York: Free Press.

Porter, M. E. 1990. *The Competitive Advantage of Nations.* NewYork: Free Press.

Powderly, T. V. 1890. *Thirty Years of Labor 1859–1889, In Which the History of the Attempts to Form Organizations of Workingmen for the Discussion of Political, Social, and Economic Questions is Traced.* Philadelphia.

Powell, W. W. 1990. "Neither market nor hierarchy: Network forms of organization." In B. Staw and L. Cummings (eds.), *Research in Organizational Behavior* 12:195–336. Greenwich, CT: JAI Press.

Powell, W. W. 1991. "Expanding the scope of institutional analysis." In W. W. Powell and P. J. DiMaggio, (eds.), *The New Institutionalism in Organizational Analysis,* 183–203. Chicago: University of Chicago Press.

Powell, W. W., and P. J. DiMaggio (eds.). 1991. *The New Institutionalism in Organizational Analysis.* Chicago: University of Chicago Press.

Powell, W. W., and P. Brantley. 1993. "Magic bullets and patent wars: New product development and the evolution of the biotechnology industry." In T. Nishiguchi, (ed.), *Competitive Product Development: Implications for Strategy, Technology, and Organization.* New York: Oxford University Press.

Prakhash, P., and A. Rappaport. 1977. "Information inductance and its significance for accounting." *Accounting, Organizations and Society* 2:29–38.

Prince, T. R. 1975. *Information Systems for Management Planning and Control.* Homewood, IL: Irwin.

Puccia, C. J., and R. Levins. 1985. *Qualitative Modeling of Complex Systems.* Cambridge, MA: Harvard University Press.

Quinn, J. B. 1980. *Strategies for Change: Logical Incrementalism.* Homewood, IL: Irwin.

Quinn, J. B. 1986. "Innovation and corporate strategy: Managed chaos." In M. Horwitch, (ed.), *Technology in the Modern Corporation: A Strategic Perspective.* Elmsford, NY: Pergamon Press.

Radcliffe, D. "The cochlear implants: Its time has come." *The Hearing Journal* 37:7–15.

Radner, R. 1976. "A behavioral model of cost reduction." *Bell Journal of Economics* 7:196–215.

Randle, Y. E. 1990. "Toward an ecological life cycle model of organizational success and failure." Ph.D. diss., University of California, Los Angeles.

Ranger-Moore, J., J. Banaszak-Holl, and M. T. Hannan. 1991."Density-dependent dynamics in regulated industries: Founding rates of banks and life insurance companies." *Administrative Science Quarterly* 36:36–65.

Rao, H. V., and J. Delacroix. 1988. "Business organizations and the limits of density dependence." Western Academy of Management Conference, Big Sky, Montana, March 24–26.

Rao, H. V., and M. Reddy. 1992. "Density and organizational mortality in technologically heterogeneous industries." Unpublished manuscript, Emory University, GA.

Rappaport, A. (ed.). 1982 *Information of Decision Making,* 3d ed. Englewood Cliffs, NJ: Prentice-Hall.

Rasmusen, E. 1989. *Games and Information.* New York: Basil Blackwell.

Ravenscraft, D. 1983. "Structure-profit relationships at the line of business and industry level." *Review of Economics and Statistics* 65:22–31.

Reich, R. 1988. "Bailout: A comparative study in law and industrial structure." In A. M. Spence and H. A. Hazard, (eds.), *International Competitiveness.* Cambridge, MA: Ballinger.

Rich, J. T., and J. A. Larson. 1984. "Why some long-term incentives fail." *Compensation Review* 16:16–26.

Richardson, G. P. 1991. *Feedback Thought in Social Science and Systems Theory.* Philadelphia: University of Pennsylvania Press.

Ridgeway, V. 1956. "Dysfunctional consequences of performance measures." *Administrative Science Quarterly* 1:240–47.

Robey, D. 1982. *Designing Organizations: A Macro Perspective.* Homewood, IL: Richard D. Irwin.

Robbins, J. 1987. "Organizational Economics." *Administrative Science Quarterly* 32:68–86.

Rose-Ackerman, S. 1988. "The market for loving kindness: Day care centers and the demand for child care." In C. Milofsky (ed.), *Community organizations: Studies in resource mobilization and exchange,* 170–82. New York: Oxford University Press.

Rosenberg, N. 1983. *Inside the Black Box: Technology and Economics.* Cambridge, England: Cambridge University Press.

Roughgarden, J. 1979a. *Perspectives in Ecological Theory.* Princeton, NJ: Princeton University Press.

Roughgarden, J. 1979b. *The Theory of Population Genetics and Evolutionary Ecology: An Introduction.* New York: Macmillan.

Roughgarden, J. 1983. "The theory of coevolution." In D. J.Futuyama and M. Slatkin, (eds.), *Coevolution,* 33–64. Sunderland,MA: Sinauer.

Romanelli, E. 1991a. "The evolution of new organizational forms."*Annual Review of Sociology* 17:79–103.

Romanelli, E. 1991b. "Organizational Imprinting: Initial Conditions as a Constraint on the Direction of Organizational Change." Unpublished manuscript, Duke University.

Ross, D. 1991. *The Origins of American Social Science.* Cambridge, England: University of Cambridge Press.

Rubel, S. M. 1982. *Guide to Venture Capital Sources,1982–83.* 6th ed. Chicago: Capital.

Rumelt, R. 1974. *Strategy, Structure, and Economic Performance.* Boston, MA: Harvard Business School Press.

Rumelt, R. 1984. "Toward a strategic theory of the firm." In R. B.Lamb, (ed.), *Competitive Strategic Management,* 557–70. Englewood Cliffs, NJ: Prentice-Hall.

Rundall, T. G., and J. O. McClain. 1982. "Environmental selection and physician supply." *American Journal of Sociology* 87:1090–1112.

Russell, C., and W. M. S. Russell. 1968. *Violence, Monkeys and Man.* London: Macmillan.

Russel, R., and R. Hanneman. 1991. "Births and deaths of Israeli cooperatives: 1948–1989: Dependency, ecological and institutional effects." Paper presented at the American Sociological Association Meeting, Cincinnati, OH, August 27.

Ruttan, V. W. 1978. "Induced institutional change." In H. P. Binswanger and V. W. Ruttan (eds.), *Induced Innovation,* Baltimore, MD: Johns Hopkins University Press.

Ruttan, V. W., and Y. Hayami. 1984. "Toward a theory of induced institutional innovation." *Journal of Development Studies* 20:302–23.

Sabel, C. 1991. "Moebius-strip organizations and open labor markets: Some consequences of the reintegration of conception and execution in a volatile economy." In P. Bourdieu and J. S. Coleman, (eds.), *Social Theory for a Changing Society,* 23–54. Boulder, CO: Westview Press and New York: Russell Sage Foundation.

Salancik, G. R., and J. Pfeffer. 1977. "Who gets power and how they hold on to it: A strategic contingency model of power."*Organizational Dynamics* 5(3):2–21.

Salthe, S. N. 1985. *Evolving Hierarchical Systems: Their Structure and Representation.* New York: Columbia University Press.

Samuelson, P. A. 1979. *Foundations of Economic Analysis.* New York: Atheneum.

SAS Institute. 1983. *SUGI Supplemental Library Users' Guide, 1983 Edition.* Cary, NC: SAS Institute.

SAS Institute. 1986. *Statistics, Version 5.* Cary, NC: SAS Institute.

Schelling, T. 1960. *The Strategy of Conflicts.* Cambridge, MA: Harvard University Press.

Schelling, T. 1978. *Micromotives and Macrobehavior.* New York: Norton.

Schmalensee, R. 1985. "Do markets differ much?" *American Economic Review* 75:341–51.

Schmitter, P., and W. Streeck. 1981. "The organization of business interests." Research proposal. *International Institute of Management,* West Berlin.

Schon, D. A. 1971. *Beyond the Stable State.* New York: Norton.

Schoonhoven, C. B., K. M. Eisenhardt, and K. Lyman. 1990. "Speeding products to market: Waiting time to first product introduction in new firms." *Administrative Science Quarterly* 35:177–207.

Schroeder, R., A. H. Van de Ven, G. D. Scudder, and D. Polley. 1989."The development of innovation ideas." In A. H. Van de Ven, H. L. Angle, M. S. Poole, (eds.), *Research on the Management of Innovation,*107–34. New York: Harper & Row.

Schumpeter, J. A. 1934. *The Theory of Economic Development.* Cambridge, MA: Harvard University Press.

Schumpeter, J. A. 1942. *Capitalism, Socialism, and Democracy.* New York: Harper.

Schwenk, C. R. 1982. "Why sacrifice rigor for relevance? A proposal for combining laboratory and field research in strategic management."*Strategic Management Journal* 3:213–55.

Scott, W. R. 1981. *Organizations: Rational, Natural, and Open Systems.* Englewood Cliffs, NJ: Prentice-Hall.

Scott, W. R. 1987a. "The adolescence of institutional theory."*Administrative Science Quarterly* 32:493–511.

Scott, W. R. 1987b. *Organizations: Rational, Natural, and Open Systems.* 2d ed. Englewood Cliffs, NJ: Prentice-Hall.

Scott, W., and J. Meyer 1983. "The organization of societal sectors 1–16." *Organizational Environments: Ritual and Ratonality.* Beverly Hills, CA: Sage.

Selznick, P. 1949. *TVA and the Grass Roots.* Berkeley, CA: University of California Press.

Shapere, D. 1977. "Scientific theories and their domains. In F.Suppe (ed.), *The Structure of Scientific Theories.* 2d ed., 518–65. Urbana, IL: University of Illinois Press.

Shapira, Z. 1993. "Risk sharing and incentive contracts: on setting compensation policy for expatriate professionals in a foreign operation."In *Coalition and Competition: Globalization of Professional Services,* 153–60. London: Routledge.

Shapira, Z. (in press). *Managerial Risk Taking.* New York: Russell Sage Foundation.

Sherman, P. W., J. U. M. Jarvis, and R. D. Alexander, (eds.). 1991. *The Biology of the Naked Mole-Rat.* Princeton, NJ: Princeton University Press.

Sherman, P. W., J. U. M. Jarvis, and S. H. Braude. 1992. "Naked mole rats." *Scientific American* 267:72–78.

Shleifer, A., and L. H. Summers. 1988. "Breach of trust in hostile takeovers." In A. J. Auerbach, (ed.), *Corporate Takeovers: Causes and Consequences.* Chicago: University of Chicago Press.

Siegel, S. 1957. "Level aspiration and decision making."*Psychology Review* 64:253–62.

Silhan, P. A., and H. Thomas. 1986. "Using simulated mergers to evaluate corporate diversification." *Strategic Management Journal* 7:523–34.

Simmons, F. B. 1985. "Some medical, social, and psychological considerations in cochlear implants." *Seminars in Hearing* 6:1–6.

Simon, H. A. 1947. *Administrative Behavior.* New York: Free Press.

Simon, H. 1951. "A formal theory of the employment relation."*Economertrica* 19:293–305.

Simon, H. A. 1955. "A behavioral model of rational choice."*Quarterly Journal of Economics* 69:99–118.

Simon, H. A. 1956. "Rational choice and the structure of the environment." *Psychological Review* 63:129–38.

Simon, H. A. 1957. *Administrative Behavior.* 2d ed. New York: Macmillan.

Simon, H. A. 1962. "The architecture of complexity."*Proceedings of the American Philosophy Society* 106:467–82.

Simon, H. A. 1987. "Satisficing." In J. Eatwell, M. Millgate, and P. Newman, (eds.), *The New Palgrave: A Dictionary of Economics* 4:243–45.

Simpson, G. G. 1944. *Tempo and Mode in Evolution.* New York: Columbia University Press.

Simpson, G. G. 1953. *The Major Features of Evolution.* NewYork: Columbia University Press.

Simpson, J. H., and E. S. C. Weiner. 1989. *Oxford English Dictionary.* 2d ed. Oxford, England: Clarendon.

Singh, J. V. 1986. "Performance, slack, and risk taking in organizational decision making." *Academy of Management Journal* 29:562–85.

Singh, J. V. (ed.). 1990. *Organizational Evolution: New Directions.* Newbury Park, CA: Sage.

Singh, J. V., R. J. House, and D. J. Tucker. 1986. "Organizational change and organizational mortality." *Administrative Science Quarterly* 31:587–611.

Singh, J. V., and C. J. Lumsden. 1990. "Theory and research in organizational ecology." *Annual Review of Sociology* 16:161–95.

Singh, J. V., D. J. Tucker, and R. J. House. 1986. "Organizational legitimacy and the liability of newness." *Administrative Science Quarterly* 31:171–93.

Singh, J. V., D. J. Tucker, and A. G. Meinhard. 1988. "Are voluntary social service organizations structurally inert? Exploring an assumption in organizational ecology." Paper presented at the Academy of Management national meetings, Anaheim, CA.

Singh, J. V., D. J. Tucker, and A. G. Meinhard. 1991. "Institutional change and ecological dynamics." In W. W. Powell and P. J. DiMaggio (eds.), *The New Institutionalism in Organizational Analysis,* 390–422. Chicago: University of Chicago Press.

Skeels, J. W. 1982. "The economic and organizational basis of early United States Strikes, 1900–1948." *Industrial and Labor Relations Review* 35:491–503.

Skinner, B. F. 1953. *Science and Human Behavior.* New York: MacMillan.

Smelser, N. J. 1963. *Theory of Collective Behavior.* New York: Free Press.

Snyder, D. 1970. "Determinants of industrial conflict: historical models of strikes in France, Italy, and United States." Ph. D. diss., Department of Sociology, University of Michigan.

Snyder, D. 1977. "Early north American strikes: A reinterpretation." *Industrial and Labor Relations Review* 30:325–41.

Sober, E. 1984. *The Nature of Selection: Evolutionary Theory in Philosophical Focus.* Cambridge, MA: MIT Press.

Social Planning Council of Metropolitan Toronto. 1968. *Day Care in Metropolitan Toronto.* Toronto: Social Planning Council of Metropolitan Toronto.

Social Planning Council of Metropolitan Toronto. 1981. *Metropolitan Social Profile: Guide to Social Planning Facts in Metropolitan Toronto,* Vol. 1. Toronto: Social Planning Council of Metropolitan Toronto.

Soltis, J., R. Boyd, and P. J. Richerson. 1992. "Can group-functional behaviors evolve by cultural group selection? An empirical test." Research Group on Biological Foundations of Human Culture at the Center for Interdisciplinary Research (1991/92), University of Bielefeld, D-4800, Bielefeld FRG.

Sommerhoff, G. 1950. "Purpose, adaptation and 'directive correlation'." In W. Buckley (ed.), *Modern Systems Research for the Behavioral Scientist,* 281–95. Chicago: Aldine.

Spence, J. 1985."Achievement American style: The rewards and costs of individualism." *American Psychologist* 40:1285–95.

Staber, U. 1982. "The organizational properties of trade associations." Ph.D. diss., Cornell University.

Staber, U. 1987. "Corporation and the governance structure of American trade associations." *Political Studies* 35:278–88.

Staber U. 1989. "Age dependence and historical effects on the failure rates of worker cooperatives." *Economic and Industrial Democracy* 10:59–80.

Stanley, S. M. 1979a. "Fossils, macroevolution, and theory." In J. Roughgarden, R. M. May, and S. A. Levin (eds.), *Perspectives in Ecological Theory,* 125–34 Princeton, NJ: Princeton University Press.

Stanley, S. M. 1979b. *Macroevolution: Pattern and Process.* San Francisco: Freeman.

Stapleford, E. M. 1976. *History of the Day Nurseries Branch.* Toronto: Ontario Ministry of Community and Social Services.

Starbuck, W. H. 1965. "Organizational Growth and Development." In J. G. March, (ed.), *Handbook of Organizations,* 451–533. Chicago: Rand-McNally.

Starbuck, W. H. 1968. "Organizational Metamorphosis." In R. W. Millman and M. P. Hottenstein (eds.) *Promising Research Directions,* Toronto: Academy of Management.

Starbuck, W. H. 1981. "A trip to view the elephants and rattlesnakes in the garden of Aston." In A. H. Van de Ven and W. F. Joyce (eds.), *Perspectives on Organization Design and Behavior,* 167–198. NewYork: Wiley-Interscience.

Starbuck, W. H. 1983. "Organizations as action generators." *American Sociological Review* 48:91–102.

Starbuck, W. H., and F. J. Milliken. 1988. "Executives' perceptual filters: What they notice and how they make sense." In D. C. Hambrick, (ed.), *The Executive Effect: Concepts and Methods for Studying Top Managers,* 35–65. Greenwich, CT: JAI Press.

Staw, B. M. 1981. "The escalation of commitment to a course of action." *Academy of Management Review* 6:577–87.

Staw, B. M., L. Sandelands, and J. E. Dutton. 1981. "Threat rigidity cycles in organizational behavior." *Administrative Science Quarterly* 26:501–24.

Stein, J. 1989. "Efficient markets, inefficient firms: a model of myopic corporate behavior." *Quarterly Journal of Economics* 104:655–69.

Stinchcombe, A. L. 1965. "Social structure and organizations." In J. G. March, (ed.), *Handbook of Organizations,* 153–93. Chicago: Rand McNally.

Stinchcombe, A. L. 1968. *Contructing Social Theories.* NewYork: Harcourt Brace Jovanovich.

Stinchcombe, A. L. 1983. *Economic Sociology.* New York: Academic Press.

Streeck, W. 1985. "Community, market, state—and associations? The prospective contribution of interest governance to social order." *European Sociological Review* 1:119–38.

Strohmeyer, J. 1986. *Crisis in Bethlehem: Big Steel's Struggle to Survive.* Bethesda, MD: Adler and Adler.

Struass, A. 1978. *Negotiations.* San Francisco: Josey-Bass.

Swaminathan, A., and J. Delacroix. 1991. "Differentiation within an organizational population: Additional evidence from the wine industry." *Academy of Management Journal* 34:679–92.

Swaminathan, A., and G. Wiedenmayer. 1991. "Does the pattern of density dependence vary across levels of analysis: Evidence from the German brewing industry." *Social Science Research* 20:45–73.

Sylos Labini, P. 1962. *Oligopoly and Technical Progress.* Cambridge, MA: Harvard University Press.

Teece, D. J. 1987. "Profiting from technological innovation: Implications for integration, collaboration, licensing and public policy." In D. Teece, (ed.), *The Competitive Challenge,* 185–219. New York: Harper & Row.

Thaler, R. 1991. *Quasi Rationality Economics.* New York: Russell Sage Foundation.

Thomas, G. M., and J. M. Meyer. 1984. "The expansion of the state." *Annual Review of Sociology* 10:461–82.

Thompson, J. D. 1967. *Organizations in Action.* New York:Academic Press.

Thirtle C. G., and V. W. Ruttan. 1986. "The role of demand and supply in the generation and diffusion of technical change." Bulletin No.86-5. University of Minnesota Economic Development Center, Minneapolis, MN.

Tilton, J. H. 1971. *International Diffusion of Technology: The Case of Semiconductors.* Washington, DC: Brookings Institution.

Tolbert, P. S. 1985. "Resource dependence and institutional environments: sources of administrative structure in institutions of higher education." *Administrative Science Quarterly* 30:1–13.

Toulmin, S. 1972. *Human Understanding.* Vol. 1 Princeton, NJ: Princeton University Press.

Travis, J., and L. D. Mueller. 1989. "Blending ecology and genetics: Progress toward a unified population biology." In J. Roughgarden, R. M. May, and S. A. Levin, (eds.), *Perspectives in Ecological Theory,* 101–124. Princeton, NJ: Princeton University Press.

Trist, E. 1981. "The evolution of sociotechnical systems as a conceptual framework and as an action research program." In A. H. Van de Ven and W. F. Joyce, (eds.), *Perspectives on Organization Design and Behavior,* 19–75. New York: John Wiley and Sons.

Trivers, R. L. 1971. "The evolution of reciprocal altruism."*Quarterly Review of Biology* 46:35–57.

Tucker, D. J., J. A. C. Baum, and J. V. Singh. 1992. "The institutional ecology of human service organizations." In Yeheskel Hasenfel, (ed.), *Human Services as Complex Organizations,* 47–72.Newbury Park, CA: Sage.

Tucker, D. J., and L. F. Hurl. 1992. "An Ecological Study of the Dynamics of Foster Home Entries." *Social Service Review* 66:617–41.

Tucker, D. J., J. V. Singh, and A. G. Meinhard. 1988. "Founding conditions, environmental selection, and organizational mortality."Unpublished manuscript, McMaster University, School of Social Work.

Tucker, D., J. V. Singh, and A. Meinhard. 1990b. "Organizational form, population dynamics, and institutional change: The founding patterns of voluntary organizations." *Academy of Management Journal* 33:151–178.

Tucker, D. J., J. V. Singh, and A. G. Meinhard. 1990a. "Founding characteristics, imprinting, and organizational change." In J. V. Singh,(ed.), *Organizational Evolution: New Directions,* 182–200. Newbury Park CA: Sage.

Tucker, D. J., J. V. Singh, A. G. Meinhard, and R. J. House. 1988. 'Ecological and institutional sources of change in organizational populations." In G. R. Carroll, (ed.), *Ecological Models of Organizations,* 127–51. Cambridge, MA: Ballinger.

Tuma, N. B. 1979/1980. *Invoking RATE.* 2d ed. Menlo Park, CA: SRI International.

Tuma, N. B., and M. T. Hannan. 1984. *Social Dynamics: Models and Methods.* New York: Acedemic Press.

Tushman, M. L., and P. Anderson. 1986. "Technological discontinuities and organizational environments." *Administrative Science Quarterly* 31:439–65.

Tushman, M. L., and E. Romanelli. 1985. "Organizational evolution: A metamorphosis model of convergence and reorientation." In L. L. Cummings and B. M. Staw, (eds.), *Research in Organizational Behavior.* 7:171–222. Greenwich, CT: JAI Press.

Tushman, M. L., and L. Rosenkopf. 1992. "Organizational determinants of technological change: Toward a sociology of technological evolution."In L. L. Cummings and B. M. Staw, (eds.), *Research in Organizational Behavior,* 14:311–47. Greenwich, CT: JAI Press.

Tushman, M. L., B. Virany, and E. Romanelli. 1985. "Executive succession, strategic reorientations, and organization evolution."*Technology in Society* 7:297–313.

Tversky, A., and D. Kahneman. 1986. "Rational choice and the framing of decisions." *Journal of Business.* 59:S251–S278.

Tyne, G. F. J. 1977. *Saga of the Vacuum Tube.* Indianapolis, IN: Howard W. Sams.

Ulrich, D., and B. McKelvey. 1990. "General organizational classification: An empirical test using the United States and Japanese electronics industries." *Organization Science* 1:99–118.

Usher, A. P. 1954. *A History of Mechanical Inventions.* Cambridge, MA: Harvard University Press.

U.S. Bureau of the Census. 1975. *Historical Statistics of the United States, Colonial Times to 1970.* Washington, DC: U.S. Government Printing Office. 1984. Statistical Abstract of the United States. Washington, DC: U.S. Government Printing Office.

U.S. Bureau of Labor Statistics. 1984. *Handbook of Labor Statistics.* Washington, DC: U. S. Government Printing Office.

U.S. Department of Commerce. 1979. *A Report on the U.S. Semiconductor Industry.* Washington, DC: U.S. Government Printing Office.

U.S. Department of Commerce. 1980. "Selected electronic and Associated products, including telephone and telegraph apparatus." In *Current Industrial Reports.* Washington, DC: Industry Division, Bureau of the Census.

U.S. Department of Commerce. 1982. "Selected electronic and associated products, including telephone and telegraph apparatus." In *Current Industrial Reports.* Washington, DC: Industry Division,Bureau of the Census.

U.S. Department of Commerce. 1983. *Annual Report of the Commissioner of Patents.* Washington, DC: U.S. Government Printing Office.

U.S. General Accounting Office. 1991. *Management Practices: U.S.Companies Improve Performance Through Quality Efforts* (GAO/NSIAD-91-190). Washington, DC: U.S. General Accounting Office.

Utterback, J. M., and W. J. Abernathy. 1975. "A dynamic model of process and product innovation." *Omega* 3:639–56.

Uwe, E. R. 1973. "Proposed changes in the organization of health care delivery: An overview and critique." *The Milbank Memorial Fund Quarterly* 51:169–22.

Van de Ven, A. H., H. L. Angle, and M. S. Poole. 1989. *Research on the Management of Innovation.* New York: Harper & Row.

Van de Ven, A. H., and R. Garud. 1989. "A framework for understanding the emergence of new industries." *Research on Technological Innovation Management and Policy* 4:295–325.

Van de Ven, A. H., and R. Garud, 1992. "The evolution of novelty in the development of cochlear implants." Working paper, Strategic Management Research Center, Minneapolis: University of Minnesota.

Van de Ven A. H., and M. S. Poole, 1990. "Methods for studying innovation development in the Minnesota Innovation Research Program."*Organization Science* 1:313–35.

Van de Ven, A. H., and M. S. Poole, 1992. "Process theories of development and change." Working paper, Strategic Management Research Center, University of Minnesota.

Van Valen, L. 1973. "A new evolutionary law." *EvolutionaryTheory* 1:1–30.

Varian, H. R. 1978. *Microeconomic Analysis.* New York: Norton.

Venture Economics. 1984. "Estimated Venture Capital Disbursements." Internal report, Wellesley Hills, MA: Capital Publications.

Von Hipple, E. 1987. "Cooperation between rivals: informal know-how trading." *Research Policy* 16:291–302.

Waddington, C. H. 1960. *The Ethical Animal.* London: Allen and Unwin.

Walker, J. L. 1969. "The diffusion of innovations among American states." *American Political Science Review* 63:880–99.

Walsh, J. P. 1990. "Knowledge structures and the management of organizations: A research review and agenda." Unpublished manuscript,Tuck School of Management.

Walton, M. 1990. *Deming Management at Work.* New York: Putnam.

Warriner, C. K. 1978. "Teleology, Ecology, and Organizations."(Revision of 1973 paper) Mimeographed. Lawerence: University of Kansas.

Webbink, D. W. 1977. *The Semiconductor Industry: A Survey of Structure, Conduct and Performance.* Washington, DC: Federal Trade Commision.

Weber, M. 1947. *Theory of Economic and Social Organization.* New York: Free Press.

Weber, M. 1958. "Bureaucracy." In H. H. Gerth and C. W. Mills, (eds.), *From Max Weber: Essays in Sociology,* 1864–1920. NewYork: Oxford University Press.

Weber, M. 1968. *On Charisma and Institution Building.* Chicago: University of Chicago Press.

Webster, J., and W. H. Starbuck. 1988. "Theory building in industrial and organizational psychology." In C. L. Cooper and I.Robertson, (eds.), *International Review of Industrial and Organizational Psychology,* 93–138. Chichester, England: Wiley.

Weick, K. E. 1969/1979. *The Social Psychology of Organizing.* Reading, MA: Addison-Wesley.

Weick, K. E. 1991. "The nontraditional quality of organizational learning." *Organization Science* 2:116–24.

Weick, K. E., and D. P. Gilfillan. 1971. "The fate of arbitrary traditions in a laboratory microculture." *Journal of Personality and Social Psychology* 17:179–91.

Wernerfelt, B. 1984. A resource view of the firm. *Strategic Management Journal* 5:171–80.

White, L. 1991. *The S&L Debacle.* New York: Oxford University Press.

Wholey, D. R., and J. W. Brittain. 1986. "Organizational ecology: Findings and implications." *Academy of Management Review* 11:513–33.

Wholey, D. R., and J. W. Brittain. 1989. "Characterizing environmental change." *Academy of Management Journal* 32:867–82.

Wholey D. R., and L. R. Burns. 1989. "Ecological events, interdependence, and organizational performance: A comparison of four HMO forms." Working paper, Department of Management, University of Arizona.

Wholey, D. R., J. B. Christianson, and S. M. Sanchez. 1991. "The diffusion of health maintenance organizations: density, competitive and institutional determinants of entry." Unpublished manuscript. University of Arizona.

Wildavsky, A. 1972. "The self evaluating organization." *Public Administration Review* 32:509–520.

Wiley, M., and M. Zald. 1968 "The growth and transformation of educational accrediting agencies: and exploratory study in the social control of institutions." *Sociology of Education* 41:36–56.

Williams, G. C. 1966. *Adaptation and Natural Selection.* Princeton, NJ: Princeton University Press.

Williamson, O. E. 1985. *The Economic Institutions of Capitalism.* New York: Free Press.

Williamson, O. E. 1991. "Comparative economic organization: the analysis of discrete structural alternatives." *Administrative Science Quarterly* 36:269–98.

Wilson, D. S. 1983. "The group selection controversy: History and current status." *Annual Review of Ecology and Systematics* 14:159–87.

Wilson, D. S., and E. Sober. 1989. "Reviving the superorganism."*Journal of Theoretical Biology* 136:337–56.

Wilson, E. O. 1968. "The ergonomics of caste in the social insects." *American Naturalist* 102:41–66.

Wilson, R. W., P. K. Ashton, and T. P. Egan. 1980. *Innovation,Competition, and Government Policy in the Semiconductor Industry.* Lexington, MA: D. C. Heath.

Windmill, I. M., S. Martinez, M. B. Nolph, and B. Eisenmenger. 1987."The downside of cochlear implants." *The Hearing Journal* 39: January:18–21.

Winter, S. G. 1971. "Satisficing, selection and the innovating remnant." *Quarterly Journal of Economics* 85:237–61.

Winter, S. G. 1987. "Knowledge and competence as srategic assets."In D. Teece, (ed.), *The Competitive Challenge,* 159–84. New York: Harper & Row.

Winter, S. G. 1990. "Survival, selection, and inheritance in evolutionary theories of organization." In J. V. Singh, (ed.),*Organizational Evolution: New Directions,* 269–97. Newbury Park CA: Sage.

Winter, Sidney G. 1993. "Routines, Cash Flows and Uncoventional Assets: Corporate Change in the 1980s." In M. Blair (ed.), *The Deal Decade: What Takeovers and Leveraged Buyouts Mean for Corporate Governance.* Washington, DC: The Brookings Institution. Forthcoming.

Wold, H. O. A. 1965. "A graphic introduction to stochastic processes." In H. O. A. Wold, (ed.), *Bibliography on Time Series and Stochastic Processes,* 7–76. Edinburgh: Oliver and Boyd.

Yin, L., and D. A. Segerson. 1986. "Cochlear implants: Overview of Safety and Effectiveness." *Otolaryngologic Clinics of North America* 19:423–33.

Young, R. C. 1988. "Is population ecology a useful paradigm for the study of organizations?" *American Journal of Sociology* 94:1–24.

Yoxen, E. 1987. "Seeing with sound: a study of the development of medical imaging." In W. Bijker, et al., (eds.), *The Social Construction of Tecnological Systems.* Cambridge, MA: MIT Press.

Zelditch, M., Jr. 1971. "Intelligible comparisons." *Comparative Methods in Sociology:* In I. Vallier, (ed.), *Essays on Trends andApplications,* 267–307. Berkeley, CA: University of California Press.

Zeldtich, M. and H. Walker. 1984. "Legitimacy and the stability of authority." In E. Lawler, (ed.), *Advances in Group Processes,* 1:1–25. Greenwich, CT: JAI Press.

Zucker, L. G. 1977. "The role of institutionalization in cultural persistence." *American Sociological Review* 42:726–43.

Zucker, L. G. 1983. "Organizations as institutions." In S. B. Backarack, (ed.), *Research in the Sociology of Organizations,* Greenwich, CT: JAI Press.

Zucker, L. G. 1986. "Production of trust: institutional sources of economic structure, 1840–1920." In L. Cummings and B. Staw (eds.) *Research in Organizational Behavior,* 8:53–111. Greenwich, CT: JAI Press.

Zucker, L. G. 1987. "Institutional theories of organization."*Annual Review of Sociology* 13:443–64.

Zucker, L. G. 1989a. "Combining institutional theory and populations ecology: no legitimacy, no history." *American Sociological Review* 54(4):542–45.

Zucker, L. G. 1989b. *NSF Data on Strikes in the 1880's: The Strike-level Data Set Codebook.* Data Archives Library, Institute for Social Science Research, UCLA.

Zucker, L. G., L. Crabbe, and A. Wu 1988. "A rejection of strike series for 1881–1886 in the U.S.: Misclassification errors and probable political motivation in the Bureau of Labor." Los Angeles: UCLA: Institute of Industrial Relations Working Paper Series.

Zucker, L. G., K. Yip, and M. Kalmijn. 1992. "Strikes as institution-building: union locals as strike outcomes and strike moderators in the 1880's." In K. L. Sokoloff, (ed.), *Studies in Labor Markets and Institutions,* 49–95. Los Angeles: UCLA: Institute of Industrial Relations, Monographs and Research Series, 56.

Index